Meet the
Southern Living® Foods Staff

With these photographs we invite you to match the names and faces
of the people behind these pages (left to right unless otherwise noted).

DONNA FLORIO, *Associate Foods Editor;*
SUSAN HAWTHORNE NASH, *Foods Editor;*
ANDRIA SCOTT HURST, *Associate Foods Editor*

(front) KAYE MABRY ADAMS, *Executive Editor;*
(back) WANDA T. STEPHENS, *Administrative Assistant;*
VICKI POELLNITZ, *Editorial Assistant*

(sitting) MARGARET MONROE, *Test Kitchens Director;* LYDA H. JONES, VANESSA A. MCNEIL, *Test Kitchens staff*
(standing) VIE WARSHAW, JAN MOON, MARY ALLEN PERRY, *Test Kitchens staff*

(sitting) LYNNMARIE P. COOK, *Assistant Foods Editor*;
(standing) CYNTHIA BRISCOE, *Assistant Foods Editor;* PEGGY SMITH,
Associate Foods Editor; SCOTT JONES, *Assistant Foods Editor*

Assistant Foods Editors:
JOY E. ZACHARIA, KATE NICHOLSON,
VANESSA TAYLOR JOHNSON

Photographers and Photo Stylists: (front) ROSE NGUYEN, CHARLES WALTON IV, BUFFY HARGETT
(back) MARY LYN H. JENKINS, TINA CORNETT, WILLIAM DICKEY, CINDY MANNING BARR, RALPH ANDERSON

Anniversary Cake, page 117

Southern Living

2000 ANNUAL RECIPES

Oxmoor House.

ISBN: 0-8487-1993-x
ISSN: 0272-2003

Printed in the United States of America
First printing 2000

WE'RE HERE FOR YOU!

We at Oxmoor House are dedicated to serving you with reliable information that expands your imagination and enriches your life. We welcome your comments and suggestions. Please write us at:

Oxmoor House, Inc.
Editor, *Southern Living*® *Annual Recipes*
2100 Lakeshore Drive
Birmingham, AL 35209

To order additional publications, call 1-205-877-6560.

We Want Your FAVORITE RECIPES!

Southern Living cooks are the best cooks of all, and we want your secrets! Please send your favorite original recipes for main dishes, desserts, and everything in between, along with any hands-on tips and a sentence about why you like each recipe. We can't guarantee we'll print them in a cookbook, but if we do, we'll send you $20 and a free copy of the cookbook. Send each recipe on a separate page with your name, address, and daytime phone number to:

Cookbook Recipes
Oxmoor House
2100 Lakeshore Drive
Birmingham, AL 35209

Southern Living®

Executive Editor: Kaye Mabry Adams
Foods Editor: Susan Hawthorne Nash
Associate Foods Editors: Donna Florio, Andria Scott Hurst, Peggy Smith, Patty M. Vann
Assistant Foods Editors: Cynthia Briscoe, Lynnmarie P. Cook, Vanessa Taylor Johnson, Scott Jones, Kate Nicholson, Joy E. Zacharia
Test Kitchens Director: Margaret Monroe
Test Kitchens Staff: Lyda H. Jones, Vanessa A. McNeil, Jan Moon, Mary Allen Perry, Vie Warshaw
Administrative Assistant: Wanda T. Stephens
Editorial Assistant: Vicki Poellnitz
Director of Photography and Color Quality: Kenner Patton
Senior Foods Photographer: Charles Walton IV
Photographers: Ralph Anderson, Tina Cornett, William Dickey
Senior Photo Stylist: Cindy Manning Barr
Photo Stylists: Buffy Hargett, Mary Lyn H. Jenkins, Rose Nguyen
Photo Services: Tracy Duncan
Production Manager: Katie Terrell
Production Assistant: Nicole Johnson

Oxmoor House, Inc.

Editor-in-Chief: Nancy Fitzpatrick Wyatt
Senior Editor, Copy and Homes: Olivia Kindig Wells
Art Director: James Boone

Southern Living® *2000 Annual Recipes*

Senior Foods Editor: Susan Carlisle Payne
Editor: Keri Bradford Anderson
Copy Editor: Catherine Ritter Scholl
Editorial Assistant: Jane E. Lorberau
Director, Production and Distribution: Phillip Lee
Books Production Manager: Theresa L. Beste
Production Assistant: Faye Porter Bonner

Contributors

Designer: Carol O. Loria
Indexer: Mary Ann Laurens
Editorial Consultant: Jean Wickstrom Liles

Cover: Twinkling Star Cake, page 306
Back Cover: Grilled Chicken Salad Sandwiches, Grilled Asparagus, Summer Vegetable-and-Orzo Salad, pages 164-165; Strawberry Custard Pie, page 81; Pork Medaillons in Mustard Sauce, Carrot-Sweet Potato Puree, Green Beans With Caramelized Onion, pages 32-33; Key Lime Pie, page 120
Page 1: Maple-Plum Glazed Turkey Tenderloins, page 285; Sweet Potato Soufflé, page 273; Butter Rolls, page 257; Garlic Green Beans, page 260; Cornbread Dressing, page 259; Cranberry-Ginger Chutney, page 253; Cranberry-Pineapple Punch, page 284

CONTENTS

OUR YEAR AT SOUTHERN LIVING®

Dear Friends,

Putting the finishing touches on our 22nd *Southern Living® Annual Recipes* completes a swift and eventful first year of a brand-new century.

As you page through this volume, we hope you'll rediscover the simple joys of food—a goal that remains constant with our Foods team. We also hope that you'll find a degree of comfort. It is, after all, each of *you* who continues to inspire these pages—whether you are a new cook, a seasoned kitchen veteran, or a first-time reader.

Knowing that time with family and friends often overrides time spent in the kitchen, we share a number of timesaving discoveries throughout this book. Take a look at our seven-ingredient recipes (page 14); innovative ways to use deli-roasted chicken (page 44); and prizewinning recipes by and for kids (page 198).

"Rediscover the simple joys of food—a goal that remains constant with our Foods Team."

Our new feature "A Taste of the South," a monthly exploration of our region's culinary traditions, includes tips for shortcutting classic Southern recipes without sacrificing great flavor. A cozy New Year's supper of black-eyed peas and cornbread (page 22); a foolproof quick-and-easy pound cake recipe (page 36); and secrets to perfect fried chicken (page 142) make their debut in this column. Another newcomer, "Top-Rated Menu," updates favored dishes from our Recipe Hall of Fame with timesaving ingredient substitutions and streamlined directions. Wine picks from Assistant Foods Editor Scott Jones accompany many of these great meal plans. "Quick & Easy" and "What's for Supper?" continue to deliver simple dinnertime solutions every month.

Our Foods pages celebrate flavor and diversity. Whether you're trying caramel recipes for the first time (page 52) or looking for a brand-new version of bread pudding (page 104), our kitchen-tested recipes, step-by-step instructions, and helpful tips provide the perfect culinary partner. Time-honored dishes—those standbys destined to become handed-down favorites—carry the *Southern Living* icon. And, our high-flavor, healthful options in "Living Light" now include expanded nutritional information.

We hope you'll stay in touch via e-mail, telephone, and letters. Let us know how you're doing and how we can help. Your thoughts are important to us.

Thank you for making our annual collection part of your cookbook library. We look forward to hearing from you.

Susan Nash

Susan Hawthorne Nash
Foods Editor

P.S. If it's been a while since you've visited us on-line, you're in for a great surprise. Our website—southernliving.com—has a brand-new look. You'll find recipe and menu suggestions, plus market orders to make mealtime even easier.

Susan joined the Foods Staff of Southern Living *in 1992 and has worked on the magazine in several different capacities, including Editorial Coordinator, before being named to the position of Foods Editor in 1997. She is a member of the International Association of Culinary Professionals and the Association of Food Journalists.*

Best Recipes of 2000

Our Foods staff gathers almost every day to taste-test and assign recipes a rating based on taste, overall appeal, ease, and even cost. Here we share this year's highest-rated recipes.

Toasted Pecan Clusters, page 14, satisfy chocolate cravings with only three ingredients: butter, pecans, and chocolate.

Parmesan Cheese Bites, page 20, are perfect party snacks because you can make them ahead of time.

Lamb Chops With Minted Apples, page 20, from the Biltmore Estate enable you to re-create this restaurant specialty at home.

Margaret's Creamy Grits, page 21, made with rich cream and two kinds of cheeses, will convert even dissenters of the South's noted grain.

1-2-3 Blackberry Sherbet, page 21, features summer's sweet berries in a refreshingly simple dessert.

Pork Medaillons in Mustard Sauce, page 32, make a simple but spectacular presentation on a dinner plate.

Carrot-Sweet Potato Puree, page 32, marries the two colorful vegetables in a smooth and creamy side dish.

Green Beans With Caramelized Onion, page 33, is a memorable accompaniment for any roasted meat or poultry.

Sour Cream Yeast Rolls, page 33, may become your family's favorite dinner roll once they try them.

Hot Chocolate Deluxe, page 33, gets a noteworthy splash of coffee liqueur for its finish.

Two-Step Pound Cake, page 36, simplifies the technique but leaves the flavor of our favorite pound cake unsurpassed.

Chicken Cakes With Rémoulade Sauce, page 44, take their shape from their crab cousins but offer simplicity and satisfaction uniquely their own.

Banana Napoleons, page 50, were created by the chefs at Walt Disney World and provide a sweet feast for the senses of young and old alike.

Caramel Sauce, page 52, glistens like gold when spooned over a scoop of vanilla ice cream.

Caramel Sticky Buns, page 52, are extrasimple to make with yeast roll dough, but no one will know it unless you tell them.

Marinated Chicken Strips and Vegetables, page 54, make a sophisticated one-dish salad supper you can prepare ahead of time.

Parmesan Bread, page 54, sports a golden crust speckled with Parmesan cheese. You can even make it ahead and freeze it, if you'd like.

Lemon Ice Cream, page 55, takes its delightfully sweet tang from fresh grated lemon rind and juice. No substitutes!

Baby Blue Salad, page 81, may steal the show next time you have company over for dinner. A balsamic vinaigrette skillfully blends the salad greens, sweet fruit, and tangy blue cheese.

Mushrooms in Sour Cream, page 106, offers rich and creamy indulgence spooned over crostini as an appetizer. You can vary the type of mushrooms to your liking.

Beef Tenderloin With Henry Bain Sauce, page 107, will garner encore samplings when sandwiched in soft dinner rolls on an appetizer buffet.

Baby Hot Browns, page 107, capture the comforting flavor of the stately sandwich in miniature for a party.

Tortilla Soup, page 110, takes a little time to make but yields ample to freeze and serve all winter long.

Chicken and Dumplings, page 111, nourishes body and soul today just like yesteryear, and Grandma would beg for this recipe.

Mushroom-Wine Sauce, page 125, makes a great steak even better. A baked potato on the side sops up the sauce nicely, too.

Stuffed Focaccia With Roasted Pepper Vinaigrette, page 134, may be the classiest sandwich you've ever served, and it takes just 20 minutes to make.

Homemade Butter Rolls, page 137, yields four dozen dinner rolls that you can bake right away or freeze and bake a few at a time.

Our Best Southern Fried Chicken, page 142, cooks up extrajuicy from a leisurely soak in a saline solution and extraflavorful from bacon drippings added to the frying oil.

Summer Fruit Salad With Blueberry Vinaigrette, page 154, doubles your menu options. Toss the combo with chopped cooked chicken for a main-dish salad.

Sachertorte Cookies, page 155, package the flavors of the classic chocolate torte in bite-size confections perfect for gift-giving.

Tangy Green Beans With Pimiento, page 170, get their irresistible flavor from a sweet-and-sour dressing and crisp bacon crumbled over the top.

Lemon Ice, page 176, was never so tasty or simple to make. This one starts with frozen lemonade concentrate.

Fresh Tomato Dressing, page 182, mellows in the refrigerator up to a month, ever ready to spoon over crisp salad greens or sliced fresh tomatoes.

Tomato Napoleon, page 182, marinates fresh mozzarella in Fresh Tomato Dressing and layers the cheese with tomato slices and basil leaves into a stately creation.

Tomato-Pesto Tart, page 195, blends several irresistible Italian flavors into a freestanding tart suitable for an appetizer or a main dish.

Grilled Four-Cheese Sandwich With Tomato, Avocado, and Bacon, page 199, may mean you'll never want a "plain" grilled cheese again. The simple flavor combination is incredible in this recipe.

Fried Okra, page 205, takes a new twist but stays distinctly Southern with red pepper in the breading and bacon drippings in the oil.

Blue Cheese Rolls, page 210, start any menu off right with their zesty Cheddar-blue cheese combination.

Curried Shrimp Salad, page 217, features the seafood favorite served with a creamy curried dressing and cool, crisp iceberg lettuce.

Caramelized Onions, page 218, have never been so easy. Just toss three ingredients in your slow cooker, and eight hours later you have sweet perfection—all without stirring!

Sweet Potato Biscuits, page 232, are so rich and tender, they'll disappear from the dinner table in just minutes.

Meatball Lasagna, page 243, offers the convenience of frozen cooked meatballs and builds its layers with egg roll wrappers instead of lasagna noodles.

Cinnamon Breakfast Rolls, page 243, will make your mornings easy—the dough rises overnight in the fridge.

Mocha Pecan Mud Pie, page 245, starts with your favorite cream-filled chocolate cookies, adds two kinds of ice cream, and transforms it all into a frozen decadent delight.

Cream of Cilantro Soup, page 249, showcases the earthy but subtle cilantro flavor in a creamy, but light, recipe.

Caramel Sauce, page 256, takes just 15 minutes to prepare, making it an ideal gift during the hectic holidays.

Sweet Onion Pudding, page 260, is a silky, smooth Thanksgiving favorite of Jan Moon in our Test Kitchens.

Caramel-Applesauce Cobbler With Bourbon-Pecan Ice Cream, page 260, caramelizes Granny Smith apples for a sweet-tart cobbler similar to an applesauce pie.

Pecan Pie Cookies, page 290, pack all the rich, buttery flavor of the pie into delectable morsels.

Texas Millionaires, page 291, will delight kids of all ages with their classic caramel-pecan-chocolate trio.

Collard Greens Soup, page 293, is a comforting and hearty dish that will warm you on even the coldest nights.

Two-Tomato Tapas, page 308, a Mediterranean-style appetizer, burst with tomato and herb flavors.

Beef Filets With Stilton-Portobello Sauce, page 309, pair bold Stilton cheese and meaty portobellos with a filet.

Shellfish Crêpes in Wine-Cheese Sauce, page 310, is an elegant make-ahead casserole featuring crab and shrimp.

Pear Salad With Raspberry Cream, page 311, joins two favorite fruits in a refreshing, sophisticated salad.

Tiramisù Toffee Trifle Pie, page 312, was inspired by the Italian classic and creates its crust with pound cake slices.

Curry-Ginger Shrimp, page 316, takes time to prepare but is worth the wait after one taste of its spicy goodness.

Buttery Blue Cheese Spread With Walnuts, page 329, provides you with perfect holiday party fare because it keeps in the freezer up to a month.

Smoky Green Chile-Cheddar Cheese With Avocado-Mango Salsa, page 328, contrasts savory cheeses with tart mango salsa for an appetizer guests will crave.

Potato Chowder With Green Chiles, page 329, spikes up the traditional soup with poblano and jalapeño peppers.

JANUARY

Simple as One, Two, Three

Imagine having a stash of favorite recipes with only three to seven ingredients. From appetizers to entrées, each is made to order for the busy cook. We've even included macaroni and cheese that's just a stir away and a dessert that's microwaveable.

GLAZED ROASTED CHICKEN

Prep: 20 minutes
Chill: 8 hours
Bake: 45 minutes

½ cup lite teriyaki sauce
¼ cup frozen orange juice concentrate, thawed and undiluted
3 tablespoons dark sesame oil
4 garlic cloves, minced
2 (3-pound) whole chickens
½ teaspoon freshly ground pepper

● **Stir** together first 4 ingredients, and reserve half of mixture.
● **Cut** each chicken in half, and sprinkle evenly with pepper.
● **Place** chicken in a large heavy-duty zip-top plastic bag, and pour remaining half of teriyaki mixture over chicken; seal bag, and chill 8 hours, turning chicken, if desired.
● **Remove** chicken from marinade, discarding marinade. Place chicken, skin side up, on an aluminum foil-lined 15- x 10-inch jellyroll pan.
● **Bake** at 450° for 45 minutes or until a meat thermometer inserted into chicken thigh registers 180°. Brush chicken with reserved teriyaki mixture. **Yield:** 6 to 8 servings.

William N. Cottrell
New Orleans, Louisiana

EASY TARRAGON FILLETS

You can use any lean, firm fish in place of the grouper in this recipe.

Prep: 10 minutes
Broil: 20 minutes

¼ cup sweet-and-spicy sauce and marinade
¼ cup butter or margarine
½ teaspoon dried tarragon
4 grouper fillets (2 pounds)
2 tablespoons fresh lemon juice

● **Cook** first 3 ingredients in a small saucepan over medium heat 5 minutes or until butter is melted.
● **Place** fish fillets on a lightly greased rack in a broiler pan. Drizzle evenly with lemon juice, and brush with tarragon sauce mixture.
● **Broil** 6 inches from heat (with electric oven door partially open) 10 minutes on each side or until fish flakes with a fork, basting fish occasionally with remaining tarragon sauce mixture. **Yield:** 4 servings.

Note: For testing purposes only, we used The Original Tiger Sauce for sweet-and-spicy sauce and marinade.

Lisa Boutwell Dumigan
Baton Rouge, Louisiana

TORTELLINI SOUP

Small cheese-filled pasta and canned diced tomatoes turn this soup into a satisfying meal in 25 minutes.

Prep: 10 minutes
Cook: 15 minutes

3 (14½-ounce) cans chicken broth
2 (9-ounce) packages refrigerated cheese-filled tortellini *
1 (14½-ounce) can diced tomatoes, undrained
4 green onions, chopped
2 garlic cloves, minced
2 teaspoons minced fresh or 1 teaspoon dried basil
Garnish: shredded Parmesan cheese

● **Bring** broth to a boil in a large saucepan over medium-high heat.
● **Add** tortellini and next 4 ingredients. Reduce heat, and simmer 10 minutes. Garnish, if desired. **Yield:** 12 cups.

★ Substitute meat-filled tortellini for cheese-filled tortellini, if desired.

Carol Y. Chastain
San Antonio, Texas

TOASTED PECAN CLUSTERS

How many ingredients? No one believes it after eating one of these nutty chocolate clusters. They've been one of our favorites since 1985.

Prep: 20 minutes
Cook: 45 minutes

3 tablespoons butter or margarine
3 cups pecan pieces
12 ounces chocolate candy coating

● **Melt** butter in a 15- x 10-inch jellyroll pan in a 300° oven. Spread pecans evenly in pan with butter.
● **Bake** at 300° for 30 minutes, stirring every 10 minutes.
● **Melt** chocolate candy coating in a heavy saucepan over low heat. Remove

from heat, and cool 2 minutes. Stir in toasted pecans. Drop mixture by rounded teaspoonfuls onto wax paper. Cool. **Yield:** about 4 dozen.

Microwave Directions: Place butter in a 1-quart glass bowl; microwave at HIGH 50 seconds or until melted. Add pecans, tossing to coat. Microwave at HIGH 6 to 8 minutes or until lightly toasted, stirring at 3-minute intervals. Place candy coating in a 1-quart glass bowl. Microwave at MEDIUM (50% power) 2 to 3 minutes or until coating is softened; stir well. Cool 2 minutes; add pecans, stirring to coat. Drop mixture by rounded teaspoonfuls onto wax paper. Cool.

QUICK-AND-EASY MACARONI AND CHEESE

Prep: 10 minutes
Bake: 25 minutes

8   ounces large elbow macaroni, cooked
1   (8-ounce) package shredded sharp Cheddar cheese*
1   (10¾-ounce) can cream of mushroom soup, undiluted*
½   cup mayonnaise*
½   cup milk*

• **Stir** together all ingredients in a lightly greased 2½-quart baking dish.
• **Bake** at 375° for 25 minutes. **Yield:** 6 servings.

*Substitute shredded reduced-fat sharp Cheddar cheese; reduced-sodium, reduced-fat cream of mushroom soup; light mayonnaise; and fat-free milk, if desired.

Kathy Bourland
Louisville, Mississippi

HONEY CHICKEN WINGS

Prep: 5 minutes
Bake: 55 minutes

1   cup salsa or picante sauce
¼   cup honey
½   teaspoon ground ginger
1½ pounds chicken wing pieces

• **Stir** together first 3 ingredients in a large bowl.
• **Add** chicken wing pieces, tossing to coat. Place on an aluminum foil-lined 15- x 10-inch jellyroll pan.
• **Bake** at 400° for 55 minutes or until chicken is done, turning once. **Yield:** 4 appetizer servings.

Teresa Hubbard
Russellville, Alabama

Reunions: Rich in Love

Everyone should have at least one family reunion," says Betty Mitchell of Burna, Kentucky. This family spreads love to family and friends each year as they gather to salute the beginning of deer-hunting season. From spicy muffins to warm, fruity dumplings, these recipes are favorites from relatives near and far.

GINGERBREAD MUFFINS

Prep: 10 minutes
Bake: 20 minutes

1   cup shortening
1   cup sugar
1   cup molasses
3   large eggs
1   cup buttermilk
3   cups all-purpose flour
1   teaspoon baking soda
½   teaspoon salt
1½ tablespoons ground ginger
1   teaspoon ground cinnamon
½   teaspoon ground nutmeg

• **Beat** shortening at medium speed with an electric mixer until fluffy; gradually add sugar, beating well.
• **Add** molasses; beat until blended.
• **Add** eggs, 1 at a time, beating until blended after each addition. Add buttermilk; beat until blended.
• **Combine** flour and next 5 ingredients. Gradually add to buttermilk mixture; beat until blended.
• **Spoon** into greased muffin pans, filling two-thirds full.
• **Bake** muffins at 350° for 20 minutes. Remove from pans immediately. **Yield:** 2½ dozen.

Elsie Davidson
Marion, Kentucky

TEMPURA VEGETABLES

Try these vegetables with zesty horseradish or a sweet-and-sour dipping sauce.

Prep: 10 minutes
Cook: 4 minutes per batch

2   medium zucchini
2   medium-size yellow squash
1   medium onion
¾   cup cornstarch
½   cup self-rising cornmeal
¼   teaspoon pepper
½   cup water
1   large egg, lightly beaten
Corn oil
½   teaspoon salt

• **Cut** zucchini, yellow squash, and onion into ¼-inch-thick slices. Separate onion slices into rings.
• **Combine** cornstarch, cornmeal, and pepper; stir in ½ cup water and egg until smooth. Dip vegetables into batter.
• **Pour** oil to a depth of ½ inch into a heavy skillet; heat to 375°.
• **Fry** vegetables, in batches, 4 minutes or until golden. Drain on paper towels; sprinkle with salt. **Yield:** 4 servings.

Janice Rogers
Smithland, Kentucky

APPLE-CRANBERRY DUMPLINGS

Prep: 20 minutes
Cook: 8 minutes
Bake: 40 minutes

5 medium Granny Smith apples, diced
1 cup whole-berry cranberry sauce
½ cup chopped walnuts, toasted
2 cups all-purpose flour
1 tablespoon baking powder
1 teaspoon salt
2 tablespoons sugar
½ cup shortening
¾ cup milk
2 cups water
2 cups sugar
½ teaspoon ground cinnamon
½ teaspoon ground cloves
½ cup butter or margarine

• **Stir** together first 3 ingredients; drain and set aside.
• **Combine** flour and next 3 ingredients. Cut in shortening with a pastry blender until crumbly; add milk, stirring until dry ingredients are moistened.
• **Turn** dough out onto a lightly floured surface; knead 3 or 4 times.
• **Roll** dough into an 18- x 12-inch rectangle. Spread apple mixture over dough. Roll up, jellyroll fashion, starting at short end.
• **Cut** into 1-inch slices, and place slices, cut side down, in a greased 13- x 9-inch pan.
• **Bring** 2 cups water and next 3 ingredients to a boil in a saucepan; boil 5 minutes. Remove from heat, and stir in butter. Pour hot syrup over dumplings.
• **Bake** at 425° for 35 to 40 minutes. Serve warm. **Yield:** 12 servings.

Janice Alsobrook
Anderson, Indiana

Sour Power

If lemons could talk, they'd holler out loud. Their scent is scintillating, their color screams "See me," and their flavor turns a pout into a pucker. A splash or slice of this yellow jewel will wipe away winter blues. Why not preserve the fruit's goodness at its fresh best to spike your meals with sunshine all year long?

LIVELY LEMON TOSSED SALAD

Preserved lemon and fresh-squeezed juice add the zing to this bright salad.

Prep: 25 minutes
Chill: 30 minutes

¼ Fresh Preserved Lemons recipe (on facing page)
3 tablespoons fresh lemon juice (1 medium lemon)
1 tablespoon extra-virgin olive oil
¼ cup minced fresh mint
2 tablespoons minced fresh parsley
1 garlic clove, pressed
¼ teaspoon freshly ground pepper
6 plum tomatoes, seeded and diced
1 green bell pepper, diced
1 purple onion, thinly sliced
1 avocado, peeled and cut into 1-inch cubes
½ cup sliced kalamata or ripe olives
4 ounces crumbled feta cheese
Mixed salad greens

• **Rinse** preserved lemon; remove and discard pulp. Cut rind into ¼-inch cubes.
• **Whisk** together lemon juice and next 5 ingredients in a large bowl; add lemon rind, tomato, and next 5 ingredients, tossing to coat. Cover and chill 30 minutes. Serve over salad greens. **Yield:** 4 servings.

Lively Lemon-Chicken Salad: Double the lemon juice mixture, reserving half for tomato mixture.

Place 4 skinned and boned chicken breast halves in a shallow dish or large heavy-duty zip-top plastic bag; pour remaining half of lemon juice mixture over chicken. Cover or seal; chill 20 minutes. Remove chicken from marinade, discarding marinade.

Cook chicken in a large nonstick skillet over medium-high heat 6 to 7 minutes on each side or until done. Serve with tomato mixture over lettuce.

Note: For peak flavor, choose bright yellow fruit that is heavy, firm, smooth-skinned, and medium to large in size. A medium lemon yields about 3 tablespoons lemon juice and 1 tablespoon grated rind.

FRESH PRESERVED LEMONS

You can layer on the flavor by adding fresh mint sprigs, bay leaves, cinnamon sticks, or peppercorns to the jar.

Prep: 15 minutes
Freeze: 8 hours
Chill: 6 days

4   medium lemons
5   tablespoons fine-grain sea salt, divided
½   cup fresh lemon juice (about 3 lemons)

• **Cut** lemons lengthwise into quarters from the top to within ½ inch of bottom, without separating quarters.
• **Sprinkle** 1 tablespoon salt into a clean 1-quart jar; pack lemons into jar. Cover jar with lid, and shake; freeze 8 hours.
• **Sprinkle** lemons with remaining 4 tablespoons salt; cover with lid, and shake to coat. Remove lid, and press lemons to release juices.
• **Add** ½ cup lemon juice to cover lemons. Cover with lid; chill 6 days, shaking jar each day. Store lemons in refrigerator up to 6 months. **Yield:** 4 lemons.

Note: Preserved lemons may have a white film; rinse the lemons under cold water prior to using. The quarters can be used with or without pulp. Lemons will darken during storage.

Seaside Salads

Salads fresh from the sea need little gilding—just great seasonings and a subtle touch. These recipes showcase the essence of the seas and the bounty of the fields. We offer some of the best ways to savor the flavor of your favorite catch.

COASTAL SHRIMP SALAD

Prep: 45 minutes

1   pound unpeeled, large fresh shrimp
1   (3-ounce) package boil-in-bag shrimp and crab boil
6   cups mixed salad greens
3   large oranges, peeled and sectioned
2   large pink grapefruit, peeled and sectioned
2   medium avocados, peeled and sliced
Sour Cream-Horseradish Dressing

• **Cook** shrimp in boil-in-bag mix according to package directions. Drain and rinse with cold water.
• **Peel** shrimp, and devein, if desired. Cover and chill.
• **Arrange** salad greens on individual plates; top with shrimp, orange sections, grapefruit sections, and avocado. Serve with Sour Cream-Horseradish Dressing. **Yield:** 4 to 6 servings.

Sour Cream-Horseradish Dressing

Prep: 5 minutes

1   (8-ounce) container sour cream
¼   cup orange juice
1   tablespoon Dijon mustard
2   teaspoons prepared horseradish
4   green onions, diced

• **Stir** together all ingredients until well blended. Cover and chill, if desired. **Yield:** 1⅓ cups.

CRAB LUNCHEON SALAD

Prep: 20 minutes
Chill: 3 hours

⅓   cup vegetable oil
½   cup water
¼   cup cider vinegar
½   teaspoon salt
½   teaspoon pepper
¼   teaspoon Worcestershire sauce
1   pound fresh lump crabmeat, drained
1   medium onion, diced
3   tomatoes, sliced
Lettuce leaves
3   hard-cooked eggs, quartered
12   ripe olives (optional)
12   pimiento-stuffed olives (optional)

• **Whisk** together first 6 ingredients. Add crabmeat and onion, tossing gently to coat. Cover and chill 3 hours. Drain.
• **Arrange** tomato on lettuce-lined plates, and top with crabmeat mixture. Place egg and, if desired, olives around crabmeat mixture. **Yield:** 4 servings.

SALAD SAVVY

■ Chilling the salad plates or serving bowl will keep salad greens crisp longer.

■ The best salads have a balance of textures, colors, and tastes. Contrast crunchy ingredients with smooth dressings, vibrant colors with muted hues, and mellow flavors with spicy or bold ones.

■ Dress for success: Resist heavy dressings that weigh down ingredients; a lighter dressing lets the freshness shine through.

SWORDFISH SALAD

Prep: 10 minutes
Grill: 12 minutes

1 (8-ounce) swordfish fillet
2 tablespoons vinaigrette
2 green onions, chopped
¼ cup sliced ripe olives
½ teaspoon dried crushed red
    pepper
2 cups mixed salad greens
Additional vinaigrette

• **Brush** fish evenly with 2 tablespoons vinaigrette.
• **Grill,** covered with grill lid, over medium-high heat (350° to 400°) 4 to 6 minutes on each side or until fish flakes easily with a fork. Cool and flake fish.
• **Toss** together fish, chopped green onions, sliced ripe olives, and pepper. Serve on mixed salad greens with additional vinaigrette. **Yield:** 2 servings.

Dan Whitehead
Jacksonville, Florida

Chuck Roasts

Dear Mom,

Today I cooked a chuck roast. I'm trying to eat at home more, and you know how I love roast and gravy. So I bought a nice three-pounder for less than $6. You were right—it's a very inexpensive cut. I browned that sucker well in a little oil, added some great ingredients (I was feeling creative), covered it, and baked it for an hour and a half. It was as tough as the sole of my loafers!

So I added a cup of water, took a nap, and let it cook for another hour and a half (guess you could say I slept on the problem). This time the roast was awesome: falling-apart tender and succulent, with plenty of gravy. I've even enclosed the recipe—Savory Chuck Roast. I know you'll be impressed; it would be great if you tried one of my recipes for a change!

Love, Frank

SAVORY CHUCK ROAST

Prep: 15 minutes
Bake: 3 hours

1 (3-pound) boneless chuck roast,
    trimmed
2 tablespoons white vinegar
1 teaspoon garlic salt
¼ cup all-purpose flour
2 tablespoons olive oil
1 (0.9-ounce) envelope dry
    onion-and-mushroom soup mix
¾ cup sweet sherry
¼ cup brewed coffee
1 cup sliced fresh mushrooms

• **Rub** roast with vinegar. Cut 8 to 10 slits in roast; sprinkle garlic salt into slits. Dredge roast in flour; brown on all sides in hot oil in a Dutch oven over medium-high heat. Combine soup mix, sherry, and coffee; pour over roast. Add mushrooms.
• **Bake,** covered, at 350° for 3 hours. Serve with steamed cabbage and carrots and parsleyed rice. **Yield:** 6 to 8 servings.

Slow Cooker Method: Cut roast into 3 roughly equal pieces. Place in a slow cooker with remaining ingredients. Cook on HIGH 2 hours; reduce temperature to LOW, and cook 7 hours.

Note: For testing purposes only, we used Lipton Dry Onion-Mushroom Soup Mix.

Mrs. M. Moody
Clearwater, Florida

FOUR-HOUR BARBECUE

Prep: 15 minutes
Bake: 4 hours

1 (3-pound) boneless chuck roast,
    trimmed
2 tablespoons vegetable oil
2 cups water
1 cup ketchup
2 small onions, chopped
1 garlic clove, minced
¼ cup white vinegar
¼ cup Worcestershire sauce
1 tablespoon chili powder
2 teaspoons salt
1 teaspoon pepper

• **Brown** roast on all sides in hot vegetable oil in a Dutch oven over medium-high heat.
• **Stir** together 2 cups water and next 8 ingredients. Pour over roast.
• **Bake,** covered, at 325° for 4 hours. **Yield:** 6 to 8 servings.

Judy Ring
Newport, Kentucky

POT ROAST WITH VEGETABLES

Prep: 10 minutes
Cook: 55 minutes

1 (3-pound) boneless chuck roast,
    trimmed
2 tablespoons vegetable oil
4 carrots, cut into 1-inch slices
3 potatoes, cut into 1½-inch cubes
1 medium onion, minced
3 cups water
1 (10½-ounce) can beef broth,
    undiluted
1 (8-ounce) can tomato sauce
1 cup dry red wine
1 teaspoon sugar
1 teaspoon hot sauce
¾ teaspoon salt

• **Brown** roast on all sides in hot oil in a pressure cooker over medium-high heat. Add carrot and remaining ingredients; close cover securely.
• **Place** pressure regulator on vent pipe; cook 45 minutes with pressure regulator rocking slowly. Remove from heat.
• **Run** cold water over pressure cooker to reduce pressure instantly; remove lid so that steam escapes away from you. **Yield:** 4 to 6 servings.

Dutch Oven Method: Brown roast on all sides in hot oil in a large Dutch oven over medium-high heat. Add carrot and remaining ingredients. Cover, reduce heat, and simmer 3 hours or until roast and vegetables are tender.

Mrs. Richard Joyner
Kelford, North Carolina

What's for Supper?

Italian cuisine is a favorite with many of us. And it's doubly good when it's fast. Meaty Stuffed Manicotti may be frozen up to one month before baking. Finish off your meal with fruit sherbet and almond cookies or with biscotti and espresso.

MEATY STUFFED MANICOTTI

Prep: 20 minutes
Bake: 40 minutes

8 ounces uncooked manicotti
   shells
½ pound hot Italian sausage
½ pound ground round
1 large egg
⅓ cup milk
2 white bread slices, cubed
2 cups (8 ounces) shredded
   mozzarella cheese
1 (16-ounce) container small-curd
   cottage cheese
1 tablespoon dried Italian
   seasoning
½ teaspoon salt
½ teaspoon garlic powder
½ teaspoon pepper
2 (16-ounce) jars spaghetti sauce
   with mushrooms, divided
¼ cup shredded Parmesan
   cheese

• **Cook** pasta according to package directions; rinse with cold water. Drain.
• **Remove** casings from sausage, and discard. Cook sausage and beef in a large skillet, stirring until meat crumbles and is no longer pink. Drain.
• **Stir** together egg and milk in a large bowl; add bread.
• **Stir** in sausage mixture, mozzarella cheese, and next 5 ingredients. Spoon into manicotti shells; arrange stuffed shells in a lightly greased 13- x 9-inch

baking dish. Pour 1½ jars spaghetti sauce over shells.
• **Bake,** covered, at 350° for 30 minutes. Uncover and pour remaining ½ jar spaghetti sauce over shells; sprinkle with Parmesan. Bake, uncovered, 10 more minutes. **Yield:** 6 to 8 servings.

Note: Casserole may be assembled and frozen up to 1 month. Thaw in refrigerator overnight; bake, covered, at 350° for 40 minutes or until heated.

Lanera Jackson
Poyen, Arkansas

ZESTY CHICKEN PARMIGIANA

Prep: 35 minutes
Bake: 38 minutes

⅔ cup Italian-seasoned
   breadcrumbs
⅔ cup grated Parmesan cheese,
   divided
8 skinned and boned chicken breast
   halves
2 large eggs, lightly beaten
¼ to ⅓ cup olive oil
1 (26-ounce) jar spaghetti sauce
1 teaspoon dried oregano, crushed
1 (6-ounce) package mozzarella
   cheese slices
16 ounces rotini, cooked
¼ cup butter or margarine
2 tablespoons minced fresh Italian
   parsley

• **Combine** breadcrumbs and ⅓ cup Parmesan cheese. Dip chicken in egg; dredge in breadcrumb mixture.
• **Brown** half of chicken in hot oil in a large skillet over medium-high heat, turning once. Remove chicken from skillet; repeat with remaining chicken.
• **Stir** together spaghetti sauce and oregano. Pour into a lightly greased 13- x 9-inch baking dish. Arrange chicken over sauce.
• **Bake,** covered, at 350° for 30 minutes. Top chicken with mozzarella slices. Sprinkle with remaining ⅓ cup Parmesan cheese.
• **Bake,** uncovered, 8 more minutes or until mozzarella is lightly browned.
• **Toss** hot pasta with butter and parsley. Serve with chicken. **Yield:** 8 servings.

Debby Clark
Johnson City, Tennessee

CAESAR SALAD

Prep: 10 minutes

¾ cup olive oil
¼ cup red wine vinegar
6 anchovy fillets
4 garlic cloves, minced
1 tablespoon lemon juice
1 tablespoon Dijon mustard
½ teaspoon pepper
1 cup freshly shredded Parmesan
   cheese
2 (10-ounce) packages chopped
   hearts of Romaine lettuce
1 (5.5-ounce) package large
   Caesar-style croutons

• **Process** first 7 ingredients in a food processor until smooth.
• **Add** Parmesan cheese; process until blended. Toss with lettuce. Top with croutons. **Yield:** 8 servings.

Terri Cohen
North Potomac, Maryland

1999 Top-Rated Menu

All of these praiseworthy dishes, published last year, are now members of our "best" hall of fame. If you didn't have a chance to try them before, enjoy this sampling as a menu.

Menu for Four
Serves 4

Parmesan Cheese Bites
Lamb Chops With Minted Apples
Margaret's Creamy Grits
Steamed baby carrots
1-2-3 Blackberry Sherbet

PARMESAN CHEESE BITES

Prep: 20 minutes
Chill: 8 hours
Bake: 15 minutes

1 cup all-purpose flour
⅔ cup grated Parmesan cheese
¼ teaspoon ground red pepper
½ cup butter or margarine, cut up
2 tablespoons milk

• **Stir** together first 3 ingredients in a medium bowl.
• **Cut** in butter with a pastry blender until crumbly. (Mixture will look very dry.) Gently press mixture together with hands, working until blended and smooth (about 2 to 3 minutes).
• **Shape** dough into 2 (4-inch-long) logs. Wrap in plastic wrap, and place in an airtight container. Chill 8 hours, or freeze up to 3 months. (Thaw overnight in refrigerator.)
• **Cut** log into ¼-inch-thick slices, and place on a lightly greased baking sheet. Brush with milk.
• **Bake** at 350° for 12 to 15 minutes or until lightly browned. Freeze cheese bites up to 1 month, if desired. **Yield:** 32 cheese bites.

Note: Dough may be rolled into a 10- x 7-inch (¼-inch-thick) rectangle on a lightly floured surface. Cut lengthwise into 8 strips and crosswise into 4 strips, using a pastry wheel or knife and forming 32 squares. Place cheese squares on a lightly greased baking sheet, and bake immediately.

Caryn Nabors
Gadsden, Alabama

LAMB CHOPS WITH MINTED APPLES

Guests will applaud when you serve this impressive entrée or its pork variation that follows. A dry rub made with rosemary, sage, and other herbs and spices seasons the succulent lamb.

Prep: 1 hour, 10 minutes
Bake: 45 minutes

1 garlic bulb
1 tablespoon olive oil
8 (2-inch-thick) lamb chops, trimmed
1 tablespoon Biltmore Dry Rub
Minted Apples

• **Cut** off pointed end of garlic bulb, and place garlic bulb on a piece of aluminum foil.
• **Drizzle** garlic with olive oil, and fold foil to seal.
• **Bake** at 425° for 30 minutes. Cool and peel 12 cloves, reserving any remaining cloves for other uses.
• **Sprinkle** lamb evenly with Biltmore Dry Rub, and place on a lightly greased rack in a broiler pan.
• **Bake** lamb at 325° for 45 minutes or until a meat thermometer inserted into thickest portion of lamb registers 145° (medium-rare). Reserve ¼ cup drippings for Minted Apples. Serve lamb with Minted Apples and roasted garlic. **Yield:** 4 servings.

Biltmore Dry Rub

Prep: 10 minutes

¼ cup salt
½ teaspoon onion powder
½ teaspoon ground celery seeds
½ teaspoon garlic powder
½ teaspoon paprika
½ teaspoon pepper
¼ teaspoon dried rosemary
¼ teaspoon ground sage
¼ teaspoon dried dillweed

• **Combine** all ingredients. Store in an airtight container up to 6 months. Use to season lamb, pork, chicken, or steak. **Yield:** about ¼ cup.

Minted Apples

Prep: 10 minutes
Cook: 12 minutes

3 tablespoons butter
2 shallots, thinly sliced
1 garlic clove, minced
2 tablespoons sugar
3 Granny Smith apples, peeled and
    sliced
⅓ cup apple cider vinegar
¼ cup reserved lamb drippings or
    bacon drippings
2 tablespoons mint jelly
2 teaspoons chopped fresh mint
    (optional)

• **Melt** butter in a large skillet over low heat; add shallots and garlic, and sauté until tender. Stir in sugar.
• **Add** apple, and cook, stirring occasionally, 3 minutes or until lightly caramelized.
• **Add** vinegar, lamb drippings, and mint jelly.
• **Cook,** stirring occasionally, 6 to 8 minutes. Serve immediately, or chill, if desired; reheat just before serving. Sprinkle with fresh mint, if desired. **Yield:** 4 servings.

Pork Chops With Minted Apples: Substitute 4 (2-inch-thick) bone-in pork chops for 8 lamb chops. Sprinkle evenly with 2 teaspoons Biltmore Dry Rub. Bake at 325° for 45 minutes or until a meat thermometer inserted into thickest portion registers 160°. Remove chops, and add ¼ cup water to pan; cook over medium heat 2 minutes, stirring to loosen browned bits. Substitute mixture for ¼ cup reserved drippings in Minted Apples. Garnish with fresh sage and rosemary, if desired.

Executive Chef Stephen Adams
Biltmore Estate

MARGARET'S CREAMY GRITS

Prep: 10 minutes
Cook: 10 minutes

2 cups half-and-half or whipping
    cream
¼ teaspoon salt
⅛ teaspoon granulated garlic
⅛ teaspoon pepper
½ cup uncooked quick-cooking
    grits
2 ounces cream cheese, cubed
¾ cup (3 ounces) shredded sharp
    Cheddar cheese
¼ teaspoon hot sauce

• **Bring** first 4 ingredients to a boil in a Dutch oven; gradually stir in grits. Return to a boil; cover, reduce heat, and simmer, stirring occasionally, 5 to 7 minutes or until thickened.
• **Add** cheeses and hot sauce, stirring until cheeses melt. Serve immediately. **Yield:** 4 servings.

1-2-3 BLACKBERRY SHERBET

Prep: 15 minutes
Stand: 30 minutes
Freeze: 11 hours

4 cups fresh blackberries *
2 cups sugar
2 cups buttermilk
Garnishes: blackberries, fresh mint
    sprigs

• **Stir** together 4 cups blackberries and sugar in a large bowl; let mixture stand 30 minutes.
• **Process** blackberry mixture in a food processor or blender until smooth, stopping to scrape down sides. Pour blackberry mixture through a fine wire-mesh strainer into a 9-inch square pan, discarding solids; stir in buttermilk. Cover mixture, and freeze 8 hours.
• **Break** frozen mixture into chunks, and place in bowl; beat at medium speed with an electric mixer until smooth. Return to pan; cover and freeze 3 hours or until firm. Garnish, if desired. **Yield:** 1 quart.

* Substitute 2 (14-ounce) packages frozen blackberries, thawed, for fresh blackberries, if desired.

Arlene P. Rogers
Louisville, Kentucky

A Taste of the South

Black-eyed peas and cornbread start the year right and inaugurate our new column celebrating classic Southern foods.

You might call them soul mates, the humble, nutritious black-eyed pea and the savory quick bread made from corn. Individually they are tasty, but together these two foods approach the sublime. Both of these recipes can be ready to cook in less than 20 minutes and make a great addition to almost any meal.

HEARTY BLACK-EYED PEAS

In a pinch, canned black-eyed peas doctored with chopped country ham or smoked sausage make a respectable 10-minute substitute for this Southern classic.

Prep: 20 minutes
Cook: 1 hour

1 (16-ounce) package dried black-eyed peas
4 cups water
1 medium onion, chopped
½ teaspoon pepper
¾ teaspoon salt
1 (1-pound) ham steak, cut into ½-inch cubes, or 1 ham hock
4 whole jalapeño peppers (optional)

• **Bring** first 6 ingredients and, if desired, jalapeño peppers to a boil in a Dutch oven.
• **Cover,** reduce heat, and simmer 1 hour or until peas are tender. **Yield:** 8 servings.

SKILLET CORNBREAD

"A well-seasoned cast-iron skillet is a must for a golden brown crust," says John Martin Taylor. Turn hot cornbread onto a plate, bottom side up, to preserve its crunchy texture.*

Prep: 10 minutes
Bake: 15 minutes

2 teaspoons bacon drippings
1 large egg
2 cups buttermilk
1¾ cups white cornmeal
1 teaspoon baking powder
1 teaspoon baking soda
1 teaspoon salt

• **Coat** bottom and sides of a 10-inch cast-iron skillet with bacon drippings. Heat in a 450° oven.
• **Stir** together egg and buttermilk. Add cornmeal, stirring well.
• **Stir** in baking powder, soda, and salt. Pour batter into hot skillet.
• **Bake** at 450° for 15 minutes or until lightly browned. **Yield:** 6 servings.

Note: This recipe is adapted from *Hoppin' John's Lowcountry Cooking* by John Martin Taylor.

A SOUTHERN TRADITION

On a chilly day, a bowl of steaming peas served with a wedge of fresh-from-the-oven cornbread is a meal few Southerners would turn down. These dishes are inexpensive standbys that have evolved with the times.

Cooks use them in inventive dishes: Black-eyed peas show up in salads and fritters, and cornbread, studded with jalapeños or dotted with herbs, is used to stuff *everything*.

Peas come fresh, frozen, dried, and canned—take your pick. We prefer fresh or dried, which require up to an hour of cooking time.

Cornbread mixes, like favorite recipes, vary in the color of cornmeal used (white is traditional), flavor, and texture. Cornbread can be a sturdy, slightly salty round with a rich buttermilk twang like the traditional version offered here, or sweet and crumbly with a cakelike texture. The latter gets its dainty, high-rising ways from flour and sugar, two hotly debated ingredients.

In his book *More Than Moonshine*, Tennessean Sidney Saylor Farr wrote, "Even if we only had soup and beans, fried potatoes and greens to eat, as long as we had a pan of hot corn bread, it was a fine meal."

Today, when most of us have all the food we want or need, we still revere these two simple heritage foods: black-eyed peas and cornbread. Perhaps it's because they connect us to our childhood, our ancestors, and our region's storied past.

Quick & Easy

Spicy chili-garlic paste is a favorite ingredient in our kitchens. Flavored with red chiles and garlic, this product adds both heat and zest, often allowing you to reduce the overall number of ingredients in recipes.

To complement the spiciness in these meal-in-one dishes, serve a salad with cool buttermilk dressing. Barbecue Pork Sandwiches pair well with creamy coleslaw.

If you are unable to find chili-garlic paste at your supermarket, call Pacific Mercantile Company at (303) 295-0293.

BARBECUE PORK SANDWICHES

Prep: 15 minutes
Bake: 30 minutes

1 (1½-pound) package pork
   tenderloins
3 cups hot water
⅔ cup ketchup
3 tablespoons soy sauce
2 tablespoons hoisin sauce
2 tablespoons honey
2 tablespoons chili-garlic paste
6 hamburger buns

- **Place** pork tenderloins on a lightly greased rack in a broiler pan; add 3 cups hot water to pan (to prevent drippings from burning).
- **Stir** together ketchup and next 4 ingredients; divide sauce in half. Reserve half of sauce to toss with cooked pork.
- **Bake** pork at 475° for 15 minutes. Turn pork, and brush with remaining half of sauce.
- **Bake** 15 more minutes or until a meat thermometer inserted into thickest portion of pork registers 160°. Cool slightly. Coarsely chop pork, and toss with reserved sauce. Serve on buns. **Yield:** 6 servings.

GARLIC-CHILI SHRIMP AND GRITS

Prep: 8 minutes
Cook: 20 minutes

1 bunch fresh asparagus
3¼ cups chicken broth, divided
1 cup uncooked quick-cooking
   grits
½ cup half-and-half
6 tablespoons butter or margarine,
   divided
1½ tablespoons chili-garlic paste,
   divided
1 bunch green onions, cut into
   ½-inch pieces
1 pound peeled, large fresh
   shrimp
2 tablespoons lemon juice
1 teaspoon salt

- **Snap** off tough ends of asparagus. Cut into 1-inch pieces, and set aside.
- **Bring** 3 cups chicken broth to a boil in a medium saucepan over medium-high heat; whisk in grits and half-and-half.
- **Cook**, whisking constantly, 7 minutes or until thickened. Remove from heat.
- **Stir** in 4 tablespoons butter and 1½ teaspoons chili-garlic paste. Set grits aside; keep warm.
- **Melt** remaining 2 tablespoons butter in a large skillet over medium-high heat. Add asparagus and green onions, and sauté 3 to 4 minutes.
- **Add** shrimp and remaining ¼ cup chicken broth, and cook mixture 2 to 3 minutes.
- **Stir** in remaining 1 tablespoon chili-garlic paste, lemon juice, and salt; cook 3 minutes or just until shrimp turn pink. Serve immediately over warm grits. **Yield:** 4 servings.

THAI CHICKEN STIR-FRY

This colorful stir-fry relies on traditional Thai ingredients—coconut milk, peanut butter, and dark sesame oil—for its fabulous flavor.

Prep: 25 minutes
Cook: 20 minutes

1 (14-ounce) can coconut milk,
   divided
1 cup water
½ teaspoon salt
1 cup uncooked long-grain rice
3 tablespoons creamy peanut
   butter
2 tablespoons soy sauce
2 teaspoons chili-garlic paste
2 tablespoons dark sesame
   oil
2 skinned and boned chicken
   breast halves, cubed
3 green onions, diagonally
   sliced
1 medium-size red bell pepper,
   cut into thin strips

- **Bring** 1 cup coconut milk, 1 cup water, and salt to a boil in a medium saucepan.
- **Stir** in rice; cover, reduce heat, and simmer 20 minutes.
- **Whisk** together remaining coconut milk, peanut butter, soy sauce, and chili-garlic paste until blended.
- **Heat** sesame oil in a large skillet or wok over medium-high heat 2 minutes.
- **Add** chicken, and stir-fry 5 minutes or until browned. Add green onions and bell pepper.
- **Cook**, covered, stirring occasionally, 10 minutes.
- **Add** peanut butter mixture, and bring to a boil.
- **Cook**, stirring constantly, 3 minutes. Serve over rice. **Yield:** 2 or 3 servings.

Living Light

Healthful foods that taste great are easy to come by here. Cook any of these delectable edibles and rejoice in the fact that they're *really* good for you. Many have even been proven to influence our well-being. We focused on a few (spinach, oranges, sweet potatoes, black-eyed peas, and carrots) and incorporated them into recipes you can easily include in your diet.

These particular foods are packed with vitamins and other important substances that help the body stay healthy. See "Powerful Foods" in the box at right to learn why they are so important.

TANGY SPINACH SALAD

Prep: 15 minutes
Cook: 7 minutes

6 turkey bacon slices
3 tablespoons lemon juice
2 tablespoons brown sugar
2 tablespoons Dijon mustard
1 (10-ounce) package fresh spinach, torn
1 (8-ounce) package sliced fresh mushrooms

• **Cook** bacon in a large skillet over medium-high heat until crisp; remove bacon, reserving drippings in skillet. Crumble bacon, and set aside.
• **Add** lemon juice, brown sugar, and mustard to skillet.
• **Cook** mixture over low heat, stirring constantly, 1 minute.
• **Toss** together spinach, mushrooms, and lemon juice mixture. Sprinkle with bacon. **Yield:** 4 servings.

Mrs. Carl M. Schmieg
Annandale, Virginia

♥ Per serving: Calories 104 (34% from fat)
Fat 4.0g (sat 0.8g, mono 1.5g, poly 1.0g)
Protein 6.2g Carb 11.3g Fiber 3.6g
Cholesterol 15mg Iron 3.1mg
Sodium 583mg Calcium 87mg

ORANGE-OATMEAL MUFFINS

Purchase extra oranges to slice and serve with these muffins.

Prep: 6 minutes
Bake: 15 minutes

1 cup all-purpose flour
1 tablespoon baking powder
½ teaspoon salt
1 cup quick-cooking oats
¼ cup sugar
1 large egg, lightly beaten
1 tablespoon grated orange rind
½ cup fresh orange juice
¼ cup fat-free milk
2 tablespoons vegetable oil
Vegetable cooking spray
2 tablespoons sugar
½ teaspoon grated orange rind
¼ teaspoon ground cinnamon

• **Combine** first 5 ingredients in a large bowl; make a well in center of mixture.
• **Stir** together egg and next 4 ingredients. Add to flour mixture, stirring just until dry ingredients are moistened.
• **Spoon** into muffin pans coated with cooking spray, filling three-fourths full.
• **Stir** together 2 tablespoons sugar, ½ teaspoon grated rind, and ¼ teaspoon cinnamon until blended.
• **Sprinkle** sugar mixture evenly over tops of muffins.
• **Bake** at 400° for 15 minutes or until muffins are lightly browned. Remove from pans immediately, and cool on a wire rack. **Yield:** 10 muffins.

Melanie Gonterman
Louisville, Kentucky

♥ Per muffin: Calories 157 (28% from fat)
Fat 4.9g (sat 0.8g, mono 1.1g, poly 2.5g)
Protein 3.5g Carb 24.8g Fiber 1.2g
Cholesterol 22mg Iron 1.2mg
Sodium 274mg Calcium 100mg

POWERFUL FOODS

■ **Black-eyed peas** contain soluble fiber, which aids in reducing blood cholesterol. They also decrease the risk of some cancers.

■ **Carrots** are rich in beta carotene and soluble fiber, which lowers blood cholesterol. They can even aid in preventing strokes.

■ **Oranges** and other citrus fruits have limonene, which boosts cancer-fighting enzymes in the body.

■ **Spinach,** high in folic acid, may help to prevent depression. Eating lots of spinach has also been shown to lessen the chances of age-related blindness.

■ **Sweet potatoes,** rich in beta carotene, reduce the risk of some forms of cancer.

OVEN-ROASTED SWEET POTATOES AND ONIONS

Prep: 10 minutes
Bake: 35 minutes

4 medium-size sweet potatoes (about 2¼ pounds)
2 medium-size sweet onions
1 tablespoon olive oil
½ teaspoon garlic pepper
¼ teaspoon salt
Vegetable cooking spray

• **Peel** sweet potatoes, and cut each into 2-inch pieces. Cut onions into 1-inch pieces.
• **Toss** together sweet potato, onion, oil, and seasonings in a 15- x 10-inch jelly-roll pan coated with cooking spray.

- **Bake** at 425° for 35 minutes or until tender, stirring mixture occasionally. **Yield:** 6 servings.

Note: For testing purposes only, we used Lawry's Garlic Pepper Blend.

Joy Howell
Anniston, Alabama

♥ Per serving: Calories 221 (13% from fat)
Fat 3.3g (sat 0.5g, mono 1.7g, poly 0.7g)
Protein 3.3g Carb 45.4g Fiber 6.0g
Cholesterol 0mg Iron 1.1mg
Sodium 145mg Calcium 47mg

NEW YEAR'S DAY SOUP

Prep: 20 minutes
Cook: 1 hour, 30 minutes

1 cup diced smoked lean ham
2 celery ribs, chopped
1 medium onion, chopped
2 carrots, chopped
2 garlic cloves, minced
2 (15-ounce) cans black-eyed peas, undrained
2 (14½-ounce) cans low-sodium, fat-free chicken broth
2 (14½-ounce) cans no-salt-added stewed tomatoes, undrained
1 (14½-ounce) can no-salt-added diced tomatoes, undrained
1 (8-ounce) can tomato sauce
1½ cups chopped fresh spinach
½ cup chopped fresh parsley
½ teaspoon pepper
Garnish: chopped fresh spinach

- **Sauté** first 5 ingredients over medium heat in a Dutch oven until vegetables are tender. Stir in peas and next 4 ingredients; bring to a boil. Cover, reduce heat, and simmer 1 hour and 30 minutes.
- **Stir** in 1½ cups chopped spinach, parsley, and pepper. Garnish, if desired. **Yield:** 10 cups.

Chris Schrang
Cumming, Georgia

♥ Per cup: Calories 144 (9% from fat)
Fat 1.4g (sat 0.5g, mono 0.4g, poly 0.3g)
Protein 9.1g Carb 24.5g Fiber 6.3g
Cholesterol 7mg Iron 2.5mg
Sodium 538mg Calcium 80mg

EXPANDED NUTRITIONAL ANALYSIS

This year we're adding more nutritional Information on "Living Light" recipes to arm you with knowledge about the foods you eat. Here's the new information we're including.

Percent of calories from fat: 30% or less is considered low fat.

Saturated fat (sat): Type of fat that increases LDL cholesterol, known as "bad" cholesterol, which contributes to heart disease. Less than 10% of total calories per day should come from saturated fat. Primary sources are animal fat, butter, stick margarine, coconut oil, and palm oil.

Monounsaturated fat (mono): Type of fat that may lower LDL cholesterol. Olive, canola, and peanut oils contain large proportions of monounsaturated fat. No more than 15% of calories per day should come from monounsaturated fat.

Polyunsaturated fat (poly): Type of fat that may lower LDL cholesterol. Sunflower, soybean, safflower, and corn oils contain large proportions of polyunsaturated fat. Omega-3 fatty acids, found in some varieties of fish, also contain large amounts of polyunsaturated fat. No more than 10% of calories should come from polyunsaturated fat.

Protein: Nutrient essential for life and dietary source of energy. Only 15% of total calories should come from protein. Meat, eggs, dairy products, and legumes are excellent sources.

Carbohydrate (Carb): Principal dietary source of energy; 55% to 60% of total calories per day should come from carbohydrates. Whole grains, fruits, vegetables, and legumes are excellent sources.

Fiber: Nondigestible carbohydrate that may reduce the incidence of colon cancer and help reduce cholesterol levels. Fiber is highest in fruits, vegetables, legumes, and whole grains; 25 to 30 grams of fiber per day is recommended.

Iron: Essential nutrient for red blood cell production. Women need about 15 milligrams per day, while men need about 10 milligrams per day. Iron-rich foods include red meat, eggs, vegetables, and fortified cereals.

Calcium: Essential nutrient for strong bones and teeth. Helps prevent osteoporosis. Both women and men need about 800 to 1,200 milligrams per day (depending on age). Dairy products and some leafy green vegetables are excellent sources.

For more information on nutrition or to contact a dietitian in your area, visit the American Dietetic Association Web site at www.eatright.org.

Spinach With Panache

Spinach is rich in vitamins A and C, plus potassium and iron. And it's higher in protein than most vegetables. Discover the goodness of spinach in these three delicious dishes.

SPINACH BURGERS

Prep: 20 minutes
Cook: 10 minutes

1 (10-ounce) package frozen chopped spinach, thawed
2 pounds lean ground beef
½ cup fine, dry breadcrumbs
½ cup (2 ounces) shredded Cheddar cheese
2 tablespoons Worcestershire sauce
1 teaspoon garlic powder
⅛ teaspoon salt
⅛ teaspoon pepper
8 hamburger buns
Leaf lettuce
Tomato slices

• **Drain** spinach well, pressing between layers of paper towels.
• **Combine** spinach, beef, and next 6 ingredients. Shape into 8 patties.
• **Cook** in a large skillet over medium-high heat 5 minutes on each side or until beef is no longer pink. Serve on hamburger buns with lettuce and tomato. **Yield:** 8 servings.

Note: Burgers may be grilled, covered with grill lid, over medium-high heat (350° to 400°) 5 minutes on each side or until beef is no longer pink.
Anna T. Rucker
Norfolk, Virginia

SPINACH-ARTICHOKE DIP

To serve a smaller group, cut the ingredients in half, and bake dip in an 8-inch square baking dish.

Prep: 15 minutes
Bake: 20 minutes

1 (10-ounce) package frozen chopped spinach, thawed
1 (14-ounce) can artichoke heart quarters, drained
1 (5.5-ounce) container garlic-and-herb soft spreadable cheese
1 cup shredded Parmesan cheese
1 (8-ounce) container sour cream
½ cup mayonnaise
1 (2-ounce) jar chopped pimiento, drained
6 bacon slices, cooked and crumbled

• **Drain** spinach well, pressing between layers of paper towels.
• **Stir** together spinach and next 6 ingredients. Spoon into a lightly greased 11-x 7-inch baking dish.
• **Bake** at 400° for 20 minutes or until bubbly. Sprinkle with bacon. Serve with crackers or chips. **Yield:** 8 servings.

Note: For testing purposes only, we used Alouette Garlic and Herbes Gourmet Spreadable Cheese for garlic-and-herb soft spreadable cheese.
Meg Culp
Chapel Hill, North Carolina

SPINACH PIE

Prep: 30 minutes
Bake: 30 minutes

½ (15-ounce) package refrigerated piecrusts
1 (10-ounce) package frozen chopped spinach, thawed
2 tablespoons butter or margarine
1 small onion, chopped
1 small red bell pepper, chopped
2 celery ribs, chopped
4 garlic cloves, minced
2 tablespoons all-purpose flour
3 large eggs, lightly beaten
1 (4-ounce) package feta cheese, crumbled
1 tablespoon dried parsley
½ teaspoon dried dillweed
¼ teaspoon salt
¼ teaspoon pepper
¼ cup grated Parmesan cheese

• **Fit** piecrust into a 9-inch pieplate according to package directions; fold edges under, and crimp.
• **Bake** crust at 400° for 7 minutes. Remove from oven. Set aside.
• **Drain** spinach well, pressing between layers of paper towels; set aside.
• **Melt** butter in a large skillet over medium heat; add onion and next 3 ingredients, and sauté 5 minutes or until tender.
• **Stir** in flour; cook, stirring constantly, 1 minute.
• **Stir** together spinach, onion mixture, eggs, and next 5 ingredients. Pour into piecrust.
• **Bake** at 350° for 25 minutes. Sprinkle evenly with Parmesan cheese, and bake 5 more minutes or until set. Cool 10 minutes. **Yield:** 8 servings.

Pudding Perfection

If you're like most people, you grew up enjoying pudding that started out from a little box. You're in for a treat here. These silky concoctions are superbly flavorful. Serve them when you want a dessert that's chic, casual, and smoothly satisfying.

PEANUT BUTTER PUDDING

Prep: 5 minutes
Cook: 12 minutes
Chill: 2 hours

½ cup sugar
2 tablespoons cornstarch
¼ teaspoon salt
1½ cups milk
½ cup half-and-half
¾ cup creamy peanut butter
1 teaspoon vanilla extract
Garnishes: whipped cream, chocolate curls

• **Combine** first 3 ingredients in a medium-size heavy saucepan; gradually whisk in milk and half-and-half.
• **Bring** to a boil over medium heat, whisking constantly.
• **Boil,** whisking constantly, 1 minute. Remove pudding from heat. (Pudding will be thin.)
• **Add** peanut butter and vanilla, whisking until smooth.
• **Pour** pudding into a bowl; place plastic wrap directly over warm pudding. Chill 2 hours. Garnish, if desired. **Yield:** 2½ cups.

Ellie Wells
Lakeland, Florida

VANILLA CREAM

This classic recipe was the filling for a fabulous vanilla cream pie in 1984. We made slight adjustments to update it.

Prep: 5 minutes
Cook: 12 minutes
Chill: 2 hours

¾ cup sugar
5 tablespoons cornstarch
⅛ teaspoon salt
3 egg yolks
3 cups milk or half-and-half
2 tablespoons butter or margarine
1 teaspoon vanilla extract

• **Combine** first 3 ingredients in a medium-size heavy saucepan.
• **Whisk** together egg yolks and milk; gradually add to sugar mixture. Whisk until smooth.
• **Bring** to a boil over medium heat, whisking constantly.
• **Boil,** whisking constantly, 1 minute. Remove from heat; whisk in butter and vanilla.
• **Pour** pudding into a bowl; place plastic wrap directly over warm pudding. Cool 30 minutes. Chill 2 hours. **Yield:** 4 cups.

Almond Cream: Decrease milk to 1 cup. Whisk together egg yolks, 2 cups half-and-half, and 1 cup milk; follow directions for Vanilla Cream. Substitute 1 teaspoon almond extract for vanilla extract. Garnish with toasted almond slices. **Yield:** 4 cups.

Coconut Cream: Decrease milk to 2 cups. Whisk together egg yolks, 2 cups milk, ½ cup cream of coconut, and ¾ cup pineapple juice; follow directions for Vanilla Cream. Omit vanilla extract, and substitute 1 (6-ounce) package frozen coconut, thawed. **Yield:** 5 cups.

Coffee Cream: Add ½ cup strong brewed coffee to egg yolk mixture; follow directions for Vanilla Cream. **Yield:** 4½ cups.

Orange Cream: Decrease milk to 2 cups. Whisk together egg yolks, 2 cups milk, 1 tablespoon grated orange rind, and 1 cup fresh orange juice; follow directions for Vanilla Cream. Substitute 2 tablespoons orange liqueur for vanilla extract. Garnish with orange rind curls. **Yield:** 4 cups.

SMOOTH MOVES

Jan Moon of our Test Kitchens developed several of the recipes for this story. Here are her tips for great results.

■ For the smoothest texture, stir with a whisk.

■ Don't boil the mixture more than a minute, or the cornstarch will break down and the pudding will be thin.

■ Be sure to chill pudding the required amount of time.

■ Don't stir the pudding after it has chilled, or it will lose its body.

From Our Kitchen

The Wonders of Rosemary

The fragrance of rosemary leaves is described as a combination of pine and nutmeg, while the flavor is somewhat peppery, warm, spicy, and resinous. It's wonderful with lamb, pork, and veal dishes, and it gives a robust boost to roasted vegetables. Use the woody stems as skewers for kabobs. Toss large, leafy stems onto hot coals for additional flavor to grilled food.

Explore the wonders of rosemary and other herbs that help you feel good while they taste good. The versatile herb is said to improve memory, help migraine headaches, retard hair loss, and stimulate the circulatory system.

Tips and Tidbits

■ Be careful what you use in your microwave oven. Unless containers and plastic wraps are labeled "microwave safe," cooking and heating in them could make you sick. Some foam containers and plastics melt in and on food when heated. Ingestion of these particles is unhealthy.

■ January is Oatmeal Month, the perfect excuse to bake dozens of oatmeal cookies. But don't stop there. Because oats are high in fiber, low in fat, and great for lowering cholesterol, take advantage of the many ways they're available.

Do You Know Your Oats?

■ **Groats** are the oat grain that has had the outer husk removed.

■ **Steel-cut oats** are groats that have been sliced one or two times.

■ **Rolled oats** are groats that have been softened by steam and flattened on rollers to form flakes.

■ **Old-fashioned oats** are rolled oats made from larger pieces of groats.

■ **Quick oats** are the smaller pieces of rolled oats.

■ **Instant oats** are even smaller pieces of rolled oats and may be cooked by mixing with very hot water.

Here are 10 tasty ways to make oats part of your diet.

1. Add oat bran, rolled oats, or oat flour to casseroles, stews, chili, and soups.

2. Use oat bran or oat flour to thicken sauces and gravies.

3. Soak rolled or steel-cut oats, and add to bread dough.

4. In bread recipes, substitute oat flour for about one-third of the flour specified.

5. Add oats to your cookies and pancakes, allowing up to ¼ cup oats per 1 cup of dough or batter.

6. Use oats instead of breadcrumbs as a binder in meat loaves.

7. Stir a spoonful of oat bran into scrambled eggs before pouring into the pan.

8. Use toasted oats as a crunchy topping on vegetables, casseroles, salads, yogurt, or fruit desserts.

9. Replace brown rice with groats. The cooking directions are the same.

10. Add oat bran to other hot cereals, allowing 2 to 4 tablespoons oat bran for each cup of grain and increasing the liquid by ½ to 1 cup.

GRATE ZEST

Have you ever omitted the grated citrus rind from a recipe because it was just too much trouble or you had unsatisfactory results? Now you can get perfect

shavings of rind with every stroke on the Microplane Stainless Steel Zester. The razor-sharp teeth shave instead of ripping and shredding. Our entire Foods staff agrees this is the best zester we've ever used.

Stroke the Microplane across the lemon as if you were playing the violin. Rind collects in the upper channel; the fine shavings are easy to collect and measure. The white pith (just under the rind) is very bitter, so stroke lightly to avoid it. This particular zester is also great for feathery grating of hard cheeses and fresh nutmeg.

The zester, and other Microplane graters, are available in kitchen shops for about $13.95. For more information or for a dealer near you, call 1-800-555-2767.

FEBRUARY

Tasting & Toasting

When Jackson, Mississippi, lawyer Charles Witt visits Dallas each spring, he takes with him a lifetime of cooking skills and a boundless passion for food. He shares both at a party where he is the star attraction. This annual event is a cooking lesson, wine tasting, and dinner party rolled into one great evening.

Dallas Dinner Party
Serves 6 to 8

Barbecue Shrimp
Smoked Chicken-and-Roasted Shallot Risotto
Crunchy Romaine Toss
Champagne Vanilla Zabaglione With Fruit

BARBECUE SHRIMP

Prep: 10 minutes
Bake: 10 minutes

16 unpeeled, jumbo fresh
     shrimp (1¼ pounds)
½ cup unsalted butter, sliced
¼ cup Worcestershire sauce
3 garlic cloves, chopped
2 tablespoons lemon juice
1 tablespoon Creole seasoning
1 tablespoon coarsely ground
     pepper
1 lemon, cut into 4 wedges

• **Stir** together all ingredients in an ovenproof skillet.
• **Bake** at 450° for 10 minutes or just until shrimp turn pink.
• **Serve** shrimp with crusty bread. **Yield:** 8 appetizer servings.

SMOKED CHICKEN-AND-ROASTED SHALLOT RISOTTO

Prep: 20 minutes
Bake: 30 minutes
Cook: 40 minutes

8 shallots, unpeeled
1 pound fresh asparagus
1½ tablespoons unsalted butter
1 medium onion, chopped
2 garlic cloves, minced
2 cups uncooked Arborio rice
½ cup dry red wine
7 cups hot chicken broth
2 cups chopped smoked chicken
1 small red bell pepper, chopped
1 (8-ounce) package sliced fresh
     mushrooms
1 cup freshly shredded Parmesan
     cheese
1 tablespoon chopped fresh
     rosemary
¼ teaspoon pepper

• **Place** shallots in an 8-inch square pan. Bake shallots at 425° for 30 minutes. Cool slightly; peel, coarsely chop, and set aside.
• **Snap** off tough ends of asparagus; cut into ¾-inch pieces.
• **Melt** butter in a Dutch oven over medium heat; add onion and garlic, and sauté 4 to 5 minutes.
• **Add** rice, and sauté 3 to 4 minutes. Add wine, and cook, stirring constantly, until liquid is absorbed.
• **Add** ½ cup broth, and cook, stirring constantly, until liquid is absorbed.
• **Repeat** with remaining broth, ½ cup at a time. (Cooking time is about 30 minutes.)
• **Add** shallots, asparagus, chicken, bell pepper, and mushrooms with last ½ cup broth. Stir in cheese, rosemary, and pepper. **Yield:** 8 servings.

CRUNCHY ROMAINE TOSS
(pictured on page 38)

Prep: 20 minutes
Bake: 10 minutes

1 (3-ounce) package ramen noodle
     soup mix
¼ cup unsalted butter
1 cup chopped walnuts
½ cup extra-virgin olive oil
¼ cup honey
⅓ cup white wine vinegar
¼ teaspoon salt
¼ teaspoon pepper
1 pound fresh broccoli, coarsely
     chopped
1 head Romaine lettuce, torn into
     pieces
4 green onions, chopped

• **Remove** flavor packet from soup mix; reserve for another use. Break noodles into ½-inch pieces.
• **Melt** butter in a pan in a 350° oven. Add noodles and walnuts.
• **Bake,** stirring occasionally, 10 minutes or until lightly browned.
• **Whisk** together oil and next 4 ingredients in a large bowl.
• **Add** walnut mixture, broccoli, lettuce, and chopped green onions, tossing to coat. **Yield:** 6 servings.

CHAMPAGNE VANILLA ZABAGLIONE WITH FRUIT

Zabaglione is a classic Italian dessert made with egg yolks, wine, and sugar. Here, champagne replaces the more traditional Marsala wine.

Prep: 10 minutes
Cook: 25 minutes
Broil: 1 minute

6 egg yolks
1 cup sugar
1 vanilla bean, cut in half
    lengthwise
1¼ cups champagne
1 cup fresh blueberries
1 cup fresh raspberries
1 cup sliced fresh strawberries
2 ripe bananas, sliced

• **Whisk** together egg yolks and sugar in top of a double boiler.
• **Scrape** vanilla bean seeds into egg mixture, and add bean halves.
• **Whisk** in champagne; bring water to a boil. Reduce heat to medium.
• **Cook,** whisking constantly, 20 minutes or until mixture is thickened. Discard vanilla bean halves.
• **Arrange** berries and banana slices in an 11- x 7-inch baking dish, or divide fruit among 8 (8-ounce) custard cups.
• **Pour** egg mixture over berries and banana in baking dish.
• **Broil** 6 inches from heat (with electric oven door partially open) 1 minute or until top is lightly browned. **Yield:** 8 servings.

"One of the things that makes this party so successful is that everyone rolls up his sleeves and gets involved."
Charles Witt

Guests to Charles Witt's annual party in Dallas know they'll enjoy great food, exceptional wines, and a chance to work alongside this agreeable gourmet.

Dallas resident Patty Blackburn, a close friend of Charles and Lynn Witt, started the tradition. "A few years ago Patty said, 'Maybe when you come to Dallas you can cook,'" Charles recalled. "So she and Anne Logan organized a gathering at Anne's home, where everyone could take part in the preparation. And the same group has come back every year."

This year, Charles selected about eight dishes to be tasted during the evening. He sent the recipes weeks earlier so that participants would know what they'd be preparing and so that Donovan Campbell, the group's wine expert, could select wines to complement the food.

The day of the party, Peter Bartholow chopped shallots with a wickedly sharp knife and a practiced hand, while Diana Macdonald admired the huge, heads-on shrimp that would be baked in a bath of spicy butter sauce.

After an afternoon of preparations, Charles' helpers headed home to freshen up, while he stopped to admire the wines. Among them was a 1983 Riesling Alsace Grand Cru that Donovan bought more than 15 years ago. "There were only four bottles left, so I brought them," Donovan said. "It's no fun having something wonderful and not sharing it."

The partygoers gradually reassembled as Charles and crew moved into high gear. The scene was one of barely controlled chaos. Charles was everywhere at once, instructing on technique, checking for doneness, sharing a laugh.

Each dish was served as it came off the stove, in no particular order. The group stood around Anne's spacious kitchen island and dug into risotto, succulent lamb, and crabmeat salad. But the last course, Champagne Vanilla Zabaglione With Fruit, garnered a toast with glasses of Muscat de Beaumes de Venise, a nectarlike dessert wine.

The guests gradually faded away, having done their share of eating, visiting, and dishwashing. At last, the cook got to put his feet up and relax with one last glass of St. Emilion 1982. He sighed and smiled broadly, "Well, I guess we can rest again until next year."

Turn to "From Our Kitchen" on page 46 to learn more about serving wines at similar gatherings in your own home.

Top-Rated Menu

Dinner's ready in 35 minutes—if you plan ahead and follow our countdown guide. These members of our hall of fame once again received high praise and make up this simple menu.

Plan-Ahead Menu
Serves 4

Crunchy Romaine Toss (recipe on page 30)
Pork Medaillons in Mustard Sauce
Carrot-Sweet Potato Puree
Green Beans With Caramelized Onion
Sour Cream Yeast Rolls
Hot Chocolate Deluxe   Pecan Toffee (recipe on page 42)

PORK MEDAILLONS IN MUSTARD SAUCE
(pictured on page 39)

Updates from 1990: Decreased oil, increased mustard, increased baking temperature.

Prep: 15 minutes
Chill: 8 hours
Bake: 30 minutes

2   tablespoons vegetable oil
2   tablespoons coarse-grained mustard
½   teaspoon salt
½   teaspoon coarsely ground pepper
1½ pounds pork tenderloin
¼   cup dry white wine or chicken broth
Mustard Sauce

• **Stir** together first 4 ingredients. Rub mixture over pork, and place in a large heavy-duty zip-top plastic bag. Seal bag; chill 8 hours. Place pork on a lightly greased rack in a shallow roasting pan.

• **Bake** at 450° for 15 minutes. Reduce temperature to 400°; bake 15 minutes or until a meat thermometer inserted into thickest portion registers 160°, basting with wine every 10 minutes. Slice and serve with Mustard Sauce. **Yield:** 4 servings.

Mustard Sauce

Prep: 5 minutes
Cook: 21 minutes

1¾ cups whipping cream
¼   cup coarse-grained mustard
¼   teaspoon salt
⅛   teaspoon ground white pepper

• **Cook** whipping cream in a heavy saucepan over medium heat until reduced to 1¼ cups (about 20 minutes). Do not boil.
• **Stir** in remaining ingredients, and cook 1 minute. **Yield:** 1¼ cups.

CARROT-SWEET POTATO PUREE
(pictured on page 39)

Updates from 1994: Substituted two cans of sweet potatoes for fresh sweet potatoes; included sour cream and grated lemon rind instead of yogurt.

Prep: 20 minutes
Cook: 17 minutes

5   carrots, sliced
¾   cup water
¼   cup butter or margarine
1   (29-ounce) can sweet potatoes, drained
1   (16-ounce) can sweet potatoes, drained
1   (8-ounce) container sour cream
1   tablespoon sugar
1   teaspoon grated lemon rind
½   teaspoon ground nutmeg
¼   teaspoon salt
¼   teaspoon ground black pepper
⅛   teaspoon ground red pepper

• **Microwave** carrot and ¾ cup water in a glass bowl at HIGH 10 to 12 minutes or until tender. Drain.
• **Process** carrot and butter in a food processor until mixture is smooth, stopping to scrape down sides. Transfer to a large bowl.
• **Process** both cans of sweet potatoes in food processor until smooth, stopping to scrape down sides. Add sweet potatoes to carrot mixture.
• **Stir** together sweet potato mixture, sour cream, and remaining ingredients.
• **Spoon** mixture into a 1½-quart glass dish. Cover and chill up to 2 days, if desired; let stand at room temperature 30 minutes.
• **Microwave** at HIGH 4 to 5 minutes or until thoroughly heated. **Yield:** 4 servings.

GREEN BEANS WITH CARAMELIZED ONION
(pictured on page 39)

Updates from 1995: Changed pearl onions to sweet onions and added a splash of balsamic vinegar.

Prep: 20 minutes
Cook: 25 minutes

1 pound fresh green beans
2 medium-size sweet onions
2 tablespoons butter or margarine
2 tablespoons brown sugar
1 to 2 teaspoons balsamic vinegar (optional)

• **Cook** green beans in boiling water to cover 15 minutes; drain and chill overnight, if desired.
• **Cut** onions into thin slices, and cut each slice in half.
• **Cook** onion in a nonstick skillet over medium-high heat 8 to 10 minutes (do not stir).
• **Cook,** stirring often, 5 to 10 minutes or until golden brown. Reduce heat to medium; stir in butter and brown sugar.
• **Add** green beans, and cook 5 minutes or until thoroughly heated. Toss green bean mixture with vinegar, if desired. **Yield:** 4 servings.

SOUR CREAM YEAST ROLLS

Update from 1990: Changed shape of roll from crescent to cloverleaf.

Prep: 45 minutes
Chill: 8 hours
Rise: 1 hour
Bake: 12 minutes

½ cup sour cream
¼ cup butter or margarine
¼ cup sugar
½ teaspoon salt
1 (¼-ounce) envelope active dry yeast
¼ cup warm water (100° to 110°)
1 large egg, lightly beaten
2 cups all-purpose flour
Melted butter

MENU PLAN

Menu Countdown

Up to 1 month ahead—Prepare, bake, and freeze rolls.

1 day ahead—Prepare Carrot-Sweet Potato Puree. Cook the green beans; chill. Marinate pork. Prepare Pecan Toffee.

35 minutes—Remove Carrot-Sweet Potato Puree from refrigerator, and remove rolls from freezer. Let stand at room temperature.

30 minutes—Place pork tenderloins in oven to bake.

28 minutes—Begin caramelizing onion for green beans. Begin preparing Crunchy Romaine Toss.

25 minutes—Begin preparing Mustard Sauce while the pork bakes and onion caramelizes.

15 minutes—Place rolls in oven with pork; microwave puree.

8 minutes—Measure ingredients for Hot Chocolate Deluxe.

5 minutes—Add cooked green beans to onion, and cook until thoroughly heated.

Wine Picks

Pork offers the flexibility to use a fuller bodied white wine or a lighter bodied red wine. These are some good selections.

White wines: Viognier, "Vin Du Mistral," Joseph Phelps; Riesling, Houge; Chardonnay, "Russian River Ranches," Sonoma-Cutrer.

Red wines: Pinot Noir, Rex Hill; Pinot Noir, Firesteed; Pinot Noir, Bridgeview Vineyard.

• **Cook** first 4 ingredients in a saucepan over low heat, stirring occasionally, until butter melts. Cool sour cream mixture to 100° to 110°.
• **Dissolve** yeast in ¼ cup warm water in a large mixing bowl; let stand 5 minutes.
• **Stir** in sour cream mixture and egg. Gradually add flour to yeast mixture, mixing well. (Dough will be wet.) Cover and chill 8 hours.
• **Punch** dough down. Shape into 36 (1-inch) balls; place 3 balls in each lightly greased muffin cup. Cover and let rise in a warm place (85°), free from drafts, 1 hour or until doubled in bulk.
• **Bake** at 375° for 10 to 12 minutes or until golden brown.
• **Brush** rolls with melted butter. Freeze up to 1 month, if desired. To reheat, wrap frozen rolls in aluminum foil, and bake at 400° for 15 minutes or until thoroughly heated. **Yield:** 1 dozen.

HOT CHOCOLATE DELUXE
(pictured on page 38)

1990 Recipe Hall of Fame

Prep: 10 minutes
Cook: 8 minutes

¼ cup boiling water
⅓ cup chocolate syrup
4 cups milk
⅓ to ½ cup coffee liqueur
Garnish: whipped cream

• **Stir** together ¼ cup boiling water and syrup in a saucepan. Add milk, stirring until blended. Cook over medium heat 6 to 8 minutes or until heated. Stir in liqueur. Garnish, if desired. **Yield:** 5 cups.

Note: For testing purposes only, we used Kahlúa for coffee liqueur.

What's for Supper?

Planning to serve chili tonight? Top it with your favorite Southwestern toppings, or try it Cincinnati style—steaming over pasta and piled high with onion, cheese, and beans. Round out the meal with crunchy raw vegetables, Quick Creamy Vegetable Dip, and crusty bread.

QUICK CREAMY VEGETABLE DIP

Prep: 20 minutes
Chill: 2 hours

½ cup mayonnaise
½ cup sour cream
1 (2-ounce) jar diced pimiento, drained
¼ cup chopped onion
¼ cup diced green bell pepper
½ teaspoon salt
⅛ teaspoon garlic powder
⅛ teaspoon pepper
⅛ teaspoon hot sauce

• **Stir** together all ingredients in a medium bowl. Cover dip, and chill 2 hours.
• **Serve** dip with raw vegetables or as a topping for chili or baked potatoes. **Yield:** about 1½ cups.

Charlotte Guttormsen
Titusville, Florida

THREE-BEAN CHILI

Prep: 10 minutes
Cook: 30 minutes

2 pounds ground chuck
1 large yellow onion, chopped
1 large green bell pepper, chopped
2 (14½-ounce) cans diced tomatoes with garlic and onion, undrained
1 (15-ounce) can tomato sauce
1 (15-ounce) can kidney beans, rinsed and drained
1 (15-ounce) can black beans, rinsed and drained
1 (15-ounce) can black-eyed peas, rinsed and drained
2 (1.6-ounce) envelopes chili seasoning
2 cups water
¼ teaspoon ground red pepper
1 tablespoon sugar (optional)
Toppings: shredded Monterey Jack-colby cheese, chopped green onions, sour cream, corn chips

• **Cook** first 3 ingredients in a large Dutch oven over high heat 10 minutes, stirring until beef crumbles and is no longer pink. Drain. Return to pan.
• **Stir** in diced tomatoes, next 7 ingredients, and, if desired, sugar. Cook over medium-high heat 20 minutes. Serve with desired toppings. **Yield:** 12 cups.

Wendy Hagen
Decatur, Alabama

CINCINNATI-STYLE CHILI

This hearty chili will delight diners with its blend of spices and cocoa.

Prep: 20 minutes
Cook: 40 minutes

1 pound ground beef
1 medium onion, chopped
2 garlic cloves, minced
2 (14½-ounce) cans Mexican-style stewed tomatoes, undrained
1 (8-ounce) can tomato sauce
1 cup water
2 tablespoons chili powder
1½ tablespoons cocoa
½ teaspoon ground cinnamon
¼ teaspoon ground allspice
8 ounces rotini or spaghetti, cooked
Toppings: chopped onion, shredded Cheddar cheese, kidney beans

• **Cook** first 3 ingredients in a Dutch oven over medium-high heat, stirring until ground beef crumbles and is no longer pink.
• **Drain** beef mixture, and return to Dutch oven.
• **Stir** stewed tomatoes and next 6 ingredients into beef mixture, and bring to a boil. Cover, reduce heat, and simmer, stirring occasionally, 30 minutes. Serve chili over hot cooked pasta with desired toppings. **Yield:** 10 cups.

Slow Cooker Cincinnati-Style Chili: Cook first 3 ingredients according to recipe directions; drain and place in a 4½-quart slow cooker.

Add tomatoes, tomato sauce, chili powder, and next 3 ingredients, omitting 1 cup water. Cover and cook at LOW 8 hours. Serve chili over hot cooked pasta with desired toppings.

Elaine C. Heintz
Staunton, Virginia

Quick & Easy

Omelets don't have to be intimidating. We offer you two easy ways to make them: a basic and a puffy method. In the basic method, the whole egg is beaten; in the puffy version, the egg yolks and whites are beaten separately. Whichever you make, you are sure to be delighted with the tasty results.

PUFFY DESSERT OMELET

When baking an omelet, be sure your pan has a handle that is ovenproof. If not, wrap the handle with aluminum foil to protect it from the heat.

Prep: 20 minutes
Cook: 6 minutes
Broil: 1 minute

1 pint fresh strawberries, sliced
2 tablespoons sugar
6 large eggs, separated
¼ teaspoon salt
¼ cup sugar
2 tablespoons all-purpose flour
2 teaspoons grated lemon rind
1 teaspoon vanilla extract
2 tablespoons butter or
    margarine
Sweetened whipped cream
Powdered sugar
Garnishes: strawberries, lemon
    twist

• **Toss** sliced strawberries with 2 tablespoons sugar; set aside.
• **Beat** egg whites and salt at high speed with an electric mixer until stiff peaks form. Beat egg yolks, ¼ cup sugar, and next 3 ingredients at medium speed until blended. Fold in beaten egg whites.
• **Melt** butter in a 10-inch ovenproof skillet over low heat.
• **Add** egg mixture to skillet.
• **Cook,** without stirring, 6 minutes or until bottom of omelet is golden. Remove skillet from heat.

• **Broil** 5½ inches from heat (with electric oven door partially open) 1 minute or until golden.
• **Invert** omelet onto a serving plate.
• **Top** with sliced sweetened strawberries, whipped cream, and powdered sugar. Garnish, if desired. **Yield:** 4 servings.

Ellie Wells
Lakeland, Florida

OMELET PIE

Prep: 15 minutes
Cook: 32 minutes
Stand: 5 minutes

2 cups frozen hash browns
1 cup chopped cooked ham
1 cup (4 ounces) shredded Cheddar
    cheese
4 green onions, thinly sliced
4 large eggs
½ cup milk
½ teaspoon salt
½ teaspoon pepper
Sour cream
Chopped fresh chives

• **Microwave** frozen hash browns in a lightly greased glass pieplate at HIGH 4 minutes or until thawed.
• **Press** hash browns into bottom of pieplate; microwave at HIGH 3 more minutes.
• **Sprinkle** hash browns with ham, cheese, and green onions.
• **Whisk** together eggs and next 3 ingredients in a bowl.
• **Pour** egg mixture over hash brown mixture. Cover pieplate with a sheet of wax paper.
• **Microwave** at MEDIUM-HIGH (70% power) 25 minutes or until omelet appears to be set. Let stand 5 minutes before serving. Top with sour cream; sprinkle with chives. **Yield:** 6 servings.

John N. Riggins
Nashville, Tennessee

SPANISH OMELET

Prep: 15 minutes
Cook: 25 minutes

¼ cup butter or margarine,
    divided
4 ounces sliced fresh mushrooms
    (1⅔ cups)
½ small onion, chopped
2 tablespoons chopped green bell
    pepper
½ (14½-ounce) can diced
    tomatoes with basil, garlic,
    and oregano
2 tablespoons tomato paste
1 bay leaf
⅛ teaspoon ground red pepper
8 large eggs
3 tablespoons milk
¼ teaspoon salt
¼ teaspoon pepper

• **Melt** 2 tablespoons butter in a saucepan over medium-high heat.
• **Add** sliced mushrooms, onion, and bell pepper, and sauté 7 minutes or until vegetables are tender.
• **Stir** in tomatoes and next 3 ingredients. Simmer, stirring occasionally, 10 minutes; discard bay leaf.
• **Melt** remaining 2 tablespoons butter in a large skillet over medium heat.
• **Whisk** together eggs and next 3 ingredients; add egg mixture to skillet.
• **Cook** 1 minute; gently lift edges of omelet with a spatula, and tilt pan so uncooked portion flows underneath. Cover and cook 6 to 8 minutes or until omelet is set.
• **Spoon** half of tomato sauce over omelet; fold in half. Transfer to a serving plate, and serve with remaining sauce. **Yield:** 3 to 4 servings.

Note: Reserve remaining ½ can tomatoes for another use.

Mariet Van den Munckhof-Vedder
Dublin, Georgia

A Taste of the South

*Few foods incite more discussion at our
tasting table than pound cake. Everyone has a
favorite recipe, and most of us have used
the same ones for decades. And that's why
we were so excited when our simplified pound
cake technique produced spectacular results.*

In fact, when we stumbled onto an extremely simple method of making our favorite pound cake, we doubted it would work twice. A procedure that broke all the rules—not adding the eggs one at a time, not alternating the milk and flour, not beating the butter and sugar together until fluffy—surely would be doomed to fail.

But we gave the method another whirl. Two additional tests produced beautiful cakes—tall, crusty on top, with a fine, velvety texture and buttery flavor. They were every bit as wonderful as their traditionally made counterparts.

TWO-STEP POUND CAKE
(pictured on facing page)

*You'll need a heavy-duty stand mixer
with a 4-quart bowl and a paddle
attachment to make this pound cake.
If you don't have the mixer, though, you
can prepare the pound cake using the
traditional method that follows.*

*Prep: 10 minutes
Bake: 1 hour, 30 minutes*

4 **cups all-purpose flour**
3 **cups sugar**
1 **pound butter, softened**
¾ **cup milk**
6 **large eggs**
2 **teaspoons vanilla extract**

• **Place** flour, sugar, butter, milk, eggs, and vanilla (in that order) in a 4-quart mixing bowl. Beat mixture at low speed with a heavy-duty electric mixer 1 minute, stopping to scrape down sides. Beat at medium speed 2 minutes. Pour batter into a greased and floured 10-inch tube pan.

• **Bake** at 325° for 1 hour and 30 minutes or until a wooden pick inserted in center comes out clean. Cool in pan on a wire rack 10 minutes. Remove cake from pan, and cool completely on wire rack. **Yield:** 1 (10-inch) cake.

Note: For testing purposes only, we used a KitchenAid mixer.

Traditional Method: Beat butter at medium speed with an electric mixer 2 minutes or until creamy; gradually add sugar, beating until light and fluffy. Add eggs, 1 at a time, beating after each addition.

Add flour to butter mixture alternately with milk, beginning and ending with flour. Beat at low speed just until blended after each addition. Stir in vanilla.

Pour batter into a greased and floured 10-inch tube pan. Bake cake as directed in two-step method.

STARTING POINTS

■ Dry measuring cups are crucial for measuring flour, sugar, and other dry ingredients.

■ To measure flour or sugar, spoon it into the dry measuring cup, and then sweep it level with the rim of the cup using the straight edge of a knife (see photo above). Do not pack flour.

■ Soften the butter to room temperature (don't melt it) before adding it to the mixture. Remove the butter from the refrigerator about 2 hours before you plan to use it. If you're in a hurry, cut it into cubes to speed the process.

■ Grease the sides and bottom of the pan with solid vegetable shortening; sprinkle it well with flour to cover the inside surfaces. Shake out any excess flour.

Two-Step Pound Cake, facing page

Crunchy Romaine Toss, page 30

Hot Chocolate Deluxe, page 33; Pecan Toffee, page 42

Pork Medaillons in Mustard Sauce,
Carrot-Sweet Potato Puree, Green Beans
With Caramelized Onion, pages 32-33

Pecan Toffee, page 42

Cream Cheese Mints, facing page

Raspberry-Fudge Truffles, facing page

Cherry-Pistachio Bark, facing page

Cupid's Confections

Flowers and cards are the expected gifts on Valentine's Day, so what about offering homemade confections instead? You can make these easy sweets ahead, and then the next time a special occasion arises, you'll have truffles and mints just a freezer step away.

CREAM CHEESE MINTS
(pictured on facing page)

Freeze in layers of wax paper in an airtight container.

Prep: 1 hour, 10 minutes
Stand: 4 hours

1 (8-ounce) package cream cheese
¼ cup butter, softened
1 (2-pound) package powdered sugar
½ teaspoon peppermint extract
6 drops red liquid food coloring (optional)
Powdered sugar

• **Cook** cream cheese and butter in a saucepan over low heat, stirring constantly, until smooth. Gradually stir in package of powdered sugar; stir in peppermint extract.
• **Divide** cream cheese mixture into 2 portions, if desired. Stir 2 drops coloring into 1 portion and remaining 4 drops coloring into second portion.
• **Shape** each portion of mixture into 1-inch balls. Dip a 2-inch round cookie stamp or bottom of a glass into powdered sugar.
• **Press** each ball to flatten. Let stand, uncovered, 4 hours or until firm. Freeze, if desired. **Yield:** 8 dozen.

Susan Cantrell
Birmingham, Alabama

CHERRY-PISTACHIO BARK
(pictured on facing page)

Lightly grease the cutter with cooking spray to make cutting easier.

Prep: 10 minutes
Cook: 10 minutes
Chill: 1 hour

1¼ cups dried cherries
2 tablespoons water
2 (12-ounce) packages white chocolate morsels
6 (2-ounce) vanilla candy coating squares
1¼ cups chopped red or green pistachios

• **Microwave** cherries and 2 tablespoons water in a small glass bowl at HIGH 2 minutes; drain.
• **Melt** chocolate morsels and candy coating in a heavy saucepan over low heat. Remove from heat; stir in cherries and pistachios. Spread into a wax paper-lined 15- x 10-inch jellyroll pan.
• **Chill** 1 hour or until firm. Cut with a 3-inch heart-shaped cookie cutter. Store in an airtight container. **Yield:** 3½ pounds.

RASPBERRY-FUDGE TRUFFLES
(pictured on facing page)

Use a sturdy wooden pick to dip well-chilled or frozen balls.

Prep: 30 minutes
Chill: 3 hours
Cook: 5 minutes

2 cups (12 ounces) semisweet chocolate morsels
2 (8-ounce) packages cream cheese, softened
1 cup seedless raspberry preserves
2 tablespoons raspberry liqueur
1½ cups vanilla wafer crumbs
10 (2-ounce) chocolate candy coating squares
3 (1-ounce) white chocolate squares
1 tablespoon shortening

• **Microwave** chocolate morsels in a 4-cup glass measuring cup at HIGH 1½ to 2½ minutes or until melted, stirring every 30 seconds.
• **Beat** cream cheese at medium speed with an electric mixer until smooth.
• **Add** melted chocolate, preserves, and liqueur, beating until blended.
• **Stir** in vanilla wafer crumbs; cover and chill 2 hours.
• **Shape** mixture into 1-inch balls; cover and freeze 1 hour or until firm.
• **Microwave** chocolate coating in a 4-cup glass measuring cup at HIGH 1½ to 2½ minutes or until melted, stirring every 30 seconds. Dip balls in coating; place on wax paper.
• **Place** white chocolate and shortening in a small heavy-duty zip-top plastic bag; seal bag. Submerge in hot water until chocolate melts; knead until smooth.
• **Snip** a tiny hole in 1 corner of bag, and drizzle mixture over truffles. Let stand until firm. Store in refrigerator or freezer, if desired. **Yield:** 6 dozen.

PECAN TOFFEE

(pictured on pages 38 and 40)

Nibble on this rich toffee and sip Hot Chocolate Deluxe as a delicious dessert for the menu on page 32.

Prep: 10 minutes
Cook: 15 minutes
Chill: 30 minutes

1½ cups chopped pecans, divided
1 cup sugar
1 cup butter, softened
⅓ cup water
5 (1.55-ounce) milk chocolate bars, broken into small pieces

• **Line** a 15- x 10-inch jellyroll pan with heavy-duty aluminum foil; lightly grease foil.
• **Sprinkle** foil with 1 cup pecans to within 1 inch of edges.
• **Bring** sugar, butter, and ⅓ cup water to a boil in a large heavy saucepan over medium heat, stirring constantly.
• **Cook** mixture over medium-high heat, stirring constantly, 12 minutes or until a candy thermometer registers 310° (hard crack stage).
• **Pour** hot mixture over pecans; sprinkle with chocolate pieces, and let stand 30 seconds.
• **Sprinkle** with remaining ½ cup pecans. Chill 30 minutes.
• **Break** up toffee using a mallet or rolling pin. Store in an airtight container. **Yield:** 1¾ pounds.

Living Light

Mix-and-match any of these dishes for a healthy and satisfying vegetable plate. Calling for inexpensive pantry items, each recipe serves four to six and easily adjusts to serve more.

TOMATO-STUFFED YELLOW SQUASH

Prep: 15 minutes
Cook: 15 minutes
Bake: 25 minutes

3 medium-size yellow squash
¼ cup chopped onion
3 garlic cloves, minced
2 teaspoons olive oil
3 plum tomatoes, peeled, seeded, and diced
2 tablespoons chopped fresh oregano
¼ teaspoon salt
¼ teaspoon freshly ground pepper
⅓ cup fine, dry breadcrumbs
1½ tablespoons shredded Parmesan cheese

• **Cook** squash in a saucepan in boiling water to cover 5 minutes or until tender; drain. Plunge into ice water to stop the cooking process, and drain. Cut squash in half lengthwise; carefully scoop out seeds, and discard. Set shells aside.
• **Sauté** onion and garlic in hot oil in a saucepan 5 minutes or until tender.
• **Stir** in tomato and next 3 ingredients; cook over medium heat just until thoroughly heated. Stir in breadcrumbs; spoon mixture into squash shells.
• **Sprinkle** with cheese, and place on a baking sheet.
• **Bake,** covered, at 375° for 25 minutes or until heated. **Yield:** 6 servings.

♥ Per serving: Calories 64 (35% from fat)
Fat 2.5g (sat 0.6g, mono 1.4g, poly 0.3g)
Protein 2.1g   Carb 9.0g   Fiber 1.4g
Cholesterol 1mg   Iron 1.1mg
Sodium 176mg   Calcium 57mg

VEGETABLE SLAW

Prep: 15 minutes
Chill: 2 hours

¼ cup light mayonnaise
¼ cup light sour cream
1 tablespoon white vinegar
1 teaspoon salt
¼ teaspoon pepper
3 cups shredded cabbage
1 cup fresh broccoli flowerets, chopped
1 cup fresh cauliflower flowerets, chopped
2 cups seeded, diced plum tomato
½ cup chopped purple onion

• **Stir** together first 5 ingredients in a large bowl.
• **Add** cabbage and remaining ingredients, tossing well. Cover and chill 2 hours. **Yield:** 6 servings.
Janice Dellinger Whisenhunt
Goldsboro, North Carolina

♥ Per serving: Calories 76 (49% from fat)
Fat 4.1g (sat 0.9g, mono 0.2g, poly 1.9g)
Protein 2.5g   Carb 8.6g   Fiber 2.4g
Cholesterol 7mg   Iron 0.8mg
Sodium 477mg   Calcium 63mg

RANCH-STYLE BEANS

This comforting vegetable dish is hearty enough to soothe cold-weather cravings.

Prep: 15 minutes
Stand: 1 hour
Cook: 2 hours

1 (1-pound) package dried pinto beans
8 cups water
1 medium onion, diced
1 small green bell pepper, diced
1 garlic clove, minced
2 tablespoons Worcestershire sauce
1 tablespoon chili powder
¾ teaspoon salt
½ teaspoon dry mustard
¼ teaspoon pepper
1 (10-ounce) can diced tomatoes and green chiles

• **Place** pinto beans in a large Dutch oven; add water 2 inches above beans. Bring to a boil.
• **Boil** pinto beans 1 minute; cover, remove from heat, and let beans stand 1 hour. Drain.
• **Bring** pinto beans and 8 cups water to a boil in Dutch oven. Cover, reduce heat, and simmer 1 hour or until beans are tender.
• **Add** onion and next 7 ingredients; simmer 30 minutes.
• **Add** tomatoes; simmer 30 minutes. **Yield:** 7 cups.

Mary Jayne Allen
Chattanooga, Tennessee

♥ Per serving: Calories 249 (4% from fat)
Fat 1.0g (sat 0.2g, mono 0.2g, poly 0.4g)
Protein 14.1g Carb 46.4g Fiber 8.7g
Cholesterol 0mg Iron 4.3mg
Sodium 482mg Calcium 100mg

CORN STICKS

Here, we transformed one of our favorite muffin batters (featured in December 1998) into festive sticks. Freeze leftover Corn Sticks to accompany a later meal.

Prep: 10 minutes
Bake: 15 minutes

1 cup all-purpose flour
1 cup yellow cornmeal
1 tablespoon baking powder
1 teaspoon salt
1 (11-ounce) can sweet whole kernel corn, drained
2 tablespoons minced red bell pepper
¼ teaspoon ground red pepper
¾ cup 1% low-fat milk
½ cup egg substitute
2 egg whites
1 tablespoon vegetable oil
Vegetable cooking spray

• **Combine** first 7 ingredients; make a well in center of mixture.
• **Stir** together milk and next 3 ingredients in a bowl.
• **Add** milk mixture to flour mixture, stirring just until moistened.
• **Heat** cast-iron corn stick pans in 450° oven 5 minutes or until hot. Remove pans from oven, and coat with vegetable cooking spray.
• **Spoon** batter into hot pans.
• **Bake** at 450° for 15 minutes. Remove from pans immediately; cool slightly on wire racks. **Yield:** 20 sticks.

♥ Per corn stick: Calories 77 (18% from fat)
Fat 1.5g (sat 0.4g, mono 1.2g, poly 1.1g)
Protein 2.8g Carb 13.9g Fiber 0.3g
Cholesterol 0mg Iron 0.6mg
Sodium 252mg Calcium 56mg

Quick Cassoulet

Cassoulet—a hearty French casse-role—can literally take days to prepare the old-fashioned way, which starts out with cooking and boning a duck. Reader Brooks Hart developed a streamlined method (minus the duck) that offers great flavor in a fraction of the time.

EASY CHICKEN CASSOULET

Prep: 25 minutes
Cook: 1 hour, 16 minutes

8 skinned and boned chicken thighs
3 tablespoons olive oil
2 cups sliced fresh mushrooms
2 to 3 teaspoons minced fresh or dried rosemary
½ cup vermouth
4 (15-ounce) cans navy beans, drained
1 cup shredded Parmesan cheese
1 cup fine, dry breadcrumbs*
1 teaspoon salt
½ teaspoon pepper
1 (12-ounce) jar mushroom gravy
2 tablespoons butter or margarine, cut up

• **Brown** chicken on both sides in hot oil in a 12-inch cast-iron skillet over medium-high heat. Add mushrooms and rosemary, and sauté 3 minutes.
• **Stir** in vermouth; cook 5 minutes. Add 2 cans beans, gently pressing into skillet.
• **Sprinkle** with ½ cup Parmesan cheese, ½ cup breadcrumbs, salt, and pepper. Drizzle with gravy. Add remaining 2 cans navy beans. Sprinkle with remaining ½ cup Parmesan and remaining ½ cup breadcrumbs; dot with butter.
• **Bake,** covered with aluminum foil, at 350° for 40 minutes. Remove foil, and bake 20 more minutes or until golden brown. **Yield:** 8 to 10 servings.

*Substitute soft breadcrumbs for fine, dry breadcrumbs, if desired.

Brooks Hart
Woodbury, Connecticut

Timesaving Chicken Dinners

Create your own "convenience food" by stocking your freezer with cooked chicken. Read the box on the facing page for tips on buying and preparing cooked chicken.

Thrill family and guests when you present flavorful Chicken Cakes that are served with zesty Rémoulade Sauce. Or delight in preparing simple and elegant Chicken Tetrazzini—it combines cooked chicken and items from your pantry. Designed to use the meat of one rotisserie chicken, each of these entrées gives you a much-needed head start so you won't have to get up with the chickens to prepare dinner.

CHICKEN CAKES WITH RÉMOULADE SAUCE

The cakes also make terrific appetizers. Simply halve the amount of mixture, and form into 18 patties.

Prep: 15 minutes
Cook: 12 minutes

2 tablespoons butter or margarine
½ medium-size red bell pepper, diced
4 green onions, thinly sliced
1 garlic clove, pressed
3 cups chopped cooked chicken
1 cup soft breadcrumbs
1 large egg, lightly beaten
2 tablespoons mayonnaise
1 tablespoon Creole mustard
2 teaspoons Creole seasoning
¼ cup vegetable oil
Rémoulade Sauce

• **Melt** butter in a large skillet over medium heat.
• **Add** bell pepper, green onions, and garlic, and sauté 3 to 4 minutes or until vegetables are tender.
• **Stir** together bell pepper mixture, chicken, and next 5 ingredients in a bowl. Shape chicken mixture into 8 (3½-inch) patties.
• **Fry** 4 patties in 2 tablespoons hot oil in a large skillet over medium heat 3 minutes on each side or until golden brown. Drain on paper towels.
• **Repeat** procedure with remaining 2 tablespoons oil and patties. Serve immediately with Rémoulade Sauce. **Yield:** 4 servings.

Rémoulade Sauce

Prep: 5 minutes

1 cup mayonnaise
3 green onions, sliced
2 tablespoons Creole mustard
2 garlic cloves, pressed
1 tablespoon chopped fresh parsley
¼ teaspoon ground red pepper
Garnish: sliced green onions

• **Stir** together first 6 ingredients until sauce is well blended. Garnish, if desired. **Yield:** about 1¼ cups.

CHICKEN COBBLER WITH CARAMELIZED ONIONS

Prep: 45 minutes
Bake: 40 minutes

⅓ cup butter or margarine
2 large sweet onions, diced
¼ cup all-purpose flour
1 (12-ounce) can evaporated milk
1 cup chicken broth
½ cup dry white wine
1 tablespoon chicken bouillon granules
¼ teaspoon pepper
3 cups coarsely chopped cooked chicken
3 tablespoons chopped fresh parsley
1 (15-ounce) package refrigerated piecrusts
½ cup finely chopped pecans, toasted
½ cup grated Parmesan cheese

• **Melt** butter in a large skillet over medium heat; add onion, and sauté 20 minutes or until caramel colored.
• **Add** flour; cook, stirring constantly, 1 minute. Gradually stir in evaporated milk, chicken broth, and wine.
• **Cook,** stirring constantly, 5 minutes or until thickened.
• **Add** bouillon granules and pepper. Remove from heat; stir in chicken and parsley. Pour chicken mixture into a lightly greased 10-inch deep-dish pieplate.
• **Unfold** piecrusts, and press out fold lines. Sprinkle 1 piecrust with pecans and Parmesan cheese. Top with remaining piecrust.
• **Roll** into a 14-inch circle; press edges to seal. Cut into ½-inch-wide strips. Arrange strips in a lattice design over filling, reserving any extra strips; fold edges under.
• **Bake** at 425° for 35 to 40 minutes or until golden brown.
• **Place** remaining strips on a lightly greased baking sheet.
• **Bake** at 425° for 10 to 12 minutes or until golden brown. Serve with cobbler. **Yield:** 6 servings.

CHICKEN ENCHILADAS

These enchiladas couldn't be easier, and you won't have to run to the store for the basic ingredients.

Prep: 15 minutes
Bake: 40 minutes

3 cups chopped cooked chicken
2 cups (8 ounces) shredded Monterey Jack cheese with peppers
½ cup sour cream
1 (4.5-ounce) can chopped green chiles, drained
⅓ cup chopped fresh cilantro
8 (8-inch) flour tortillas
Vegetable cooking spray
1 (8-ounce) container sour cream
1 (8-ounce) bottle green taco sauce
Toppings: diced tomato, chopped avocado, chopped green onions, sliced ripe olives, chopped fresh cilantro

• **Stir** together first 5 ingredients. Spoon chicken mixture evenly over tortillas, and roll up.
• **Arrange** in a lightly greased 13- x 9-inch baking dish. Coat tortillas with vegetable cooking spray.
• **Bake** at 350° for 35 to 40 minutes or until golden brown.
• **Stir** together sour cream and taco sauce in a bowl.
• **Spoon** sour cream mixture over hot enchiladas; sprinkle with desired toppings. **Yield:** 4 servings.

COST AND CONVENIENCE: A BALANCING ACT

Busy schedules peck away at time we can spend in the kitchen. Get a jump on dinner by using precooked chicken. Review these poultry options and decide what your time is worth.

Type of Chicken	Average Cost Per Pound
Cooked at home (whole chicken)	$1.48*
Rotisserie from deli	$2.36
Canned	$6.32
Fully cooked, prepackaged	$7.09

*A 4½-pound chicken loses about 33 percent of its original weight during cooking; cost per pound increases from 99 cents to $1.48.

Spending an hour or more cooking an entire chicken may not be part of your preferred plan, so we've come up with this surefire way to buy you precious prep time.

Remove the meat from the bones while the chicken is still warm, and then chop, shred, or cube the meat and freeze it in a heavy-duty freezer bag. Each pound of cooked chicken yields about half a pound of pulled meat or 3 cups chopped meat. Refrigerate cooked chicken up to three days or freeze up to three months.

And remember, cooking your own chicken may be more economical, but convenience weighs in heavily for the store-bought rotisserie chicken. Watch for in-store sales when you can buy several chickens to freeze.

CHICKEN TETRAZZINI

Prep: 20 minutes
Bake: 25 minutes

3 cups chopped cooked chicken
1 cup shredded Parmesan cheese, divided
1 (10¾-ounce) can cream of mushroom soup, undiluted *
1 (10-ounce) container refrigerated Alfredo sauce *
1 (3½-ounce) can sliced mushrooms, drained
½ cup slivered almonds, toasted
½ cup chicken broth
¼ cup dry sherry
¼ teaspoon freshly ground pepper
7 ounces vermicelli, cooked

• **Stir** together chicken, ½ cup Parmesan cheese, and next 7 ingredients; stir in pasta.
• **Spoon** mixture into 6 lightly greased 6-ounce baking dishes or an 11- x 7-inch baking dish.
• **Sprinkle** with remaining ½ cup Parmesan cheese.
• **Bake** at 350° for 25 minutes or until thoroughly heated. **Yield:** 6 servings.

*Substitute reduced-sodium, reduced-fat cream of mushroom soup and light Alfredo sauce, if desired.

From Our Kitchen

Not Just Scrambled Eggs

Our "Quick & Easy" column on page 35 this month spotlights omelets. Whether you make them flat or fluffy, rolled or folded, it's important to use fresh eggs and the right pan. Although special omelet pans are available, you can achieve beautiful results with what you have on hand. Choose a sturdy 6- to 10-inch pan with sloping sides and a long handle.

Also, be sure to select the right pan size for the amount of ingredients. If you cook a few eggs in a large pan, they'll be thin and tough. Too many eggs in a small pan will cook too slowly and become scrambled eggs as you try to cook the middle. Remember, it's much easier to make several three-egg omelets than to manage one 12-egg omelet.

On the Road to Wellness

Phytochemicals, antioxidants, and flavonoids are words we hear a lot. They're present in foods that taste good, and they work to keep you well. Here's what they mean.

- **Phytochemicals** are protective chemicals in plants that have been found to prevent some forms of cancer.

- **Antioxidants** are substances in plants that keep foods from becoming rancid or discolored. These help reduce the risk of cancer and heart disease. Citrus fruit, nuts, sweet potatoes, broccoli, and brussels sprouts are all good sources of antioxidants.

- **Flavonoids** are any group of phytochemicals that act as antioxidants in preventing some kinds of cancers, clogged arteries, and blood clots. Flavonoids are present in red wine, tea, and most fruits and vegetables.

So cruise the produce section, and you'll find everything you need. Then look forward to our recipes for wonderful ways to prepare these fruits and vegetables.

ALL ABOUT WINE

Wine Tips and Tidbits

Remember when we had wine only with dinner in restaurants on special occasions? Things have really changed; now we're enjoying wines anytime and we don't have to be experts. Here are some tips.

- Don't cook with a wine you wouldn't also drink.

- When recipes call for a small amount of wine, small bottles—called splits—are the best buy.

- You can store open bottles of wine corked and chilled up to one week.

- Don't throw out leftover wine. Freeze it in ice cube trays, and store in zip-top plastic bags for use in soups, stews, sauces, and casseroles.

- You can substitute broth or fruit juice for wine in some recipes, but be aware that doing so may lessen the full-bodied flavor of the dish.

There's no reason to be intimidated when you shop for wine. These four steps will make it easy for you to find the wines you like.

1. Tell the salesperson the price you want to pay.

2. Describe the type of wine you prefer—crisp, dry, fruity, light, full-bodied, etc.

3. Tell what foods you plan to serve with the wine.

4. Ask for a sample if it is available. Weekly wine tastings at supermarkets and wine shops are a great way to discover what you do and don't like.

Dine With Wine and Make the Meal Shine

At an annual dinner in Dallas (see story on page 30), Donovan Campbell serves wines from his private collection to complement each course of the meal. When you select wines to accompany the recipes, consider Pinot Noir, Sauvignon Blanc, and Riesling.

Here's a crash course to help you make your selection.

- Pinot Noir is a spicy, rich red wine. American Pinot Noirs are inexpensive and pair well with almost any food.

- Sauvignon Blanc's crisp, grassy flavors pair well with spicy dishes and grilled fish. This light- to medium-bodied wine is acidic and dry.

- Riesling—sometimes called White Riesling or Johannisberg Riesling—has aromas and flavors that range from flowery to fruity to hints of minerals. Although Riesling is generally considered a sweet wine, many selections are dry. It's a light-bodied, refreshing choice during any course of the meal.

MARCH

Buttermilk: A Perfect Partner

Terrific flavor and old-fashioned goodness come easy when buttermilk finds its way into a recipe. Discover the versatility of this classic Southern ingredient in these no-fuss dishes.

BUTTERMILK BAKED CHICKEN

Prep: 10 minutes
Bake: 45 minutes

¼ cup butter or margarine *
4 bone-in chicken breast halves, skinned
½ teaspoon salt
½ teaspoon pepper
1½ cups buttermilk, divided *
¾ cup all-purpose flour
1 (10¾-ounce) can cream of mushroom soup, undiluted *
Hot cooked rice

• **Melt** butter in a lightly greased 13- x 9-inch baking dish in a 425° oven.
• **Sprinkle** chicken with salt and pepper. Dip chicken in ½ cup buttermilk, and dredge in flour.
• **Arrange** chicken, breast side down, in baking dish.
• **Bake** at 425° for 25 minutes. Turn chicken, and bake 10 more minutes.
• **Stir** together remaining 1 cup buttermilk and soup; pour over chicken, and bake 10 more minutes, shielding with aluminum foil to prevent excessive browning, if necessary. Serve over rice. **Yield:** 4 servings.

*Substitute light butter; nonfat buttermilk; and reduced-sodium, reduced-fat cream of mushroom soup, if desired.
Susan B. McCombs
Dallas, Texas

BASIC BUTTERMILK BISCUITS

Prep: 6 minutes
Bake: 14 minutes

⅓ cup butter or margarine, cut up
2 cups self-rising soft wheat flour
¾ cup buttermilk
Butter or margarine, melted

• **Cut** ⅓ cup butter into flour with a pastry blender until crumbly; add buttermilk, stirring just until dry ingredients are moistened.
• **Turn** dough out onto a lightly floured surface; knead 3 or 4 times.
• **Pat** or roll dough to ¾-inch thickness; cut with a 2½-inch round cutter, and place on a lightly greased baking sheet.
• **Bake** at 425° for 12 to 14 minutes. Brush biscuits with melted butter. **Yield:** 10 biscuits.

Note: For testing purposes only, we used Martha White Self-Rising Soft Wheat Flour.

BUTTERMILK LAYER CAKE

Part of the beauty of this rich cake is that the ingredients are basic pantry staples.

Prep: 10 minutes
Bake: 22 minutes

1 cup shortening
2 cups sugar
3 large eggs
2½ cups all-purpose flour
½ teaspoon salt
½ teaspoon baking soda
1½ cups buttermilk
2 teaspoons vanilla extract
Caramel Frosting (recipe on page 52)

• **Beat** shortening at medium speed with an electric mixer until fluffy. Gradually add sugar, beating well.
• **Add** eggs, 1 at a time, beating until blended after each addition.
• **Combine** flour, salt, and soda; add to shortening mixture alternately with buttermilk, beginning and ending with flour mixture. Beat at low speed until blended after each addition. Beat at medium-high speed 2 minutes.
• **Stir** in vanilla, and pour batter into 3 greased and floured 8-inch round cakepans.
• **Bake** at 350° for 22 minutes or until a wooden pick inserted in center comes out clean. Cool in pans on wire racks 10 minutes; remove from pans. Cool completely on wire racks.
• **Spread** Caramel Frosting between layers and on top and sides of cake. **Yield:** 1 (3-layer) cake.

Chocolate-Buttermilk Cake: Substitute ½ cup cocoa for ½ cup flour. Pour batter into a lightly greased 13- x 9-inch pan. Bake at 350° for 40 minutes or until a wooden pick inserted in center comes out clean.

Whole Wheat Quick Bread

Prep: 5 minutes
Bake: 45 minutes

1½ cups whole wheat flour
1½ cups all-purpose flour
1 teaspoon salt
1 teaspoon baking soda
1½ cups buttermilk
1 large egg
3 tablespoons honey
2 tablespoons butter or margarine, melted
¾ cup chopped pecans, toasted (optional)
3 tablespoons uncooked regular oats (optional)

• **Combine** first 4 ingredients in a large bowl. Combine buttermilk and next 3 ingredients; add to dry ingredients, stirring until blended.
• **Stir** in pecans, if desired. Spread batter into a well-greased 9- x 5-inch loafpan. Sprinkle with oats, if desired.
• **Bake** at 375° for 45 minutes or until a wooden pick inserted in center comes out clean. Cool in pan on a wire rack 10 minutes. Remove from pan, and cool completely on wire rack. **Yield:** 1 loaf.

Berry-Banana Buttermilk Smoothie

Replace the strawberries with other fresh fruit for a change of flavor.

Prep: 5 minutes

2 large bananas, sliced and frozen
¾ cup frozen apple juice concentrate, thawed
2½ cups buttermilk
2 teaspoons vanilla extract
10 large fresh strawberries, frozen
Garnish: fresh strawberries

• **Process** first 4 ingredients in a blender until smooth.
• **Add** 10 strawberries, 2 at a time, pulsing until smooth.
• **Pour** into glasses. Garnish, if desired; serve immediately. **Yield:** 5 cups.

BUTTERMILK BASICS

The tangy liquid we know as buttermilk may not be the most alluring beverage in the dairy case, but it's certainly a hard worker. Stirred into quick breads and cake batters or used hand in hand with convenience products, buttermilk adds tenderness and flavor usually expected only in scratch cooking.

In days past, "real" buttermilk was the butter-flecked liquid left after hours of butter churning. Today's refrigerated versions—both full fat and fat free—are made thick and tart by special cultures added to milk.

You'll be pleased any way you pour buttermilk. Try it in main dishes, salad dressings, soups, beverages, or desserts. For some salad dressing ideas, turn to this month's "From Our Kitchen" on page 66.

Buttermilk Pralines

Our staff judged these sugary wafers from Grandmother's kitchen "the best."

Prep: 5 minutes
Cook: 10 minutes
Cool: 12 minutes

½ cup buttermilk
½ teaspoon baking soda
2 cups firmly packed light brown sugar
2 tablespoons butter or margarine
2 tablespoons light corn syrup
1 cup toasted pecans, chopped
1 teaspoon vanilla extract

• **Stir** together buttermilk and baking soda in a large heavy saucepan until blended. Add brown sugar, butter, and corn syrup.
• **Cook** over medium-high heat 8 to 10 minutes or until a candy thermometer registers 234° (soft ball stage). Remove from heat; cool 10 to 12 minutes.
• **Beat** with a wooden spoon until mixture thickens slightly.
• **Stir** in pecans and vanilla. Working rapidly, drop by rounded tablespoonfuls onto lightly greased wax paper. Let stand until firm. **Yield:** 2 dozen.

Lila McElroy
Shreveport, Louisiana

Tomato-Basil Bisque

Canned tomato soup gets a boost from buttermilk in this satisfying version. Serve the bisque warm or cold.

Prep: 5 minutes
Cook: 8 minutes

2 (10¾-ounce) cans tomato soup, undiluted
1 (14½-ounce) can diced tomatoes
2½ cups buttermilk
2 tablespoons chopped fresh basil
¼ teaspoon freshly ground pepper
Garnish: shredded fresh basil

• **Cook** first 5 ingredients in a 3-quart saucepan over medium heat, stirring often, 6 to 8 minutes or until mixture is thoroughly heated. Garnish, if desired; serve immediately, or serve chilled. **Yield:** about 7 cups.

The Magic of Disney

Disney restaurant experiences are magic. Sure, you can find plenty of great hamburgers, hot dogs, and pizza at Walt Disney World. But a visit with Chef Mickey and his sidekicks shouldn't stop with expected theme park fare. Stellar dining destinations offer a feast for the senses. Come along for a taste.

BANANA NAPOLEONS

Prep: 45 minutes
Bake: 55 minutes
Chill: 2 hours
Cook: 18 minutes

3 egg yolks
2½ cups whipping cream, divided
1⅓ cups sugar, divided
1 vanilla bean
¾ cup butter or margarine, divided
5 frozen phyllo pastry sheets, thawed
½ cup powdered sugar
2 bananas, cut into ¼-inch-thick slices
Garnishes: sweetened whipped cream, grated chocolate

• **Whisk** together egg yolks and ¼ cup whipping cream; set aside.
• **Combine** 1¼ cups whipping cream and ⅓ cup sugar in a heavy saucepan.
• **Cut** vanilla bean in half lengthwise; scrape seeds into saucepan, and add vanilla bean halves.
• **Bring** vanilla mixture to a boil over medium-high heat. Remove from heat; discard vanilla bean.
• **Whisk** about one-fourth of hot mixture gradually into yolk mixture; add to remaining hot mixture, whisking constantly. Skim air bubbles from top of mixture.
• **Pour** mixture into an 8-inch square pan. Place pan into a 13- x 9-inch pan.

Add hot water to larger pan to depth of 1 inch.
• **Bake** at 300° for 35 minutes. Remove pan from water, and cool. Cover and chill at least 2 hours.
• **Melt** ½ cup butter. Stack phyllo, brushing each sheet with butter and sprinkling with powdered sugar. Cut phyllo stack into 16 (3-inch) squares.
• **Place** squares on a parchment paper-lined baking sheet. Cover with a sheet of parchment paper and a baking sheet.
• **Bake** at 375° for 20 minutes or until golden. Remove from oven, and cool to room temperature.
• **Cook** remaining 1 cup sugar and remaining ¼ cup butter in a small heavy saucepan over medium heat, stirring until butter melts. Slowly add remaining 1 cup whipping cream; cook, stirring constantly, 8 to 10 minutes or until caramel color. Set caramel sauce aside.
• **Cut** chilled custard into 6 squares. Place 1 square on each of 6 dessert plates. Top each custard square with 1 phyllo square. Drizzle a small amount of caramel sauce around custard.
• **Stir** together banana and remaining caramel sauce. Spoon evenly over phyllo squares on plates.
• **Top** each with a second phyllo square, and garnish, if desired. Reserve remaining phyllo squares for another use. **Yield:** 6 servings.

Chef John State
Flying Fish Café
Orlando, Florida

CRISP RICE CEREAL SUSHI

Once you show them how, older kids can make this whimsical treat themselves.

Prep: 25 minutes
Cook: 8 minutes

8 chewy fruit rolls
¼ cup butter or margarine
1 (10-ounce) package miniature marshmallows
6 cups crisp rice cereal
16 worm-shaped chewy candies or 24 fish-shaped chewy candies

• **Unroll** fruit rolls, and place, with plastic sheet side down, on a cutting board.
• **Melt** butter in a Dutch oven over medium heat.
• **Add** marshmallows, stirring until melted; remove from heat. Stir in rice cereal until blended.
• **Spread** about ½ cup cereal mixture quickly over each fruit roll, leaving a 1-inch border on 1 long side.
• **Arrange** 2 worm-shaped candies or 3 fish-shaped candies lengthwise down center of cereal mixture.
• **Roll** up, starting at side without border. Press to seal securely. Repeat procedure with remaining fruit rolls, cereal mixture, and candies.
• **Cut** each roll into 4 slices. Serve with chopsticks, if desired. **Yield:** 32 rolls.

Sushi Bars: Press cereal mixture into a buttered 13- x 9-inch pan. Let stand 15 minutes, and cut into 2½- x 1-inch rectangles. Top each bar with a fish-shaped candy.

Confetti Sushi Bars: Substitute fruity sweetened corn puffs cereal for crisp rice cereal. Press into a buttered 13- x 9-inch pan. Let stand 15 minutes before cutting into 1½-inch squares. (For testing purposes only, we used Trix corn puffs cereal.)

Chef Cliff Pleau
California Grill
Orlando, Florida

LOBSTER-AND-ROASTED CORN BEIGNETS

Prep: 1 hour
Rise: 30 minutes
Cook: 30 minutes

2 cups fresh or frozen corn kernels
  (4 ears)
3 tablespoons vegetable oil,
  divided
1 teaspoon salt, divided
½ teaspoon freshly ground pepper,
  divided
1 (8-ounce) bottle clam juice
⅓ cup dark amber beer
¾ teaspoon active dry yeast
½ cup milk
1 cup all-purpose flour
2 tablespoons butter or margarine
2 to 3 tablespoons hot sauce
1 cup finely chopped cooked
  lobster
3 egg whites
Vegetable oil
Sweet chili sauce

• **Toss** together corn kernels, 2 tablespoons oil, ½ teaspoon salt, and ¼ teaspoon pepper.
• **Arrange** corn in a single layer in a large shallow pan.
• **Bake** at 400° for 17 to 20 minutes or until corn is tender and golden. Set aside.
• **Cook** clam juice in a small saucepan over high heat 20 minutes or until reduced to 1 tablespoon.
• **Heat** amber beer in a small saucepan to 105° to 115°.
• **Add** yeast to warm beer, and let stand 5 minutes.
• **Stir** in remaining 1 tablespoon oil, remaining ½ teaspoon salt, remaining ¼ teaspoon pepper, corn, clam juice, milk, and next 4 ingredients.
• **Cover** and let rise in a warm place (85°), free from drafts, 30 minutes.
• **Beat** egg whites in a mixing bowl at medium speed with an electric mixer until stiff peaks form.
• **Fold** beaten egg whites into yeast mixture. Spoon into a large pastry bag fitted with a large (½-inch) round tip.
• **Pour** oil to a depth of 2 inches into a Dutch oven; heat to 360°.
• **Pipe** batter, in batches, into oil; fry 2 minutes or until golden.

• **Serve** beignets immediately with sweet chili sauce. **Yield:** 8 to 10 appetizer servings.

Note: For testing purposes only, we used Blackened Voodoo dark amber beer, Tabasco sauce, and Mae Ploy Sweet Chili Sauce (available in Asian markets). Beignets can also be dropped by tablespoonfuls into hot oil.

Chef John Clark
Coral Reef Restaurant
Orlando, Florida

PENNE WITH PANCETTA

Prep: 20 minutes
Cook: 20 minutes

4 ounces pancetta or bacon, diced
¼ cup olive oil
2 medium onions, diced
2 to 3 garlic cloves, minced
3 (14-ounce) cans whole tomatoes,
  crushed
¼ teaspoon salt
1 to 1½ teaspoons dried crushed red
  pepper
¼ teaspoon ground black pepper
12 ounces penne, cooked
Garnishes: shaved Romano or
  Parmesan cheese,
  minced fresh chives

• **Cook** pancetta in hot oil in a Dutch oven over medium heat until crisp; drain pancetta on paper towels, reserving 1 tablespoon drippings in pan.
• **Sauté** onion in hot drippings 3 to 4 minutes.
• **Add** garlic, and sauté 2 to 3 minutes. Stir in tomatoes, salt, and red and black pepper.
• **Cook,** stirring occasionally, 10 minutes or until thickened.
• **Add** pasta, and cook until thoroughly heated. Sprinkle with pancetta. Garnish, if desired. **Yield:** 4 to 6 servings.

Chef Bart Hosmer
Spoodles at Disney's Boardwalk Resort
Orlando, Florida

SPICED PEACH JAM

Cardamom, cumin, and a
bevy of other spices pack this
simple jam with flavor.

Prep: 10 minutes
Cook: 2 hours
Chill: 2 hours

2 (16-ounce) packages frozen sliced
  peaches
1 (16-ounce) package light brown
  sugar
½ cup dry white wine
½ teaspoon salt
⅛ teaspoon freshly ground
  pepper
⅛ teaspoon dried crushed red
  pepper
⅛ teaspoon ground cardamom
⅛ teaspoon ground ginger
⅛ teaspoon ground coriander
⅛ teaspoon ground cumin
⅛ teaspoon ground cinnamon
⅛ teaspoon ground cloves
½ cup chunky applesauce

• **Bring** peaches and brown sugar to a boil in a large saucepan over medium heat; reduce heat, and simmer, stirring occasionally, 1 hour.
• **Stir** wine and next 9 ingredients into saucepan.
• **Cook** over low heat, stirring occasionally, 45 minutes or until thickened. Cool slightly.
• **Process** mixture in a food processor until smooth.
• **Stir** in applesauce. Cover jam, and chill at least 2 hours or up to 1 month. **Yield:** 4 cups.

Chef Anette Grecchi
Artist Point Restaurant at
Disney's Wilderness Lodge
Orlando, Florida

Caramel: One of Life's Golden Opportunities

Like honey from a spoon, this classic mixture of sugar, butter, and cream swirls deliciously into many recipes.

You can awake to the aroma of Caramel Sticky Buns and have extra sauce for ice cream. Our frosting takes a little effort, but Assistant Foods Editor Peggy Smith says "beating the frosting until spreading consistency is all in the feel." If you're a new cook, don't be intimidated. The step-by-step photos in "From Our Kitchen" on page 66 will guide you to perfection.

CARAMEL FROSTING

This frosting is fabulous on Buttermilk Layer Cake (page 48).

Prep: 18 minutes
Cook: 20 minutes

3¾ cups sugar, divided
1½ cups whipping cream
¼ cup butter
¼ teaspoon baking soda

• **Bring** 3 cups sugar, cream, butter, and baking soda to a boil in a heavy saucepan. Remove from heat, and keep warm.
• **Sprinkle** remaining ¾ cup sugar in a heavy saucepan.
• **Cook** over medium heat, stirring constantly, until sugar melts and syrup is light golden brown. (Sugar will clump before melting.) Gradually pour into whipping cream mixture. (Mixture will bubble.) Stir until smooth.
• **Cook** over medium heat, stirring often, 10 to 12 minutes or until a candy thermometer registers 240° (soft ball stage). Remove from heat.
• **Beat** at high speed with an electric mixer until spreading consistency (8 to 10 minutes). **Yield:** 3 cups.

CARAMEL SAUCE

Prep: 10 minutes
Cook: 30 minutes

2 cups whipping cream
¼ cup butter
½ teaspoon baking soda
2 cups sugar
½ cup water
2 teaspoons lemon juice

• **Cook** first 3 ingredients in a Dutch oven over medium heat, stirring occasionally, until butter melts; remove mixture from heat.
• **Bring** sugar, water, and lemon juice to a boil in a Dutch oven over high heat, stirring occasionally.
• **Reduce** heat to medium-high, and boil, stirring occasionally, 8 minutes or until mixture begins to brown. Reduce heat to medium, and cook, stirring occasionally, 5 minutes or until caramel colored.
• **Pour** sugar mixture gradually into whipping cream mixture. Remove from heat; let stand 1 minute. Whisk until smooth.
• **Cook** over medium-low heat, stirring occasionally, until a candy thermometer registers 230° (thread stage); cool. **Yield:** 2½ cups.

Lois M. Clonts
Bakersfield, California

CARAMEL STICKY BUNS

Prep: 25 minutes
Rise: 30 minutes
Bake: 16 minutes

1 (16-ounce) package hot roll mix
1½ cups Caramel Sauce (recipe at left)
1 cup chopped pecans, toasted
3 tablespoons butter, softened
¼ cup sugar
2 teaspoons ground cinnamon

• **Prepare** roll dough according to package directions. Let stand 5 minutes.
• **Pour** Caramel Sauce into a lightly greased 13- x 9-inch pan or into 2 lightly greased 8-inch square pans. Sprinkle with pecans.
• **Roll** dough into a 15- x 10-inch rectangle. Spread with butter; sprinkle with sugar and cinnamon.
• **Roll** up, starting at a long edge. Cut into 1-inch-thick slices. Arrange slices, cut side down, over Caramel Sauce.
• **Cover** and let rise in a warm place (85°), free from drafts, 30 minutes or until doubled in bulk.
• **Bake** at 375° for 16 minutes. Let stand on wire rack 5 minutes. Invert onto serving dish. **Yield:** 15 buns.

Note: Buns may be frozen before rising. Remove from freezer, and let thaw at room temperature; continue as directed above.

Overnight Caramel Sticky Buns: Allow dough to rise in refrigerator overnight. Remove dough from refrigerator, and let stand 30 minutes. Bake as directed above.

Green Is Gold

Chock-full of vitamins and minerals, broccoli is an excellent source of calcium, perfect for those who are lactose intolerant. In addition, researchers at Johns Hopkins University say broccoli is loaded with a cancer-fighting agent called sulforophane.

Despite its healthful qualities, broccoli still gets a bum rap from many folks, because they simply don't know how to cook it properly. While testing these recipes, we discovered one important rule: Quicker is better. Steaming or quickly boiling retains color and texture.

Several of these recipes work just as easily with frozen broccoli if fresh is unavailable. As for the stems and stalks, when given a little extra cooking time, they can be used right along with the flowerets.

BROCCOLI CUPS

Prep: 15 minutes
Bake: 25 minutes

1 (16-ounce) package fresh broccoli
   flowerets *
1 (12-ounce) container 2% low-fat
   small-curd cottage cheese
1 small onion, minced
⅓ cup shredded Parmesan cheese
⅓ cup fine, dry breadcrumbs
2 large eggs, lightly beaten
¼ cup butter or margarine,
   melted
½ teaspoon salt
¼ teaspoon pepper
½ cup shredded Parmesan
   cheese

● **Arrange** broccoli in a steamer basket over boiling water.
● **Cover** and steam 8 minutes or until tender; chop broccoli.
● **Stir** together broccoli, cottage cheese, and next 7 ingredients.
● **Spoon** evenly into 12 lightly greased 6-ounce custard cups or muffin pans.

● **Bake** at 400° for 20 minutes. Sprinkle with ½ cup Parmesan cheese. Bake 5 more minutes. **Yield:** 12 servings.

* Substitute 1 (16-ounce) package frozen chopped broccoli, thawed, if desired. Omit steaming.

Corile W. Wilhelm
Terra Alta, West Virginia

BROCCOLI MAC 'N' CHEESE

Prep: 20 minutes
Cook: 10 minutes

2 cups fresh broccoli flowerets *
2 tablespoons butter or
   margarine
1 (8-ounce) loaf pasteurized prepared
   cheese product, cubed
1 cup milk
2 cups chopped cooked chicken
8 ounces elbow macaroni,
   cooked
1 garlic clove, minced
1 cup (4 ounces) shredded Cheddar
   cheese

● **Arrange** broccoli in a steamer basket over boiling water.
● **Cover** and steam 8 minutes or until tender.
● **Melt** butter and pasteurized cheese cubes in a large skillet over low heat, stirring often. Stir in milk until well blended.
● **Add** broccoli, chicken, macaroni, and garlic; cook over medium heat, stirring occasionally, until thoroughly heated.
● **Sprinkle** each serving with shredded Cheddar cheese, and serve immediately. **Yield:** 4 to 6 servings.

Note: For testing purposes only, we used Velveeta for pasteurized prepared cheese product.

* Substitute 1 (10-ounce) package frozen chopped broccoli, thawed, if desired. Omit steaming.

BROCCOLI-CHICKEN SALAD

Cranberries, red bell pepper, green onions, and Chutney Dressing give this salad rich color, texture, and flavor.

Prep: 20 minutes
Cook: 15 minutes
Chill: 1 hour

4 skinned and boned chicken breast
   halves
4 cups water
¼ cup soy sauce
2 garlic cloves, minced
1 (16-ounce) package fresh broccoli
   flowerets
4 green onions, chopped
1 medium-size red bell pepper,
   chopped
1 cup sweetened dried cranberries
Chutney Dressing
¼ cup chopped peanuts

● **Bring** first 4 ingredients to a boil in a medium saucepan. Boil 15 minutes or until chicken is done; drain.
● **Cool** chicken, and cut into bite-size pieces.
● **Toss** together chicken, broccoli, and next 4 ingredients. Chill 1 hour. Sprinkle with peanuts before serving. **Yield:** 6 servings.

Chutney Dressing

Prep: 5 minutes

1 (9-ounce) jar mango chutney
½ cup mayonnaise
2 garlic cloves, minced
¼ teaspoon dried crushed red pepper

● **Stir** together all ingredients in a bowl. **Yield:** 1¾ cups.

Note: For testing purposes only, we used Major Grey Chutney.

Top-Rated Menu

This menu lends itself to outdoor entertaining. Served on beds of mixed greens, the marinated chicken and vegetables creates a sophisticated yet easy main-dish salad. For dessert, serve a refreshingly simple ice cream.

Easy Make-Ahead Menu
Serves 6

Marinated Chicken Strips and Vegetables
Parmesan Bread
Lemon Ice Cream

MARINATED CHICKEN STRIPS AND VEGETABLES
(pictured on page 78)

1990 Recipe Hall of Fame

Prep: 25 minutes
Chill: 2 hours
Bake: 15 minutes

¾ cup lite soy sauce
⅔ cup honey
⅓ cup dry sherry*
½ teaspoon garlic powder
¼ teaspoon ground ginger
1½ pounds fresh asparagus spears
6 skinned and boned chicken breast halves, cut into ¼-inch strips
¼ cup stone-ground mustard
2 tablespoons sesame seeds, toasted
3 medium tomatoes, cut into wedges
8 cups mixed salad greens
Honey-Mustard Dressing

• **Stir** together first 5 ingredients; set ½ cup mixture aside.

• **Pour** remaining soy sauce mixture evenly into 2 heavy-duty zip-top plastic bags. Snap off tough ends of asparagus; place asparagus spears in 1 bag. Add chicken to remaining bag. Seal and chill at least 2 hours.
• **Drain** chicken and asparagus, discarding marinade. Place chicken on a lightly greased roasting pan. Place asparagus in a lightly greased 13- x 9-inch pan.
• **Stir** together reserved ½ cup soy sauce mixture, mustard, and sesame seeds. Pour ½ cup mixture over chicken and remaining ¼ cup over asparagus.
• **Bake** chicken at 425° for 5 minutes. Place asparagus in oven, and bake chicken and asparagus 10 minutes or until chicken is done. Cool, if desired. If desired, place separately in zip-top plastic bags and chill 8 hours.
• **Arrange** chicken, asparagus, and tomato over salad greens, and drizzle with Honey-Mustard Dressing. **Yield:** 6 servings.

*Substitute ⅓ cup pineapple juice for sherry, if desired.

Honey-Mustard Dressing

Prep: 5 minutes

1 (8-ounce) container light sour cream
¼ cup light mayonnaise
½ cup honey
2 tablespoons stone-ground mustard
2 tablespoons Dijon mustard
2 tablespoons lemon juice

• **Stir** together all ingredients; cover and chill up to 3 days. **Yield:** 2 cups.

PARMESAN BREAD
(pictured on page 78)

1992 Recipe Hall of Fame

Prep: 10 minutes
Rise: 55 minutes
Bake: 30 minutes

1 cup water
¼ cup butter or margarine
3 cups all-purpose flour
1 (¼-ounce) envelope rapid-rise yeast
2 tablespoons sugar
2 teaspoons dried onion flakes
½ teaspoon salt
½ to 1 teaspoon dried Italian seasoning
½ teaspoon garlic salt
1 large egg
⅔ cup grated Parmesan cheese, divided
1 tablespoon butter or margarine, melted

• **Heat** 1 cup water and ¼ cup butter in a small saucepan until butter melts. Cool to 120° to 130°.
• **Combine** 2 cups flour and next 6 ingredients in a large mixing bowl. Gradually add liquid mixture to flour mixture, beating at high speed with an electric mixer 1 minute. Add egg; beat at medium speed 2 minutes. Gradually stir in ⅓ cup cheese and remaining 1 cup flour.
• **Cover** and let rest 10 minutes. Place dough in a greased 2-quart round baking dish. Brush with melted butter, and sprinkle with remaining ⅓ cup cheese. Cover and let rise in a warm place (85°), free from drafts, 45 minutes (bread will not double in bulk).
• **Bake** at 350° for 30 minutes or until golden. Cool bread in dish 10 minutes.

Remove to a wire rack. Serve warm or at room temperature. **Yield:** 8 servings.

Note: Freeze bread up to 1 month. Thaw, wrapped in foil, at room temperature; bake at 350° for 25 minutes.

LEMON ICE CREAM
(pictured on page 79)

1991 Recipe Hall of Fame

Prep: 8 minutes
Freeze: 6 hours

2 cups sugar
2 cups milk
2 cups half-and-half
2 teaspoons grated lemon rind
1 cup fresh lemon juice
6 drops yellow liquid food coloring
Garnish: fresh mint sprigs

• **Combine** first 6 ingredients. Pour into a 13- x 9-inch pan; freeze at least 2 hours.
• **Process** half of mixture in a food processor until smooth. Remove from processor. Repeat procedure with remaining mixture. Return all of mixture to pan. Freeze 4 hours or until firm. Garnish, if desired. **Yield:** 1½ quarts.

WINE PICKS

■ Von Simmern, Riesling, Spätlese (from Rheingau, Germany, about $10). The crisp acidity contrasts with the fullness of the chicken's soy sauce-honey marinade; the wine's apple/pear characteristic complements the sweet dressing.

■ Fetzer Vineyards Bonterra Chardonnay (from Mendocino, California, about $10). This relatively dry wine's fruity flavor contrasts with the marinade's acidic and assertive flavors without overpowering the chicken's flavor.

Quick & Easy

Ground beef isn't just for hamburgers. Not only are these recipes quick, easy, and satisfying, but they're also economical. All have a pound of ground beef and other items you likely have on hand. Take your pick and perk up everyday family dinners. Add a green salad or fruit salad to round out the meal.

SHEPHERD'S PIE

Prep: 15 minutes
Bake: 30 minutes

1 (22-ounce) package frozen mashed potatoes
1 pound ground beef
1 onion, chopped
½ cup frozen sliced carrot, thawed
2 tablespoons all-purpose flour
2 teaspoons salt, divided
½ teaspoon pepper, divided
1 cup beef broth
1 large egg, lightly beaten
½ cup (2 ounces) shredded Cheddar cheese
Garnish: chopped fresh parsley

• **Cook** potatoes according to package directions; set aside.
• **Cook** beef and onion in a large skillet over medium-high heat 5 to 6 minutes, stirring until beef crumbles and is no longer pink. Drain and return to skillet; add carrot.
• **Stir** in flour, 1 teaspoon salt, and ¼ teaspoon pepper.
• **Add** broth, and cook, stirring constantly, 3 minutes or until slightly thickened. Spoon mixture into a lightly greased 11- x 7-inch baking dish.
• **Stir** together potatoes, egg, remaining 1 teaspoon salt, and remaining ¼ teaspoon pepper. Spoon over beef mixture.
• **Bake** at 350° for 25 minutes. Sprinkle with cheese, and bake 5 more minutes. Garnish, if desired. **Yield:** 6 servings.
Jill Rose
Royston, Georgia

CHILI AND ENCHILADAS

Prep: 15 minutes
Bake: 25 minutes

1 medium onion
1 pound ground chuck
1 (1¾-ounce) envelope chili seasoning mix
½ cup water
1 (16-ounce) can kidney beans, rinsed and drained
1 (14½-ounce) can diced tomatoes
1 (8-ounce) can tomato sauce
1 (4.5-ounce) can chopped green chiles, divided
2 cups (8 ounces) shredded sharp Cheddar cheese, divided
8 to 10 (6-inch) flour tortillas

• **Chop** onion, reserving half for filling. Cook beef and remaining onion in a large skillet over medium-high heat 5 to 6 minutes, stirring until beef crumbles and is no longer pink; drain and return to skillet.
• **Stir** in seasoning mix, next 4 ingredients, and half of green chiles.
• **Cook** over low heat, stirring occasionally, 8 minutes. Reserve 1 cup meat mixture; spoon remaining meat mixture into an 11- x 7-inch baking dish.
• **Stir** together 1½ cups cheese, reserved onion, and remaining chiles. Spoon evenly down centers of tortillas.
• **Roll** up tortillas; place, seam side down, over meat mixture. Top evenly with reserved meat mixture.
• **Bake** at 350° for 20 minutes or until thoroughly heated. Sprinkle with remaining ½ cup cheese, and bake 5 more minutes. **Yield:** 4 to 6 servings.
Adelyn P. Whiting
Albany, Georgia

LAYERED PASTA FLORENTINE

Prep: 20 minutes
Bake: 30 minutes

1 (10-ounce) package frozen chopped
    spinach, thawed
1 pound ground chuck
1 medium onion, chopped
1 garlic clove, pressed
1 (15½-ounce) jar spaghetti sauce
    with mushrooms
1 (8-ounce) can tomato sauce
1 (6-ounce) can tomato paste
½ teaspoon salt
Dash of pepper
8 ounces small shell pasta, cooked
1 tablespoon vegetable oil
1 cup (4 ounces) shredded sharp
    Cheddar cheese
½ cup Italian-seasoned breadcrumbs
2 large eggs, lightly beaten
Shredded Parmesan cheese (optional)

• **Place** spinach in a fine wire-mesh
strainer over a bowl; press spinach with
back of spoon to remove juice. Measure
juice, and add enough water to measure
1 cup. Set spinach aside.
• **Cook** beef, onion, and garlic in a skillet
over medium-high heat 5 to 6 minutes,
stirring until beef crumbles and is no
longer pink. Drain and return to skillet.
• **Stir** in spinach liquid, spaghetti sauce,
and next 4 ingredients; bring to a boil.
Reduce heat, and simmer 10 minutes.
• **Toss** pasta with vegetable oil. Stir in
spinach, Cheddar cheese, breadcrumbs,
and eggs. Spread into a lightly greased
13- x 9-inch baking dish. Top with beef
mixture.
• **Bake,** covered, at 350° for 30 minutes
or until thoroughly heated. Sprinkle
with Parmesan cheese, if desired.
Yield: 8 to 10 servings.

Ouida Hamilton
Birmingham, Alabama

And the Winner Is ...

*Invite a group of movie fans to watch the
Academy Awards at your house. While you
cheer for your favorite stars, serve an
assortment of these terrific appetizers.*

Oscar-Night Open House
Serves 10

Blue Cheese-Walnut Wafers
Taco Cheesecake
Sesame-Maple Chicken Wings

BLUE CHEESE-WALNUT WAFERS

*Be sure to use butter—it makes
these wafers wonderfully short and
the dough easy to handle.*

Prep: 6 minutes
Chill: 1 hour, 5 minutes
Bake: 12 minutes

1 (4-ounce) package blue cheese,
    softened
½ cup butter, softened
1¼ cups all-purpose flour
⅓ cup finely chopped walnuts

• **Process** first 3 ingredients in a food
processor until smooth, stopping to
scrape sides. (Mixture will be sticky.)
Spoon into a bowl; stir in nuts. Cover;
chill 5 minutes. Divide in half. Shape
each portion into an 8-inch log. Wrap in
heavy-duty plastic wrap; chill 1 hour.
• **Slice** dough into ¼-inch-thick slices;
place on ungreased baking sheets.
• **Bake** at 350° for 12 minutes or until
lightly browned. Store in an airtight
container up to a week. **Yield:** 4 dozen.

TACO CHEESECAKE

*Make this cheesecake a day ahead.
Heat and add toppings before serving.*

Prep: 35 minutes
Bake: 25 minutes

1 cup crushed tortilla chips
1 tablespoon butter or margarine,
    melted
1 pound ground round
1 (1¼-ounce) envelope taco
    seasoning mix, divided
2 tablespoons water
2 (8-ounce) packages cream cheese,
    softened
2 large eggs
2 cups (8 ounces) shredded sharp
    Cheddar cheese
1 (8-ounce) container sour
    cream
2 tablespoons all-purpose flour
Toppings: shredded lettuce, chopped
    tomato, chopped green bell pepper

• **Stir** together crushed tortilla chips and
butter; press into bottom of a 9-inch
springform pan.

- **Bake** at 325° for 10 minutes. Cool on a wire rack.
- **Cook** beef in a large skillet over medium heat, stirring until it crumbles and is no longer pink; drain and pat dry with paper towels. Return beef to skillet. Reserve 1 teaspoon taco seasoning mix.
- **Stir** remaining taco seasoning mix and 2 tablespoons water into beef. Cook over medium heat, stirring occasionally, 5 minutes or until liquid evaporates.
- **Beat** cream cheese at medium speed with an electric mixer until fluffy; add eggs and reserved 1 teaspoon taco seasoning mix, beating until blended. Add Cheddar cheese; beat until blended.
- **Spread** cream cheese mixture evenly over crust and 1 inch up sides of pan. Spoon in beef mixture. Spread cream cheese mixture from around sides of pan over beef mixture, forming a 1-inch border. Combine sour cream and flour; spread over cheesecake.
- **Bake** at 325° for 25 minutes. Cool in pan on a wire rack 10 minutes. Run a knife around edges; release sides. Serve warm with toppings. Store in refrigerator. **Yield:** 12 appetizer servings.

SESAME-MAPLE CHICKEN WINGS

Prep: 20 minutes
Chill: 2 hours
Cook: 6 minutes
Bake: 54 minutes

⅓ cup maple syrup
¼ cup soy sauce
3 tablespoons sesame oil
1 tablespoon chopped fresh ginger
1 tablespoon chili oil
3 garlic cloves
4 pounds chicken wing pieces
2 tablespoons sesame seeds

- **Process** first 6 ingredients in a blender or food processor until smooth, stopping to scrape down sides.
- **Place** chicken in a shallow dish or large heavy-duty zip-top plastic bag; pour marinade over chicken. Cover or seal; chill 2 hours.
- **Remove** chicken from marinade, reserving marinade. Arrange chicken in a

single layer on a lightly greased 15- x 10-inch jellyroll pan.
- **Bring** reserved marinade to a boil in a small saucepan; boil 1 minute.
- **Bake** chicken at 375° for 25 minutes; turn chicken, and bake 15 more minutes. Baste with marinade, and bake 7 minutes. Turn and baste with remaining marinade.
- **Sprinkle** with sesame seeds, and bake 7 minutes or until seeds are golden. **Yield:** 8 to 10 appetizer servings.

Jeanne Wood
New Orleans, Louisiana

What's for Supper?

These pots will boil—watched or not. But they'll boil faster if you start with unsalted water and cover the pot with a lid. Cook the pasta uncovered at a rapid boil, stirring often. At the last minute, add the vegetables to the pot of boiling pasta for Garden Pasta Toss. This will save steps and time—only one pot to wash.

CHICKEN FETTUCCINE ALFREDO

Prep: 5 minutes
Cook: 20 minutes

1 quart water
3 skinned and boned chicken breast halves, cut into bite-size pieces
2 (9-ounce) packages refrigerated fettuccine
1 (17-ounce) jar Alfredo sauce with mushrooms
¾ cup light sour cream

- **Bring** 1 quart water to a boil in a Dutch oven.
- **Add** chicken, and cook 12 minutes or until done. Remove chicken from water with a slotted spoon, and set aside.

- **Add** pasta, and cook 2 to 3 minutes or until tender; drain. Return chicken and pasta to Dutch oven. Stir in Alfredo sauce and sour cream.
- **Cook** over medium heat, stirring occasionally, 1 to 2 minutes or until thoroughly heated. Serve immediately. **Yield:** 6 to 8 servings.

Angela Randle
Cordova, Tennessee

GARDEN PASTA TOSS

Prep: 5 minutes
Cook: 13 minutes
Chill: 2 hours

3 cups uncooked bow-tie pasta
3 quarts water
1 cup broccoli flowerets
2 small carrots, thinly sliced
1 (14-ounce) can artichoke heart quarters, drained
1 cup cherry tomatoes, halved
4 green onions, sliced
¼ teaspoon dried oregano
¼ teaspoon dried basil
½ cup Italian Parmesan dressing
Shredded Parmesan cheese (optional)

- **Cook** pasta in 3 quarts boiling water in a Dutch oven 12 minutes.
- **Add** broccoli and carrot, and cook 1 minute; drain. Rinse with cold water to stop the cooking process; drain. Return pasta mixture to Dutch oven.
- **Stir** in artichokes and next 4 ingredients. Add dressing, tossing to coat. Cover and chill 2 hours. Sprinkle with Parmesan cheese, if desired. **Yield:** 4 to 6 servings.

Patsy Bell Hobson
Liberty, Missouri

SALSA SPAGHETTI

Prep: 10 minutes
Cook: 5 minutes

7 ounces vermicelli, cooked
1 tablespoon olive oil
1½ (24-ounce) jars thick-and-chunky
   salsa
1 (15-ounce) can black beans, rinsed
   and drained
½ teaspoon salt
¼ teaspoon pepper
Toppings: shredded Monterey Jack
   cheese, chopped fresh cilantro

• **Toss** together pasta and oil in a Dutch oven; drain.
• **Add** salsa and next 3 ingredients; cook over medium heat, stirring occasionally, 5 minutes or until thoroughly heated. Serve with desired toppings. **Yield:** 4 servings.

Kay Higgins
Gadsden, Alabama

ONE-POT SPAGHETTI

Prep: 5 minutes
Cook: 20 minutes

1 pound ground chuck
1 small onion, chopped
2 (14½-ounce) cans chicken
   broth
1 (6-ounce) can tomato paste
½ teaspoon salt
½ teaspoon dried oregano
⅛ teaspoon garlic powder
¼ teaspoon pepper
7 ounces uncooked spaghetti, broken
   into 3-inch pieces
Grated Parmesan cheese

• **Cook** ground beef and onion in a large skillet over medium-high heat, stirring until beef crumbles and is no longer pink; drain. Return to skillet.
• **Stir** in broth and next 5 ingredients. Bring to a boil; add pasta. Reduce heat, and simmer, stirring often, 15 minutes or until pasta is tender. Sprinkle with cheese. **Yield:** 4 servings.

Elaine McVinney
Alexandria, Virginia

Living Light

These sandwiches are worthy of taking center stage at the table. Using different types of bread, we offer sandwiches that are meaty and meatless; hot and cold; and open-faced, stacked, and rolled.

Sandwich bread is often slathered with a high-fat spread, such as mayonnaise. These sandwiches are served with low-fat spreads and sauces. To keep your meal low calorie, see "Sides Under 50 Calories" for ideas other than the usual potato chips.

GARBANZO-VEGETABLE PITAS

Prep: 20 minutes

1 (20-ounce) can garbanzo beans,
   rinsed and drained
1 garlic clove, minced
¼ cup lemon juice
3 tablespoons water
2 tablespoons light sour cream
½ teaspoon lemon pepper
4 cups bean sprouts
1 cup grated carrot
1 red bell pepper, chopped
½ cup diced kalamata olives
¼ cup chopped purple onion
2 pepperoncini salad peppers, chopped
3 tablespoons chopped fresh parsley
½ teaspoon dried oregano
6 (6-inch) pita bread rounds
Garnish: fresh parsley sprigs

• **Process** first 6 ingredients in a food processor until smooth, stopping to scrape down sides. Chill.
• **Toss** together bean sprouts and next 7 ingredients.
• **Spread** garbanzo bean mixture evenly on bread rounds. Top evenly with bean sprouts mixture, and roll up. Garnish, if desired. **Yield:** 6 servings.

Clara Watkins
Garden Ridge, Texas

♥ Per serving: Calories 355 (12% from fat)
Fat 4.8g (sat 1.0g, mono 1.7g, poly 1.6g)
Protein 15.4g Carb 65.3g Fiber 6.5g
Cholesterol 2mg Iron 5.4mg
Sodium 707mg Calcium 130mg

CRAB BURGERS

Prep: 25 minutes
Chill: 1 hour
Cook: 10 minutes

1 pound fresh crabmeat
2 cups soft breadcrumbs
1 small onion, chopped
½ green bell pepper, chopped
⅓ cup light mayonnaise
1 large egg
¼ teaspoon salt
¼ teaspoon pepper
Vegetable cooking spray
6 lettuce leaves
3 English muffins, split
Roasted Red Pepper Sauce
Garnish: fresh Italian parsley sprigs

• **Drain** and flake crabmeat, removing any bits of shell.
• **Stir** together crabmeat, breadcrumbs, and next 6 ingredients. Shape into 6 (3½-inch) patties. Chill 1 hour.
• **Cook** patties in a nonstick skillet coated with cooking spray over medium-high heat 5 minutes on each side or until lightly browned.
• **Place** lettuce on muffin halves. Top with crab burgers; spoon Roasted Red Pepper Sauce over burgers. Garnish, if desired; serve with tomato wedges. **Yield:** 6 servings.

Roasted Red Pepper Sauce

Prep: 5 minutes

1 (7-ounce) jar roasted sweet red
   peppers, drained
3 tablespoons light mayonnaise
1 garlic clove
⅛ teaspoon dried crushed red pepper

• **Process** first 3 ingredients in a food processor until smooth. Stir in crushed red pepper. **Yield:** ⅔ cup.

♥ Per serving: Calories 287 (31% from fat)
Fat 10.2g (sat 1.7g, mono 0.9g, poly 4.9g)
Protein 20.4g Carb 28.8g Fiber 1.8g
Cholesterol 121mg Iron 2.2mg
Sodium 725mg Calcium 157mg

TURKEY AND HAM PINE-BERRY SANDWICHES

Prep: 8 minutes

1 (3-ounce) package light cream
    cheese, softened
⅓ cup drained crushed pineapple
12 raisin bread slices
1 (6-ounce) package low-fat smoked
    turkey breast slices
6 tablespoons cranberry-orange relish,
    drained
1 (6-ounce) package low-fat cooked
    ham slices

• **Stir** together softened cream cheese and pineapple.
• **Spread** 2 teaspoons cream cheese mixture on each bread slice. Top 6 bread slices with turkey.
• **Spread** relish over turkey slices. Top with ham and remaining bread slices. **Yield:** 6 servings.

Nancy B. Hall
Calvert City, Kentucky

❤ Per serving: Calories 272 (21% from fat)
Fat 6.2g (sat 2.5g, mono 1.3g, poly 0.6g)
Protein 15.2g Carb 41.4g Fiber 2.4g
Cholesterol 33mg Iron 1.7mg
Sodium 878mg Calcium 57mg

SIDES UNDER 50 CALORIES

1 cucumber, sliced
12 baby carrots
16 celery sticks
1 large tomato, cut into
    wedges
30 small pretzel sticks
4 (3-inch) dill pickles
1½ cups broccoli flowerets
½ apple, sliced
12 radishes
5 low-fat crackers

BROILED CHICKEN SANDWICHES WITH FRESH SALSA

Prep: 10 minutes
Chill: 3 hours
Cook: 10 minutes

4 (4-ounce) skinned and boned
    chicken breast halves
1 garlic clove, minced
½ teaspoon ground cumin
½ teaspoon chili powder
⅛ teaspoon ground red pepper
2 teaspoons lime juice
Olive oil cooking spray
4 Red Leaf lettuce leaves
8 (¾-ounce) slices reduced-calorie
    whole wheat bread, toasted
Fresh Salsa, drained

• **Place** chicken between 2 sheets of heavy-duty plastic wrap, and flatten to ¼-inch thickness using a meat mallet or rolling pin.
• **Stir** together garlic and next 4 ingredients. Rub mixture on chicken. Place in a shallow dish or heavy-duty plastic bag; cover or seal, and chill 3 hours.
• **Place** chicken on a rack coated with cooking spray in a broiler pan.
• **Broil** 5½ inches from heat (with electric oven door partially open) 5 minutes on each side or until done.
• **Place** lettuce leaves on half of bread slices; top with chicken.
• **Spoon** ¼ cup Fresh Salsa over each chicken breast; top with remaining bread slices. **Yield:** 4 servings.

Fresh Salsa

Prep: 5 minutes
Chill: 2 hours

1 large tomato, peeled, seeded, and
    chopped
2½ tablespoons diced purple
    onion
1 jalapeño pepper, seeded and
    minced
1½ teaspoons chopped fresh
    cilantro
1 garlic clove, minced
½ teaspoon red wine vinegar
½ teaspoon salt
¼ teaspoon pepper

• **Stir** together all ingredients; cover and chill 2 hours. **Yield:** about 1¼ cups.

Brenda Russell
Signal Mountain, Tennessee

❤ Per serving: Calories 245 (13% from fat)
Fat 3.5g (sat 0.7g, mono 0.6g, poly 1.3g)
Protein 31.8g Carb 24.2g Fiber 1.0g
Cholesterol 67mg Iron 1.5mg
Sodium 608mg Calcium 62mg

GRILLED FLANK STEAK WITH MOLASSES BARBECUE GLAZE

Prep: 3 minutes
Chill: 2 hours
Grill: 12 minutes

½ cup molasses
¼ cup coarse-grained mustard
1 tablespoon olive oil
1 (1½-pound) flank steak
6 (8-inch) flour tortillas
1 cup shredded lettuce
1 large tomato, chopped
¾ cup (3 ounces) shredded reduced-
    fat Cheddar cheese
½ cup light sour cream

• **Whisk** together first 3 ingredients.
• **Place** steak in a shallow dish or large heavy-duty zip-top bag.
• **Pour** molasses mixture over steak, reserving ¼ cup for basting. Cover or seal, and chill 2 hours, turning occasionally. Remove meat from marinade, discarding marinade.
• **Grill,** covered with grill lid, over medium-high heat (350° to 400°) 6 minutes on each side or to desired degree of doneness, brushing often with reserved marinade.
• **Cut** steak diagonally across the grain into very thin strips.
• **Serve** steak with remaining ingredients. **Yield:** 6 servings.

❤ Per serving: Calories 283 (30% from fat)
Fat 9.4 (sat 3.0g, mono 3.9g, poly 1.3g)
Protein 9.5g Carb 40.7g Fiber 1.4g
Cholesterol 14mg Iron 2.8mg
Sodium 376mg Calcium 181mg

A Taste of the South

You can't get more basic than chess pie. Remarkable in its simplicity, timeless in appeal, this is the ultimate pantry pie. Here's our favorite recipe, plus some easy variations, ches' for you.

Of course, you can get fancy with flavorings such as lemon juice and vanilla extract. Or add a dash of nutmeg, ginger, or cinnamon. Sprinkle in some flaked coconut or toasted chopped pecans. Some believe a splash of buttermilk makes it better; others swear by a tablespoon of vinegar. To double the already-decadent richness, stir in cocoa powder.

CLASSIC CHESS PIE

Chess pie, as simple or as fancy as you please, never fails to bring a smile.

Prep: 23 minutes
Bake: 55 minutes

½ (15-ounce) package refrigerated piecrusts
2 cups sugar
2 tablespoons cornmeal
1 tablespoon all-purpose flour
¼ teaspoon salt
½ cup butter or margarine, melted
¼ cup milk
1 tablespoon white vinegar
½ teaspoon vanilla extract
4 large eggs, lightly beaten

• **Fit** piecrust into a 9-inch pieplate according to package directions; fold edges under, and crimp.
• **Line** pastry with aluminum foil, and fill with pie weights or dried beans.
• **Bake** at 425° for 4 to 5 minutes. Remove weights and foil.

• **Bake** 2 more minutes or until golden. Cool completely.
• **Stir** together sugar and next 7 ingredients until blended.
• **Add** eggs, stirring well. Pour filling into piecrust.
• **Bake** at 350° for 50 to 55 minutes, shielding edges with aluminum foil after 10 minutes to prevent excessive browning. Cool completely on a wire rack. **Yield:** 1 (9-inch) pie.

Coconut Chess Pie: Prepare filling as directed above; stir in 1 cup toasted flaked coconut before pouring into piecrust. Bake as directed above.

Chocolate-Pecan Chess Pie: Prepare filling as directed above; stir in 3½ tablespoons cocoa and ½ cup toasted chopped pecans before pouring into piecrust. Bake as directed above.

Lemon Chess Pie: Prepare filling as directed above; stir in ⅓ cup lemon juice and 2 teaspoons grated lemon rind before pouring into piecrust. Bake as directed above.

A SIMPLE TRADITION

Chess pie may be a chameleon confection, but at its heart are always the basic four ingredients—flour, butter, sugar, and eggs. And the preparation is never much more than a little stirring and about an hour in the oven.

"There are a lot of similar desserts that share the same ingredients," explains cookbook author Jeanne Voltz. "That's because the South was at one time agrarian, and a farm woman had to cook with what was there—things like eggs, butter, sugar, and cornmeal. She'd put it all together and try to make something out of it, and when it was good she'd try to remember what she did."

Though no one's certain how the sweet got its start, John Egerton offers two possibilities in his book, *Southern Food.* Chess pie may have been called "chest pie" because it held up well in the pie chest, a piece of furniture common in the early South.

His second story has to do with a creative cook who served the pie to her husband.

"What kind of pie is this?" her spouse is said to have exclaimed. She just shrugged, smiled, and replied, "I don't know. It's ches' pie."

In the Mardi Gras Spirit

If you can't make it to the French Quarter for the Mardi Gras festivities, create your own Fat Tuesday celebration. Serve red beans and rice with King Cake and Hurricane Punch—and let the good times roll.

KING CAKE

A fitting end to any traditional Mardi Gras celebration, this highly recommended recipe originally appeared in January 1990.

Prep: 50 minutes
Rise: 1 hour, 20 minutes
Bake: 15 minutes

¼ cup butter or margarine
1 (16-ounce) container sour cream
⅓ cup sugar
1 teaspoon salt
2 (¼-ounce) envelopes active dry yeast
1 tablespoon sugar
½ cup warm water (100° to 110°)
2 large eggs
6 to 6½ cups all-purpose flour
½ cup sugar
1½ teaspoons ground cinnamon
⅓ cup butter or margarine, softened
Colored Frostings
Colored Sugars

• **Cook** first 4 ingredients in a saucepan over low heat, stirring often, until butter melts. Cool mixture to 100° to 110°.
• **Dissolve** yeast and 1 tablespoon sugar in ½ cup warm water in a large bowl; let stand 5 minutes.
• **Add** butter mixture, eggs, and 2 cups flour; beat at medium speed with an electric mixer 2 minutes or until smooth. Gradually stir in enough remaining flour to make a soft dough.
• **Turn** dough onto a lightly floured surface; knead until smooth and elastic, about 10 minutes.
• **Place** dough in a well-greased bowl, turning to grease top. Cover and let rise in a warm place (85°), free from drafts, 1 hour or until doubled in bulk.
• **Stir** together ½ cup sugar and cinnamon; set aside.
• **Punch** dough down; divide in half. Roll each portion to a 28- x 10-inch rectangle. Spread each rectangle evenly with softened butter, and sprinkle with cinnamon mixture.
• **Roll** dough, jellyroll fashion, starting at long side.
• **Place** dough rolls, seam side down, on a lightly greased baking sheet. Bring ends of rolls together to form an oval ring, moistening and pinching edges together to seal.
• **Cover** and let rise in a warm place, free from drafts, 20 minutes or until doubled in bulk.
• **Bake** at 375° for 15 minutes or until golden. Decorate with bands of Colored Frostings; sprinkle with Colored Sugars. **Yield:** 2 cakes.

Note: Once the cake has cooled, randomly insert a plastic baby doll into cake before frosting, if desired.

Colored Frostings

Prep: 15 minutes

3 cups powdered sugar
3 tablespoons butter, melted
3 to 6 tablespoons milk
¼ teaspoon vanilla extract
1 or 2 drops each of green, yellow, red, and blue liquid food coloring

• **Stir** together powdered sugar and melted butter. Add milk to reach desired consistency for drizzling; stir in vanilla.
• **Divide** frosting into 3 batches, tinting 1 green, 1 yellow, and combining red and blue food coloring for purple frosting. **Yield:** about 1½ cups.

Colored Sugars

Prep: 20 minutes

1½ cups sugar
1 or 2 drops each of green, yellow, red, and blue liquid food coloring

• **Place** ½ cup sugar and drop of green food coloring in a jar or zip-top plastic bag; seal. Shake vigorously to evenly mix color with sugar.
• **Repeat** procedure with ½ cup sugar and yellow food coloring. For purple, combine 1 drop red and 1 drop blue food coloring before adding to remaining ½ cup sugar. **Yield:** ½ cup of each colored sugar.

HURRICANE PUNCH

Prep: 10 minutes

½ (64-ounce) bottle red fruit punch
1 (6-ounce) can frozen limeade concentrate, thawed
1 (6-ounce) can frozen orange juice concentrate, thawed
1⅔ cups light rum
1⅔ cups dark rum

• **Stir** together all ingredients. Serve over ice. **Yield:** 8¼ cups.

Kathy Bowes
Metairie, Louisiana

Cooking Up a Mystery

Author Lou Jane Temple infuses her novels with intrigue, creative characters, and a passion for cooking. Here are some of her favorite culinary creations.

SWEET-AND-SOUR RED CABBAGE AND APPLES

From Bread on Arrival, *published by St. Martin's Press*

Prep: 20 minutes
Cook: 40 minutes

- 2 tablespoons butter or margarine
- 2 tablespoons olive oil
- 1 large red cabbage, thinly sliced
- 3 Granny Smith apples, cut into ½-inch wedges
- 1 cup sugar
- 1 cup red wine vinegar
- ¼ teaspoon kosher salt or table salt
- ¼ teaspoon pepper

• **Melt** butter with oil in a large skillet over medium-high heat; add cabbage, and sauté 10 minutes. Stir in apple, and set aside.
• **Melt** sugar in a heavy saucepan over medium heat, stirring constantly; stir in vinegar (mixture will bubble, and sugar will clump), and bring to a boil.
• **Cook,** stirring often, until sugar dissolves and mixture is caramel colored.
• **Stir** in cabbage mixture; cook over medium heat, stirring occasionally, 20 minutes. Stir in salt and pepper. **Yield:** 6 servings.

Lou Jane Temple
Kansas City, Missouri

BRAISED LAMB SHANKS

From A Stiff Risotto, *published by St. Martin's Press*

Prep: 30 minutes
Bake: 3 hours

- 4 lamb shanks (6 pounds)
- ½ cup all-purpose flour
- ¼ cup olive oil
- 2 (12-ounce) cans stout ale
- 2 (11.5-ounce) cans apricot nectar
- 2 garlic bulbs, halved
- 5 fresh rosemary sprigs
- 1½ teaspoons kosher salt or table salt
- ½ teaspoon pepper
- Mashed potatoes
- Garnish: fresh rosemary sprigs

• **Dredge** lamb shanks in flour; brown on all sides in hot oil in a large skillet. Place lamb in a large roasting pan; add ale and next 5 ingredients.
• **Bake,** covered, at 375° for 2 hours. Uncover and bake 1 more hour. Skim fat from drippings
• **Serve** lamb shanks and drippings with mashed potatoes. Garnish, if desired. **Yield:** 4 servings.

Note: For testing purposes only, we used Guinness Stout.

Lou Jane Temple
Kansas City, Missouri

PANZANELLA

Serve this Italian bread salad for a light, refreshing main course. From Bread on Arrival, *published by St. Martin's Press*

Prep: 20 minutes
Chill: 1 hour

- 1 (16-ounce) stale French or Italian bread loaf
- 10 plum tomatoes, halved and sliced
- ½ teaspoon salt, divided
- ½ teaspoon pepper, divided
- 2 purple onions, halved and thinly sliced
- 1 cup firmly packed basil leaves, shredded
- 1 cup kalamata olives, pitted
- 1 cup walnuts, toasted
- 1 cucumber, seeded and sliced
- 1 red bell pepper, quartered and thinly sliced
- 1 green bell pepper, quartered and thinly sliced
- 1 cup (4 ounces) crumbled Gorgonzola cheese
- 4 garlic cloves, minced
- 1 cup red wine vinegar, divided
- 1 cup extra-virgin olive oil, divided

• **Cut** bread into 1-inch cubes, and place on a baking sheet.
• **Bake** bread cubes at 350° for 10 to 15 minutes or until toasted.
• **Place** bread cubes in a large bowl. Top with tomato; sprinkle with ¼ teaspoon salt and ¼ teaspoon pepper.
• **Layer** with onions and next 4 ingredients, and sprinkle with remaining ¼ teaspoon salt and ¼ teaspoon pepper.
• **Layer** with red bell pepper and next 3 ingredients. Drizzle with ½ cup red wine vinegar and ½ cup olive oil. Cover and chill 1 hour.
• **Drizzle** with remaining ½ cup vinegar and ½ cup olive oil; serve immediately. **Yield:** 6 to 8 servings.

Lou Jane Temple
Kansas City, Missouri

> *"Life has led me down some interesting paths, and I'm still anxious to learn every day. Every time you turn a corner, there's something new to discover."*
>
> Lou Jane Temple

The voice on Lou Jane Temple's answering machine is smoky and playful: "Hi, this is Lou Jane," it purrs, "and I don't want to miss *a thing*! So please leave a message." The Kansas City, Missouri, mystery writer, caterer, and script supervisor is also, it appears, a character.

An Eclectic Career

Lou Jane hasn't missed much in her life. She started on her adventuresome career path when she passed up law school in favor of becoming a caterer—to rock stars.

"I was married to a musician in the seventies, when rock 'n' roll began to be big business and performers started demanding food backstage," Lou Jane recalls. It was challenging work. "No one is pickier than the English rock stars. [The experience] taught me to think on my feet and be inventive."

In the eighties, between cooking stints and raising her three children, she sold vintage clothing and antique quilts. That led to work as a props person for movies and commercials. From there, she graduated to script supervisor. And now? Lou Jane has achieved her goal of working as an assistant director.

From Restaurateur to Writer

In the early nineties, Lou Jane opened a restaurant, Cafe Lulu. "It was a great artistic success but not a good business venture," she says. After the restaurant closed, she wrote a regular wine column and occasional food features for the *Kansas City Star.*

An article she wrote on culinary mystery writers piqued her interest in the genre. "When I was done with the piece, I decided to write a novel of my own." *Death by Rhubarb, Revenge of the Barbeque Queens, A Stiff Risotto, Bread on Arrival,* and the newly published *The Cornbread Killer* were the results.

Her books are peppered with recipes that Lou Jane (in the guise of Heaven Lee, her protagonist) develops. "That's how I went from cooking food to killing people with it," she laughs heartily.

She gets ideas everywhere. "Every day I think of either an article I want to write about food or wine, or a mystery. I clip things from the newspaper that might be an idea I can use. Actually sitting down and writing is the troublesome part." She still cooks professionally from time to time—to promote her books, during television appearances, and once at the prestigious James Beard House in New York.

All in the Family

Lou Jane passed her love of food and writing on to two of her three children. A son worked as a kitchen manager in Colorado, and her daughter, Reagan Walker, is a food writer for the *Atlanta Journal–Constitution.*

Lou Jane still sees her future as an adventure. "Life has led me down some interesting paths," she muses. "And I'm still anxious to learn every day. Every time you turn a corner, there's something new to discover."

Popping Over the Top

Deep-cupped popover pans produce tall, airy popovers. Standard muffin pans and 8-ounce custard cups work well as substitutes.

Piercing basic Popovers and Cheddar Popovers prevents a soggy puff. The Parmesan and Yorkshire variations do not require this step.

Popovers deflate quickly, so serve them immediately.

Popovers, with their crusty exteriors and soft centers, command attention. Steam and eggs help these whisk-together rolls rise to grand proportions and live up to their names. You can create any one of our variations in just a few easy steps. "Popover Pointers" (left) offers you tips for success. Try a batch with butter and jam, or eat them alongside soup or supper. You'll win instant status as a baking wizard.

POPOVERS

Prep: 10 minutes
Bake: 35 minutes

½ cup milk
2 large eggs
1 tablespoon vegetable oil
¾ cup all-purpose flour

• **Whisk** together first 3 ingredients in a medium bowl.
• **Add** flour, whisking until mixture is smooth.
• **Place** well-greased popover pans or 8-ounce custard cups in a 450° oven 3 minutes or until a drop of water sizzles when dropped in them. Remove pans from oven; spoon batter into hot pans, filling three-fourths full.
• **Bake** on lowest oven rack at 450° for 15 minutes. Reduce temperature to 350°, and bake 15 minutes. Turn oven off. Cut a small slit in popover tops; return to oven, and let stand 5 minutes with oven door closed. Serve immediately. **Yield:** 6 servings.

Herbed Popovers: Add ½ teaspoon crushed dried thyme to batter.

Patsy Bell Hobson
Liberty, Missouri

CHEDDAR POPOVERS

Prep: 10 minutes
Bake: 30 minutes

1 cup all-purpose flour
½ teaspoon salt
¼ teaspoon paprika
⅛ teaspoon ground red pepper
2 large eggs
1 cup milk
½ cup (2 ounces) shredded Cheddar cheese

• **Combine** first 4 ingredients. Whisk together eggs and milk; add to flour mixture, whisking until smooth. Stir in cheese.
• **Place** well-greased popover pans or 8-ounce custard cups in a 450° oven 3 minutes or until a drop of water sizzles when dropped in them. Remove pans from oven; spoon batter into hot pans, filling three-fourths full.
• **Bake** on lowest oven rack at 450° for 15 minutes. Reduce temperature to 350°, and bake 10 minutes. Turn oven off. Cut a small slit in popover tops; return to oven, and let stand 5 minutes with oven door closed. Serve immediately. **Yield:** 8 servings.

Jill Snelson Shaw
Fort Worth, Texas

PARMESAN POPOVERS

Prep: 15 minutes
Bake: 45 minutes

2 tablespoons grated Parmesan cheese
1 cup all-purpose flour
1 cup milk
2 large eggs
2 egg whites
1 tablespoon butter or margarine, melted
2 teaspoons Worcestershire sauce
½ teaspoon salt
¼ teaspoon garlic powder

• **Sprinkle** bottom and sides of well-greased popover pans or 8-ounce custard cups with Parmesan cheese.
• **Whisk** together flour and next 7 ingredients until blended. Spoon into pans, filling three-fourths full.

• **Bake** on lowest oven rack at 450° for 15 minutes. Reduce temperature to 350°, and bake 30 minutes or until golden brown. Serve immediately. **Yield:** 6 servings.

YORKSHIRE POPOVERS

Prep: 15 minutes
Stand: 1 hour
Bake: 45 minutes

1 cup all-purpose flour
1 cup water
Dash of salt
2 large eggs
2 tablespoons bacon drippings

• **Beat** first 3 ingredients at low speed with an electric mixer 2 minutes. Let stand 1 hour. Add eggs, beating 1 minute.
• **Place** drippings in muffin pans or 8-ounce custard cups, and heat in a 475° oven 3 minutes or until a drop of water sizzles when dropped in them. Remove pans from oven, and spoon batter into hot pans, filling half full.
• **Bake** on lowest oven rack at 475° for 15 minutes. Reduce temperature to 350°, and bake 30 minutes. Serve immediately. **Yield:** 8 servings.

Beccie Seaman
Opelika, Alabama

Baked (in) Alaska

A laska brings to mind magnificent mountains, the contrast of untouched land and areas where wildlife roam freely, and the peculiar light in summer when the sun never sets. And once you sample food from the Princess Wilderness Lodges, Denali and Kenai, Alaska will also make you think of delicious food—a combination of sophisticated cuisine and familiar Southern fare. Try these dishes for a taste of Alaska—you'll feel right at home.

SMOKED SALMON-WHISKEY BISQUE

Prep: 30 minutes
Cook: 40 minutes

¼ cup unsalted butter
⅓ cup all-purpose flour
1 quart Fish Stock
1 quart half-and-half
¼ cup whiskey
2 tablespoons unsalted butter
1 tablespoon Worcestershire sauce
2 teaspoons lemon juice
1 teaspoon hot sauce
½ teaspoon salt
¼ teaspoon Old Bay seasoning
¼ teaspoon ground white pepper
2 (4-ounce) packages smoked salmon, chopped
2 tablespoons dry sherry (optional)
Garnishes: smoked salmon, fresh tarragon sprigs

• **Melt** ¼ cup butter in a Dutch oven over medium heat; whisk in flour until smooth.
• **Cook,** whisking constantly, 5 minutes. Gradually whisk in Fish Stock.
• **Bring** mixture to a boil; reduce heat, and simmer 30 minutes.
• **Whisk** in half-and-half and next 8 ingredients. Cook until thoroughly heated.
• **Stir** in chopped smoked salmon, and, if desired, dry sherry. Garnish each serving, if desired. **Yield:** 3 quarts.

Fish Stock

Prep: 15 minutes
Cook: 2 hours, 30 minutes

1 carrot, chopped
1 small onion, chopped
1 celery rib, chopped
2 tablespoons olive oil
2 quarts water
1 (6-ounce) can tomato paste
¼ cup whiskey
2 garlic cloves, pressed
1 extra-large fish bouillon cube
1 bay leaf
1 teaspoon dried tarragon

• **Sauté** first 3 ingredients in hot oil in a large Dutch oven over medium-high heat until lightly browned.

• **Stir** in 2 quarts water and remaining ingredients.
• **Bring** to a boil; reduce heat, and simmer, stirring occasionally, 2 hours and 30 minutes.
• **Pour** mixture through a wire-mesh strainer into a large bowl, discarding solids. Refrigerate up to 3 days, if desired. **Yield:** 1 quart.

Note: For testing purposes only, we used Knorr Fish Bouillon and Jack Daniel's whiskey.

POT ROAST

Prep: 15 minutes
Bake: 4 hours
Cook: 35 minutes

1 (5-pound) beef brisket
1 teaspoon salt
1 teaspoon coarsely ground pepper
3 carrots, cut into 2-inch pieces
2 celery ribs, cut into 1-inch pieces
3 medium onions, chopped
3 garlic cloves, minced
1 tomato, quartered
2 bay leaves
½ teaspoon dried thyme
3 (14½-ounce) cans beef broth
¼ cup butter or margarine
¾ cup all-purpose flour
Garlic mashed potatoes

• **Sprinkle** brisket with salt and pepper, and place in a large roasting pan. Add carrot and next 7 ingredients.
• **Bake,** covered, at 325° for 4 hours or until brisket is tender. Remove brisket, and keep warm. Remove vegetables with a slotted spoon, and keep warm. Discard bay leaves. Reserve 3 cups drippings.
• **Melt** butter in a medium saucepan over medium-high heat; whisk in flour until smooth.
• **Cook,** whisking constantly, 1 minute. Gradually whisk in reserved 3 cups drippings until smooth. Reduce heat, and simmer, whisking occasionally, 30 minutes or until thickened. Serve with brisket, vegetables, and garlic mashed potatoes. **Yield:** 6 servings.

From Our Kitchen

Shake Up a Salad

Buttermilk and a dash of chopped green onions and herbs or spices give garden-fresh flavor to prepared salad dressings. Blend equal parts of nonfat buttermilk with a bottled dressing; then add a few tablespoons of green onions and/or your favorite herb.

For other ideas using buttermilk, see our story on page 48. If it's not a staple at your home, you can get the flavor from a powder. Find SACO Cultured Buttermilk Blend—in 12- and 16-ounce containers among other dry milk products on your grocer's shelves. It's ideal for cooking and baking. Use it in any recipe that calls for liquid buttermilk or sour milk. One advantage is you can store the powder for two to three years in the refrigerator after opening. For 1 cup of full-strength liquid buttermilk, stir 4 level tablespoons of powder into 1 cup water.

When a recipe calls for a cup of buttermilk and you have neither liquid nor dry, substitute an equal amount of plain yogurt, or 1 tablespoon vinegar or lemon juice added to enough milk to measure 1 cup (let mixture stand 5 minutes).

Tips and Tidbits

■ **Grand Marnier** is one brand of orange liqueur. We like its smooth flavor with no bitter aftertaste. For alcohol-free cooking, substitute orange juice for the liqueur.

■ **Sherry** can be substituted with apple juice (in sweet dishes) or chicken broth (in savory dishes).

■ **Lavosh** is a round, thin bread that looks and tastes like water crackers. It is available both soft (for rolling) and crisp (for dipping). Middle Eastern markets and specialty grocery stores carry it.

■ **Artichokes** provide great flavor as well as vitamins A and C, folate, and potassium. They're fat free and low in sodium.

CARAMEL STEP-BY-STEP

Now that you're craving the luscious caramel described on page 52, see how easy it is to make with these simple steps.

1. Cook sugar over medium-high heat until it turns a rich caramel color. As the sugar melts, the color progresses from pale yellow to brown. We recommend a large cast-iron skillet or heavy saucepan to achieve even browning. And for best results, use a wooden spoon; it can take the heat, and the handle doesn't get hot.

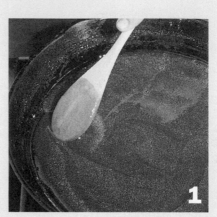

2. Carefully pour caramelized sugar into the whipping cream mixture. Be sure to use a large pot, because the mixture will bubble as the cream and sugar combine.

3. There's no guesswork when you use a thermometer that signals when proper temperature is reached.

Cleanup is a snap when you soak the utensils in hot water to remove all hardened caramel. Protect your thermometer by allowing it to cool completely before placing it in warm water.

You can make caramel sauce on a humid day, but save caramel frostings for a clear, dry day.

APRIL

An Easy Easter Brunch

Celebrate the season with these creative ideas that combine traditional holiday fare and a few fun surprises.

Festive Easter Menu
Serves 12 to 15

Curried Chicken Salad Spread with crackers

Honey ham on biscuits with Beehive Butter

Fresh Fruit Salad With Celery Seed Dressing

Steamed Asparagus With Tomato-Basil Dip

Double-Stuffed Eggs

Sunny Spring Lemonade

Awaken this spring to all things new, to gardens revived and friendships revisited after a long and languid winter. Celebrate the glorious gift of Easter with a wonderful brunch. Most of the menu can be made ahead and includes purchased foods. Mary Allen Perry of our Test Kitchens coordinated this celebration menu using an artful collection of traditional dishes with ingenious twists.

The centerpiece (pictured on pages 74-75) is simple to create with an abundance of flower, herb, and vegetable transplants. Arranged to look like a spring garden, the collection can later be transferred to containers and flowerbeds. Read the box on facing page for instructions.

Assemble the table garden on Friday or Saturday so that Sunday's schedule is relaxed and easy.

CURRIED CHICKEN SALAD SPREAD
(pictured on pages 74 and 75)

Prep: 30 minutes
Chill: 8 hours

4 cups finely chopped cooked chicken
3 (8-ounce) packages cream cheese, softened*
¾ cup golden raisins, chopped
½ cup flaked coconut, toasted
2 celery ribs, diced
6 green onions, minced
1 (2¼-ounce) package slivered almonds, toasted
1 tablespoon curry powder
½ teaspoon salt
½ teaspoon pepper
1 tablespoon freshly grated ginger
Garnishes: green onion stems, minced green onions, toasted flaked coconut, pistachios, fresh dill sprigs, yellow squash wedges, fresh chives, salad greens, pansies, cucumber slices

• **Stir** together first 11 ingredients. Form into an egg shape.
• **Cover** and chill 8 hours. Garnish, if desired. Serve with crackers. **Yield:** 20 to 25 appetizer servings.

*Substitute reduced-fat cream cheese for regular cream cheese, if desired.

BEEHIVE BUTTER
(pictured on pages 74 and 75)

Prep: 20 minutes
Chill: 2 hours

1½ cups butter, softened
½ cup spicy brown mustard
1 cup finely chopped pecans, toasted
1 pecan half
Garnishes: fresh herbs, edible flower petals

• **Stir** together first 3 ingredients.
• **Form** butter mixture into a beehive shape. Smooth mound with a spatula or rounded knife.
• **Form** grooves around mound with tines of a fork.
• **Insert** pecan half near the base for a door; cover and chill 2 hours or up to 2 days. Garnish, if desired. **Yield:** 3 cups.

FRESH FRUIT SALAD WITH CELERY SEED DRESSING
(pictured on page 74)

Prep: 15 minutes

⅔ cup sugar
⅓ cup honey
5 tablespoons white vinegar
1 tablespoon fresh lemon juice
1 teaspoon dry mustard
1 teaspoon paprika
1 teaspoon celery seeds or poppy seeds
¼ teaspoon salt
1 cup vegetable oil, chilled
8 cups assorted fresh fruit (melon cubes, strawberry halves, pineapple chunks)

• **Process** first 8 ingredients in a blender until smooth, stopping to scrape down sides. With blender running, add oil in a slow, steady stream.

• **Cover** and chill 8 hours, if desired. Serve with assorted fruit. **Yield:** 12 to 15 servings.

Note: No time to cut up fruit? Stop by the deli or supermarket salad bar Saturday night. Toss the fruit with lemon juice to keep it looking fresh.

Nena Gibson
Mooresville, North Carolina

STEAMED ASPARAGUS WITH TOMATO-BASIL DIP
(pictured on pages 74 and 75)

Make the dip up to two days ahead, and chill until ready to serve with crisp asparagus.

Prep: 20 minutes
Cook: 3 minutes

1   cup mayonnaise
½   cup sour cream
½   cup chopped fresh basil
1   tablespoon tomato paste
1   tablespoon grated lemon rind
4   pounds fresh asparagus
Garnish: fresh basil

• **Whisk** together first 5 ingredients until blended. Cover and chill up to 2 days, if desired.
• **Snap** off tough ends of asparagus.
• **Cook** in boiling water to cover 3 minutes or until crisp-tender; drain.
• **Plunge** asparagus into ice water to stop the cooking process; drain. Cover and chill until ready to serve with dip. Garnish dip, if desired. **Yield:** 12 to 15 servings.

EASTER GARDEN CENTERPIECE

Celebrate spring flowers, vegetables, and herbs with an easy Easter centerpiece. An arrangement is as simple as a trip to the garden shop. Follow our instructions below for materials and assembly.

Materials

2 nonpartitioned flats
green sheet moss
glue gun
foil
scissors
flowers, herbs, and vegetables

Shop for Color

Choose a color scheme that complements your table linens and decor. Select bright flowers in cell packs and several 3- or 4-inch pots. Your spring centerpiece can include small calla lilies, dianthus, stock, sweet alyssum, and violas. This will provide diversity in height and fullness. Check out herbs and vegetables as well. Pots of fresh lettuce, parsley, and fennel make good choices for texture.

Purchase enough flowers, vegetables, and herbs to fill one flat. Many flats have built in dividers; use one without partitions for this project. To add extra stability, place one flat inside another.

Put It Together

Use a glue gun to carefully attach sheet moss to the flat's outer edge. Trim the bottom of the moss with scissors so that the flat will sit evenly on the table.

Line the container with aluminum foil, covering the bottom in one continuous sheet; press foil up the sides. Tuck edges down so that the foil is not visible over the flat's edge.

Water all plant material prior to arranging. Choose a starting point in a back corner of the flat. Place the tallest flowers and herbs in this location, and arrange the others, stepping down in height to the edges of the container. Bedding plants may be cut apart or removed from their containers to snuggle roots more closely. Cluster flowers of like kinds together, adding lettuces and herbs intermittently for textural interest.

After the Party

The arrangement may stay in the flat for several days. Then you can transplant the contents into the garden. Keep in mind the individual light and water requirements for each seedling, and plant them in the appropriate place. The flat and foil can be used again. Repair any moss that has come loose, and store the flat away from direct light. It will be ready to fill for the next occasion.

DOUBLE-STUFFED EGGS
(pictured on pages 74 and 75)

*The potato flakes make a
full-bodied filling, perfect for
piping. One basic recipe makes
two variations to chill overnight.*

Prep: 30 minutes

1 dozen hard-cooked eggs, peeled
¾ cup light mayonnaise
1 tablespoon Dijon mustard
¼ teaspoon salt
¼ teaspoon pepper
½ cup instant potato flakes
Garnish: fresh dill sprigs

• **Cut** eggs in half lengthwise. Remove yolks. Process egg yolks, mayonnaise, and next 4 ingredients in a food processor until smooth, stopping to scrape down sides.
• **Spoon** or pipe filling into egg whites. Cover and chill up to 8 hours. Garnish, if desired. **Yield:** 2 dozen.

Bacon-Stuffed Eggs: Stir ⅔ cup (8 slices) crumbled cooked bacon, 3 tablespoons pickle relish, and ¼ cup chopped fresh chives into yolk mixture. Proceed as directed.

Shrimp-Stuffed Eggs: Stir ¾ pound shrimp, cooked, peeled, and chopped; 2 tablespoons prepared horseradish; and 6 green onions, minced, into yolk mixture. Proceed as directed.

SUNNY SPRING LEMONADE

Prep: 5 minutes

6 cups white grape juice, chilled
1 (12-ounce) can frozen lemonade
   concentrate, thawed and
   undiluted
5½ cups club soda, chilled

• **Stir** together all ingredients in a 1-gallon pitcher or punch bowl. Serve over ice. **Yield:** 3 quarts.

*Ann Quenelle
Birmingham, Alabama*

A Taste of the South

You know you're in the South when you see iced tea on the breakfast menu. And when the waitress says, "Tell me, hon, would you like that sweet or unsweet?"

And how much sugar does it take? "A mere sprinkle of sweetness won't do. It has to be more like a thundershower of sugar," writes syndicated food columnist Rob Kasper. "A good glass of real ice tea, the stuff with a sugar edge, doesn't just pick a person up. It throws him back into the ring, and gets him ready to take some more licks."

Here's our best version of the heat-fighting elixir.

SOUTHERN SWEETENED TEA

*Prep: 2 minutes
Cook: 5 minutes
Steep: 10 minutes*

6 cups water
4 family-size tea bags
1 to 1¾ cups sugar

• **Bring** 6 cups water to a boil in a saucepan; add tea bags.
• **Boil** 1 minute; remove from heat. Cover and steep 10 minutes. Remove tea bags, squeezing gently.
• **Add** sugar, stirring until dissolved. Pour into a 1-gallon pitcher, and add enough water to fill pitcher. Serve over ice. **Yield:** 1 gallon.

TIME FOR TEA

Some say sweet tea made its debut at the 1904 World's Fair, but food historian John Egerton traces its roots to 1868, the start of commercial ice manufacturing. The moment some thirsty sipper poured freshly brewed hot tea over chipped ice, "Shazam! The greatest thirst quencher in all history explodes like a clap of thunder on the dark surface of Southern consciousness," Egerton writes.

Tea evangelist Jay Grelen has sought to spread the word through Sweet Tea Sip-Offs in Mobile. His only male winner, Jamie Price, is quick to spill the secrets of his success: "It's just good ol' sweet tea, strong and sweet, just like my grandmother made it."

New York Times reporter Rick Bragg says, "In the vernacular of the South of not so long ago, there was no such thing as sweet iced tea. There was just tea, always sweetened in a jug or pitcher with cane sugar, always poured over ice."

Speaking of vernacular, is it ice tea or iced tea? Gary Doc, an iced tea man who's married to a soft drink lover, writes, "The only time I heard anyone say iced tea was on the Lipton Tea commercials."

For lack of consensus we'll dodge the "d" issue, as long as it's fresh, cold, and sweet.

Top-Rated Menu

Honor a graduate, a bride, or expectant parents with this appetizer menu. There's reason to celebrate—all of these long-favored recipes have fewer than 10 ingredients. These memorable hors d'oeuvres are guaranteed to please when served for any occasion.

Make-Ahead Appetizer Menu
Serves 20

Shrimp Tartlets

Asparagus With Garlic Cream

Tomato-Cheese Torte   Assorted crackers

Chocolate-Almond Petits Fours

SHRIMP TARTLETS

To streamline this recipe, we substituted prepared phyllo pastry shells for homemade cream puffs.

Prep: 30 minutes
Chill: 8 hours
Bake: 15 minutes

2¼ cups water
¾ pound unpeeled, medium-size fresh shrimp
½ cup grated Parmesan cheese, divided
1 (3-ounce) package cream cheese, softened
¼ cup sour cream
1 green onion, minced
½ teaspoon Cajun seasoning
2 (2.1-ounce) packages frozen mini phyllo pastry shells

• **Bring** 2¼ cups water to a boil; add shrimp, and cook 3 to 5 minutes or just until shrimp turn pink.

• **Drain** shrimp, and rinse with cold water.
• **Peel** shrimp, and devein, if desired; finely chop.
• **Stir** together ¼ cup Parmesan cheese and next 4 ingredients; stir in shrimp. Cover and chill 8 hours.
• **Bake** pastry shells according to package directions; cool completely. Store in an airtight container 8 hours, if desired.
• **Fill** baked pastry shells with shrimp mixture. Place on baking sheets, and sprinkle evenly with remaining ¼ cup Parmesan cheese.
• **Bake** at 325° for 10 to 15 minutes or until thoroughly heated. Serve immediately. **Yield:** 2 dozen.

Note: To serve tartlets chilled, do not bake after filling. Cover and chill 1 hour. Sprinkle with Parmesan before serving.

ASPARAGUS WITH GARLIC CREAM
(pictured on page 73)

When selecting asparagus, look for firm, thin stalks that are bright green and have tight tips.

Prep: 20 minutes
Cook: 3 minutes
Chill: 8 hours

1 (8-ounce) container sour cream
2 tablespoons milk
1 tablespoon white wine vinegar
1 tablespoon olive oil
2 garlic cloves, minced
¼ teaspoon salt
¼ teaspoon freshly ground pepper
2 pounds fresh asparagus
Freshly ground pepper (optional)

• **Stir** together first 7 ingredients in a medium bowl. Cover garlic cream, and chill 8 hours.
• **Snap** off tough ends of asparagus, and cook asparagus in boiling water to cover 3 minutes or until asparagus is crisp-tender; drain.
• **Plunge** asparagus into ice water to stop the cooking process; drain. Cover and chill 8 hours, if desired.
• **Serve** chilled asparagus with chilled garlic cream. Sprinkle with additional pepper, if desired. **Yield:** 16 to 20 appetizer servings.

TOMATO-CHEESE TORTE
(pictured on facing page)

Prep: 20 minutes
Chill: 8 hours

½ cup dried tomatoes in oil, drained
   and chopped
1½ cups shredded Parmesan cheese,
   divided
1 (8-ounce) package cream cheese,
   softened
4 ounces goat cheese, crumbled
¼ cup butter or margarine,
   softened
2 to 3 garlic cloves, minced
¼ cup minced fresh parsley
1 tablespoon minced fresh
   basil
½ teaspoon freshly ground
   pepper

• **Line** a 3-cup mold or 4-cup glass measuring cup with plastic wrap, allowing 5 to 6 inches to hang over edges; coat wrap with cooking spray.
• **Sprinkle** chopped dried tomato into prepared mold.
• **Beat** 1 cup Parmesan cheese and next 4 ingredients with an electric mixer until mixture is smooth. Reserve 1 cup mixture; spread remaining mixture over tomato.
• **Beat** reserved 1 cup cheese mixture, remaining ½ cup Parmesan cheese, minced parsley, basil, and ground pepper until smooth; spread over cheese mixture in mold.
• **Fold** plastic wrap over torte, and chill up to 8 hours.
• **Unmold** chilled torte, and serve with assorted crackers. **Yield:** 20 appetizer servings.

CHOCOLATE-ALMOND PETITS FOURS
(pictured on facing page)

Almond paste is a mixture of blanched ground almonds, sugar, and glycerin. You can find it in most large supermarkets.

Prep: 15 minutes
Bake: 10 minutes
Chill: 30 minutes

¾ cup butter or margarine,
   softened
2 (8-ounce) cans almond paste
1½ cups sugar
8 large eggs
1½ cups all-purpose flour
1 (12-ounce) can apricot filling *
Chocolate Ganache
Garnishes: almond slices, dried
   apricots

• **Grease** bottom and sides of 2 (15- x 10-inch) jellyroll pans, and line with wax paper; grease and flour wax paper. Set aside.
• **Beat** softened butter and almond paste at medium speed with an electric mixer until mixture is creamy. Gradually add sugar to creamed mixture, beating well. Add eggs, 1 at a time, beating after each addition.
• **Stir** in flour, and spread batter into prepared pans.
• **Bake** at 400° for 8 to 10 minutes. Cool in pans on wire racks.
• **Turn** 1 cake out onto a flat surface; remove wax paper, and spread with apricot filling.

• **Top** with remaining cake, and cut with a 1½-inch round cutter.
• **Place** cakes on a wire rack in a large shallow pan.
• **Using** a squeeze bottle, coat top and sides of cakes with warm Chocolate Ganache. (Spoon up any excess frosting that drips through rack; reheat and refill bottle, and use to continue frosting cakes.)
• **Chill** petits fours at least 30 minutes. Freeze up to 3 months. Garnish, if desired. **Yield:** 3 dozen.

* Substitute 1 (10-ounce) jar apricot spreadable fruit for canned apricot filling, if desired.

Chocolate Ganache

Prep: 5 minutes

1 cup whipping cream
2 cups (12 ounces) semisweet
   chocolate morsels

• **Microwave** whipping cream in a 2-cup glass measuring cup at HIGH 2 minutes.
• **Add** chocolate morsels, stirring until melted. **Yield:** 2 cups.

Chocolate-Almond Petits Fours,
facing page

Asparagus With Garlic Cream, page 71;
Tomato-Cheese Torte, facing page

Honey ham
on biscuits with
Beehive Butter,
page 68

Clockwise from top: Fresh Fruit Salad With
Celery Seed Dressing, honey ham on biscuits
with Beehive Butter, Steamed Asparagus
With Tomato-Basil Dip, Double-Stuffed
Eggs, pages 68-70

*Double-Stuffed Eggs,
page 70*

*Steamed Asparagus With
Tomato-Basil Dip, page 69*

*Beehive Butter,
page 68*

*Curried Chicken Salad
Spread, page 68*

Southwestern Grilled Gazpacho, page 84

Veggie Pancakes, page 85

Dilled Peas and Potatoes Vinaigrette, page 102

Marinated Chicken Strips and Vegetables, Parmesan Bread, page 54

Lemon Ice Cream, page 55

Double-Berry Milk Shakes, facing page

Baby Blue Salad, facing page

Strawberry Custard Pie, facing page

Strawberries

Take your pick of recipes using the sweetheart of fruits. Whether you go to a pick-them-yourself farm or to the local market to select your own berries, don't pass up these succulent recipes.

Strawberries, available year-round, are at their peak from April to June. For the most flavorful berries, choose those that are brightly colored, plump, and uniform in size. Don't wash them until you're ready to use them. For a new take on an old favorite, sample Strawberry Custard Pie. Between the berries and the crust hides a layer of custard.

STRAWBERRY CUSTARD PIE
(pictured on facing page)

A creamy filling and sweet glaze make this pie delightful.

Prep: 30 minutes
Cook: 12 minutes
Chill: 4 hours

1⅓ cups sugar, divided
7 tablespoons cornstarch, divided
¼ teaspoon salt
2 cups milk
2 egg yolks, lightly beaten
1 tablespoon butter or margarine
1 teaspoon vanilla extract
1 baked 9-inch pastry shell
1 cup water, divided
1 tablespoon lemon juice
½ teaspoon liquid red food coloring
6 cups fresh strawberries, halved
Garnishes: sweetened whipped cream, fresh strawberry

• **Combine** ⅔ cup sugar, 4 tablespoons cornstarch, and salt in a saucepan; stir in milk. Bring to a boil over medium heat.
• **Cook,** stirring constantly, 1 minute.
• **Whisk** milk mixture gradually into egg yolks until blended. Return mixture to saucepan.
• **Cook** over medium heat, whisking constantly, 1 minute or until thickened. Remove from heat.
• **Stir** in butter and vanilla. Spoon hot filling into pastry shell.
• **Stir** together remaining ⅔ cup sugar, remaining 3 tablespoons cornstarch, and 2 tablespoons water.
• **Bring** remaining water to a boil in a medium saucepan.
• **Whisk** in sugar mixture; cook, whisking constantly, 2 to 3 minutes or until thickened and clear. Remove from heat.
• **Stir** in lemon juice and food coloring; cool. Fold strawberries into syrup mixture. Spoon over custard mixture; chill 4 hours. Garnish, if desired. **Yield:** 1 (9-inch) pie.

DOUBLE-BERRY MILK SHAKE
(pictured on facing page)

Prep: 5 minutes

1 pint fresh strawberry halves, frozen
¾ cup milk
¼ cup powdered sugar
½ teaspoon vanilla extract
1 pint strawberry ice cream
Garnishes: sweetened whipped cream, fresh strawberries

• **Process** first 4 ingredients in a blender until smooth.
• **Add** ice cream; process until blended. Garnish, if desired. **Yield:** 4 cups.

BABY BLUE SALAD
(pictured on facing page)

Prep: 10 minutes

¾ pound mixed salad greens
Balsamic Vinaigrette
4 ounces blue cheese, crumbled
2 oranges, peeled and thinly sliced
1 pint fresh strawberries, quartered
Sweet-and-Spicy Pecans

• **Toss** greens with Balsamic Vinaigrette and blue cheese. Place on 6 plates.
• **Arrange** orange slices over greens. Sprinkle with berries, top with Sweet-and-Spicy Pecans. **Yield:** 6 servings.

Balsamic Vinaigrette

Prep: 5 minutes

½ cup balsamic vinegar
3 tablespoons Dijon mustard
3 tablespoons honey
2 garlic cloves, minced
2 small shallots, minced
¼ teaspoon salt
¼ teaspoon pepper
1 cup olive oil

• **Whisk** together first 7 ingredients until blended. Gradually whisk in olive oil. **Yield:** 1⅔ cups.

Sweet-and-Spicy Pecans

Prep: 5 minutes
Bake: 10 minutes

¼ cup sugar
1 cup warm water
1 cup pecan halves
2 tablespoons sugar
1 tablespoon chili powder
⅛ teaspoon ground red pepper

• **Stir** together ¼ cup sugar and warm water until sugar dissolves. Add pecans; soak 10 minutes. Drain, discarding syrup.
• **Combine** 2 tablespoons sugar, chili powder, and pepper. Add pecans, tossing to coat. Place pecans on a lightly greased baking sheet. Bake at 350° for 10 minutes, stirring once. **Yield:** 1 cup.
Chef Franklin Biggs
Homewood, Alabama

STRAWBERRY TART

Prep: 45 minutes
Bake: 35 minutes
Chill: 30 minutes

3 **tablespoons butter or margarine, softened**
3 **tablespoons granulated sugar, divided**
2 **tablespoons almond paste**
½ **teaspoon grated lemon rind**
1 **large egg, separated**
⅔ **cup all-purpose flour**
1 **teaspoon unflavored gelatin**
2 **tablespoons all-purpose flour**
⅛ **teaspoon salt**
½ **cup milk**
2 **tablespoons rum or ½ teaspoon rum extract**
⅔ **cup whipping cream**
1 **tablespoon powdered sugar**
1 **teaspoon vanilla extract**
1½ **pints fresh strawberry halves**
Currant Jelly Glaze
Garnish: fresh mint leaves

• **Beat** butter at medium speed with an electric mixer until creamy; add 1 tablespoon granulated sugar, almond paste, and lemon rind, beating well.
• **Add** egg white, and beat at high speed until smooth. Gradually add ⅔ cup flour, and beat until blended.
• **Pat** dough into a 6-inch circle on a lightly greased baking sheet, lightly flattening top.
• **Bake** at 300° for 30 to 35 minutes or until lightly browned. Cool on pan on a wire rack 15 minutes. Remove from pan, and cool completely on wire rack.
• **Whisk** together remaining 2 tablespoons granulated sugar, yolk, gelatin, and next 4 ingredients in a saucepan.
• **Cook** over medium heat, whisking constantly, 3 to 5 minutes or until thickened. Cool slightly.
• **Beat** whipping cream at high speed with electric mixer until foamy; gradually add powdered sugar, beating until stiff peaks form. Whisk into gelatin mixture until blended; stir in vanilla. Spread over pastry. Chill 30 minutes or until set.
• **Arrange** strawberries over filling; brush with Currant Jelly Glaze. Garnish, if desired. **Yield:** 4 servings.

Currant Jelly Glaze

Prep: 15 minutes

½ **cup red currant jelly**
1 **tablespoon cherry brandy**

• **Cook** jelly in a small saucepan over medium heat until melted. Remove from heat.
• **Stir** in brandy. (If glaze is too thick, add a small amount of water, and cook over low heat.) **Yield:** ½ cup.

Mrs. Michael Dryden
Pollock, Louisiana

LAYERED STRAWBERRY CAKE

Prep: 30 minutes
Bake: 20 minutes

1 **(18.5-ounce) package butter recipe golden cake mix**
⅔ **cup buttermilk**
½ **cup butter or margarine, softened**
3 **large eggs**
½ **cup strawberry preserves, divided**
2 **cups whipping cream**
3 **tablespoons powdered sugar**
2 **quarts fresh strawberries, sliced**
Garnish: fresh strawberries

• **Beat** first 4 ingredients at low speed with an electric mixer until cake mix is moistened. Beat at medium speed 4 minutes. Pour batter into 2 greased and floured 9-inch round cakepans.
• **Bake** at 350° for 18 to 20 minutes or until a wooden pick inserted in center comes out clean. Cool on wire racks 10 minutes; remove from pans. Brush top of each cake layer with 2 tablespoons preserves. Cool on wire racks.
• **Beat** remaining preserves with cream and powdered sugar at high speed with electric mixer until stiff peaks form.
• **Place** 1 cake layer on a serving plate. Arrange half of strawberries over layer; top with half of whipped cream mixture. Repeat procedure with remaining layer, strawberries, and whipped cream mixture. Garnish, if desired. **Yield:** 1 (2-layer) cake.

STRAWBERRY-BROWN SUGAR SHORTCAKE

Prep: 35 minutes
Bake: 15 minutes

3 **cups all-purpose flour**
1½ **tablespoons baking powder**
½ **teaspoon salt**
⅓ **cup firmly packed brown sugar**
2 **teaspoons ground cinnamon, divided**
¼ **cup shortening**
¼ **cup butter or margarine, cut up**
1⅓ **cups buttermilk**
2 **tablespoons butter or margarine, melted**
2 **tablespoons brown sugar**
1 **tablespoon granulated sugar**
4 **cups sliced fresh strawberries**
½ **cup firmly packed brown sugar**
1 **cup whipping cream**
2 **tablespoons powdered sugar**

• **Stir** together first 4 ingredients and 1 teaspoon cinnamon in a large bowl.
• **Cut** shortening and ¼ cup butter into flour mixture with a pastry blender until crumbly.
• **Add** buttermilk, stirring until dry ingredients are moistened.
• **Turn** dough out onto a lightly floured surface; knead 3 or 4 times.
• **Pat** or roll dough to ¾-inch thickness; cut dough into 8 circles with a 3½-inch scalloped cutter, and place on a lightly greased baking sheet.
• **Bake** at 400° for 15 minutes or until golden. Brush shortcakes with 2 tablespoons melted butter.
• **Combine** ½ teaspoon cinnamon, 2 tablespoons brown sugar, and 1 tablespoon granulated sugar; sprinkle evenly over shortcakes.
• **Stir** together strawberries, ½ cup brown sugar, and remaining ½ teaspoon cinnamon. Cover and chill.
• **Beat** whipping cream at high speed with an electric mixer until foamy; gradually add powdered sugar, beating until soft peaks form.
• **Cut** shortcakes in half horizontally, and serve with strawberries and sweetened whipped cream. **Yield:** 8 servings.

Patsy Taylor
Russellville, Alabama

An Enriching Passover

Passover at Jami Gaudet's home is as creative as her work in television. "I love this holiday. The focus is food, family, and friends," says Jami, a television host and writer/producer. "There's no definitive Passover Seder. In our home, the key is participation by everyone at the table."

Passover Dinner
Serves 6

Saucy Brisket
Mushroom Matzo Kugel
Buttered brussels sprouts

SAUCY BRISKET

Jami's tip: "For a healthier version, I prepare this a day or two ahead. Just before reheating, I skim off the fat and place the brisket in a low oven (250° to 300°) until heated through."

Prep: 10 minutes
Bake: 3 hours

1 (4- to 5-pound) beef brisket
2 tablespoons vegetable oil
1 (8-ounce) package sliced fresh
    mushrooms
½ cup firmly packed brown sugar
½ cup barbecue sauce
½ cup ketchup
½ cup cider vinegar
½ cup duck sauce
1 (1-ounce) envelope dry onion soup mix
1 cup water
4 bay leaves
4 large baking potatoes, each cut into
    8 wedges (optional)

• **Brown** brisket on both sides in hot vegetable oil in a Dutch oven over medium-high heat; place brisket in a large roasting pan.
• **Stir** together mushrooms and next 6 ingredients in a bowl; spread mixture over brisket.
• **Bake,** covered, at 350° for 1 hour.
• **Add** 1 cup water and bay leaves to Dutch oven, and bake, covered, 1 hour and 30 minutes.
• **Add** potato wedges, if desired.
• **Bake,** uncovered, 30 more minutes or until potato wedges are tender. Discard bay leaves.
• **Cut** brisket diagonally across the grain into thin slices. Serve brisket with sauce and potato wedges. **Yield:** 8 servings.

Note: Duck sauce is found in the Asian section of the supermarket.
Jami Gaudet
Macon, Georgia

MUSHROOM MATZO KUGEL

Jami's tip: "I always double this recipe, because it freezes well."

Prep: 20 minutes
Bake: 30 minutes

1 small onion, diced
3 celery ribs, diced
1 (8-ounce) package sliced fresh
    mushrooms
⅓ cup canola oil
3½ cups matzo farfel
2 large eggs, lightly beaten
1 (10½-ounce) can chicken broth,
    undiluted
1¼ cups hot water
1 teaspoon salt
¼ teaspoon pepper
Garnish: celery leaves

• **Sauté** first 3 ingredients in hot canola oil in a large skillet until tender; remove from heat.
• **Stir** matzo farfel and next 5 ingredients into mushroom mixture.
• **Spoon** into a lightly greased 1½-quart baking dish.
• **Bake** at 375° for 30 minutes. Garnish, if desired. **Yield:** 6 servings.
Jami Gaudet
Macon, Georgia

Fresh Suppers

As the warm months arrive, colorful produce begins appearing in the market. Put an end to the winter blahs by adding these bright recipes to your menu. These unexpected ingredient combinations will expand your repertoire. You can mix-and-match any of these vegetable creations for a sensational meal.

SPICY BEAN BURGERS

Prep: 10 minutes
Cook: 12 minutes

2 (15-ounce) cans pinto beans with jalapeño peppers, rinsed and drained
1 (16-ounce) can black beans, rinsed and drained
1 cup uncooked quick-cooking oats
4 green onions, chopped
1 large egg, lightly beaten
½ cup ketchup
1 teaspoon garlic salt
1 teaspoon Worcestershire sauce
½ teaspoon liquid smoke
¼ cup vegetable oil

• **Mash** beans in a large bowl. Stir in oats and next 6 ingredients.
• **Shape** bean mixture into 10 (4-inch) patties.
• **Cook** half of patties in 2 tablespoons hot oil in a large skillet over medium-high heat 2 to 3 minutes on each side or until lightly browned.
• **Repeat** procedure with remaining patties and oil. **Yield:** 10 servings.

ASPARAGUS SOUP

Prep: 15 minutes
Cook: 12 minutes

1 pound fresh asparagus
½ cup water
3 tablespoons butter or margarine
1 medium onion, chopped
3 tablespoons all-purpose flour
3 cups milk
1 teaspoon salt
½ teaspoon pepper
3 tablespoons sour cream

• **Snap** off tough ends of asparagus. Cut into 2-inch pieces.
• **Cook** asparagus in ½ cup boiling water 3 to 5 minutes or until tender; drain, reserving liquid. Set aside.
• **Melt** butter in a Dutch oven over medium-high heat; add onion, and sauté 4 minutes or until tender.
• **Add** flour; cook, stirring constantly, 5 minutes. Stir in reserved liquid until smooth.
• **Add** asparagus, milk, salt, and pepper; bring to a boil. Stir in sour cream. Cool slightly.
• **Process** asparagus mixture, in batches, in a blender until smooth, stopping to scrape down sides. Return to Dutch oven; cook until thoroughly heated (do not boil). **Yield:** 5 cups.

Carolyne M. Carnevale
Ormond Beach, Florida

SOUTHWESTERN GRILLED GAZPACHO
(pictured on page 76)

Serve half of this recipe as a soup; toss the remainder with pasta, or use as a salsa.

Prep: 1 hour
Grill: 20 minutes
Chill: 8 hours

1 garlic bulb
12 plum tomatoes
4 medium-size sweet onions, quartered
2 zucchini, cut in half lengthwise
1 red bell pepper, cut in half and seeded
1 jalapeño pepper
1 (32-ounce) can vegetable juice
2 (10-ounce) cans diced tomatoes and green chiles
⅓ cup chopped fresh cilantro
3 tablespoons lime juice
1 teaspoon salt
1 teaspoon sugar
1 teaspoon dried chervil
1 teaspoon ground cumin
½ teaspoon pepper
1 cucumber, seeded and diced
Garnishes: sour cream, chopped avocado

• **Cut** off pointed end of garlic bulb. Arrange garlic bulb, tomatoes, and onion in a lightly greased grill basket.
• **Place** zucchini, bell pepper halves, and jalapeño on lightly greased grill rack.
• **Grill,** covered with grill lid, over medium-high heat (350° to 400°), 15 to 20 minutes or until lightly charred, turning occasionally. Place bell pepper in a heavy-duty zip-top plastic bag; seal. Let stand 10 minutes. Peel pepper.
• **Cut** jalapeño pepper in half lengthwise; discard stem and seeds.
• **Pulse** grilled vegetables, in batches, in a food processor until coarsely chopped, stopping to scrape down sides.
• **Combine** vegetables, vegetable juice, and next 8 ingredients in a bowl. Stir in cucumber. Cover and chill 8 hours. Garnish, if desired. **Yield:** 4 quarts.

Note: Vegetable mixture may be frozen up to 12 months, omitting cucumber. Thaw; stir in cucumber before serving.

Cindie Hackney
Longview, Texas

SPINACH AND DUMPLINGS

Prep: 20 minutes
Cook: 10 minutes

1 medium onion, chopped
1 garlic clove, pressed
2 tablespoons olive oil
4 (14½-ounce) cans chicken
    broth
1 (10-ounce) package fresh spinach,
    shredded
1 (14½-ounce) can diced tomatoes
    with basil, garlic, and oregano
½ teaspoon salt
½ teaspoon pepper
6 (8-inch) flour tortillas
Fresh Parmesan cheese, shaved
    (optional)

• **Sauté** chopped onion and garlic in hot olive oil in a large Dutch oven over medium-high heat 5 to 6 minutes or until tender.
• **Stir** in broth and next 4 ingredients; bring to a boil.
• **Cut** tortillas into 2- x 1-inch strips; add to broth mixture.
• **Cook** 8 to 10 minutes, stirring often. Top each serving with Parmesan cheese, if desired. **Yield:** 4 to 6 servings.

POTATO TORTILLA

Prep: 20 minutes
Cook: 21 minutes

2 large potatoes, peeled and cut into
    ¼-inch-thick slices
⅓ cup olive oil
1 teaspoon salt
1 small onion, thinly sliced
1 small red bell pepper, chopped
6 large eggs
½ teaspoon pepper
2 tablespoons chopped fresh
    parsley
Salsa

• **Cook** potato, in batches, in hot oil in a large nonstick skillet over medium-high heat, stirring often, 5 minutes or until lightly browned. Drain on paper towels; sprinkle with salt.

• **Sauté** onion and bell pepper in skillet over medium-high heat 7 to 8 minutes or until tender; remove from heat.
• **Arrange** potato over onion mixture.
• **Whisk** together eggs and pepper; pour over potato and onion. Cover and cook over medium-low heat 5 minutes or until set.
• **Invert** onto a large plate; return to skillet, top side down.
• **Cook** 1 minute or until lightly browned; sprinkle with parsley. Cut into wedges. Serve warm with salsa. **Yield:** 8 servings.

VEGGIE PANCAKES
(pictured on page 76)

Cornmeal mix and buttermilk give these pancakes unbeatable flavor and texture.

Prep: 10 minutes
Cook: 16 minutes

1 (6-ounce) package self-rising white
    cornmeal mix
1 (11-ounce) can whole kernel corn,
    drained
½ large red bell pepper, diced
½ cup all-purpose flour
7 green onions, thinly sliced
1 large carrot, shredded
⅔ cup buttermilk
1 large egg, lightly beaten
½ teaspoon dried crushed red
    pepper
¼ cup vegetable oil, divided
Toppings: sour cream, salsa
Garnish: chopped fresh cilantro

• **Stir** together first 9 ingredients.
• **Heat** 2 tablespoons oil in a large non-stick skillet.
• **Drop** half of batter by ⅓ cupfuls into hot oil, and cook 3 to 4 minutes on each side or until golden.
• **Repeat** procedure with remaining oil and batter. Serve pancakes with sour cream and salsa. Garnish, if desired. **Yield:** 10 servings.

FIESTA PIZZA

Prep: 20 minutes
Bake: 15 minutes

1 to 1½ tablespoons cornmeal
1 (10-ounce) can refrigerated pizza
    crust
1 (15-ounce) can black beans, rinsed
    and drained
½ teaspoon ground cumin
½ teaspoon chili powder
¼ teaspoon garlic powder
1 (4.5-ounce) can chopped green
    chiles, drained
½ cup salsa
½ cup pizza sauce
1 small onion, chopped
½ green bell pepper, chopped
1 cup (4 ounces) shredded Cheddar
    cheese
3 tablespoons sliced ripe olives
    (optional)
Chopped tomato (optional)

• **Sprinkle** cornmeal onto a lightly greased 12-inch pizza pan; press pizza crust into pan.
• **Bake** at 450° for 10 to 12 minutes or until lightly browned.
• **Stir** together black beans and next 3 ingredients; mash with a fork or potato masher. Stir in chiles; spread mixture over crust.
• **Combine** salsa and pizza sauce; spread over bean mixture. Sprinkle with onion, bell pepper, cheese, and, if desired, olives.
• **Bake** at 450° for 12 to 15 minutes or until cheese melts. Sprinkle with tomato, if desired. **Yield:** 4 servings.

Kim Papenfuss
Louisville, Kentucky

Start With a Mix

Cake mixes can shorten a recipe without compromising flavor. Use your imagination and stir in favorite additions—a dash of creativity is the perfect ingredient.

PINEAPPLE-COCONUT CAKE

Prep: 55 minutes
Chill: 9 hours

1 (3.4-ounce) package French vanilla instant pudding mix
1 (18.25-ounce) package white cake mix
1 (20-ounce) can crushed pineapple, drained well
1 cup flaked coconut
1 cup chopped pecans or macadamia nuts, toasted
1 (8-ounce) container frozen whipped topping, thawed

• **Prepare** pudding according to package directions; cover pudding, and chill 1 hour.
• **Bake** cake according to package directions in a 13- x 9-inch pan; cool in pan on a wire rack.
• **Spread** pudding over cake. Spoon pineapple over pudding.
• **Sprinkle** cake with coconut and half of pecans. Spread with whipped topping, and sprinkle with remaining half of pecans. Cover and chill 8 hours. **Yield:** 8 to 10 servings.

Helen Fields
Newport News, Virginia

OOEY-GOOEY BUTTER CAKE

Prep: 15 minutes
Bake: 40 minutes

1 (16-ounce) package pound cake mix
½ cup butter or margarine, melted
4 large eggs, divided
1 (8-ounce) package cream cheese, softened
1¼ cups powdered sugar, divided
1 cup chopped pecans
1 cup (6 ounces) semisweet chocolate morsels

• **Beat** cake mix, butter, and 2 eggs at medium speed with an electric mixer until smooth.
• **Pour** batter into a lightly greased 13- x 9-inch pan.
• **Beat** remaining 2 eggs, cream cheese, and 1 cup powdered sugar at medium speed until smooth. Pour over cake batter. Sprinkle evenly with pecans and chocolate morsels.
• **Bake** at 350° for 30 to 40 minutes or until a wooden pick inserted in center comes out clean. Cool cake in pan on a wire rack.
• **Sprinkle** cake evenly with remaining ¼ cup powdered sugar. **Yield:** 12 to 15 servings.

Jean M. Lumley
Pfafftown, North Carolina

MILK CHOCOLATE BAR CAKE

A chocoholic's dream come true, this scrumptious cake blends cream cheese, candy bars, and chocolate cake from a mix.

Prep: 20 minutes
Bake: 25 minutes

1 (18.25-ounce) package Swiss chocolate cake mix
1 (8-ounce) package cream cheese, softened
1 cup powdered sugar
½ cup granulated sugar
10 (1.5-ounce) milk chocolate candy bars with almonds, divided
1 (12-ounce) container frozen whipped topping, thawed

• **Prepare** cake batter according to package directions.
• **Pour** batter into 3 greased and floured 8-inch round cakepans.
• **Bake** at 325° for 20 to 25 minutes or until a wooden pick inserted in center comes out clean.
• **Cool** layers in pans on wire racks 10 minutes. Remove from pans, and cool completely on wire racks.
• **Beat** cream cheese, powdered sugar, and granulated sugar at medium speed with an electric mixer until mixture is creamy.
• **Chop** 8 candy bars finely. Fold cream cheese mixture and chopped candy into whipped topping.
• **Spread** icing between layers and on top and sides of cake.
• **Chop** remaining 2 candy bars.
• **Sprinkle** half of chopped candy bars over cake. Press remaining chopped candy along bottom edge of cake. Store in refrigerator. **Yield:** 1 (3-layer) cake.

Note: For testing purposes only, we used Duncan Hines Swiss Chocolate Cake Mix and Hershey's Milk Chocolate Bars with Almonds.

Janet Hunter
Broadway, North Carolina

Baby Elephant Ears

Traditional elephant ears—also known by their French name, *palmiers*—are huge, crisp pastries found in bakeries. Glittering with a generous topping of sugar crystals, they are tantalizing delicacies.

Our elephant ears go against the grain. Their petite size makes them less likely to shed buttery flakes everywhere. They're also savory rather than sweet, making them delightful appetizers and perfect accompaniments to salads and soups. Or grab one of these babies for a melt-in-your-mouth snack.

GARLIC-AND-HERB BABY ELEPHANT EARS

Frozen puff pastry makes these elegant crisps easy to prepare.

Prep: 15 minutes
Bake: 15 minutes

1 (17¼-ounce) package frozen puff pastry, thawed
3 tablespoons butter or margarine, melted
2 garlic cloves, minced
½ teaspoon salt
1 to 1½ tablespoons minced fresh chives, divided
1 to 1½ tablespoons minced fresh parsley, divided
1 egg yolk
1 tablespoon water

• **Roll** 1 pastry sheet into a 13- x 11-inch rectangle.
• **Stir** together butter, garlic, and salt in a bowl.
• **Brush** half of butter mixture over pastry. Sprinkle with half of minced chives and parsley.
• **Roll** up, jellyroll fashion, starting with each short side and ending at middle of pastry sheet.

• **Repeat** procedure with remaining pastry sheet, butter mixture, and herbs.
• **Cut** rolls crosswise into ⅓-inch-thick slices. Place on lightly greased baking sheets.
• **Whisk** together egg yolk and 1 tablespoon water, and brush mixture evenly over pastries.
• **Bake** at 375° for 10 to 15 minutes or until golden brown. **Yield:** 5½ dozen.

Note: Basil and oregano or other fresh herb combinations may be substituted for chives and parsley.

Southwestern Baby Elephant Ears: Omit garlic; substitute 1 tablespoon chili powder and 2 tablespoons minced fresh cilantro for minced herbs.

Parmesan-Pepper Baby Elephant Ears: Omit garlic; substitute ¼ cup grated Parmesan cheese, 2 teaspoons paprika, and ½ teaspoon black pepper for minced herbs.

Baby Elephant Ears Provençale: Substitute 3 tablespoons olive oil for melted butter. Sauté 3 tablespoons minced onion in 1 tablespoon olive oil.

Stir in 2 tablespoons chopped ripe olives, 2 tablespoons chopped dried tomatoes, and 1 tablespoon minced fresh parsley. Substitute olive mixture for minced herbs.

Mushroom-and-Brie Petite Elephant Ears: Omit garlic and minced herbs. Sauté 1⅓ cups finely chopped shiitake mushrooms in 1 tablespoon butter until tender. Spread over pastry, and proceed as directed.

Top each pastry with a ½-inch cube of Brie in last 3 minutes of baking.

Rosy Rhubarb

Sugar and spice are key for enhancing rhubarb's tartness. This old-fashioned upside-down cake relies on a mix to make preparation easy.

RHUBARB UPSIDE-DOWN CAKE

¼ cup butter or margarine
½ cup chopped pecans
¼ cup firmly packed dark brown sugar
1 tablespoon candied ginger, chopped *
4 rhubarb stalks (about ½ pound)
1 (16-ounce) package pound cake mix
¾ cup milk
2 large eggs
½ cup sour cream
1 teaspoon vanilla extract
Vanilla ice cream (optional)

• **Melt** butter in a 10½-inch cast-iron skillet over medium heat.
• **Stir** in pecans, brown sugar, and candied ginger until sugar dissolves. Remove pecans from pan.
• **Cut** 2 rhubarb stalks into 4 (4-inch) pieces; cut each piece lengthwise into thin strips.
• **Chop** remaining 2 stalks. Place rhubarb strips in bottom of skillet in a spoke design. Top with pecans and chopped rhubarb.
• **Prepare** pound cake batter according to package directions using ¾ cup milk and 2 large eggs; add sour cream and vanilla. Spoon over rhubarb.
• **Bake** at 350° for 35 minutes or until a wooden pick inserted in center of cake comes out clean. Let stand in pan 5 minutes on a wire rack.
• **Turn** cake out onto a serving platter; serve with ice cream, if desired. **Yield:** 1 (10½-inch) cake.

*Substitute ½ teaspoon ground ginger for candied ginger, if desired.

Sizzling Affair

"There's something warm and soothing about the smell of a fire, and then the reward of flavorful food," Bill Wellborn says. "It's a social, gastronomic experience." Try his recipes, and you'll agree.

JAMAICAN JERK RASPBERRY CHICKEN

Hickory chips give this chicken an extrasmoky flavor. Store extra rub in an airtight container for use on all cuts of chicken and pork.

Prep: 15 minutes
Chill: 6 hours
Grill: 42 minutes

4 pounds chicken drumettes*
2 tablespoons olive oil
3 tablespoons Jamaican Jerk Rub
2 cups hickory chips
Raspberry Glaze

• **Rub** chicken with oil, and sprinkle with desired amount of Jamaican Jerk Rub. Cover and chill 4 to 6 hours.
• **Soak** wood chips in water 30 minutes.
• **Prepare** fire by piling charcoal or lava rocks on each side of grill, leaving center empty.
• **Drain** chips and place on a square of heavy-duty aluminum foil. Fold foil to seal and cut several slits in top of packet. Place foil packet on 1 side of coals. Place drip pan between coals. Place rack on grill.
• **Arrange** chicken over medium-hot coals (350° to 400°), and grill, covered with grill lid, 10 to 15 minutes on each side. Place chicken over drip pan, and grill, covered with grill lid, 5 to 6 minutes on each side, brushing often with Raspberry Glaze. **Yield:** 30 appetizer servings.

*Substitute 4 pounds chicken wings for drumettes, if desired. Cut off wingtips, and discard; cut wings in half at joint. Continue as directed.

Jamaican Jerk Rub

Prep: 5 minutes

⅓ cup freeze-dried chives
1 tablespoon fine-grain sea salt
1 tablespoon onion powder
1 tablespoon dried onion flakes
1 tablespoon garlic powder
1 tablespoon ground ginger
1 tablespoon dried thyme
1 tablespoon light brown sugar
1 tablespoon ground red pepper
2 teaspoons ground allspice
2 teaspoons coarsely ground black pepper
2 teaspoons ground coriander
1 teaspoon ground cinnamon
½ teaspoon ground nutmeg
½ teaspoon ground cloves

• **Process** all ingredients in a blender until ground and well blended. **Yield:** about ¾ cup.

Raspberry Glaze

Prep: 10 minutes
Cook: 30 minutes

2 tablespoons butter or margarine
½ medium-size sweet onion, diced
½ (18-ounce) jar raspberry preserves
1½ teaspoons Jamaican Jerk Rub
1 tablespoon olive oil
2 tablespoons dry red wine
1½ teaspoons red wine vinegar
1 tablespoon lemon juice

• **Melt** butter in a saucepan over medium-high heat; add onion, and sauté until tender. Stir in preserves, Jamaican Jerk Rub, and olive oil.
• **Cook,** stirring often, 5 minutes or until preserves are melted.
• **Stir** in wine and vinegar. Bring to a boil; reduce heat, and simmer 15 minutes. Add lemon juice. **Yield:** 1 cup.

Jamaican Jerk Raspberry Ribs: Substitute 4 pounds pork back ribs, cut into pieces, for 4 pounds chicken drumettes. Grill as directed or until ribs are tender.

Bill Wellborn
Roanoke, Virginia

GRILLED BREAD

Prep: 10 minutes
Grill: 7 minutes

2 cups hickory chips
1 (18.5-ounce) package hoagie rolls, split
3 tablespoons olive oil
1 (4½-ounce) can chopped ripe olives, drained
6 plum tomatoes, thinly sliced
6 ounces Gruyère cheese, shredded or sliced
⅓ cup coarsely chopped fresh basil

• **Soak** wood chips in water 30 minutes.
• **Drain** chips; place on a square of heavy-duty aluminum foil. Fold foil to seal; cut several slits in top of packet. Place packet on coals or lava rocks; ignite. Let charcoal burn 30 minutes, or let a gas grill preheat over medium heat (300° to 350°) 15 minutes.
• **Brush** cut sides of rolls with olive oil; sprinkle evenly with olives. Top with tomato slices, cheese, and basil.
• **Coat** food rack with cooking spray; place rack on grill.
• **Place** rolls, cut side up, on rack; grill, covered with grill lid, 5 to 7 minutes or until cheese melts. **Yield:** 6 servings.

Note: Gruyère cheese is a Swiss-style cheese with a rich, sweet, nutty flavor.

Bill Wellborn
Roanoke, Virginia

HICKORY-SMOKED BARBECUE SHRIMP

For easier cleanup, cover the dish inside and out with aluminum foil.

Prep: 40 minutes
Grill: 20 minutes

2 cups hickory chips
3 pounds unpeeled, large fresh shrimp
3 lemons, sliced
½ to ⅔ cup hickory-flavored barbecue sauce
½ cup dry shrimp-and-crab boil seasoning
1 teaspoon pepper
1 teaspoon hot sauce
¾ cup butter or margarine, cut up
¾ cup dry white wine

• **Soak** wood chips in water 30 minutes.
• **Prepare** charcoal fire in grill; let burn 15 to 20 minutes.
• **Drain** chips, and place on coals.
• **Place** layers of shrimp and lemon slices alternately in baking dish; brush with barbecue sauce.
• **Sprinkle** with shrimp-and-crab boil seasoning, pepper, and hot sauce; dot with butter. Add wine to dish.
• **Place** dish on grill rack, and cook, covered with grill lid, 15 to 20 minutes or just until shrimp turn pink, stirring once. **Yield:** 8 to 10 servings.

Note: For testing purposes only, we used Kraft Thick 'n' Spicy Hickory Smoked Barbecue Sauce and McCormick Shrimp-and-Crab Boil Seasoning.

Bill Wellborn
Roanoke, Virginia

BE PREPARED

Bill Wellborn's love for outdoor cooking began during childhood camp-outs. "We built a circle of rocks, mounded charcoal in the middle, and topped it with a grate from an old grill." The Wellborns, who live in Roanoke, Virginia, favor grilling year-round.

Bill's hints for outdoor cooking ensure great times with the grill.

■ Get organized before you begin. Have side dishes ready to serve before you start grilling any main dishes.

■ Experiment with different wood chips. Try hickory for a strong, hearty smoke. Apple and cherry woods lend mild, fruity tones that are well suited for poultry. Add sprigs of rosemary for an herb-scented smoke.

■ Allow additional time for the grill to preheat, or lengthen cooking time in cooler weather.

■ Be sure to coat food racks, cooking grates, and low-fat foods such as fish and vegetables with vegetable cooking spray or oil to eliminate sticking.

■ Keep a spray bottle of water close by when you are grilling in case of flare-ups.

GRILLED PORTOBELLO PIZZAS

Prep: 10 minutes
Grill: 10 minutes

1 cup tomato-basil pasta sauce
1 garlic clove, minced
1 tablespoon Worcestershire sauce
½ cup chopped fresh basil, divided
8 large portobello mushroom caps
1 (8-ounce) bottle Italian dressing
1 cup (4 ounces) shredded Italian cheese blend

• **Stir** together first 3 ingredients and ¼ cup basil. Set aside.
• **Combine** mushroom caps and Italian dressing in a heavy-duty zip-top plastic bag, turning to coat mushrooms. Let stand 2 to 3 minutes.
• **Remove** mushrooms from marinade, discarding marinade.
• **Coat** food rack with vegetable cooking spray, and place rack on grill over medium-high heat (350° to 400°).
• **Place** mushroom caps, stem side up, on rack, and grill, covered with grill lid, 3 to 4 minutes on each side.
• **Turn** mushroom caps, stem side up, and spoon sauce mixture evenly into each cap.
• **Grill,** covered, 2 more minutes or until thoroughly heated.
• **Sprinkle** evenly with shredded Italian cheese blend and remaining ¼ cup chopped basil; serve immediately. **Yield:** 8 servings.

Note: For testing purposes only, we used Classico Tomato-Basil Pasta Sauce.

Grilled Portobello Pizza Burgers: Serve Grilled Portobello Pizzas on warm, toasted hamburger buns with desired toppings.

Bill Wellborn
Roanoke, Virginia

Quick & Easy

Whether you're dashing off to exercise or taking the children to dance or baseball practice, it's hard to find time to put a nutritious meal on the table. Let the baking and chilling times in these entrées and sides work to your advantage.

Reader Amy Turnbow of Gardendale, Alabama, has shared some of her quick-to-assemble family favorites. Check the tips after each recipe and let Amy help you with dinner.

LEMON-HERB CHICKEN

Prep: 15 minutes
Bake: 1 hour, 15 minutes

1 (2½-pound) chicken, cut up
2 tablespoons fresh lemon juice
1½ teaspoons grated lemon rind
½ teaspoon salt
½ teaspoon cracked pepper
4 sprigs fresh rosemary, sage, or thyme
Hot cooked wild rice

• **Arrange** chicken in a lightly greased 13- x 9-inch baking dish.
• **Drizzle** chicken with lemon juice, and sprinkle with lemon rind, salt, and pepper. Place fresh herbs over chicken.
• **Bake**, covered, at 375° for 1 hour. Uncover and bake 15 more minutes. Serve with wild rice. **Yield:** 4 servings.

Tip: Place chicken in baking dish in the morning; cover with plastic wrap, and chill. Remove plastic wrap; drizzle with lemon juice, and proceed with recipe. Bake while you're running errands.
Amy Turnbow
Gardendale, Alabama

BROCCOLI-CAULIFLOWER SALAD

Prep: 20 minutes
Chill: 4 hours

1 cucumber, peeled
1 cup mayonnaise
2 tablespoons white wine vinegar
1 garlic clove, pressed
1 tablespoon sugar
1 teaspoon salt
1 pound cauliflower, coarsely chopped
1 pound broccoli, coarsely chopped
4 green onions, sliced

• **Cut** cucumber in half lengthwise, and thinly slice.
• **Whisk** together mayonnaise and next 4 ingredients in a large bowl.
• **Add** cucumber, cauliflower, broccoli, and green onions, tossing well. Cover and chill at least 4 hours. **Yield:** 6 servings.

Tip: Prepare Broccoli-Cauliflower Salad a day ahead, if desired.
Amy Turnbow
Gardendale, Alabama

EASY SWISS STEAK

Prep: 15 minutes
Cook: 1 hour

¼ cup all-purpose flour
½ teaspoon salt
½ teaspoon lemon pepper
1¼ pounds cube steak, cut into strips
Vegetable oil
1 large onion, cut in half and thinly sliced
1 green bell pepper, cut into 1-inch pieces
2 (11.5-ounce) cans tomato juice
Hot cooked rice

• **Combine** first 3 ingredients. Dredge steak in flour mixture.
• **Pour** oil to a depth of 1 inch into a large heavy skillet.
• **Cook** steak in hot oil, in batches, over medium-high heat 1 to 2 minutes on each side or until golden. Remove meat from skillet, and set aside; reserve 1 teaspoon oil in skillet.
• **Add** onion and bell pepper, and sauté in hot oil until tender.
• **Stir** in tomato juice, and bring mixture to a boil. Cover, reduce heat, and simmer 30 minutes.
• **Add** steak; cook 10 minutes. Serve with hot cooked rice. **Yield:** 4 servings.

Tip: Prepare recipe through sautéing step; remove from heat. Go to planned activity; return, add tomato juice, and proceed with recipe. (Cooking time may be a few minutes longer.)
Amy Turnbow
Gardendale, Alabama

GARLIC BUTTER

Prep: 15 minutes
Bake: 30 minutes
Chill: 8 hours

1 garlic bulb
2 tablespoons olive oil
2 tablespoons fresh lemon juice
1½ teaspoons grated lemon rind
½ teaspoon pepper
1 sprig fresh rosemary
1 sprig fresh thyme
1 cup butter, softened

• **Cut** off pointed end of garlic; place garlic bulb on a piece of aluminum foil. Drizzle bulb with oil and lemon juice; sprinkle with lemon rind and pepper. Top with rosemary and thyme sprigs; fold foil to seal.
• **Bake** at 425° for 30 minutes; cool. Squeeze pulp from garlic cloves; mash with a fork in a medium bowl.
• **Stir** in butter. Cover and chill 8 hours. Serve with potatoes, baguette slices, or fish. **Yield:** 1 cup.

Tip: Prepare Garlic Butter a day ahead, if desired.
Amy Turnbow
Gardendale, Alabama

Sharing the Greens

Mild greens, such as Swiss chard and kale, retain their flavor better when cooked quickly, just until tender. Stronger flavored yet revered turnip and collard greens tend to please the palate when they're cooked just a bit longer, usually in a seasoned broth to tame any bitter taste.

GREEN AND GOLD

Prep: 25 minutes
Cook: 30 minutes

1½ pounds Yukon gold potatoes
1 tablespoon salt
2 bunches Swiss chard (about 1 pound)
3 to 4 tablespoons olive oil, divided
1 small onion, diced
⅛ teaspoon dried crushed red pepper
2 garlic cloves, minced
⅛ teaspoon salt
⅛ teaspoon ground black pepper
2 to 3 tablespoons grated Parmesan cheese

• **Peel** potatoes, and cut in half. Cook potato and 1 tablespoon salt in boiling water to cover 15 minutes or until tender; drain. Cool slightly; cut potato into ¼-inch-thick slices, and set aside.
• **Remove** and discard ribs from Swiss chard. Rinse chard with cold water; drain and chop.
• **Sauté** potato in 2 tablespoons hot oil in a large nonstick skillet 8 minutes.
• **Add** remaining 1 to 2 tablespoons oil, onion, and red pepper, and sauté 5 minutes or until golden brown.
• **Add** garlic, and sauté 1 minute. Add Swiss chard; cover and cook 3 minutes or until greens are wilted.

• **Sprinkle** with ⅛ teaspoon salt, black pepper, and Parmesan cheese. **Yield:** 4 servings.

Tamara Robinson
Olive Branch, Mississippi

HOMESTYLE KALE

Prep: 25 minutes
Cook: 15 minutes

2 bunches fresh kale (about 1 pound)
6 bacon slices, chopped
1 small onion, chopped
1 to 2 tablespoons cider vinegar

• **Remove** stems and discolored spots from kale; rinse with cold water, and drain. Tear kale into bite-size pieces.
• **Place** in a steamer basket over boiling water. Cover and steam 5 minutes.
• **Cook** bacon in a skillet until crisp; remove and drain on paper towels, reserving 2 tablespoons drippings in skillet.
• **Sauté** onion in hot drippings until onion is tender.
• **Stir** in kale and bacon. Drizzle with vinegar. **Yield:** 4 to 6 servings.

Stacia Ewing
Hillsboro, Maryland

CREAMY PASTA WITH GREENS

Turnip greens and bacon add a flavorful touch to to this creamy pasta dish.

Prep: 25 minutes
Cook: 30 minutes

1 (16-ounce) package fresh turnip or collard greens, chopped *
6 to 8 bacon slices, diced
1 large onion, diced
2 garlic cloves, minced
1 (7-ounce) jar roasted sweet red peppers, drained and diced
½ teaspoon salt
¼ teaspoon ground black pepper
¼ teaspoon dried crushed red pepper
2 cups whipping cream
1 (5-ounce) package shredded Parmesan cheese, divided
12 ounces linguine, cooked
Garnish: shaved Parmesan cheese

• **Cook** greens in boiling water to cover in a Dutch oven 10 minutes. Drain and set aside.
• **Cook** bacon in Dutch oven until crisp; remove and drain on paper towels, reserving 2 tablespoons bacon drippings in skillet. Set bacon aside.
• **Sauté** onion and garlic in hot drippings until tender.
• **Add** greens, roasted red peppers, and next 3 ingredients; cook over medium heat, stirring occasionally, 5 minutes or until thoroughly heated.
• **Heat** cream in a small saucepan over medium heat 5 minutes or until thoroughly heated (do not boil). Set aside 2 tablespoons shredded Parmesan cheese.
• **Stir** in remaining shredded cheese until melted. Toss together cream mixture and pasta.
• **Top** pasta with greens mixture, and sprinkle with bacon and reserved cheese. Garnish, if desired. **Yield:** 4 servings.

* Substitute 16 ounces mustard greens for turnip greens, if desired. Cook 10 to 15 more minutes.

Elbows on the Table

"Keep your elbows off the table" rates high on the dos and don'ts list for table manners. Exception to this rule—elbow macaroni with plenty of cheese. A big bowl of one of these favorites can almost make you forget your manners.

TEX-MEX MACARONI AND CHEESE

Prep: 35 minutes
Bake: 25 minutes

1 (16-ounce) package ground pork
    sausage
1 small onion, chopped
3 tablespoons all-purpose
    flour
½ teaspoon ground cumin
2 cups milk
1 (16-ounce) loaf Mexican
    pasteurized prepared cheese
    product, cubed
1 (4.5-ounce) can chopped green
    chiles, drained
16 ounces elbow macaroni, cooked
1 (8-ounce) package shredded
    Southwestern cheese blend
Salsa (optional)

• **Cook** sausage and onion in a large nonstick skillet over medium-high heat until sausage crumbles and is no longer pink; drain.
• **Add** flour, cumin, and milk, stirring constantly, until thickened.
• **Add** cheese product and chiles, stirring until cheese is melted. Add macaroni.
• **Spoon** mixture into a lightly greased 13- x 9-inch baking dish.
• **Bake** at 350° for 25 minutes or until thoroughly heated.
• **Sprinkle** with shredded cheese blend, and serve with salsa, if desired. **Yield:** 8 servings.

SOUPER MACARONI AND CHEESE

For a less cheesy flavor, substitute cream of mushroom soup for nacho cheese soup.

Prep: 10 minutes
Bake: 30 minutes

1 (10¾-ounce) can nacho cheese
    soup, undiluted
1 (8-ounce) package shredded
    Cheddar and American cheese
    blend
½ cup milk
½ teaspoon prepared mustard
¼ teaspoon black pepper
8 ounces elbow macaroni,
    cooked
1 (3-ounce) can French-fried onions

• **Stir** together first 5 ingredients until blended. Stir in macaroni.
• **Spoon** macaroni mixture into a lightly greased 11- x 7-inch baking dish.
• **Bake** at 350° for 25 minutes or until casserole is thoroughly heated.
• **Top** evenly with French-fried onions, and bake 5 more minutes. **Yield:** 6 to 8 servings.

Mrs. E. R. White
Smyrna, Georgia

EXTRA CHEESY MACARONI

Prep: 33 minutes
Bake: 25 minutes

1 (16-ounce) loaf pasteurized prepared
    cheese product, cubed
1 (12-ounce) can evaporated milk
1 (10¾-ounce) can Cheddar cheese
    soup, undiluted
1 cup (4 ounces) shredded Cheddar
    cheese
12 ounces elbow macaroni, cooked
20 saltines, crushed
2 tablespoons butter or margarine,
    melted

• **Cook** first 4 ingredients in a medium saucepan over medium heat, stirring constantly, until smooth.

• **Stir** in macaroni; spoon into a lightly greased 11- x 7-inch baking dish.
• **Toss** together cracker crumbs and butter. Sprinkle mixture over macaroni.
• **Bake** at 350° for 25 minutes or until lightly browned. **Yield:** 6 servings.

Note: For testing purposes only, we used Velveeta cheese product.

Dorothy Davis
Slater, Missouri

THREE-CHEESE MACARONI

Prep: 30 minutes
Bake: 30 minutes

3 tablespoons butter or margarine,
    divided
¼ cup all-purpose flour
1 quart milk
2 teaspoons dry mustard
¾ teaspoon salt
⅛ teaspoon ground red pepper
1 cup (4 ounces) shredded sharp
    Cheddar cheese
1 cup (4 ounces) shredded mozzarella
    cheese
¼ cup shredded Parmesan cheese
8 ounces elbow macaroni, cooked
1 cup soft breadcrumbs
1 tablespoon chopped fresh parsley

• **Melt** 2 tablespoons butter in a large heavy saucepan over low heat; whisk in flour until smooth.
• **Cook,** whisking constantly, 1 minute. Gradually whisk in milk and next 3 ingredients. Cook over medium heat, whisking constantly, until mixture is thickened and bubbly. Remove from heat, and whisk in cheeses until melted.
• **Stir** macaroni into cheese mixture, and spoon into a lightly greased 2-quart baking dish.
• **Melt** remaining 1 tablespoon butter in a glass bowl in microwave at HIGH 30 seconds. Stir in breadcrumbs and parsley. Sprinkle mixture over macaroni.
• **Bake** at 375° for 30 minutes or until top is lightly browned. Let stand 10 minutes. **Yield:** 8 servings.

Lilann Taylor
Savannah, Georgia

Swirl and Twirl

Most Asian noodles are made from the same basics as their Italian counterparts—flour, water, and, occasionally, egg. These recipes feature soba and udon noodles—two of the more widely available Japanese noodles.

Soba noodles are made with buckwheat flour and have a brownish tint, while udon noodles, made with wheat or corn flour, are similar to linguine. These recipes also work with vermicelli or fettuccine. See "From Our Kitchen" on page 100 for tips on Asian ingredients.

TEMPURA UDON

Crispy fried shrimp makes an ideal partner for silky udon noodles.

Prep: 45 minutes
Cook: 9 minutes

16 unpeeled, medium-size fresh
    shrimp
6 cups water
2 (6-ounce) packages udon
    noodles, uncooked
1½ tablespoons dashi soup
    stock*
¼ cup mirin*
2 tablespoons soy sauce
1½ cups all-purpose flour
1¼ cups ice water
1 large egg
1 egg white
5 cups vegetable oil
1 cup thinly sliced shiitake
    mushrooms
1 cup shredded savoy cabbage*
1 bunch green onions, sliced

• **Peel** shrimp, and devein, if desired.
• **Bring** 6 cups water to a boil in a large stockpot. Add noodles, and cook 6 to 8 minutes. Remove noodles with a slotted spoon, reserving boiling water. Rinse noodles; drain and set aside.
• **Add** soup stock, mirin, and soy sauce to boiling water. Reduce heat, and simmer 5 minutes. Keep warm.
• **Stir** together flour and next 3 ingredients. Coat shrimp with mixture.
• **Pour** oil into a Dutch oven; heat to 375°. Fry shrimp, in batches, in hot oil over medium-high heat 3 minutes or until golden brown.
• **Drain** shrimp on paper towels, and keep warm.
• **Cook** mushrooms in hot broth 2 minutes. Add cabbage, and cook 2 minutes.
• **Divide** noodles evenly into 4 large bowls; top with broth mixture, and sprinkle with green onions. Serve with fried shrimp. **Yield:** 4 servings.

*If desired, substitute fish bouillon granules for dashi, 4 teaspoons sugar for ¼ cup mirin, and napa cabbage for savoy cabbage.

Will Uhlhorn
Boston, Massachusetts

GRILLED CHICKEN WITH SPICY SOBA NOODLES

Prep: 30 minutes
Chill: 4 hours
Grill: 12 minutes

3 tablespoons soy sauce
2 teaspoons grated fresh ginger
2 garlic cloves, minced
4 skinned and boned chicken breast
    halves
2 (6-ounce) packages soba noodles,
    uncooked
1 red bell pepper, cut into thin strips
1 cup snow pea pods, cut into thin
    strips
5 green onions, sliced
Asian Dressing
2 tablespoons sesame seeds, toasted

• **Combine** first 3 ingredients in a shallow dish or large heavy-duty zip-top plastic bag; add chicken. Cover or seal, and chill 4 hours, turning occasionally.
• **Remove** chicken from marinade, discarding marinade.
• **Grill,** covered with grill lid, over medium-high heat (350° to 400°) 6 minutes on each side or until chicken is done. Cool; slice thinly, and set aside.
• **Cook** noodles in boiling salted water 6 to 8 minutes; drain. Rinse and drain.
• **Combine** chicken, noodles, bell pepper, snow peas, and green onions.
• **Drizzle** with Asian Dressing, tossing to coat. Sprinkle with sesame seeds. **Yield:** 4 servings.

Asian Dressing

Prep: 5 minutes

2 tablespoons light brown sugar
2 tablespoons chili-garlic paste
2½ tablespoons rice vinegar
2½ tablespoons soy sauce
2 tablespoons vegetable oil
2 tablespoons sesame oil

• **Whisk** together all ingredients in a bowl. **Yield:** ¾ cup.

Living Light

You don't have to put much thought into menu planning when the entire meal is served from one dish. It's economical, because meat can go farther when served with vegetables and starches. And best of all, cleanup is a snap.

CHICKEN WITH BLACK BEANS AND ORANGES

Prep: 40 minutes
Cook: 10 minutes

1   (10-ounce) package yellow
      rice mix
1   teaspoon olive oil
4   skinned and boned chicken breast
      halves
1   medium onion, chopped
2   garlic cloves, minced
⅓   cup orange juice
3   tablespoons lime juice
2   (15-ounce) cans black beans, rinsed
      and drained
1   cup low-sodium, fat-free chicken
      broth
2   oranges, sectioned
2   tablespoons chopped fresh
      cilantro

• **Prepare** rice according to package directions, omitting oil. Set aside.
• **Heat** oil in a large nonstick skillet over medium-high heat; add chicken, and cook 3 minutes on each side or until browned. Remove chicken, reserving drippings in skillet. Set aside.
• **Sauté** onion and garlic in hot drippings 3 to 4 minutes or until tender.
• **Add** orange juice and lime juice, and cook 2 minutes, stirring to loosen particles from bottom of skillet.
• **Stir** in black beans and broth, and add chicken. Bring to a boil. Reduce heat, and simmer 10 minutes or until chicken is done.

• **Remove** chicken breasts from bean mixture, and slice. Serve bean mixture over rice; top with chicken slices and orange sections, and sprinkle with cilantro. **Yield:** 8 servings.

Merle Dunson
Taylor, South Carolina

♥ Per serving: Calories 341 (5% from fat)
Fat 1.9g (sat 0.41g)   Protein 24.8g
Carb 56.3g   Fiber 6.2g
Cholesterol 34mg   Iron 3.4mg
Sodium 646mg   Calc 71mg

TANGY MARINATED LENTILS

Prep: 15 minutes
Cook: 45 minutes

1   cup dried lentils
2   cups low-sodium, fat-free chicken
      broth
1   medium-size purple onion, diced
1   celery rib, diced
1   medium carrot, diced
3   tablespoons olive oil, divided
½   small red bell pepper, diced
½   cup diced mozzarella cheese
1   tablespoon minced fresh or frozen
      chives
1   tablespoon minced fresh or
      1 teaspoon dried basil
2   tablespoons white vinegar
2   tablespoons lemon juice
½   teaspoon salt
¼   teaspoon freshly ground
      pepper

• **Bring** lentils and broth to a boil in a medium saucepan; reduce heat, and simmer 25 minutes or until tender. Drain and set aside.
• **Sauté** onion, celery, and carrot in 1 tablespoon hot oil in saucepan over medium-high heat 5 minutes.
• **Add** red bell pepper, and sauté 2 minutes. Stir in lentils and remaining 2 tablespoons oil; cool.
• **Stir** in cheese and remaining ingredients. Serve immediately, or cover and chill. **Yield:** 6 servings.

Valerie Stutsman
Norfolk, Virginia

♥ Per serving: Calories 218 (35% from fat)
Fat 8.7g (sat 1.9g, mono 5.5g, poly 0.8g)
Protein 12g   Carb 23.8g   Fiber 4.7g
Cholesterol 5mg   Iron 3.2mg
Sodium 255mg   Calc 91mg

QUICK 3-CHEESE PIZZA

Serving this pizza is an easy way to sneak in nutritious vegetables.

Prep: 25 minutes
Bake: 15 minutes

1   (10-ounce) can refrigerated pizza
      crust
Vegetable cooking spray
1   large red bell pepper, cut into thin
      strips
½   (8-ounce) package sliced fresh
      mushrooms
1   teaspoon olive oil
4   plum tomatoes, sliced
½   (10-ounce) package fresh spinach,
      torn
½   (14-ounce) can artichoke hearts,
      drained and coarsely chopped
3   ounces goat cheese, crumbled
1   cup (4 ounces) shredded reduced-fat
      mozzarella cheese
2   tablespoons shredded Parmesan
      cheese
1   teaspoon dried Italian seasoning
½   (10-ounce) package Canadian
      bacon, cut into thin strips (optional)

• **Unroll** pizza dough, and press into a 15- x 10-inch jellyroll pan coated with vegetable cooking spray.

- **Bake** at 425° for 5 to 7 minutes.
- **Sauté** bell pepper and mushrooms in hot oil in a large nonstick skillet over medium-high heat 5 to 7 minutes or until tender.
- **Sprinkle** bell pepper mixture, plum tomato, next 6 ingredients, and, if desired, Canadian bacon over pizza crust.
- **Bake** at 425° for 6 to 10 minutes or until cheese melts. Let stand 5 minutes before serving. **Yield:** 4 servings.

♥ Per serving: Calories 382 (34% from fat)
Fat 12.9g (sat 6.7g) Protein 29g
Carb 47g Fiber 4g
Cholesterol 33mg Iron 1.5mg
Sodium 750mg Calc 321mg

SHRIMP RISOTTO

Prep: 20 minutes
Cook: 1 hour, 30 minutes

¾ pound unpeeled, medium-size fresh shrimp
1 small onion, diced
1 garlic clove, minced
1 tablespoon olive oil
1½ cups uncooked Arborio rice
⅔ cup dry white wine
4 cups low-sodium, fat-free chicken broth
1 (8-ounce) package sliced fresh mushrooms
⅔ cup fresh sugar snap peas
¼ teaspoon salt
½ teaspoon freshly ground pepper
½ cup shredded Parmesan cheese

- **Peel** shrimp, and devein, if desired.
- **Sauté** onion and garlic in hot olive oil in a medium saucepan 10 minutes or until tender.
- **Add** rice, and sauté 2 minutes. Reduce heat to medium.
- **Add** wine and 1 cup broth.
- **Cook,** stirring constantly, until liquid is absorbed (about 30 minutes).
- **Repeat** procedure with remaining broth, ½ cup at a time. (Cooking time is 30 to 45 minutes.) When adding the last ½ cup broth, stir in mushrooms and sugar snap peas.

- **Cook,** stirring constantly, 10 minutes.
- **Add** shrimp, and cook, stirring constantly, 5 minutes or just until shrimp turn pink. Remove from heat, and stir in salt and pepper. Sprinkle with cheese. **Yield:** 5 cups.

♥ Per serving: Calories 498 (16.3% from fat)
Fat 8.2g (sat 2.7g, mono 3.7g, poly 1g)
Protein 24.7g Carb 71g Fiber 3.1g
Cholesterol 104mg Iron 6.4mg
Sodium 438mg Calc 199mg

Reunions

The aromas of fried chicken, baked ham, biscuits, and other delights drift over the town park of Reedsville, West Virginia, signaling the annual Brown family reunion. The event has been going strong for more than 100 years.

A silver dollar prize spurs a friendly competition between the masters of the art of baking in the Brown family. Makeshift tables groan under the weight of cakes with sumptuous frostings, luscious pies, and nutty cookies. Here's a taste of what the group has been enjoying for years.

CREAMY COCO-NANA PIE

The pudding filling in this creamy pie is enriched with coconut.

Prep: 9 minutes
Cook: 20 minutes
Bake: 20 minutes

¾ cup sugar
¼ cup cornstarch
½ teaspoon salt
2 cups milk
3 large eggs, separated
1 cup flaked coconut, toasted and divided
1¼ teaspoons vanilla extract, divided
2 bananas, sliced
Pastry
¼ teaspoon cream of tartar
⅛ teaspoon salt
⅓ cup sugar

- **Combine** first 3 ingredients in a heavy saucepan.
- **Whisk** in milk and egg yolks until blended. Bring mixture to a boil over medium heat.
- **Boil,** whisking constantly, 16 minutes or until thickened. Remove from heat; stir in ½ cup coconut and 1 teaspoon vanilla.
- **Arrange** banana slices in bottom of baked Pastry; pour custard over banana.
- **Beat** egg whites, cream of tartar, and ⅛ teaspoon salt at high speed with an electric mixer until foamy.
- **Add** ⅓ cup sugar, 1 tablespoon at a time, beating until stiff peaks form and sugar dissolves (2 to 4 minutes).
- **Stir** in remaining ¼ teaspoon vanilla. Spread meringue over hot filling, sealing to edge of Pastry.
- **Bake** at 325° for 20 minutes or until golden brown. Sprinkle with remaining ½ cup coconut. **Yield:** 1 (9-inch) pie.

Pastry

Prep: 6 minutes
Bake: 22 minutes

1 cup all-purpose flour
1 tablespoon sugar
¼ teaspoon salt
½ cup shortening
¼ cup cold water

- **Combine** first 3 ingredients; cut in shortening with a pastry blender until crumbly.
- **Sprinkle** ¼ cup cold water, 1 tablespoon at a time, over surface; stir with a fork until dry ingredients are moistened. Shape into a ball; chill.
- **Roll** pastry to ⅛-inch thickness on a lightly floured surface. Fit into a 9-inch pieplate; trim off excess pastry along edges. Fold edges under, and crimp.
- **Prick** bottom and sides of pastry shell generously with a fork.
- **Bake** at 350° for 22 minutes or until golden. **Yield:** 1 (9-inch) pastry shell.

Louis Overfield
Reedsville, West Virginia

APPLE DUMPLINGS

Prep: 21 minutes
Bake: 40 minutes

1½ cups sugar
2 cups water
½ teaspoon ground cinnamon, divided
½ teaspoon ground nutmeg, divided
¼ cup butter or margarine
2¼ cups all-purpose flour
2 teaspoons baking powder
½ teaspoon salt
⅔ cup shortening
½ cup milk
6 small Rome apples, peeled and cored
⅓ cup sugar
¼ cup butter or margarine, cut up

• **Bring** 1½ cups sugar, 2 cups water, ¼ teaspoon cinnamon, and ¼ teaspoon nutmeg to a boil in a saucepan. Reduce heat; simmer 5 minutes.
• **Remove** from heat, and stir in ¼ cup butter. Set aside.
• **Combine** flour, baking powder, and salt. Cut in shortening with a pastry blender until crumbly.
• **Add** milk, stirring until dry ingredients are moistened. Shape into a ball.
• **Turn** dough out onto a lightly floured surface, and roll into an 18- x 12-inch rectangle. Cut into 6 (6-inch) squares. Place 1 apple in center of each square.
• **Combine** ⅓ cup sugar, remaining cinnamon, and remaining nutmeg; sprinkle over apples. Top evenly with ¼ cup butter.
• **Moisten** dough edges with water; pull corners over apples, pinching to seal.
• **Place** dumplings in a lightly greased 13- x 9-inch dish. Pour syrup over dumplings.
• **Bake** at 375° for 40 minutes or until golden brown. **Yield:** 6 servings.

Darla Brown
Arthurdale, West Virginia

No-Fuss Dinner for Eight

There's no denying that Southerners love to entertain, and this menu is designed to make it easy.

Easy Company Dinner
Serves 8

Herb-Roasted Pork Tenderloins
Easy Romaine Toss
Best Hot Rolls

To get started, prepare and chill the marinade and vinaigrette up to one week ahead. Bake and freeze the rolls up to three months ahead. On the big night, roast the pork while guests mingle. Toss the salad just before serving. Reheat the rolls after you've removed the pork.

HERB-ROASTED PORK TENDERLOINS

Prep: 8 minutes
Stand: 30 minutes
Bake: 40 minutes

¼ cup soy sauce
¼ cup Worcestershire sauce
¼ cup vegetable oil
1 teaspoon dried thyme
1 teaspoon dried marjoram
1 teaspoon rubbed sage
1 teaspoon garlic powder
1 teaspoon onion powder
1 teaspoon ground ginger
1 teaspoon salt
1 teaspoon pepper
2 (1½-pound) packages pork tenderloins

• **Stir** together first 11 ingredients in a shallow dish or heavy-duty zip-top plastic bag.
• **Prick** pork with a fork, and place in marinade, turning to coat.
• **Cover** dish, or seal bag; let pork stand at room temperature 30 minutes, or chill 2 hours.
• **Remove** from marinade, discarding marinade. Place pork on a rack in a roasting pan.
• **Bake** at 350° for 40 minutes or until a meat thermometer inserted into thickest portion of pork registers 160°. **Yield:** 8 servings.

Betty W. Hayes
Conroe, Texas

EASY ROMAINE TOSS

*Blend this dressing ahead
and store it in the refrigerator to
get a jump start on the salad.*

Prep: 15 minutes

⅓ cup sherry vinegar
¼ cup balsamic vinegar
2 teaspoons Dijon mustard
1 garlic clove, minced
½ teaspoon salt
¼ teaspoon coarsely ground pepper
½ cup walnut oil*
½ cup olive oil
8 cups torn romaine lettuce or mixed
    salad greens
Toasted walnuts (optional)
Tomato wedges (optional)

• **Process** first 6 ingredients in a blender
or food processor until smooth.
• **Turn** blender on high, and add oils in a
slow, steady stream. Cover and chill
dressing, if desired.
• **Serve** dressing at room temperature
with torn lettuce and, if desired, toasted
walnuts and tomato wedges. **Yield:** 8
servings.

*Substitute ½ cup olive oil for walnut
oil, if desired.

*Beverle Greico
Houston, Texas*

BEST HOT ROLLS

*Make these ahead and freeze;
then you can have hot homemade
rolls in minutes.*

*Prep: 1 hour, 45 minutes
Chill: 8 hours
Bake: 20 minutes*

½ cup sugar
½ cup shortening
1¾ cups cold water
2 teaspoons salt
1 (¼-ounce) envelope active dry
    yeast
¼ cup warm water (100° to 110°)
1 large egg
5 to 5½ cups all-purpose flour

• **Cook** first 4 ingredients in a medium
saucepan over medium heat, stirring
mixture constantly, until shortening
melts. Cool to 110°.
• **Stir** together yeast and ¼ cup warm
water in a 2-cup glass measuring cup;
let stand 5 minutes.
• **Beat** yeast mixture, sugar mixture,
egg, and 4 cups flour in a large mixing
bowl at medium speed with an electric
mixer until blended. Gradually stir in
enough remaining flour to make a soft
dough.
• **Turn** dough out onto a lightly floured
surface, and knead until smooth and
elastic (about 5 minutes).
• **Place** in a well-greased bowl, turning
to grease top.
• **Cover** and let rise in a warm place
(85°), free from drafts, 1 hour or until
doubled in bulk.
• **Punch** dough down; cover and chill
dough 8 hours.
• **Pinch** off small pieces of dough (with
well-greased hands), and shape into
1-inch balls.
• **Arrange** balls in 2 greased 9-inch
square pans.
• **Cover** and let rise in a warm place,
free from drafts, 30 minutes or until
doubled in bulk.
• **Bake** at 400° for 20 minutes or until
golden. **Yield:** 50 rolls.

Note: To make Best Hot Rolls ahead of
time, bake rolls at 400° for 12 to 15
minutes or until just browned. Cool.
Freeze up to 3 months. To reheat, bake
rolls at 400° for 5 to 7 minutes or until
golden.

*Roberta Harding Wells
Liberty, Kentucky*

Previously Served

Pantry staples and those untouched
helpings from last night can give you
a break. Let leftover turkey, roast beef, or
chicken give you a jump on dinner.

Here's help for putting a new face on that
everyday entrée or on the extras from a
special-occasion feast. No leftovers? No
problem. Simply make a quick stop at the
supermarket deli. You can get 3 to 3½ cups
chopped chicken from a whole roasted
bird. That's enough for the pot pie and a
batch of chicken salad for the next day.

So make the most of what you've got.
Even family members who don't think
they like leftovers will compliment you
on these dishes.

TURKEY "FRIED" RICE

*Prep: 10 minutes
Cook: 22 minutes*

1¼ cups water
1½ cups uncooked instant brown
    rice
2 tablespoons butter or margarine
3 tablespoons soy sauce
2 cups chopped cooked turkey or
    chicken
½ cup frozen sweet green peas
2 small carrots, coarsely
    shredded
2 green onions, thinly sliced
1 small green bell pepper, coarsely
    chopped
1 large egg, lightly beaten

• **Bring** 1¼ cups water to a boil in a
medium saucepan; stir in rice, and cook
according to package directions. Set
aside.
• **Melt** butter in a large nonstick skillet
or wok over low heat; stir in soy sauce.
• **Add** turkey; cover and cook 5 minutes. Increase heat to medium; add peas
and next 3 ingredients, and stir-fry 3
minutes. Stir in egg; stir-fry 1 minute.
Remove from heat, and stir in rice.
Yield: 5 servings.

HOT BEEF SANDWICHES

If you don't have leftover roast and gravy, you can use 12 ounces deli roast beef and 1 (1.2-ounce) package beef gravy mix instead.

Prep: 15 minutes
Cook: 19 minutes

1 large onion, sliced
1 tablespoon vegetable oil
1½ cups leftover beef gravy
12 ounces roast beef, thinly sliced
1⅓ cups shredded iceberg lettuce
4 (6-inch) French bread loaves, split and toasted
2 tomatoes, sliced

• **Sauté** onion in hot oil in a large skillet over medium-high heat 10 minutes or until golden brown.
• **Stir** in beef gravy. Add roast beef to gravy mixture.
• **Cook** over medium heat 5 minutes or until thoroughly heated.
• **Place** lettuce on bottom halves of loaves.
• **Top** with roast beef mixture, tomato slices, and remaining bread. **Yield:** 4 servings.

Suzan L. Wiener
Spring Hill, Florida

CHICKEN-AND-EGG POT PIE

Leftover chicken, canned vegetables, and crescent roll dough allow you to whip up this old-fashioned favorite in record time.

Prep: 20 minutes
Bake: 35 minutes

2 cups chopped cooked chicken
2 hard-cooked eggs, chopped
1 (15¼-ounce) can whole kernel corn, rinsed and drained
1 (15¼-ounce) can sweet green peas, rinsed and drained
1 (10¾-ounce) can cream of chicken soup, undiluted
1 cup (4 ounces) shredded Cheddar cheese
1 (2-ounce) jar diced pimiento, drained
¼ teaspoon pepper
2 (8-ounce) cans refrigerated crescent roll dough, divided

• **Stir** together first 8 ingredients in a large bowl until mixture is blended.
• **Unroll** 1 can crescent roll dough, and press dough into a lightly greased 9-inch square baking dish.
• **Bake** at 350° for 15 minutes. Remove from oven.
• **Spoon** chicken mixture over crescent roll dough in dish.
• **Unroll** remaining can crescent roll dough, and roll dough into a 9-inch square.
• **Place** dough over chicken mixture, pressing edges of top and bottom crusts to dish to seal.
• **Bake** 18 to 20 more minutes or until golden. **Yield:** 4 to 6 servings.

Ethel C. Jernigan
Savannah, Georgia

TORTILLA SOUP

Prep: 10 minutes
Cook: 58 minutes

Vegetable oil
1 (11.5-ounce) package corn tortillas, cut into ½-inch strips
2 (14½-ounce) cans chicken broth
1 large onion, chopped
4 cups chopped cooked turkey or chicken
2 (14½-ounce) cans stewed tomatoes
1 (10-ounce) can diced tomatoes with green chiles
1 (16-ounce) jar salsa
1 (10¾-ounce) can cream of chicken soup, undiluted
1 tablespoon chili powder
1 teaspoon garlic powder
1 teaspoon ground cumin
1 medium zucchini, chopped
½ cup chopped fresh cilantro
2 cups (8 ounces) shredded Monterey Jack cheese

• **Pour** vegetable oil to a depth of ½ inch into a Dutch oven, and heat oil to 350°.
• **Fry** tortilla strips, in batches, 2 minutes or until golden brown. Drain on paper towels.
• **Bring** chicken broth and chopped onion to a boil in a large Dutch oven over medium-high heat; boil 5 minutes.
• **Stir** chopped cooked turkey and next 7 ingredients into Dutch oven; return mixture to a boil. Reduce heat, and simmer 30 minutes.
• **Add** chopped zucchini and cilantro; simmer, stirring occasionally, 10 minutes or until zucchini is tender.
• **Top** each serving with cheese and tortilla strips. **Yield:** 3½ quarts.

Carolyn Gregory
Hendersonville, Tennessee

What's for Supper?

This lemony couscous and colorful vegetable-topped fish is a healthful combo. If you'd like to serve wine, Chardonnay complements this menu nicely.

Just a reminder: Store fresh fish in the coldest part of the refrigerator. Be sure to use it within a day or two of purchase.

Quick Weeknight Supper
Serves 6

Creole Flounder With
Lemon Couscous

Stir-Fried Broccoli

Salad greens with
Cucumber-Radish Dressing

CREOLE FLOUNDER WITH LEMON COUSCOUS

Minimum preparation and fast cooking make this a perfect weekday entrée.

Prep: 20 minutes
Bake: 10 minutes

2 pounds flounder fillets
1 large tomato, seeded and
      chopped
1 medium-size green bell pepper,
      chopped
2 tablespoons chopped fresh
      basil
1 tablespoon dried minced
      onion
1 teaspoon Creole seasoning
⅓ cup fresh lemon juice
1 tablespoon olive oil
¼ teaspoon hot sauce
Lemon Couscous
Garnish: lemon slices

• **Cut** fish into 6 pieces. Place in a lightly greased 13- x 9-inch pan.
• **Stir** together tomato and next 7 ingredients; spoon over fish.
• **Bake** at 500° for 7 to 10 minutes or until fish flakes easily with a fork. Serve with Lemon Couscous. Garnish, if desired. **Yield:** 6 servings.

Lemon Couscous

Prep: 5 minutes
Cook: 5 minutes

10 ounces couscous, cooked
2 tablespoons fresh lemon juice

• **Stir** together couscous and lemon juice. **Yield:** 6 servings.

Linda Morten
Katy, Texas

STIR-FRIED BROCCOLI

Prep.: 10 minutes
Cook: 7 minutes

2 slices peeled fresh ginger
3 tablespoons vegetable oil
1 (16-ounce) package fresh broccoli
      flowerets
½ teaspoon salt
¼ teaspoon sugar
½ cup water
½ teaspoon chicken bouillon
      granules
1 tablespoon sesame oil
1 tablespoon sesame seeds,
      toasted

• **Sauté** ginger in hot vegetable oil in a large skillet over medium-high heat 1 minute. Add broccoli; stir-fry 2 minutes. Sprinkle with salt and sugar.
• **Stir** together ½ cup water and bouillon granules until dissolved. Pour over broccoli mixture. Cover, reduce heat to medium, and cook 2 to 3 minutes.
• **Drizzle** with sesame oil; sprinkle with sesame seeds. **Yield:** 6 servings.

Sherida Eddlemon
Memphis, Tennessee

CUCUMBER-RADISH DRESSING

Prep: 10 minutes
Chill: 1 hour

½ cup sour cream
⅓ cup mayonnaise
⅓ cup finely chopped peeled
      cucumber
3 small radishes, diced
¼ teaspoon salt
¼ teaspoon pepper

• **Stir** together all ingredients; cover and chill 1 hour. Serve with mixed salad greens. **Yield:** 1 cup.

Mrs. Thomas Lee Adams
Kingsport, Tennessee

MARKET ORDER

Staples on Hand
Salt, pepper, sugar
Dried minced onion
Creole seasoning
Mayonnaise
Olive oil, vegetable oil
Hot sauce
Chicken bouillon granules

Grocery List
1 small cucumber
3 small radishes
1 large tomato
1 medium-size green bell
      pepper
Fresh basil
4 lemons
1 small gingerroot
1 (16-ounce) package fresh
      broccoli flowerets
Mixed salad greens
½ cup sour cream
2 pounds flounder fillets
Sesame oil
Sesame seeds
1 (10-ounce) package couscous

From Our Kitchen

Cut It Out

As our readers know, we like using cookie cutters of all sorts. But sometimes they have a difficult time locating the sizes and shapes we use. We have a terrific source for every cutter imaginable.

The Little Fox Factory makes a huge selection of handcrafted tinplate sheet steel cookie cutters. Most shapes cost $1.25 each. For a free brochure, send a business-size, self-addressed, stamped envelope to The Little Fox Factory, 931 Marion Road, Bucyrus, OH 44820, or call (419) 562-5420.

Garlic

To add garlic in the right form and amount, here's a quick reference guide.

- A garlic **bulb** is the whole head, consisting of several sections enclosed in papery white skin.

- A **clove** of garlic is one of the individual sections of the bulb.

- Garlic **powder** is made by grinding dried garlic flakes.

- Garlic **salt** is a blend of garlic powder and salt. With this one, you'll have as much salt as garlic. It's not an even substitute for the powder alone.

- Garlic **juice** comes from pressed fresh garlic cloves.

- Don't overlook minced and chopped garlic in jars in the grocery produce section. There are even jars of **roasted** minced garlic available.

- **Shallots** resemble garlic bulbs but have a mild, sweet onion flavor. There are two or three large cloves joined under a purplish papery skin.

- Substitute onions—not garlic—for shallots in recipes.

NOODLE KNOWLEDGE

You won't wheel past bundles of Japanese noodles once you see just how easy they are to cook and how great they taste. Treat yourself to bowls of steaming goodness with the Japanese noodle recipes on page 93. Japanese cooks use an "add water" technique to ensure perfectly cooked noodles and to prevent starchy foam from gathering on the water. This traditional method takes more time, but purists swear quality is improved.

If you want to try it, here goes: For 1 pound dried noodles, bring 4 quarts salted water to a boil in a 6-quart stockpot; add noodles. When the water returns to a boil, stir in 1 cup cold water, and return to a boil. Repeat procedure three times; the noodles will be tender. A pound of noodles feeds 6 to 8.

- Japanese noodles should be served *al dente*, or tender "to the tooth," like their Italian cousins. Japanese cooks prefer to rinse cooked noodles to remove the excess starch. For hot or room-temperature dishes, rinse in warm water. For chilled dishes, such as salads, rinse in cold.

- If the long noodles are unmanageable, snip cooked, rinsed noodles into smaller lengths.

Additional ingredients:

- **Dashi** (DA-shee)—the base for most Japanese soups—is made with dried bonito tuna flakes, a seaweed called kombu (KOHM-boo), and water. Dashi is sold in granulated and powdered forms.

- **Mirin** (MIHR-ihn), a low-alcohol, sweet wine made from rice, is related to sake (SAH-key), the national alcoholic drink of Japan. Mirin is also referred to simply as rice wine, not to be confused with rice wine vinegar.

Take Note

When you freeze food, you may not always be sure you'll remember what it is and when you froze it. If you've thawed many mysterious packages and have been surprised come mealtime, Ruth McMillen of Colorado suggests using Fresh Notes—labels that stick on refrigerator and freezer containers to identify the contents and the date when they were stored.

Attach the colorful, magnetized board, which contains labels, a permanent marker, and food storage guidelines, to your refrigerator door so that you'll have labels and pen at your fingertips.

To place an order, call 1-888-686-8883 or visit www.freshnotes.com. For $7.95 plus $3 shipping, you will receive 102 labels. Refill labels are also available.

Tips and Tidbits

Here are some of our Test Kitchens staff's favorite ingredients that can take you to a lighter level.

- Fat-free half-and-half performs the same as its heavier cousin. Cook with it and discover there's no difference in taste or texture in any recipe.

- Reduced-sodium, reduced-fat chicken broth is one of our pantry basics.

- Ham bouillon cubes become a pot full of flavor without the fat.

- While vegetable broth perks up soups and stews, it also adds great flavor to rice, grits, and mashed potatoes.

MAY

Best of Spring

You don't have to have a green thumb—or spend a day in the kitchen—to capture a bumper crop of fine flavors. Whether you head to the supermarket or a nearby garden to harvest seasonal bounty, these fresh, no-fuss vegetable dishes deliver field-fresh flavor to your table in a snap.

DILLED PEAS AND POTATOES VINAIGRETTE
(pictured on page 77)

Served warm or cold, these peas and potatoes put a crisp new spin on satisfying side dish options.

*Prep: 30 minutes
Chill: 2 hours*

- 8 small red potatoes (about 1½ pounds)
- 1 pound sugar snap peas *
- ½ cup olive oil
- 6 tablespoons white wine vinegar
- 2 tablespoons minced fresh dill
- ½ teaspoon salt
- ½ teaspoon freshly ground pepper
- 6 green onions, chopped

• **Cook** potatoes in a Dutch oven in boiling water to cover 25 to 30 minutes or until tender; drain. Thinly slice.
• **Cook** snap peas in boiling water 2 minutes or until crisp-tender; drain. Plunge peas into ice water to stop the cooking process; drain.
• **Whisk** together oil and next 4 ingredients in a large bowl. Add sliced potato, snap peas, and onions, tossing gently to coat. Cover and chill 2 hours, or serve immediately. **Yield:** 6 to 8 servings.

*Substitute 1 (16-ounce) package frozen sugar snap peas for fresh, if desired.
*La Juan Coward
Jasper, Texas*

GRILLED YELLOW SQUASH AND TOMATOES

*Prep: 25 minutes
Chill: 2 hours
Grill: 12 minutes*

- ¼ cup sugar
- 1 teaspoon salt
- ½ teaspoon freshly ground pepper
- ⅓ cup olive oil
- ¼ cup balsamic vinegar
- 6 small yellow squash, cut in half lengthwise
- 6 plum tomatoes, cut in half lengthwise
- ¼ cup chopped fresh chives (optional)
- ¼ cup chopped fresh basil (optional)

• **Whisk** together first 5 ingredients until blended.
• **Place** squash in a large heavy-duty zip-top plastic bag. Pour marinade over squash. Seal bag and chill 2 hours, turning bag occasionally. Remove squash from marinade, reserving marinade.
• **Cook** reserved marinade in a small saucepan over medium-high heat 5 to 7 minutes or until reduced to ½ cup.
• **Grill** squash, covered with grill lid, over medium-high heat (350° to 400°) 5 to 6 minutes on each side or until squash is crisp-tender.
• **Add** tomato halves to grill, and grill 2 minutes on each side.
• **Sprinkle** with chives and basil, if desired. Serve with marinade. **Yield:** 6 to 8 servings.

ASPARAGUS-VERMICELLI TOSS

Cook pasta and asparagus together to bring this main dish to your table in less than half an hour.

Prep: 25 minutes

- 1 pound fresh asparagus
- 7 ounces uncooked vermicelli
- 1 cup grape tomato halves
- 4 green onions, sliced
- 2 tablespoons chopped fresh basil
- 1½ teaspoons minced fresh thyme
- ¼ teaspoon salt
- ½ teaspoon freshly ground pepper
- ⅔ cup Italian dressing
- 2 tablespoons lemon juice

• **Snap** off tough ends of asparagus, and cut into 2-inch pieces.
• **Cook** pasta according to package directions, adding asparagus for last minute of cooking; drain. Rinse with cold water; drain.
• **Place** pasta and asparagus in a large bowl. Add remaining ingredients, toss to coat. Chill, if desired. **Yield:** 6 servings.
*Valerie G. Stutsman
Norfolk, Virginia*

BAKED VIDALIA ONIONS

*Prep: 10 minutes
Bake: 1 hour*

- 4 large Vidalia onions
- ¼ cup butter, cut into pieces
- 1 teaspoon salt
- ¼ teaspoon freshly ground pepper
- 1 cup shredded Parmesan cheese

• **Peel** onions, leaving root ends intact. Cut each onion into eighths, cutting to, but not through, root ends.
• **Place** each onion on a lightly greased 12-inch square of aluminum foil.
• **Press** cut butter evenly into onions; sprinkle with salt, pepper, and cheese.
• **Wrap** onions in foil, and arrange in a 13- x 9-inch pan.
• **Bake** onions at 400° for 1 hour. **Yield:** 4 servings.

*Michelle Ettenger
Alpharetta, Georgia*

SIMPLE ROASTED ASPARAGUS

Prep: 5 minutes
Broil: 4 minutes

1 pound fresh asparagus
3 tablespoons olive oil
½ teaspoon sugar
¼ teaspoon salt
¼ teaspoon freshly ground pepper

• **Snap** off tough ends of asparagus. Arrange in a 15- x 10-inch jellyroll pan. Drizzle with olive oil.
• **Broil** 5½ inches from heat (with electric oven door partially open) 4 minutes. Sprinkle with sugar, salt, and pepper. **Yield:** 3 to 4 servings.

Shirley Corriher
Atlanta, Georgia

SWEET ONION CASSEROLE

Prep: 15 minutes
Bake: 25 minutes

1½ pounds (about 3 large) Vidalia onions, sliced and separated into rings
1 cup whipping cream
1 large egg
¾ teaspoon salt
½ teaspoon pepper
½ cup (2 ounces) shredded sharp Cheddar cheese
½ teaspoon paprika

• **Cook** onion in a Dutch oven in boiling water to cover 1 minute; drain.
• **Place** onion in a lightly greased 8-inch square baking dish.
• **Whisk** together whipping cream and next 3 ingredients. Pour over onion. Sprinkle with cheese and paprika.
• **Bake** at 350° for 25 minutes. **Yield:** 4 servings.

Marge Hanley
Palm Harbor, Florida

CRUNCHY PEA SALAD

Prep: 20 minutes
Chill: 1 hour

¾ cup water
1 teaspoon sugar
1 pound shelled fresh sweet green peas
6 green onions, sliced
2 celery ribs, diced
1 cup chopped cauliflower
1 cup cashews, chopped
1 cup Ranch-style dressing
½ cup sour cream
8 bacon slices, cooked and crumbled

• **Bring** ¾ cup water and sugar to a boil in a medium saucepan.
• **Add** peas, and cook over medium-high heat 10 minutes; drain. Stir together peas and next 6 ingredients. Cover and chill 1 hour. Sprinkle with bacon, and serve immediately. **Yield:** 6 servings.

Lori Cook
Wichita Falls, Texas

NEW POTATOES WITH LEMON-BUTTER SAUCE

Prep: 30 minutes
Cook: 25 minutes

3 pounds small new potatoes
½ cup butter or margarine
¼ cup olive oil
3 tablespoons minced fresh chives
2 tablespoons minced fresh parsley
1 tablespoon grated lemon rind
0 tablespoons fresh lemon juice
½ teaspoon salt
½ teaspoon pepper
¼ teaspoon ground nutmeg

• **Peel** each potato, leaving a 1½-inch band of peel around middle.
• **Cook** potatoes in a Dutch oven in boiling water to cover 20 minutes or until tender; drain. Place in a large bowl.
• **Bring** butter and next 8 ingredients to a boil in a saucepan over medium heat. Remove from heat. Drizzle over potatoes, tossing to coat. **Yield:** 8 servings.

Hilda Marshall
Front Royal, Virginia

Rags to Riches

Having risen from humble beginnings, bread pudding is now the darling of many a fancy meal. Its alluring, baked-in goodness is tough to resist.

Mouths water at the mention of bread pudding, with its crusty exterior and custardlike texture. This is soothing comfort food at its best.

Traditionally a dessert, it is now showing up with ingredients such as cheese, onions, ham, and garlic, like in Rosemary-Tasso Bread Pudding. Another update is the use of fresh rather than stale bread. (See "From Our Kitchen" on page 128 for more tips.) In addition to the more contemporary savory pudding, try one of the sweet recipes. Whether you're in the mood for a simple dessert or a sumptuous finale, these creations will not disappoint.

ROSEMARY-TASSO BREAD PUDDING

Prep: 1 hour
Chill: 1 hour
Bake: 45 minutes

1 **garlic bulb**
½ **cup finely chopped tasso ***
1½ **cups half-and-half**
4 **large eggs**
1 **tablespoon chopped fresh rosemary**
½ **teaspoon salt**
½ **teaspoon rubbed sage**
¼ **teaspoon pepper**
6 **cups French bread cubes**

• **Cut** off pointed end of garlic bulb; place garlic on a piece of aluminum foil. Fold foil to seal.
• **Bake** at 400° for 1 hour; cool. Squeeze pulp from garlic cloves. Set aside.
• **Cook** tasso in a small skillet over medium-high heat until lightly browned.
• **Whisk** together half-and-half and eggs in a large bowl.

• **Whisk** in garlic pulp, tasso, chopped rosemary, and next 3 ingredients. Gently stir in bread cubes. Cover mixture, and chill 1 hour.
• **Spoon** mixture evenly into 4 lightly greased 8-ounce custard cups.
• **Bake** at 350° for 40 to 45 minutes or until pudding is set. **Yield:** 4 servings.

*Substitute ½ cup finely chopped Cajun-style kielbasa, if desired.

Note: Bread pudding mixture may be prepared in an 11- x 7-inch baking dish. Bake as directed.

Chef John Currance
Oxford, Mississippi

WHITE CHOCOLATE BREAD PUDDING

Prep: 30 minutes
Bake: 35 minutes
Chill: 1 hour

½ **(16-ounce) French bread loaf, cut into ½-inch cubes**
1½ **cups half-and-half**
½ **cup whipping cream**
1 **large egg**
4 **egg yolks**
¼ **cup sugar**
1½ **teaspoons vanilla extract**
4 **(1-ounce) white chocolate baking squares**
White Chocolate Sauce
Semisweet Chocolate Sauce

• **Bake** bread cubes on a baking sheet at 350° for 10 minutes or until golden brown. Arrange evenly in 6 lightly greased 6-ounce custard cups; set aside.

• **Cook** half-and-half and whipping cream in a saucepan over medium heat until hot. (Do not boil.)
• **Whisk** together egg, egg yolks, and sugar. Gradually whisk about one-fourth of hot mixture into egg mixture; add to remaining hot mixture, whisking constantly. Whisk in vanilla until blended.
• **Microwave** white chocolate in a large glass bowl at HIGH 1½ minutes or until melted, stirring twice. Gradually whisk in cream mixture; pour through a wire-mesh strainer evenly into prepared custard cups.
• **Place** cups in a 13- x 9-inch pan; add boiling water to pan to depth of 1 inch.
• **Bake** at 350° for 35 minutes or until a knife inserted in center comes out clean. Cover and chill 1 hour. Loosen edges of puddings with a knife; remove and place on serving plates. Serve with chilled White Chocolate Sauce and warm Semisweet Chocolate Sauce. **Yield:** 6 servings.

White Chocolate Sauce

Cook: 10 minutes
Chill: 30 minutes

1 **cup whipping cream**
4 **(1-ounce) white chocolate baking squares, chopped**

• **Cook** cream in a saucepan over medium heat, stirring often, until hot. (Do not boil.) Whisk in chocolate until smooth. Cover and chill. **Yield:** 1 cup.

Semisweet Chocolate Sauce

Cook: 10 minutes

1 **cup whipping cream**
1 **(8-ounce) package semisweet chocolate squares, chopped**

• **Cook** cream in a saucepan over medium heat, stirring often, until heated. (Do not boil.) Whisk in chocolate until smooth. **Yield:** 1½ cups.

Note: Bread pudding may be prepared in an 11- x 7-inch baking dish. Bake as directed.

David Walser
Anaheim, California

OLD-FASHIONED BREAD PUDDING

Prep: 15 minutes
Bake: 50 minutes

3 tablespoons butter or margarine, melted
¾ cup sugar
2 cups milk
3 large eggs
2 teaspoons vanilla extract
3 (1-inch-thick) French bread slices, torn into small pieces

• **Drizzle** butter into an 8-inch square pan. Whisk together sugar and next 3 ingredients. Stir in bread. Spoon into pan.
• **Bake** at 350° for 15 minutes; stir. Bake 35 more minutes or until pudding is set. **Yield:** 4 to 6 servings.

Libby Jones
Apopka, Florida

Quick & Easy

When it comes to versatility and economy, cabbage rates high. Whether served raw in slaw or cooked in other dishes, it deserves accolades. Store raw cabbage properly to retain nutrients and texture. Wrap the head in a moist paper towel; place in a zip-top plastic bag, seal, and store up to two weeks.

GERMAN CABBAGE SLAW

Prep: 10 minutes
Cook: 10 minutes

1 medium cabbage, shredded
3 tablespoons minced onion
1 teaspoon salt, divided
¼ teaspoon pepper
6 bacon slices, chopped
⅓ cup sugar
⅓ cup water
¼ cup white vinegar

• **Combine** cabbage, onion, ½ teaspoon salt, and pepper.
• **Cook** bacon in a skillet until crisp. Drain bacon, reserving drippings in skillet.
• **Stir** sugar, ⅓ cup water, vinegar, and remaining ½ teaspoon salt into reserved drippings. Bring to a boil, and remove from heat.
• **Stir** in bacon; drizzle over cabbage mixture, and toss. Serve immediately. **Yield:** 6 servings.

Joyce Woods
Edmond, Oklahoma

ASIAN SHRIMP AND CABBAGE

Prep: 35 minutes
Cook: 5 minutes

6 cups water
1½ pounds unpeeled, medium-size fresh shrimp
4 cups shredded napa cabbage
1 red bell pepper, cut into thin strips
1 cup alfalfa sprouts
5 green onions, chopped
1 ripe avocado, peeled and chopped
Asian Vinaigrette

• **Bring** 6 cups water to a boil; add shrimp.
• **Cook** 3 minutes or until shrimp turn pink. Drain and peel shrimp; devein.
• **Combine** shrimp, cabbage, and next 4 ingredients in a large bowl; toss with Asian Vinaigrette. Serve immediately. **Yield:** 4 to 6 servings.

Asian Vinaigrette

Prep: 5 minutes

⅓ cup vegetable oil
¼ cup rice vinegar
2 tablespoons hot sesame oil
2 tablespoons minced fresh ginger
1 tablespoon lite soy sauce
2 garlic cloves, minced
½ teaspoon freshly ground pepper

• **Whisk** together all ingredients in a bowl. **Yield:** ¾ cup.

Mrs. Shelby J. Barton
Carpentersville, Illinois

CREOLE CABBAGE

Prep: 12 minutes
Cook: 55 minutes

3 bacon slices, chopped
1 large cabbage, coarsely shredded (about 12 cups)
2 (28-ounce) cans chopped tomatoes with bell pepper and onion
⅓ cup white vinegar
2 teaspoons salt
2 teaspoons salt-free Creole seasoning
¼ teaspoon ground red pepper

• **Cook** bacon in a large Dutch oven until crisp. Drain. Reserve drippings in skillet. Crumble bacon; set aside.
• **Stir** cabbage and next 5 ingredients into hot bacon drippings; bring to a boil. Cover, reduce heat, and simmer 45 minutes. Top with bacon. **Yield:** 8 to 10 servings.

Janice Hodges
Scottsboro, Alabama

PASTA WITH CABBAGE AND CHEESE SAUCE

Prep: 10 minutes
Cook: 19 minutes

1 cup (4 ounces) shredded fontina or provolone cheese
⅔ cup butter or margarine, divided
⅔ cup whipping cream
4 cups finely shredded cabbage
2 cups bow-tie pasta, cooked
¼ teaspoon salt
¼ teaspoon pepper

• **Cook** cheese, ⅓ cup butter, and whipping cream in a saucepan over low heat, stirring often, until cheese melts.
• **Melt** remaining ⅓ cup butter in a Dutch oven over medium heat; add cabbage. Cook 2 minutes.
• **Add** pasta, cheese mixture, salt, and pepper. Cook until thoroughly heated. **Yield:** 4 servings.

And They're Off . . .

Anticipation builds in Kentucky the first Saturday in May, as three-year-old contenders gather at the post. Steeped in Derby fashion are polished silver, long-stemmed red roses, and elaborate hats. Many folks enjoy brunch before leaving for a day at the track. Others partake in elegant to casual home parties. Listen to the call of the race and create your own jubilee with these traditional recipes.

Kentucky Derby Appetizer Party
Serves 12 to 16

Strawberry-Cheese Horseshoe   Crackers

Curried Chicken Pâté   Beaten biscuits

Mushrooms in Sour Cream (double recipe)   Crostini

Beef Tenderloin With Henry Bain Sauce

Dinner rolls

Baby Hot Browns

Kentucky Derby Tartlets

STRAWBERRY-CHEESE HORSESHOE

Prep: 20 minutes
Chill: 8 hours

1 (1-pound) block sharp Cheddar
   cheese, shredded
1 cup mayonnaise
½ cup chopped onion
¼ teaspoon salt
¼ teaspoon pepper
¼ to ½ teaspoon ground red pepper
1 cup chopped pecans, toasted
1 (12-ounce) jar strawberry
   preserves

• **Beat** first 6 ingredients at medium speed with an electric mixer until blended; stir in pecans.
• **Shape** mixture into a horseshoe shape, or spoon into a 5-cup mold. Cover and chill 8 hours.
• **Spoon** preserves over cheese mixture, and serve immediately with crackers or bread rounds. **Yield:** 12 to 16 appetizer servings.

Note: Cheese mixture may be prepared up to 2 days ahead, if desired. Store in refrigerator.

Jean and John Briscoe
Louisville, Kentucky

CURRIED CHICKEN PÂTÉ

Prep: 15 minutes
Chill: 8 hours

2 cups chopped cooked chicken
   breast
½ Granny Smith apple, peeled and
   quartered
1 large shallot, quartered
½ cup butter or margarine, softened
½ teaspoon salt
½ teaspoon curry powder
1 teaspoon lemon juice
Hot mango chutney
Garnishes: Italian parsley sprig,
   chopped pimiento

• **Process** first 3 ingredients in a food processor until smooth, stopping to scrape down sides. Add butter and next 3 ingredients; process until smooth.
• **Spoon** mixture into a lightly greased 6- x 3-inch loafpan. Cover and chill 8 hours. Unmold and serve with hot mango chutney and beaten biscuits or crackers. Garnish, if desired. **Yield:** 3 cups.

Jean and John Briscoe
Louisville, Kentucky

MUSHROOMS IN SOUR CREAM

Prep: 20 minutes
Cook: 12 minutes

¼ cup butter or margarine
1 pound assorted fresh mushrooms,
   coarsely chopped
2 garlic cloves, minced
½ cup dry white wine *
½ teaspoon salt
¼ teaspoon pepper
1 tablespoon all-purpose flour
1 (8-ounce) container sour cream
¼ cup chopped fresh parsley

• **Melt** butter in a large skillet over medium-high heat; add mushrooms and garlic, and sauté 5 minutes.
• **Add** wine, salt, and pepper.
• **Cook,** stirring often, 4 to 5 minutes or until wine is reduced by half. Stir in flour, and cook 1 minute.
• **Add** sour cream and parsley, stirring until thoroughly heated. Cover and chill

8 hours, if desired. Serve warm with crostini or in a round bread shell. **Yield:** 6 to 8 appetizer servings.

* Substitute Marsala wine for white wine, if desired.

Note: Crostini may be cut with a horse-head cookie cutter, if desired.

Jean and John Briscoe
Louisville, Kentucky

BEEF TENDERLOIN WITH HENRY BAIN SAUCE

Henry Bain Sauce originated with the head waiter at the Pendennis Club in Louisville.

Prep: 10 minutes
Chill: 2 hours
Bake: 35 minutes

1 (8-ounce) bottle chutney
1 (14-ounce) bottle ketchup
1 (12-ounce) bottle chili sauce
1 (11-ounce) bottle steak sauce
1 (10-ounce) bottle Worcestershire sauce
1 teaspoon hot sauce
¼ cup butter or margarine, softened
2 teaspoons salt
1 teaspoon freshly ground pepper
1 (4½- to 5-pound) beef tenderloin, trimmed

● **Process** chutney in a food processor until smooth. Add ketchup and next 4 ingredients, and process until blended. Chill at least 2 hours.
● **Stir** together butter, salt, and pepper; rub over beef. Place on a lightly greased rack in a 15- x 10-inch jellyroll pan. Fold under 4 to 6 inches of narrow end of beef to fit onto rack. Bake at 500° for 30 to 35 minutes or to desired doneness. Let stand 15 minutes before serving.
● **Serve** beef with sauce and dinner rolls. **Yield:** 3 dozen appetizer servings.

Note: For testing purposes only, we used Major Grey's Chutney and A-1 Steak Sauce.

Jean and John Briscoe
Louisville, Kentucky

THE CALL OF THE RACE PACES THE PARTY

They enter the first turn and pass the stands for the first time. Family and friends of Louisville natives Jean and John Briscoe enjoy their 28th annual Derby party with a festive table of Jean's favorite dishes that have endured the test of time.

Down the backstretch and turning for home. Guests turn their attention to the race as they enjoy traditional Baby Hot Browns and tenderloin-stuffed rolls dabbed with renowned Henry Bain Sauce.

And down the stretch they come. Hold on to your racing guides and mint juleps while cheering on your favorite Thoroughbred.

BABY HOT BROWNS

Prep: 35 minutes
Bake: 2 minutes

24 pumpernickel party rye bread slices
3 tablespoons butter or margarine
3 tablespoons all-purpose flour
½ cup (2 ounces) shredded sharp Cheddar cheese
1 cup milk
1½ cups diced cooked turkey
¼ teaspoon salt
¼ teaspoon ground red pepper
½ cup freshly grated Parmesan cheese
6 bacon slices, cooked and crumbled

● **Arrange** bread slices on a lightly greased baking sheet. Bake at 500° for 3 to 4 minutes.
● **Melt** butter in a saucepan over low heat; add flour, and cook, whisking constantly, until smooth.
● **Add** Cheddar cheese, whisking until cheese melts. Gradually whisk in milk; cook over medium heat, whisking constantly, until thickened and bubbly.
● **Stir** in turkey, salt, and pepper. Cover and chill, if desired.
● **Top** bread slices evenly with warm cheese mixture. Sprinkle evenly with Parmesan cheese and bacon.
● **Bake** at 500° for 2 minutes or until Parmesan is melted. **Yield:** 2 dozen.

Jean and John Briscoe
Louisville, Kentucky

KENTUCKY DERBY TARTLETS

These bite-size tartlets are filled to the brim with chocolate, pecans, and bourbon.

Prep: 20 minutes
Bake: 20 minutes

36 frozen mini phyllo pastry shells
⅓ cup semisweet chocolate mini-morsels
1 cup finely chopped pecans, toasted
¾ cup firmly packed light brown sugar
1 tablespoon butter or margarine, softened
¼ cup bourbon
1 large egg, lightly beaten

● **Arrange** shells on a lightly greased 15- x 10-inch jellyroll pan. Sprinkle chocolate mini-morsels into shells.
● **Stir** together pecans and next 4 ingredients. Spoon evenly into shells.
● **Bake** at 350° for 20 minutes or until golden brown. Store in an airtight container up to 3 days, or freeze up to 1 month. **Yield:** 3 dozen.

Note: For testing purposes only, we used Athens Foods Mini Fillo Dough Shells.

Jean and John Briscoe
Louisville, Kentucky

Anniversary Celebration

Treat your best friends to "an evening out" at home with festive yet simple dishes and decorations to commemorate their special day.

Celebration Menu
Serves 8

Prosciutto Bruschetta and Cantaloupe Chutney
Spinach Salad With Hot Citrus Dressing
Bourbon Peppered Beef in a Blanket
Creamy Chive Potatoes
Steamed green beans
Anniversary Cake (recipe on page 117)

PROSCIUTTO BRUSCHETTA AND CANTALOUPE CHUTNEY

Prep: 5 minutes
Broil: 3 minutes

12 (¼-inch-thick) baguette slices
2 tablespoons olive oil
12 thin prosciutto slices*
Cantaloupe Chutney

• **Place** baguette slices on a baking sheet, and brush tops with oil.
• **Broil** 3 inches from heat (with electric oven door partially open) until toasted, turning once.
• **Top** toasted baguette slices with prosciutto and Cantaloupe Chutney. Serve with remaining chutney. **Yield:** 12 appetizer servings.

*Substitute thinly sliced country ham for prosciutto, if desired.

Cantaloupe Chutney

Prep: 15 minutes
Cook: 45 minutes

½ cantaloupe, peeled, seeded and diced
1 small shallot, diced
½ cup firmly packed light brown sugar
¼ cup white wine vinegar
1 tablespoon minced fresh ginger or
    ¼ teaspoon ground ginger
2 garlic cloves, minced
¼ teaspoon salt
¼ teaspoon ground cloves
⅛ teaspoon ground red pepper (optional)

• **Combine** first 8 ingredients and, if desired, red pepper, in a large nonaluminum saucepan. Cook over medium-low heat, stirring often, 45 minutes or until thickened. Cool. **Yield:** 1½ cups.

Keevin Chavis
Charleston, South Carolina

SPINACH SALAD WITH HOT CITRUS DRESSING

Prep: 20 minutes

2 pounds fresh spinach
4 oranges, peeled and sectioned
1 large purple onion, thinly sliced and
    separated into rings
3 ounces goat cheese, crumbled
1 cup sweetened dried cranberries
½ cup chopped pecans, toasted
Hot Citrus Dressing

• **Remove** stems from spinach; wash leaves thoroughly, and pat dry.
• **Arrange** spinach and next 5 ingredients on 8 salad plates. Drizzle with Hot Citrus Dressing. **Yield:** 8 servings.

Hot Citrus Dressing

Prep: 15 minutes
Cook: 12 minutes

1 (6-ounce) can frozen orange juice
    concentrate, thawed
1 small onion, diced
⅓ cup red wine vinegar
1 cup firmly packed light brown sugar
1 tablespoon grated orange rind
1 teaspoon dry mustard
1 teaspoon salt
1 teaspoon hot sauce
1 cup peanut oil

• **Process** first 3 ingredients in a blender until smooth.
• **Add** brown sugar and next 4 ingredients; process until smooth. Turn blender on high; add oil in a slow, steady stream.
• **Bring** mixture to a boil in a medium-size nonaluminum saucepan.
• **Cook** over medium heat 10 minutes. **Yield:** 2½ cups.

Doyle Haeussler
Muncie, Indiana

BOURBON PEPPERED BEEF IN A BLANKET

Prep: 25 minutes
Chill: 8 hours
Bake: 13 minutes

8 (6- to 8-ounce) beef tenderloin
    steaks (1½ inches thick)
2 leeks, chopped
¾ cup bourbon
¼ cup freshly cracked black pepper
1 pound portobello mushrooms,
    thinly sliced
3 tablespoons Worcestershire sauce
2 (8-ounce) cans refrigerated crescent
    rolls
1 egg white, lightly beaten
Garnish: fresh chives

• **Combine** first 3 ingredients in a shallow dish or large heavy-duty zip-top plastic bag. Cover or seal, and chill 8 hours, turning occasionally.
• **Remove** steaks from marinade, reserving marinade. Press pepper evenly onto both sides of steaks.
• **Cook** steaks in a large nonstick skillet over medium-high heat 4 to 5 minutes on each side. Set aside; cool completely.
• **Bring** reserved marinade to a boil in a medium saucepan over medium heat.
• **Stir** in mushrooms and Worcestershire sauce; reduce heat, and simmer 10 minutes. Keep warm.
• **Unroll** crescent rolls, and separate into 8 rectangles; press perforations to seal. Roll rectangles to 6-inch squares.
• **Place** 1 steak in center of each pastry square. Bring corners of 1 pastry square to center, pinching to seal. Repeat with remaining steaks and pastry. Brush evenly with egg white.
• **Bake,** seam side down, on a lightly greased rack in a broiler pan at 375° for 13 minutes.
• **Spoon** warm sauce evenly onto serving plates; top with steaks. Garnish, if desired. **Yield:** 8 servings.

Note: Steaks and sauce can be prepared 1 day ahead. Follow above directions up to baking the steaks. Remove steaks and sauce from refrigerator; let stand 30 minutes before completing the recipe.

Irene R. Smith
Covington, Georgia

CREAMY CHIVE POTATOES

These can be made ahead and refrigerated. To reheat, cook over low heat, stirring in additional whipping cream, if needed.

Prep: 20 minutes
Cook: 25 minutes

5 pounds russet potatoes, peeled and
    quartered
½ cup butter or margarine
1 (8-ounce) container sour cream
¼ to ½ cup whipping cream
3 tablespoons minced fresh chives
1½ teaspoons salt
1 teaspoon onion powder
½ teaspoon pepper

• **Cook** potato in a Dutch oven in boiling water to cover 25 minutes or until tender; drain.
• **Add** butter and remaining ingredients to potato; mash with a potato masher until smooth. **Yield:** 8 servings.

Mike Towle
Ormond Beach, Florida

Supper Club Specialties

Once a month, 11 food-loving friends in Smithfield, North Carolina, gather to dine, dish, and laugh. The group, called The Supper Club, has been going strong since 1994. Nine of the members prepare an assigned dish to bring to the home of that month's host, who doesn't cook. The previous month's host also enjoys a break from the kitchen. These recipes are from one of their Asian-themed meals.

SHRIMP TOAST

This deep-fried Asian appetizer can be made ahead and frozen. Just remove it from the freezer and fry as directed.

Prep: 1 hour
Chill: 1 hour
Cook: 30 minutes

8 very thin white sandwich bread slices
1 pound unpeeled, medium-size fresh
    shrimp
1 medium onion, coarsely chopped
1 (¼-inch) piece fresh ginger, peeled
    and coarsely chopped
½ teaspoon salt
½ teaspoon freshly ground pepper
2 egg whites
½ cup fine, dry breadcrumbs
Vegetable oil

• **Trim** crusts from bread; cut each slice into 4 triangles. Set aside.
• **Peel** shrimp, and devein, if desired.
• **Process** shrimp and next 4 ingredients in a blender or food processor until smooth, stopping to scrape down sides. With blender or processor running, add egg whites, and process until blended.
• **Spread** mixture over bread; coat with breadcrumbs. Cover and chill 1 hour.
• **Pour** oil to a depth of 2 inches in a large heavy skillet. Fry, in batches, 3 minutes on each side or until golden brown. Drain on paper towels. **Yield:** 32 appetizers.

Lisa McMillen
Smithfield, North Carolina

SWEET-AND-SOUR PORK

Prep: 30 minutes
Chill: 30 minutes
Cook: 15 minutes

1 tablespoon cornstarch
2 tablespoons soy sauce
½ teaspoon cold water
1 egg yolk
1 pound pork tenderloins, cut into
   ½-inch cubes
½ cup cornstarch
½ cup peanut oil
2 green bell peppers, cubed
1 (15.4-ounce) can pineapple chunks,
   drained
Seasoning Sauce
Hot cooked rice

• **Whisk** together first 4 ingredients;
add pork. Cover and chill 30 minutes.
• **Remove** pork from marinade, discarding marinade. Dredge pork in ½ cup
cornstarch.
• **Pour** oil to a depth of ¼ inch in a
heavy skillet or wok.
• **Fry** pork in hot oil over medium-high
heat 2 minutes or until lightly browned.
Remove pork from skillet.
• **Reheat** oil, and fry pork 2 more minutes. Drain on paper towels. Reserve 2
tablespoons oil in skillet or wok.
• **Stir-fry** bell pepper and pineapple
over high heat 2 minutes.
• **Add** Seasoning Sauce; stir-fry until
thickened. Stir in pork; cook 1 minute.
Serve with rice. **Yield:** 4 servings.

Seasoning Sauce

Prep: 5 minutes

¼ cup sugar
1 tablespoon cornstarch
½ teaspoon salt
¼ cup ketchup
¼ cup cold water
3 tablespoons white vinegar
1 teaspoon sesame oil
1 teaspoon soy sauce

• **Combine** all ingredients. **Yield:** 1 cup.
Ann Wilson
Smithfield, North Carolina

Top-Rated Recipes

*This month we offer two favorite one-pot members
of our "best" hall of fame. These highly praised recipes
have been retested and simplified, and justify spending
an afternoon in the kitchen. We added options for
preparing the dishes partway and then refrigerating
up to three days or freezing up to three months.*

TORTILLA SOUP

*This soup, from the 1993 recipe hall of
fame, is best made ahead and frozen,
allowing its flavors to blend.*

Prep: 45 minutes
Cook: 1 hour, 15 minutes

Mesquite chips
8 skinned and boned chicken breast
   halves
16 medium tomatoes (about 8½
   pounds)
2 large onions, peeled and cut into
   eighths
1 tablespoon vegetable oil
2 poblano chile peppers
3 garlic cloves, minced
2 (10-ounce) packages 6-inch corn
   tortillas, cut into thin strips and
   divided
5 (14½-ounce) cans chicken broth
4 (14½-ounce) cans beef broth
1 (8-ounce) can tomato sauce
1 tablespoon ground cumin
1 tablespoon chili powder
1 bay leaf
½ teaspoon salt
½ teaspoon ground red pepper
½ cup vegetable oil
2 cups (8 ounces) shredded
   colby-Monterey Jack cheese
   blend
1 avocado, peeled and diced

• **Wrap** mesquite chips in heavy-duty
aluminum foil; punch holes in top of
foil. (Soak chips if using charcoal grill.)
Place foil packet over medium-high
heat (350° to 400°).
• **Grill** chicken, covered with grill lid, 6
minutes on each side or until done. Remove chicken; chop and set aside.
• **Place** tomatoes and onion on a large
piece of heavy-duty aluminum foil.
Brush with 1 tablespoon oil; fold foil to
seal. Place on food rack.
• **Grill,** covered with grill lid, 10 minutes. Place chile peppers on food rack
with foil-wrapped vegetables, and grill,
covered with grill lid, 10 minutes.
• **Peel** peppers, remove seeds, and chop.
• **Process** one-third tomato and onion
mixture in a food processor until
smooth. Press through a wire-mesh
strainer into a bowl, discarding solids;
transfer to a Dutch oven.
• **Repeat** procedure twice with remaining tomato and onion mixture. Stir in
chopped peppers and garlic.
• **Add** half of tortilla strips and next 8
ingredients to tomato mixture. Bring to
a boil. Cover, reduce heat, and simmer
30 minutes. Remove from heat. Discard
bay leaf.
• **Stir** in chicken. Refrigerate up to 3
days, or freeze up to 3 months, if desired. Thaw in refrigerator overnight.
• **Pour** ½ cup oil into a large skillet. Fry
remaining tortilla strips in hot oil until
crisp. Drain on paper towels.
• **Top** servings with crisp tortilla strips,
cheese, and avocado. **Yield:** 22 cups.

CHICKEN AND DUMPLINGS

1997 Recipe Hall of Fame

Prep: 40 minutes
Cook: 1 hour, 50 minutes

1 (3-pound) whole chicken, cut up
¼ cup chicken bouillon granules
1 teaspoon pepper
2 cups all-purpose flour
1 tablespoon baking powder
½ teaspoon salt
¼ cup shortening
⅔ to ¾ cup milk
4 hard-cooked eggs, chopped
   (optional)
Chopped fresh parsley (optional)

• **Cover** chicken with water and bring to a boil in a large Dutch oven; reduce heat, and simmer 1 hour or until tender. Remove chicken; cool.
• **Pour** broth through a wire-mesh strainer into a large saucepan, discarding solids. Skim off fat. Return broth to Dutch oven.
• **Skin,** bone, and coarsely chop chicken. Add chicken, bouillon granules, and pepper to broth. Refrigerate up to 3 days, or freeze up to 3 months, if desired. Thaw in refrigerator overnight.
• **Combine** flour, baking powder, and salt in a bowl. Cut shortening into flour mixture with a pastry blender until crumbly. Add milk, stirring until dry ingredients are moistened.
• **Turn** dough out onto a lightly floured surface; knead 3 or 4 times.
• **Roll** dough to ⅛-inch thickness; sprinkle lightly with flour, and cut into 3- x 2-inch strips.
• **Bring** broth mixture to a boil. Drop strips, 1 at a time, into boiling broth, stirring gently. Reduce heat, and simmer, stirring often, 20 minutes.
• **Stir** in egg, and sprinkle with parsley, if desired. **Yield:** 6 to 8 servings.

Dinner for Two

This cozy menu is the perfect way for a couple to celebrate a first Mother's Day. It is designed to maximize both stove space and precious alone time. Plus, these recipes have been selected with the husband in mind, so they're easy. Many of the ingredients will already be in your refrigerator and pantry.

**Mother's Day Dinner
for Two**
Serves 2

Asian Glazed Cornish Hens
Three-Cheese Mashed Potatoes
Warm Spinach-Orange Salad
Caramel-Toffee Bombe

ASIAN GLAZED CORNISH HENS
(pictured on page 113)

Prep: 15 minutes
Chill: 8 hours
Bake: 1 hour, 15 minutes

1½ tablespoons soy sauce
1½ tablespoons teriyaki sauce
1 tablespoon honey
2 teaspoons lemon juice
⅛ teaspoon ground ginger
⅛ teaspoon pepper
1 garlic clove, minced
2 (1½-pound) Cornish hens *

• **Combine** first 7 ingredients in a large heavy-duty zip-top plastic bag; add hens. Seal and chill 8 hours.
• **Remove** Cornish hens from marinade, reserving marinade. Tie ends of legs together, if desired, and place on a lightly greased rack in a roasting pan. Bring marinade to a boil in a small saucepan, remove from heat.
• **Bake** Cornish hens at 400° for 1 hour and 15 minutes or until hens are done, basting occasionally with marinade. Cover Cornish hens loosely with aluminum foil after 1 hour to prevent browning, if necessary.
• **Remove** hens from oven, and cover with foil; let stand 5 minutes. **Yield:** 2 servings.

*Substitute 4 bone-in chicken breast halves for 2 Cornish hens, if desired. Marinate 2 hours, and bake at 400° for 40 minutes.

Dawn Snow
Lavergne, Tennessee

THREE-CHEESE MASHED POTATOES

(pictured on facing page)

Prep: 35 minutes
Bake: 20 minutes

2 large potatoes, peeled and cubed*
½ cup sour cream
1 (3-ounce) package cream cheese, softened
2 tablespoons butter or margarine, softened
⅓ cup milk
¼ cup (1 ounce) shredded Cheddar cheese
¼ cup (1 ounce) shredded Muenster cheese
1 teaspoon salt
½ teaspoon pepper
1 tablespoon butter or margarine, cut up
Garnish: minced fresh chives

• **Cook** potato in boiling water to cover 15 minutes or until tender. Drain.
• **Beat** potato, sour cream, cream cheese, and 2 tablespoons butter at medium speed with an electric mixer until smooth.
• **Stir** in milk and next 4 ingredients. Spoon into a lightly greased 1-quart baking dish; dot with 1 tablespoon butter. Cover and chill 8 hours, if desired; remove from refrigerator, and let stand 30 minutes.
• **Bake** at 400° for 15 to 20 minutes or until thoroughly heated. Garnish, if desired. **Yield:** 2 servings.

*Substitute frozen mashed potatoes, if desired. Prepare potatoes according to package directions for 4 servings. Use leftover potatoes for breaded and fried potato pancakes.

Marcia Phillips
Oradea, Romania

WARM SPINACH-ORANGE SALAD

(pictured on facing page)

Prep: 15 minutes

½ (10-ounce) package fresh spinach, stems removed
1 orange, peeled and sectioned
¼ cup sliced almonds
2 tablespoons cider vinegar
1½ tablespoons orange juice
1½ tablespoons olive oil
1½ tablespoons honey

• **Combine** first 3 ingredients in a large serving bowl.
• **Bring** vinegar and next 3 ingredients to a boil in a small saucepan over medium heat. Pour over spinach mixture, and toss. Serve immediately. **Yield:** 2 servings.

CARAMEL-TOFFEE BOMBE

Prep: 25 minutes
Freeze: 8 hours

¾ cup gingersnap cookie crumbs (about 10 cookies)
2 tablespoons butter or margarine, melted
1 pint vanilla ice cream, softened
2 (1.4-ounce) English toffee candy bars, crushed
1 (12-ounce) jar caramel sauce

• **Line** a 2-quart bowl with heavy-duty plastic wrap.
• **Stir** together cookie crumbs and butter; press into prepared bowl.
• **Stir** together ice cream and candy; spoon over crumbs. Cover and freeze 8 hours.
• **Invert** bowl onto a serving plate. Carefully remove bowl and plastic wrap. Cut into wedges, and serve immediately with warm caramel sauce. **Yield:** 4 to 6 servings.

Note: For testing purposes only, we used Skor candy bars.

Asian Glazed Cornish Hen, page 111;
Three-Cheese Mashed Potatoes,
Warm Spinach-Orange Salad,
facing page

Grilled Pineapple With Vanilla-Cinnamon Ice Cream, page 127

Key Lime Pie, page 120

Pear Preserves Cake, page 139

115

*Four-Layer Coconut Cake,
facing page*

Layers of Flavor

Nothing says celebration like a tall cake spread with homemade frosting. Here are two cakes to help you launch the season's festivities.

Some say a tender, moist layer cake is the test of a good cook. We say cake baking shouldn't be a test. It can be a deliciously rewarding experience. All you need is time and a great recipe. Pound cakes, Bundt cakes, and loaf cakes are fine, but layer cakes are lofty combinations of textures, flavors, and tradition. We've even given new bakers a jump start on beautiful Anniversary Cake by using a mix. (To join the party, see "Anniversary Celebration" on page 108.) To ensure your sweet success, read our cake tips in "From Our Kitchen" on page 128.

FOUR-LAYER COCONUT CAKE
(pictured on facing page)

Prep: 12 minutes
Bake: 20 minutes

3 cups all-purpose flour
1 teaspoon baking powder
½ teaspoon salt
2⅔ cups sugar
1 cup shortening
½ cup butter or margarine, softened
1 cup milk
2 teaspoons coconut extract
1 teaspoon vanilla extract
5 large eggs
1 (6-ounce) package frozen flaked coconut, thawed
Coconut Filling
2 cups whipping cream
¼ cup powdered sugar
Garnish: toasted coconut shavings

• **Beat** first 7 ingredients at medium speed with an electric mixer until well blended. Add flavorings, beating mixture well.
• **Add** eggs, 1 at a time, beating until blended after each addition.
• **Stir** in coconut. Pour batter into 4 greased and floured 9-inch round cakepans.
• **Bake** at 400° for 20 minutes or until a wooden pick inserted in center comes out clean. Cool in pans on wire racks 10 minutes, and remove from pans. Cool completely on racks.
• **Spread** Coconut Filling between layers. Beat whipping cream at high speed until foamy. Gradually add powdered sugar, beating until soft peaks form. Spread on top and sides of cake. Garnish, if desired. **Yield:** 1 (4-layer) cake.

Coconut Filling

Cook: 15 minutes

2 cups sugar
¼ cup all-purpose flour
2 cups milk
4 large eggs, lightly beaten
2 (6-ounce) packages frozen flaked coconut, thawed
2 teaspoons vanilla extract

• **Cook** first 4 ingredients in a large saucepan over medium-low heat, whisking constantly, 12 to 15 minutes or until thickened and bubbly. Remove from heat.
• **Stir** in coconut and vanilla. Cool completely. **Yield:** 5½ cups.

Mava S. Vass
Hillsville, Virginia

ANNIVERSARY CAKE
(pictured on page 4)

Prep: 45 minutes
Bake: 40 minutes

2 (1-pound, 2.25-ounce) packages white cake mix with pudding
2½ cups buttermilk
½ cup butter or margarine, melted
4 large eggs
2 tablespoons grated lemon rind
1 tablespoon vanilla extract
1 teaspoon almond extract
Coconut Milk Frosting

• **Grease** and flour 2 (6-inch) and 2 (9-inch) round cakepans; set aside.
• **Beat** first 4 ingredients at low speed with an electric mixer just until dry ingredients are moistened. Beat at medium speed 3 to 4 minutes or until batter is smooth. Stir in rind and flavorings.
• **Spoon** 1¾ cups batter into each 6-inch pan. Divide remaining batter into 9-inch pans. Bake at 350° for 35 to 40 minutes or until a wooden pick inserted in center comes out clean. Cool in pans on wire racks 10 minutes; remove layers from pans. Cool completely on wire racks.
• **Spread** Coconut Milk Frosting between 9-inch layers and between 6-inch layers. Frost top and sides of 9-inch cake. Position 6-inch cake in center of 9-inch cake. Frost top and sides of 6-inch cake. Decorate with edible flowers and ribbon. **Yield:** 20 to 25 servings.

Coconut Milk Frosting

Prep: 10 minutes

1½ cups butter or margarine, softened
¼ teaspoon salt
2 teaspoons vanilla extract
½ teaspoon almond extract
3 (16-ounce) packages powdered sugar
1 cup canned coconut milk

• **Beat** first 4 ingredients at medium speed with an electric mixer until fluffy.
• **Add** sugar alternately with coconut milk, beating until smooth. **Yield:** 9 cups.

Note: For testing purposes only, we used Pillsbury Moist Supreme Pudding in the Mix white cake mix.

Elegant Spring Luncheon

This stylish menu is a guaranteed treat for you and your guests. We've taken some of the best produce the season has to offer and created a delicious and colorful midday menu. All of the recipes are easy to prepare, but no one will ever suspect it.

Elegant Spring Luncheon Menu
Serves 4

Gazpacho
Pesto-Chicken Cheesecakes
Quick Flatbread
Iced tea

GAZPACHO

Prep: 20 minutes
Chill: 2 hours

1½ cups low-sodium tomato juice
½ cup low-fat, low-sodium beef broth
1 medium cucumber, diced
2 tomatoes, chopped
1 green bell pepper, diced
2 tablespoons red wine vinegar
1 tablespoon lemon juice
4 green onions, chopped
½ teaspoon Worcestershire sauce
2½ teaspoons hot sauce
½ teaspoon garlic powder
2 tablespoons chopped fresh basil

• **Stir** together all ingredients; chill 2 hours. **Yield:** 5¼ cups.

Sudi DaCosta-Hatfield
Edison, New Jersey

PESTO-CHICKEN CHEESECAKES

These savory cheesecakes are filled with chicken and basil-packed pesto. Serve them individually on beds of salad greens.

Prep: 15 minutes
Bake: 30 minutes

2 (8-ounce) packages cream cheese, softened
2 large eggs
3 tablespoons all-purpose flour, divided
3 tablespoons Pesto *
1 cup chopped cooked chicken
1 (8-ounce) container sour cream
Mixed salad greens
Garnish: chopped fresh chives

• **Beat** cream cheese at medium speed with an electric mixer until smooth.
• **Add** eggs, 2 tablespoons flour, and Pesto, beating until blended.
• **Stir** in chicken. Pour into 4 (4-inch) springform pans.
• **Bake** at 325° for 20 minutes.
• **Stir** together remaining 1 tablespoon flour and sour cream.
• **Spread** over cheesecakes; bake 10 more minutes. Cool on a wire rack 10 minutes. Gently run a knife around edges of cheesecakes, and release sides.
• **Serve** individual cheesecakes hot or cold atop salad greens. Garnish, if desired. **Yield:** 4 servings.

Note: Cheesecake mixture may be baked in a 9-inch springform pan. Add 5 minutes to the initial baking time, and an additional 5 minutes after adding the flour and sour cream.

Pesto

Pecans take the place of traditional pine nuts in this easy make-ahead recipe.

Prep: 6 minutes

1½ cups firmly packed fresh basil leaves
½ cup pecan pieces, toasted
½ cup olive oil
3 garlic cloves
3 tablespoons lemon juice
½ teaspoon salt

• **Process** all ingredients in a food processor until smooth. Refrigerate leftover Pesto up to 5 days, or freeze up to 3 months. **Yield:** 1 cup.

＊Substitute 3 tablespoons prepared pesto for homemade pesto, if desired.

Quick Flatbread

Commercial pizza dough is the secret to this fast flatbread.

Prep: 10 minutes
Bake: 17 minutes

1 (10-ounce) can refrigerated pizza
   crust
¼ cup olive oil, divided
1 large sweet onion
2 garlic cloves, minced
1½ teaspoons dried Italian
   seasoning
⅛ teaspoon salt
¼ teaspoon pepper
¾ cup (3 ounces) shredded Asiago
   or Parmesan cheese

• **Unroll** pizza dough, and place on a baking sheet.
• **Press** handle of a wooden spoon into dough to make indentations at 1-inch intervals; brush with 2 tablespoons olive oil.
• **Bake** at 425° for 10 to 12 minutes.
• **Cut** onion into thin slices; cut each slice in half.
• **Sauté** onion in remaining 2 tablespoons olive oil over medium heat about 8 minutes or until browned.
• **Add** garlic and next 3 ingredients, and sauté 1 minute.
• **Top** pizza crust with onion mixture, and sprinkle with cheese.
• **Bake** at 425° for 5 minutes or until cheese is melted. Serve immediately.
Yield: 4 to 6 servings.

Crazy for Cola

From its start in 1886, Coca-Cola has been a thirst cure. When we're hungry, cola adds distinctive flavor to food—from sauces to salads, dinner to dessert. Enjoy these new recipes featuring your favorite fizz.

Nutty Cream Cheese Party Sandwiches

Prep: 30 minutes
Bake: 1 hour
Chill: 8 hours

1¼ cups cola soft drink
1 cup firmly packed light brown sugar
1 cup raisins
2 tablespoons vegetable oil
2 cups all-purpose flour
1 teaspoon baking powder
1 teaspoon baking soda
¼ teaspoon salt
½ teaspoon ground nutmeg
1 cup chopped walnuts
1 large egg, lightly beaten
1 teaspoon vanilla extract
1 (8-ounce) container soft cream
   cheese
2 tablespoons honey
½ teaspoon ground cinnamon

• **Bring** cola to a boil in a medium saucepan; remove from heat. Stir in sugar, raisins, and oil. Combine flour and next 4 ingredients. Stir in cola mixture, walnuts, egg, and vanilla.
• **Pour** batter into a greased and floured 9- x 5-inch loafpan.
• **Bake** at 350° for 1 hour or until a wooden pick inserted in center comes out clean. Cool in pan on a wire rack 20 minutes; remove from pan, and cool completely on wire rack. Cover and chill 8 hours.
• **Slice** bread into ¼-inch-thick slices.
• **Stir** together cream cheese, honey, and cinnamon. Spread on half of slices; top with remaining slices. Cut sandwiches into thirds. **Yield:** 30 sandwiches.

Sweet-and-Tangy Barbecue Sauce

Cola's the secret to this picnic-perfect barbecue sauce.

Prep: 5 minutes
Cook: 1 hour

1 large onion, finely chopped
1 teaspoon vegetable oil
¾ cup cola soft drink
¾ cup chili sauce
1 tablespoon brown sugar
½ teaspoon salt
1 tablespoon dry mustard
1 tablespoon paprika
⅛ teaspoon ground red
   pepper
2 tablespoons white vinegar

• **Cook** onion in oil in a large saucepan over low heat, stirring often, 15 minutes or until onion is caramel colored.
• **Stir** in cola and remaining ingredients. Bring to a boil over medium heat. Cover, reduce heat, and simmer, stirring occasionally, 45 minutes. **Yield:** 2 cups.

COLA CAKE

Prep: 20 minutes
Bake: 35 minutes

2 cups all-purpose flour
2 cups sugar
1 teaspoon baking soda
1 cup cola soft drink
1 cup butter or margarine
2 tablespoons cocoa
1½ cups miniature marshmallows
½ cup buttermilk
2 large eggs, lightly beaten
1 teaspoon vanilla extract
Cola Frosting
1 cup finely chopped pecans

• **Stir** together first 3 ingredients. Bring cola, butter, and cocoa to a boil over medium heat, stirring constantly. Gradually stir into flour mixture.
• **Stir** in marshmallows and next 3 ingredients. Pour into a greased and floured 13- x 9-inch pan. Bake at 350° for 30 to 35 minutes or until a wooden pick inserted in center comes out clean.
• **Spread** frosting over warm cake; top with pecans. **Yield:** 15 servings.

Cola Frosting

½ cup butter or margarine
6 tablespoons cola soft drink
3 tablespoons cocoa
1 (16-ounce) package powdered sugar
1 teaspoon vanilla extract

• **Bring** first 3 ingredients to a boil over medium heat, stirring until butter melts; remove from heat. Stir in sugar and vanilla until smooth. **Yield:** 2¼ cups.

Quick Cola Cake: Omit first 10 ingredients. Beat 1 (18.25-ounce) package Swiss chocolate cake mix, 1 (3.9-ounce) package chocolate instant pudding mix, 1 (10-ounce) bottle cola soft drink, ½ cup vegetable oil, and 4 large eggs at low speed with mixer until blended. Beat at medium speed 3 minutes; pour into prepared 13- x 9-inch pan. Bake at 350° for 45 minutes. Frost cake; top with pecans.

Chocolate-Peanut Butter Frosting: Substitute ½ cup peanut butter for ½ cup butter in Cola Frosting.

A Taste of the South

Just as Memphis is known for barbecue and New Orleans is celebrated for gumbo, Key West is internationally famous for Key lime pie.

If fresh Key limes aren't available in your area, you can opt for bottled juice. Nellie & Joe's Key lime juice is a popular brand that does not contain the preservative sulfur dioxide, which some believe gives the pie a sulfurlike aftertaste. You can order bottled juice from Key West Key Lime Shoppe at 1-800-376-0806 or www.keylimeshop.com; or from Key West Key Lime Pie Company at 1-800-872-2714 or www.keylimepiecompany.com.

KEY LIME PIE
(pictured on page 114)

Prep: 30 minutes
Bake: 28 minutes
Chill: 8 hours

1¼ cups graham cracker crumbs
¼ cup firmly packed light brown sugar
⅓ cup butter or margarine, melted
2 (14-ounce) cans sweetened condensed milk
1 cup fresh Key lime juice
2 egg whites
¼ teaspoon cream of tartar
2 tablespoons sugar
Garnish: lime slices

• **Combine** first 3 ingredients. Press into a 9-inch pieplate. Bake at 350° for 10 minutes; cool. Stir together milk and lime juice until blended. Pour into crust.
• **Beat** egg whites and cream of tartar at high speed with an electric mixer just until foamy. Add sugar, 1 tablespoon at a time, beating until soft peaks form and sugar dissolves (2 to 4 minutes).
• **Spread** meringue over filling.
• **Bake** at 325° for 25 to 28 minutes. Chill 8 hours. Garnish, if desired. **Yield:** 1 (9-inch) pie.

Mike Smith
Kissimmee, Florida

What's for Supper?

Whether you choose Prime, Choice, or Select grades of steak, there's one to fit any menu or budget.

SPICY BEEF FILETS

If beef tenderloin is too pricey, try boneless top sirloin.

Prep: 10 minutes
Cook: 15 minutes

6 (6-ounce) beef tenderloin steaks
   (1½ inches thick)
¼ teaspoon salt
¼ teaspoon pepper
¼ cup butter or margarine
2 garlic cloves, pressed
2 tablespoons all-purpose
   flour
1 cup beef broth
1 cup dry red wine *
¼ cup bourbon *
2 tablespoons Dijon mustard
1 teaspoon Worcestershire
   sauce

• **Sprinkle** steaks with salt and pepper.
• **Melt** butter in a large skillet over medium heat.
• **Add** steaks, and cook 5 to 7 minutes on each side or to desired degree of doneness. Remove steaks from pan, and keep warm.
• **Add** garlic and flour to pan drippings; cook over medium heat, stirring constantly, 1 minute. Gradually add broth, wine, and bourbon, stirring to loosen particles from bottom; bring to a boil.
• **Stir** in mustard and Worcestershire sauce; reduce heat, and simmer 5 minutes. Top steaks with sauce. **Yield:** 6 servings.

*Substitute 1¼ cups cranberry juice for red wine and bourbon, if desired.
Vikki D. Sturm
Rossville, Georgia

FLANK STEAKS WITH MUSHROOMS

Less tender steaks, such as boneless chuck, skirt steak, or eye of round, work well with this marinade.

Prep: 5 minutes
Chill: 3 hours
Grill: 20 minutes

¼ cup firmly packed light brown sugar
¼ teaspoon freshly ground pepper
1 cup lite soy sauce
2 tablespoons sesame oil
1 tablespoon minced fresh ginger or
   ¼ teaspoon ground ginger
2 garlic cloves, minced
2 (1-pound) flank steaks, trimmed
1 tablespoon butter or margarine
1 pound fresh mushrooms, sliced

• **Combine** first 6 ingredients in a shallow dish; add steaks. Cover and chill 3 to 6 hours, turning steaks occasionally.
• **Remove** steaks from marinade, discarding marinade.
• **Grill,** covered with grill lid, over medium-high heat (350° to 400°) 10 minutes on each side or to desired degree of doneness.
• **Melt** butter in a large skillet over medium heat. Add mushrooms; sauté until liquid evaporates.
• **Cut** steaks diagonally across the grain into thin strips. Serve with mushrooms. **Yield:** 6 servings.

Note: To broil steaks, place on a lightly greased rack in a broiler pan. Broil steaks 5½ inches from heat (with electric oven door partially open) 10 minutes on each side or to desired degree of doneness.

Pam Rappaport
Pembroke Pines, Florida

STATELY STEAKS

Substitute T-bone/porterhouse or rib steaks for rib eyes, if desired.

Prep: 7 minutes
Chill: 2 hours
Grill: 10 minutes

4 (10-ounce) rib-eye or beef strip
   steaks (1 inch thick)
2 tablespoons olive oil
2 teaspoons garlic powder
2 teaspoons coarsely ground
   pepper
½ cup lite soy sauce
½ cup Worcestershire sauce

• **Rub** steaks with olive oil; sprinkle with garlic powder and pepper.
• **Combine** soy sauce and Worcestershire sauce.
• **Pour** ¾ cup soy sauce mixture in a shallow dish or large heavy-duty zip-top plastic bag; add steaks. Cover or seal. Chill 2 hours, turning occasionally.
• **Remove** steaks from marinade, discarding marinade.
• **Grill,** covered with grill lid, over medium-high heat (350° to 400°) 5 minutes on each side or to desired degree of doneness, basting with remaining ¼ cup soy sauce mixture. **Yield:** 4 servings.

Susan H. Price
Greensboro, North Carolina

STEAK GUIDE

Steak labels vary from region to region. The following will help guide you in your selection for these recipes.

■ Flank—Flank Steak Filet, Jiffy Steak, London Broil

■ Rib eye—Beauty Steak, Delmonico Steak, Filet, Spencer

■ Tenderloin—Filet Mignon, Filet de Boeuf, Filet, Tender Steak

Southwest Fiesta Brunch

Host a hands-on tamale brunch to celebrate Cinco de Mayo. Make-ahead recipe options put this fiesta within easy reach.

Cinco de Mayo Brunch
Serves 8 to 10

Sangría or orange juice

Fresh Mango Salsa or Black Bean Salsa
Tortilla chips

Breakfast Tamales

Huevos con Queso (double recipe)

Santa Fe Grits Bake   Polvorones

SANGRÍA

Pre-party hint: Garnish glasses, and cover until serving time.

Prep: 10 minutes
Chill: 8 hours

2 (750-milliliter) bottles Beaujolais
¼ cup sugar
¼ cup brandy
1 orange, sliced
1 lemon, sliced
1 lime, sliced
1 (1-liter) bottle club soda, chilled
Additional brandy (optional)
Additional sugar (optional)

• **Stir** together first 6 ingredients. Chill 8 hours. Stir in soda; serve immediately. To garnish glasses, moisten rims with brandy, and dip in sugar. **Yield:** 2 quarts.

Jerrie Brumbloe
Maylene, Alabama

FRESH MANGO SALSA

Prep: 20 minutes
Chill: 3 hours

2 ripe mangoes, peeled and finely chopped★
½ red bell pepper, finely chopped
½ purple onion, finely chopped
2½ tablespoons chopped fresh cilantro
2 to 3 tablespoons chopped fresh mint
1 jalapeño pepper, seeded and minced
2 tablespoons fresh lime juice
½ teaspoon salt
¼ teaspoon pepper

• **Stir** together all ingredients. Cover and chill 3 hours. **Yield:** 2 cups.

★Substitute 1 (26-ounce) jar mango slices, drained and finely chopped, or papayas, pineapple, or citrus, if desired.

Mildred Bickley
Bristol, Virginia

BLACK BEAN SALSA

Prep: 30 minutes
Chill: 8 hours

2 medium tomatoes
1 red bell pepper
1 green bell pepper
1½ cups fresh or frozen corn kernels (3 ears fresh corn)
¼ cup finely chopped purple onion
1 serrano chile pepper, seeded and minced
1 (15-ounce) can black beans, rinsed and drained
⅓ cup fresh lime juice
¼ cup olive oil
⅓ cup chopped fresh cilantro
1 teaspoon salt
½ teaspoon ground cumin
¼ teaspoon ground red pepper

• **Chop** tomatoes and bell peppers.
• **Stir** together tomato, bell pepper, corn, and remaining ingredients. Cover and chill 8 hours. Serve with tortilla chips. **Yield:** 7 cups.

Joy Kloess
Birmingham, Alabama

BREAKFAST TAMALES

Prep: 1 hour, 15 minutes
Cook: 30 minutes

1 (8-ounce) package dried cornhusks
2 cups masa harina mix
1 teaspoon salt
½ teaspoon baking powder
½ teaspoon baking soda
1 tablespoon paprika
2 cups water
½ (12-ounce) package ground pork sausage
3 green onions, chopped
1 cup medium or hot salsa, divided
9 large eggs, lightly beaten
½ cup (2 ounces) shredded Cheddar cheese
Garnishes: fresh cilantro sprigs, chile peppers, lime wedges

- **Soak** cornhusks in hot water 1 hour.
- **Combine** masa mix and next 4 ingredients in a large bowl; stir in 2 cups water.
- **Cook** sausage and green onions in a large skillet over medium-high heat, stirring until sausage crumbles and is no longer pink; drain well. Stir in ½ cup salsa.
- **Add** eggs, and cook over medium heat, stirring often, until eggs are almost set. Add cheese, and stir until melted.
- **Drain** cornhusks, and press between paper towels.
- **Spread** about 1 tablespoon masa mixture over half of each cornhusk. Top with 1 tablespoon sausage mixture. Roll up, starting at a long side. Fold in half. Tie in groups of four, if desired.
- **Arrange** tamales, open end up, in a steamer basket over boiling water. Cover and cook 30 minutes. Serve with remaining ½ cup salsa. Garnish, if desired. **Yield:** 36 tamales.

Pam Traylor
Brenham, Texas

HUEVOS CON QUESO

Prep: 30 minutes
Cook: 12 minutes

1 (12-ounce) package 6-inch corn
   tortillas
¾ cup vegetable oil
3 tablespoons butter or margarine
1 small onion, finely chopped
½ medium-size red bell pepper,
   chopped
½ teaspoon ground cumin
2 tablespoons all-purpose flour
1 (8-ounce) container sour cream
1 (8-ounce) loaf Mexican pasteurized
   prepared cheese product, cubed
1 cup (4 ounces) shredded Monterey
   Jack cheese with peppers
6 large eggs, lightly beaten
1 (4-ounce) can tomatillo salsa

- **Cut** tortillas into ¼-inch strips.
- **Pour** oil into a Dutch oven; heat to 375°. Fry tortilla strips, in batches, until crisp and golden. Set aside.
- **Melt** butter in a large skillet over medium heat; add onion, bell pepper, and cumin, and sauté until vegetables are tender. Add flour, and cook, stirring constantly, 1 minute; reduce heat to low.
- **Stir** in sour cream and cheeses. Cook, stirring constantly, until cheeses melt; keep warm.
- **Cook** eggs in a large, lightly greased skillet over medium heat, stirring occasionally, until set.
- **Divide** tortilla strips onto 6 serving plates. Top evenly with cheese mixture and eggs. Drizzle with salsa, and serve immediately. **Yield:** 6 servings.

Note: For testing purposes only, we used Mexican Velveeta.

SANTA FE GRITS BAKE

Pre-party hint: Assemble recipe
the day before, and chill.

Prep: 20 minutes
Bake: 45 minutes
Stand: 10 minutes

5 cups water
1 teaspoon salt
½ teaspoon hot sauce
1⅓ cups uncooked regular grits
1 (16-ounce) loaf pasteurized prepared
   cheese product, cubed
½ cup butter or margarine
3 large eggs, lightly beaten
2 (4.5-ounce) cans chopped green
   chiles, undrained

- **Bring** first 3 ingredients to a boil in a Dutch oven; gradually stir in grits. Reduce heat, and simmer, stirring occasionally, 15 to 20 minutes or until thickened. Remove grits from heat; add cheese and butter, stirring until cheese melts. Stir in eggs and chiles.
- **Pour** into a lightly greased 13- x 9-inch baking dish. Cover and chill 8 hours, if desired; remove grits from refrigerator, and let stand 30 minutes.
- **Bake** at 350° for 45 minutes or until puffed and golden. Remove from oven, and let stand 10 minutes. **Yield:** 8 to 10 servings.

Joyce Sauls
DeRidder, Louisiana

POLVORONES

Serve polvorones—Mexican
shortbread cookies—with coffee
as a light dessert. Guests will love
these sweet little treasures hidden
inside colorful paper.

Prep: 20 minutes
Bake: 15 minutes

2 cups all-purpose flour
½ teaspoon baking soda
1 cup ground peanuts or
   almonds
1 cup powdered sugar
1 cup butter or margarine,
   cut up
Powdered sugar
Colored tissue paper squares (4 x 4
   inches)
Wax paper squares (4 x 4 inches)

- **Combine** first 4 ingredients. Cut in butter with a pastry blender until mixture is crumbly.
- **Turn** dough onto a lightly floured surface. Roll into an 8- x 6-inch rectangle (½ inch thick).
- **Cut** dough into 24 (2- x 1-inch) pieces, and arrange on a lightly greased baking sheet.
- **Bake** at 350° for 15 minutes or until cookies are lightly browned. Remove to wire racks to cool.
- **Roll** polvorones in powdered sugar.
- **Top** each tissue paper square with 1 wax paper square.
- **Place** a polvorone in center of squares. Wrap in paper, gently twisting ends of paper to seal. **Yield:** 2 dozen.

Surf and Turf

For some of us, surf and turf is a one-way ticket down memory lane. Back before mango salsa or Brie were dots on America's culinary horizon, the combination of steak and lobster was the ultimate night-on-the-town splurge. An evening of dinner and dancing . . . well, some things just don't lose their charm. Add timely updates—Mango Salsa, for example—to travel down a fresh path.

STEAK-AND-SHRIMP KABOBS

Prep: 25 minutes
Chill: 2 hours, 20 minutes
Grill: 12 minutes

16 unpeeled, jumbo fresh shrimp
½ cup dry sherry
½ cup olive oil
¼ cup grated orange rind
½ cup fresh orange juice
¼ cup soy sauce
4 garlic cloves, minced
2 tablespoons minced fresh ginger
½ teaspoon dried crushed red pepper
   (optional)
1½ pounds rib-eye steak, cut into
   1-inch cubes
Mixed salad greens

• **Peel** shrimp, and devein, if desired.
• **Whisk** together sherry, next 6 ingredients, and, if desired, crushed red pepper. Reserve 1 cup sherry mixture. Pour remaining mixture into a shallow dish or large heavy-duty zip-top plastic bag; add steak. Cover or seal, and chill 2 hours. Add shrimp; cover or seal, and chill 20 minutes.
• **Remove** beef and shrimp from marinade, discarding marinade. Thread beef and shrimp alternately onto 4 (12-inch) skewers.
• **Grill,** covered with grill lid, over medium-high heat (350° to 400°) 10 to 12 minutes or until done. Serve over salad greens with reserved 1 cup sherry mixture. **Yield:** 4 servings.

BEEFY CRAB QUESADILLAS WITH MANGO SALSA

Prep: 15 minutes
Cook: 16 minutes

½ pound round steak, thinly sliced
¼ teaspoon salt
½ teaspoon ground cumin
⅛ teaspoon pepper
1 tablespoon olive oil
2 tablespoons fresh lime juice
8 (8-inch) flour tortillas
½ pound fresh crabmeat, drained
2 teaspoons chopped fresh chives
1 (8-ounce) block Monterey Jack
   cheese with peppers, shredded
Mango Salsa

• **Sprinkle** beef slices with salt, cumin, and pepper.
• **Brown** beef in hot oil in a large skillet over medium-high heat; remove from skillet. Sprinkle with lime juice.
• **Arrange** beef evenly on 4 tortillas; top evenly with crabmeat, chopped chives, and cheese. Top with remaining tortillas. Cook quesadillas in a lightly greased skillet over medium heat 2 minutes on each side or until cheese melts. Serve with Mango Salsa. **Yield:** 4 servings.

Mango Salsa

Prep: 10 minutes

2 mangoes, peeled and chopped *
½ cup diced green or red bell pepper
3 green onions, sliced
2 tablespoons fresh lime juice
1 jalapeño pepper, seeded and diced
¼ teaspoon salt

• **Stir** together all ingredients. Chill, if desired. **Yield:** 2¼ cups.

*Substitute 1½ cups chopped bottled mango slices for fresh mango, if desired.
Rosie Mellis
Charleston, South Carolina

STUFFED BEEF TENDERLOIN

Prep: 30 minutes
Chill: 2 hours
Bake: 45 minutes
Cook: 20 minutes

2 tablespoons juniper berries
¼ cup chopped fresh rosemary
¼ cup chopped fresh thyme
2 garlic cloves
10 black peppercorns
1 (4½-pound) beef tenderloin, trimmed
3 (4-ounce) fresh or frozen lobster
   tails, thawed
¼ cup butter or margarine, melted
2 tablespoons lemon juice
2 teaspoons chopped fresh thyme
½ teaspoon ground red pepper
6 thick bacon slices
½ cup butter or margarine
3 large shallots, chopped
1 cup dry red wine or beef broth

• **Bake** berries in a shallow pan at 400° for 5 minutes. Pulse berries, rosemary, and next 3 ingredients in a food processor 6 or 7 times. Spread mixture over beef. Cover and chill 1 to 2 hours.
• **Cut** shell of lobster tail segments lengthwise on the top and underside. Pry open tail segments; remove meat.
• **Make** a lengthwise cut down center of tenderloin, cutting to, but not through, bottom; press to flatten. Arrange lobster tails down center of tenderloin. Drizzle lobster with ¼ cup melted butter, and sprinkle with lemon juice, 2 teaspoons thyme, and red pepper. Fold beef over lobster; tie with string at 1-inch intervals. Place in a roasting pan.
• **Bake** at 425° for 30 minutes. Arrange bacon slices over beef, and bake 10 more minutes or until a meat thermometer inserted into thickest portion of beef registers 145° (medium-rare).
• **Melt** ½ cup butter in a skillet over medium heat; add shallots, and sauté until tender. Stir in wine; bring to a boil. Reduce heat; simmer 20 minutes or until reduced to ½ cup. Slice beef; serve with wine sauce. **Yield:** 6 to 8 servings.

Note: You can find juniper berries in the spice section of most supermarkets.
Julie Wesson
Hainesville, Illinois

Golden Shallots

Although small in size, shallots add a real wallop of flavor. Looking like overgrown garlic, dried shallots have a thin paper skin like onions do. Available year-round, shallots have an off-white flesh and mild onion flavor. This assortment of recipes shows off shallots at their best.

TOMATO-AND-HERB SAUCE

Prep: 10 minutes
Cook: 15 minutes

4 large shallots, finely chopped
1 tablespoon olive oil
1 (35-ounce) can peeled whole plum
    tomatoes
1 (6-ounce) can tomato paste
1 tablespoon Worcestershire
    sauce
½ cup chopped fresh basil *
1 tablespoon chopped fresh or
    1 teaspoon dried oregano *
½ teaspoon garlic salt
½ teaspoon freshly ground pepper
1 bay leaf
2 teaspoons sugar (optional)

• **Sauté** shallots in hot oil in a Dutch oven over medium-high heat 3 minutes or until tender.
• **Add** tomatoes, and crush with back of a wooden spoon; bring to a boil.
• **Stir** in tomato paste, next 6 ingredients, and, if desired, sugar. Reduce heat; simmer 15 minutes. Discard bay leaf. Serve over pasta. **Yield:** 5 cups.

*Substitute 2 teaspoons dried Italian seasoning for basil and oregano, if desired.

SHRIMP BOURBON

Prep: 30 minutes
Cook: 14 minutes

2 pounds unpeeled, medium-size
    fresh shrimp
2 tablespoons butter or
    margarine
8 large shallots, chopped
2 garlic cloves, minced
1 cup chicken broth
½ cup bourbon
1 cup half-and-half
½ teaspoon ground red pepper
Hot cooked fettuccine
Shredded Parmesan cheese (optional)

• **Peel** shrimp, and devein, if desired.
• **Melt** butter in a Dutch oven over medium-high heat; add shallots and garlic. Sauté 3 minutes or until tender.
• **Stir** in chicken broth and next 3 ingredients. Cook, stirring occasionally, 5 minutes or until slightly thickened.
• **Add** shrimp; cook 3 minutes or until shrimp turn pink. Remove from heat, and serve over fettuccine. Sprinkle with Parmesan cheese, if desired. **Yield:** 8 servings.

Cyndi Christensen
Virginia Beach, Virginia

SHALLOT SAVVY

■ Choose dry-skinned shallots that are plump and firm with no sign of wrinkling or sprouting.

■ Store dry shallots in a cool, dry, well-ventilated place up to a month.

■ Refrigerate fresh shallots up to a week.

■ Before cooking fresh shallots, cut off tops and roots, wash white part, separate layers, and let water run between them to remove dirt.

MUSHROOM-WINE SAUCE

This sauce tastes great over steak.

Prep: 15 minutes
Cook: 13 minutes

½ cup butter or margarine
12 shallots, chopped
4 green onions, chopped
1 garlic clove, minced
1 (8-ounce) package fresh mushrooms,
    sliced
¼ cup all-purpose flour
2 (10¾-ounce) cans beef consommé,
    undiluted
½ cup dry red wine

• **Melt** butter in a skillet over medium-high heat. Add shallots, onions, and garlic; sauté 2 minutes. Add mushrooms; sauté 5 minutes. Add flour; cook, stirring constantly, 1 minute. Gradually stir in consommé and wine.
• **Cook,** stirring constantly, 5 minutes until slightly thickened. **Yield:** 4 cups.

Nina Page Winkler
Ocoee, Florida

ROASTED VEGETABLES WITH FRESH SAGE

This makes a flavorful side dish for chicken, beef, or pork.

Prep: 30 minutes
Bake: 25 minutes

6 small zucchini (about 2 pounds)
1 large red bell pepper, cut into ½-inch
    strips
20 shallots
6 garlic cloves
3 tablespoons olive oil
½ teaspoon salt
½ teaspoon freshly ground pepper
¼ cup chopped fresh sage

• **Cut** each zucchini lengthwise into quarters; cut quarters in half crosswise.
• **Arrange** zucchini and next 3 ingredients in a greased shallow foil-lined roasting pan. Drizzle with oil. Bake at 500° for 25 minutes. Sprinkle with salt, pepper, and sage. **Yield:** 6 servings.

Living Light

Why mess up your kitchen? Prepare a meal on the grill while you savor a beautiful warm afternoon.

HONEY-GRILLED TENDERLOINS

Brown sugar, honey, and sesame oil lend this simple pork dish distinctive flair.

Prep: 10 minutes
Chill: 3 hours
Grill: 20 minutes

2 (¾-pound) pork tenderloins
¼ cup lite soy sauce
5 garlic cloves, minced
½ teaspoon ground ginger
2 tablespoons brown sugar
3 tablespoons honey
2 teaspoons dark sesame oil

• **Make** a lengthwise cut down center of each tenderloin to within ¼ inch of opposite side; press to open.
• **Combine** soy sauce, garlic, and ginger in a shallow dish.
• **Add** tenderloins. Cover and chill 3 hours, turning meat occasionally.
• **Stir** together brown sugar, honey, and sesame oil.
• **Grill** tenderloins, covered with grill lid, over medium-high heat (350° to 400°) 20 minutes or until a meat thermometer inserted into thickest portion registers 160°, turning occasionally and basting with honey mixture. **Yield:** 6 servings.

Tammy Goff
Norfolk, Virginia

❤ Per serving: Calories 139 (28.1% from fat)
Fat 4.3g (sat 1.2g, mono 1.9g, poly 0.9g)
Protein 24.8g Carb 12.1g Fiber 0g
Chol 74mg Iron 1.8mg
Sodium 408mg Calc 20mg

GRILLED POLENTA

Prep: 20 minutes
Chill: 1 hour
Grill: 6 minutes

1¼ cups water
1 (14.25-ounce) can reduced-sodium chicken broth
2 garlic cloves, minced
1½ cups stone-ground cornmeal
½ cup (2 ounces) shredded reduced-fat Swiss cheese
2 tablespoons minced fresh thyme
½ teaspoon salt
¼ teaspoon freshly ground pepper
¼ teaspoon ground red pepper
Olive oil-flavored cooking spray

• **Bring** first 3 ingredients to a boil in a medium saucepan; reduce heat to medium.
• **Add** cornmeal, 1 tablespoon at a time, stirring constantly, until smooth.
• **Cook,** stirring constantly with a wooden spoon, 5 minutes or until mixture is very thick; remove from heat. Stir in cheese and next 4 ingredients.
• **Spoon** mixture into an 8-inch square baking dish coated with cooking spray. Cover and chill 1 hour.
• **Cut** polenta into 6 pieces. Coat both sides of polenta with cooking spray.
• **Grill,** covered with grill lid, over medium-high heat (350° to 400°) 3 minutes on each side or until browned. Serve immediately. **Yield:** 6 servings.

❤ Per serving: Calories 169 (16.1% from fat)
Fat 3.1g (sat 1g, mono 0.2g, poly 0.3g)
Protein 6.9g Carb 28.3g Fiber 1.9g
Chol 6mg Iron 1.9mg
Sodium 234mg Calc 116mg

MARINATED GRILLED VEGETABLES

Prep: 20 minutes
Chill: 30 minutes
Grill: 24 minutes

10 large fresh mushrooms
2 zucchini
2 yellow squash
1 green bell pepper
1 red bell pepper
½ cup balsamic vinegar
2 tablespoons olive oil
3 garlic cloves, minced
½ teaspoon salt
1 teaspoon minced fresh thyme
1 teaspoon freshly ground pepper
Vegetable cooking spray

• **Remove** mushroom stems, and discard. Cut zucchini and yellow squash into ½-inch slices. Cut bell peppers into 1-inch strips.
• **Combine** vegetables, vinegar, and next 5 ingredients in a large heavy-duty zip-top plastic bag; seal and chill 30 minutes. Remove vegetables with a slotted spoon, reserving marinade.

• **Coat** a grill wok with cooking spray; arrange vegetables in basket. Grill, covered with grill lid, over medium heat (300° to 350°) 12 minutes on each side or until crisp-tender. Place vegetables in a large bowl; drizzle with reserved marinade, tossing to coat. **Yield:** 6 servings.

Karen C. Greenlee
Lawrenceville, Georgia

♥ Per serving: Calories 100 (48.1% from fat)
Fat 5.3g (sat 0.7g, mono 3.5g, poly 0.6g)
Protein 2.1g Carb 9.3g Fiber 2.3g
Chol 0mg Iron 2.4mg
Sodium 201mg Calc 42mg

GRILLED PINEAPPLE WITH VANILLA-CINNAMON ICE CREAM

(pictured on page 114)

Prep: 15 minutes
Grill: 14 minutes

1 **fresh pineapple**
3 **tablespoons brown sugar**
½ **teaspoon ground cinnamon**
1 **tablespoon grated fresh ginger**
Vegetable cooking spray
Vanilla-Cinnamon Ice Cream ∗

• **Cut** pineapple lengthwise into quarters; discard core. Remove pineapple pulp, discarding shell.
• **Combine** brown sugar and cinnamon. Sprinkle evenly over pineapple pulp, and sprinkle with ginger.
• **Coat** a food rack with cooking spray; place on grill over medium-high heat (350° to 400°). Place pineapple on rack.
• **Grill,** covered with grill lid, 5 to 7 minutes on each side. Remove pineapple from grill; cut into chunks. Serve with ice cream. **Yield:** 6 servings.

∗ Substitute low-fat or fat-free vanilla frozen yogurt, if desired.

♥ Per serving (pineapple):
Calories 73 (6% from fat)
Fat 0.5g (sat 0g, mono 0.1g, poly 0.1g)
Protein 0.4g Carb 18.7g Fiber 1.3g
Chol 0mg Iron 0.5mg
Sodium 3.3mg Calc 14mg

LIGHT NOTES

Outdoor grilling can become a healthy obsession. Your kitchen will stay cool and clean . . . and you'll stay lean. Grilling adds wonderful flavor and color without adding fat and calories. So brush off that grill rack, fill up the tank, and discover a whole new way of creating light and delicious suppers.

30-Minute Countdown

30 minutes—Place marinated vegetables in grill wok; place wok on grill rack.

25 minutes—Place pork tenderloins on grill rack.

20 minutes—Place pineapple on lower grill rack.

10 minutes—Arrange polenta squares on lower grill rack.

5 minutes—Place pineapple on upper grill rack (if you have a single rack grill, remove pineapple from grill, and keep warm). Remove pork and vegetables from grill. Slice pork; remove polenta from grill.

Smart Bites

We know that eating 25 to 30 grams of fiber per day is recommended, but how do we accomplish this without carrying around a calculator? Simply eat at least two servings of fruit and three servings of vegetables. Here are some simple tricks.

■ Enjoy grilled fruit and vegetables with your lunch and supper.

■ Spread fat-free refried beans on corn tortillas instead of fatty ground beef.

■ Try a new grain every week. Bulghur, quinoa, and barley are high in fiber as well as delicious.

■ Snack on fresh fruit instead of chips while watching TV.

■ Eat the skin on your washed apples, pears, and potatoes.

■ Look for 100% whole wheat as the first ingredient in your bread.

■ Choose brown rice instead of white rice.

Vanilla-Cinnamon Ice Cream

While this delicious ice cream contains no fat, it is not a low-calorie dessert.

Prep: 1 hour

2 **(14-ounce) cans fat-free sweetened condensed milk**
1 **quart fat-free half-and-half**
1 **tablespoon vanilla extract**
1 **teaspoon ground cinnamon**
Garnish: cinnamon sticks

• **Stir** together first 4 ingredients. Pour mixture into freezer container of a 1-gallon electric freezer.
• **Freeze** according to manufacturer's instructions. Serve immediately, or place in freezer. Garnish, if desired. **Yield:** 7½ cups.

♥ Per ½-cup serving:
Calories 189 (0% from fat)
Fat 0g Protein 4.1g Carb 38g
Fiber 0g Chol 0mg Iron 0mg
Sodium 117mg Calc 143mg

From Our Kitchen

The Rise of Bread Pudding

The bread pudding we know today is a direct descendant of England's famous hasty pudding, which is made from flour, milk, eggs, butter, and spices. Our savory and sweet bread puddings on pages 104 and 105 use leftover bread instead of flour.

Stale bread makes the best pudding, but soft, fresh bread ages beautifully when you give it a little heat. Trim and discard crust from bread. Cut to desired size, and place on a baking sheet. Bake in a 300° oven until pieces begin to lose some of their moisture, about 15 to 20 minutes, stirring after 10 minutes. Be careful not to brown or overdry the bread or you'll have croutons.

Refrigerator Fresh

We recently tried a new product that we like—the FoodBuddy from Anamac, Inc. It's a small plastic container (won't leak or spill) that holds an active mineral that ensures a drier, fresher environment in the refrigerator. FoodBuddy helps eliminate odors, mold, and bacteria from the freezer and the fridge. Keep one on the top shelf, one in the crisper drawer, and one in the freezer.

FoodBuddy keeps working up to six months with a monthly zap in the microwave. To order a package of three for $14.95 plus shipping and handling, call 1-800-655-3990.

Spatulas and Spoons

Spatulas are multipurpose kitchen tools. We use them for everything from folding ingredients together to scrambling eggs to stir-frying. Our Test Kitchens staff likes Le Creuset spatulas, because they can take the heat and cold. They don't chip, split, or melt under our demanding circumstances. These spatulas can be pricey, so let your cooking style direct your choices. Several heat-resistant brands of spatulas are available, so browse around before you buy.

The Lore Behind the Layers

A *Lane cake* contains a mixture of coconut, nuts, and dried fruits between its layers. Although the layers may be white or yellow, it's always covered with white frosting. Emma Rylander Lane of Clayton, Alabama, is said to be its creator; she won a prize for it in the state fair.

Lady Baltimore cake is a three-layer white cake with a fruit-and-nut filling under a blanket of fluffy white frosting. Owen Wister ignited the popularity of the cake. After he tasted the wonderful confection, he wrote about it in his 1906 novel *Lady Baltimore*.

Fragrant, fruity layers are the likely reason folks call it a *hummingbird cake*. It's believed that the aromas of bananas, pineapple, cinnamon, and vanilla are heavenly to the flying sweet-seekers. Hummingbirds and bakers alike find this cake irresistible . . . it is our most requested recipe.

In the Pan

We know you'll be eager to get that oven preheated when you read our layer cake recipes on page 117, but first take an inventory of your cabinet.

Before you begin mixing, measure to make sure you have the correct pan size. If pans are 1 inch larger than recommended, you'll get thinner layers that may be dry. Pans smaller than recommended will yield thicker layers. Both instances alter cooking times and/or temperatures.

Fill your pans no more than three-fourths full to have uniform layers and to prevent batter from overflowing as the cake rises.

TIPS AND TIDBITS

"Living Light," beginning on page 126, offers a great meal on the grill. Consider these bits of advice before grilling any foods.

■ Weber has improved its product line to simplify outdoor cooking. If you have any questions, call the Grill-Line Monday-Friday April 1 through Labor Day at 1-800-474-5568. Or e-mail your questions year-round to grillout@weber.com.

■ Susan Markuske of Charlotte, North Carolina, adds crushed fresh herbs to warm water when soaking wooden kabob skewers. The food picks up a hint of herbs from inside out. Susan suggests soaking skewers in the same water used to soak mesquite or hickory chips to impart an intense wood flavor.

■ Don't sacrifice food to the wrong charcoal. Natural coals are slow burning and hold a consistent temperature longer. Fast-lighting coals work well for quick-cooking foods, such as hot dogs and hamburgers, but they burn away too quickly for slow cooking. Choose odorless lighter fluid when you need to ignite the coals immediately. Otherwise, a charcoal starter "chimney" gets a great fire going in no time with just newspaper, coals, and a long match.

JUNE

Southern Setting

Enjoy a meal reminiscent of old-fashioned Sunday dinners that epitomize Southern style and hospitality.

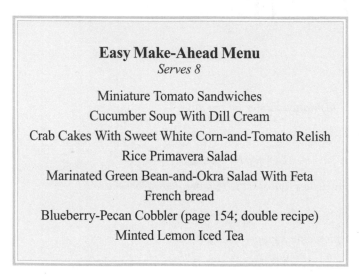

Easy Make-Ahead Menu
Serves 8

Miniature Tomato Sandwiches
Cucumber Soup With Dill Cream
Crab Cakes With Sweet White Corn-and-Tomato Relish
Rice Primavera Salad
Marinated Green Bean-and-Okra Salad With Feta
French bread
Blueberry-Pecan Cobbler (page 154; double recipe)
Minted Lemon Iced Tea

MINIATURE TOMATO SANDWICHES

Prep: 10 minutes

¼ cup mayonnaise
1 (3-ounce) package cream cheese, softened
2 teaspoons chopped fresh basil
¼ teaspoon salt, divided
¼ teaspoon pepper, divided
1 baguette
4 plum tomatoes, sliced

• **Stir** together mayonnaise, cream cheese, basil, ⅛ teaspoon salt, and ⅛ teaspoon pepper; cover and chill 8 hours, if desired.
• **Cut** baguette into 16 slices.
• **Spread** cheese mixture on baguette slices. Top with tomato, and sprinkle with remaining salt and pepper. **Yield:** 16 appetizer servings.

CUCUMBER SOUP WITH DILL CREAM

Prep: 15 minutes
Chill: 8 hours

2 cups half-and-half, divided
4 cucumbers, peeled, seeded, and chopped
2 green onions, sliced
1 tablespoon lemon juice
1 (16-ounce) container sour cream
½ teaspoon salt
½ teaspoon hot sauce
½ cup sour cream
1 tablespoon chopped fresh dill

• **Process** 1 cup half-and-half and next 3 ingredients in a blender until smooth, stopping to scrape down sides.
• **Combine** cucumber mixture, remaining half-and-half, 16 ounces sour cream, salt, and hot sauce. Cover; chill 8 hours.
• **Stir** together ½ cup sour cream and dill; dollop on each serving. **Yield:** 1½ quarts.

CRAB CAKES WITH SWEET WHITE CORN-AND-TOMATO RELISH

Prep: 20 minutes
Cook: 16 minutes

6 tablespoons butter, divided
1 small sweet onion, chopped
2 garlic cloves, minced
1 pound fresh lump crabmeat, drained
3 cups soft breadcrumbs, divided
¼ cup mayonnaise
1 large egg, lightly beaten
2 tablespoons chopped fresh parsley
1 tablespoon Dijon mustard
1 tablespoon Worcestershire sauce
¼ teaspoon salt
¼ teaspoon pepper
¼ teaspoon hot sauce
1 teaspoon lemon juice
Sweet White Corn-and-Tomato Relish

• **Melt** 2 tablespoons butter in a large skillet over medium heat; add onion and garlic, and sauté until tender. Remove from heat; stir in crabmeat, 2 cups breadcrumbs, and next 9 ingredients.
• **Shape** mixture into 8 patties; dredge in remaining 1 cup breadcrumbs.
• **Melt** 2 tablespoons butter in a large skillet over medium-high heat; cook 4 crab cakes 3 to 4 minutes on each side or until golden. Drain on paper towels. Repeat procedure with remaining 2 tablespoons butter and crab cakes.
• **Serve** with Sweet White Corn-and-Tomato Relish. Serve immediately, or cover and chill up to 4 hours. **Yield:** 8 servings.

Sweet White Corn-and-Tomato Relish

Prep: 15 minutes
Cook: 1 minute
Chill: 3 hours

4 ears fresh sweet white corn
2 large tomatoes, peeled and chopped
3 green onions, sliced
2 tablespoons lemon juice
1 tablespoon olive oil
½ teaspoon salt
½ teaspoon pepper
¼ teaspoon garlic salt
⅛ teaspoon hot sauce

- **Cook** corn in boiling water to cover 1 minute; drain and cool. Cut kernels from cobs.
- **Stir** together corn, tomato, and remaining ingredients; cover and chill 3 hours. **Yield:** 3 cups.

Note: For sweet white corn, we used Silver Queen.

RICE PRIMAVERA SALAD

Prep: 15 minutes
Chill: 8 hours

2 zucchini
2 yellow squash
1 large red bell pepper, chopped
1 medium-size purple onion, chopped
5 cups cooked long-grain rice
¾ cup mayonnaise
⅓ cup buttermilk
2 tablespoons Dijon mustard
2 tablespoons white vinegar
1½ teaspoons salt
½ teaspoon pepper

- **Cut** zucchini and yellow squash in half lengthwise; cut into slices.
- **Stir** together vegetables, rice, and remaining ingredients; cover and chill 8 hours. **Yield:** 8 cups.

MARINATED GREEN BEAN-AND-OKRA SALAD WITH FETA

Prep: 15 minutes
Cook: 3 minutes
Chill: 3 hours

1½ pounds fresh green beans, trimmed
1½ pounds small fresh okra
¾ cup olive oil
6 tablespoons white wine vinegar
1 tablespoon chopped fresh basil
½ teaspoon salt
½ teaspoon pepper
¼ teaspoon dry mustard
¼ cup crumbled feta cheese

A CELEBRATION OF SUMMER

Remember the days when your grandmother's table exemplified the talents of an accomplished host? Everyone would eat in style and relax into the evening. For many grandmothers, such entertaining was second nature. Today, however, those gracious traditions are lost under a pile of busy schedules. Yet Southern style and gentle hospitality can still exist. The key is using modern conveniences.

A Gracious Setting

The beauty of a well-prepared table lies in the details. It's not about having the biggest house or the most manicured yard. Just start with basic elements—a few things you find hidden in the top of your pantry or in a cedar-lined hope chest you've pushed to the back of the closet.

- Position the table and chairs in the shade of a tree.

- Colored and clear glass jars serve as great centerpiece containers. Add some fresh-cut gardenias for seasonal fragrance.

- Pull out those starched white linens you inherited. If they need ironing, save time and effort by taking them to the dry cleaner.

A Simple, Elegant Menu

Our make-ahead menu fits right in with an atmosphere of tailored simplicity. Because all the recipes can be served chilled, you'll have plenty of time to sip Minted Lemon Iced Tea with guests and share a taste of those bygone days when setting a table for friends was not a chore, but standard practice.

Even though preparation time for each of the recipes in our menu is less than 35 minutes, sometimes you may not have even that much time. Here are a couple of quick substitutions.

- Purchase pasta salad from a deli for Rice Primavera Salad.

- Substitute jarred corn relish for Sweet White Corn-and-Tomato Relish. Stir in 2 or 3 chopped plum tomatoes.

- **Cook** beans and okra in boiling water to cover 3 minutes.
- **Plunge** beans and okra into ice water to stop the cooking process; drain.
- **Whisk** together olive oil and next 5 ingredients in a bowl.
- **Pour** oil mixture over beans and okra. Cover and chill 3 hours. Sprinkle salad with feta cheese. **Yield:** 8 servings.

MINTED LEMON ICED TEA

Prep: 10 minutes
Steep: 5 minutes
Chill: 2 hours

2 quarts boiling water
10 lemon zinger tea bags
1 to 1½ cups sugar
1 cup fresh mint leaves

- **Pour** boiling water over tea bags. Stir in sugar and mint; steep 5 minutes. Remove tea bags and mint leaves. Chill 2 hours. Serve over ice. **Yield:** 2 quarts.

Summer's Heat

Sweet or hot, large or small, peppers perk up your taste buds and add vibrant color to a world of different dishes.

These reader recipes use three popular peppers—the yellow banana pepper, which can vary from sweet to hot; the sweet red bell, which is a green bell pepper ripened longer on the vine; and the fiery habanero, one of the world's hottest chile peppers. To reduce the habanero pepper's heat, cut off the stem and remove the seeds and potent ribs.

STUFFED HUNGARIAN YELLOW BANANA PEPPERS

Banana peppers are also referred to as Hungarian wax chiles. Smelling banana peppers gives you a good idea of how hot they will be.

Prep: 15 minutes
Bake: 20 minutes

6 large banana peppers
1 cup crumbled feta cheese
1 (3-ounce) package cream cheese, softened
½ teaspoon dried oregano
2 tablespoons olive oil

• **Scoop** seeds and membrane from banana peppers.
• **Stir** together feta cheese, cream cheese, and dried oregano. Carefully spoon cheese mixture into peppers.
• **Place** stuffed peppers on an aluminum foil-lined jellyroll pan. Drizzle with olive oil.
• **Bake** at 400° for 20 minutes or until peppers are tender. **Yield:** 6 appetizer servings.

Lynda Liollio
Memphis, Tennessee

RED PEPPER HUMMUS

Prep: 10 minutes
Broil: 10 minutes

1 large red bell pepper *
1 (15-ounce) can chickpeas, rinsed and drained
1 garlic clove
¼ cup lemon juice
3 tablespoons tahini
2 tablespoons olive oil
2 tablespoons chopped fresh parsley
1 tablespoon lite soy sauce
1½ teaspoons ground cumin
½ teaspoon ground red pepper
⅛ teaspoon salt
Garnishes: fresh cilantro sprig, red bell pepper strips

• **Broil** bell pepper on an aluminum foil-lined baking sheet 5 inches from heat (with electric oven door partially open) about 5 minutes on each side or until pepper looks blistered.
• **Place** pepper in a heavy-duty zip-top plastic bag; seal and let stand 10 minutes to loosen skin. Peel pepper, and discard seeds.
• **Process** pepper and next 10 ingredients in a food processor until smooth, stopping to scrape down sides.
• **Serve** hummus with assorted crackers or pita chips. Garnish, if desired. **Yield:** 2 cups.

* Substitute ½ (7-ounce) jar roasted sweet red peppers, drained and chopped, for red bell pepper, if desired.

Sharlie G. Rigby
Little Rock, Arkansas

DIPSY DEVIL

Habanero chiles are extremely hot, so adjust the heat to suit your taste.

Prep: 10 minutes
Chill: 8 hours

½ (8-ounce) package cream cheese, softened
1 cup mayonnaise
1 (2.5-ounce) can deviled ham
1 (2-ounce) jar diced pimiento, drained
½ small habanero pepper, seeded and finely chopped *
1 shallot, finely chopped
2 tablespoons minced fresh parsley
1 tablespoon finely chopped onion

• **Beat** all ingredients at medium speed with an electric mixer until blended. Cover and chill 8 hours. Serve with crackers or tortilla chips. **Yield:** 1 cup.

* Substitute 4 drops hot sauce for habanero pepper, if desired.

DeLea Lonadier
Montgomery, Louisiana

PEPPER POINTERS

■ Peppers peak during warm months, showing up in abundance in our gardens, local farmers markets, and grocery stores. Be sure to look for peppers that are firm, shiny, and smooth.

■ When working with hot chile peppers, wear disposable gloves, if possible, and never touch your face or eyes. Always wash your hands immediately after handling hot peppers.

■ Store raw peppers in the freezer up to six months by covering them in wax paper and then wrapping in plastic wrap.

PICKLED CONFETTI VEGETABLES

Prep: 45 minutes
Chill: 8 hours
Process: 10 minutes

½ small cabbage, chopped
1½ large onions, chopped
6 medium-size ripe tomatoes, chopped
8 medium-size green tomatoes, chopped
1½ red bell peppers, chopped
1½ green bell peppers, chopped
1 cup chopped celery
1 medium cucumber, chopped
¼ cup salt
6 cups white vinegar (5% acidity)
2 (16-ounce) packages light brown sugar
2 teaspoons dry mustard

• **Combine** first 8 ingredients in a large bowl; sprinkle with salt. Cover and chill 8 hours.
• **Drain** and rinse with cold water. Pack vegetables evenly into hot jars.
• **Bring** vinegar, brown sugar, and mustard to a boil; pour over vegetables, filling to ½ inch from top. Remove air bubbles; wipe jar rims. Cover at once with metal lids, and screw on bands.
• **Process** in boiling-water bath 10 minutes. **Yield:** 4 quarts.

Marion Hall
Knoxville, Tennessee

Quick & Easy

Mom always appreciates helping hands in the kitchen, but Dad will be happy this Father's Day when you serve him these sweet and savory treats.

SNACK CRACKERS

Prep: 5 minutes
Bake: 15 minutes

½ cup vegetable oil
1 (1-ounce) envelope Ranch-style dressing mix
1 (10-ounce) package oyster crackers
½ (10-ounce) package bite-size Cheddar cheese crackers (2 cups)

• **Whisk** together oil and dressing mix; pour over crackers, tossing to coat. Spread on a lightly greased baking sheet.
• **Bake** at 350° for 15 minutes, stirring after 7 minutes. **Yield:** 6 cups.

Glenna Wilson
Florence, Alabama

EASY COOKIES

Prep: 5 minutes
Bake: 10 minutes

1 (18.25-ounce) package chocolate or yellow cake mix
½ cup vegetable oil
2 large eggs
1 cup (6 ounces) semisweet chocolate morsels
½ cup chopped pecans

• **Beat** first 3 ingredients at medium speed with an electric mixer until smooth. Stir in chocolate morsels and pecans. Drop by heaping teaspoonfuls onto ungreased baking sheets. Bake at 350° for 8 to 10 minutes. Remove to wire racks to cool. **Yield:** 4½ dozen.

Abby Hogan
Cartersville, Georgia

POPCORN DELIGHT

Prep: 15 minutes
Chill: 30 minutes

8 cups popped popcorn
3 cups corn chips, coarsely crushed
2 cups crispy corn puffs cereal
1 pound white chocolate, chopped
2 cups candy-coated chocolate pieces (optional)

• **Combine** first 3 ingredients in a large bowl. Microwave white chocolate in a glass bowl at HIGH 2 to 3 minutes, stirring every minute, until chocolate melts. Drizzle over popcorn mixture, tossing to coat.
• **Stir** in candy-coated chocolate pieces, if desired.
• **Spread** in a wax paper-lined 15- x 10-inch jellyroll pan; chill 30 minutes. Break into pieces; store in an airtight container. **Yield:** 15 cups.

Note: For testing purposes only, we used Kix cereal.

Denise Schwartz
Brighton, Michigan

BACON-CHEESE FINGERS

Prep: 15 minutes
Bake: 10 minutes

1 cup (4 ounces) shredded Swiss cheese
8 bacon slices, cooked and crumbled*
¼ cup mayonnaise
1 tablespoon grated onion
½ teaspoon celery salt
10 white bread slices, crusts removed

• **Stir** together first 5 ingredients, and spread over bread slices. Cut each slice into 3 strips. Place on a lightly greased baking sheet.
• **Bake** at 325° for 10 minutes. **Yield:** 30 appetizer servings.

*Substitute 1 (2.5-ounce) package fully cooked bacon pieces, if desired.

Ashley Hogan
Knoxville, Tennessee

What's for Supper?

Supper is extraeasy when you start with ingredients from your grocer's deli. You can prepare each of these recipes in half an hour or less.

SUMMER REUBENS

Purchase coleslaw, onion rolls, cheese, and corned beef. Complete the meal with potato salad.

Prep: 15 minutes
Bake: 5 minutes

1　pound prepared coleslaw
4　green onions, sliced
6　onion rolls, cut in half
⅓　cup spicy brown mustard
1　pound thinly sliced lean corned beef
6　(1-ounce) slices Monterey Jack
　　cheese with peppers

• **Stir** together coleslaw and green onions; drain and set aside.
• **Place** rolls, cut sides up, on a baking sheet. Spread with mustard. Top bottom halves of rolls with corned beef and cheese slices. Bake at 425° for 5 minutes.
• **Spoon** coleslaw mixture evenly over cheese. Cover with top halves of rolls. **Yield:** 6 servings.

CHICKEN PARMESAN PIZZA

Chicken fingers, garlic bread, and a green salad make a terrific meal.

Prep: 5 minutes
Bake: 20 minutes

1　(8-ounce) loaf garlic bread
4　large chicken fingers
½　cup marinara sauce
1　cup (4 ounces) shredded Italian
　　cheese blend
2　tablespoons chopped fresh basil
　　(optional)

• **Place** garlic bread, butter side up, on a baking sheet. Arrange chicken fingers on baking sheet.
• **Bake** at 425° for 10 minutes or until bread is lightly browned. Spread marinara sauce over garlic bread.
• **Cut** chicken fingers into ½-inch strips; arrange over marinara sauce. Sprinkle with cheese and, if desired, basil.
• **Bake** at 425° for 5 to 10 minutes or until cheese melts. **Yield:** 2 to 4 servings.

OPEN-FACED CHEESY CHICKEN SALAD MELTS

Buy chicken salad and serve with fresh fruit salad.

Prep: 15 minutes
Bake: 15 minutes

1½　pounds chicken salad
4　English muffins, split and lightly
　　toasted
3　large eggs, separated
1½　cups (6 ounces) shredded sharp
　　Cheddar cheese
¼　teaspoon salt
¼　teaspoon ground red pepper
1　to 2 tablespoons chopped fresh
　　parsley (optional)

• **Spread** chicken salad evenly over English muffin halves.
• **Beat** egg whites at high speed with an electric mixer until stiff peaks form.
• **Stir** together egg yolks, cheese, salt, and pepper; fold in egg whites. Spoon egg mixture evenly over chicken salad.
• **Bake** at 350° for 15 minutes or until puffed and golden. Sprinkle with parsley, if desired. **Yield:** 4 servings.

STUFFED FOCACCIA WITH ROASTED PEPPER VINAIGRETTE

Pick up a rotisserie chicken, roasted red peppers, and diced fresh fruit from the deli to create a quick meal.

Prep: 20 minutes

1　(9-inch) round loaf focaccia
Roasted Pepper Vinaigrette, divided
1　(3-ounce) goat cheese log,
　　crumbled
¼　cup pine nuts or slivered almonds
1　rotisserie chicken
3　cups mixed lettuces
½　pint grape or cherry tomatoes,
　　halved

• **Cut** focaccia in half horizontally, using a serrated knife; place, cut sides up, on a baking sheet.
• **Drizzle** evenly with 1 cup Roasted Pepper Vinaigrette. Sprinkle with goat cheese and pine nuts.
• **Bake** at 400° for 6 to 8 minutes or until lightly browned.
• **Remove** meat from chicken, and coarsely chop. Sprinkle chicken over bottom half of bread. Top with lettuce and tomato; cover with top of bread. Cut into 6 wedges. Serve immediately with remaining vinaigrette, if desired. **Yield:** 6 servings.

Roasted Pepper Vinaigrette

1　cup oil-and-vinegar dressing
1　(5.2-ounce) jar roasted sweet red
　　peppers, drained

• **Process** dressing and roasted pepper in a blender or food processor until smooth. **Yield:** 1½ cups.

Note: For testing purposes only, we used focaccia topped with bell peppers, onions, mushrooms, and cheese.

Spreading the Flavor

Constructing the perfect sandwich isn't difficult, but it does require a little culinary engineering. If bread is the foundation upon which the sandwich is built, then the spread is the glue that holds everything together.

Whether you're using delicate grilled vegetables or assembling a hardy Dagwood piled high with meat and cheese, a complementary spread can add that touch that completes your work of art.

All of these recipes, along with our suggestions for bread and meat pairings, will garner rave reviews at your next summertime outing.

CUCUMBER-YOGURT SPREAD

Serve this refreshing spread on soft rolls with grilled chicken, sliced turkey, or fresh tomato slices.

Prep: 15 minutes
Chill: 24 hours

1 (16-ounce) container plain nonfat yogurt
2 small cucumbers, peeled, seeded, and finely chopped
2 garlic cloves, pressed
6 small mint leaves, minced
¼ teaspoon salt
¼ teaspoon pepper
Garnishes: cucumber slices, fresh mint sprigs

• **Line** a mesh strainer with a paper coffee filter. Spoon yogurt into filter, and place strainer over a bowl. Cover with plastic wrap, and chill 24 hours.
• **Spoon** yogurt into a bowl, discarding liquid (yogurt will have a very thick consistency).
• **Stir** in chopped cucumber and next 4 ingredients. Cover and chill up to 3 days. Garnish, if desired. **Yield:** 2 cups.
Augusta Duffey
Atlanta, Georgia

TAPENADE

Try this classic olive spread with grilled fish or vegetables on sliced focaccia.

Prep: 10 minutes

1 (6-ounce) jar pitted kalamata olives, drained
1 anchovy fillet, rinsed
2 garlic cloves, chopped
1 small shallot, chopped
1 teaspoon capers
¼ cup olive oil
1 tablespoon lemon juice
1 tablespoon chopped fresh parsley
Garnishes: olives, lemon slice, fresh parsley

• **Process** first 5 ingredients in a food processor until smooth. With processor running, pour oil through food chute, stopping to scrape down sides.
• **Stir** in lemon juice and chopped parsley. Garnish, if desired. **Yield:** 1 cup.

HERBED FETA SPREAD

This spread is perfect on pita bread filled with grilled vegetables or on BLTs.

Prep: 10 minutes

1 (8-ounce) package feta cheese, softened
1 (8-ounce) package cream cheese, softened
3 tablespoons chopped fresh basil
3 tablespoons chopped fresh chives
2 tablespoons olive oil
2 tablespoons balsamic vinegar
⅓ cup pine nuts, toasted
Garnish: fresh basil sprigs

• **Stir** together first 6 ingredients until smooth. Cover and chill up to 7 days.
• **Stir** in pine nuts just before serving. Garnish, if desired. **Yield:** 2½ cups.
Eva Jones
Tower Hill, Illinois

BÉARNAISE MAYONNAISE

Spread your choice of these mayonnaise variations over hard rolls with sliced roast beef, on hamburgers, or on tomato sandwiches.

Prep: 20 minutes

⅓ cup dry white wine
1 tablespoon white wine vinegar
2 shallots, minced
1 cup mayonnaise
2 tablespoons chopped fresh tarragon
1 teaspoon grated lemon rind
⅛ teaspoon pepper
Garnish: fresh tarragon sprig

• **Cook** first 3 ingredients over medium-high heat 5 minutes or until liquid is reduced to 1 tablespoon. Remove from heat, and cool.
• **Stir** together mayonnaise and next 3 ingredients; stir in wine reduction. Cover and chill up to 7 days. Garnish, if desired. **Yield:** 1 cup.

Tomato-Basil Mayonnaise: Stir together 1 cup mayonnaise, 2 tablespoons tomato paste, and 2 tablespoons chopped fresh basil until blended.

Gremolata Mayonnaise: Stir together 1 cup mayonnaise, 2 tablespoons chopped fresh parsley, 2 tablespoons grated lemon rind, and 1 garlic clove, pressed.

Firefly Picnic

Head out to the patio, fire up the grill, and savor this satisfying menu.

Summer Picnic
Serves 4

Garlic-and-Wine Grilled Chicken
Vegetable Salad
Homemade Butter Rolls

We all remember catching fireflies in jelly jars while the sky caught smoke from our parents' grills. Joyce Metevia of Baton Rouge says outdoor rituals of fun and food are for all ages. This retired schoolteacher and principal finds that the hospitable atmosphere of the South is conducive to entertaining.

GARLIC-AND-WINE GRILLED CHICKEN

Prep: 8 minutes
Chill: 4 hours
Grill: 55 minutes

¾ cup dry white wine
½ cup butter or margarine, melted
½ cup minced fresh parsley
6 garlic cloves, minced
4 green onions, chopped
2 tablespoons lemon juice
1 teaspoon salt
½ teaspoon pepper
½ teaspoon paprika
1 (3- to 4-pound) package chicken pieces

• **Stir** together first 9 ingredients, and reserve ½ cup. Pour remaining mixture into a large heavy-duty zip-top plastic bag, and add chicken. Seal and chill 4 hours, turning occasionally.
• **Remove** chicken from marinade, discarding marinade. Prepare fire by piling charcoal or lava rocks on 1 side of grill, leaving other side empty. Place rack on grill. Arrange chicken over side with charcoal, and grill, covered with grill lid, 5 minutes on each side. Place chicken over empty side. Grill, covered with grill lid, 45 minutes, turning 3 times and basting often with reserved ½ cup wine mixture. **Yield:** 4 servings.

Joyce Metevia
Baton Rouge, Louisiana

VEGETABLE SALAD

Prep: 10 minutes
Chill: 4 hours

1 small zucchini
½ small purple onion
1 small red bell pepper
1 medium tomato
1 small jalapeño pepper
1 ear fresh corn
¼ cup Ranch-style dressing
¼ teaspoon salt
¼ teaspoon pepper
2 large yellow bell peppers

- **Cut** zucchini in half lengthwise; thinly slice zucchini, onion, and red bell pepper. Seed and chop tomato; seed jalapeño, and cut into thin strips.
- **Cut** corn from cob into a bowl; add cut vegetables, dressing, salt, and pepper, tossing to coat. Cover and chill at least 4 hours.
- **Cut** bell peppers in half lengthwise; discard seeds and membrane. Stuff with vegetable mixture. **Yield:** 4 servings.

Joyce Metevia
Baton Rouge, Louisiana

HOMEMADE BUTTER ROLLS

Prep: 20 minutes
Chill: 8 hours
Rise: 2 hours
Bake: 10 minutes

2 (¼-ounce) envelopes active dry yeast
1 cup sugar, divided
2 cups warm water (100° to 110°)
1 cup butter or margarine, melted
6 large eggs, lightly beaten
1½ teaspoons salt
8½ to 9½ cups all-purpose flour

- **Stir** together yeast, 2 tablespoons sugar, and 2 cups warm water in a 4-cup glass measuring cup; let stand 5 minutes.
- **Stir** together yeast mixture, butter, and remaining sugar; stir in eggs and salt. Gradually stir in enough flour to make a soft dough. Cover and chill 8 hours.
- **Divide** dough into 4 equal portions. Turn each portion out on a lightly floured surface, and roll into a 12-inch circle. Cut each circle into 12 wedges. Roll up wedges, starting at wide end; place on greased baking sheets. (Rolls may be frozen at this point.) Cover and let rise in a warm place (85°), free from drafts, 2 hours or until doubled in bulk.
- **Bake** at 400° for 10 minutes or until golden. **Yield:** 4 dozen.

Note: If unbaked rolls are frozen, place frozen rolls on ungreased baking sheets. Cover and let rise in a warm place, free from drafts, 2 hours or until doubled in bulk. Bake as directed.

Joyce Metevia
Baton Rouge, Louisiana

Colors of the Season

Squash and zucchini, thin-skinned cousins,
are easy to find and even easier to prepare.
Here we make the most of their fresh flavors.

Look for squash that have firm, bright-colored skin free of spots and bruises. In general, the smaller the squash, the more tender it is. Store squash in a plastic bag in the refrigerator for no more than four days.

GRILLED MARINATED VEGETABLES

Prep: 15 minutes
Chill: 1 hour
Grill: 20 minutes

3 medium-size yellow squash, sliced diagonally
3 medium zucchini, sliced diagonally
1 red bell pepper, cut into 6 pieces
1 large purple onion, cut into ½-inch-thick slices
⅓ cup olive oil
1 tablespoon lemon juice
1 garlic clove, pressed
½ teaspoon dried marjoram
¼ teaspoon salt
¼ teaspoon pepper

- **Place** first 4 ingredients in a heavy-duty zip-top plastic bag.
- **Whisk** together oil and next 5 ingredients. Pour over vegetables. Chill 1 hour. Remove vegetables from marinade, reserving marinade.
- **Arrange** vegetables evenly in a grill basket.
- **Grill,** covered with grill lid, over medium-high heat (350° to 400°) 20 minutes or until crisp-tender, turning and brushing occasionally with marinade. **Yield:** 6 servings.

Mitchelann Rayas
Gainesville, South Carolina

SOUTH-OF-THE-BORDER SQUASH

Prep: 12 minutes
Bake: 30 minutes

1 pound yellow squash, sliced
1 pound zucchini, sliced
2 cups crushed tortilla chips
1 (10¾-ounce) can Cheddar cheese soup, undiluted
1 (10¾-ounce) can cream of mushroom soup, undiluted
1 (4.5-ounce) can chopped green chiles
¼ cup chopped onion
2 large eggs, lightly beaten
2 tablespoons taco seasoning
1 cup (4 ounces) shredded sharp Cheddar cheese
4 bacon slices, cooked and crumbled

- **Cook** yellow squash and zucchini, covered, in a small amount of boiling water in a medium saucepan 8 minutes or until tender; drain. Press between layers of paper towels to remove excess moisture.
- **Combine** vegetables, tortilla chips, and next 6 ingredients; spoon into a lightly greased 13- x 9-inch baking dish. Sprinkle with cheese and bacon.
- **Bake** at 450° for 30 minutes. **Yield:** 8 servings.

SUMMER VEGETABLE SKILLET

Prep: 12 minutes
Cook: 40 minutes

1   medium zucchini
1   medium-size yellow squash
½   pound fresh okra
½   pound potatoes, peeled
1   cup cornmeal
1   teaspoon salt
1   teaspoon ground red pepper
4   bacon slices
½   cup vegetable oil

• **Cut** first 4 ingredients into 1-inch cubes. Combine cornmeal, salt, and ground red pepper in a large heavy-duty zip-top plastic bag. Add vegetables; seal and shake to coat.
• **Cook** bacon in a large heavy skillet until crisp; remove bacon, and crumble, reserving drippings in skillet.
• **Add** oil to drippings, and place over medium-high heat until hot. Add half of vegetable mixture; cook over high heat, stirring often, 15 minutes. Cover, reduce heat to low, and cook 5 more minutes. Remove from skillet; keep warm.
• **Repeat** procedure with remaining half of vegetable mixture. Sprinkle with bacon. **Yield:** 4 to 6 servings.

Mary Abrams
Springville, Alabama

HERBED VEGETABLE MEDLEY

(pictured on page 191)

Prep: 10 minutes
Cook: 10 minutes

3   small zucchini
3   small yellow squash
1   medium-size red bell pepper
2   medium carrots
2   tablespoons butter or vegetable oil
3   garlic cloves, pressed
1   teaspoon salt
1   teaspoon lemon pepper
⅓   cup chopped green onions
2   tablespoons chopped fresh basil
Garnish: fresh basil sprig

• **Cut** first 4 ingredients into thin strips; set aside.

• **Melt** butter in a large skillet over medium-high heat; add garlic, and sauté 1 to 2 minutes. Add carrot, salt, and lemon pepper, and sauté 2 to 3 minutes.
• **Add** remaining vegetable strips, green onions, and basil. Sauté 3 minutes or until crisp-tender. Garnish, if desired. **Yield:** 8 servings.

RISOTTO PRIMAVERA

Prep: 25 minutes
Cook: 45 minutes

4½ cups chicken broth
½   carrot, cut into thin strips
2   tablespoons butter or margarine, divided
1   medium zucchini, thinly sliced
1   small yellow squash, thinly sliced
1   small onion, diced
1   garlic clove, minced
1¼ cups uncooked Arborio rice
1   teaspoon dried Italian seasoning
¼   teaspoon pepper
3   tablespoons chopped walnuts, toasted
⅓   cup crumbled blue cheese

• **Bring** broth to a boil in a medium saucepan over medium heat. Add carrot, and cook 2 minutes. Remove with a slotted spoon. Keep broth hot.
• **Melt** 1 tablespoon butter in a large saucepan; add carrot, zucchini, and squash. Sauté 5 minutes or until tender. Remove from pan, and set aside.
• **Melt** remaining 1 tablespoon butter in saucepan; add onion and garlic. Sauté 1 minute.
• **Add** rice, and cook, stirring constantly, 5 minutes or until translucent. Reduce heat to medium; add ½ cup hot chicken broth.
• **Cook,** stirring constantly, until liquid is absorbed.
• **Repeat** procedure with remaining broth, ½ cup at a time. Remove from heat, and stir in zucchini mixture, Italian seasoning, and pepper. Sprinkle with walnuts and cheese. Serve immediately. **Yield:** 4 servings.

Reunions

Lumber City, Georgia's Shelton Chapel hosts one of the South's largest family reunions. What started out in the 1940s with a handful of Brewer family members has grown to more than 400 guests. "This is one big family get-together," says Sheila Brewer Gratham.

Tradition is something these folks know all too well. A reading of the minutes and a recap of the year's news officially mark the beginning of each celebration. Covered dishes grace chapel grounds, with some ambitious cooks bringing up to four dishes. The day passes quickly, but an exchange of addresses and phone numbers keeps everyone in touch until the same time next year.

Join us in sampling these wonderfully flavorful selections from family members.

EASY BRUNSWICK STEW

Prep: 30 minutes
Cook: 3 hours, 45 minutes

1   (4- to 5-pound) Boston butt pork roast
4   cups frozen cubed hash brown potatoes
3   (14½-ounce) cans diced tomatoes with garlic and onion
1   (14½-ounce) can whole kernel corn, drained
1   (14½-ounce) can cream-style corn
1   (15¼-ounce) can sweet green peas, drained
1   (16-ounce) bottle barbecue sauce
1   tablespoon hot sauce
1   teaspoon salt
1   teaspoon pepper

• **Cook** pork roast in boiling water to cover in a stockpot 2½ hours or until tender; drain, reserving 4 cups liquid. Cool slightly; shred meat with a fork.
• **Return** reserved liquid to stockpot; add hash brown potatoes, and bring to a boil. Reduce heat; simmer 15 minutes.
• **Add** shredded pork, tomatoes, and remaining ingredients. Bring mixture to a boil; cover, reduce heat, and simmer 1 hour. **Yield:** 5 quarts.

COLORFUL CORN SALAD

Prep: 7 minutes
Chill: 2 hours

1 (16-ounce) package frozen whole
   kernel corn, thawed
1 small sweet onion, chopped
1 large tomato, seeded and chopped
1 large green bell pepper, chopped
¼ cup mayonnaise
½ teaspoon salt
½ teaspoon coarsely ground black
   pepper
¼ cup seeded and chopped cucumber
   (optional)

• **Stir** together first 7 ingredients until blended; cover and chill 2 hours. Serve with a slotted spoon. Top with chopped cucumber, if desired. **Yield:** 5 cups.

PEAR PRESERVES CAKE
(pictured on page 115)

Spicy flavor and dense texture make this cake a homey dessert.

Prep: 20 minutes
Bake: 1 hour, 20 minutes

1 cup shortening
2½ cups sugar
4 large eggs
1 teaspoon vanilla extract
3¼ cups all-purpose flour
¾ teaspoon baking soda
1 teaspoon ground cinnamon
1 teaspoon ground cloves
1 teaspoon ground allspice
1 cup buttermilk
1 (11.5-ounce) jar pear preserves
1 cup chopped pecans
Powdered sugar

• **Beat** shortening and sugar at medium speed with an electric mixer until fluffy. Add eggs, beating well. Stir in vanilla.
• **Combine** flour and next 4 ingredients; add to shortening mixture alternately with buttermilk, beginning and ending with flour mixture. Beat at low speed just until blended after each addition.
• **Fold** in preserves and pecans. Pour into a greased and floured 10-inch tube pan.

• **Bake** at 325° for 1 hour and 20 minutes or until a long wooden pick inserted in center of cake comes out clean. Cool in pan on a wire rack 10 minutes; remove from pan, and cool completely on wire rack. Dust top of cake with powdered sugar. **Yield:** 1 (10-inch) cake.

Just Right on Ice

Few things are as rejuvenating as a thirst-quenching drink on a steamy afternoon. Two of these drinks—Rice-and-Cinnamon Cooler and Watermelon Punch (recipe on page 140)—are based on classic beverages enjoyed throughout Spain and Mexico. With make-ahead ease, these recipes are the perfect pick-me-ups. So sit back, put your feet up, and pour any of these delicious drinks over ice.

CITRUS ICED TEA

Prep: 30 minutes
Chill: 2 hours

3 cups water
2 whole cloves
1 family-size tea bag
1½ cups pineapple juice
½ cup orange juice
2 to 4 tablespoons fresh lemon
   juice
⅔ cup sugar
Garnishes: fresh mint sprigs, orange
   slices

• **Bring** 3 cups water and cloves to a boil over medium heat; reduce heat, and simmer 10 minutes. Remove from heat, and add tea bag; steep 10 minutes.
• **Discard** tea bag and cloves. Add fruit juices and sugar, stirring until sugar dissolves. Chill 2 hours; serve over crushed ice. Garnish, if desired. **Yield:** 5 cups.

Marcia Porch
Winter Park, Florida

RICE-AND-CINNAMON COOLER

This milky-looking drink, adapted from the Spanish and Mexican horchata, is delightfully sweet, yet surprisingly light.

Prep: 10 minutes
Cook: 5 minutes
Chill: 4 hours

1 (3-inch) cinnamon stick
2 (32-ounce) containers rice milk
3 cups 2% reduced-fat milk
1 cup sugar
Cinnamon sticks (optional)

• **Break** 1 cinnamon stick into small pieces. Cook in a small skillet over high heat 6 minutes or until lightly browned.
• **Process** cinnamon pieces, rice milk, and 3 cups milk, in batches, in a blender or food processor until smooth.
• **Pour** mixture through a fine wire-mesh strainer into a saucepan, discarding cinnamon pieces.
• **Stir** in sugar, and cook over low heat, stirring occasionally, 5 minutes or until sugar dissolves. Chill 2 to 4 hours. Serve over crushed ice with cinnamon sticks, if desired. **Yield:** 2½ quarts.

FRESH LEMONADE

This recipe originally appeared in The Ultimate SOUTHERN LIVING *Cookbook.*

Prep: 10 minutes

1½ cups sugar
½ cup boiling water
1½ cups fresh lemon juice (6 to 8
   large lemons)
5 cups cold water
Garnishes: lemon slices, fresh mint
   sprigs

• **Stir** together sugar and ½ cup boiling water until sugar dissolves.
• **Stir** in lemon juice and 5 cups cold water. Garnish, if desired. **Yield:** 8 cups.

Fresh Limeade: Substitute fresh lime juice for lemon juice.

WATERMELON PUNCH

*Adapted from the Mexican
agua fresca, this variation
on a fresh fruit "ade" is
refreshing and nutritious.*

Prep: 25 minutes
Chill: 2 hours

2½ cups water
⅔ cup fresh lemon juice (3 large
    lemons)
⅔ cup sugar
2 cups fresh orange juice (6 to 8
    oranges)
1 small watermelon
Garnish: lime wedges

• **Bring** first 3 ingredients to a boil in a saucepan; boil 3 minutes. Cool completely, and stir in orange juice.
• **Peel,** seed, and cube watermelon.
• **Process** cubed watermelon in a blender until smooth. Pour through a wire-mesh strainer into a bowl, reserving 3 cups juice; discard watermelon pulp.
• **Stir** together watermelon juice and sugar mixture; chill thoroughly. Serve over crushed ice. Garnish, if desired. **Yield:** 8 cups.

Cantaloupe Punch: Substitute cantaloupe for watermelon, and use lime juice instead of lemon juice.

*Margaret Latchaw
Macon, Georgia*

Living Light

New spouse, new house, and new pots and pans. So what do you do with your new kitchen accoutrements? Make those first steps into your new life together healthful ones with our simple menu for two.

Newlywed Menu
Serves 2

Cherry Tomato-Caper Salad
Cracked Pepper Salmon Fillets
Veggie Wild Rice
Easy Tropical Bananas

CHERRY TOMATO-CAPER SALAD

*Reduce sodium by rinsing
capers well and omitting salt.*

Prep: 15 minutes
Stand: 15 minutes

1 tablespoon drained small capers
1 tablespoon balsamic vinegar
2 teaspoons olive oil
¼ teaspoon salt
¼ teaspoon pepper
8 large cherry tomatoes, halved
3 fresh basil leaves, shredded
Bibb lettuce leaves (optional)

• **Combine** first 5 ingredients. Drizzle over tomatoes, tossing to coat. Let stand at least 15 minutes or up to 1 hour. Sprinkle with basil. Serve over lettuce, if desired. **Yield:** 2 servings.

*Patsy Bell Hobson
Liberty, Missouri*

♥ Per serving: Calories 65 (64% from fat)
Fat 4.5g (sat 0.6g, mono 3.2g, poly 0.5g)
Protein 1.2g Carb 4g Fiber 0.9g
Chol 0mg Iron 0.5mg
Sodium 747mg Calc 10mg

CRACKED PEPPER SALMON FILLETS

Prep: 10 minutes
Cook: 15 minutes

2 tablespoons chopped fresh
    parsley
1 garlic clove, minced
1 teaspoon coarsely ground
    pepper
1 teaspoon blackened seasoning
2 (6-ounce) salmon fillets
Vegetable cooking spray
Green Tomato-Cranberry Chutney

• **Combine** first 4 ingredients in a shallow dish. Coat both sides of fillets with parsley mixture.
• **Cook** fillets, skin side down, in a large nonstick skillet coated with cooking spray over medium-high heat 10 minutes. Cover and cook 5 minutes or until fish flakes with a fork. Serve with Green Tomato-Cranberry Chutney. **Yield:** 2 servings.

♥ Per serving (without chutney):
Calories 264 (38% from fat)
Fat 10.9g (sat 1.9g, mono 3.6g, poly 2.8g)
Protein 37.4g Carb 2.1g Fiber 0.9g
Chol 66mg Iron 2.4mg
Sodium 277mg Calc 27mg

Green Tomato-Cranberry Chutney

*Chutney, from the East Indian word
chatni, is a versatile condiment usually
made of fruit, vinegar, sugar, and spices.*

Bake: 35 minutes
Cook: 10 minutes

1 jalapeño pepper
3 medium-size green tomatoes,
    chopped
1 large pear, chopped
1 golden apple, chopped
1 (16-ounce) can whole-berry
    cranberry sauce
1 tablespoon lime juice

• **Bake** jalapeño pepper in a small pan at 400° for 20 minutes, turning once; cool pepper to touch, remove seeds, and mince.

• **Cook** jalapeño and next 3 ingredients in a large skillet over medium-high heat, stirring often, 5 minutes or until most of the liquid is absorbed.
• **Stir** in cranberry sauce, and cook 5 minutes or until most of the liquid is absorbed. Stir in lime juice. Serve with meat, fish, or poultry. **Yield: 2 cups.**

Sharon Bradberry
Tallahassee, Florida

♥ Per ¼-cup serving: Calories 125 (2% from fat)
Fat 0.4g (sat 0g, mono 0.1g, poly 0.1g)
Protein 0.8g Carb 32g Fiber 1.9g
Chol 0mg Iron 0.5mg
Sodium 23mg Calc 13mg

VEGGIE WILD RICE

Prep: 10 minutes
Cook: 36 minutes

1 (14-ounce) can vegetable broth
¾ cup water
1 (6-ounce) package long-grain and
     wild rice mix
3 tablespoons chopped walnuts
Vegetable cooking spray
½ medium-size red bell pepper, chopped
1 cup sliced fresh mushrooms
1 garlic clove, minced
3 green onions, sliced
¼ teaspoon salt
½ teaspoon freshly ground pepper

• **Bring** broth and ¾ cup water to a boil in a medium saucepan; add rice mix, discarding seasoning packet. Cover, reduce heat, and simmer 30 minutes.
• **Sauté** walnuts in a large nonstick skillet coated with cooking spray over medium-high heat 5 minutes. Remove from pan; set aside. Add bell pepper, mushrooms, and garlic to skillet coated with cooking spray; sauté over medium-high heat 5 minutes or until tender.
• **Stir** in cooked rice, green onions, salt, and pepper; sprinkle with walnuts. Serve immediately. **Yield: 4½ cups.**

♥ Per cup: Calories 198 (27% from fat)
Fat 6g (sat 0.4g, mono 1.2g, poly 3.6g)
Protein 6g Carb 31g Fiber 1g
Chol 0mg Iron 1.8mg
Sodium 166mg Calc 27mg

SMART BITES

Avoid the newlywed spread with these snacks under 150 calories.

Snack	Serving Size	Calories
Almondina Biscuits*	3 biscuits	90
Fresh broccoli flowerets with reduced-fat Ranch-style dressing	1 cup broccoli plus 2 tablespoons dressing	135
Light whole grain bread	1 slice	40
Healthy Choice garden vegetable soup	1 cup	120
Rold Gold honey mustard pretzels	16 pretzels	110
Orville Redenbacher Smart Pop popcorn	7 cups popped	120
Frozen grapes	1 cup	58
Healthy Choice smoked ham	6 slices	60
Sunkist fruit rolls	1 roll	70
Dannon Light Yogurt	8 ounces	120

* A crunchy cookie similar to biscotti. Great with hot tea or coffee, or crumbled over nonfat yogurt. Visit www.almondina.com.

EASY TROPICAL BANANAS

Prep: 10 minutes
Cook: 13 minutes

1½ cups angel food cake cubes
1 tablespoon light butter
2 tablespoons dark brown sugar
2 cups pineapple juice
3 tablespoons dark rum
1 teaspoon vanilla extract
¼ teaspoon ground cinnamon
2 bananas, each cut into 8 pieces
6 macadamia nuts, toasted and
     chopped
Nonfat vanilla frozen yogurt (optional)

• **Bake** cake cubes in an 11- x 7-inch pan at 350° for 5 minutes or until lightly toasted. Set aside.

• **Melt** butter in a large nonstick skillet over medium-high heat.
• **Add** sugar, and cook, stirring often, 5 minutes.
• **Stir** in pineapple juice and rum; cook 3 minutes.
• **Stir** in vanilla and ground cinnamon. Add banana, and cook 3 minutes.
• **Arrange** cake on individual plates. Spoon banana mixture over cake.
• **Drizzle** cake with any remaining sauce, and sprinkle with nuts. Serve warm with frozen yogurt, if desired. **Yield: 2 servings.**

♥ Per serving: Calories 533 (16% from fat)
Fat 9.5g (sat 3g, mono 4.4g, poly 0.3g)
Protein 5.1g Carb 99.4g Fiber 3.3g
Chol 10mg Iron 1.6mg
Sodium 262mg Calc 100mg

A Taste of the South

Fried chicken is simple food that goes to the heart of what's good about the South. A sprinkle of salt and pepper, a dance in flour, and a skillet of hot grease turn ordinary chicken into heavenly food.

Our Best Southern Fried Chicken

Prep: 25 minutes
Chill: 8 hours
Cook: 30 minutes

3 quarts water
1 tablespoon salt
1 (2- to 2½-pound) broiler-fryer, cut up
1 teaspoon salt
1 teaspoon pepper
1 cup all-purpose flour
2 cups vegetable oil
¼ cup bacon drippings

• **Combine** 3 quarts water and 1 tablespoon salt in a large bowl; add chicken. Cover; chill 8 hours. Drain chicken, and rinse with cold water; pat dry.
• **Combine** 1 teaspoon salt and pepper; sprinkle half of mixture over chicken.
• **Combine** remaining salt-and-pepper mixture and flour in a large heavy-duty zip-top bag. Place 2 pieces of chicken in bag; seal. Shake to coat. Remove chicken; repeat with remaining chicken.
• **Combine** oil and bacon drippings in a 12-inch cast-iron skillet or chicken fryer; heat to 360°. Add chicken, a few pieces at a time, skin side down. Cover; cook 6 minutes. Uncover and cook 9 minutes.
• **Turn** chicken pieces; cover and cook 6 minutes. Uncover and cook 5 to 9 minutes, turning pieces during the last 3 minutes for even browning, if necessary. Drain chicken on paper towels; keep warm. **Yield:** 4 servings.

Note: For best results, keep the oil temperature between 300° to 325°. Substitute 2 cups buttermilk for the saltwater solution, if desired.

A TASTE OF THE PAST

Fried chicken is on the menu of most gatherings that celebrate Southern life. Eating it for breakfast was a treat for me when we visited my grandparents in Atmore, Alabama. Granny Scott served the usual grits, eggs, and biscuits with a variety of her homemade preserves, but the focus of the meal was the huge platter of hot, crisp fried chicken.

Little white clouds escaped from the brown paper bag she shook to flour the pieces. Chicken tasted different at Granny Scott's house. Maybe because it was cooked on a woodburning stove or fried in fresh lard. Maybe her own corn-fed, yard-raised birds made the difference. Or the way she needed me to sample a wing while she fried the rest. Whatever the reasons, hers was the best.

When I fry chicken, it's hot, crisp, tender, and juicy. A zip-top bag holds the flour, and a deep cast-iron pot is my frying vessel. As I savor the wings, I can taste years of memories.

Family food rituals inform and warm the heart. I laughed till I cried when my mom announced, "When we were little, we'd eat the rough pieces first—such as the backs—then we'd have our choice of legs, breasts, or wings." Even now, she still prefers the bony pieces.

A friend remembers, "In the good ole days some referred to chicken as the 'gospel bird,' because it was the traditional Sunday meal. When the preacher came to dinner, he got his pick of the chick first."

If most of your fried chicken dinners involve trips to the drive-through, make some new memories with your kids. Buy a whole chicken and cut it up or choose a package of your favorite pieces. And please leave the skin on—that's a delicious part of the experience.

Here are some more pointers.

■ We tried several very good recipes before we proclaimed this one the best. We prefer a cast-iron skillet, because it maintains a consistent temperature. Plan to fry in batches; too many pieces crowd the skillet, lower the oil temperature, and increase grease absorption.

■ How you eat it is as important as how you cook it. It's a delicious hands-on activity—all you need are napkins and a hearty appetite.

■ Don't let times and temperatures discourage you. Get the oil sizzling hot but not smoking. Ease no more than 4 large, floured chicken pieces into hot oil at a time. Fry the chicken until it is cooked through, evenly browned and crisp, using tongs to turn the pieces. You may need to test a wing for doneness (one of the perks of being the cook).

—*Andria Scott Hurst*

Homemade Scoops

If you've never made ice cream before, June is a good time to start. All you have to do is make the custard—electric freezers have taken the hard work out of the process.

Make sure you have 3 to 4 cups rock salt and 20 pounds crushed ice on hand. Remember to use enough salt, because the ice can't do the job alone.

Ask one helper to time and another to assemble the napkins, cones, bowls, and spoons. That way you won't waste a minute before enjoying the frosty creation.

TOASTED COCONUT ICE CREAM

Prep: 40 minutes
Chill: 3 hours
Freeze: 20 minutes

2 cups flaked coconut
4 cups milk
1 cup sugar
6 egg yolks
2 cups half-and-half
1 (16-ounce) can cream of coconut
2 teaspoons vanilla extract
Garnish: toasted flaked coconut

• **Bake** 2 cups coconut in a shallow pan at 350°, stirring occasionally, 10 minutes or until toasted.
• **Whisk** together milk, sugar, and egg yolks in a heavy saucepan.
• **Cook** over medium heat, whisking constantly, 20 minutes or until mixture thickens and coats a spoon. (Do not boil.) Remove from heat.
• **Whisk** in coconut, half-and-half, cream of coconut, and vanilla. Cover and chill 3 hours.
• **Pour** mixture into freezer container of a 1-gallon hand-turned or electric freezer. Freeze according to manufacturer's instructions.
• **Pack** freezer with additional ice and rock salt, let stand 1 hour before serving. Garnish, if desired. **Yield:** 2½ quarts.

PEANUT BUTTER ICE CREAM

Prep: 15 minutes
Freeze: 25 minutes

1 (12-ounce) jar chunky peanut butter
1½ quarts half-and-half
6 large eggs
1 (14-ounce) can sweetened condensed milk
1 cup milk
1 tablespoon vanilla extract
2 cups sugar
2 tablespoons all-purpose flour

• **Cook** peanut butter, 2 cups half-and-half, and eggs in a Dutch oven over low heat, whisking constantly, 7 minutes or until a thermometer registers 160°.
• **Whisk** in remaining 4 cups half-and-half, condensed milk, milk, and vanilla.
• **Combine** sugar and flour; whisk into hot mixture until sugar dissolves.
• **Pour** into freezer container of a 5-quart hand-turned or electric freezer. Freeze according to manufacturer's instructions.
• **Pack** freezer with additional ice and rock salt, and let stand 1 hour before serving. **Yield:** 1 gallon.

Elizabeth Hicks
Birmingham, Alabama

BANANA-NUT ICE CREAM

*Roasting the bananas adds
a caramelized sweetness.*

Prep: 30 minutes
Bake: 30 minutes
Chill: 2 hours
Freeze: 20 minutes

4 ripe bananas, unpeeled
3 cups whipping cream
2 cups milk
2 cups sugar
8 egg yolks, lightly beaten
1½ cups chopped pecans, toasted

• **Place** bananas on a baking sheet. Bake at 350° for 30 minutes; cool and peel. Process in a food processor until smooth.
• **Cook** whipping cream and next 3 ingredients in a heavy saucepan over medium heat, whisking constantly, about 25 minutes or until mixture thickens and coats a spoon. (Do not boil.)
• **Fold** in bananas and pecans; cool slightly. Place plastic wrap directly on surface; chill until completely cooled.
• **Pour** mixture into freezer container of a 1-gallon hand-turned or electric freezer. Freeze according to manufacturer's instructions.
• **Pack** freezer with additional ice and rock salt, and let stand 1 hour before serving. **Yield:** about 2 quarts.

VANILLA CUSTARD ICE CREAM

Look for vanilla beans on the spice aisle. If you can't find them, substitute 1 tablespoon vanilla extract.

Prep: 40 minutes
Chill: 1 hour
Freeze: 20 minutes

2 cups milk
1 vanilla bean, split
8 egg yolks
¾ cup sugar
½ teaspoon salt
¼ cup (2 ounces) vanilla extract
2 cups whipping cream
Topping: crumbled pralines

• **Cook** milk in a heavy saucepan over medium heat, stirring often, just until bubbles appear; remove from heat. Add vanilla bean; cover and let stand 20 minutes. Discard vanilla bean.
• **Whisk** together yolks and next 3 ingredients in a large bowl until thick and pale. Gradually whisk warm milk mixture into yolk mixture; return to saucepan.
• **Cook** over very low heat, stirring constantly, 5 minutes or until mixture thickens and coats a spoon. Remove from heat; pour through a wire-mesh strainer into a bowl. Cool, stirring occasionally.
• **Stir** in cream; cover and chill 1 hour.
• **Pour** mixture into freezer container of a 1-gallon hand-turned or electric freezer. Freeze according to manufacturer's instructions.
• **Pack** freezer with additional ice and rock salt; let stand 1 hour before serving. Top with pralines. **Yield:** 2 quarts.

Cool Soups

It's time to chill the soup bowls and cool the palates. These frosty concoctions can be served as a first course, a light meal, or an icy dessert. Here we offer two savory and two sweet interpretations.

CURRIED CHICKEN BISQUE

Make this easy but elegant soup as a perfect first course on a steamy night.

Prep: 15 minutes
Cook: 15 minutes
Chill: 1 hour

5 cups chicken broth
4 egg yolks
2 cups whipping cream
2 teaspoons curry powder
2 teaspoons lemon pepper
¼ teaspoon salt
⅛ teaspoon ground red pepper
1 cup finely chopped cooked
   chicken

• **Bring** chicken broth to a boil in a large heavy saucepan.
• **Whisk** together egg yolks, whipping cream, and next 4 ingredients in a medium bowl; whisk in ½ cup hot chicken broth.
• **Whisk** mixture into remaining hot broth; cook, whisking constantly, 5 minutes or until slightly thickened. Cool.
• **Stir** in chicken. Cover and chill at least 1 hour. **Yield:** 6½ cups.

Bebe May
Pensacola, Florida

INSTANT GAZPACHO

Prep: 15 minutes

5 green onions, sliced
1 small red or green bell pepper,
   diced
1 small cucumber, diced
2 plum tomatoes, diced
1 cup Bloody Mary mix
¼ teaspoon salt
¼ teaspoon pepper
⅓ cup sour cream
½ teaspoon prepared horseradish
⅓ cup croutons

• **Stir** together first 7 ingredients. Chill 1 hour, if desired. Stir together sour cream and horseradish; chill, if desired.
• **Sprinkle** each serving with croutons, and dollop with sour cream mixture. **Yield:** 2⅓ cups.

Carol Emmerth
Allentown, Pennsylvania

PLUM-AND-WINE SOUP

Prep. 45 minutes
Cook: 20 minutes

4 to 5 small plums, halved and pitted
   (about 8 ounces)
¼ cup sugar, divided
1¼ cups water, divided
2 cups dry red wine
⅛ teaspoon ground cinnamon
2 whole cloves
Rind of 1 lemon, cut into strips
3 tablespoons cornstarch
8 small coconut macaroons

• **Sprinkle** plums with 3 tablespoons sugar, and let stand 30 minutes.
• **Bring** 1 cup water, wine, remaining 1 tablespoon sugar, cinnamon, cloves, and lemon rind to a boil in a large saucepan; reduce heat, and simmer, stirring occasionally, 10 minutes.
• **Add** plums, and cook 5 minutes. Remove from heat. Discard cloves and lemon rind.
• **Process** half of mixture at a time in a blender until smooth. Return mixture to saucepan.
• **Stir** together cornstarch and remaining ¼ cup water until smooth. Stir into plum mixture.
• **Bring** to a boil, stirring constantly; boil, stirring constantly, 1 minute or until slightly thickened.
• **Remove** from heat; cool slightly. Cover and chill. Top each serving with macaroons. **Yield:** 3⅔ cups.

Mike Singleton
Memphis, Tennessee

RASPBERRY SOUP

Prep: 5 minutes

1 cup fresh or frozen raspberries,
   thawed
½ cup rosé or dry white wine
½ cup firmly packed brown
   sugar
½ cup sour cream
Garnishes: lime slices, fresh
   raspberries

• **Process** raspberries and next 3 ingredients in a blender until smooth, stopping to scrape down sides.
• **Pour** mixture through a wire-mesh strainer into serving bowls. Garnish, if desired. **Yield:** 2⅓ cups.

Sherida Eddlemon
Memphis, Tennessee

Magical Marjoram

Early Greeks considered marjoram a symbol of happiness and believed its enchanting scent reminded mortals of their own beauty. The scent of marjoram, a member of the mint family, conjures up images of sunshine. Sweet marjoram, the most popular type, flourishes in the South. This versatile herb works well in salads, vinaigrettes, and marinades and happily pairs with herbs such as thyme and basil.

MEDITERRANEAN FLANK STEAK

Prep: 10 minutes
Chill: 8 hours
Grill: 12 minutes

½ cup lemon juice
½ cup olive oil
¼ cup dry red wine
2 shallots, minced
2 garlic cloves, minced
2 tablespoons chopped fresh
    marjoram *
2 teaspoons hot sauce
1 (1¾-pound) flank steak
½ teaspoon salt
½ teaspoon pepper

• **Combine** first 7 ingredients in a shallow dish or large heavy-duty zip-top plastic bag; add flank steak. Cover or seal; chill 8 hours, turning occasionally.
• **Remove** steak from marinade, discarding marinade. Sprinkle steak with salt and pepper.
• **Grill,** covered with grill lid, over medium-high heat (350° to 400°) 4 to 6 minutes on each side or to desired degree of doneness. Let stand 5 minutes.
• **Cut** steak diagonally across the grain into thin strips. **Yield:** 6 servings.

*Substitute 2 teaspoons dried marjoram for fresh, if desired.

Denise Bagley
Orlando, Florida

MAKING THE MOST OF HERBS

Marjoram Matters

■ Marjoram is often mistakenly interchanged with its more assertive cousin oregano. But if you taste them, you'll understand the difference. Marjoram has a mild taste that is sweeter than the almost peppery flavor of oregano.

■ A little marjoram goes a long way. Also, because of its delicate nature, it should be added toward the end of cooking.

■ Dried marjoram holds flavor well and can be substituted for fresh by decreasing the amount called for by one-third.

■ For best results, rub dried marjoram between your fingers to release the flavor before using it.

Herb Hints

Drying herbs: Place herb leaves between two paper towels. Microwave at HIGH, turning every 30 seconds, until leaves are crumbly, about 2 minutes. Crush and store in an airtight container.

Herb vinegars: Wash and clean a handful of herbs; add them to a sterilized jar. Fill jar with white vinegar, and store in a cool, dry, dark place for at least a month.

Herb pestos: For variety, combine different herbs in your favorite pesto recipe; add other ingredients like chopped garlic, peppers, and lemon juice. Freeze leftover pesto in ice cube trays; pop cubes into soups, stews, and pasta dishes. The thawed pesto also makes a quick topping for grilled meat.

HERBED MUSTARD DRESSING

Prep: 15 minutes
Chill: 1 hour

½ cup olive oil
2 tablespoons honey mustard
2 tablespoons white wine vinegar
1 shallot, chopped
¼ teaspoon salt
2 tablespoons shredded Parmesan
    cheese
2 teaspoons chopped fresh marjoram
⅛ teaspoon pepper

• **Blend** first 5 ingredients with a handheld blender until smooth. Stir in cheese, marjoram, and pepper. Cover and chill 1 hour. Serve over salad greens. **Yield:** 1 cup.

Note: A standard blender may be used in place of the handheld blender.

James Brady
New Orleans, Louisiana

ZESTY MARJORAM BUTTER

Prep: 10 minutes
Chill: 1 hour

1 cup butter, softened
1 tablespoon minced fresh
    marjoram
1 tablespoon minced dried
    tomatoes
1½ teaspoons minced fresh thyme
1 teaspoon chopped fresh chives
1 tablespoon lemon juice

• **Stir** together all ingredients. Cover and chill 1 hour. Serve with grilled chicken, steak, or vegetables. **Yield:** 1 cup.

Top-Rated Menu

Rub on a seasoning mixture, stir in roasted garlic,
and add a splash of molasses to turn ordinary steak,
mashed potatoes, and vegetables into extraordinary fare.

No-Fuss Company Fare
Serves 6

Peppered Rib-Eye Steaks
Roasted Garlic-Parmesan Mashed Potatoes
Grilled Vegetable Salad
Blackberry Pudding Tarts

PEPPERED RIB-EYE STEAKS
(pictured on page 150)

1997 Hall of Fame

Prep: 15 minutes
Chill: 1 hour
Grill: 20 minutes

2½ teaspoons freshly ground black
    pepper
1 tablespoon dried thyme
1½ teaspoons salt
4½ teaspoons garlic powder
1½ teaspoons lemon pepper
1½ teaspoons ground red pepper
1½ teaspoons dried parsley
    flakes
6 (1½-inch-thick) rib-eye steaks
3 tablespoons olive oil
Garnish: fresh thyme sprigs

• **Combine** first 7 ingredients. Brush steaks with oil; rub with pepper mixture. Cover and chill 1 hour.
• **Grill,** covered with grill lid, over medium-high heat (350° to 400°) 8 to 10 minutes on each side or to desired degree of doneness. Garnish, if desired. **Yield:** 6 servings.

ROASTED GARLIC-PARMESAN MASHED POTATOES
(pictured on page 150)

1997 Hall of Fame

Prep: 20 minutes
Bake: 30 minutes
Cook: 25 minutes

2 garlic bulbs
Olive oil (optional)
3 pounds potatoes, peeled and
    quartered
2 teaspoons salt, divided
¼ cup whipping cream
¼ cup shredded Parmesan
    cheese
3 tablespoons butter or margarine,
    softened
⅓ cup chopped fresh parsley
½ teaspoon pepper
Garnish: fresh thyme sprigs

• **Cut** off pointed ends of garlic bulbs; place garlic on a piece of aluminum foil, and drizzle with oil, if desired. Fold foil to seal.
• **Bake** at 425° for 30 minutes; cool. Squeeze pulp from garlic cloves; set aside.
• **Bring** potato, 1 teaspoon salt, and water to cover to a boil in a Dutch oven; boil 20 to 25 minutes or until potato is tender. Drain.
• **Mash** potato, or press through a ricer. Stir in garlic pulp, remaining 1 teaspoon salt, whipping cream, and next 4 ingredients. Garnish, if desired. **Yield:** 6 servings.

GRILLED VEGETABLE SALAD
(pictured on page 150)

1994 Hall of Fame

Prep: 25 minutes
Grill: 20 minutes

⅓ cup white balsamic vinegar
2 tablespoons olive oil
2 shallots, finely chopped
1 teaspoon dried Italian seasoning
¼ teaspoon salt
¼ teaspoon pepper
1½ teaspoons molasses
½ pound baby carrots
1 red bell pepper, seeded
1 yellow bell pepper, seeded
2 zucchini
2 yellow squash
1 large onion

• **Stir** together first 7 ingredients in a large bowl. Set aside.
• **Cut** carrots and next 5 ingredients into large pieces.
• **Add** vegetables to vinegar mixture. Let vegetables stand 30 minutes, stirring occasionally.
• **Drain** vegetables, reserving vinegar mixture. Arrange vegetables evenly in a grill basket.
• **Grill,** covered with grill lid, over medium-high heat (350° to 400°) 15 to 20 minutes or until crisp-tender, turning occasionally.
• **Toss** vegetables in reserved vinegar mixture. Serve salad immediately, or cover and chill up to 8 hours. **Yield:** 6 servings.

Note: Vegetables may be roasted at 400° in a shallow roasting pan for 15 minutes or until crisp-tender, stirring occasionally.

The day before:
- Bake tart shells, and prepare blackberry pudding; fill shells, and chill.
- Cut up vegetables and make the marinade for the vegetable salad; seal the marinade and vegetables separately in zip-top plastic bags.

Two hours before:
- Rub steaks with seasoning mixture, and chill.
- Place garlic in oven to bake. Toss together marinade and vegetables.
- Set table.

One hour before:
- Drain vegetables, reserving marinade.
- Peel and quarter potatoes; place in water to cover with salt. Set aside.
- Beat whipping cream, sugar, and vanilla; dollop on tarts. Chill.
- Grill vegetables; toss with the reserved marinade.
- Bring potatoes to a boil, and cook 20 to 25 minutes.
- Grill steaks while potatoes cook. Remove from grill, and keep warm.
- Drain potatoes; mash with other ingredients.

King of Quesadillas

While the breakfast specials, great sandwiches, and baked goods keep Arthur Elizalde's customers coming back to Arturo's in Austin, quesadillas are the specialty of the house. Here are some of his favorites, along with a sauce and a pesto that you can make ahead.

SESAME-GINGER CHICKEN QUESADILLAS

Prep: 15 minutes
Cook: 4 minutes

3 tablespoons Sesame-Ginger Sauce (recipe on following page)
1 cup chopped cooked chicken ∗
3 carrots, shredded
¼ cup diced purple onion
4 (8-inch) flour tortillas
1 (8-ounce) package shredded Mexican cheese blend ∗

• **Heat** Sesame-Ginger Sauce in a large skillet over medium heat; add chicken, carrot, and onion.
• **Cook,** stirring occasionally, 2 to 4 minutes or until thoroughly heated.
• **Spoon** chicken mixture evenly on half of each tortilla; sprinkle with shredded cheese. Wipe skillet clean.
• **Cook,** tortilla side down, in lightly greased skillet over medium-high heat 1 minute or until lightly browned.
• **Fold** tortillas over filling, and serve immediately. **Yield:** 4 servings.

∗ Substitute frozen chopped cooked chicken, thawed, if desired. Substitute 1 (8-ounce) package shredded Monterey Jack cheese for Mexican cheese blend, if desired.

Arthur Elizalde
Austin, Texas

BLACKBERRY PUDDING TARTS
(pictured on page 150)

1993 Hall of Fame

These berry tarts begin with convenient tart shells from the grocery.

Prep: 20 minutes
Cook: 25 minutes

1 (10-ounce) package frozen tart shells
2 quarts fresh blackberries ∗
1 cup water
1¾ cups sugar, divided
½ cup self-rising flour
¼ cup butter or margarine
2⅛ teaspoons vanilla extract, divided
1 cup whipping cream
Garnishes: fresh blackberries, fresh mint sprigs

• **Bake** tart shells according to package directions; cool completely.
• **Bring** blackberries and 1 cup water to a boil over medium heat. Reduce heat, and simmer 5 minutes or until blackberries are soft.
• **Mash** blackberries with a fork; pour through a wire-mesh strainer into a 4-cup liquid measuring cup, using the back of a spoon to squeeze out 2 cups juice. Discard pulp and seeds. (Boil blackberry juice to reduce to 2 cups, if necessary.)
• **Stir** together 1½ cups sugar and flour in a saucepan; gradually add blackberry juice to pan, whisking constantly until smooth.
• **Bring** to a boil over medium heat, whisking constantly.
• **Reduce** heat, and simmer 3 minutes or until mixture is thickened. Remove from heat.
• **Stir** in butter and 2 teaspoons vanilla.
• **Spoon** filling into prepared tart shells. Cool completely.
• **Beat** whipping cream at high speed with an electric mixer until foamy; gradually add remaining ¼ cup sugar, beating until stiff peaks form.
• **Fold** remaining ⅛ teaspoon vanilla into whipped cream.
• **Dollop** whipped cream over tarts; garnish, if desired. **Yield:** 8 tarts.

∗ Substitute 2 (16-ounce) packages frozen blackberries, thawed, for fresh blackberries, if desired.

SESAME-GINGER SAUCE

Arthur also uses this sauce as a marinade for roasted chicken.

Prep: 10 minutes

⅓ cup rice wine vinegar
½ cup soy sauce
⅓ cup canola oil
⅓ cup sesame oil
3 tablespoons honey
2 tablespoons minced fresh ginger
1 garlic clove, minced

• **Whisk** together all ingredients until well blended. Store in refrigerator up to 1 week. **Yield:** 1½ cups.

Arthur Elizalde
Austin, Texas

QUICK QUESADILLAS

Arthur Elizalde creates his specialty by combining the flavors of his Southwest heritage and extensive travels. He and his crew make the quesadillas to order on a large grill. When you make them at home, keep the first batch warm in the oven while the others are cooking.

"One of the great things about quesadillas," Arthur says, "is that everything is ready in five minutes."

Cilantro Pesto and Sesame-Ginger Sauce are easy to make and keep well in the fridge. Once you have the other ingredients, it's just a matter of assembling and toasting the sandwiches.

If you get the chance to travel to Austin, visit Arturo's restaurant at 314 West 17th Street; (512) 469-0380. Hours are 6:30 a.m. to 4 p.m. Monday through Friday.

CHORIZO, BLACK BEAN, AND CORN QUESADILLAS
(pictured on facing page)

Prep: 15 minutes
Cook: 4 minutes

4 (4-inch) chorizo sausage links, chopped
1 (15-ounce) can black beans, rinsed and drained
½ cup frozen whole kernel corn, thawed
½ teaspoon ground cumin
2 tablespoons Cilantro Pesto (recipe at right)
4 (8-inch) flour tortillas
1 (8-ounce) package shredded Mexican cheese blend ✱
Garnish: fresh cilantro sprigs

• **Cook** sausage in a large skillet over medium heat 5 minutes or until browned.
• **Add** black beans, corn, and cumin, and cook, stirring occasionally, 3 to 4 minutes or until thoroughly heated.
• **Spread** Cilantro Pesto evenly on tortillas. Spoon chorizo mixture on half of each tortilla; sprinkle with cheese. Wipe skillet clean.
• **Cook,** tortilla side down, in lightly greased skillet over medium-high heat 1 minute or until lightly browned.
• **Fold** tortillas over filling. Serve immediately. Garnish, if desired. **Yield:** 4 servings.

✱ Substitute 1 (8-ounce) package shredded Monterey Jack cheese for Mexican cheese blend, if desired.

Arthur Elizalde
Austin, Texas

CILANTRO PESTO

Prep: 10 minutes

6 bunches fresh cilantro, stems removed
2 tablespoons fresh lime juice
3 tablespoons olive oil
2 garlic cloves
1 teaspoon salt

• **Process** all ingredients in a food processor until smooth, stopping to scrape down sides. Store in refrigerator up to 1 week. **Yield:** 1¼ cups.

Arthur Elizalde
Austin, Texas

SPINACH, MUSHROOM, AND CILANTRO QUESADILLAS

Prep: 15 minutes
Cook: 8 minutes

1 (10-ounce) package frozen chopped spinach, thawed
1 (8-ounce) package sliced fresh mushrooms
¼ cup Cilantro Pesto (recipe above)
1 teaspoon salt
8 (8-inch) flour tortillas
2 (8-ounce) packages shredded Mexican cheese blend ✱

• **Drain** spinach well, pressing between paper towels.
• **Sauté** spinach and mushrooms in a large lightly greased skillet 5 minutes or until mushrooms are tender.
• **Stir** in Cilantro Pesto and salt.
• **Spread** spinach mixture evenly on half of each tortilla, and sprinkle with shredded cheese blend. Wipe skillet clean.
• **Cook,** tortilla side down, in lightly greased skillet over medium-high heat 1 minute or until lightly browned.
• **Fold** tortillas over filling, and serve immediately. **Yield:** 8 servings.

✱ Substitute 2 (8-ounce) packages shredded Monterey Jack cheese for Mexican cheese blend, if desired.

Arthur Elizalde
Austin, Texas

Chorizo, Black Bean, and Corn Quesadillas, facing page

Blackberry Pudding Tart, page 147

Peppered Rib-Eye Steak, Roasted Garlic-Parmesan Mashed Potatoes, Grilled Vegetable Salad, page 146

Fried Catfish, Home-Style Baked Beans,
Buttermilk Hush Puppies,
Creamy Sweet Slaw, page 172

Blueberry Cheesecake, facing page

Blueberry-Peach Ice Cream with fresh fruit, facing page

Best of the Blues

Fresh blueberries are one of summer's sweet treasures. These deep blue-violet orbs get the prize for perfect packaging, from their refreshing, frosty appearance to the fact that they're packed with vitamins A and C, potassium, and phosphorus. Turn to "From Our Kitchen" on page 156 for more on blueberries.

BLUEBERRY-PEACH ICE CREAM
(pictured on facing page)

Prep: 25 minutes
Freeze: 10 minutes

3 medium peaches, peeled and sliced
2 cups milk
1 (14-ounce) can sweetened
   condensed milk
1 (12-ounce) can evaporated milk
3 large eggs, lightly beaten
1 cup sugar
3 cups whipping cream
1 pint fresh or frozen blueberries
Garnishes: peach slices, blueberries,
   fresh mint sprigs

• **Process** peach slices in a blender until smooth; set aside. Whisk together 2 cups milk and next 4 ingredients in a large heavy saucepan. Cook over medium heat, whisking constantly, until mixture reaches 160° (about 10 minutes). Remove from heat; cool 30 minutes.
• **Beat** whipping cream at high speed with an electric mixer until soft peaks form. Let whipped cream stand 30 minutes. Stir whipped cream, pureed peach, and blueberries into milk mixture.
• **Pour** mixture into freezer container of a 1-gallon electric freezer. Freeze according to manufacturer's instructions.
• **Pack** freezer with additional ice and rock salt; let stand 1 hour before serving. Garnish, if desired. **Yield:** 3 quarts.
Kelly Davis
Calabash, North Carolina

BLUEBERRY CHEESECAKE
(pictured on facing page)

Prep: 30 minutes
Bake: 1 hour, 10 minutes
Stand: 30 minutes
Chill: 8 hours

1½ cups finely ground almonds
¼ cup sugar
3 tablespoons butter or margarine,
   softened
1 tablespoon all-purpose flour
3 (8-ounce) packages cream cheese,
   softened
1¼ cups sugar
3 tablespoons all-purpose flour
½ teaspoon salt
4 large eggs
1 (8-ounce) container sour cream
1 teaspoon vanilla extract
1 tablespoon grated lemon rind
1½ cups fresh or frozen blueberries
1 cup whipping cream
2 teaspoons sugar
2 tablespoons sour cream
Garnishes: blueberries, lemon rind
   strips

• **Combine** first 4 ingredients in a small bowl. Press mixture into bottom and 1½ inches up sides of a lightly greased 9-inch springform pan; set aside.
• **Beat** cream cheese at medium speed with an electric mixer until smooth.
• **Combine** 1¼ cups sugar, 3 tablespoons flour, and salt. Add to cream cheese, beating until blended.

• **Add** eggs, 1 at a time, beating well after each addition.
• **Add** 8 ounces sour cream, vanilla, and lemon rind, beating just until blended. Gently stir in blueberries. Pour mixture into prepared pan.
• **Bake** at 300° for 1 hour and 10 minutes or until center of cheesecake is firm. Turn off oven, and let cheesecake stand in oven, with oven door partially open, 30 minutes.
• **Remove** cheesecake from oven; cool in pan on a wire rack 30 minutes. Cover and chill 8 hours. Release sides of pan.
• **Beat** whipping cream at high speed until foamy; gradually add 2 teaspoons sugar, beating until stiff peaks form.
• **Fold** in 2 tablespoons sour cream. Spread over cheesecake, and garnish, if desired. **Yield:** 12 servings.

♥ Per serving: Calories 664 Fat 51g
Jan Downs
Shreveport, Louisiana

Reduced-fat Blueberry Cheesecake: Omit first 4 ingredients; substitute 1 cup graham cracker crumbs, 3 tablespoons melted butter, and 1 tablespoon sugar; press into pan as directed. Bake at 350° for 5 minutes.

Substitute 2 (8-ounce) packages reduced-fat cream cheese and 1 (8-ounce) package fat-free cream cheese for 3 packages cream cheese. Reduce 1¼ cups sugar to 1 cup. Substitute 2 whole eggs plus 2 egg whites for 4 eggs. Substitute 1 (8-ounce) container light sour cream. Omit whipping cream and next 2 ingredients; substitute mixture of 1 (8-ounce) container reduced-fat frozen whipped topping and ¼ cup light sour cream. Proceed as directed. Garnish, if desired. **Yield:** 12 servings.

♥ Per serving: Calories 313 Fat 14.6g

BLUEBERRY CHUTNEY

*Serve this as a condiment
with grilled chicken or pork.*

*Prep: 15 minutes
Cook: 40 minutes*

1 large Granny Smith apple, peeled
    and diced
½ cup sugar
½ cup orange juice
1 tablespoon grated orange rind
1 teaspoon ground ginger
¼ to ½ teaspoon dried crushed red
    pepper
¼ teaspoon ground black pepper
4 cups fresh or frozen blueberries
3 tablespoons balsamic vinegar

• **Bring** first 7 ingredients to a boil in a
medium saucepan. Reduce heat to low;
simmer, stirring occasionally, 15 minutes or until apple is tender.
• **Stir** in blueberries and vinegar; bring
to a boil. Reduce heat to medium; cook,
stirring occasionally, 40 minutes or
until thickened. **Yield:** 3 cups.

*Leanne McMullen
Natchez, Mississippi*

SUMMER FRUIT SALAD WITH BLUEBERRY VINAIGRETTE

*Prep: 10 minutes
Chill: 1 hour*

2 cups fresh or frozen
    blueberries
1 cup fresh strawberries, halved
2 nectarines, sliced
8 cups mixed salad greens
Blueberry Vinaigrette
½ cup slivered almonds, toasted
    (optional)

• **Combine** first 4 ingredients in a large
bowl. Cover and chill 1 hour.
• **Drizzle** with ⅓ cup Blueberry Vinaigrette, tossing to coat. Sprinkle with almonds, if desired. **Yield:** 4 servings.

**Summer Fruit-Chicken Salad With
Blueberry Vinaigrette:** Add 2 cups
chopped cooked chicken.

Blueberry Vinaigrette

Prep: 5 minutes

¼ cup Blueberry Chutney (left)
¼ cup minced onion
⅓ cup balsamic vinegar
1 teaspoon salt
½ teaspoon pepper
⅔ cup vegetable oil

• **Whisk** together first 5 ingredients.
Gradually whisk in oil until blended.
Refrigerate leftover vinaigrette up to 2
weeks. **Yield:** 1½ cups.

SOUR CREAM-BLUEBERRY COFFEE CAKE

*Prep: 15 minutes
Bake: 40 minutes*

½ cup butter or margarine, softened
½ cup sugar
2 large eggs
1 (8-ounce) container sour cream
1 teaspoon vanilla extract
2 teaspoons grated lemon rind
1½ cups all-purpose flour
1 teaspoon baking powder
½ teaspoon salt
1 pint fresh or frozen blueberries
½ cup chopped pecans
¼ cup sugar
1 teaspoon ground cinnamon
1 cup powdered sugar
4 teaspoons milk

• **Beat** butter at medium speed with an
electric mixer 2 minutes or until creamy.
Gradually add ½ cup sugar, beating 2 to
3 minutes. Add eggs and next 3 ingredients, beating until smooth.
• **Combine** flour, baking powder, and
salt. Gradually add to butter mixture,
beating until blended. Pour batter into a
lightly greased 9-inch springform pan.
• **Combine** berries and next 3 ingredients; sprinkle over batter. Bake at 350° for
35 to 40 minutes or until a wooden pick
inserted in center comes out clean. Cool
in pan on a wire rack 10 to 15 minutes; remove from pan. Cool on rack 10 minutes.
• **Whisk** sugar and milk until smooth.
Drizzle over cake. **Yield:** 1 (9-inch) cake.

BLUEBERRY-PECAN COBBLER

*Each bite of this old-fashioned
cobbler contains two layers of crust
and plenty of plump berries. We loved it
with and without ice cream. Double this
recipe to serve as part of the "Southern
Setting" menu on page 130.*

*Prep: 15 minutes
Bake: 20 minutes*

4 pints fresh or frozen blueberries
1½ cups sugar
½ cup all-purpose flour
½ teaspoon ground cinnamon
⅓ cup water
2 tablespoons lemon juice
1 teaspoon vanilla extract
1 (15-ounce) package refrigerated
    piecrusts
½ cup chopped pecans, toasted
Vanilla ice cream
Garnish: fresh mint sprigs

• **Bring** first 7 ingredients to a boil in a
saucepan over medium heat, stirring
until sugar melts. Reduce heat to low;
cook, stirring occasionally, 10 minutes.
• **Spoon** half of blueberry mixture into
a lightly greased 8-inch square pan.
• **Roll** 1 piecrust to ⅛-inch thickness on
a lightly floured surface; cut into an 8-
inch square. Place over blueberry mixture; sprinkle with pecans.
• **Bake** at 475° for 10 minutes.
• **Spoon** remaining blueberry mixture
over baked crust.
• **Roll** remaining piecrust to ⅛-inch
thickness, and cut into 1-inch strips.
Arrange in lattice design over blueberry
mixture.
• **Bake** at 475° for 10 minutes or until
golden.
• **Serve** cobbler with vanilla ice cream;
garnish, if desired. **Yield:** 4 servings.

Chocolate Favorites

If you love chocolate, these creations are for you. They make enough to freeze, and each freezes well. Just layer the goodies between wax paper in airtight containers and store in the freezer up to three months.

SACHERTORTE COOKIES

Prep: 10 minutes
Bake: 15 minutes

1 cup butter or margarine, softened
1 (3.9-ounce) package chocolate instant pudding mix
1 large egg
2 cups all-purpose flour
3 tablespoons sugar
½ cup seedless raspberry jam
½ cup (3 ounces) semisweet chocolate morsels
3 tablespoons butter or margarine

• **Beat** 1 cup butter and pudding mix at medium speed with an electric mixer until fluffy. Add egg, beating until blended. Gradually add flour, beating at low speed until blended.
• **Shape** into 1-inch balls; roll in sugar. Place 2 inches apart on lightly greased baking sheets. Press thumb in center of each cookie, making an indentation.
• **Bake** at 325° for 12 to 15 minutes. Remove to wire racks to cool. Spoon about ½ teaspoon jam into each indentation.
• **Place** chocolate morsels and 3 tablespoons butter in a small heavy-duty zip-top plastic bag; seal. Submerge in hot water until chocolate melts; knead mixture until blended. Snip a tiny hole in 1 corner of bag, and drizzle chocolate mixture over cookies. **Yield:** 3 dozen.

Note: Chocolate mixture and jam may be omitted. While cookies are warm, place a milk chocolate kiss in each indentation.

Betty Garrison
Elmer, New Jersey

CHOCOLATE PIXIES

Prep: 15 minutes
Chill: 2 hours
Bake: 18 minutes

4 (1-ounce) unsweetened chocolate squares
¼ cup unsalted butter
4 large eggs
2 cups sugar
2 teaspoons vanilla extract
2 cups all-purpose flour
2 teaspoons baking powder
½ teaspoon salt
½ cup chopped pecans, toasted (optional)
½ cup powdered sugar

• **Microwave** chocolate and butter in a large glass bowl at HIGH 1½ to 2 minutes or until melted, stirring once.
• **Add** eggs, 1 at a time, beating at medium speed with an electric mixer after each addition. Gradually add 2 cups sugar, beating until blended. Stir in vanilla.
• **Combine** flour, baking powder, and salt. Gradually add to chocolate mixture, beating at low speed until blended.
• **Stir** in pecans, if desired. Cover and chill 2 hours.
• **Shape** dough into 1-inch balls; roll in powdered sugar, and place on lightly greased baking sheets.
• **Bake** at 300° for 15 to 18 minutes. Remove to wire racks to cool. **Yield:** 5 dozen.

Roevis McKay
New York, New York

FROSTED PEANUT BUTTER BROWNIES

Pop a jar of peanut butter in the microwave for the middle layer of these brownies.

Prep: 20 minutes
Bake: 20 minutes
Chill: 50 minutes

1½ cups butter or margarine, divided
⅓ cup cocoa
2 cups sugar
1½ cups all-purpose flour
½ teaspoon salt
4 large eggs
1 teaspoon vanilla extract
1 (18-ounce) jar chunky peanut butter
⅓ cup milk
10 large marshmallows
¼ cup cocoa
1 (16-ounce) package powdered sugar

• **Cook** 1 cup butter and ⅓ cup cocoa in a saucepan over low heat until butter melts, stirring often. Remove from heat, and cool slightly.
• **Combine** sugar, flour, and salt in a large mixing bowl. Add chocolate mixture, and beat at medium speed with an electric mixer until blended.
• **Add** eggs and vanilla, beating until blended. Spread mixture into a greased 15- x 10-inch jellyroll pan.
• **Bake** at 350° for 20 minutes or until a wooden pick inserted in center comes out clean.
• **Remove** lid from peanut butter jar; microwave peanut butter at MEDIUM (50% power) 2 minutes, stirring once. Spread over warm brownies. Chill 30 minutes.
• **Cook** remaining ½ cup butter, milk, and marshmallows in a large saucepan over medium heat, stirring often, until marshmallows melt. Remove from heat.
• **Whisk** in ¼ cup cocoa. Gradually stir in powdered sugar until smooth. Spread over peanut butter, and chill 20 minutes. Cut into squares. **Yield:** 6 dozen.

From Our Kitchen

Frozen Sweets

If you're an ice cream fanatic, you'll love preparing a luscious batch of the ice creams on page 143. But when you want it fast, there's always something tempting in the grocer's freezer. Let these reminders help you grab the one you need.

• Ice cream is a rich mixture of cream, milk, at least 10 percent milk fat, and sugar or other sweeteners.

• Ice milk contains less milk fat and milk solids than ice cream does, making it lighter and lower in calories than its heavier cousin.

• Frozen yogurt can be made from whole milk or low-fat and fat-free milk sweetened with sugar or artificial sweeteners. These products can be lower in fat but not necessarily lower in calories.

• Sherbet is usually made from sweetened fruit juice, milk, and water.

• Sorbet contains no milk, so it's a good choice for those who need to stay away from dairy products.

• Granita is water and sugar combined with fruit juice, wine, or coffee. This one is a firm slush of icy crystals.

Just the Right Size

Get ready to preserve a bit of summer when the abundance of fresh produce fills farmers markets and roadside stands. Large canning jars are great for the big jobs, but you need tiny jars, such as those made by Ball, for saving goodies from backyard gardens. Their wide-mouth, one-piece, screw-on lids make it easy to save small batches, and the size is right for gifts from your kitchen. Pick up a carton of them as soon as they appear in stores—they get away quickly. That way, when the spirit hits to can a little something you'll be set.

TIPS AND TIDBITS

■ We always want you to have success with our recipes, so we give you as much information as possible. When a recipe states "For testing purposes only, we used. . ." that means not all brands work equally well for that dish. We mention brand names when a recipe works best with a specific product.

■ When preparing the quesadilla recipes on pages 147 and 148, our Test Kitchens staff misted the flour tortillas with vegetable cooking spray for extra crispness. Also, we prefer to use nonrefrigerated flour tortillas; they're thinner and easier to work with, and they don't dry out or split as fast.

■ Near the end of cooking time, stir in a jar of salsa to perk up bean soup.

■ Suzan L. Wiener of Spring Hill, Florida, writes, "A little chili powder adds a wonderful Mexican taste to meat loaf, meatballs, roast chicken, scrambled eggs, and cheese sauces."

■ Suzan suggests using the juice from canned fruit as part of the liquid when making fruit gelatin. And using juice frozen in ice cube trays is a good way to chill and flavor beverages.

■ Mint-flavored chocolate morsels are wonderful in recipes but can sometimes be difficult to find. If they're not available when you need them, make your own.
   Pour a bag of semisweet chocolate morsels into a heavy-duty zip-top plastic bag, and add ½ teaspoon mint extract. Close the bag, and toss to coat the chocolate morsels. Remove as much air from the bag as possible, and seal. Leave the morsels on the counter overnight. They'll absorb the mint flavor and will be ready for use in any recipe.

Clues for Blues

You're sure to enjoy the harvest of blueberry recipes beginning on page 153. They're so delicious, you'll soon forget the tiny, watery impostors that come packed in a muffin mix or bagged in the supermarket freezer case.

Here are a few nuggets of information for making the most of this glorious fruit.

■ Blueberries belong to the same family as the wild huckleberry or azalea.

■ Blueberries do not ripen further after they're picked.

■ The powdery gray-blue bloom on the surface of the skin helps the small berry retain its moisture after harvest.

■ Blueberries aren't as perishable as other berries and will keep about a week if handled properly. Place them in a plastic container and refrigerate as soon as possible. Don't wash berries until you're ready to use them. (Added moisture will hasten growth of mold.)

■ Washing blueberries before freezing results in toughening of their skin.

■ A quart of blueberries serves four people generously.

JULY

Peas & Chowchow

Southern peas served with sweet-and-spicy chowchow are the stuff memories are made of. These recipes offer fresh variations on several popular pea varieties. Our flavorful Chowchow is the perfect companion to A Mess of Peas.

A MESS OF PEAS

"My grandmother always made what she called a 'mess' of peas," says Assistant Foods Editor Peggy Smith, "because at the end of the growing season, you never had enough of any one kind to cook."

Prep: 5 minutes
Cook: 1 hour

1 quart water
1 (8- to 10-ounce) smoked ham hock
8 cups fresh field peas
4 to 6 hot peppers in vinegar, drained
1 teaspoon sugar
1 teaspoon salt
1 teaspoon pepper

• **Bring** 1 quart water and smoked ham hock to a boil in a large Dutch oven over medium-high heat. Reduce heat to low, and simmer 30 minutes.
• **Stir** in peas and remaining ingredients; cover and simmer 25 to 30 minutes or until peas are done. **Yield:** 10 to 12 servings.

Note: For testing purposes only, we used a variety of peas.

CHOWCHOW
(pictured on page 190)

Cabbage, green tomatoes, and onions are the basic ingredients for all chowchows. For more heat, add chopped jalapeño to the vegetables.

Prep: 2 hours
Chill: 8 hours
Process: 15 minutes

5 green bell peppers
5 red bell peppers
2 large green tomatoes
2 large onions
½ small cabbage
¼ cup pickling salt
3 cups sugar
2 cups white vinegar (5% acidity)
1 cup water
1 tablespoon mustard seeds
1½ teaspoons celery seeds
¾ teaspoon turmeric

• **Chop** first 5 ingredients.
• **Stir** together chopped vegetables and salt in a large Dutch oven. Cover and chill 8 hours. Rinse and drain; return mixture to Dutch oven. Stir in sugar and remaining ingredients. Bring to a boil; reduce heat, and simmer 3 minutes.
• **Pack** hot mixture into hot jars, filling to ½ inch from top. Remove air bubbles; wipe jar rims. Cover at once with metal lids, and screw on bands.
• **Process** in boiling-water bath 15 minutes. **Yield:** 5½ pints.

Mavis Faulkner
Henderson, North Carolina

FIELD PEA PATTIES

Prep: 18 minutes
Cook: 8 minutes

2 cups cooked, drained field peas or black-eyed peas
½ large yellow bell pepper, finely chopped
¼ cup all-purpose flour
¼ cup ketchup
6 green onions, finely chopped
1 large egg, lightly beaten
½ teaspoon salt
½ teaspoon freshly ground pepper
3 tablespoons vegetable oil
Chowchow (recipe at left)

• **Coarsely** mash peas. Stir in bell pepper and next 6 ingredients. Shape mixture into 8 patties.
• **Cook** 4 patties in 1½ tablespoons hot oil in a large skillet over medium-high heat 2 minutes on each side or until golden brown. Repeat with remaining patties and oil. Serve with Chowchow. **Yield:** 8 servings.

PINK-EYED PEA SALSA
(pictured on page 190)

This salsa will pump up the flavor of a grilled pork chop and brilliant vine-ripened tomatoes.

Prep: 15 minutes
Chill: 1 hour

2 cups cooked, drained pink-eyed peas
1 cup fresh corn kernels
½ large purple onion, finely chopped
½ red bell pepper, finely chopped
2 tablespoons chopped fresh cilantro
¼ cup olive oil
¼ cup fresh lime juice
¼ teaspoon salt

• **Stir** together all ingredients; cover and chill 1 hour. Serve with grilled pork or chicken. **Yield:** about 4 cups.

PEPPERED TUNA WITH CROWDER PEAS

Prep: 25 minutes
Cook: 55 minutes

1 quart water
1 (6- to 8-ounce) smoked ham hock
3 cups fresh crowder peas
3 or 4 hot peppers in vinegar, drained
2 teaspoons Cajun seasoning
1 (0.9-ounce) package béarnaise
    sauce mix
4 (6-ounce) tuna steaks
2 teaspoons olive oil
½ teaspoon salt
¼ to ½ teaspoon ground red pepper
1 tablespoon coarsely ground black
    pepper
4 cups mixed salad greens
Garnish: fresh tarragon sprigs

• **Bring** 1 quart water and smoked ham hock to a boil in a Dutch oven over medium-high heat.
• **Cook** 30 minutes or until mixture is reduced by half. Discard ham hock.
• **Stir** in peas, hot peppers, and Cajun seasoning; bring to a boil. Cover, reduce heat, and simmer 25 minutes or until peas are tender.
• **Prepare** béarnaise sauce according to package directions; keep warm.
• **Coat** tuna steaks evenly with 2 teaspoons olive oil. Sprinkle evenly with salt, red pepper, and black pepper.
• **Cook** tuna in a large hot skillet over high heat 5 minutes on each side or to desired degree of doneness.
• **Divide** mixed salad greens onto 4 serving plates. Top with tuna steaks and ¼ cup drained peas. Drizzle with béarnaise sauce, and garnish, if desired. **Yield:** 4 servings.

Note: For testing purposes only, we used Knorr béarnaise sauce mix.

PEA APPEAL

At the Curb Market in Montgomery, a stall named Pea Heaven sums up the market's bounty. It is high season for Southern peas. Folks here know this is the place to find them. Bags of purple hulls are stacked on crates of crowders; mounds of shelled black-eyed peas fill bins; delicate lady creams delight an elderly shopper.

The people here are particular about their peas. Some prefer the hearty, dark-meated types such as black-eyeds, crowders, and pink-eyeds; others cherish pale lady creams and butter peas. Margaret Still, who works at the market, favors pink-eyeds. "They make a dark soup," she says. "I cook them with a little piece of fat meat. My family loves 'em with cornbread."

At Pea Heaven, Whipporwills are the specialty of the day. These peas are small, dark, and speckled. "They cook up darker than a crowder," says Vivian Tatum, who operates the stall. She also offers lady cream peas, which resemble kernels of corn cut from the cob. "I like to cook them with some butter or bouillon," she says.

Though answers may differ on which pea is preferred, few disagree about what to serve with them—chowchow. The condiment's sweet spiciness perks up Southern peas. While a mound of chowchow with a dish of peas is a staple, which type to serve can be hotly contested. But whether one prefers sweet or hot is a moot point as long as all agree that peas call for chowchow.

SPINACH WITH CROWDER PEAS

Cookbook author Ronni Lundy writes richly of peas in Butter Beans to Blackberries *(North Point Press, 1999). We adapted this recipe from her book.*

Prep: 10 minutes
Cook: 40 minutes

2 cups fresh or frozen crowder
    peas
1 cup chicken, ham, or vegetable
    broth
¾ teaspoon salt, divided
2 tablespoons butter or margarine
1 small sweet onion, chopped
1 bunch green onions, chopped
2 garlic cloves, minced
1 (10-ounce) package fresh
    spinach
½ teaspoon dried crushed red
    pepper

• **Bring** peas, broth, and ½ teaspoon salt to a boil in a saucepan over high heat. Reduce heat to low; cover and simmer 30 minutes or until peas are tender. Set aside.
• **Melt** butter in a large skillet over medium heat. Add sweet onion, green onions, and minced garlic; sauté 2 minutes.
• **Stir** in spinach, remaining ¼ teaspoon salt, and crushed red pepper; sauté 1 to 2 minutes or until spinach wilts. Serve immediately with peas. **Yield:** 4 servings.
Ronni Lundy
Louisville, Kentucky

Salute to Fruit

Fresh fruit is one of the great pleasures of summer. Serve it as a refreshing dessert, as a side with your favorite sandwich, or as a cooling complement to a spicy entrée. To enhance fruit's vitamin-packed sweetness, keep the dressing simple. Include a touch of fresh herbs for an aromatic spark to these juicy jewels.

FROZEN FRUIT SALAD

Prep: 15 minutes
Freeze: 4 hours

1 (15-ounce) can pitted dark sweet cherries, drained
1 (15-ounce) can apricot halves, drained
1 (8-ounce) container sour cream
1 (3-ounce) package cream cheese, softened
½ cup sugar
2 tablespoons lemon juice
1 (8-ounce) can crushed pineapple, drained
1 banana, coarsely chopped
½ cup chopped pecans

• **Coarsely** chop cherries and apricots.
• **Stir** together sour cream and next 3 ingredients in a large bowl until blended. Stir in fruit and pecans. Spoon into 18 aluminum foil-lined muffin cups.
• **Freeze** 4 hours or until firm. Remove from freezer 10 minutes before serving. **Yield:** 18 servings.

Deborah Eichhorn
Dayton, Ohio

WHITE GRAPE JUICE FRUIT BOWL

Prep: 25 minutes
Chill: 2 hours

2 apples, cubed
2 pears, peeled and cubed
¼ cup orange juice
2 tablespoons lemon juice
2 fresh peaches, peeled and sliced
2 fresh nectarines, sliced
2 plums, sliced
1 cup seedless green grapes
1 cup fresh raspberries
1 cup fresh blueberries
3 tablespoons sugar
2 teaspoons grated orange rind
¾ cup white grape juice, chilled
1 tablespoon chopped fresh mint
⅓ cup sliced almonds, toasted

• **Stir** together first 4 ingredients in a large bowl.
• **Add** peach slices and next 7 ingredients; tossing gently to combine. Cover and chill 2 hours.
• **Stir** together grape juice and chopped mint; pour over fruit.
• **Sprinkle** with almonds. **Yield:** 10 to 12 servings.

Dottie B. Miller
Jonesborough, Tennessee

STUFFED PINEAPPLE

Prep: 15 minutes

1 fresh pineapple
3 oranges, sectioned
1 banana, sliced
1 kiwifruit, peeled and sliced
½ cup seedless red grapes
1 star fruit, sliced
¼ cup sugar
1 tablespoon lemon juice
1 tablespoon dark rum
Garnish: chopped macadamia nuts, toasted

• **Cut** pineapple in half lengthwise, leaving green tops attached; remove and discard core. Remove pineapple pulp, and cut into 1-inch pieces, leaving ½-inch-thick shells.
• **Combine** pineapple pulp, orange sections, and next 7 ingredients; spoon into shells. Garnish, if desired. **Yield:** 2 servings.

Valerie G. Stutsman
Norfolk, Virginia

FRUIT SALAD WITH CITRUS-CILANTRO DRESSING

Prep: 10 minutes

1 cup cantaloupe chunks
1 cup honeydew chunks
½ cup fresh blueberries
½ cup halved strawberries
Citrus-Cilantro Dressing

• **Combine** all ingredients, tossing to coat fruit. **Yield:** 4 servings.

Citrus-Cilantro Dressing

Prep: 5 minutes

¼ cup orange juice
1½ tablespoons lime juice
1 tablespoon honey
1½ teaspoons minced fresh cilantro
1½ teaspoons minced fresh mint

• **Stir** together all ingredients in a bowl. **Yield:** ½ cup.

Summer Suppers.

*Summer offers adventure at every turn. Visit a dude ranch,
cycle the back roads, or pick a bounty of vegetables.
We share these journeys—and more—in this special section.*

Best of the West

At Bald Eagle Ranch in Bandera, Texas, the dudes are treated to great food as well as high adventure. After a day of riding through the Hill Country, hiking, or shooting archery targets, guests from as far away as England and Germany are ready to chow down (even if they have to stand up to do it). They enjoy everything from baby back ribs, blackened salmon, and chicken breasts topped with crawfish and crabmeat. Here are a few Bald Eagle specialties to help you dream of ridin', ropin', and relaxin'. For more information call Bald Eagle Ranch at (830) 460-3012.

CHOCOLATE TORTE WITH FIREWATER CREAM

Prep: 20 minutes
Bake: 50 minutes
Chill: 8 hours

1 cup semisweet chocolate
   morsels
1 cup whipping cream
¼ cup butter
5 large eggs
¼ cup sugar

- **Wrap** outside of a greased 6-inch springform pan with aluminum foil. Set pan aside.
- **Cook** first 3 ingredients in a medium saucepan over low heat, stirring occasionally, until chocolate melts; remove pan from heat.
- **Whisk** together eggs and sugar. Gradually whisk about one-fourth of hot mixture into egg mixture; add to remaining hot mixture, whisking constantly. Pour into prepared pan. Place in a larger baking pan; pour water to a depth of 1½ inches into larger pan.
- **Bake** at 350° for 50 minutes or until set. Cool and chill 8 hours. Serve with Firewater Cream or sweetened whipped cream. **Yield:** 6 servings.

Firewater Cream

Cook: 40 minutes

2 cups sugar
2 cups whipping cream
¼ cup bourbon
2 tablespoons vanilla extract

- **Bring** all ingredients to a boil in a saucepan over medium heat. Boil 30 to 40 minutes or until mixture is reduced by half. Serve warm. **Yield:** 2 cups.

Note: For testing purposes only, we used Jack Daniel's whiskey.

Bald Eagle Ranch
Bandera, Texas

CHILE MASHED POTATOES

Prep: 10 minutes
Cook: 30 minutes

6 large red potatoes, peeled and
   quartered (about 4 pounds)
2 carrots, finely chopped
2 (4.5-ounce) cans chopped green
   chiles, drained
½ cup sour cream
¼ cup butter or margarine,
   softened
1 teaspoon salt
¾ teaspoon pepper
¼ to ½ teaspoon ground cumin

- **Cook** potato in boiling salted water to cover 25 minutes.
- **Add** carrot; cook 5 minutes or until potato is tender. Drain; stir in chiles.
- **Beat** potato mixture, sour cream, and remaining ingredients at medium speed with an electric mixer until smooth. **Yield:** 4 servings.

Bald Eagle Ranch
Bandera, Texas

Freewheeling in the Virginia Wine Country

Cycle your way to adventure this summer on the back hills of southwestern Virginia. About 40 miles outside of Roanoke lies one of Virginia's largest wineries, Château Morrisette. Stop here to savor the fine cuisine and tour the winery. If time doesn't allow for dining, order a box lunch to enjoy wherever the road takes you. Once home, you can relive the experience with these recipes.

RANCH HOUSE SALAD WITH PECAN VINAIGRETTE

Prep: 5 minutes

1 (8-ounce) package mixed salad greens
1 cup finely shredded red cabbage
½ cup (2 ounces) shredded Monterey Jack cheese
1 tomato, cut into wedges
1 avocado, sliced
Vegetable oil
2 corn tortillas, cut into thin strips
Pecan Vinaigrette

• **Divide** greens evenly onto 4 salad plates; top with cabbage and cheese. Arrange tomato wedges and avocado over greens.
• **Pour** oil to depth of ½ inch in a skillet; heat to 350°.
• **Fry** tortilla strips in hot oil 1 minute or until crisp. Drain on paper towels.
• **Drizzle** salads with Pecan Vinaigrette; top evenly with tortilla strips. **Yield:** 4 servings.

Pecan Vinaigrette

Prep: 5 minutes

¼ cup white wine vinegar
2 tablespoons Dijon mustard
2 garlic cloves
½ teaspoon salt
½ teaspoon pepper
2 tablespoons dry sherry (optional)
1 cup olive oil
¼ cup chopped pecans, toasted

• **Process** first 5 ingredients and, if desired, sherry in a blender until smooth, stopping to scrape down sides. Turn blender on high; gradually add oil in a slow, steady stream until thickened. Stir in pecans. **Yield:** 1¼ cups.

Bald Eagle Ranch
Bandera, Texas

POTATO-AND-GREEN BEAN SALAD

Prep: 30 minutes
Cook: 32 minutes
Chill: 30 minutes

2 pounds small red potatoes, quartered
1 teaspoon salt, divided
1 pound thin fresh green beans, trimmed
1 large purple onion, finely chopped
1 teaspoon sugar
1 tablespoon olive oil
2 garlic cloves, minced
1 teaspoon chopped fresh or dried rosemary
½ cup white vinegar
¼ cup stone-ground mustard
½ teaspoon pepper

• **Cook** potato and ½ teaspoon salt in boiling water to cover 20 to 25 minutes. Remove with a slotted spoon; drain and set aside.
• **Add** green beans, and cook 5 to 7 minutes; drain and set aside.
• **Cook** onion and sugar in hot oil in a large skillet over medium-high heat, stirring occasionally, 15 to 20 minutes.
• **Stir** in garlic and rosemary; cook 2 minutes. Add vinegar, and cook 2 minutes, stirring to loosen particles from bottom of skillet. Remove from heat, and let stand 10 minutes.
• **Stir** mustard into onion mixture; add potatoes, tossing to coat. Sprinkle with remaining ½ teaspoon salt and pepper; chill 30 minutes. Stir in green beans. **Yield:** 6 servings.

Chef John Bradstreet
Château Morrisette, Inc.
Meadows of Dan, Virginia

Summer Suppers

GRILLED CHICKEN BREASTS WITH FIG-AND-MELON COMPOTE

Prep: 30 minutes
Chill: 8 hours
Grill: 12 minutes

1 cup milk
⅓ cup honey
8 skinned and boned chicken breast
   halves
1 cantaloupe, peeled, seeded, and
   finely chopped
1 honeydew melon, peeled, seeded,
   and finely chopped
1 papaya, finely chopped
¾ cup fig preserves
1 tablespoon chopped fresh
   mint
1 tablespoon lime juice
½ teaspoon salt
½ teaspoon pepper
Garnish: fresh mint sprigs

• **Combine** milk and honey in a shallow dish or large heavy-duty zip-top plastic bag; add chicken. Cover or seal, and chill 8 hours, turning occasionally.
• **Stir** together cantaloupe and next 5 ingredients in a bowl; cover and chill 2 hours.
• **Remove** chicken from marinade, discarding marinade. Sprinkle with salt and pepper.
• **Grill,** covered with grill lid, over medium-high heat (400° to 450°) 6 minutes on each side or until done.
• **Top** chicken with fruit mixture. Garnish, if desired. **Yield:** 8 servings.

Chef John Bradstreet
Château Morrisette, Inc.
Meadows of Dan, Virginia

GOURMET GREENS WITH RASPBERRY VINAIGRETTE

Prep: 15 minutes

2½ cups olive oil
2 tablespoons finely chopped purple onion
2 tablespoons stone-ground mustard
3 garlic cloves
1 teaspoon minced fresh or
   ¼ teaspoon dried basil
1 teaspoon minced fresh or
   ¼ teaspoon dried oregano
1 teaspoon minced fresh cilantro
½ teaspoon salt
½ teaspoon pepper
½ cup raspberry vinegar
¼ cup honey
8 cups gourmet greens
1 (6-ounce) package fresh raspberries
1 (2-ounce) package slivered almonds,
   toasted
¼ cup crumbled feta cheese

• **Process** first 4 ingredients in a blender until smooth, stopping to scrape down sides. Stir in basil and next 6 ingredients.
• **Top** greens with raspberries, almonds, and feta cheese; drizzle with raspberry vinaigrette. **Yield:** 6 servings.

Chef John Bradstreet
Château Morrisette, Inc.
Meadows of Dan, Virginia

SAUTÉED TOMATO WITH FRESH MOZZARELLA

Prep: 20 minutes
Cook: 16 minutes

4 large tomatoes
12 ounces fresh mozzarella cheese,
   cut into 12 slices
2 tablespoons chopped fresh basil
1 cup soft breadcrumbs
1 tablespoon grated Romano cheese
1 teaspoon minced fresh oregano
½ teaspoon salt
½ teaspoon pepper
½ cup chopped ruby Swiss chard
3 tablespoons basil-infused or plain
   olive oil
2 tablespoons balsamic vinegar

• **Cut** each tomato into 3 slices. Top 6 slices evenly with mozzarella cheese. Sprinkle evenly with basil, and top with remaining tomato slices.
• **Combine** breadcrumbs and next 4 ingredients. Dredge each tomato stack in breadcrumb mixture.
• **Cook,** in batches, in a lightly greased nonstick skillet over medium heat 3 to 4 minutes on each side. Serve over Swiss chard, and drizzle evenly with oil and vinegar. **Yield:** 6 servings.

Chef John Bradstreet
Château Morrisette, Inc.
Meadows of Dan, Virginia

Summer Suppers

A Movable Feast

Few things can top dining outdoors with nature as the backdrop. Although some of these recipes may require a few minutes in the kitchen the night before, the time is minimal and the rewards are plentiful.

A Bountiful Picnic
Serves 4

Minted Tea Punch   Cheese Wafers

Corn Salsa   Tortilla chips

Grilled Chicken Salad Sandwiches

Summer Vegetable-and-Orzo Salad

Grilled Asparagus

White Chocolate Tropical Macaroons

MINTED TEA PUNCH
(pictured on pages 186 and 187)

Prep: 20 minutes
Chill: 2 hours

4 cups boiling water
4 family-size decaffeinated tea bags
½ cup loosely packed fresh mint leaves
¾ cup sugar
1 (6-ounce) can frozen lemonade concentrate, thawed and undiluted
4 cups cold water
Garnishes: lemon slices, fresh mint sprigs

• **Pour** 4 cups boiling water over tea bags and mint leaves. Cover; steep 3 minutes. Discard tea bags and mint. Stir in sugar until dissolved. Stir in concentrate and 4 cups cold water; chill. Serve over ice. Garnish, if desired. **Yield:** 9 cups.

Judy Johnson
Knoxville, Tennessee

CHEESE WAFERS
(pictured on pages 186 and 187)

Prep: 30 minutes
Chill: 10 hours
Bake: 15 minutes per batch

2 cups butter or margarine, softened
1 (1-pound) block sharp Cheddar cheese, shredded
4 cups all-purpose flour
½ teaspoon salt
1 to 2 teaspoons ground red pepper
½ teaspoon paprika

• **Beat** butter and cheese at medium speed with an electric mixer until blended; add flour and remaining ingredients, beating until blended. Cover and chill 2 hours.
• **Shape** dough into 4 (8-inch) logs; cover and chill 8 hours. Cut into ¼-inch slices, and place on ungreased baking sheets.
• **Bake** at 350° for 15 minutes. Remove to wire racks to cool. Store in an airtight container. **Yield:** 10 dozen.

Ann P. Porter
Jefferson City, Tennessee

CORN SALSA
(pictured on page 186)

Prep: 20 minutes
Chill: 2 hours

3 large ears fresh corn
1 large tomato, finely chopped
1 (7-ounce) jar roasted sweet red peppers, drained and chopped
2 green onions, finely chopped
1 jalapeño pepper, seeded and minced
3 tablespoons minced fresh cilantro
2 tablespoons fresh lime juice
1 tablespoon white wine vinegar
½ teaspoon salt
¼ teaspoon pepper
¼ teaspoon ground cumin
2 avocados, chopped (optional)

• **Cut** corn from cobs. Stir together corn, next 10 ingredients and, if desired, avocado. Cover; chill at least 2 hours. Serve with tortilla chips. **Yield:** 2½ cups.

Cindi Hackney
Longview, Texas

GRILLED CHICKEN SALAD SANDWICHES
(pictured on page 187)

Prep: 10 minutes
Grill: 14 minutes

4 skinned and boned chicken breast halves
Vegetable cooking spray
2 teaspoons Creole seasoning*
¼ cup mayonnaise
¼ cup sour cream
Lettuce leaves
8 tomato slices
4 sourdough rolls, split

Summer Suppers

- **Coat** chicken with cooking spray; sprinkle with Creole seasoning.
- **Grill** chicken, covered with grill lid, over medium-high heat (350° to 400°) 7 minutes on each side or until done. Cool slightly; coarsely chop.
- **Stir** together mayonnaise and sour cream; stir in chicken. Cover and chill, if desired.
- **Place** lettuce and 2 tomato slices on bottom half of each roll. Top evenly with chicken mixture; cover with tops of rolls. **Yield:** 4 servings.

*Substitute blackened seasoning for Creole seasoning, if desired.

Angela Williams
Montgomery, Alabama

SUMMER VEGETABLE-AND-ORZO SALAD

(pictured on pages 186 and 187)

Prep: 20 minutes
Cook: 10 minutes
Chill: 2 hours

1 medium-size sweet onion, chopped
3 tablespoons olive oil
1 cup orzo, cooked
4 large carrots, coarsely shredded
1 large red bell pepper, chopped
1 large zucchini, chopped
3 to 4 tablespoons white balsamic vinegar*
2 tablespoons honey
¾ teaspoon salt
½ teaspoon freshly ground pepper
Lettuce leaves (optional)

- **Sauté** onion in 1 tablespoon hot olive oil 10 minutes or until browned. Remove from heat.
- **Stir** in orzo, remaining 2 tablespoons olive oil, carrot, and next 6 ingredients. Cover and chill at least 2 hours. Serve on lettuce leaves, if desired. **Yield:** 4 servings.

*Substitute white wine vinegar for white balsamic vinegar, if desired.

PERFECT PICNIC

The South's diverse topography offers an almost endless variety of picnic sites. A sunny afternoon is the ideal time to pick a beautiful location and relax with a scrumptious meal. Talk about getting the "perfect table."

Even if you don't have a place in mind, simply loading up the car and driving until you find your dining destination is worth the adventure. So perhaps the best way to enjoy the day is to have no plan at all.

And if the weather is good enough to play outside, then chances are you're not going to want to spend a lot of time in the kitchen. In many cases the food plays second fiddle to the location. But this menu allows you to have the best of both worlds.

You'll pack a basket that is portable, creative, and most importantly, delicious—the perfect accompaniment to the picnic spot that you choose to visit.

Here are a few suggestions and basic food-handling tips to help you keep the good times rolling.

- Keep a picnic kit ready. Include disposable dinnerware, cups, and utensils; paper towels; a knife; a bottle opener; and a trash bag for easy cleanup.

- Keep cooked and raw food in separate containers. If you're going to be cooking, pack additional clean plates to avoid contaminating cooked meats. Don't put cooked food on a plate that held raw food. Make sure that meats are thawed completely before cooking and cooked to the proper temperature.

- One hour is the maximum time food should be left unrefrigerated if the outside temperature is above 85 degrees. Pack your cooler directly from the refrigerator or freezer (placing food to be kept the coolest on the bottom), and store the cooler in the shade, if possible, with the lid sealed tight.

GRILLED ASPARAGUS

(pictured on page 187)

Prep: 10 minutes
Grill: 4 minutes
Chill: 2 hours

1 pound fresh asparagus
3 tablespoons olive oil
¼ cup lemon juice
½ teaspoon salt
¼ teaspoon freshly ground pepper
Garnish: lemon slices

- **Snap** off tough ends of asparagus. Drizzle asparagus with oil.
- **Grill,** covered with grill lid, over medium-high heat (350° to 400°) 2 minutes on each side or until asparagus is crisp-tender.
- **Drizzle** with lemon juice, and sprinkle with salt and pepper. Cover and chill at least 2 hours. Garnish, if desired. **Yield:** 4 servings.

That's Italian

If you can't spend the summer dining under the Tuscan sun, we'll bring the adventure to you. Enjoy this authentic Italian menu without ever leaving your kitchen. These soul-saving dishes focus on easy assembly with few ingredients.

WHITE CHOCOLATE TROPICAL MACAROONS

Prep: 30 minutes
Bake: 17 minutes

4 ounces white chocolate, coarsely chopped
1 cup sugar
¼ teaspoon ground ginger
¼ teaspoon ground cinnamon
4 egg whites
2 cups flaked coconut
1 cup finely chopped dried pineapple
½ cup finely chopped macadamia nuts *

• **Microwave** chopped white chocolate in a small glass bowl at HIGH 1½ minutes or until melted, stirring once. Set aside.
• **Stir** together sugar, ground ginger, and cinnamon.
• **Beat** egg whites at high speed with an electric mixer until foamy.
• **Add** sugar mixture, 1 tablespoon at a time, beating until stiff peaks form and sugar dissolves (2 to 4 minutes).
• **Fold** in white chocolate, coconut, pineapple, and macadamia nuts.
• **Drop** mixture by rounded tablespoonfuls 2 inches apart onto parchment paper-lined baking sheets.
• **Bake** at 350° for 13 to 17 minutes or until edges begin to brown. Remove to wire racks to cool. Store in an airtight container. **Yield:** 4 dozen.

*Substitute chopped pecans for the macadamia nuts, if desired.

Note: Bake 13 to 14 minutes for chewy cookies.

Edwina Gadsby
Great Falls, Montana

Italian Repast
Serves 4

Veal Scaloppine in Lemon Sauce
Italian Tossed Salad
Easy Tiramisù

VEAL SCALOPPINE IN LEMON SAUCE

Lemon juice and capers add a zesty flair to the buttery sauce that tops the tender veal cutlets.

Prep: 15 minutes
Cook: 10 minutes

1¼ pounds veal cutlets
⅓ cup all-purpose flour
½ teaspoon salt
¼ teaspoon freshly ground pepper
3 tablespoons butter or margarine, divided
1 tablespoon olive oil
½ cup dry white wine
3 tablespoons lemon juice
2 tablespoons chopped fresh parsley
1 large garlic clove, pressed
2 tablespoons capers
Garnishes: fresh parsley sprigs, lemon slices

• **Place** veal between 2 sheets of heavy-duty plastic wrap, and flatten veal to ¼-inch thickness, using a meat mallet or rolling pin.
• **Combine** flour, salt, and pepper; dredge veal in mixture.
• **Melt** 2 tablespoons butter with oil in a large skillet over medium-high heat; add veal, and cook, in batches, 1 minute on each side or until golden. Remove from skillet, and keep warm.
• **Add** remaining 1 tablespoon butter, wine, and lemon juice to skillet, stirring to loosen browned particles. Cook until thoroughly heated.
• **Stir** in parsley, garlic, and capers; spoon over veal. Garnish, if desired. Serve immediately. **Yield:** 4 servings.

Chicken Scaloppine in Lemon Sauce: Substitute 4 skinned and boned chicken breast halves. Cook chicken 3 minutes on each side.

Michele Baker
Richardson, Texas

Summer Suppers

ITALIAN TOSSED SALAD

Prep: 15 minutes

1 (14-ounce) can hearts of palm
    pieces, rinsed and drained
1 head Romaine lettuce, torn
1 (8-ounce) jar marinated artichoke
    hearts, undrained
½ cup small pitted ripe olives
⅓ cup shredded Parmesan cheese
Pimiento Vinaigrette

• **Cut** hearts of palm into thin slices; toss with Romaine lettuce and remaining ingredients. Serve salad immediately. **Yield:** 4 servings.

Pimiento Vinaigrette

Prep: 5 minutes

½ cup olive oil
3 tablespoons red wine vinegar
1 tablespoon minced purple onion
1 garlic clove
1 (2-ounce) jar diced pimiento, drained

• **Process** first 4 ingredients in a blender or food processor until smooth; stir in pimiento. **Yield:** ⅔ cup.

Fran Pointer
Kansas City, Missouri

EASY TIRAMISÙ

Prep: 20 minutes
Chill: 8 hours

1 (16-ounce) package mascarpone
    cheese*
1¼ cups whipping cream
¼ cup powdered sugar
1½ teaspoons vanilla extract
1 cup brewed espresso
2 tablespoons dark rum
2 (3-ounce) packages ladyfingers
4 (1-ounce) bittersweet chocolate
    squares, grated

• **Beat** first 4 ingredients at high speed with an electric mixer 30 seconds or just until blended.

• **Stir** together espresso and rum. Arrange 1 package ladyfingers in bottom of a 3-quart bowl or trifle dish; brush with half of espresso mixture. Layer half of mascarpone cheese mixture over ladyfingers; sprinkle with half of grated chocolate. Repeat layers. Cover and chill 8 hours. **Yield:** 8 servings.

*If desired, substitute the following for 16 ounces mascarpone cheese: 2 (8-ounce) packages cream cheese, softened; ⅓ cup sour cream; and ¼ cup whipping cream, beaten until blended.

Rose Clark Weems
Shreveport, Louisiana

Cruising With Friends

As members of the Bay Point Yacht Club in Panama City, Florida, Al and Beth Barron of Birmingham enjoy regular "Raft-Up" trips. Seven to eight boats hook together at a favorite destination. Weekends are easy—no planned agenda, just shorts, swimsuits, and great food. "The party is always great," Beth says. "When you wake in the morning, the boats have shifted, and so has the scenery."

CRUISING DRINK

Prep: 5 minutes

¾ cup dark rum
¾ cup orange juice
2 cups ginger ale, chilled
1 lime, cut into wedges

• **Stir** together first 3 ingredients in a pitcher. Pour over crushed ice, and serve with lime wedges. **Yield:** 3½ cups.

Dan Alexander
Panama City, Florida

WHITE DIPPING SAUCE

This sauce tastes great served with peeled, steamed shrimp; crunchy raw vegetables; or spicy hot wings.

Prep: 10 minutes
Chill: 8 hours

1½ cups mayonnaise
¼ cup prepared horseradish
3 tablespoons lemon juice
2 tablespoons Worcestershire sauce
1 teaspoon salt
1 teaspoon onion juice*
1 teaspoon minced fresh parsley
¼ teaspoon hot sauce
1 garlic clove, minced
Garnish: fresh parsley sprig

• **Stir** together first 9 ingredients; cover and chill 8 hours. Serve with peeled, steamed shrimp, and garnish, if desired. **Yield:** 2 cups.

*Substitute 1 tablespoon minced onion for onion juice, if desired.

Jane Wesson
Panama City, Florida

GROUPER FINGERS

Prep: 6 minutes
Cook: 16 minutes

1 pound grouper
2 large eggs, lightly beaten
18 saltine crackers, crushed
Canola oil
¼ teaspoon salt

• **Cut** fish into 5- x 1½-inch strips. Dip in egg, and dredge in saltine cracker crumbs.
• **Pour** oil to a depth of 1½ inches into a heavy skillet; heat oil to 375°.
• **Fry** fish, in batches, 2 minutes on each side. Drain on paper towels; sprinkle with salt. **Yield:** 5 appetizer servings.

Mary Perry
Panama City, Florida

QUICK PIZZA DIP

Prep: 10 minutes
Cook: 3 minutes

1 (8-ounce) package cream cheese, softened
1 teaspoon dried Italian seasoning
1 (14-ounce) jar pasta sauce
1 (3-ounce) package sliced pepperoni, chopped
1 small green bell pepper, chopped
¼ cup minced onion
1 (2¼-ounce) can sliced ripe olives, drained
½ cup shredded Parmesan cheese
½ cup (2 ounces) shredded mozzarella cheese

• **Stir** together cream cheese and dried Italian seasoning; spread into a lightly greased 9-inch pieplate.
• **Spoon** pasta sauce over cream cheese mixture; top with pepperoni and next 3 ingredients.
• **Sprinkle** evenly with Parmesan and mozzarella cheeses.
• **Microwave** at HIGH 2 to 3 minutes or until dip is thoroughly heated. Serve with corn chips. **Yield:** 8 appetizer servings.

Sherry Alexander
Panama City, Florida

Summer's Just Ripe for Picking

If tomatoes still warm from the sun and the crunch of just-picked corn fill your thoughts of summer, you'll love these recipes. Add a soundtrack of uncontainable giggles of pleasure and pride, and culinary musing becomes a priceless memory.

Eight-year-old Catherine Poellnitz and her older sister, Elizabeth, asked us to join them on a beautiful sun-washed morning at Willow Creek Farm near Jemison, Alabama, for a picking adventure. Catherine promised us the outing would be "totally fun," while 10-year-old Elizabeth suggested the picking would be "pretty cool."

"It's not like in the grocery store," Elizabeth continued. "On the farm you can pick the ripest ones. . . . In the movies it looks like there's corn everywhere. Here it takes time."

Our day at Willow Creek produced several bushels of produce—inspiration enough for our Test Kitchens to transform the farm-fresh bounty into fine fare. Take a peek at these recipes—results of Catherine and Elizabeth's day at Willow Creek. Then grab your sun hat and head for the country. You still have plenty of time to pick your own adventure.

ZUCCHINI JAM

Prep: 15 minutes
Cook: 25 minutes
Process: 15 minutes

6 medium zucchini, peeled and shredded
6 cups sugar
½ cup lemon juice
1 (15½-ounce) can crushed pineapple, drained
1 (6-ounce) package orange gelatin
1 to 2 teaspoons grated orange rind

• **Cook** zucchini in boiling water to cover 15 minutes. Drain well.
• **Bring** zucchini, sugar, lemon juice, and pineapple to a boil over medium heat, stirring often; reduce heat, and cook 6 minutes.
• **Remove** from heat, and stir in gelatin and orange rind until gelatin dissolves.
• **Pack** hot mixture into hot jars, filling to within ½ inch from top. Remove air bubbles; wipe jar rims. Cover at once with metal lids, and screw on bands.
• **Process** in a boiling-water bath 15 minutes, or refrigerate up to 1 month. **Yield:** 4 pints.

Nora Henshaw
Okemah, Oklahoma

Summer Suppers

SAVING FRUITS AND VEGETABLES

Perfect Pickles, Jams, and Jellies

Follow our hints for storing, freezing, and canning fruits and vegetables, and you'll have a bumper crop to enjoy now and later.

■ Select tender vegetables and firm fruits for making relishes or pickles.

■ Pickle fruits or vegetables within 24 hours after they're picked. If produce can't be used immediately, refrigerate or spread out the produce in a well-ventilated area.

■ Wash and sort fruits and vegetables just before preparing for pickling, canning, or freezing. Remove a 1/16-inch slice from blossom end of vegetables.

■ "Pickling" or "canning" salt yields the clearest brine. Use fresh spices for best quality and flavor.

■ Use canning jars and pre-treated lids.

■ Check jars and lids. Discard cracked or chipped jars and any lids with blemished sealing surfaces. Wash, rinse, and then boil jars and lids for about 10 minutes to sterilize before filling. Jars should be hot when filled.

■ Before filling jars, skim off any foam that collects during the boiling process.

■ Place filled jars in canner—or large Dutch oven with cooling rack—and cover with at least 1 inch of water. Start timing as soon as water begins to boil.

■ At altitudes of more than 1,000 feet, add 1 minute to processing time for each additional 1,000 feet of altitude.

■ Cool filled, processed jars; remove screw-on bands after 12 hours. Store in a dry, cool place. The shorter the storage time, the better the product.

■ Examine jars closely before opening homemade relishes and jams. A bulging lid, leakage, disagreeable odor, spurting liquid, or change in color of vegetables may mean contents are spoiled. Do not taste the contents.

Deep Freeze

■ Select the best quality fruits and vegetables at their peak of maturity for freezing. Fruit should be firm, yet ripe. Vegetables should be young, tender, and unwilted. Sort for size, ripeness, and color.

■ Use rigid plastic freezer containers or heavy-duty freezer bags to store fruits and vegetables.

■ Work in small quantities; fill a few containers at a time to maintain peak quality and nutrients.

■ Wash and drain all fruit, handling gently to prevent bruising. Do not let produce soak.

■ Blanching locks in color, crispness, and flavor. Use about 1 gallon of water for each pound of produce. Place the vegetables in a metal steaming basket; lower the basket into rapidly boiling water, and cover. Blanch green beans for 3 minutes; corn on the cob for 7 to 11 minutes; okra for 3 to 4 minutes; field peas for 2 minutes; and summer squash for 3 minutes.

■ Cool promptly to stop the cooking process by plunging vegetables into ice water. Cool the vegetables for the same amount of time they were blanched.

■ Drain thoroughly and package, leaving 1/2-inch headspace. Remove as much air from container as possible; seal and freeze.

■ To freeze produce in individual pieces, after blanching, cooling, and draining, spread the produce in a single layer on trays or baking sheets. Place in freezer until frozen firm. Package quickly, leaving no headspace, and seal. Produce remains loose and can be poured from the container and the package reclosed.

■ Wash tomatoes, and dip in boiling water for 30 seconds to loosen skin. Core and peel. Freeze whole or in pieces. Pack in containers, leaving 1-inch headspace.

■ To freeze green tomatoes, wash, core, and cut the tomatoes into 1/4-inch-thick slices. Pack the tomato slices into containers, with freezer wrap between slices. Leave 1/2-inch headspace.

SAVORY SQUASH PIE

Prep: 25 minutes
Bake: 40 minutes

3   medium-size yellow squash,
      sliced
3   medium zucchini, sliced
1   yellow bell pepper, sliced
1   small onion, sliced and separated
      into rings
1   teaspoon olive oil
1   garlic clove, pressed
2   teaspoons minced fresh marjoram
¼   teaspoon salt
¼   teaspoon pepper
Pastry
½   cup shredded Parmesan cheese,
      divided
1½ cups cherry tomatoes, halved
1   large egg, lightly beaten

• **Sauté** first 4 ingredients in hot oil in a large nonstick skillet over medium heat 7 minutes or until crisp-tender.
• **Stir** in garlic and next 3 ingredients. Set aside.
• **Roll** Pastry to a 13-inch round on a lightly floured surface; transfer to a parchment paper-lined or lightly greased baking sheet. Sprinkle with half of cheese, leaving a 2-inch border.
• **Spoon** squash mixture over cheese; top with tomato halves. Fold edge of Pastry over filling, and brush with egg.
• **Bake** at 400° for 35 to 40 minutes or until golden. Sprinkle with remaining cheese, and cool 30 minutes on a wire rack. **Yield:** 6 to 8 servings.

Pastry

Prep: 10 minutes
Chill: 20 minutes

1¼ cups all-purpose flour
½   cup butter, cut into pieces
¼   teaspoon salt
¼   teaspoon pepper
½   teaspoon grated lemon rind
2   tablespoons fresh lemon juice
2   tablespoons buttermilk

• **Pulse** first 5 ingredients in a food processor 7 to 8 times or until mixture is crumbly. With processor running, gradually add lemon juice and buttermilk; process until dough forms a ball and leaves sides of bowl. Cover and chill 20 minutes. **Yield:** pastry for 13-inch pie.

Louise Bodziony
Gladstone, Missouri

TANGY GREEN BEANS WITH PIMIENTO
(pictured on page 188)

A sweet-sour dressing and crisp bacon give these green beans irresistible flavor appeal.

Prep: 10 minutes
Cook: 20 minutes

1½ pounds fresh green beans,
      trimmed
3   bacon slices
1   large onion, chopped
3   garlic cloves, minced
1   (2-ounce) jar diced pimiento,
      drained
¼   cup red wine vinegar
1   teaspoon sugar
½   teaspoon salt
½   teaspoon pepper
½   teaspoon cumin seeds

• **Cook** green beans in boiling water to cover 4 to 5 minutes.
• **Drain** and plunge beans into ice water to stop the cooking process; drain and set aside.
• **Cook** bacon in a large skillet until crisp; remove bacon, and drain on paper towels, reserving 2 tablespoons drippings in skillet.
• **Crumble** bacon, and set aside.
• **Sauté** onion and garlic in hot bacon drippings over medium-high heat until tender. Stir in pimiento and next 5 ingredients. Stir in green beans; cover, reduce heat, and simmer 5 minutes. Sprinkle with bacon. **Yield:** 6 servings.

Kitty Pettus
Huntsville, Alabama

FRESH BASIL CORN ON THE COB

Prep: 15 minutes
Cook: 7 minutes

4   ears fresh corn with husks
¼   cup butter or margarine, softened
½   teaspoon grated orange rind
2   tablespoons chopped fresh basil

• **Remove** heavy outer husks from corn; pull back inner husks. Remove and discard silks. Pull husks back over corn; arrange, spoke fashion, on a glass plate.
• **Microwave** at HIGH 7 minutes, turning corn after 3½ minutes.
• **Stir** together butter, orange rind, and basil. Pull back husks; brush butter mixture evenly over corn. **Yield:** 4 servings.

Charlotte Bryant
Greensburg, Kentucky

TOMATO MARMALADE

Prep: 25 minutes
Bake: 1 hour

1   medium onion, finely chopped
1   tablespoon olive oil
4   large tomatoes, peeled and finely
      chopped
2   garlic cloves, minced
3   tablespoons minced fresh basil*
½   teaspoon salt
½   to 1 teaspoon fennel seeds
¼   teaspoon pepper

• **Sauté** onion in hot oil in a Dutch oven over medium-high heat until tender. Remove from heat, and stir in tomato and remaining ingredients.
• **Bake,** covered, at 400° for 1 hour or until thick and bubbly, stirring occasionally. Serve with grilled meat or crab cakes. **Yield:** 1½ cups.

*Substitute 2 teaspoons dried basil for fresh basil, if desired.

Caroline Kennedy
Lighthouse Point, Florida

Food Fun

Try these three fun responses to the age-old statement, "Mom, I'm bored."

Looking for fun kids' activities? We've adapted some ideas from *Fun at Home With Dian Thomas* (Dian Thomas Communications, 1993).

Invite a group of children over for a Kick-the-Can Ice Cream party. This five-ingredient ice cream requires no cooking—only plenty of fancy footwork. Pick partners or kick alone. (Just remember this isn't a game for open-toed shoes.) Each team can prepare a different flavor, and even adults can participate.

Little hands can create works of art with Peanut Butter Fun Dough. Just pat and cut out the dough with a cookie cutter, or shape it into imaginative creations—animals and flowers, plants and planets. Chefs of any age will enjoy these recipes and the good times.

KICK-THE-CAN ICE CREAM

Prep: 5 minutes
Freeze: 15 minutes

1 cup whipping cream
¾ cup milk
⅓ cup sugar
¼ cup egg substitute
½ teaspoon vanilla extract
1 (1-pound) coffee can with plastic lid
1 (3-pound) coffee can with plastic lid
Crushed ice
¾ cup rock salt, divided
Masking tape
Waffle bowls (optional)
Candy-coated milk chocolate sprinkles (optional)

• **Stir** together first 5 ingredients; pour into 1-pound can, and seal with lid. Place small can inside large can. Fill large can with ice and half of rock salt. Secure small can in place with masking tape. Seal large can with lid.
• **Roll** large can with your foot 5 minutes. Remove lid from large can; drain off water. Add more ice and remaining rock salt. Replace lid; roll can 10 minutes. Let stand 5 minutes before serving. (Ice cream will be soft.) If desired, serve in waffle bowls, and decorate with chocolate sprinkles. **Yield:** 3 cups.

Note: For testing purposes only, we used Keebler Waffle Bowls and Hershey's Chocolate Shoppe Sprinkles.

PEANUT BUTTER FUN DOUGH

Prep: 6 minutes

2 cups nonfat dry milk powder
2 cups powdered sugar
1¾ cups creamy peanut butter
1¾ cups honey

• **Beat** all ingredients at medium speed with an electric mixer until smooth. Mold or shape mixture as desired. **Yield:** 5 cups.

HAMBURGER COOKIES

1 cup flaked coconut
4 drops green liquid food coloring
1 (4¼-ounce) tube white decorator icing
1 (12-ounce) package vanilla wafers
1 (10-ounce) package chocolate mint-flavored cookies
1 (4¼-ounce) tube yellow decorator icing
1 (4¼-ounce) tube red decorator icing
1 tablespoon water
2 teaspoons light corn syrup
Sesame seeds

• **Combine** 1 cup flaked coconut and 4 drops food coloring in a zip-top plastic bag; seal and shake until evenly colored. Set aside.
• **Squeeze** about ½ teaspoon white icing onto flat side of a vanilla wafer. Top with a mint-flavored cookie, pressing gently to show icing around edges.
• **Squeeze** about ½ teaspoon yellow icing and ½ teaspoon red icing over mint-flavored cookie; sprinkle with 1 teaspoon coconut.
• **Squeeze** about ½ teaspoon of any color icing onto flat side of a vanilla wafer.
• **Place** vanilla wafer, icing side down, over coconut, pressing gently to show icing around edges.
• **Combine** 1 tablespoon water and corn syrup; brush lightly over top of cookie; sprinkle with sesame seeds, and let glaze dry.
• **Repeat** procedure with remaining ingredients. **Yield:** 3 dozen.

Note: For testing purposes only, we used Keebler Grasshopper Fudge Mint Cookies for chocolate mint-flavored cookies.

Gone Fishin'

Every year, members of Rock Mountain Lakes Baptist Church in McCalla, Alabama, participate in a spirited fishing tournament. Fish are caught, cleaned, and taken to the church for an old-fashioned fish fry.

Summer Fish Fry
Serves 8

Fried Catfish
Home-Style Baked Beans
Creamy Sweet Slaw
Buttermilk Hush Puppies

CREAMY SWEET SLAW
(pictured on page 151)

Prep: 20 minutes

1 large cabbage, shredded, or 2 (10-ounce) bags angel hair cabbage
4 celery ribs, chopped
1 small green bell pepper, finely chopped
1 (2-ounce) jar diced pimiento, drained
½ cup sugar
¼ cup white vinegar
¾ cup mayonnaise
⅓ cup evaporated milk
1 teaspoon salt
½ teaspoon black pepper

• **Combine** first 4 ingredients in a large bowl. Stir together sugar and next 5 ingredients; spoon over cabbage mixture, tossing to coat. **Yield:** 8 servings.
Sherry Sims
McCalla, Alabama

FRIED CATFISH
(pictured on page 151)

Prep: 15 minutes
Cook: 12 minutes per batch

5 large eggs
1 cup milk
1 teaspoon salt
¼ teaspoon pepper
1 (1-pound) package saltine crackers
8 catfish fillets (3½ to 4 pounds)
Vegetable oil

• **Whisk** together first 4 ingredients; set aside. Process saltine crackers in a food processor until finely crushed.
• **Dip** fish in egg mixture; dredge in cracker crumbs.
• **Pour** oil to a depth of 5 inches in a Dutch oven; heat to 375°. Fry fish, in batches, 4 to 6 minutes on each side or until fish flakes with a fork. Drain on paper towels. **Yield:** 8 servings.
Sherry Lewis
McCalla, Alabama

HOME-STYLE BAKED BEANS
(pictured on page 151)

Prep: 10 minutes
Bake: 46 minutes

2 (28-ounce) cans baked beans with tangy sauce, bacon, and brown sugar
1 sweet onion, quartered
1 cup ketchup
½ to ¾ cup prepared mustard
2 tablespoons light brown sugar
4 bacon slices

• **Stir** together first 5 ingredients; pour into a lightly greased 11- x 7-inch baking dish. Top with bacon. Bake at 400° for 45 minutes. Broil 5 inches from heat (with electric oven door partially open) 1 minute. **Yield:** 6 to 8 servings.

Note: For testing purposes only, we used Bush's Original Baked Beans.
Carol Beck
McCalla, Alabama

BUTTERMILK HUSH PUPPIES
(pictured on page 151)

Prep: 20 minutes
Cook: 7 minutes per batch

2 cups self-rising flour
2 cups self-rising white cornmeal
1 teaspoon sugar
½ teaspoon salt
½ teaspoon pepper
1 large onion, grated
1 jalapeño pepper, seeded and minced (optional)
2 cups buttermilk
1 large egg
Vegetable oil

• **Combine** first 5 ingredients; stir in onion and, if desired, jalapeño pepper.
• **Whisk** together buttermilk and egg; add to flour mixture.
• **Pour** oil to a depth of 3 inches in a Dutch oven; heat to 375°. Drop batter by level tablespoonfuls into oil; fry, in batches, 5 to 7 minutes or until golden. Drain on paper towels. **Yield:** 5 dozen.
Nell Grantham
McCalla, Alabama

Trailblazer Treats

Want to ensure that everyone remains a happy camper on your next outing? Then organize your equipment and plan the meals before you head out. These dishes are sure to delight. Just remember—everything takes longer to cook when you're at higher altitudes. So take an outdoor trip and escape life's hectic pace. Happy camping!

CAMPFIRE CASSEROLE

The aroma of this casserole will lure sleepyheads to breakfast.

Prep: 10 minutes
Cook: 24 minutes

½ pound bacon
2 pounds potatoes, diced
1 medium onion, diced
1 teaspoon salt, divided
½ teaspoon pepper, divided
12 large eggs
1½ cups (6 ounces) shredded
    Cheddar cheese (optional)
Salsa or ketchup

• **Cook** bacon in a large skillet until crisp. Drain bacon on paper towels, reserving 2 tablespoons drippings in skillet. Crumble bacon; set aside.
• **Sauté** potato, onion, ½ teaspoon salt, and ¼ teaspoon pepper in hot bacon drippings, stirring occasionally, 20 minutes or until browned.
• **Whisk** together eggs, remaining ½ teaspoon salt, and remaining ¼ teaspoon pepper; pour over potato in skillet.
• **Cook** over medium heat 4 minutes or until eggs are set, stirring if necessary. Sprinkle with bacon and, if desired, Cheddar cheese.
• **Serve** with salsa or ketchup. **Yield:** 6 servings.

Mindi Goddard
Yukon, Oklahoma

ONE-POT PASTA DINNER

Backpackers will find this a convenient dinner.

Prep: 5 minutes
Cook: 15 minutes

4 cups water
2 cups uncooked rotini or tortellini
2 tablespoons dried minced
    onion
2 tablespoons freeze-dried red bell
    pepper flakes
½ teaspoon salt
1 (2.4-ounce) package tomato-with-
    basil soup mix
1 teaspoon dried oregano
1 teaspoon dried minced garlic
½ cup grated Parmesan cheese
¼ teaspoon ground red pepper

• **Bring** 4 cups water to a boil in a Dutch oven.
• **Add** pasta and next 3 ingredients; cook 10 minutes or until tender. Add soup mix, oregano, and garlic; cook 5 minutes. Stir in cheese and red pepper. Serve immediately. **Yield:** 2 servings.

Note: For testing purposes only, we used Knorr Tomato With Basil Soup and Recipe Mix.

Lisa Beckham
Atlanta, Georgia

BANANA BOATS

Prep: 10 minutes
Cook: 5 minutes

4 firm ripe bananas, unpeeled
¼ cup miniature marshmallows
¼ cup semisweet chocolate
    mini-morsels

• **Peel** back, but do not remove, a 1-inch-wide strip of each banana peel. Cut a lengthwise slit in each banana, being careful not to cut through banana.
• **Place** marshmallows and chocolate morsels evenly inside bananas. Replace 1-inch strip of banana peel, and wrap each "boat" in aluminum foil. Place over hot coals about 5 minutes or until marshmallows and chocolate melt. Serve immediately in banana peel. **Yield:** 4 servings.

Terri Preston
Piedmont, Oklahoma

The Lure of Shrimp

*These firm, flavorful shellfish are a Southern
favorite, and our dishes offer new mealtime sensations.
Most types of shrimp can be used interchangeably in
these recipes, but size will affect the cooking time.
Be sure to cook them until they turn pink.*

GARLIC SHRIMP-AND-GOAT CHEESE PASTA

*Prep: 20 minutes
Cook: 15 minutes*

1 pound unpeeled, large fresh shrimp
1 medium onion, diced
2 tablespoons olive oil
1 garlic clove, minced
½ cup milk
4 ounces goat cheese
8 ounces rotini, cooked
1 tablespoon chopped fresh parsley
½ teaspoon salt
⅛ teaspoon pepper

• **Peel** shrimp, and devein, if desired.
• **Sauté** onion in hot oil in a large skillet over medium-high heat until tender.
• **Stir** in shrimp and garlic; sauté 4 minutes or until shrimp turn pink. Remove from heat.
• **Cook** milk and goat cheese in a saucepan over low heat 5 to 7 minutes or until cheese melts.
• **Stir** into shrimp mixture. Toss with pasta, and sprinkle with parsley, salt, and pepper. Serve immediately. **Yield:** 3 to 4 servings.

*Debbie Pringle
Delray Beach, Florida*

SHRIMP RELLENOS

*Prep: 25 minutes
Cook: 5 minutes*

3 (4-ounce) cans whole green chiles
6 cups water
¾ pound unpeeled, medium-size fresh shrimp
1 small red apple, diced
½ cup (2 ounces) shredded sharp Cheddar cheese
2 jalapeño peppers, seeded and minced
4 green onions, thinly sliced
½ teaspoon grated lime rind
2 teaspoons fresh lime juice
3½ tablespoons mayonnaise
6 cups mixed salad greens

• **Cut** green chiles lengthwise on 1 side; remove and discard seeds. Drain well on paper towels.
• **Bring** 6 cups water to a boil; add shrimp, and cook 3 to 5 minutes or just until shrimp turn pink. Drain and rinse with cold water. Chill.
• **Peel** shrimp, and devein, if desired. Dice shrimp.
• **Stir** together shrimp, diced apple, and next 6 ingredients.
• **Spoon** shrimp mixture evenly into green chiles, and arrange on mixed salad greens. **Yield:** 6 servings.

*Denise Halferty Neff
Imperial Beach, California*

FROGMORE STEW

*Prep: 10 minutes
Cook: 27 minutes*

5 quarts water
¼ cup Old Bay seasoning
4 pounds small red potatoes
2 pounds kielbasa or hot smoked link sausage, cut into 1½-inch slices
6 ears fresh corn, halved
4 pounds unpeeled, large fresh shrimp
Additional Old Bay seasoning
Cocktail sauce
Melted butter

• **Bring** 5 quarts water and ¼ cup Old Bay seasoning to a boil in a large stockpot. Add potatoes; return to a boil, and cook 10 minutes.
• **Add** sausage and corn, and return to a boil. Cook 10 minutes or until potatoes are tender. Remove potatoes, corn, and sausage with a slotted spoon.
• **Add** shrimp to stockpot; cook 3 to 5 minutes or until shrimp turn pink. Remove shrimp with a slotted spoon. Serve with additional Old Bay seasoning, cocktail sauce, and butter. **Yield:** 12 servings.

DAUFUSKIE SHRIMP

This recipe originated on Daufuskie Island and was passed down to Dianne Brown's family.

*Prep: 35 minutes
Cook: 1 hour, 5 minutes*

2 pounds unpeeled, medium-size fresh shrimp
7 bacon slices, chopped
2 medium onions, diced
1 large green bell pepper, diced
3 jalapeño peppers, seeded and minced
4 garlic cloves, minced
2 (28-ounce) cans diced tomatoes
¼ cup cocktail sauce
½ teaspoon salt
⅛ teaspoon pepper
Hot cooked grits

- **Peel** shrimp, and devein, if desired. Chill until time to add to soup.
- **Cook** bacon in a large skillet until crisp; remove bacon, and drain on paper towels, reserving 3 tablespoons drippings in skillet.
- **Sauté** onion in hot drippings 5 to 7 minutes. Stir in bell pepper, jalapeño peppers, and garlic; sauté 7 to 9 minutes or until tender.
- **Stir** in tomatoes and next 3 ingredients. Reduce heat, and simmer, stirring occasionally, 1 hour.
- **Stir** in shrimp, and cook 5 minutes. Serve over hot cooked grits, and sprinkle with bacon. **Yield:** 8 servings.

Dianne Brown
Augusta, Georgia

COCONUT SHRIMP

If you're a fried shrimp lover, this recipe will top your list of favorites.

Prep: 30 minutes
Chill: 1 hour
Cook: 4 minutes

1   **pound unpeeled, large fresh shrimp**
½   **cup cream of coconut**
3   **tablespoons cornstarch**
1   **tablespoon mayonnaise**
1   **tablespoon lemon juice**
1   **teaspoon Worcestershire sauce**
1   **cup cornstarch**
1¼ **cups flaked coconut**
½   **cup fine, dry breadcrumbs**
Vegetable oil

- **Peel** shrimp, leaving tails intact; devein, if desired.
- **Stir** together cream of coconut and next 4 ingredients until smooth.
- **Coat** shrimp with 1 cup cornstarch; dip in cream of coconut mixture; drain on a wire rack.
- **Dredge** shrimp in coconut; dredge in breadcrumbs. Place on a baking sheet; cover and chill 1 hour.
- **Pour** oil to a depth of 2 inches into a Dutch oven; heat to 375°. Fry shrimp, in batches, until golden. Drain. **Yield:** 4 appetizer servings.

Vikki D. Sturm
Rossville, Georgia

A Taste of the South

Count yourself lucky if neighbors or friends offer you some of their fig harvest. Louise Floyd does. "Figs can be real scarce," says the Selma, Alabama, native. When a neighbor shares, Louise captures the flavor by preparing her husband's favorite preserves. "We eat them every morning with toast or biscuits," Louise says.

Lera Townley of Roanoke, Alabama, bottles figs using a sugar syrup. "I like this recipe for what it is," says Lera, "figs, pure and simple."

Shop for figs from late June through October. Handle fresh ones gently, and store them in the refrigerator up to two or three days.

FIG PRESERVES

Prep: 10 minutes
Stand: 8 hours
Cook: 2 hours
Process: 15 minutes

2   **quarts fresh figs (about 4 pounds)**
8   **cups sugar**

- **Layer** figs and sugar in a Dutch oven. Cover and let stand 8 hours.
- **Cook** over medium heat 2 hours, stirring occasionally, until syrup thickens and figs are clear.
- **Pack** hot figs into hot jars, filling to ½ inch from top. Cover fruit with boiling syrup, filling to ½ inch from top. Remove air bubbles; wipe jar rims. Cover jars at once with metal lids, and screw on bands.
- **Process** in boiling-water bath 15 minutes. Cool completely; chill, if desired. **Yield:** 4 quarts.

Lera Townley
Roanoke, Alabama

Quick & Easy

Take time to chill with these salads and desserts. It's easy to savor long evenings and make weeknight meals less harrowing. Just plan ahead and use these recipes that are prepared quickly and chilled or frozen.

Having this kind of head start might even entice you to invite spur-of-the-moment guests for dinner. Allow standing time for Ice Cream-Toffee Dessert and Paper Cup Frozen Salads.

ICE CREAM-TOFFEE DESSERT

Prep: 20 minutes
Freeze: 8 hours
Stand: 30 minutes

2 (3-ounce) packages ladyfingers
2 tablespoons instant coffee
     granules
¼ cup hot water
6 (1.4-ounce) toffee candy bars,
     divided
½ gallon vanilla ice cream,
     softened*
3 tablespoons coffee liqueur (optional)
1 (8-ounce) container frozen whipped
     topping, thawed

• **Stand** ladyfingers around edge of a 9-inch springform pan; line bottom of pan with remaining ladyfingers.
• **Combine** coffee granules and ¼ cup hot water in a small bowl, stirring until dissolved; let cool completely.
• **Chop** 5 candy bars into small pieces. Stir chopped candy and coffee into ice cream. Spoon into prepared pan. Cover with plastic wrap, and freeze 8 hours.
• **Stir** liqueur into whipped topping, if desired. Dollop around edge of ice-cream mixture.

• **Chop** remaining candy bar; sprinkle evenly over top. Let stand 30 minutes before serving. **Yield:** 8 servings.

*Substitute ½ gallon coffee ice cream for vanilla ice cream, if desired; omit coffee granules and water.

Note: For testing purposes only, we used Skor candy bars.

Mrs. Bill Baker
Richardson, Texas

LEMON ICE

Prep: 15 minutes
Freeze: 8 hours, 45 minutes

1 (12-ounce) can frozen lemonade
     concentrate, thawed
3 cups ice cubes
1 cup water
⅓ cup sugar

• **Process** all ingredients in a food processor or blender until smooth. Pour mixture into a 13- x 9-inch pan, and freeze 45 minutes.
• **Process** mixture in a food processor or blender until smooth. Return to pan, and freeze 8 hours. **Yield:** 4 cups.

Agnes L. Stone
Ocala, Florida

PAPER CUP FROZEN SALADS

Prep: 15 minutes
Freeze: 8 hours
Stand: 15 minutes

2 cups sour cream
1 (8-ounce) can crushed pineapple,
     drained
½ cup sugar
2 tablespoons lemon juice
Dash of salt
4 drops red liquid food coloring
¼ cup chopped pecans,
     toasted
1 (16-ounce) can pitted cherries,
     drained

• **Stir** together first 5 ingredients in a large bowl.
• **Stir** in food coloring, pecans, and cherries.
• **Place** paper baking cups in a muffin pan; spoon fruit mixture evenly into paper cups.
• **Cover** and freeze 8 hours. Remove from freezer, and let stand 15 minutes before serving. **Yield:** 1 dozen.

Margaret Jahns
Tarpon Springs, Florida

APPLE SALAD

Prep: 35 minutes
Chill: 3 hours

2 cups boiling water
1 (3-ounce) package lemon gelatin
20 large marshmallows
½ cup cold water
2 Red Delicious apples, diced
½ cup chopped pecans
Frozen whipped topping, thawed

• **Stir** together first 3 ingredients until blended. Add ½ cup cold water, and chill 30 minutes or until consistency of unbeaten egg white.
• **Stir** in apple and pecans. Pour mixture into a 9-inch square dish. Cover and chill 3 hours or until firm. Serve with whipped topping. **Yield:** 6 servings.

Bunnie George
Birmingham, Alabama

All-American Cookout

A good, old-fashioned outdoor get-together with family and friends is a great way to celebrate America's Independence Day. These recipes include new twists on familiar Fourth favorites, such as ribs and steak, that will satisfy hungry party-goers.

ADAMS' RIBS

Perfect for any gathering, this spicy-sweet recipe originally appeared in Southern Living in September 1995.

Prep: 30 minutes
Grill: 2 hours, 30 minutes

Hickory chunks
1 tablespoon garlic powder
1 tablespoon Creole seasoning
2 tablespoons pepper
1 tablespoon Worcestershire sauce
5 pounds spareribs
Grill Basting Sauce
The Sauce

• **Soak** wood chunks in water to cover 30 minutes. Drain.
• **Prepare** a hot fire by piling charcoal on 1 side of grill, leaving other side empty. Place wood chunks on charcoal. Place food rack on grill.
• **Combine** garlic powder and next 3 ingredients, and rub on all sides of ribs. Arrange ribs over unlit side of grill.
• **Grill,** covered with grill lid, 2 to 2½ hours, basting with Grill Basting Sauce during last 30 minutes. Turn once after basting. Serve with The Sauce. **Yield:** 10 to 12 servings.

Note: For testing purposes only, we used Zatarain's Creole seasoning.

Grill Basting Sauce

Prep: 5 minutes
Cook: 1 hour

2¾ cups red wine vinegar
1¾ cups water
¾ cup dry white wine
¾ cup ketchup
¼ cup prepared mustard
¼ cup Worcestershire sauce
¼ cup firmly packed brown sugar
2 to 4 tablespoons salt
2 tablespoons dried crushed red pepper
2 tablespoons ground black pepper

• **Cook** all ingredients in a saucepan over medium heat, stirring occasionally, 1 hour. **Yield:** 6 cups.

The Sauce

Prep: 5 minutes
Cook: 18 minutes

1 tablespoon butter or margarine
1 medium onion, finely chopped
4 garlic cloves, minced
1 cup ketchup
½ cup white vinegar
¼ cup lemon juice
¼ cup steak seasoning
2 tablespoons brown sugar
1 tablespoon Cajun seasoning
2 tablespoons liquid smoke

• **Melt** butter in a large skillet over medium-high heat; add onion, and sauté until tender.
• **Add** garlic and remaining ingredients; reduce heat, and simmer 15 minutes. **Yield:** 2½ cups.

Note: For testing purposes only, we used Dale's for steak seasoning and Luzianne Cajun seasoning.

FLANK STEAK WITH CHILI BUTTER

Prep: 10 minutes
Chill: 8 hours
Grill: 16 minutes

1 (2-pound) flank steak
Southwestern Marinade
Chili Butter
Garnish: red jalapeño peppers

• **Place** flank steak in a shallow dish or heavy-duty zip-top plastic bag, and add Southwestern Marinade. Cover or seal, and chill 8 hours, turning occasionally.
• **Remove** steak from marinade, discarding marinade.
• **Grill,** covered with grill lid, over medium-high heat (350° to 400°) 7 to 8 minutes on each side or to desired degree of doneness. Cut steak diagonally across the grain into thin strips. Serve with Chili Butter. Garnish, if desired. **Yield:** 8 servings.

Southwestern Marinade

Prep: 5 minutes

1 small onion, finely chopped
3 garlic cloves, minced
2 tablespoons chopped fresh cilantro
½ cup olive oil
¼ cup lime juice
2 tablespoons Worcestershire sauce
2 teaspoons sugar
1 teaspoon salt
1 teaspoon ground cumin
1 teaspoon pepper

• **Stir** together all ingredients in a bowl. **Yield:** 1¼ cups.

Chili Butter

Prep: 5 minutes

1 cup butter or margarine, softened
1 garlic clove, minced
2 tablespoons chili powder
¼ teaspoon ground cumin
¼ teaspoon hot sauce

• **Combine** all ingredients. **Yield:** 1 cup.

What's for Supper?

When it's too hot to step into the kitchen, try these tasty solutions. Add a crisp salad and sandwich to the menu, and declare it a No-Cook Day.

Keep items on hand such as deli-sliced turkey and canned navy beans for sandwich fixings. Marinate leftover potatoes, pasta, or grilled chicken in Italian dressing to use for salads. Serve an antipasto tray, supermarket-steamed shrimp, and fruit for a refreshing meal. And check the deli for prepared items that you can quickly dress up.

WHITE BEAN SPREAD WITH CREAMY CUCUMBER SAUCE

Shredded lettuce may be added to this pita. No-bake cookies and lemonade complete the cooling effect.

Prep: 25 minutes
Chill: 2 hours

1 small cucumber, peeled, seeded, and chopped
1 (8-ounce) container sour cream
¼ teaspoon salt
1 garlic clove, pressed
3 (16-ounce) cans navy beans, rinsed and drained
1 (4-ounce) package crumbled feta cheese
¼ cup uncooked regular oats
½ teaspoon salt
½ teaspoon freshly ground pepper
½ teaspoon minced fresh rosemary
6 pita rounds, quartered

• **Stir** together first 4 ingredients; cover and chill 2 hours.
• **Beat** beans and next 5 ingredients at medium speed with an electric mixer until blended. Spread on pita bread; top with cucumber sauce. **Yield:** 6 servings.

MARINATED GARDEN SALAD

Prep: 15 minutes
Chill: 1 hour

3 medium tomatoes
1 green bell pepper
1 small purple onion
1 medium cucumber
1 cup kalamata olives
¼ cup olive oil
2 tablespoons red wine vinegar
½ teaspoon salt
¼ teaspoon pepper
¼ teaspoon dried oregano
2 (4-ounce) packages crumbled feta cheese
1 (2-ounce) can anchovies, drained (optional)
Lettuce leaves (optional)

• **Cut** each tomato into 8 wedges. Slice bell pepper and onion into rings. Peel and slice cucumber.
• **Combine** tomato, bell pepper, onion, cucumber, and olives.
• **Whisk** together oil and next 4 ingredients; drizzle over vegetables, and toss. Serve immediately, or cover and chill 1 hour. Sprinkle with cheese; top with anchovies, if desired. Serve salad on lettuce leaves, if desired. **Yield:** 6 to 8 servings.

Mary Pappas
Richmond, Virginia

TURKEY-SPINACH ROLLUPS

Cut rollups into 1-inch pieces to serve as appetizers or small snacks.

Prep: 12 minutes

1 (8-ounce) package cream cheese, softened
3 tablespoons chutney
2 tablespoons mayonnaise
8 (8-inch) flour tortillas
1 pound thinly sliced cooked turkey
1 bunch green onions, chopped
1 (6-ounce) package fresh spinach

• **Stir** together first 3 ingredients, and spread evenly over tortillas. Top with turkey, onions, and spinach.
• **Roll** tortillas tightly, and cut in half. **Yield**: 8 servings.

Merle Dunson
Taylors, South Carolina

SHRIMP WITH TARTAR SAUCE

Serve this sauce with fish or chicken or as a spread on roast beef sandwiches.

Prep: 5 minutes
Chill: 1 hour

1 cup mayonnaise
1½ tablespoons Dijon mustard
1 (3-ounce) jar green peppercorns, drained
2 garlic cloves, pressed
¾ pound unpeeled, medium-size fresh shrimp, steamed

• **Process** first 4 ingredients in a blender or food processor until smooth. Cover and chill 1 hour. Serve with shrimp. **Yield:** 2 to 3 servings.

Glenwood Wilkes
Lillington, North Carolina

Living Light

Trying to eat less and lose weight? You can just skip breakfast and lunch and then eat a big supper, right? Wrong. Eating a nutritious breakfast is one of the most important things you can do (besides exercising) to rev up your metabolism. Simply put, if you burn more calories than you eat, weight loss will follow. Eating a nutritious breakfast promotes mental alertness and sets a healthy standard for the rest of the day. Here are some quick breakfast ideas for rushed weekdays and light treats for relaxed weekends.

ENGLISH MUFFIN FRENCH TOAST

Serve this with your favorite fruit for a satisfying start to the day.

Prep: 5 minutes
Chill: 8 hours
Cook: 18 minutes

1 cup egg substitute
1 cup fat-free milk
1 teaspoon vanilla extract
6 English muffins, split
Vegetable cooking spray
Chopped kiwifruit, blueberries, nectarines, strawberries (optional)
Garnish: fresh mint sprigs

• **Stir** together first 3 ingredients. Place in a gallon-size zip-top plastic bag; add English muffins. Seal and chill 8 hours, turning occasionally. Remove muffins from bag, discarding remaining liquid.
• **Cook** English muffins, in batches, in a large skillet coated with cooking spray over medium-high heat 2 to 3 minutes on each side or until muffins are golden. Serve with light pancake syrup and, if desired, kiwifruit, blueberries, nectarines, and strawberries. Garnish, if desired. **Yield:** 6 servings.

♥ Per serving: Calories 326 (8% from fat)
Fat 3g (sat 0.7g, mono 0.4g, poly 0.2g)
Protein 15.2g Carb 60g Fiber 2.3g
Chol 5mg Iron 3mg
Sodium 468mg Calc 309mg

BREAKFAST-STUFFED POTATOES

Prep: 1 hour
Bake: 15 minutes

6 (4-ounce) Yukon gold potatoes
¼ cup fat-free half-and-half
4 ounces fat-free cream cheese, softened
2 tablespoons grated Parmesan cheese
¼ teaspoon garlic salt
¼ teaspoon freshly ground pepper
4 turkey bacon slices, diced
½ small sweet onion, chopped
½ (10-ounce) package frozen chopped broccoli, thawed and drained
¼ cup (1 ounce) reduced-fat shredded Cheddar cheese

• **Bake** potatoes at 400° for 35 to 40 minutes or until tender; cool slightly.
• **Cut** potatoes in half crosswise; gently scoop out pulp, leaving a ¼-inch-thick shell and reserving pulp. Stand potato shells, cut side up, in miniature muffin pan cups.
• **Stir** together reserved pulp, half-and-half, and next 4 ingredients.
• **Cook** bacon in a nonstick skillet over medium-high heat 2 to 3 minutes or until browned.
• **Add** onion and broccoli; sauté 4 to 5 minutes or until tender. Stir into potato mixture.
• **Stuff** mixture evenly into potato shells. Sprinkle with Cheddar cheese.
• **Bake** stuffed potatoes at 350° for 15 minutes. **Yield:** 6 servings.

♥ Per serving: Calories 239 (30% from fat)
Fat 7.9g (sat 3.1g, mono 2.7g, poly 1.4g)
Protein 15g Carb 24.4g Fiber 2.5g
Chol 36mg Iron 1.1mg
Sodium 840mg Calc 211mg

GET-UP-AND-GO SHAKE

Prep: 5 minutes

2 cups low-fat soy milk *
1 (8-ounce) container vanilla low-fat yogurt
½ cup frozen apple juice concentrate, thawed
4 large peaches, diced and frozen (about 2 cups)
½ teaspoon vanilla extract

• **Process** all ingredients in a blender until smooth, stopping to scrape down sides. **Yield:** about 5 cups.

♥ Per cup: Calories 162 (7% from fat)
Fat 1.3g (sat 0.4g) Protein 5.9g
Carb 31g Fiber 1.1g
Chol 2mg Iron 0.5mg
Sodium 67mg Calc 184mg

Double Strawberry Shake: Substitute strawberry yogurt for vanilla yogurt and 2 cups frozen strawberries for 4 large peaches.

Tropical Shake: Substitute piña colada yogurt for vanilla yogurt, 2 cups frozen pineapple chunks for peaches, and pineapple-orange juice concentrate for apple juice concentrate.

* Substitute fat-free milk for soy milk, if desired.

Note: For testing purposes only, we used White Wave Silk Plain Soymilk.

From Our Kitchen

Peas Under Pressure

Fresh and dried Southern peas cook quickly in a pressure cooker. Try this method with fresh pink-eyed, black-eyed, field, or crowder peas. Place ½ cup water and 2½ cups peas in a pressure cooker over medium-high heat. Close lid securely. Following manufacturer's directions, bring to high pressure (about 10 to 12 minutes); cook 3 minutes. For dried peas, reduce heat to low after cooker has reached high pressure; cook 15 minutes. Remove from heat; cool and open according to manufacturer's directions. After you open the pressure cooker, bring the peas to a boil for a few minutes to cook down the broth and enhance the flavor.

Tips and Tidbits

■ Vanessa McNeil of our Test Kitchen staff removes the gills—the dark brown fibers on the underside of the cap—from portobello mushrooms before cooking. This keeps the juices and other ingredients in the recipe from turning black.

■ Dottie Wicklund of Largo, Florida, shares this tip for those who store flour in the freezer. "When you plan to bake," she writes, "measure out the flour, bring it to room temperature, and measure again. When you remeasure you'll have flour leftover. Cold flour is more dense and does not give a true measure."

■ Jan Moon of our Test Kitchen staff likes no-cook lasagna noodles because they're a great time-saver. You'll find them on the shelves with regular dried pasta. But sometimes the pasta may still be slightly undercooked. Jan advises, "While you gather ingredients, soak noodles in warm water for 3 to 4 minutes. This allows the pasta to absorb just enough moisture to make the noodles flexible and easy to handle, so they bake consistently. The lasagna can be baked uncovered, and the noodles will be perfectly cooked."

ALL ABOUT SHRIMP

Shrimp Stats

"The Lure of Shrimp" (pages 174-175) gives terrific ways to prepare this seafood. Here are a few tips for handling it.

■ Shrimp with heads are more perishable than those without. Keep them iced, and use soon after purchase. Remove heads, then follow recipe instructions.

■ Buy only as much shrimp as you need. However, when you must store them, follow these tips. Rinse raw shrimp under cold running water, and drain. Store in an airtight container or heavy-duty zip-top plastic bag in the refrigerator up to two days. You may safely keep cooked shrimp up to three days in the refrigerator.

■ Freeze shrimp in airtight containers or heavy-duty zip-top freezer bags. (Frozen shrimp start to lose quality after three months.) Thaw them under cold running water or in the refrigerator overnight. Drain and pat dry with paper towels.

■ Large shrimp have large veins you'll want to remove. Cut a tiny slit down the back of the shrimp—near the vein—for fast and easy removal. This is especially quick if done under cold running water.

■ One pound of shrimp in the shell serves two for a main course or four as an appetizer. Without the shells, 1 pound serves two to three as a main course or four to six as a first course.

Boiled Shrimp—Not Exactly

■ To serve perfectly cooked, tender shrimp, don't boil them. Drop them into a large pot of boiling water, and bring water back to a boil. Cover and remove pot from heat; let shrimp stand 3 to 5 minutes (depending on size) or until shrimp turn pink. Timing is everything; overcooked shrimp are tough and rubbery.

■ If you're serving the shrimp hot, drain and transfer them to a serving dish. If you like them chilled, drain and transfer them to a large heavy-duty zip-top plastic bag; surround the bag with ice. Don't rinse or drop shrimp in cold water because you'll wash away the seasonings.

■ Take your pick from a large selection of shrimp boils and seafood seasonings. They typically have a mild spicy flavor with a hint of pickling spices. You may substitute beer for some of the water for a richer flavor. Some liquid seasonings range from medium to hot, so use sparingly. Old Bay seafood seasoning is a favorite because of its spicy heat and onion and celery flavors. Try several brands and types before you settle on one. Read the packages carefully; some need no additional salt.

Bottled Barbecue Sauces

If you don't make your own sauce, try these: **Mad Dog Original BBQ Sauce,** Ashley Food Company, Inc., 1-800-378-4359 or www.ashleyfood.com. When you want one that rocks with a grilled steak, try **Virginia Gentleman Bourbon Steak Sauce,** Ashman Manufacturing Company, 1-800-641-9924 or www.ashmanco.com.

AUGUST

Legacy of Summer

With a perfect balance of sweet and tart, heirloom tomatoes possess an invigorating taste like nothing else—a flavor we dream of for most of the year.

FRESH TOMATO DRESSING
(pictured on page 191)

Mix-and-match a variety of heirlooms such as the sweet and fruity Sun Gold or Snow White with a more tart variety such as Green Zebra.

Prep: 20 minutes
Stand: 1 hour
Chill: 8 hours

1 cup olive oil
½ cup balsamic vinegar
3 garlic cloves, sliced
1 tablespoon sugar
1 tablespoon salt
1 teaspoon pepper
4 large tomatoes, peeled and chopped
2 tablespoons fresh thyme leaves or 4 thyme sprigs

• **Whisk** together first 6 ingredients in a large glass bowl.
• **Stir** in tomato and thyme. Cover and let stand at room temperature 1 hour, stirring occasionally. Cover and chill 8 hours. **Yield:** 4 cups.

Note: Dressing may be stored in refrigerator up to 1 month. Stir additional fresh chopped tomato into dressing after each use.

TOMATO NAPOLEON
(pictured on page 191)

An Amish heirloom since 1885, the pink-red Brandywine is a terrific choice for this salad because of its rich and spicy flavor.

Prep: 30 minutes
Chill: 1 hour

8 ounces fresh mozzarella cheese, cut into 8 slices
¾ cup Fresh Tomato Dressing (recipe at left)
3 large tomatoes, each cut into 4 slices
1 teaspoon salt
1 teaspoon pepper
24 fresh basil leaves, shredded

• **Place** mozzarella cheese in a shallow dish. Pour Fresh Tomato Dressing over cheese; cover and chill 1 hour.
• **Remove** cheese slices, reserving Fresh Tomato Dressing marinade.
• **Sprinkle** tomato slices evenly with salt and pepper.
• **Place** 1 tomato slice on each of 4 salad plates, and top each with 1 cheese slice and 2 shredded basil leaves. Repeat with tomato slice, cheese slice, and basil leaves.
• **Top** with remaining tomato slice and basil. Drizzle evenly with reserved Fresh Tomato Dressing marinade. **Yield:** 4 servings.

FLOYD'S FAVORITE TOMATO SANDWICH

Large heirloom beefsteak varieties such as Red Brandywine and Aunt Ginny's Purple slice well for sandwiches and have a classic rich and juicy tomato flavor.

Prep: 10 minutes
Chill: 8 hours

1 large ripe tomato, peeled
1 large onion
3 tablespoons mayonnaise
1 tablespoon prepared mustard
16 sandwich bread slices
⅛ teaspoon salt
⅛ teaspoon pepper

• **Cut** tomato and onion into 8 (¼-inch-thick) slices each. Layer in a shallow dish. Cover; chill 8 hours. Discard onion.
• **Stir** together mayonnaise and mustard; spread on 1 side of bread slices. Place 1 tomato slice on each of 8 bread slices; sprinkle lightly with salt and pepper. Top with remaining bread slices. Cover and chill up to 2 days. **Yield:** 8 sandwiches.

TOMATOES AND OKRA

Smaller amounts of seeds and juice make the meaty yet flavorful Oxheart varieties such as Jefferson Giant and Anna Russian perfect for sautéing.

Prep: 30 minute
Cook: 15 minutes

1 large sweet onion, chopped
2 tablespoons bacon drippings or olive oil
3 large tomatoes, chopped
1 pound fresh okra, chopped
1 teaspoon salt
1 teaspoon pepper

• **Sauté** onion in hot bacon drippings in a Dutch oven over medium-high heat 5 minutes or until tender.
• **Stir** in tomato and remaining ingredients. Reduce heat, and cook, stirring often, 10 minutes or until okra is tender. **Yield:** 8 servings.

SCALLOPED TOMATOES

With its sweet and tangy flavor, the red, banana pepper-shaped Opalka tomato is great for baking and sauce-making.

Prep: 10 minutes
Bake: 30 minutes

2 medium-size red bell peppers, halved
4 large tomatoes, peeled and cut into ¼-inch-thick slices
1 teaspoon salt
½ teaspoon pepper
1 cup Italian-seasoned breadcrumbs
½ cup grated Parmesan cheese
1 tablespoon fresh thyme leaves
½ cup olive oil

• **Place** bell pepper halves, cut sides down, on an aluminum foil-lined baking sheet.
• **Bake** at 425° for 10 minutes or until peppers look blistered.
• **Place** peppers in a heavy-duty zip-top plastic bag; seal bag, and let stand 10 minutes to loosen skins. Peel peppers; remove and discard seeds.
• **Sprinkle** tomato slices evenly with salt and pepper; sprinkle ¼ cup breadcrumbs in bottom of a lightly greased 9-inch deep-dish pieplate, and top with one-fourth of tomato slices.
• **Sprinkle** tomatoes with ¼ cup breadcrumbs and one-third of cheese. Repeat layer with tomatoes, breadcrumbs, and cheese.
• **Top** with roasted peppers, remaining breadcrumbs, and cheese; sprinkle with thyme leaves, and drizzle with oil.
• **Bake** at 475° for 30 minutes. Cool to room temperature. Chill, if desired. **Yield:** 8 servings.

SOWING THE SEEDS

Heirlooms are handed down from generation to generation in an effort to preserve part of our heritage and history. We cherish such things as old family photos, special pieces of furniture, lovely sets of china and crystal, and in the South even tomato seeds.

Bearing odd-sounding names such as Banana Legs, Cape Gooseberry, and German Johnson, heirloom tomatoes burst with flavors that many of us have only heard about from our parents and grandparents.

Unlike the commercially produced hybrids—those year-round stand-ins developed to tolerate shipping, to be perfectly shaped, and to ripen after harvest—these summer gems are purebred, prized for their diversity in tastes and singular shapes.

Vanessa McNeil, a member of our Test Kitchens staff, found a way to capture the essence of the season in her Fresh Tomato Dressing and Tomato Napoleon— both received our highest rating. Even if heirloom tomatoes aren't available in your area, you can still enjoy these delicious recipes by using vine-ripened garden tomatoes from your favorite produce stand. **Tip:** To save time when peeling tomatoes, give them a quick dip in boiling water followed by a plunge in ice water to loosen their skins.

If you don't grow your own heirloom vegetables, or they aren't available in your local market, contact The Chef's Garden at 1-800-289-4644.

You can order heirloom seeds by telephone or on the Internet from the following companies.

■ Shepherd's Garden Seeds: (860) 482-3638
www.shepherdseeds.com

■ The Cook's Garden: 1-800-457-9703
www.cooksgarden.com

■ Southern Exposure Seed Exchange: (540) 894-9480
www.southernexposure.com

■ Tomato Growers Supply Company: 1-888-478-7333 (toll free)
www.tomatogrowers.com

STEWED TOMATOES

Perfect for cooking and canning, Bradley and Box Car Willie heirloom varieties have the right balance of size, sweet flavor, and subtle acidity.

Prep: 10 minutes
Cook: 1 hour

4 large tomatoes, peeled, seeded, and chopped *
½ cup butter or margarine
¾ cup sugar

• **Bring** all ingredients to a boil in a non-aluminum 3-quart saucepan; reduce heat, and simmer, stirring often, 1 hour or until thickened. Serve hot over black-eyed peas, turnip greens, or cornbread, if desired. **Yield:** 2 cups.

*Substitute 2 (14½-ounce) cans diced tomatoes for fresh, if desired.

Martha Sharpe
Humboldt, Tennessee

Top-Rated Menu

For a scrumptious summer meal, combine these winning recipes from our 1996 Recipe Hall of Fame with your favorite cornbread. Try a juicy slice of watermelon for dessert.

Summer Vegetable Supper
Serves 4

Butterbeans, Bacon, and Tomatoes
Buttermilk Fried Corn   Edna's Greens
Cornbread   Watermelon slices

BUTTERBEANS, BACON, AND TOMATOES
(pictured on facing page)

1996 Recipe Hall of Fame

Prep: 20 minutes
Cook: 1 hour

3 bacon slices, chopped
1 medium onion, finely chopped
1 small green bell pepper, chopped
3 garlic cloves, minced
1 bay leaf
3 medium-size tomatoes, chopped
4 cups chicken broth
4 cups fresh or frozen butterbeans, thawed
2 tablespoons minced fresh parsley
1 teaspoon salt
1 teaspoon pepper
1 teaspoon Worcestershire sauce
½ teaspoon hot sauce

• **Cook** bacon in a Dutch oven until crisp. Stir in onion and next 3 ingredients; sauté until vegetables are tender. Stir in tomato, and cook 3 minutes.

• **Stir** in broth and butterbeans; bring to a boil. Cover, reduce heat, and simmer, stirring occasionally, 30 minutes.

• **Simmer,** uncovered, 20 minutes, stirring often. Stir in parsley and remaining ingredients. Cook, stirring often, 5 minutes. Discard bay leaf. **Yield:** 6 servings.

BUTTERMILK FRIED CORN
(pictured on facing page)

1996 Recipe Hall of Fame

Prep: 15 minutes
Stand: 30 minutes
Cook: 16 minutes

3 cups fresh corn kernels
2¼ cups buttermilk
1 cup all-purpose flour
1 cup cornmeal
1 teaspoon salt
1½ teaspoons pepper
Corn oil

• **Stir** together corn and buttermilk; let stand 30 minutes. Drain.

• **Combine** flour and next 3 ingredients in a large heavy-duty zip-top plastic bag. Add corn to flour mixture, a small amount at a time, and shake bag to coat.

• **Pour** oil to a depth of 1 inch in a Dutch oven; heat to 375°. Fry corn, in small batches, 2 minutes or until golden. Drain on paper towels. Serve immediately. **Yield:** 3 cups.

EDNA'S GREENS
(pictured on facing page)

1996 Recipe Hall of Fame

Prep: 5 minutes
Cook: 1 hour, 20 minutes

¾ pound salt pork (streak of lean) or smoked pork shoulder
3 quarts water
¼ teaspoon freshly ground pepper
3 (16-ounce) bags frozen collard or turnip greens ✱

• **Slice** pork at ¼-inch intervals, cutting to, but not through, the skin. Bring pork, 3 quarts water, and pepper to a boil in a large Dutch oven. Cover, reduce heat, and simmer 1 hour. Add greens, and cook 20 minutes or until tender. Serve using a slotted spoon. **Yield:** 4 servings.

✱ Substitute 4½ pounds fresh greens (collard, turnip, or mustard), if desired. Remove stems and discolored spots from greens. Wash greens thoroughly; drain and cut into strips. Cook according to above directions.

PLAN AHEAD

Cooking a main plate of vegetables takes time (about 1 hour and 30 minutes) and an empty dishwasher. You'll agree, though, that this meal is well worth the effort and a few dirty pots and pans.

Edna's Greens; Buttermilk Fried Corn;
Butterbeans, Bacon, and Tomatoes
served with cornbread, facing page

From top: Minted Tea Punch, Summer Vegetable-and-Orzo Salad, Corn Salsa, Cheese Wafers, pages 164-165

Summer Vegetable-and-Orzo Salad, page 165

Minted Tea Punch, page 164

Cheese Wafers, page 164

Grilled Chicken Salad Sandwiches, Grilled Asparagus, Summer Vegetable-and-Orzo Salad, pages 164-165

Fried Okra, page 205

Tangy Green Beans With Pimiento, page 170

Polly's Baked Brisket, Potato Salad
served with a mixed green salad and
dinner roll, pages 194-195

Chowchow, page 158

Pink-Eyed Pea Salsa served with a grilled
pork chop and tomato slices, page 158

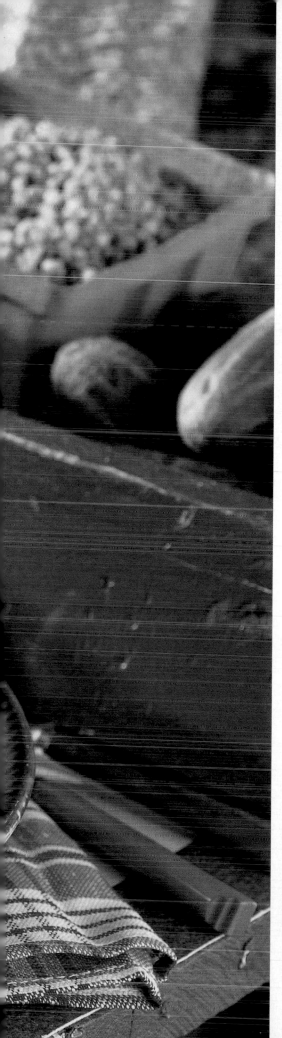

Tomato Napoleon, Fresh Tomato Dressing, page 182

Herbed Vegetable Medley, page 138

191

Cinnamon Toasty Fruity Delight, facing page

Breakfast for Supper

Soccer practice ran late, a neighbor stopped to chat, and choir practice starts in an hour. One child needs homework help, another needs a bath, and the boss expects that big assignment tomorrow. Sound familiar? We've got an answer. Treat yourself to breakfast for supper.

There's something about French toast that brings a certain comfort to crazy days. Nothing fussy or complicated, just straightforward goodness from your pantry to the table. So, when life becomes a blur, breakfast for supper may be just the break you need. When your life is racing ninety-to-nothing, these meals are ready in no time flat.

BREAKFAST PIZZA

Prep: 8 minutes
Bake: 20 minutes

1 (8-ounce) package shredded Italian cheese blend, divided
1 (16-ounce) Italian bread shell
8 bacon slices, cooked and crumbled
4 plum tomatoes, sliced
½ teaspoon freshly ground pepper
2 large eggs
½ cup milk
¼ cup chopped fresh basil

• **Sprinkle** half of cheese over Italian bread shell; top with bacon, tomato, and pepper.
• **Whisk** together eggs, milk, and basil; pour in center of pizza (it will spread to edges). Sprinkle with remaining cheese.
• **Bake** at 425° for 20 minutes or until set. **Yield:** 4 to 6 servings.

Katie Moon
Birmingham, Alabama

STUFFED FRENCH TOAST

Prep: 20 minutes
Stand: 10 minutes
Bake: 25 minutes

1 (16-ounce) French bread loaf, cut into 18 slices
1 pound thinly sliced cooked ham, diced
9 (¾-ounce) Swiss cheese slices
6 large eggs
1½ cups milk
2 tablespoons orange juice
1 teaspoon vanilla extract
¼ cup butter or margarine
¼ cup powdered sugar (optional)

• **Place** 9 bread slices in a single layer in a lightly greased 13- x 9-inch baking dish; top evenly with ham, cheese, and remaining bread slices.
• **Whisk** together eggs and next 3 ingredients; pour over bread slices. Let stand 10 minutes, turning once.
• **Melt** 2 tablespoons butter in a large skillet over medium-high heat; add half of French toast, and cook 1 to 2 minutes on each side. Place on a lightly greased 15- x 10-inch jellyroll pan. Repeat procedure with remaining butter and French toast.
• **Bake** at 375° for 20 to 25 minutes or until golden. Sprinkle with powdered sugar, if desired. **Yield:** 9 servings.

Judith Reilly
Amherst, Virginia

CINNAMON TOASTY FRUITY DELIGHT
(pictured on facing page)

Prep: 15 minutes
Cook: 16 minutes

2 cups pancake mix
1½ cups water
1 teaspoon vanilla extract
¼ teaspoon ground cinnamon
2 tablespoons butter or margarine
2 tablespoons vegetable oil
8 cinnamon bread slices
2 bananas, sliced
¼ cup chopped pecans, toasted
Maple syrup
Garnish: fresh strawberries

• **Whisk** together first 4 ingredients.
• **Melt** ½ tablespoon butter and ½ tablespoon oil in a large skillet over medium heat. Dip 2 bread slices in batter; cook 2 to 3 minutes on each side or until golden. Repeat procedure with remaining butter, oil, bread slices, and batter.
• **Top** with bananas and pecans. Serve with maple syrup. Garnish, if desired. **Yield:** 4 servings.

Note: For testing purposes only, we used Pepperidge Farm Cinnamon Swirl Bread.

Zita Wilensky
North Miami, Florida

SPICED BREAKFAST APPLES

Prep: 10 minutes
Cook: 20 minutes

¼ cup butter or margarine
5 large Granny Smith apples, peeled, cored, and sliced
1 cup sugar
1 teaspoon ground cinnamon
¼ teaspoon ground nutmeg

• **Melt** butter in a large skillet over medium-high heat; add apple and remaining ingredients. Sauté 15 to 20 minutes or until apple is tender. **Yield:** 4 to 6 servings.

Ellen Miller Crow
Texarkana, Texas

MEXICAN BREAKFAST

This hearty breakfast casserole will have your family lining up for seconds. And its savory sauce takes only five minutes to make!

Prep: 30 minutes
Bake: 30 minutes

1 pound ground pork sausage
2 tablespoons butter or margarine
6 eggs, lightly beaten
¼ cup cottage cheese
3 green onion tops, chopped
1 tablespoon chopped fresh parsley
Sour Cream Sauce
8 (7-inch) flour tortillas
1 cup (4 ounces) shredded Cheddar cheese
1 cup (4 ounces) shredded Monterey Jack cheese

• **Cook** sausage in a large skillet, stirring until it crumbles and is no longer pink; drain and wipe skillet clean.
• **Melt** butter in a large skillet over medium heat; add eggs and next 3 ingredients to skillet.
• **Cook,** without stirring, until eggs begin to set on bottom.
• **Draw** a spatula across bottom of skillet to form large curds. Continue cooking until eggs are thickened but still moist. Remove from heat.
• **Stir** in sausage and 2 tablespoons Sour Cream Sauce.
• **Spread** 1 cup Sour Cream Sauce evenly into a lightly greased 13- x 9-inch baking dish.
• **Spoon** egg mixture evenly down centers of tortillas; roll up.
• **Place** tortillas, seam side down, in prepared dish.
• **Pour** remaining Sour Cream Sauce over tortillas; sprinkle with Cheddar and Monterey Jack cheeses.
• **Bake,** covered, at 325° for 30 minutes or until tortillas are thoroughly heated. **Yield:** 4 to 6 servings.

Sour Cream Sauce

Prep: 5 minutes

1 (10¾-ounce) can cream of mushroom soup, undiluted
1 (8-ounce) container sour cream
1 (4.5-ounce) can chopped green chiles, undrained
2 tablespoons green chile salsa
2 tablespoons chopped fresh cilantro
¼ teaspoon ground cumin

• **Whisk** together all ingredients. **Yield:** 2½ cups.

Lisa Cobb
College Station, Texas

GARLIC GRITS

Prep: 20 minutes
Bake: 1 hour

4 cups water
2 garlic cloves, pressed
1 teaspoon salt
½ teaspoon ground red pepper
1 cup uncooked quick-cooking grits
1 (16-ounce) loaf pasteurized prepared cheese product, cubed
½ cup butter or margarine
2 large eggs
½ cup milk
1 cup cornflake crumbs

• **Bring** first 4 ingredients to a boil in a Dutch oven; gradually stir in grits. Return to a boil; cover, reduce heat, and simmer, stirring occasionally, 5 minutes or until thickened.
• **Add** cheese product and butter, stirring until melted.
• **Whisk** together eggs and milk; stir into grits mixture. Pour into a lightly greased 13- x 9-inch baking dish. Sprinkle with cornflake crumbs.
• **Bake** at 350° for 1 hour or until set. **Yield:** 8 to 10 servings.

Arlene Cox
Elizabethton, Tennessee

Reunions

Their names read like a Who's Who of Cajun culture—Guidry, Hebert, Broussard, Thibodeaux—and their family members are farflung. But during the three weeks of Congrès Mondial last August, thousands of Acadians made their way to Lafayette, Louisiana, and surrounding areas to celebrate family reunions. About 60 families gathered in parks, school auditoriums, relatives' backyards, and even the Cajun Dome. They convened to celebrate a heritage that has sustained them since they were banished from their homes in Acadia in 1755.

And as is typical whenever Cajuns gather, food took center stage—even if the reunion groups were often too large for home cooking. Enjoy these favorite family recipes that members of the Mouton and Richard clans shared with us.

Acadian-Style Supper
Serves 4 to 6

Polly's Baked Brisket
Potato Salad
Mixed green salad   Dinner rolls
Iced tea

POLLY'S BAKED BRISKET
(pictured on page 189)

Prep: 12 minutes
Bake: 3 hours

1 (4.5-pound) untrimmed beef brisket
3 tablespoons olive oil
¼ cup white wine vinegar
2 tablespoons vegetable oil
2 tablespoons ketchup
1 teaspoon salt
2 teaspoons garlic powder
2 teaspoons pepper
1 (1.4-ounce) envelope dry onion soup mix
1 cup water

- **Brown** brisket in hot olive oil over high heat 5 minutes on each side.
- **Place** brisket in a lightly greased 13- x 9-inch pan.
- **Stir** together vinegar and next 6 ingredients; pour over brisket. Add 1 cup water to pan.
- **Bake,** covered, at 350° for 2 hours, basting every hour.
- **Reduce** oven temperature to 300°, and bake brisket 1 more hour.
- **Skim** fat from drippings, discarding fat; serve drippings with brisket. **Yield:** 4 to 6 servings.

Polly Richard
Scott, Louisiana

POTATO SALAD
(pictured on page 189)

Prep: 15 minutes
Cook: 10 minutes
Chill: 2 hours

4 pounds red potatoes (8 large)
5 hard-cooked eggs, separated
1 teaspoon salt, divided
3 green onions, sliced (optional)
1 cup mayonnaise
2 tablespoons sweet pickle relish
1 tablespoon prepared mustard
½ teaspoon pepper

- **Cook** potatoes in boiling water to cover 40 minutes or until tender; drain and cool. Peel potatoes, and cut into 1-inch cubes.
- **Chop** egg whites. Stir together potato cubes, egg whites, ½ teaspoon salt, and, if desired, green onions.
- **Mash** egg yolks; add remaining ½ teaspoon salt, mayonnaise, and next 3 ingredients, stirring until blended. Gently stir into potato mixture. Cover and chill 2 hours. **Yield:** 8 servings.

Louise Mouton Cousin
New Iberia, Louisiana

Quick & Easy

Pesto, a sauce originating in Genoa, Italy, traditionally combines fresh basil, garlic, pine nuts, Parmesan, and olive oil. Today we offer new options, including one with dried tomatoes and sweet red peppers.

Any pesto can be tossed with pasta, spread on sandwiches and pizzas, or served as dip. Mary Jane Bone of El Reno, Oklahoma, even spreads basil pesto on each side of steak before grilling.

If you have an abundance of basil in your garden, make the pesto from Basil Pesto Focaccia to freeze for later. But don't fret if you can't make your own. You'll find pesto at your local grocery.

BASIL PESTO FOCACCIA

Prep: 12 minutes
Bake: 13 minutes

2 tablespoons cornmeal
1 (10-ounce) can refrigerated pizza crust
1 cup fresh basil leaves
½ cup walnuts or pine nuts
1 tablespoon olive oil
1 garlic clove
¼ teaspoon salt
¼ teaspoon pepper
10 cherry tomatoes, halved
½ cup (2 ounces) shredded provolone cheese

- **Sprinkle** cornmeal onto a lightly greased baking sheet. Unroll pizza crust over cornmeal.
- **Bake** at 450° for 8 minutes or until golden brown.
- **Process** basil and next 5 ingredients in a food processor or blender until blended, stopping to scrape down sides. Spread mixture over crust.

- **Arrange** tomato halves, cut side up, over basil mixture. Sprinkle with cheese.
- **Bake** at 450° for 5 minutes or until cheese is melted. Serve immediately. **Yield:** 6 to 8 servings.

Veronica Callaghan
Glastonbury, Connecticut

TOMATO-PESTO TART

Prep: 20 minutes
Bake: 35 minutes

½ (15-ounce) package refrigerated piecrusts
2 cups (8 ounces) shredded mozzarella cheese, divided
5 plum tomatoes, sliced
½ cup mayonnaise
¼ cup grated Parmesan cheese
2 tablespoons basil pesto
½ teaspoon freshly ground pepper
3 tablespoons chopped fresh basil

- **Unfold** piecrust on a lightly greased baking sheet. Roll into a 12-inch circle. Brush outer 1 inch of crust with water. Fold edges up and crimp. Prick bottom.
- **Bake** at 425° for 8 to 10 minutes. Remove from oven. Sprinkle with 1 cup mozzarella cheese; cool 15 minutes. Arrange tomato slices over cheese.
- **Stir** together remaining 1 cup mozzarella cheese, mayonnaise, and next 3 ingredients. Spread over tomato slices.
- **Bake** at 375° for 20 to 25 minutes. Sprinkle with basil. **Yield:** 4 main-dish or 8 appetizer servings.

Pamela Iaquinta
Lancaster, Pennsylvania

CREAMY TOMATO PESTO DIP WITH TORTELLINI

Prep: 30 minutes

4 quarts water
1 (9-ounce) package refrigerated mushroom tortellini
1 (9-ounce) package refrigerated spinach tortellini
1 (9-ounce) package refrigerated tomato tortellini
12 dried tomatoes
1 (8-ounce) package cream cheese, softened
1 (7-ounce) jar roasted sweet red peppers, drained
½ cup shredded Parmesan cheese
2 garlic cloves, minced
6 fresh basil leaves
2 tablespoons olive oil
1 tablespoon lemon juice
¾ teaspoon salt
¼ teaspoon dried crushed red pepper
Green and ripe olives (optional)

• **Bring** 4 quarts water to a boil in a stockpot.
• **Add** pasta, and cook over medium-high heat 5 minutes. Rinse with cold water. Drain; chill, if desired.
• **Place** dried tomatoes in a bowl, and cover with boiling water. Let stand 20 minutes. Drain.
• **Process** tomatoes, cream cheese, and next 8 ingredients in a food processor or blender until smooth, stopping to scrape down sides. Spoon pesto into a bowl, and sprinkle with olives, if desired. Serve with tortellini. **Yield:** 20 appetizer servings.

Liz Barclay
Annapolis, Maryland

The Brothers Rathbun

Kent and Kevin Rathbun share a passion for making good food that keeps their restaurants on the short list of the South's best places to eat. Scrumptious food, accompanied by their wonderful stories, gave us a peek into the hearts of this talented duo.

Award-winning chefs/restaurateurs, these talented brothers are bright stars on the culinary horizon. In their separate kitchens in Atlanta and Dallas, they are serious, no-nonsense perfectionists. But when together, they play with their food during constant good-natured teasing and uncontrollable laughter. If you can't get to one of their restaurants, have a taste of their food with these recipes.

RIB EYES WITH RED PEPPER-POLENTA FRIES AND CHILE CORN JUS

Prep: 45 minutes
Cook: 13 minutes
Chill: 2 hours

8 (10-ounce) rib-eye steaks
1 tablespoon vegetable oil
½ teaspoon salt
½ teaspoon pepper
Red Pepper-Polenta Fries
Chile Corn Jus

• **Rub** steaks evenly with oil. Sprinkle with salt and pepper.
• **Grill** steaks, covered with grill lid, over medium-high heat (350° to 400°) 5 minutes on each side or to desired degree of doneness. Serve steaks with Red Pepper-Polenta Fries and Chile Corn Jus. **Yield:** 8 servings.

Red Pepper-Polenta Fries

Prep: 20 minutes
Chill: 2 hours
Fry: 3 minutes per batch

1 tablespoon butter or margarine
1 small onion, diced
1 small red bell pepper, minced
1 cup whipping cream
1 cup chicken broth
1½ cups yellow cornmeal, divided
3 tablespoons shredded Monterey Jack cheese
1 tablespoon chopped fresh cilantro
3 cups peanut oil
1 teaspoon salt

• **Melt** butter in a large skillet over medium-high heat; add onion and bell pepper, and sauté 3 minutes or until tender. Stir in cream and broth; bring to a boil. Add 1 cup cornmeal; cook, whisking often, 3 to 5 minutes or until mixture is very thick. Remove from heat. Stir in cheese and cilantro.
• **Spoon** polenta into a lightly greased 9- x 5-inch loafpan. Cover; chill 2 hours.
• **Cut** polenta into ½-inch-thick slices; cut each slice into 4 strips. Sprinkle evenly with remaining ½ cup cornmeal.
• **Pour** peanut oil into a Dutch oven, and heat to 375°. Add polenta strips, and fry, in batches, 3 minutes or until golden brown. Drain on paper towels. Sprinkle with salt. **Yield:** 8 servings.

Chile Corn Jus

Prep: 15 minutes
Cook: 5 minutes

1   ear fresh corn
2   plum tomatoes, diced
2   tablespoons minced onion
¼   medium ancho chile pepper,
     chopped
2   tablespoons butter or margarine
¼   cup chicken broth
1   teaspoon chopped fresh cilantro
¼   teaspoon salt
¼   teaspoon pepper

• **Cut** corn kernels from cob.
• **Cook** corn in a lightly greased skillet over medium-high heat 3 minutes.
• **Stir** in tomato and remaining ingredients. Reduce heat, and simmer 2 minutes. **Yield:** 1 cup.

Kevin Rathbun
Atlanta, Georgia

Lobster Scallion Shooters

Prep: 1 hour
Cook: 20 minutes

2   (10-ounce) lobster tails,
     steamed
4   garlic cloves, minced
2   shallots, minced
1   stalk lemongrass, minced*
1   tablespoon minced fresh
     ginger
1   tablespoon sesame oil
¼   cup soy sauce
2   tablespoons chili sauce
1   bunch scallions or green onions,
     chopped
2   tablespoons chopped fresh mint
2   tablespoons chopped fresh basil
1   (16-ounce) package won ton
     wrappers
2   large eggs, lightly beaten
6   cups peanut oil
Red Curry-Coconut Cream

• **Cut** shell of lobster tail lengthwise on the underside, using kitchen shears. Pry open tail segments; remove meat, and finely chop.

• **Sauté** garlic and next 3 ingredients in hot sesame oil in a large skillet over medium-high heat, stirring constantly, 2 minutes or until lightly browned. Remove from heat.
• **Stir** in lobster, soy sauce, and next 4 ingredients.
• **Brush** wrappers lightly with egg. Spoon 1 teaspoon lobster mixture onto center of each. Bring corners together, pressing edges to seal.
• **Pour** peanut oil into a large Dutch oven; heat to 400°.
• **Fry** won tons, in batches, 1 minute or until golden. Serve with Red Curry-Coconut Cream. **Yield:** 12 appetizer servings.

Red Curry-Coconut Cream

Prep: 25 minutes
Cook: 40 minutes
Stand: 25 minutes

3   garlic cloves, chopped
1   large shallot, chopped
2   tablespoons chopped fresh
     ginger
1   stalk lemongrass, chopped*
1   tablespoon sesame oil
1   tablespoon grated lime rind
¼   cup rice wine vinegar
¼   cup rice wine
¾   cup coconut milk
1   tablespoon red curry paste
¼   cup loosely packed cilantro,
     coarsely chopped
2   tablespoons fresh lime juice

• **Sauté** first 4 ingredients in hot sesame oil in a small saucepan over medium-high heat 2 to 3 minutes or until tender.
• **Stir** in lime rind, vinegar, and wine; cook 30 minutes or until liquid is reduced by half. Add coconut milk and curry paste; bring to a boil.
• **Cook,** stirring often, 2 minutes. Stir in cilantro and lime juice. Let stand 25 minutes. Pour mixture through a wire-mesh strainer into a bowl, discarding solids. **Yield:** ¾ cup.

* Substitute 1 to 2 teaspoons grated lemon rind for lemongrass, if desired.

Kent Rathbun
Dallas, Texas

These Kids Are Cookin'

Although these great recipes are by kids for kids, adults can enjoy them too.

Finalists in our annual "I Can Do It Myself" recipe contest showed they really can do it themselves. From French toast to smoothies, their recipes were inventive, easy, and delicious. Whether you're six or 66, we think you'll agree these recipes are *all* winners.

CINNAMON-CHIP ICE CREAM BALLS

Grand prize: 9- to 12-year-old category

Prep: 12 minutes
Freeze: 3 hours

1 cup cinnamon-sugar whole
    wheat-and-rice cereal
1 cup granola
½ cup semisweet chocolate mini-morsels
6 scoops of vanilla ice cream
Toppings: chocolate syrup, caramel
    syrup

• **Crush** cereal and granola in a heavy-duty zip-top plastic bag using a rolling pin. Add chocolate morsels; seal and shake. Pour into a large bowl.
• **Shape** each ice cream scoop into a ball; roll in crumb mixture, coating evenly. Place in a 9-inch square pan; freeze until firm. Drizzle with syrups before serving. **Yield:** 6 servings.

Note: For testing purposes only, we used Cinnamon Toast Crunch cereal for cinnamon-sugar whole wheat-and-rice cereal.

Mark Conrad, age 10
Pewaukee, Wisconsin

CINNAMON-APPLE BREAKFAST BUNS

Grand prize: 5- to 8-year-old category

Prep: 8 minutes
Bake: 22 minutes

1 (12.4-ounce) can refrigerated
    cinnamon rolls
1 Granny Smith apple, peeled, cored,
    and cut into 8 rings
1 (1.62-ounce) package instant
    cinnamon and spice oatmeal
¼ cup firmly packed brown sugar
¼ cup chopped pecans
¼ teaspoon ground cinnamon
Dash of ground nutmeg
1 tablespoon butter or margarine,
    melted

• **Separate** cinnamon rolls, and place in a lightly greased 8- or 9-inch round cakepan; set icing aside.
• **Place** 1 apple ring on each cinnamon roll. Stir together oatmeal and next 5 ingredients; sprinkle mixture evenly over cinnamon rolls.
• **Bake** at 400° for 20 to 22 minutes.
• **Remove** top to icing. Microwave icing at LOW (10% power) 20 seconds; drizzle evenly over rolls. **Yield:** 8 rolls.

Robert Pritchett, age 8
League City, Texas

PEANUT BUTTER AND JELLY FRENCH TOAST

Prep: 10 minutes
Cook: 5 minutes per batch

8 white sandwich bread slices
4 teaspoons peanut butter
4 teaspoons grape jelly
2 large eggs
¼ cup milk
1 tablespoon sugar
Dash of ground cinnamon
1 tablespoon butter or margarine

• **Spread** each of 4 bread slices with 1 teaspoon peanut butter. Spread remaining bread slices with 1 teaspoon grape jelly, and place jelly side down on top of slices with peanut butter. Cut each sandwich in half diagonally.
• **Stir** together eggs and next 3 ingredients in a shallow dish.
• **Melt** butter in a large nonstick skillet over medium heat. Dip sandwiches into egg mixture, evenly coating both sides.
• **Cook** sandwich halves, in batches, 2½ minutes on each side or until golden brown. **Yield:** 4 servings.

Jessica Dickson, age 10
Louisville, Mississippi

TURKEY SCHOOLWICH SANDWICHES

Prep: 5 minutes

1 (8-ounce) container cream cheese
    with chives and onions
4 hamburger buns, split
4 cranberry sauce slices
8 ounces thinly sliced turkey breast
Lettuce leaves

• **Spread** cream cheese evenly on cut side of each bun.
• **Place** cranberry sauce slices, turkey, and lettuce evenly on bottom halves of buns; cover with bun tops. Chill sandwiches, if desired. **Yield:** 4 servings.

Kevin Bradley, age 10
Bolingbrook, Illinois

GRILLED FOUR-CHEESE SANDWICH WITH TOMATO, AVOCADO, AND BACON

Prep: 30 minutes
Cook: 6 minutes per batch

8 microwave bacon slices
2 large tomatoes, each cut into 4 slices
¼ teaspoon salt
¼ teaspoon pepper
1 large avocado, cut into 8 slices *
1 tablespoon rice vinegar
¼ cup butter, softened
1 teaspoon grated Parmesan cheese
2 tablespoons mayonnaise
8 sourdough bread slices
4 ounces sharp Cheddar cheese, sliced
4 ounces Monterey Jack cheese with peppers, sliced
4 ounces white Cheddar cheese, sliced
¼ cup Thousand Island dressing

• **Cook** bacon according to package directions; drain and set aside.
• **Sprinkle** tomatoes evenly with salt and pepper; sprinkle avocado with vinegar. Stir together butter and Parmesan cheese. Set aside.
• **Spread** mayonnaise on 1 side of 4 bread slices; layer each with 1 sharp Cheddar cheese slice, 1 tomato slice, 2 avocado slices, 2 bacon slices, 1 Monterey Jack cheese slice, 1 tomato slice, and 1 white Cheddar cheese slice.
• **Spread** remaining 4 bread slices with dressing, and place on top of sandwich with dressing side down.
• **Spread** half of butter mixture evenly on 1 side of sandwiches.
• **Cook** 2 sandwiches, buttered side down, in a hot nonstick skillet or griddle over medium heat 2 to 3 minutes.
• **Spread** remaining butter mixture evenly on ungrilled sides of sandwiches; turn and cook 2 to 3 minutes. Repeat procedure with remaining sandwiches. **Yield:** 4 sandwiches.

*Substitute ½ cup guacamole for avocado and rice vinegar, if desired.
Katherine Weisbrod, age 8
Chatsworth, California

BIRTHDAY PARTY BROWNIE CAKES

Prep: 10 minutes
Bake: 20 minutes

1 (21-ounce) package brownie mix
½ cup vegetable oil
¼ cup cranberry juice
2 large eggs
Toppings: semisweet chocolate morsels, candy-coated chocolate pieces, chopped pecans, candy sprinkles
Powdered sugar (optional)
Ice cream (optional)

• **Stir** together first 4 ingredients until smooth.
• **Spoon** batter into 12 lightly greased muffin cups, and sprinkle with desired toppings.
• **Bake** at 350° for 20 minutes or until a wooden pick inserted in center comes out clean. Remove from pan, and cool on a wire rack. If desired, sprinkle with powdered sugar and serve with ice cream. **Yield:** 12 servings.

Danielle Stallings, age 6
Wilmington, North Carolina

MEXICAN PIGS IN A BLANKET

Prep: 10 minutes
Bake: 7 minutes

1 cup canned refried beans
8 (10-inch) flour tortillas
4 (1-ounce) process American cheese slices
½ cup mild salsa
1 (16-ounce) package hot dogs
2 tablespoons vegetable oil

• **Spread** refried beans evenly on 1 side of each tortilla. Place half of a cheese slice on each tortilla; top with 1 tablespoon salsa and 1 hot dog.
• **Roll** up tightly, jellyroll fashion, and place, seam side down, on a baking sheet. Brush with oil.
• **Bake** at 400° for 5 to 7 minutes. **Yield:** 8 servings.

Samantha Hartman, age 7
Oshkosh, Wisconsin

SUPEREASY TORTILLA SOUP

Prep: 8 minutes
Cook: 30 minutes

4 celery ribs, chopped
3 medium carrots, chopped
1 (10-ounce) can mild enchilada sauce
4 cups water
6 chicken bouillon cubes
½ teaspoon lemon pepper
2 cups chopped cooked chicken
Crushed corn tortilla chips
Toppings: shredded Cheddar cheese, sour cream

• **Bring** first 6 ingredients to a boil in a saucepan over medium heat. Reduce heat, and simmer, stirring occasionally, 20 minutes. Stir in chicken, and cook until thoroughly heated.
• **Place** tortilla chips in four bowls; spoon soup evenly over chips. Serve immediately with desired toppings. **Yield:** 4 servings.

Mark Kohlhoff, age 10
Houston, Texas

EASY PINEAPPLE SMOOTHIE

Prep: 5 minutes
Freeze: 5 minutes

½ cup chopped fresh or canned pineapple
1 frozen raspberry-flavored juice pop or ¼ cup grape juice
3 tablespoons sugar
1 teaspoon pink lemonade drink mix
¼ teaspoon vanilla extract
1 cup orange juice
1 cup ice cubes
Vanilla ice cream (optional)

• **Process** first 7 ingredients and, if desired, ice cream in a blender until smooth, stopping to scrape down sides. Freeze 5 minutes. **Yield:** 1 serving.

Note: For testing purposes only, we used Welch's Fruit Juice Bars.

Jennie Scott, age 13
Elkview, West Virginia

TOASTY MARSHMALLOW TREAT

Prep: 2 minutes
Broil: 1 minute

1   white bread slice
1   tablespoon creamy peanut butter
½   cup miniature marshmallows
12 to 15 candy-coated chocolate pieces
    or semisweet chocolate morsels

• **Spread** 1 side of bread slice with peanut butter; top evenly with marshmallows. Arrange chocolate pieces in a smiley face pattern over marshmallows. Place bread on a baking sheet.
• **Broil** bread 5½ inches from heat (with electric oven door partially open) 1 minute or until marshmallows are golden brown. **Yield:** 1 serving.

Aaron Alcorn, age 8
Garland, Texas

Can-Do Kabobs

In the South when we can't stand the heat, we get out of the kitchen and make a meal outdoors. There's less stress, less mess, and more fun for everyone. From veggies to chicken to pork, everything tastes good when it's hot off the grill. So this weekend, gather together your friends and family, and hobnob over these delicious kabobs. You can't beat them for casual entertaining.

SKEWERED PORK TENDERS

Prep: 20 minutes
Chill: 8 hours
Grill: 14 minutes

2   pounds pork tenderloins
¾   cup firmly packed brown sugar
¾   cup water
½   cup French dressing
½   cup Italian dressing
⅓   cup red wine vinegar

• **Cut** pork tenderloins in half crosswise; cut each portion lengthwise into thin strips.
• **Combine** ¾ cup brown sugar and next 4 ingredients in a shallow dish or a heavy-duty zip-top plastic bag; remove ½ cup marinade, and chill until ready to grill.
• **Add** pork tenderloin strips to remaining marinade. Cover or seal, and chill 8 hours.
• **Remove** pork from marinade, discarding marinade.
• **Thread** pork strips onto 26 (12-inch) skewers.
• **Grill,** covered with grill lid, over medium-high heat (350° to 400°) 5 to 7 minutes on each side or until done, basting with reserved ½ cup marinade. **Yield:** 6 servings.

Julie Orlowski
Dubuque, Iowa

CHICKEN-PINEAPPLE KABOBS

Prep: 10 minutes
Chill: 2 hours
Grill: 20 minutes

¼   cup firmly packed light brown sugar
¼   cup soy sauce
1   tablespoon chopped fresh cilantro
1   tablespoon vegetable oil
1   teaspoon minced fresh ginger
½   teaspoon dried crushed red pepper
2   garlic cloves, minced
4   skinned and boned chicken breast halves, cut into strips
1   small cored pineapple, cut into 2-inch pieces
Hot cooked rice
Garnishes: chopped green onions, fresh cilantro sprigs

• **Combine** first 7 ingredients in a shallow dish or large heavy-duty zip-top plastic bag; add chicken strips. Cover or seal; chill 2 hours, turning chicken occasionally.
• **Remove** chicken from marinade, discarding marinade.
• **Thread** chicken onto 3 (6-inch) skewers and pineapple pieces onto 3 (6-inch) skewers.
• **Grill** chicken, covered with grill lid, over medium-high heat (350° to 400°) 15 to 20 minutes or until done, turning occasionally.
• **Grill** pineapple 5 to 7 minutes or until thoroughly heated. Serve over rice, and garnish, if desired. **Yield:** 6 servings.

BEEF TENDERLOIN SHISH KABOBS

Prep: 20 minutes
Chill: 2 hours
Grill: 14 minutes

½   cup dry sherry or beef broth
¼   cup olive oil
2   tablespoons soy sauce
1   garlic clove, minced
¼   teaspoon pepper
1   pound beef tenderloin steaks or boneless top sirloin steaks, cut into 1-inch cubes
8   large mushrooms
1   red bell pepper, cut into 1-inch pieces
8   cherry tomatoes
2   small onions, quartered
1   green bell pepper, cut into 1-inch pieces

• **Combine** first 5 ingredients in a shallow dish or large heavy-duty zip-top plastic bag; add steak and remaining ingredients. Cover or seal; chill 2 hours, turning steak occasionally.
• **Remove** steak and vegetables from marinade, discarding marinade.
• **Thread** steak and vegetables onto 4 (12-inch) skewers.
• **Grill** kabobs, covered with grill lid, over medium-high heat (350° to 400°) 5 to 7 minutes on each side or until desired degree of doneness. **Yield:** 4 servings.

Rubie M. Walker
Lynchburg, Virginia

Living Light

On sultry days, we often opt for cold food and beverages to cool us off. Believe it or not, spicy food has the same effect. That's why so many tropical dishes are fiery. So when you're in need of a heat reprieve, choose these dishes that are a breeze to prepare.

CURRIED NAVY BEANS

Spoon these hearty beans over Coconut Rice (recipe at right) for a quick, filling meal.

Prep: 30 minutes

2 medium russet potatoes, peeled and cut into ½-inch pieces
¾ teaspoon dried crushed red pepper
2 (19-ounce) cans navy beans, rinsed, drained, and divided
2 cups low-sodium fat-free chicken broth
2 teaspoons minced fresh ginger
¼ to ½ teaspoon turmeric (optional)
1 large onion, chopped
2 teaspoons olive oil
1 tablespoon hot curry powder
¾ teaspoon salt
¾ teaspoon black pepper
1 large tomato, chopped
¼ cup chopped fresh cilantro

• **Cook** potato and red pepper in boiling water to cover 15 minutes or until tender. Drain and set aside.
• **Process** 1 cup beans, broth, ginger, and, if desired, turmeric in a food processor or blender until smooth.
• **Sauté** onion in hot oil in a Dutch oven over medium-high heat 5 minutes or until tender.
• **Add** curry powder; cook 1 minute.
• **Stir** in potato, pureed bean mixture, remaining beans, salt, and black pepper. Reduce heat to low; simmer, stirring occasionally, 5 minutes or until thickened.
• **Sprinkle** with tomato and cilantro. Serve over Coconut Rice, if desired. **Yield:** 8 cups.

Don Mauer
Cary, North Carolina

♥ Per 1-cup serving: Calories 176 (11% from fat)
Fat 2.2g (sat 0.4g, mono 1g, poly 0.4g)
Protein 9.5g Carb 30.6g Fiber 5.8g
Chol 0mg Iron 3.9mg
Sodium 230mg Calc 91mg

COCONUT RICE

Prep: 10 minutes
Cook: 20 minutes

¾ cup lite coconut milk, divided
1½ cups water
1 garlic clove, minced
½ teaspoon salt
1 cup uncooked basmati rice
2 tablespoons chopped fresh basil

• **Place** coconut milk in a medium saucepan, reserving 2 tablespoons. Add 1½ cups water, garlic, and salt. Bring to a boil over medium-high heat; stir in rice. Cover, reduce heat, and simmer 20 minutes or until liquid is absorbed. Stir in reserved coconut milk, and sprinkle with basil. **Yield:** 3 cups.

♥ Per ½-cup serving: Calories 131 (12% from fat)
Fat 1.7g (sat 1g, mono 0.1g, poly 0.1g)
Protein 2.7g Carb 26g Fiber 0.4g
Chol 0mg Iron 1.3mg
Sodium 200mg Calc 17mg

KIWI-PEACH SLUSHY

Prep: 5 minutes

4 kiwifruit, peeled
4 peaches, peeled and frozen*
1 (6-ounce) can pineapple juice
¼ cup powdered sugar
¼ cup frozen limeade concentrate, undiluted
¼ teaspoon coconut extract (optional)
1 cup ice cubes

• **Process** all ingredients in batches in a blender until smooth, stopping to scrape sides. Serve immediately. **Yield:** 6 cups.

*Substitute 1 (1-pound) package frozen peaches for fresh peaches, if desired.

Carly Druda
Clearwater, Florida

♥ Per 1-cup serving: Calories 124 (2% from fat)
Fat 0.3g (sat 0g, mono 0g, poly 0.2g)
Protein 1.2g Carb 31.6g Fiber 3.4g
Chol 0mg Iron 0.4mg
Sodium 3mg Calc 23mg

SMART BITES

Cookbook author Don Mauer has come a long way. In 1990 he weighed 308 pounds and realized it was time to lose it. He lost 100 pounds by cooking lighter, eating less, and exercising.

Don says the desire to eat healthfully without compromising great flavor drove him to develop delicious, lower calorie recipes during his weight loss journey. Don's books offer recipes that are hearty enough for the big guys, with portion sizes that'll keep them satisfied. We adapted his recipes from *A Guy's Guide to Great Eating.* (Don Mauer & Associates, Inc., 1999; reprinted by permission of Houghton Mifflin Company.)

One-Bean Salad With Lime-Mustard Dressing

This dressing may also be tossed with steamed broccoli.

Prep: 20 minutes
Stand: 30 minutes

1 pound fresh green beans, trimmed
2 tablespoons coarse-grained Dijon mustard
2 tablespoons rice vinegar or white wine vinegar
½ teaspoon grated lime rind
2 to 3 tablespoons fresh lime juice
½ tablespoon olive oil
½ teaspoon honey
1 garlic clove, minced
1 large shallot, minced
¼ teaspoon salt
½ teaspoon freshly ground pepper

• **Cook** beans in boiling water to cover 3 to 4 minutes or until crisp-tender. Drain. Plunge beans into ice water to stop the cooking process; drain.
• **Whisk** together mustard and next 9 ingredients; pour over green beans, tossing to coat. Let stand 30 minutes. **Yield:** 6 servings.

Don Mauer
Cary, North Carolina

♥ Per serving: Calories 44 (33% from fat)
Fat 1.6g (sat 0.2g, mono 0.9g, poly 0.2g)
Protein 1.5g Carb 6.9g Fiber 1.7g
Chol 0mg Iron 0.8mg
Sodium 243mg Calc 31mg

In the Wings

If you're looking for a fast and inexpensive alternative for supper, look no further than chicken wings. Buffalo "wings," developed more than 30 years ago at the Anchor Bar in Buffalo, New York, are now a fixture on menus throughout America.

Traditionally thought of as snack food, the meat's mild flavor provides the perfect canvas for a wide variety of seasonings that are sure to spice up the dinner table. A quick cut through the joint of the wing's two larger sections makes it easier to handle.

Chicken Wings With Spanish Rice

Prep: 15 minutes
Cook: 52 minutes

2 pounds chicken wings
Vegetable oil
1 cup uncooked long-grain rice
2 tablespoons olive oil
2 celery ribs, chopped
1 medium onion, chopped
1 green bell pepper, chopped
1 garlic clove, minced
1 (14½-ounce) can chicken broth
1 (14½-ounce) can diced tomatoes, undrained
1 teaspoon salt
½ teaspoon paprika
½ teaspoon chili powder
½ teaspoon ground cumin
½ teaspoon pepper

• **Cut** off wingtips, and discard; cut wings in half at joint, if desired.
• **Pour** oil to depth of 2 inches into a Dutch oven; heat to 375°. Fry wings, in batches, 12 minutes. Drain; set aside.
• **Sauté** rice with olive oil in Dutch oven over medium-high heat 3 minutes. Add celery and next 3 ingredients; sauté 5 minutes or until vegetables are tender.
• **Add** wings, chicken broth, and next 6 ingredients. Cover, reduce heat, and simmer 40 minutes or until tender. **Yield:** 4 main-dish or 10 appetizer servings.

Carrie M. Treichel
Johnson City, Tennessee

Sweet-and-Hot Citrus Wings

Prep: 20 minutes
Chill: 1 hour
Bake: 45 minutes

3 pounds chicken wings
2 tablespoons grated orange rind
1 cup fresh orange juice
1 cup honey
¼ cup soy sauce
¼ cup ketchup
6 garlic cloves, minced
2 tablespoons minced fresh ginger
2 teaspoons grated lemon rind
2 tablespoons fresh lemon juice
2 teaspoons hot sauce
6 green onions, chopped

• **Cut** off wingtips, and discard; cut wings in half at joint, if desired.
• **Whisk** together orange rind and next 9 ingredients.
• **Place** wings in a shallow dish or heavy-duty zip-top plastic bag. Add 1 cup orange juice mixture; reserve

remaining mixture. Cover or seal; chill 1 hour.
- **Remove** wings from marinade, discarding marinade. Arrange wings on a wire rack in a baking pan.
- **Bake** at 400° for 45 minutes. Sprinkle with green onions.
- **Bring** reserved 2 cups orange juice mixture to a boil in a saucepan. Reduce heat; simmer 20 minutes or until reduced to 1 cup. Serve with wings. **Yield:** 6 main-dish or 12 appetizer servings.

Miriam Baroga
Fircrest, Washington

BUFFALO WINGS

Prep: 15 minutes
Cook: 12 minutes per batch
Bake: 20 minutes

3 pounds chicken wings
1 cup all-purpose flour
Vegetable oil
½ cup hot sauce
⅓ cup butter or margarine, melted
2 tablespoons orange juice
2 tablespoons honey
Celery sticks
Carrot sticks
1 (8-ounce) bottle blue cheese dressing

- **Cut** off wingtips, and discard; cut wings in half at joint, if desired.
- **Dredge** wings lightly in flour.
- **Pour** oil to depth of 2 inches into a Dutch oven, and heat to 375°. Fry wings, in batches, 12 minutes or until golden. Drain.
- **Stir** together hot sauce and next 3 ingredients in a large bowl.
- **Add** wings, tossing to coat. Remove wings, reserving sauce. Arrange wings on a wire rack in a baking pan.
- **Bake** at 350° for 20 minutes. Bring reserved sauce to a boil in a small saucepan; boil 1 minute.
- **Serve** wings with reserved sauce, celery, carrots, and dressing. **Yield:** 6 main-dish or 12 appetizer servings.

Note: For testing purposes only, we used Frank's Hot Sauce.

Cyndi Christensen
Virginia Beach, Virginia

What's for Supper?

Want an easy yet satisfying meal? Try one of these three refreshing salads for supper. To keep them cool, serve in chilled bowls or on chilled plates lined with crisp greens. For extra crunch, soak jícama strips in ice water for a few minutes, but don't forget to drain them well. And rinse cooked pasta under cold running water to cool it quickly, preventing it from becoming gummy.

Your favorite frosty beverage, crusty breadsticks, and ice cream will round out the meal perfectly.

GAZPACHO-CHICKEN SALAD

Leftover grilled chicken works well in this recipe.

Prep: 20 minutes
Chill: 1 hour

1 red bell pepper
1 yellow bell pepper
1 green bell pepper
1 small onion
½ cup olive oil
¼ cup white balsamic vinegar
2 garlic cloves, minced
½ teaspoon salt
¼ teaspoon ground cumin
¼ teaspoon pepper
1 (16-ounce) package roasted chicken breast, cut into thin strips
4 cups shredded green leaf lettuce (optional)
Garnish: chopped green onions

- **Chop** first 4 ingredients.
- **Whisk** together oil and next 5 ingredients in a bowl. Add chopped vegetables, tossing to coat. Cover and chill 1 hour.
- **Top** bell pepper mixture with chicken strips. If desired, serve over lettuce and garnish. **Yield:** 4 servings.

Margaret Pache
Mesa, Arizona

FRUIT-JÍCAMA SALAD

You can substitute any leftover jícama for water chestnuts in stir-fries.

Prep: 15 minutes
Chill: 1 hour

1 cup red seedless grapes
1 cup green seedless grapes
1 cup cubed cantaloupe
1 cup cubed fresh pineapple
1 (11-ounce) can mandarin oranges, drained
1 nectarine, cut into ½-inch pieces
½ cup halved strawberries
½ cup thin jícama strips
¼ cup orange juice
1 (8-ounce) container orange low-fat yogurt
1 tablespoon chopped fresh basil
Garnish: fresh basil sprig

- **Combine** first 9 ingredients in a large bowl. Cover and chill 1 hour.
- **Stir** together yogurt and chopped basil. Spoon over fruit mixture; garnish, if desired. **Yield:** 6 servings.

R. Murphy
Dallas, Texas

BAYOU PASTA SALAD

Prep: 10 minutes

¼ cup mayonnaise
¼ cup olive oil
1 tablespoon lemon juice
1 to 1½ tablespoons Greek seasoning
8 ounces vermicelli, cooked
1 (2-ounce) jar diced pimiento, drained
1 (2¼-ounce) can sliced ripe olives, drained
3 green onions, sliced
1 cup chopped cooked chicken (optional)
Garnishes: fresh parsley sprigs, grape tomatoes

- **Whisk** together first 4 ingredients in a large bowl. Add pasta and next 3 ingredients, tossing to coat. If desired, stir in chicken and garnish. **Yield:** 4 servings.

Sandi Pichon
Slidell, Louisiana

A Cheesecake for Everyone

Delight your guests with the decadent flavor of one of these tempting desserts. Whether you're looking for a very dense cheesecake, one that requires no baking, one with a hint of citrus, or one that has an ingredient with proven healthful benefits, we have them all.

TROPICAL TOFU CHEESECAKE

This tofu cheesecake was a hit in our Test Kitchens, and we bet your family will be none the wiser. In fact, it may become their cheesecake of choice. And for those who just can't do tofu, we have included a cream cheese substitution.

Prep: 45 minutes
Bake: 1 hour, 36 minutes
Chill: 8 hours

1 (12.3-ounce) package reduced-fat firm silken tofu ✱
1⅓ cups graham cracker crumbs
2 tablespoons brown sugar
3 tablespoons butter, melted
1 cup 2% reduced-fat cottage cheese
1 (8-ounce) package fat-free cream cheese
1½ cups sugar, divided
⅓ cup all-purpose flour
1 (15-ounce) can cream of coconut
1 teaspoon vanilla extract
2 large eggs
1 egg white
1 (15¼-ounce) can unsweetened crushed pineapple
1¼ cups low-fat sour cream
½ cup flaked coconut, toasted

• **Drain** tofu on several layers of paper towels 45 minutes.

• **Stir** together cracker crumbs, brown sugar, and butter; press into bottom and 1 inch up sides of a lightly greased 9-inch springform pan.
• **Bake** crust at 350° for 8 minutes. Cool on a wire rack.
• **Process** cheeses and tofu in a food processor until smooth, stopping to scrape down sides.
• **Add** 1 cup sugar, flour, and next 4 ingredients; process until smooth, stopping to scrape down sides. Pour into prepared crust.
• **Bake** at 325° for 1 hour and 20 minutes or until almost set. Cool cheesecake on wire rack.
• **Drain** pineapple, and pat dry with paper towels. Sprinkle over cheesecake.
• **Stir** together remaining ½ cup sugar and sour cream; spread over pineapple.
• **Bake** at 325° for 8 minutes. Sprinkle cheesecake with coconut; cool on a wire rack. Cover and chill 8 hours. **Yield:** 12 servings.

♥ Per serving: Calories 451 Fat 16.2g

✱ Substitute 1 (8-ounce) package reduced-fat cream cheese and 1 (3-ounce) package regular cream cheese for tofu, if desired.

♥ Per serving: Calories 515 Fat 22.7g

Note: For testing purposes only, we used Mori-Nu Tofu.

LIME CHEESECAKE WITH RASPBERRY SAUCE

Prep: 20 minutes
Bake: 1 hour, 25 minutes
Cool: 1 hour, 10 minutes
Chill: 11 hours

2 cups gingersnap crumbs
2½ cups sugar, divided
½ cup butter or margarine, melted
4 (8-ounce) packages cream cheese, softened
5 large eggs
1 tablespoon grated lime rind
⅓ cup fresh lime juice
1⅛ teaspoons vanilla extract, divided
1 (16-ounce) container sour cream
1 (10-ounce) package frozen raspberries, thawed

• **Stir** together gingersnap crumbs, ¼ cup sugar, and butter.
• **Press** crumb mixture into bottom and 1 inch up sides of a lightly greased 10-inch springform pan. Chill 1 hour.
• **Beat** cream cheese at medium speed with an electric mixer until smooth.
• **Add** eggs, 1 at a time, beating until blended after each addition. Gradually add 1¾ cups sugar, beating until blended.
• **Stir** in lime rind, lime juice, and 1 teaspoon vanilla. Pour mixture into prepared crust.
• **Bake** at 325° for 1 hour and 15 minutes or until center is almost set. Remove cheesecake from oven; cool on a wire rack 10 minutes.
• **Stir** together remaining ½ cup sugar, ⅛ teaspoon vanilla, and sour cream; spread evenly over cheesecake.
• **Bake** at 325° for 10 minutes. Cool cheesecake on wire rack 1 hour. Cover and chill 10 hours.
• **Process** raspberries in a blender until smooth, stopping to scrape down sides.
• **Press** raspberry puree through a wire-mesh strainer; discard seeds. Serve raspberry sauce with cheesecake. **Yield:** 14 servings.

NEW YORK-STYLE CHEESECAKE
(pictured on page 226)

Prep: 15 minutes
Bake: 1 hour, 15 minutes
Chill: 8 hours

1¾ cups graham cracker crumbs
⅓ cup butter, melted
¼ cup sugar
5 (8-ounce) packages cream cheese, softened
1 cup sugar
3 tablespoons all-purpose flour
1 tablespoon vanilla extract
3 large eggs
1 (8-ounce) container sour cream
Garnishes: chopped fresh strawberries, whole strawberries

• **Stir** together first 3 ingredients. Press crumb mixture into bottom and 1½ inches up sides of a lightly greased 9-inch springform pan.
• **Bake** crust at 350° for 10 minutes. Cool on a wire rack.
• **Beat** cream cheese at medium speed with an electric mixer until smooth. Gradually add 1 cup sugar, flour, and vanilla, beating until blended.
• **Add** eggs, 1 at a time, beating until blended after each addition. Add sour cream, and beat just until blended. Pour mixture into prepared crust.
• **Bake** at 350° for 1 hour and 5 minutes or until center is almost set. Remove cheesecake from oven; cool on wire rack. Cover and chill 8 hours. Gently run a knife around edge of cheesecake, and release sides; garnish, if desired. **Yield:** 12 servings.

Alyson M. Haynes
Birmingham, Alabama

NO-BAKE AMARETTO CHEESECAKES

Prep: 30 minutes
Chill: 8 hours or Freeze: 45 minutes

1 envelope unflavored gelatin
½ cup cold water
3 (8-ounce) packages cream cheese, softened
1¼ cups sugar
1 (5-ounce) can evaporated milk, chilled
¾ cup whipping cream
⅓ cup almond liqueur *
1 teaspoon lemon juice
1 teaspoon vanilla extract
2 (6-inch) graham cracker crusts

• **Sprinkle** gelatin over ½ cup cold water in a saucepan, and let stand 1 minute. Cook over low heat, stirring until gelatin dissolves (about 2 minutes). Set aside.
• **Beat** cream cheese and sugar at medium speed with an electric mixer until light and fluffy.
• **Add** evaporated milk; beat at high speed. Gradually add gelatin, beating until blended.
• **Add** whipping cream and next 3 ingredients, beating until blended. Spoon evenly into piecrusts. Cover and chill 8 hours, or freeze 45 minutes until firm. **Yield:** 2 (6-inch) cheesecakes.

* Substitute 1 teaspoon almond extract for almond liqueur, if desired.

Note: For flavor variations, substitute ⅓ cup coffee liqueur, hazelnut liqueur, or praline liqueur for almond liqueur.

Judi Nicholson
Monroe, Louisiana

A Taste of the South

Deep-fat frying, a no-no today, isn't the problem when serving fried okra. The main concern is fending off the folks waiting to eat the crispy morsels.

Louis Van Dyke of Blue Willow Inn in Social Circle, Georgia, says, "We use only fresh okra. It's cut, dipped in buttermilk and egg, salted and peppered, dredged in cornmeal, and then deep-fried." Louis laughs and admits, "Fried okra and okra cooked in soup are the only ways I like it. No boiled or steamed okra for me."

Clearly, okra connoisseurs all have their favorite recipe. If bacon drippings aren't used, try adding them. We did here and made a great product even better.

FRIED OKRA
(pictured on page 188)

Prep: 12 minutes
Chill: 45 minutes
Cook: 4 minutes per batch

1 pound fresh okra
2 cups buttermilk
1 cup self-rising cornmeal
1 cup self-rising flour
1 teaspoon salt
¼ teaspoon ground red pepper
Vegetable oil
¼ cup bacon drippings

• **Cut** off and discard tip and stem ends from okra; cut okra into ½-inch-thick slices. Stir into buttermilk; cover and chill 45 minutes. Combine cornmeal and next 3 ingredients. Remove okra from buttermilk with a slotted spoon; discard buttermilk. Dredge okra, in batches, in cornmeal mixture.
• **Pour** oil to depth of 2 inches into a Dutch oven or cast-iron skillet; add bacon drippings. Heat to 375°. Fry okra, in batches, 4 minutes or until golden; drain on paper towels. **Yield:** 4 servings.

Fried Okra Pods: Trim stem end; do not trim tips or slice okra. Proceed as directed.

From Our Kitchen

Shop Wisely

If your trips to the grocery store cost much more than you intended, let these tips help you spend less and enjoy shopping more.

■ Make and *follow* a list to eliminate too many stops at the store.

■ Buy luncheon meats at the deli counter. They usually cost less per pound than prepackaged meats, and you buy only as much as you need.

■ Buy fresh vegetables unpeeled, unwashed, and unpackaged.

■ Remember that single servings and snack-size packages are more expensive.

Pesto Info

■ When making pesto, keep a bit of the crunchy texture of the pine nuts. Don't overprocess the nuts, or they'll turn into butter.

■ Drizzle a thin film of olive oil over pesto to prevent discoloration when the pesto is refrigerated.

■ Stir sour cream or softened cream cheese into pesto to use as a sandwich spread or as a vegetable dip. Pesto also makes a great marinade for chicken and fish. For more pesto ideas, see "Quick & Easy" on pages 195-196.

■ Pesto will maintain its quality in the freezer up to two months.

Tomato Catch Up

When you read about heirloom tomatoes in "Legacy of Summer" on page 182, you'll start to crave the flavor of these prized fruits. Once you find them, be sure to buy plenty and treat them kindly. The refrigerator is the last place you want to

store tomatoes; they get soft and mealy, and they lose flavor. While they may look pretty on a windowsill, tomatoes last longer when stored in indirect light at room temperature. A pinch of sugar rounds out the flavor of tomatoes that are too acidic.

Give It a Squeeze

Betty, Pat's friend of Reynolds Wrap fame, makes her great pound cakes grand with a kiss of lemon. She drizzles the top of the cooled cake with the juice of one lemon. The hint of citrus enhances the buttery goodness of the cake. The next time you bake a pound cake, follow Betty's lead and give it a squeeze.

Tips and Tidbits

■ Fresh basil loses flavor in the refrigerator. It's better to put it in a glass of cold water and keep it out on a countertop. Make sure all stems are submerged. Chop or cut fresh basil at the last minute before adding to recipes to prevent it from turning brown and losing flavor.

■ When your fresh salsa has lost its punch, cook and puree the leftovers for a spicy appetizer soup.

■ Save a dish when oven-frying potatoes. Pour 2 teaspoons olive oil onto a baking

sheet; add thinly sliced potatoes, and toss until well coated with the oil. Sprinkle with salt and pepper. Bake at 400° for 25 minutes.

■ Stir chopped fresh herbs into mayonnaise for tasty salad binders and sandwich spreads.

■ Nut crusts and breadings hold onto meats, fish, or vegetables better when they are chilled in the refrigerator. Coat the items, place them in a single layer on a platter or baking sheet. Cover the dish with plastic wrap and refrigerate up to two hours. When you're ready to roast or fry, most of the coating will stay put.

■ Keep a small ice chest/cooler in your car to transport your groceries from the refrigerated and freezer sections of the market to your home. The produce won't wilt, and ice cream will stay firm while you make other stops.

■ If the cantaloupe and honeydew melons looked great at the store but have little or no flavor, don't throw them down the disposal. Scoop the melon into balls, and toss with the juice of one lime and five or six chopped fresh mint leaves. Refrigerate the mixture in an airtight container for a few hours or overnight. Or for a fresh dessert, add a splash of rum or liqueur to give bland melons a new attitude.

September

Comfort and Joy

Foods that lift your spirit and hug your soul spread cheer and kindness from one family to another. Savor these recipes meant for sharing as well as the heartwarming stories behind them in "Treasured Traditions" on the facing page.

There's no denying that food expresses feelings words just can't convey—and in no other place is this more deeply understood than in the South. Last year we asked readers to send their favorite recipes they prepare when honoring the blessings of family and friends or consoling the same folks when befallen by hardship and misfortune. The abundant responses made one thing clear—a gift of food is a profound gesture of caring.

CUCUMBER SANDWICHES

Prep: 10 minutes

1 large cucumber, peeled, seeded, and grated
1 (8-ounce) package cream cheese, softened
1 tablespoon mayonnaise
1 small shallot, minced
¼ teaspoon seasoned salt
1 (16-ounce) loaf sandwich bread
Garnish: cucumber slices

• **Drain** cucumber well, pressing between layers of paper towels.
• **Stir** together cucumber and next 4 ingredients. Spread mixture evenly over half of bread slices. Top with remaining bread slices.
• **Trim** crusts from sandwiches; cut in half diagonally. Store sandwiches in an airtight container. Garnish, if desired. **Yield:** 16 sandwiches.

Carolyn Pedison
Marshall, Texas

EASY BEEF CASSEROLE

You won't leave out the kids when you serve this yummy casserole.

Prep: 20 minutes
Bake: 30 minutes

1 pound ground beef
¼ teaspoon salt
½ (16-ounce) package frozen mixed vegetables
1 (10¾-ounce) can cream of chicken soup, undiluted
1 cup (4 ounces) shredded Cheddar cheese
½ (32-ounce) package frozen seasoned potatoes, thawed

• **Cook** ground beef and salt in a large skillet over medium heat, stirring until meat crumbles and is no longer pink; drain. Spoon ground beef into a lightly greased 2½-quart shallow baking dish.
• **Layer** frozen vegetables, soup, and cheese over ground beef. Top casserole with potatoes.
• **Bake** casserole at 400° for 30 minutes or until potatoes are golden. **Yield:** 4 to 6 servings.

Note: For testing purposes only, we used Ore-Ida Tater Tots for potatoes.

Becky Reaves
Summerfield, Florida

RASPBERRY JELLY TARTS

These treats are great for young and old alike. They take a little time, so prepare ahead.

Prep: 45 minutes
Chill: 1 hour
Bake: 15 minutes

2 cups all-purpose flour
½ cup powdered sugar
½ cup butter or margarine, softened
½ cup shortening
1 tablespoon cornstarch
½ cup raspberry jelly
¾ cup flaked coconut
⅓ cup sugar
1 large egg, lightly beaten
1½ tablespoons butter or margarine, melted
2 teaspoons lemon juice
½ teaspoon cornstarch
½ teaspoon vanilla extract
⅛ teaspoon salt

• **Combine** first 5 ingredients, and knead until blended. Shape dough into 24 (1-inch) balls.
• **Place** miniature paper baking cups in miniature (1¾-inch) muffin pans. Place balls in cups; press evenly into bottoms and up sides. Chill 1 hour.
• **Spoon** 1 teaspoon raspberry jelly into each tart.
• **Stir** together coconut and next 7 ingredients, and spoon mixture evenly into tarts.
• **Bake** at 375° for 15 minutes. Cool in pans on a wire rack. **Yield:** 2 dozen.

Note: Freeze tarts up to 1 month, if desired. Thaw at room temperature.

Brenda King
Weyburn, Saskatchewan, Canada

LESLIE'S FAVORITE CHICKEN-AND-WILD RICE CASSEROLE

Prep: 30 minutes
Bake: 35 minutes

2 (6.2-ounce) packages fast-cooking long-grain and wild rice mix
¼ cup butter or margarine
2 medium onions, chopped
4 celery ribs, chopped
2 (8-ounce) cans sliced water chestnuts, drained
5 cups chopped cooked chicken
4 cups (1 pound) shredded Cheddar cheese, divided
2 (10¾-ounce) cans cream of mushroom soup, undiluted
2 (8-ounce) containers sour cream
1 cup milk
½ teaspoon salt
½ teaspoon pepper
½ cup soft breadcrumbs (optional)

• **Prepare** rice mixes according to package directions; set aside.
• **Melt** butter in a large skillet over medium heat; add onion, celery, and water chestnuts. Sauté 10 minutes or until tender.
• **Stir** in rice, chicken, 3 cups cheese, and next 5 ingredients.
• **Spoon** mixture into a lightly greased 15- x 10-inch baking dish or a 4-quart casserole. Top casserole with breadcrumbs, if desired.
• **Bake** casserole at 350° for 30 minutes. Sprinkle with remaining 1 cup cheese; bake 5 more minutes. **Yield:** 6 to 8 servings.

Note: Freeze casserole up to 1 month, if desired. Let stand at room temperature 1 hour. Bake, covered, at 350° for 30 minutes. Uncover casserole, and bake 55 more minutes. Sprinkle with cheese, and bake 5 more minutes.

Leslie Flemister
Dunwoody, Georgia

TREASURED TRADITIONS

Simplicity Speaks Volumes

When Carolyn Pedison's mother died unexpectedly a few years ago, in true Southern tradition, food began arriving almost immediately. Carolyn reflects, "I had deep gratitude for this outpouring of love, but, unfortunately, no appetite. However, the day of the funeral, one of my mother's friends, Jewel Robbins, brought a platter of beautiful little cold Cucumber Sandwiches. I'll never forget how good they tasted and how good they made me feel—or how many I ate."

Consider the Children

Several years ago Becky Reaves found the simple, savory recipe for Easy Beef Casserole in a church cookbook, and it quickly became a family favorite. The meal is also a terrific casserole for families in need—especially those with children. Becky explains, "It's inexpensive, easy to make, and even easier to transport. But the great thing about this all-in-one meal is that kids love it—something that can't be said for a lot of casseroles you receive."

Kindness North of the Border

Brenda King, a resident of the Saskatchewan province of Canada, was quick to point out to us that delivering food to folks in times of happiness and sorrow is not just a Southern tradition. "It happens everywhere there are caring people who know that food is a thoughtful expression of sympathy and jubilation," notes Brenda. With their raspberry filling and coconut topping, her Raspberry Jelly Tarts will brighten even the bluest of days.

Helping Hand for a New Mom

Cooking was the last thing Leslie Flemister wanted to worry about in the weeks following the birth of her daughter. Fortunately, her friends recognized this, and soon the meals started to roll in—30 days' worth. "The generosity was overwhelming. Many of the women who graciously brought me meals soon became pregnant themselves, so it was nice to reciprocate the gesture and fix them a delicious, home-cooked meal," says Leslie. Leslie's Favorite Chicken-and-Wild Rice Casserole warms the stomachs and souls of her friends who receive it.

A Sweet Tradition

When Laura and Don Wallace were married 36 years ago, they were given a unique wedding present—three blueberry bushes. Since that day, love has passed from their home to others through the blueberries they grow. Laura explains, "We pick blueberries all summer and freeze them for the Blueberry Sweet Muffins recipe, which I make all year long to celebrate happy occasions and to help people who aren't feeling well." Turn the page to find her muffin recipe.

Good things come in small packages—like these delicious blueberry muffins.

Prep: 10 minutes
Bake: 25 minutes

1½ cups all-purpose flour
½ cup sugar
2 teaspoons baking powder
½ teaspoon salt
⅓ cup milk
¼ cup vegetable oil
1 large egg
1 cup fresh or frozen blueberries
2 tablespoons sugar

• **Combine** first 4 ingredients in a large bowl, and make a well in center of mixture.
• **Stir** together milk, oil, and egg; add to dry ingredients, stirring just until dry ingredients are moistened. Fold in blueberries.
• **Spoon** batter into greased muffin pans, filling two-thirds full.
• **Sprinkle** batter evenly with 2 tablespoons sugar.
• **Bake** at 400° for 20 to 25 minutes or until muffins are golden. Remove from pans immediately, and cool on wire racks. **Yield:** 6 muffins.

Note: Freeze muffins up to 1 month, if desired. Thaw muffins at room temperature 2 hours.

Laura Wallace
Albany, Oregon

Kick Off the Season

Gather the gang, invite your neighbors, or surprise your family with a festive fall spread.

Game-Day Spread
Serves 12

Blue Cheese Rolls   Assorted crackers
Fried Chicken Fingers With Come Back Sauce
Black Bean Wraps   Salsa
Sweet 'n' Hot Green Beans and Carrots (double recipe)
Dark Chocolate Brownies

Simple, make-ahead fare and creative entertaining ideas guarantee that this menu will be a winner. Play classic Fried Chicken Fingers With Come Back Sauce against the other sporty snacks. This spread is sure to please any crowd.

BLUE CHEESE ROLLS

Serve these zesty cheese rolls with assorted crackers.

Prep: 15 minutes
Chill: 1 hour

2 (8-ounce) packages cream cheese, softened
1 (8-ounce) package sharp Cheddar cheese slices, cut up
2 (4-ounce) packages crumbled blue cheese
½ small onion, diced
1½ tablespoons Worcestershire sauce
½ teaspoon ground red pepper
1½ cups finely chopped toasted pecans, divided
1½ cups finely chopped fresh parsley, divided

• **Place** first 6 ingredients in a food processor; pulse 1 to 2 minutes, stopping to scrape down sides.
• **Stir** together cheese mixture, 1 cup pecans, and ½ cup parsley. Cover and chill 1 hour.
• **Shape** cheese mixture into 4 (7-inch-long) logs.
• **Combine** remaining ½ cup pecans and 1 cup parsley.
• **Roll** logs in parsley mixture; cover and chill. Serve with crackers. **Yield:** 4 (7-inch) logs.

Note: For testing purposes only, we used Old English cheese slices. If desired, prepare cheese rolls ahead, and freeze. Thaw in refrigerator overnight.

Suzan L. Wiener
Spring Hill, Florida

FRIED CHICKEN FINGERS WITH COME BACK SAUCE

Prep: 12 minutes
Chill: 4 hours
Fry: 6 minutes per batch

8 skinned and boned chicken breast
   halves
2 cups milk
1 teaspoon salt
½ teaspoon lemon pepper
½ teaspoon black pepper
2 cups all-purpose flour
Vegetable oil
Garnish: gourmet salad greens
Come Back Sauce

• **Cut** each breast half into 4 strips.
• **Combine** chicken strips, milk, and next 3 ingredients in a shallow dish or heavy-duty zip-top plastic bag. Cover or seal, and chill 4 hours.
• **Remove** chicken, discarding marinade; dredge in flour.
• **Pour** oil to a depth of 2 inches into a large Dutch oven; heat to 350°.
• **Fry** chicken, in batches, 5 to 6 minutes or until golden. Drain on paper towels. Garnish, if desired. Serve with Come Back Sauce. **Yield:** 16 appetizer servings.

Come Back Sauce

Prep: 10 minutes
Chill: 1 hour

1 cup mayonnaise
½ cup olive oil
⅓ cup chili sauce
¼ cup ketchup
2 tablespoons water
4 teaspoons Worcestershire
   sauce
4 teaspoons prepared mustard
2 teaspoons coarsely ground
   pepper
⅛ teaspoon paprika
¼ teaspoon hot sauce
1 medium onion, minced
2 garlic cloves, minced

• **Stir** together all ingredients in a bowl. Cover sauce, and chill at least 1 hour. **Yield:** 3 cups.

BLACK BEAN WRAPS

Prep: 35 minutes

2 (8-ounce) packages cream cheese,
   softened
2 cups (8 ounces) shredded Monterey
   Jack cheese with peppers
½ cup sour cream
1 teaspoon onion salt
2 (15-ounce) cans black beans, rinsed
   and drained
¼ cup salsa
12 (8-inch) flour tortillas
1 (10-ounce) package fresh spinach
2 (7-ounce) jars roasted sweet red
   peppers, drained and coarsely
   chopped
2 carrots, shredded (optional)

• **Beat** first 4 ingredients in a large bowl at medium speed with an electric mixer until thoroughly blended. Set cheese mixture aside.
• **Process** beans and salsa in a food processor until smooth, stopping to scrape down sides.
• **Spread** bean mixture evenly over tortillas; top each evenly with cheese mixture, spinach, peppers, and, if desired, carrot. Roll tortillas tightly; wrap each in plastic wrap. Chill, if desired. Serve with salsa. **Yield:** 12 servings.

Note: If desired, prepare Black Bean Wraps up to 4 hours ahead; chill until ready to serve.

Diane Sparrow
Osage, Iowa

SWEET 'N' HOT GREEN BEANS AND CARROTS

Prep: 15 minutes
Stand: 5 hours
Cook: 1 minute

½ cup sugar
½ cup white wine vinegar
¼ to ½ teaspoon dried crushed red
   pepper
1 garlic clove, minced
½ pound fresh green beans, trimmed
½ pound carrots, cut into 4- x ½-inch
   strips

• **Whisk** together sugar and vinegar until sugar dissolves. Stir in crushed red pepper and minced garlic; cover and let stand 4 hours.
• **Cook** green beans and carrot in boiling water 1 minute; drain.
• **Plunge** into ice water to stop cooking process; drain.
• **Pour** vinegar mixture over vegetables, tossing to coat. Let stand 1 hour before serving. **Yield:** 4 to 6 appetizer servings.

Amy Morse
Birmingham, Alabama

DARK CHOCOLATE BROWNIES

Butter, walnuts, and chocolate morsels enrich these delectable brownies.

Prep: 10 minutes
Bake: 40 minutes

1 cup butter or margarine
6 ounces bittersweet chocolate
2 cups sugar
4 large eggs
1 tablespoon vanilla extract *
1 cup all-purpose flour, divided
1½ cups chopped walnuts
1 cup (6 ounces) semisweet
   chocolate morsels
⅛ teaspoon salt

• **Microwave** butter and bittersweet chocolate in a 2-quart glass bowl at HIGH 1½ minutes or until chocolate is melted, stirring mixture twice.
• **Whisk** in 2 cups sugar, eggs, and vanilla.
• **Toss** together 1 tablespoon flour, walnuts, and chocolate morsels.
• **Stir** remaining flour and salt into sugar mixture. Add walnut mixture.
• **Spread** batter into a lightly greased 13- x 9-inch pan.
• **Bake** at 350° for 30 to 40 minutes. (A wooden pick inserted in center will not come out clean.) Cool on a wire rack. **Yield:** 2 dozen.

*Substitute bourbon for vanilla extract, if desired.

Sharon Walker Howard
Mayfield, Kentucky

A Handful of Goodness

There's nothing fancy about fried pies, but these old favorites are sure to be welcome at any gathering—especially with our new twists. Baked or fried . . . you decide, but be sure to make these tender and flaky desserts.

Dried fruit is still the basic ingredient, but with the wide variety now available, you can try some wonderful combinations—ginger-peach and cherry-pear just to name two. Today's ready-made piecrusts mean these creative recipes are a breeze.

Make them any size you like. If you prefer, you can bake them instead of frying. They taste fabulous hot and are great lunchbox treats when cold. Either way, they're a delectable handful of goodness that's perfect with tonight's supper.

GINGER-PEACH FRIED PIES

Prep: 30 minutes
Stand: 1 hour
Cook: 30 minutes
Chill: 30 minutes
Fry: 20 minutes

1½ cups water
1 (6-ounce) package dried peaches, chopped
½ cup sugar
2 tablespoons minced crystallized ginger
¾ teaspoon vanilla extract
1 (15-ounce) package refrigerated piecrusts
Vegetable oil

● **Combine** 1½ cups water and peaches in a saucepan; let stand 1 hour.
● **Stir** in sugar, ginger, and vanilla; bring to a boil over medium heat. Reduce heat, and simmer, stirring often, 30 minutes or until peaches are tender and liquid has evaporated.
● **Process** peach mixture in a food processor until smooth, stopping to scrape down sides. Cover and chill 30 minutes.
● **Roll** piecrusts into 12-inch circles; cut each crust into 9 (4-inch) circles.
● **Spoon** 2 rounded teaspoonfuls peach mixture onto half of each pastry circle. Moisten edges with water; fold dough over fruit mixture, pressing edges to seal. Crimp edges of dough with a fork dipped in flour.
● **Pour** oil to a depth of ½ inch into a large heavy skillet; heat to 350°.
● **Fry** pies, in batches, 2 minutes on each side. **Yield:** 1½ dozen.

Note: To bake, place on lightly greased baking sheets at 425° for 12 minutes.

APRICOT CREAM FRIED PIES

Prep: 30 minutes
Cook: 30 minutes
Fry: 20 minutes

1⅓ cups water
1 (6-ounce) package dried apricots
¼ cup sugar
2 tablespoons cream cheese
1 (15-ounce) package refrigerated piecrusts
Vegetable oil

● **Bring** 1⅓ cups water and apricots to a boil over medium heat.
● **Cook** 30 minutes; drain. Mash apricots with a potato masher until smooth. Cool completely.
● **Process** sugar and cream cheese in a food processor until smooth.
● **Add** apricots; pulse 2 or 3 times or until blended.
● **Roll** piecrusts into 12-inch circles; cut each crust into 9 (4-inch) circles.
● **Spoon** 2 rounded teaspoonfuls apricot mixture onto half of each pastry circle. Moisten edges with water; fold dough over fruit mixture, pressing edges to seal. Crimp edges of dough with a fork dipped in flour.
● **Pour** oil to a depth of ½ inch into a large heavy skillet; heat to 350°.
● **Fry** pies, in batches, 2 minutes on each side. **Yield:** 1½ dozen.

Note: To bake, place on lightly greased baking sheets at 425° for 12 minutes.

Albert Noble
Bristol, Tennessee

DRIED CHERRY-AND-PEAR FRIED PIES

(pictured on page 228)

*These fried pies delight
the senses with bursts
of fruity flavor.*

*Prep: 25 minutes
Cook: 25 minutes
Chill: 1 hour
Fry: 20 minutes*

3 large pears, peeled and
    chopped
2 (3-ounce) packages dried
    cherries
½ cup sugar
1 (15-ounce) package refrigerated
    piecrusts
Vegetable oil

• **Cook** first 3 ingredients in a saucepan over medium heat 5 minutes. Reduce heat, and simmer, stirring occasionally, 20 minutes or until pears are tender. Cover and chill 1 hour. Drain pear mixture, discarding liquid.
• **Roll** piecrusts into 12-inch circles; cut each crust into 9 (4-inch) circles.
• **Spoon** 1 rounded tablespoonful pear mixture onto half of each pastry circle. Moisten edges with water; fold dough over fruit mixture, pressing edges to seal. Crimp edges of dough with a fork dipped in flour.
• **Pour** oil to a depth of ½ inch into a large heavy skillet; heat to 350°.
• **Fry** pies, in batches, 2 minutes on each side. **Yield:** 1½ dozen.

Note: To bake, place on lightly greased baking sheets at 425° for 12 minutes. To make larger pies, cut piecrusts into 5 (7-inch) circles. Spoon filling evenly onto circles.

A Good Cause for Celebration

With a fine-tuned plan, 32 women hosted about 200 for the annual Circle for Children's New Member Party to benefit the education and welfare of Georgia's children. Each member brought a dish that could be served at room temperature within two hours of arrival, multiplied for large quantities, and served in plastic cups or on small plates. Whether you're serving 12 or 200, you'll enjoy this easy menu.

A Simple Celebration
Serves 12

Stuffed Pork Tenderloin
Pasta Salad
Broccoli Salad

STUFFED PORK TENDERLOIN

*Prep: 40 minutes
Bake: 25 minutes*

4 (¾-pound) pork tenderloins
2 tablespoons Creole seasoning
2 (12-ounce) packages andouille
    sausage or smoked sausage
4 to 8 bacon slices
Creole mustard (optional)

• **Place** tenderloins between 2 sheets of heavy-duty plastic wrap; flatten to ½-inch thickness, using a meat mallet. Sprinkle with Creole seasoning. Pierce sausage with a fork; place 2 sausages in center of each tenderloin. Wrap tenderloin around sausage; tie with twine. Top with 1 to 2 bacon slices. (Wrap in foil and freeze up to 2 weeks, if desired; thaw in refrigerator.) Place tenderloin,

seam side down, on a lightly greased rack in a broiler pan. Bake at 450° for 15 minutes. Reduce temperature to 400°.
• **Bake** 10 minutes or until a meat thermometer registers 155°. Remove from oven; cover with foil. Let stand 10 minutes. Remove twine; slice. Serve with mustard, if desired. **Yield:** 12 servings.

*Dottie Rachels
Marietta, Georgia*

PASTA SALAD

*Prep: 10 minutes
Cook: 13 minutes
Chill: 8 hours*

1 (16-ounce) package bow tie pasta
1 medium-size red bell pepper, chopped
1 (8-ounce) bottle Caesar dressing
½ cup grated Parmesan cheese
¼ cup shredded fresh basil
⅛ teaspoon salt

• **Cook** pasta according to package directions. Drain; rinse with cold water.
• **Combine** pasta and remaining ingredients in a large bowl, tossing to coat. Cover; chill 8 hours. **Yield:** 12 servings.

*Charlotte Brand
Marietta, Georgia*

BROCCOLI SALAD

*Prep: 15 minutes
Chill: 8 hours*

¾ cup mayonnaise
¼ cup sugar
1½ tablespoons white vinegar
1 (16-ounce) package broccoli
    flowerets
1 (11-ounce) can mandarin oranges,
    drained
1 small purple onion, chopped
½ cup golden raisins
½ cup sliced almonds, toasted

• **Combine** first 3 ingredients; add broccoli and next 3 ingredients. Chill 8 hours. Top with almonds. **Yield:** 12 servings.

*Debbie Russell
Alpharetta, Georgia*

Living Light

A cheesy casserole or other fattening favorite may seem impossible to lighten. But a little tweaking and some healthful stand-ins can turn such a dish into a delicious lower calorie choice.

Many of you have asked us to slim down favorite recipes. Here's a classic meal made lighter and a quesadilla so good, no one will ever know it's healthy.

Favorite Family Fare
Serves 6

Individual Meat Loaves
Smoky Mashed Potato Bake
Steamed green beans

INDIVIDUAL MEAT LOAVES
(pictured on page 227)

Reduce sodium by omitting seasoned salt and using only half a bottle of chili sauce.

Prep: 20 minutes
Bake: 1 hour

2 pounds lean ground beef
1 tablespoon reduced-sodium Worcestershire sauce
½ teaspoon seasoned salt
½ teaspoon seasoned pepper
1 medium onion, minced
5 white bread slices, crusts removed
½ cup fat-free milk
¼ cup egg substitute
1½ cups soft breadcrumbs
Vegetable cooking spray
1 (12-ounce) bottle chili sauce
½ cup boiling water

• **Combine** first 5 ingredients; set aside.
• **Cut** bread into small pieces. Place bread, milk, and egg substitute in a large bowl. Beat at medium speed with an electric mixer until blended.
• **Stir** meat mixture into egg mixture.
• **Shape** mixture into 6 loaves; roll in breadcrumbs.
• **Arrange** loaves in a 13- x 9-inch pan coated with cooking spray. Spread chili sauce over loaves. Pour ½ cup boiling water into pan. Bake at 350° for 1 hour. **Yield:** 6 servings.

♥ Per serving: Calories 386 (21% from fat)
Fat 9g (sat 3g, mono 3.9g, poly 0.6g)
Protein 39.5g Carb 38.5g Fiber 1.7g
Chol 88mg Iron 5.1mg
Sodium 1,186mg Calc 88mg

SMOKY MASHED POTATO BAKE
(pictured on page 227)

Prep: 50 minutes
Bake: 30 minutes

3 garlic cloves, minced
1 teaspoon olive oil
Vegetable cooking spray
3½ pounds new potatoes, cut into 1-inch pieces
¾ cup (3 ounces) shredded smoked Gouda cheese, divided
1 cup fat-free half-and-half
2 to 3 chipotle peppers in adobo sauce, minced
½ cup light margarine
½ (8-ounce) package fat-free cream cheese, softened
¼ teaspoon salt

• **Sauté** garlic in hot olive oil in a small skillet coated with cooking spray over medium-high heat 2 to 3 minutes or until tender.
• **Cook** potatoes in a Dutch oven in boiling water to cover 30 minutes or until tender; drain.
• **Mash** potatoes in a large bowl.
• **Stir** in garlic, ¼ cup Gouda cheese, half-and-half, and next 4 ingredients until blended.
• **Spoon** mixture into a 13- x 9-inch baking dish coated with cooking spray. Sprinkle evenly with remaining ½ cup Gouda cheese.
• **Bake** casserole at 350° for 30 minutes or until Gouda cheese melts. **Yield:** 10 servings.

Michelle Zacharia
Omaha, Nebraska

♥ Per ½ cup: Calories 245 (32% from fat)
Fat 8.8g (sat 1.6g, mono 1g, poly 0.2g)
Protein 7.3g Carb 32g Fiber 2.9g
Chol 12mg Iron 2.1mg
Sodium 369mg Calc 152mg

SHRIMP-AND-ROASTED PEPPER QUESADILLAS

Prep: 30 minutes
Bake: 5 minutes

2 green bell peppers
1 red bell pepper
1 pound unpeeled, medium-size fresh
   shrimp
2 to 3 garlic cloves, minced
3 green onions, sliced
2 teaspoons olive oil
½ teaspoon salt
¼ teaspoon pepper
4 (10-inch) fat-free flour tortillas
1 cup (4 ounces) shredded reduced-fat
   Monterey Jack cheese with
   peppers
½ cup chopped fresh cilantro
½ cup light sour cream
½ cup salsa

• **Broil** bell peppers on an aluminum foil-lined baking sheet 5 inches from heat about 5 minutes on each side or until peppers look blistered.
• **Place** peppers in a heavy-duty zip-top plastic bag; seal and let stand 10 minutes to loosen skins. Peel peppers; remove and discard seeds. Cut into 1-inch pieces, and set aside.
• **Peel** shrimp; devein, if desired.
• **Sauté** garlic, green onions, and shrimp in hot oil in a large skillet over medium-high heat 3 minutes or just until shrimp turn pink. Sprinkle with salt and pepper.
• **Spoon** shrimp mixture evenly on half of each tortilla. Top evenly with bell pepper, shredded cheese, and cilantro. Fold in half, pressing edges gently to seal. Place quesadillas on a baking sheet.
• **Bake** at 350° for 4 to 5 minutes or until cheese melts. Top quesadillas with sour cream and salsa. **Yield:** 4 servings.
Pamela Hanlin
Louisville, Colorado

❤ Per serving: Calories 380 (31% from fat)
   Fat 13g (sat 6g, mono 2.9g, poly 1.2g)
   Protein 34g Carb 35g Fiber 2.5g
   Chol 145mg Iron 4mg
   Sodium 674mg Calc 333mg

A Taste of the South

Through the years grits have been the workhorse of the Southern table. Enlisted to fill plates when more expensive ingredients were scarce, grits also acted as a foundation for flavorful items such as gravy or overeasy eggs. However, in the past decade or so, grits have experienced a renaissance, appearing on upscale menus with ingredients such as peppers, cheese, and shrimp.

Most folks enjoy grits made with more than just water, salt, and pepper, so we're showcasing traditional Creamy Grits and topping them with either Tomato Gravy or Country Ham With Redeye Gravy (recipes on next page) for an authentic and delicious Deep South twist.

CREAMY GRITS

Prep: 5 minutes
Cook: 45 minutes

2 cups milk
2 cups water
1 to 1½ teaspoons salt
1 cup uncooked regular grits
1 cup whipping cream
¼ cup butter or margarine
1 to 2 teaspoons freshly ground pepper

• **Bring** first 3 ingredients to a boil in a large saucepan; gradually stir in grits. Reduce heat; simmer, stirring occasionally, 30 to 40 minutes or until thickened.
• **Stir** in whipping cream, butter, and pepper; simmer, stirring occasionally, 5 minutes. **Yield:** 6 servings.

Note: For thinner grits, stir in additional milk. To lighten, use 1% milk, substitute fat-free half-and-half for cream, and reduce butter to 2 tablespoons.

GARLIC-CHEESE GRITS

Prep: 30 minutes
Bake: 1 hour

4 cups water
1 teaspoon salt
2 garlic cloves, pressed
1 cup uncooked regular grits
1 (12-ounce) block sharp Cheddar
   cheese, shredded
½ cup butter or margarine
1 teaspoon seasoned pepper
1 teaspoon Worcestershire
   sauce
¼ teaspoon hot sauce
3 large eggs, lightly beaten
Paprika

• **Bring** first 3 ingredients to a boil in a large saucepan; gradually stir in grits. Return to a boil; reduce heat, and simmer, stirring occasionally, 15 minutes or until thickened.
• **Add** cheese and next 4 ingredients, stirring until cheese melts. Remove from heat; let stand 10 minutes.
• **Stir** in eggs, and pour into a lightly greased 11- x 7-inch baking dish. Sprinkle with paprika.
• **Bake** at 350° for 1 hour or until set. **Yield:** 8 to 10 servings.
Carolyn Flournoy
Shreveport, Louisiana

TOMATO GRAVY

Prep: 5 minutes
Cook: 8 minutes

2 tablespoons butter or margarine
2 tablespoons minced shallots or
     onion
1 (14½-ounce) can diced tomatoes,
     undrained
½ cup whipping cream
1 teaspoon chicken bouillon granules
½ teaspoon sugar
¼ teaspoon pepper

● **Melt** butter in a large skillet over medium heat; add shallots, and sauté until tender.
● **Stir** in tomatoes; bring to a boil. Reduce heat, and simmer, stirring constantly, 2 to 3 minutes.
● **Stir** in whipping cream and remaining ingredients; simmer, stirring often, 3 minutes or until mixture is thickened. **Yield:** 2 cups.

COUNTRY HAM WITH REDEYE GRAVY

Prep: 5 minutes
Cook: 25 minutes

2 cups hot strong brewed coffee
¼ cup firmly packed brown sugar
1 pound center-cut country ham slices

● **Stir** together coffee and sugar.
● **Cook** ham in a large cast-iron skillet over medium heat 5 minutes on each side or until browned. Remove ham; reserve drippings in skillet.
● **Add** coffee mixture to skillet, stirring to loosen particles from bottom; bring coffee mixture to a boil.
● **Boil**, stirring occasionally, until reduced by half (about 15 minutes). Serve with ham. **Yield:** 6 servings.

TRUE GRITS

Confusion abounds over what grits actually are. Commercially produced grits are made from ground, degerminated, dried white or yellow corn kernels that have been soaked in a solution of water and lye. The only grits for purists are produced by the old-fashioned method of stone grinding with a water-turned stone. These grits retain a more natural texture and rich flavor. Stone-ground grits are sometimes labeled as "speckled heart," because the remaining germ—or heart of the kernel—looks like a tiny black fleck. See "From Our Kitchen" on page 224 for more information on grits.

If your grocery store doesn't carry stone-ground grits, several companies offer them by mail. Shipping can be more expensive than the grits themselves, but for many folks there's no substitute. Raw stone-ground grits freeze well, so a great way to beat the cost of shipping is to buy in bulk with family and friends.

Here are some places you can order stone-ground grits.

■ Nora Mill Granary
1-800-927-2375
www.noramill.com

■ Falls Mill and Country Store
(931) 469-7161
www.fallsmill.com

■ Callaway Gardens Country Store
1-800-280-7524
www.callawaygardens.com

■ Hoppin' John's
1-800-828-4412
www.hoppinjohns.com

Iceberg at Its Peak

Iceberg lettuce is on a roll as the comeback story of this year. It's one of those faithful foods we crave. With its versatility and value, coolness and crunch, there's just no topping the iceberg.

To prepare iceberg lettuce in advance, remove the core and soak the lettuce in ice water for a couple of hours. Blot thoroughly with paper towels, seal in a zip-top plastic bag, and chill until time to prepare the salad. The leaves will look crisp and perky for the party.

And what if your good-looking lettuce goes limp? Our foods veteran Peggy Smith says she plunges the leaves into ice water and then lets them soak for a few more minutes. She guarantees, "They'll come right back, good as new."

LEMON-BASIL CHICKEN SALAD WRAPS

Prep: 35 minutes

1 (3.5-ounce) package peanut
     sauce mix
8 cups chopped cooked chicken
2 cups mayonnaise
6 green onions, sliced
4 celery ribs, diced
⅔ cup chopped fresh basil
1 tablespoon grated lemon rind
2 tablespoons fresh lemon juice
½ teaspoon garlic salt
½ teaspoon freshly ground pepper
8 (10-inch) flour tortillas
½ head iceberg lettuce, shredded

● **Prepare** peanut sauce according to package directions; cover and chill sauce until ready to use.
● **Combine** chopped chicken and next 8 ingredients in a large bowl. Spread 2 to 3 tablespoons peanut sauce over each tortilla. Top with chicken salad and lettuce; roll up. **Yield:** 8 servings.

Note: For testing purposes only, we used A Taste of Thai Peanut Sauce Mix.

CURRIED SHRIMP SALAD

Prep: 30 minutes

6 cups water
2 pounds medium-size fresh shrimp ✱
1 head iceberg lettuce, shredded
4 celery ribs, diced
4 green onions, diced
1¾ cups Curried Dressing
Toppings: toasted slivered almonds,
    toasted coconut, golden raisins,
    sliced green onions

• **Bring** 6 cups water to a boil; add shrimp, and cook 3 to 5 minutes or just until shrimp turn pink. Drain and rinse with cold water.
• **Peel** shrimp; devein, if desired.
• **Combine** lettuce, celery, and diced green onions, and place on a large platter. Arrange shrimp over lettuce mixture. Cover and chill, if desired.
• **Serve** with Curried Dressing and desired toppings. **Yield:** 6 to 8 servings.

✱Substitute 4 cups chopped cooked chicken for fresh boiled shrimp, if desired.

Curried Dressing

Prep: 5 minutes

1 cup mayonnaise
½ cup hot mango chutney
2 teaspoons curry powder
2 tablespoons tarragon vinegar
2 tablespoons vegetable oil

• **Process** all ingredients in a blender or food processor until smooth. **Yield:** about 1¾ cups.

Eleanor K. Brandt
Arlington, Texas

HAM-AND-PEA PASTA SALAD

Prep: 20 minutes

8 ounces uncooked small shell pasta
2 cups diced cooked ham
1 (10-ounce) package frozen baby
    sweet green peas, thawed
1 small purple onion, diced
1 cup shredded Parmesan cheese
1 cup Mayonnaise Dressing
½ small head iceberg lettuce,
    shredded

• **Cook** pasta according to package directions. Drain.
• **Sauté** ham in a lightly greased skillet over medium-high heat 3 to 5 minutes or until lightly browned. Toss together pasta, ham, and remaining ingredients. Serve immediately. **Yield:** 6 servings.

Mayonnaise Dressing

Prep: 5 minutes

1 cup mayonnaise
3 tablespoons sugar
2 tablespoons red wine vinegar
½ teaspoon seasoned salt
½ teaspoon seasoned pepper

• **Whisk** together all ingredients until blended. **Yield:** about 1 cup.

Note: Prepare salad ahead, if desired. Toss with lettuce just before serving.

ICEBERG LETTUCE WEDGES WITH BLUE CHEESE DRESSING

Prep: 15 minutes

12 bacon slices, cooked and crumbled
½ cup shredded Parmesan cheese
¼ cup chopped fresh chives
1 large head iceberg lettuce, cut into
    6 wedges
Blue Cheese Dressing

• **Stir** together first 3 ingredients.
• **Top** each lettuce wedge with Blue Cheese Dressing, and sprinkle dressing evenly with bacon mixture. **Yield:** 6 servings.

Blue Cheese Dressing

Prep: 5 minutes

1 cup mayonnaise
1 (8-ounce) container sour cream
4 ounces blue cheese, crumbled
¼ teaspoon salt
1 tablespoon Worcestershire sauce
1 teaspoon lemon juice

• **Stir** together all ingredients. **Yield:** about 2½ cups.

Laura Morris
Bunnell, Florida

What's for Supper?

Now you can simplify supper and satisfy a craving for richly flavored caramelized onions at the same time. Caramelizing onions can be as easy as taking five minutes to toss a few ingredients into a slow cooker.

CARAMELIZED ONIONS

With a supply of this golden mixture on hand, you'll be able to throw together a delicious meal in no time.

Prep: 5 minutes
Cook: 8 hours

2 extra-large sweet onions (about 3 pounds)
1 (10½-ounce) can chicken or beef broth, undiluted
¼ cup butter or margarine

• **Cut** onions in half; cut each half into ½-inch-thick slices.
• **Combine** all ingredients in a 3½-quart slow cooker. Cook, covered, at HIGH 8 hours or until golden brown and very soft. Store in an airtight container; chill up to 2 weeks, or, if desired, freeze up to 2 months. **Yield:** 2 cups.

PEPPER BURGERS WITH CARAMELIZED ONIONS

Prep: 11 minutes
Grill: 10 minutes

1 pound ground beef
¼ teaspoon salt
¼ teaspoon ground white pepper
¼ teaspoon freshly ground black pepper
¼ teaspoon ground red pepper
¼ teaspoon paprika
1 cup Caramelized Onions (recipe above)
2 teaspoons white balsamic vinegar
Lettuce leaves
4 kaiser rolls, split

• **Shape** beef into 4 patties.
• **Combine** salt and next 4 ingredients; sprinkle mixture evenly over both sides of patties.
• **Grill,** covered with grill lid, over medium-high heat (350° to 400°) 5 minutes on each side or until beef is no longer pink.
• **Cook** Caramelized Onions and vinegar in a saucepan over medium heat 5 minutes or until thoroughly heated. Spoon over burgers. Top with lettuce, and serve on rolls. **Yield:** 4 servings.

Adelyne Smith
Dunnville, Kentucky

CARAMELIZED ONION MAYONNAISE

This mayonnaise adds incredible flavor to sandwiches. You can also use it as a sauce for fish or shrimp.

Prep: 5 minutes
Chill: 30 minutes

1 cup mayonnaise
1 cup Caramelized Onions, chopped (recipe at left)
1 to 2 garlic cloves, minced
¼ teaspoon salt
¼ teaspoon pepper

• **Stir** together all ingredients. Cover and chill at least 30 minutes. Serve with fish, with steamed shrimp, or as a sandwich spread. **Yield:** 2 cups.

CARAMELIZED FRENCH ONION SOUP
(pictured on page 226)

Prep: 5 minutes
Cook: 2 hours, 30 minutes
Broil: 5 minutes

1 recipe Caramelized Onions (recipe at left)
1 (10½-ounce) can beef consommé, undiluted
1 (10½-ounce) can beef broth, undiluted
2 cups water
½ teaspoon dried thyme
¼ cup dry white wine
6 cups large croutons
1 cup (4 ounces) shredded Swiss cheese

• **Combine** first 5 ingredients in a 3½-quart slow cooker.
• **Cook,** covered, at HIGH 2½ hours or until thoroughly heated. Stir in wine.
• **Ladle** soup into 6 ovenproof bowls, and top evenly with croutons and cheese. Place bowls on a jellyroll pan.
• **Broil** 3 inches from heat 5 minutes or until cheese is melted. Serve immediately. **Yield:** 6 servings.

TIMELY TIPS FOR SLOW COOKING

■ Avoid removing the slow cooker lid during the first three-quarters of the cooking time to prevent heat loss.

■ Cooking time may be longer during extreme humidity.

■ You may have to cook foods for longer periods at altitudes higher than 3,500 feet.

Quick & Easy

Chicken's versatility makes it a staple in our meals and ideal for many convenient cooking methods. Although fried chicken will always reign supreme on Southern tables, there are countless other ways to prepare the main dish. Intense flavors abound in these three recipes.

ITALIAN CHICKEN AND ARTICHOKES

Prep: 20 minutes
Cook: 15 minutes

2 tablespoons butter or margarine
1 garlic clove, minced
6 skinned and boned chicken breast halves
1 (10¾-ounce) can cream of chicken soup, undiluted
1 (8-ounce) container sour cream
½ cup (2 ounces) shredded mozzarella cheese
¼ cup dry white wine or chicken broth
2 tablespoons grated Parmesan cheese
1 (6-ounce) jar marinated artichoke hearts, drained and chopped
Hot cooked fettuccine
2 tablespoons chopped fresh parsley

● **Melt** butter in a large skillet over medium-high heat; add garlic, and sauté 15 seconds.
● **Add** chicken, and cook 2 to 3 minutes on each side or until lightly browned.
● **Stir** together soup and next 4 ingredients; spoon over chicken. Reduce heat, and simmer 5 to 7 minutes or until chicken is done. Remove chicken from skillet, and keep warm.
● **Stir** artichokes into sauce; cover and cook 1 to 2 minutes or until thoroughly heated. Place chicken on pasta, and spoon sauce over chicken. Sprinkle with parsley. **Yield:** 6 servings.

Note: To lighten recipe, use light butter; reduced-fat chicken soup; light sour cream; reduced-fat mozzarella cheese; and 1 (14-ounce) can artichoke hearts, drained.

Debbie Collard Anderson
Elizabethtown, Kentucky

SESAME-GINGER CHICKEN

Prep: 10 minutes
Grill: 12 minutes

1 tablespoon sesame seeds, toasted
2 tablespoons soy sauce
2 tablespoons honey
2 teaspoons grated fresh ginger
Vegetable cooking spray
4 skinned and boned chicken breast halves

● **Stir** together first 4 ingredients.
● **Coat** food rack with cooking spray; place on grill over medium-high heat (350° to 400°). Place chicken on rack; grill 6 minutes on each side or until done, basting often with sauce mixture. **Yield:** 4 servings.

Note: Soy sauce mixture may also be basted on pork.

Judith L. Mason
Raleigh, North Carolina

CHICKEN PARMESAN

Prep: 15 minutes
Cook: 20 minutes

4 skinned and boned chicken breast halves
1 large egg, lightly beaten
⅓ cup Italian-seasoned breadcrumbs
2 tablespoons butter or margarine
1¾ cups spaghetti sauce
½ cup (2 ounces) shredded mozzarella cheese
1 tablespoon grated Parmesan cheese

● **Place** chicken between 2 sheets of heavy-duty plastic wrap; flatten to ¼-inch thickness using a meat mallet or rolling pin. Dip in egg; dredge in crumbs.
● **Melt** butter in a skillet over medium-high heat; add chicken. Cook 2 minutes on each side or until browned.
● **Pour** spaghetti sauce over chicken. Cover, reduce heat, and simmer 10 minutes. Top with cheeses. Cover; simmer 5 minutes or until mozzarella melts. **Yield:** 4 servings.

Julie Pyron
Birmingham, Alabama

CHICKEN IN A HURRY

The cooking method below is ideal for recipes that call for chopped cooked chicken. When time is short, your family's meals can be swift and savory.

Arrange 3 celery ribs, cut into 4-inch pieces; 2 carrots, sliced; and 1 medium onion, sliced, in a lightly greased 13- x 9-inch pan. Top with 6 skinned and boned chicken breast halves. Sprinkle chicken with ½ teaspoon salt and ¼ teaspoon pepper. Bake, covered, at 400° for 25 to 30 minutes or until chicken is done. Cool chicken slightly; chop and store in plastic bags in freezer. Reserve broth, if desired.

Quiche Quest

These easy quiches are a great solution for mealtime. With the help of ready-made crusts and pantry ingredients, you can prepare this recipe on the spot or up to two days ahead.

TRIPLE-CHEESE SPINACH QUICHES

Prep: 30 minutes
Bake: 45 minutes
Stand: 15 minutes

1 (15-ounce) package refrigerated
   piecrusts
2 tablespoons Dijon mustard
2 (10-ounce) packages frozen
   chopped spinach, thawed
¼ cup butter or margarine,
   divided
4 green onions, minced
2 (15-ounce) containers ricotta
   cheese
1 cup whipping cream
6 large eggs, lightly beaten
1 teaspoon salt
¼ teaspoon ground nutmeg
¼ teaspoon pepper
2 cups (8 ounces) shredded Cheddar
   cheese
½ cup (2 ounces) shredded Swiss
   cheese

• **Fit** piecrusts into 2 (9-inch) pieplates; fold edges under, and crimp. Line each with aluminum foil, and fill with pie weights or dried beans.
• **Bake** at 425° for 10 minutes. Remove foil and weights; cool.
• **Brush** cooled pastry shells evenly with mustard.
• **Drain** spinach well, pressing between layers of paper towels.
• **Melt** 2 tablespoons butter in a large skillet over medium heat.
• **Add** green onions; sauté 2 minutes or until tender.
• **Add** spinach; cook 2 minutes. Remove from heat.

• **Stir** in ricotta and next 5 ingredients. Pour evenly into pastry shells. Sprinkle with shredded cheeses. Dot with remaining 2 tablespoons butter.
• **Bake** at 375° for 40 to 45 minutes or until set, shielding quiche with aluminum foil to prevent excessive browning, if necessary.
• **Let** quiche stand 10 to 15 minutes before serving. **Yield:** 12 to 15 servings.

Paula Kay Wilson
Texarkana, Texas

Oregano Adds Flavor

With gray-green leaves and a sturdy, spreading form, oregano is as visually appealing as it is aromatic. This versatile herb works well in many different dishes. Try a sprinkle in omelets, frittatas, marinated vegetables, tomato salad, chili, or beef stew.

LAMB KABOBS

These kabobs pair oregano and lamb—a divine duo, especially when grilling.

Prep: 25 minutes
Chill: 8 hours
Grill: 8 minutes

½ cup olive oil
¼ cup minced onion
3 tablespoons chopped fresh oregano
2 tablespoons red wine vinegar
1 teaspoon salt
¼ teaspoon pepper
2 garlic cloves, minced
1½ pounds lean boneless lamb, cut
   into 2-inch pieces
1 green bell pepper, cut into 2-inch
   pieces
1 purple onion, cut into wedges
4 to 6 plum tomatoes, quartered

• **Combine** first 7 ingredients in a large heavy-duty zip-top plastic bag.

• **Add** lamb, bell pepper, and onion. Seal; chill 8 hours, turning occasionally.
• **Remove** lamb and vegetables from marinade; reserve marinade. Thread lamb and vegetables alternately onto 6 (12-inch) skewers. Thread tomato onto 4 (12-inch) skewers.
• **Bring** reserved marinade to a boil over medium heat; boil 1 minute.
• **Grill** kabobs, covered with grill lid, over high heat (400° to 450°) 2 minutes on each side for tomato kabobs and 4 minutes on each side for lamb kabobs. Baste kabobs frequently with marinade. **Yield:** 4 to 6 servings.

Beatriz Swirsky
Sunrise, Florida

GRILLED VEGETABLES WITH HERBS

Prep: 20 minutes
Grill: 25 minutes

1 tablespoon chopped fresh parsley
2 tablespoons olive oil
½ teaspoon salt
¼ teaspoon pepper
8 new potatoes, quartered
3 medium-size yellow squash, cut into
   1-inch pieces
1 large onion, cut into 8 pieces
1 large green bell pepper, cut into
   8 pieces
2 tablespoons butter or margarine,
   softened
1 tablespoon chopped fresh
   oregano

• **Stir** together first 4 ingredients. Toss 1 tablespoon olive oil mixture with potato. Toss remaining olive oil mixture with squash, onion, and bell pepper.
• **Place** potato quarters in a lightly greased grill wok.
• **Grill,** covered with grill lid, over medium-high heat (350° to 400°) 10 minutes. Add squash, onion, and bell pepper; cook, tossing occasionally, 15 more minutes or until potato is tender.
• **Stir** together butter and oregano; add to vegetables, tossing to coat. Serve immediately. **Yield:** 4 servings.

Mike Miller
Charleston, South Carolina

SHRIMP WITH FETA CHEESE

(pictured on page 225)

*This shrimp recipe blends
a trio of herbs with shrimp for a
great entrée. Enjoy it year-round
as an appetizer or main dish.*

*Prep: 20 minutes
Cook: 30 minutes*

1 pound unpeeled, large fresh
   shrimp
1 tablespoon butter or margarine
1 teaspoon lemon juice
1 medium onion, halved and thinly
   sliced
2 tablespoons olive oil
½ cup dry white wine
½ cup clam juice
1 garlic clove, minced
3 to 4 plum tomatoes, coarsely
   chopped
2 teaspoons chopped fresh
   oregano
1 teaspoon chopped fresh
   basil
1 teaspoon chopped fresh
   parsley
1 cup crumbled feta cheese
Garnish: fresh oregano sprig

• **Peel** shrimp, and devein, if desired.
Set aside.
• **Melt** butter in a large skillet over
medium heat.
• **Add** shrimp and lemon juice, and
sauté 2 to 3 minutes or just until shrimp
turn pink.
• **Remove** shrimp from skillet.
• **Sauté** onion in hot oil until tender.
Add wine, clam juice, and garlic. Re-
duce heat, and simmer 10 minutes.
• **Add** chopped tomato, and simmer 5
more minutes.
• **Stir** in shrimp, oregano, basil, and
parsley.
• **Sprinkle** shrimp mixture with feta
cheese. Serve over hot cooked pasta or
with crusty bread. Garnish, if desired.
Yield: 4 servings.

OREGANO FLAVOR SAVERS

■ Oregano retains its flavor when
frozen—use the same amount
as you would fresh. Freeze 2
tablespoons chopped leaves,
covered with water, in sections
of an ice-cube tray or muffin tin.
Thaw under cold running water
before adding to soups, stews,
or sauces for a pungent burst of
flavor.

■ Blend chopped fresh oregano
into softened butter, form into
a log, wrap tightly, and freeze.
Slice the frozen herb butter,
and use it to top hot cooked
fish or pork chops. Or soften
the butter, and spread it on
French bread.

■ Place the stems of fresh
oregano in a jar or glass filled
with water, top with a plastic
bag, and store in the refrigerator. Change the water every few
days, and the oregano will stay
fresh for up to 1 month.

Great Gumbo

Enjoy the goodness of gumbo in this
light version made with an oil-free
roux and low-fat sausage.

CHICKEN-AND-SAUSAGE GUMBO

*Prep: 45 minutes
Cook: 1 hour, 10 minutes*

½ cup all-purpose flour
1 pound reduced-fat smoked sausage,
   cut into ¼-inch slices
Vegetable cooking spray
2 onions, chopped
2 celery ribs, chopped
1 small green bell pepper, chopped
4 garlic cloves, minced
½ teaspoon dried thyme
¼ to ½ teaspoon ground red pepper
8 skinned and boned chicken breast
   halves, chopped
2 (32-ounce) containers chicken broth
1 (14½-ounce) can diced tomatoes,
   undrained
½ pound peeled fresh shrimp
1 (10-ounce) package frozen sliced
   okra, thawed (optional)
Hot cooked rice
Garnish: fresh celery leaves

• **Cook** flour in a Dutch oven over
medium heat, stirring constantly, 10
minutes or until golden. Remove flour
from Dutch oven.
• **Sauté** sausage in Dutch oven coated
with cooking spray over medium-high
heat. Add onion and next 5 ingredients;
sauté 5 minutes.
• **Add** chicken, and sauté 3 minutes.
Stir in flour until blended. Gradually
add broth and tomatoes; reduce heat to
low, and simmer 30 minutes.
• **Add** shrimp and, if desired, okra; simmer 20 minutes. Serve over rice; garnish, if desired. **Yield:** 3½ quarts.

♥ Per cup with ½ cup rice: Calories 317
Fat 9.1g Cholesterol 83mg Sodium 736mg

In Praise of Leeks

Leeks may look like giant green onions, but these mild members of the onion family add subtle flavor to other foods and even taste great on their own.

Roasted, leeks present a crisp sweetness; creamed, they are silken and sensational. Toss them in salads, use them as a bed for roasting meats or poultry, or add them to mashed potatoes. Gentle though they may be, they pack a giant flavor boost.

CREAMED LEEKS

Prep: 10 minutes
Cook: 25 minutes

6 small leeks
2 tablespoons butter or margarine
5 garlic cloves, minced
¼ cup dry white wine or chicken broth
½ cup chicken broth
¼ cup whipping cream
⅛ teaspoon salt
¼ teaspoon pepper

● **Remove** root, tough outer leaves, and tops from leeks, leaving 2 inches of dark leaves. Cut into quarters lengthwise; rinse well, and drain. Cut into 1-inch pieces.
● **Melt** butter in a large Dutch oven over medium heat; add garlic, and sauté 1 minute.
● **Add** leeks, and sauté 1 minute. Add wine, and cook 5 minutes or until mixture is reduced by half.
● **Stir** in chicken broth; cover, reduce heat, and simmer 10 minutes. Uncover and cook 5 more minutes or until liquid evaporates.
● **Stir** in whipping cream, salt, and pepper. **Yield:** 3 to 4 servings.

LEEKS WITH BRUSSELS SPROUTS AND ALMONDS

An unexpected combination of flavors and textures makes this a superb side dish.

Prep: 15 minutes
Cook: 14 minutes

3 large leeks
½ pound small fresh brussels sprouts
2 to 3 tablespoons butter or margarine
1 large Granny Smith apple, diced
¼ cup water
¼ teaspoon salt
¼ teaspoon pepper
½ cup sliced almonds, toasted
2 bacon slices, cooked and crumbled

● **Remove** root, tough outer leaves, and tops from leeks, leaving 2 inches of dark leaves. Thinly slice leeks; rinse well, and drain.
● **Remove** discolored leaves from brussels sprouts. Cut off stem ends, and cut a shallow X in the bottom of each sprout.
● **Cook** brussels sprouts in boiling water to cover 3 to 4 minutes; drain.
● **Melt** butter in a large skillet over medium-high heat; add leeks, and sauté 5 minutes.
● **Add** brussels sprouts, apple, and next 3 ingredients; sauté 5 minutes or until apple and brussels sprouts are crisp-tender. Stir in almonds and bacon. Serve immediately. **Yield:** 4 servings.

Cindie Hackney
Longview, Texas

ROASTED LEEKS

Prep: 10 minutes
Bake: 25 minutes

6 small leeks
1 to 2 tablespoons olive oil
¼ teaspoon salt
¼ teaspoon pepper
½ teaspoon chopped fresh thyme
Dijon Vinaigrette

● **Remove** root, tough outer leaves, and tops from leeks, leaving 2 inches of dark leaves. Cut leeks in half lengthwise; rinse well, and drain.
● **Stir** together oil and next 3 ingredients; toss with leeks. Place, cut side down, on a lightly greased 15- x 10-inch jellyroll pan.
● **Bake** at 450° for 25 minutes or until wilted and lightly browned. Serve with Dijon Vinaigrette. **Yield:** 6 servings.

Dijon Vinaigrette

Prep: 5 minutes

2 tablespoons balsamic vinegar
2 tablespoons coarse-grained Dijon mustard
¼ teaspoon sugar
¼ cup olive oil

● **Whisk** together first 3 ingredients in a small bowl; gradually whisk in olive oil. **Yield:** ¾ cup.

DEEP DOWN CLEAN

Leeks need a lot of rinsing to get the sand out from between their layers. Hold split leeks under cold running water until all the sand is gone, or immerse them in water, swish them around, and then rinse. Pat the leeks dry, and store them in a sealed plastic bag in the refrigerator. They'll last up to a week.

Snacks That Pop

The sweet and savory pleasures of crunchy puffs of corn are irresistible. Rosemary Popcorn With Pine Nuts from Chef Sheri Clark of Dish Restaurant in Atlanta will make you want to revisit the fun of transforming humble kernels of dried corn into a snappy treat. Her recipe begins by soaking grains of corn in an oil-and-herb mixture. We liked it so much, we developed two variations.

DELICIOUS CHOCOLATE POPCORN

Prep: 10 minutes
Bake: 1 hour

12 cups popped popcorn
1 cup sugar
⅔ cup dark corn syrup
2 tablespoons butter or margarine
1 cup (6 ounces) semisweet chocolate morsels
1 teaspoon vanilla extract

• **Place** popcorn on a lightly greased 15- x 10-inch jellyroll pan; set aside.
• **Bring** sugar, syrup, and butter to a boil in a saucepan over medium heat, stirring constantly. Remove from heat; add chocolate morsels and vanilla, stirring until melted.
• **Drizzle** chocolate mixture over popcorn, stirring to coat.
• **Bake** at 250° for 1 hour, stirring occasionally. Transfer popcorn to a wax paper-lined pan to cool, stirring occasionally. **Yield:** 14 cups.

Agnes L. Mixon
Ocala, Florida

ROSEMARY POPCORN WITH PINE NUTS

Fresh rosemary gives flavor power to this savory popcorn.

Prep: 5 minutes
Stand: 48 hours
Cook: 4 minutes

1 cup olive oil
½ cup unpopped popcorn kernels
12 (6-inch) rosemary sprigs, cut into 2-inch pieces
1½ teaspoons sea salt, divided
½ cup pine nuts, toasted
2 tablespoons coarsely chopped fresh rosemary

• **Cook** oil in a small saucepan over low heat 3 minutes.
• **Add** popcorn kernels, rosemary sprigs, and 1 teaspoon sea salt. Remove from heat; cover and let stand at room temperature 48 hours.
• **Drain** kernels, reserving oil; discard rosemary sprigs.
• **Place** 3 tablespoons herb-flavored oil and popcorn kernels in a Dutch oven.
• **Cook** kernels, covered, over high heat, shaking pan often for 4 minutes until popping begins to slow. Remove popcorn from heat, and let stand 2 minutes or until popping stops.
• **Place** popcorn in a large bowl. Add remaining salt, pine nuts, and chopped rosemary, and toss. Serve immediately. **Yield:** 14 cups.

Chef Sheri Clark
Dish Restaurant
Atlanta, Georgia

Note: For testing purposes only, we used Kraft Parm Plus Garlic Herb cheese.

Quick-and-Easy Asian Popcorn: Omit steeping kernels step. Substitute 2½ tablespoons dark sesame oil plus ½ tablespoon hot chili oil for olive oil, garlic salt for sea salt, and roasted cashew pieces for pine nuts.

Basil, Garlic, and Parmesan Popcorn: Substitute basil for rosemary and ½ cup grated garlic-and-herb Parmesan cheese for pine nuts.

CHILI POPCORN

Prep: 15 minutes

2 (3.5-ounce) packages butter-flavored microwave popcorn
1 tablespoon grated Parmesan cheese
¼ teaspoon salt
⅛ teaspoon garlic powder
1 teaspoon paprika
½ teaspoon chili powder
Pinch of ground red pepper

• **Prepare** popcorn according to package directions.
• **Combine** cheese and next 5 ingredients. Open popcorn bags carefully; sprinkle cheese mixture evenly in both. Close bags; shake to coat. Serve immediately, or store in an airtight container. **Yield:** 8 cups.

Madeline Gibbons
Sherwood, Arkansas

CARAMEL-NUT POPCORN CLUSTERS

Prep: 6 minutes
Bake: 1 hour

1 (14-ounce) package caramels
2 tablespoons whipping cream
12 cups popped popcorn
1 cup dry-roasted peanuts

• **Combine** caramels and whipping cream in a glass bowl. Microwave at HIGH 3 minutes or until melted, stirring mixture once.
• **Place** popcorn and peanuts in a large bowl. Drizzle with caramel sauce, tossing gently to coat.
• **Place** popcorn mixture on a lightly greased 15- x 10-inch jellyroll pan.
• **Bake** at 250° for 1 hour. Cool. **Yield:** about 13 cups.

Howard Wiener
Spring Hill, Florida

From Our Kitchen

In the Lunchbox

Use these easy tips to get a head start on school lunches.

■ Help your kids make their own lunch combination packs using their favorite cold cuts, cheese, crackers, and sweet snacks. These lunches will be less expensive than the packaged versions, and the kids will have what they like.

■ Remove the crusts from bread, and cut sandwiches into cute shapes. (This works especially well for picky eaters or those entering school for the first time.)

■ Tuck in a little surprise: a love note, a candy kiss, or the promise of a special after-school treat.

Tortillas

September is National Tortilla Month. The flat, round bread—food of the ancient Aztecs—has become a mainstream ingredient in American menus. Whether tortillas are made from wheat flour or corn, we wrap, stack, fry, bake, and stuff them. Tortillas are possibly the world's most versatile bread. And for the record, both corn and flour tortillas are low in fat; it's what you put inside that adds fat and calories.

Large red, yellow, and green flour tortillas get their appearance and flavor from vegetable ingredients such as tomatoes, roasted corn, garlic, and spinach. You'll find these in the produce section of specialty grocery stores. Use them for sandwiches, or cut them into strips and fry for crisp salad toppings.

Look for regular tortillas in the refrigerated section, the ethnic food section, or in the bakery at the supermarket.

This Grain Has Grit

■ Instant, quick, and regular grits have the germ removed, which gives them a much longer shelf life. Stone-ground grits

---

MEASURE FOR MEASURE

Get a handle on the right measurements with these heavy spoons and cups from Cuisipro. The sturdy, dent-resistant, stainless steel utensils may be the last ones you'll have to buy. The oval-shaped cups fit easily into narrow containers and into drawers for storage. The spoon handles curl under to allow each to rest on the counter without falling over. Hang both sets on the wall or a tool bar within easy reach. The spoons cost around $10 and the cups around $26.

Call Browne & Co. at (302) 326-4802 for a store near you that sells Cuisipro products.

Another handy item to have hanging around is Kuhn Rikon's Cheese and Chocolate Grater. It's designed to give fluffy flakes of Parmesan cheese and decorative chocolate shavings, and there are no sharp edges to scrape fingers. The grater is available at nationwide retailers such as Professional Cutlery Direct (1-800-859-6994).

---

contain the oily germ, requiring storage in either the refrigerator or freezer. See "A Taste of the South" on page 215 for recipes.

■ Scholars argue that grits were America's first food, and they just might be right. The Powhatan Indians (of the Tidewater area of Virginia) served the earliest Virginia settlers a hot substance made from ground corn. In any case, grits have certainly been a part of Southern cooking for centuries.

■ In the past, grits were the ultimate tool of the thrift-conscious family. Not only were they served at the table, they were also used to kill fire ants, and wrapped in cheesecloth and placed in closets to absorb moisture.

Tips and Tidbits

■ The natural moisture in popcorn is what causes it to pop; dried-out kernels won't budge. If you're getting too many unpopped kernels (widows), don't throw away the rest of the bag. You can restore moisture by placing 3 cups popcorn and 1 tablespoon water in a jar. Secure the lid, and shake well every 15 minutes or so until all the liquid is absorbed. Store the jar in a cool, dry place for a few days before using it. When in a hurry, soak the dry kernels in cold water for about 5

minutes. Pat dry with paper towels, and pop as usual. For tasty popcorn treats, see page 223.

■ Anne Verret of Lutz, Florida, freezes fresh shrimp (peeled or unpeeled) in water. She says they taste fresher and maintain their firm texture better when stored this way. Anne doesn't worry about freezer burn because the shrimp are not exposed to air. This method will consume a bit more space in your freezer, but you'll be pleased with the results.

■ Nora Henshaw of Okemah, Oklahoma, wakes up the flavor of coffee with a variety of spices. She suggests stirring in ¼ teaspoon of *either* ground ginger, coriander, or cinnamon or adding ⅛ teaspoon black pepper into a cup of coffee for a hot new brew. Nora also says 2 teaspoons vanilla ice cream can turn a cup of coffee into dessert.

■ Flea markets and yard sales are great places to find bowls, platters, casseroles, and serving dishes at giveaway prices. Buy several pretty pieces to use whenever you give gifts of food to comfort neighbors and friends. Aside from creating a lovely presentation, neither of you has to worry about having the dish returned. (See "Comfort and Joy" on page 208 for recipes to give as gifts.)

Shrimp With Feta Cheese, page 221

New York-Style Cheesecake, page 205

*Caramelized French
Onion Soup, page 218*

Individual Meat Loaf, Smoky Mashed Potato Bake
served with steamed green beans, page 214

Dried Cherry-and-Pear
Fried Pies, page 213

OCTOBER

Harvest of Memories

Dark, thick sorghum is as rich in tradition as it is in flavor. The syrup tastes sweet and pungent, with an earthiness that proclaims its homespun heritage. For the Holland family of West Blocton, Alabama, sorghum flows like a ribbon to a past of love, joy, and rich traditions. Read "Sweet Traditions" on the facing page for more about sorghum's rich heritage.

TANGY BARBECUE SAUCE

For a flavorful glaze, brush this sauce on ribs, pork chops, or chicken the last 15 minutes of cooking time.

Prep: 5 minutes
Cook: 10 minutes

1 (8-ounce) can tomato sauce
¾ cup steak sauce
½ to ¾ cup sorghum
¼ cup ketchup
¼ cup lemon juice
2 tablespoons brown sugar
2 tablespoons Worcestershire sauce
2 to 4 dashes of hot sauce
Dash of seasoned salt
2 tablespoons pineapple marmalade
   (optional)

• **Cook** first 9 ingredients and, if desired, marmalade in a medium saucepan over low heat, stirring occasionally, 10 minutes or until thoroughly heated. **Yield:** about 3 cups.

Cathy Kinlaw
White Lake, North Carolina

GLAZED FALL VEGETABLES

Prep: 20 minutes
Bake: 50 minutes

2 large sweet potatoes
1 large russet potato
½ pound baby carrots
1 acorn squash, peeled and cut into
   cubes
½ cup firmly packed brown sugar
¼ cup butter or margarine,
   melted
¼ cup sorghum
¼ cup water
½ teaspoon salt
1 teaspoon ground cinnamon
1 teaspoon vanilla extract

• **Cut** potatoes in half lengthwise; cut into ½-inch-thick slices.
• **Place** potato slices, carrots, and squash in a lightly greased 13- x 9-inch baking dish. Stir together sugar and next 6 ingredients. Drizzle over potato mixture, tossing to coat.
• **Bake,** covered, at 425° for 30 minutes. Uncover and gently stir vegetables.
• **Bake** 15 to 20 more minutes or until vegetables are tender. **Yield:** 6 to 8 servings.

Karen C. Greenlee
Lawrenceville, Georgia

GINGER-OATMEAL SORGHUM COOKIES

These cookies are wonderful, old-fashioned treats.

Prep: 30 minutes
Bake: 10 minutes per batch

4 cups all-purpose flour
1 tablespoon baking soda
1½ teaspoons salt
4 cups quick-cooking oats
1¼ cups sugar
1½ teaspoons ground ginger
1½ cups raisins
1 cup butter or margarine,
   melted
1 cup sorghum
1 cup chopped walnuts
2 tablespoons hot water
2 large eggs, lightly beaten
1 to 2 tablespoons water
½ cup sugar

• **Combine** first 7 ingredients in a large bowl; add butter and next 4 ingredients, stirring until blended.
• **Shape** dough into 36 (2½-inch) balls. Place 2 inches apart on lightly greased baking sheets; flatten each to ¼-inch thickness.
• **Brush** tops with 1 to 2 tablespoons water, and sprinkle with sugar.
• **Bake** at 375° for 8 to 10 minutes or until lightly browned. **Yield:** 3 dozen.

Elaine S. Carter
Suffolk, Virginia

SWEET TRADITIONS

A Syrup Maker's Legacy

A light rain falls on David Holland's small sorghum shed near West Blocton, Alabama. Outside, the syrup maker's family and friends, their hair slicked down by the drizzle, feed sorghum cane into a motorized mill that extracts the juice. Inside, juice from an earlier pressing boils furiously in a large copper pan, billowing steam that mimics the sky's heavy clouds.

David is a soft-spoken man committed to keeping this family tradition alive. He plants a small field of sorghum each year and spends days in October harvesting and processing it. When he's ready to cook, he calls some friends and puts a sign out on the road reading "syrup mill."

"A lot of people know when they see the sign that they can come pick up some sorghum—and watch it being made," David says. "People still say, 'I hope the sorghum's as good as your daddy's,'" he says wryly, "even though I'd been making it for about 20 years before he passed away." David skims impurities from the surface of the bubbling liquid, moving with practiced ease. "I sorta took it up as a young fella, but my father had been making it all his life. In later years, he was the PR man who sat around and talked to people. Once in awhile, though, he'd say to me, 'It's getting too done—you better watch it!'"

A retired employee of Alabama Power Company, David sells a little of the sorghum to help cover costs, but mainly he makes syrup for the memories.

"I enjoyed doing it the last years of my father's life because it was such a joy for him to watch it," David says. "He really loved teaching people about how sorghum is made."

David says that his parents were strong figures in his and his siblings' lives. His father, Huron, was a farmer who produced sorghum and sugarcane as subsistence crops in lean times. The elder Holland encouraged his children to learn to sing when they were young. "About the time we were teenagers, we began singing in a family quartet," David recalls.

But the joyful music ended on January 16, 1997, when the Holland homeplace burned down, killing Huron and his daughter Helen Prickett. "We lost everything," David says sadly. "All the mementos in the house that are impossible to replace—pictures and letters—we didn't save one thing." Except the legacy of making this sharply sweet syrup, which the region relied on during times of hardship—especially during the Depression and World War II, when sugar was scarce.

The glassy syrup is done and ready to be poured into jars. David and his wife, Sharon, strain it through a fine linen cloth into quart- and pint-size jars. David talks about his father as he works. "I had a little plaque made with his name and date of death, and I mounted it on the back of the seat where he always sat. It says, 'Dad has a better seat now.' I left his same cushion and the little bottle of syrup he kept sitting next to him on the bench."

Making syrup helps David remember it all. He says softly, "Thank goodness those memories carry us on."

Sorghum Memories

Here are a few tidbits from readers who shared sorghum thoughts and recipes with us.

■ "When I was a kid during the Depression, sometimes you didn't have enough ribbon cane, so you used sorghum. That sorghum we had would bite you back as soon as you'd bite it!"
Clarence Culpepper
Chunky, Mississippi

■ "You had to have a good substantial biscuit to begin with, and then you pressed a finger through the side about halfway. Then you poured sorghum in the hole."
Sadye C. Hawke
Pensacola, Florida

■ "Sorghum making was a social outlet where each family brought their own load of cane and a load of special dried wood. The sorghum was ready when it began to 'hog eye' and had turned to a golden amber."
Betty and Gil Stevens
Seymour, Missouri

■ "It was usually a cold winter day [when Daddy brought sorghum home]. That sorghum would be thick enough to cut with a knife."
Dorothy Tucker
Woodruff, South Carolina

■ "I keep a jar [of sorghum] to use in baked beans. The older and blacker it gets, the better flavor it gives the beans."
Helen Anderson
Calhoun, Kentucky

Sweet & Classic

Always popular at the Southern table, sweet potatoes are good for not only the time-honored pie, but also a few other surprising recipes.

Sweet potatoes are available year-round and in abundance from September through June. They lend themselves to cooking methods such as boiling and sautéing. However, baking develops the sweet, syrupy flavor.

At the market or grocery store, look for firm, small- to medium-size sweet potatoes with smooth and unblemished skin; avoid any with bruising or decay. Never refrigerate uncooked sweet potatoes. (The cold temperature will keep them from being sweet.) Instead, store them in a cool, dark, well-ventilated room for no more than a week.

In all these recipes, except for Smoky Potato Gratin, you can substitute canned sweet potatoes for fresh—just remember that one sweet potato equals about half a cup of canned.

SWEET POTATO-STUFFED APPLES

Prep: 20 minutes
Bake: 45 minutes

5 medium-size cooking apples
3 tablespoons slivered almonds, divided
2 cups cooked mashed sweet potato
3 tablespoons brown sugar
3 tablespoons maple syrup
1 tablespoon butter or margarine, melted
½ teaspoon ground cinnamon
¼ teaspoon salt

• **Core** apples, starting at stem end, without cutting through opposite end. Scoop out pulp to enlarge opening to 2 inches. Chop pulp, and set aside.

• **Place** each apple shell on a 7-inch square of aluminum foil.
• **Stir** together chopped apple, 2 tablespoons almonds, and next 6 ingredients.
• **Spoon** evenly into apple shells; top with remaining almonds.
• **Pull** foil up around sides of apples, and place in a lightly greased 11- x 7-inch baking dish.
• **Bake** at 350° for 45 minutes or until tender. **Yield:** 5 servings.

Suzan L. Wiener
Spring Hill, Florida

SWEET POTATO BISCUITS

Prep: 15 minutes
Bake: 15 minutes

4 cups all-purpose flour
2 tablespoons baking powder
2 teaspoons salt
1 cup butter or margarine
1 cup cooked mashed sweet potato
¾ to 1 cup buttermilk

• **Combine** first 3 ingredients. Cut in butter with a pastry blender until mixture is crumbly.
• **Stir** together sweet potato and buttermilk; add to dry ingredients, stirring just until moistened.
• **Turn** dough out onto a lightly floured surface, and knead 3 or 4 times. Pat or roll to ½-inch thickness.
• **Cut** dough with a 3-inch round cutter, and place biscuits on a lightly greased baking sheet.
• **Bake** at 425° for 10 to 15 minutes or until golden. **Yield:** 14 biscuits.

SWEET POTATO PIE

Prep: 1 hour, 15 minutes
Bake: 1 hour, 35 minutes

2 large sweet potatoes
½ (15-ounce) package refrigerated piecrusts
1¼ cups sugar
1 cup milk
¼ cup pineapple juice
¼ cup butter or margarine, melted
3 large eggs
1 teaspoon vanilla extract
¼ teaspoon salt
¼ teaspoon ground nutmeg
Garnish: chopped toasted pecans

• **Bake** sweet potatoes at 350° for 1 hour or until tender; cool.
• **Fit** piecrust into a 9-inch pieplate according to package directions; fold edges under, and crimp.
• **Peel** potatoes, and beat potato pulp at medium speed with an electric mixer until smooth.
• **Add** sugar and next 7 ingredients, beating until blended. Pour filling into piecrust.
• **Bake** at 425° for 15 minutes. Reduce oven temperature to 350°.
• **Bake** 1 hour and 20 minutes or until a knife inserted in center comes out clean. (Shield crust with aluminum foil to prevent excessive browning, if necessary.) Garnish, if desired. **Yield:** 1 (9-inch) pie.

Beverly Pafford
Nashville, Georgia

SMOKY POTATO GRATIN

Prep: 15 minutes
Bake: 1 hour, 10 minutes
Stand: 15 minutes

1 garlic clove, minced
1 cup whipping cream
1 cup milk
1½ tablespoons all-purpose flour
2 teaspoons adobo sauce
1 teaspoon mashed chipotle pepper
¼ teaspoon salt
¼ teaspoon pepper
2 medium-size sweet potatoes, peeled and thinly sliced
1 medium-size baking potato, peeled and thinly sliced

• **Sprinkle** minced garlic in bottom of a buttered 11- x 7-inch baking dish.
• **Whisk** together whipping cream and next 6 ingredients.
• **Layer** half of potato slices over garlic; top with half of cream mixture. Repeat procedure with remaining potato slices and cream mixture.
• **Bake,** covered, at 350° for 40 minutes. Uncover and bake 30 more minutes or until gratin is golden brown. Let stand 15 minutes before serving. **Yield:** 6 to 8 servings.

Note: For testing purposes, we used canned chipotle peppers in adobo sauce. They may be found in the ethnic section of the grocery store.

SWEET POTATO BITES

A Southern Treasure

Sweet potatoes come in a variety of colors and shapes, but the one we cherish in the South—the Beauregard—possesses smooth, copper-colored skin; soft, orange flesh; and an inherent sweet flavor. Even though commercially grown types, such as the Hernandez and Jewel, are better suited to some of our Southern soil, the Beauregard continues to be, by far, the most popular type.

Mike Cannon, director of LSU AgCenter's Sweet Potato Research Station, explains, "It has more than a 70 percent share of the market. Folks simply demand the classic characteristics of the Beauregard."

What's in a Name?

Most folks have a difficult time differentiating between sweet potatoes and yams. "They're not even kissing cousins," says Sue Johnson-Langdon of the North Carolina Sweet Potato Commission. In fact, they are from different botanical families: A sweet potato is a root; the yam is a tropical-vine tuber.

A staple for much of Asia, Africa, and Latin America, yams are generally grown in the Caribbean and imported here. Much of the confusion stems from fresh and canned sweet potatoes being sold as "American" or "Louisiana Yams," although the USDA requires they also be correctly labeled as sweet potatoes.

SOUTHERN SWEET POTATO SOUP

Prep: 30 minutes
Cook: 40 minutes

2 tablespoons butter or margarine
1 medium onion, chopped
1 celery rib, chopped
1 garlic clove, minced
2 cups chicken broth
1 large sweet potato, peeled and sliced
1½ tablespoons peanut butter
1 (1¼-inch) cinnamon stick
1½ cups whipping cream ✱
¼ teaspoon salt
¼ cup whipping cream
2 teaspoons molasses
Pinch of salt
Pinch of ground nutmeg
Garnishes: chopped dry-roasted peanuts, fresh thyme sprigs

• **Melt** butter in a large saucepan over medium heat; add onion and celery, and sauté 10 minutes or until tender. Add garlic, and sauté 1 minute.
• **Stir** in broth and next 3 ingredients. Bring to a boil; reduce heat, and simmer 15 to 20 minutes or until potato is tender. Remove and discard cinnamon stick. Process sweet potato mixture in a blender or food processor until smooth.
• **Return** mixture to Dutch oven; stir in 1½ cups whipping cream and ¼ teaspoon salt.
• **Cook** over medium heat, stirring constantly, until thoroughly heated.
• **Beat** ¼ cup whipping cream, molasses, pinch of salt, and nutmeg until soft peaks form. Serve with soup. Garnish, if desired. **Yield:** 1 quart.

✱Substitute 1½ cups fat-free half-and-half for 1½ cups whipping cream, if desired.

Kirby Farmer
Red Hook, New York

Goblins Are Gathering

This Halloween we have nothing for you but treats. Whether you're inviting lots of guests or just having your family over, we've assembled all the fixin's for a spooktacular party.

Halloween Bash
Serves 12

Bat Sandwiches
Jack-O'-Lantern Cheeseburger Pie (double recipe)
Ghosts on a Stick
Candy Corn Chocolate Cakes
Fudgy Hot Cocoa

Smiling Jack-O'-Lantern Cheeseburger Pie is not only savory, but it's also cute enough for even tiny terrors to enjoy it. And although it might require patience, let children join in the preparation, decorating the cookies for Ghosts on a Stick or rolling out marshmallows for Fudgy Hot Cocoa. Sugar is easy to clean up later, and it's a great opportunity to teach some kitchen duties.

Depending on the size of your gathering, you may need to double some of the recipes. If you do, be extra careful. You'll be doubling the frightening fun.

BAT SANDWICHES

Prep: 30 minutes

3 cups (12 ounces) shredded sharp Cheddar cheese
1 (8-ounce) container chive-and-onion flavored cream cheese, softened
1 (4-ounce) jar diced pimiento, drained
½ cup chopped pecans, toasted
24 whole wheat or pumpernickel bread slices

• **Stir** together first 4 ingredients. Using a 3- to 4-inch bat-shaped cutter, cut 2 bats from each bread slice.
• **Spread** about 2 tablespoons cheese filling over 24 bats. Top with remaining 24 bats. **Yield:** 24 sandwiches.

JACK-O'-LANTERN CHEESEBURGER PIE

Prep: 30 minutes
Bake: 30 minutes

1 pound ground beef
1 medium onion, chopped
2 garlic cloves, pressed
¾ teaspoon salt
½ teaspoon pepper
¼ cup ketchup
1 teaspoon Worcestershire sauce
1 (15-ounce) package refrigerated piecrusts
1 tablespoon prepared mustard
3 cups (12 ounces) shredded Monterey Jack cheese, divided
2 tablespoons water
1 large egg
Red and yellow liquid food coloring

• **Cook** first 5 ingredients in a large skillet over medium-high heat, stirring until beef crumbles and is no longer pink; drain. Stir in ketchup and Worcestershire sauce; cool.
• **Unfold** 1 piecrust, and place on a lightly greased baking sheet. Spread mustard evenly over crust.
• **Stir** together meat mixture and 2 cups cheese; spoon onto center of crust, leaving a 2-inch border.
• **Unfold** remaining piecrust, and cut out a jack-o'-lantern face, reserving pastry cutouts to use as a stem.
• **Place** crust over meat mixture; crimp edges of crust, and fold under. Place stem on top of jack-o'-lantern face.
• **Whisk** together 2 tablespoons water, egg, and 1 drop each of red and yellow food coloring; brush over crust.
• **Bake** at 425° for 20 minutes; remove from oven, and brush again with egg mixture.
• **Fill** eyes, nose, and mouth with remaining 1 cup cheese. Bake 5 to 10 more minutes or until crust is golden brown. **Yield:** 6 to 8 servings.

Martha Jordan Newberry
Palm Bay, Florida

GHOSTS ON A STICK

Prep: 25 minutes
Chill: 1 hour
Bake: 10 minutes per batch

½ cup butter or margarine, softened
½ cup shortening
1½ cups powdered sugar
1 large egg
2 teaspoons vanilla extract
2¾ cups all-purpose flour
1 teaspoon cream of tartar
½ teaspoon baking soda
Wooden craft sticks
1 (16-ounce) container ready-to-spread vanilla frosting
Toppings: colored sugars, mini-morsels, candy sprinkles, 1 (4.25-ounce) tube black or brown decorator frosting

• **Beat** butter and shortening at medium speed with an electric mixer until blended.
• **Add** powdered sugar, egg, and vanilla to butter mixture; beat well. Gradually add flour, cream of tartar, and baking soda, beating well.
• **Cover** and chill dough 1 hour. Roll dough to ¼-inch thickness, and cut with a 3-inch ghost-shaped cutter.
• **Place** cookies 2 inches apart on lightly greased baking sheets.
• **Place** a craft stick under each cookie, pressing stick lightly into cookie.
• **Bake** at 375° for 10 minutes or until cookies are lightly browned. Cool cookies on baking sheets 5 minutes; remove to wire racks to cool completely.
• **Microwave** frosting in a 2-quart glass bowl at HIGH 1 minute or until frosting melts. Spread melted frosting over cookies in batches of 3. (Frosting hardens quickly.) Decorate rapidly with desired toppings. **Yield:** 2 dozen.

Martha Wall
Birmingham, Alabama

CANDY CORN CHOCOLATE CAKES

Prep: 40 minutes
Bake: 40 minutes
Freeze: 30 minutes

2 cups sugar
2 cups all-purpose flour
1 cup cocoa
1 cup vegetable oil
1 teaspoon salt
2 large eggs
1 cup buttermilk
1 cup hot water
2 teaspoons baking soda
2 teaspoons vanilla extract
Buttercream Frosting

• **Beat** first 6 ingredients in a large bowl at medium speed with an electric mixer until blended. Stir in buttermilk.
• **Stir** together 1 cup hot water and baking soda; stir into batter.
• **Stir** in vanilla. Pour into 2 greased and floured 9-inch round cakepans.
• **Bake** at 350° for 30 to 40 minutes or until a wooden pick inserted in center comes out clean. Cool in pans on wire racks 10 minutes; remove from pans, and cool completely on wire racks.
• **Freeze** layers 30 minutes. Cut each layer into 8 wedges.
• **Pipe** Buttercream Frosting on top and sides of cake wedges to resemble candy corn. Using a medium star tip, pipe white frosting on the small end of each cake, yellow frosting on center, and orange on wide end. **Yield:** 16 servings.

Buttercream Frosting

Prep: 10 minutes

1 cup butter or margarine, softened
1 (2-pound) package powdered sugar
⅓ cup milk
1 teaspoon vanilla extract
Orange paste food coloring
Yellow paste food coloring

• **Beat** butter at medium speed with an electric mixer until fluffy; gradually add powdered sugar, beating until mixture is light and fluffy.

• **Add** milk, beating until spreading consistency. Stir in vanilla.
• **Stir** orange food coloring into 1½ cups frosting.
• **Stir** yellow food coloring into 1¼ cups frosting. **Yield:** 3½ cups.

Hazel Arnold
Eads, Tennessee

FUDGY HOT COCOA

Prep: 10 minutes
Cook: 10 minutes

10 cups milk
1 cup chocolate syrup
⅔ cup cocoa
⅔ cup hot fudge topping
2 teaspoons vanilla extract
½ teaspoon almond extract
Sugar
24 large marshmallows
Black decorator frosting

• **Cook** first 6 ingredients in a Dutch oven over medium-low heat, stirring occasionally, 10 minutes or until thoroughly heated. (Do not boil.)
• **Sprinkle** sugar onto wax paper, and place marshmallows 2 inches apart on paper.
• **Sprinkle** marshmallows with sugar, and top with wax paper. Flatten marshmallows with a rolling pin.
• **Remove** top sheet of wax paper, and cut marshmallows with Halloween cutters. Decorate with frosting, and serve in hot cocoa. **Yield:** 10 to 12 servings.

Christien Harden

What's for Supper?

Rice—rich in complex carbohydrates, low in fat, and packed with vitamins, minerals, and fiber—is one great staple food. It stands up to frying, boiling, baking, and reheating.

Rice is also a time-saver, requiring no peeling, washing, sorting, or chopping. Uncooked, it stores well, takes up little space, and has a long shelf life. And it goes a long way—expanding to three times its size when cooked. Add your favorite salad or steamed vegetables to any of these easy recipes for a balanced meal.

PORK SAUSAGE-SEASONED RICE

Prep: 12 minutes
Cook: 30 minutes

1 pound ground mild pork sausage
2 large onions, chopped
2 celery ribs, diced
½ small red bell pepper, chopped
½ small green bell pepper, chopped
2 cups uncooked long-grain rice
4½ cups chicken broth
½ teaspoon salt
½ teaspoon sugar
¾ teaspoon seasoned salt
¾ teaspoon pepper
4 green onions, diced

• **Cook** first 5 ingredients in a large skillet over medium-high heat until sausage crumbles and is no longer pink; drain.
• **Add** rice; cook 5 minutes, stirring often. Stir in broth and next 4 ingredients; bring to a boil. Cover, reduce heat, and simmer 20 minutes or until liquid is absorbed. Uncover and cook 5 more minutes. Stir in green onions. **Yield:** 4 to 6 servings.

Gina S. Ginn
Valrico, Florida

SAVANNAH PORK CHOPS AND RICE

Prep: 12 minutes
Cook: 25 minutes

4 (¾-inch-thick) boneless pork loin chops
2 tablespoons vegetable oil
¼ cup diced onion
1 celery rib, sliced
2 (8-ounce) cans tomato sauce
1 cup uncooked long-grain rice
1½ cups water
2 tablespoons brown sugar
1 teaspoon salt
½ teaspoon dried basil

• **Cook** pork chops in hot oil in a large skillet over medium-high heat 4 minutes on each side or until browned. Remove pork from skillet.
• **Sauté** onion and celery in skillet over medium-high heat 2 minutes. Drain, if necessary.
• **Stir** in tomato sauce and next 5 ingredients; top mixture with pork, and bring to a boil.
• **Cover,** reduce heat, and simmer 25 minutes. **Yield:** 4 servings.

Pam Clark
Fayetteville, Tennessee

HAMBURGER-RICE SKILLET

This is an easy one-dish meal with a taco twist.

Prep: 18 minutes
Cook: 30 minutes

1 pound ground chuck
1 small onion, chopped
1 small green bell pepper, chopped
1 (10-ounce) can mild diced tomato and green chiles
1½ cups water
1 cup uncooked long-grain rice
1 (1.25-ounce) envelope mild taco seasoning mix
½ teaspoon salt
2 cups chopped lettuce
3 green onions, chopped
1 tomato, chopped
1 avocado, sliced
1 (2¼-ounce) can sliced black olives, drained
1 cup (4 ounces) Mexican cheese blend
Tortilla chips
Salsa

• **Cook** first 3 ingredients in a large skillet over medium-high heat, stirring until beef crumbles and is no longer pink; drain.
• **Stir** in tomato and green chiles and next 4 ingredients.
• **Cook,** covered, over medium heat 15 minutes, stirring occasionally. Uncover and cook 15 more minutes; remove skillet from heat.
• **Sprinkle** lettuce and next 5 ingredients over meat mixture. Stand tortilla chips around edge of skillet; serve with chips and salsa. **Yield:** 6 servings.

Connie Dardenne
Humphrey, Arkansas

A Taste of the South

You don't have to go to the county fair to stir up childhood memories of sugar and spice. Make jars of apple butter year-round. As the season approaches, take your own road trip through the Appalachian Mountains and stop at community festivals and quaint crossroads stores. Purchase a jar of the sweet preserve or buy some Granny Smith apples and prepare this easy oven recipe. Then you can enjoy the tastes of fall all year long.

OVEN APPLE BUTTER
(pictured on page 264)

Prep: 25 minutes
Cook: 30 minutes
Bake: 4 hours, 30 minutes

**8 Granny Smith apples, peeled and
     diced**
1 cup apple juice
1 cup sugar
1 teaspoon ground cinnamon

• **Cook** apple and apple juice in a Dutch oven over medium heat 30 minutes or until apple is tender. Stir until apple is mashed.
• **Stir** in sugar and cinnamon.
• **Pour** apple mixture into a lightly greased 11- x 7-inch baking dish.
• **Bake** at 275° for 4½ hours, stirring every hour, or until spreading consistency. Cover and chill. **Yield:** 3 cups.

Spiced Oven Apple Butter: Increase cinnamon to 2 teaspoons and add ½ teaspoon ground cloves and ¼ teaspoon ground allspice.

Mark Sohn
Pikeville, Kentucky

AN AUTUMN RITUAL

This time of year, follow the two-lane roads through eastern Kentucky and you'll notice more than just changing leaves. Roadside stands signal the start of the season with the fragrance of simmering apple butter. This tradition has long been a symbol of fall, but as we discovered, the methods and tastes are as varied as the cooks themselves.

On the first weekend of October at the Kentucky Apple Festival of Johnson County, you'll find open kettles filled to the rim with bubbling apple butter. This 38-year-old tradition has changed very little. "It's like a big country homecoming," says festival board member Barbara Daniel. "Everyone comes out. Grown children return with their families to spend vacation time, and we still cook apple butter in the street."

Rev. Hubert Slone of the Whitaker Free Will Baptist Church teams up with 20 parish members to do the honors. "We cook apple butter the old-fashioned way, stirring all day. It splatters so bad, there's a reason for those long-handled wooden stirrers," he says. "The meat of the apple is key. You need sour, tangy apples such as Cortland or Wolf River, but we use whatever is available."

"Apple butter is as individual as the person making it," declares Buddy Hall of Applecreek Farms in Lexington, where the recipe is more a savory relish than a sweet spread. "Ours is an old Shaker recipe using dried apples." How does this compare to fresh, crisp apples? "It's a little chunky but smooth eating," says Buddy. "We often refer to it as ketchup."

Some folks prefer to cook the entire apple, straining out the peel and seeds. But the pectin in the peel thickens this fruit preserve, and that's how it's done at Cooper's Mill in Bucyrus, Ohio. "We've been making apple butter since 1969 with an old German recipe," says David Cooper. "Apples harvested late in the season have a sweeter taste than those harvested at the beginning. We use a couple of varieties too. Our apple butter begins with an apple cider reduction in a copper kettle, the addition of crisp apples, and slow cooking. A touch of cinnamon heightens the apple flavor and contributes to its rich color."

Mark Sohn, author of *Hearty Country Cooking*, offers a four-step oven recipe—Oven Apple Butter—that eliminates the need for continual stirring and makes for easy cleanup. Achieving the correct consistency is just as important as the cooking procedure. When done, the mixture should cling to the spoon, although this depends on how juicy your apples are. Mark offers both a mild and a spicy version; either tastes great on eggs, fried potatoes, or eaten straight from the jar. However, the most popular way is to eat it on biscuits.

Some folks have a fondness for spreading apple butter between layers of graham crackers, a dessert similar to an apple stack cake. But truth be told, nothing can beat tender flaky biscuits hot from the oven and slathered with freshly made apple butter.

A Toast to Oktoberfest

An integral part of any Oktoberfest celebration, beer doesn't just have to be served in a mug. It's also fabulous in batters, sauces, breads, and soups.

The two basic classes of beer—ales and lagers—range from light to dark. Ales are best in heartier recipes such as soups and stews, while lagers are terrific in batters and breads. However, don't get bogged down over having the right kind—experiment with these recipes. In the end, your favorite beer will do just fine. Turn to "From Our Kitchen" on page 250 for more on selecting beers.

BEER BREAD

Prep: 5 minutes
Bake: 1 hour

3 cups self-rising flour
¼ cup sugar
1 (12-ounce) bottle light or dark beer

• **Stir** together all ingredients; spoon dough into a lightly greased 8½- x 4½-inch loafpan.
• **Bake** at 375° for 55 to 60 minutes or until golden brown. Cool in pan on wire rack 5 minutes. Remove from pan, and cool on wire rack. **Yield:** 1 loaf.

Note: For testing purposes only, we used Honey Brown beer.
Alexis Culton Gibson
Baton Rouge, Louisiana

GAME-DAY CHILI

Prep: 25 minutes
Cook: 3 hours

2 pounds ground chuck
1 medium onion, chopped
3 to 4 garlic cloves, minced
2 (15-ounce) cans pinto beans, rinsed and drained
3 (8-ounce) cans tomato sauce
1 (12-ounce) bottle dark beer
1 (14½-ounce) can beef broth
1 (6-ounce) can tomato paste
1 (4.5-ounce) can chopped green chiles
2 tablespoons chili powder
1 tablespoon Worcestershire sauce
2 teaspoons ground cumin
1 to 2 teaspoons ground red pepper
1 teaspoon paprika
1 teaspoon hot sauce
Garnish: pickled jalapeño pepper slices

• **Cook** first 3 ingredients in a Dutch oven over medium heat, stirring until meat crumbles and is no longer pink. Drain well.
• **Combine** meat mixture, beans, and next 11 ingredients in Dutch oven; bring to a boil. Reduce heat; simmer 3 hours or until thickened. Garnish, if desired. **Yield:** 13 cups.

Note: For testing purposes only, we used Sierra Nevada Pale Ale.
Courtney Bush
Austin, Texas

SHRIMP FRITTERS

Prep: 20 minutes
Chill: 2 hours
Fry: 5 minutes per batch

6 cups water
1 pound unpeeled, medium-size fresh shrimp
1 cup all-purpose flour
1 teaspoon baking powder
1 teaspoon salt
1 teaspoon pepper
2 large eggs
¼ cup light or dark beer
1 medium onion, minced
1 jalapeño pepper, seeded and minced
4 garlic cloves, minced
½ teaspoon dried thyme
Vegetable oil

• **Bring** 6 cups water to a boil; add shrimp, and cook 3 to 5 minutes or just until shrimp turn pink. Drain and rinse with cold water. Chill.
• **Peel** shrimp; devein, if desired. Coarsely chop shrimp.
• **Beat** flour and next 5 ingredients at medium speed with an electric mixer until smooth.
• **Stir** in shrimp, onion, and next 3 ingredients. Cover and chill 2 hours.
• **Pour** oil to a depth of 5 inches into a Dutch oven; heat to 375°.
• **Drop** batter by rounded tablespoonfuls, and fry, in batches, 5 minutes or until golden. Drain fritters on paper towels. **Yield:** 8 appetizer servings.

Pineapple Fritters: Substitute 1 (8-ounce) can pineapple chunks, drained and coarsely chopped, for shrimp. Omit onion, jalapeño, garlic, and thyme. Proceed as directed.

Note: For testing purposes only, we used Honey Brown beer.
Caroline Kennedy
Lighthouse Point, Florida

WELSH RAREBIT

Prep: 12 minutes
Broil: 30 seconds

3 tablespoons butter or
   margarine
3 tablespoons all-purpose flour
¾ cup light or dark beer
3 cups (12 ounces) shredded sharp
   Cheddar cheese
½ teaspoon salt
1½ tablespoons dry mustard
1 teaspoon paprika
¼ teaspoon pepper
1 teaspoon Worcestershire
   sauce
6 English muffins, buttered and
   toasted
Tomato slices (optional)

• **Melt** butter in a saucepan over low heat; add flour, whisking until smooth.
• **Cook**, whisking constantly, 2 to 3 minutes.
• **Whisk** in beer; cook, whisking constantly, 3 minutes.
• **Stir** in Cheddar cheese and next 5 ingredients.
• **Cook** 3 to 4 minutes or just until cheese melts. Spoon sauce over toasted English muffins.
• **Broil** 5½ inches from heat 30 seconds or until browned. Serve with tomato slices, if desired. **Yield:** 6 servings.

Note: For testing purposes only, we used Sierra Nevada Pale Ale.
Cedrick Lawson
Columbia, South Carolina

Fall for Breakfast

Whether you're fixing breakfast for family or for friends, these flavorful recipes will suit the occasion.

DATE MUFFINS

Prep: 10 minutes
Stand: 1 hour
Bake: 30 minutes

1 cup finely chopped dates
1 cup boiling water
1 tablespoon shortening
1 large egg, lightly beaten
1 teaspoon vanilla extract
1½ cups all-purpose flour
1 cup sugar
1 teaspoon baking powder
½ teaspoon salt
1 cup chopped pecans

• **Combine** first 3 ingredients; let stand 1 hour. Stir in egg and vanilla.
• **Combine** flour and next 4 ingredients in a bowl; make a well in center of mixture. Add date mixture, stirring just until moistened. Spoon into greased muffin pans, filling three-fourths full.
• **Bake** at 350° for 25 to 30 minutes. **Yield:** 1 dozen.
Kay Savage
Knoxville, Tennessee

DROP SCONES

Prep: 8 minutes
Bake: 14 minutes

½ cup milk
1½ teaspoons white vinegar
½ cup butter or margarine, softened
½ cup sugar
2 cups all-purpose flour
1 teaspoon baking soda
2 teaspoons cream of tartar
¼ teaspoon salt
Sugar

• **Stir** together milk and vinegar, and set aside.
• **Stir** together butter and ½ cup sugar in a large bowl.
• **Combine** flour and next 3 ingredients; stir into butter mixture alternately with milk mixture, beginning and ending with flour mixture, until dry ingredients are moistened.
• **Drop** by rounded 2 tablespoonfuls onto an ungreased baking sheet; sprinkle with additional sugar.
• **Bake** at 450° for 12 to 14 minutes or until golden. **Yield:** 10 scones.
Jean Campbell
Titusville, Florida

JALAPEÑO-CHEESE GRITS

Prep: 10 minutes
Cook: 15 minutes
Bake: 30 minutes

2 (14½-ounce) cans chicken
   broth
1¾ cups uncooked quick-cooking
   grits
½ cup butter or margarine
1 medium onion, chopped
2 red or green jalapeño peppers,
   seeded and diced
1 large green bell pepper, chopped
2 cups (8 ounces) shredded sharp
   Cheddar cheese
2 cups (8 ounces) shredded Monterey
   Jack cheese
4 large eggs, lightly beaten
¼ teaspoon salt

• **Bring** chicken broth to a boil in a large saucepan; stir in grits. Reduce heat, and simmer, stirring occasionally, 5 minutes. Cover.
• **Melt** butter in a large skillet; add onion and peppers, and sauté 5 minutes or until tender.
• **Stir** in grits, Cheddar cheese, and remaining ingredients.
• **Pour** into a lightly greased 13- x 9-inch baking dish.
• **Bake** at 350° for 30 minutes or until set; serve grits immediately. **Yield:** 8 to 10 servings.
LaJuan Coward
Jasper, Texas

SPINACH-AND-BACON QUICHE

Prep: 20 minutes
Bake: 45 minutes

1 (10-ounce) package frozen chopped
    spinach, thawed
4 large eggs, lightly beaten
1½ cups half-and-half
1 (1.8-ounce) envelope leek
    soup mix
¼ teaspoon pepper
10 bacon slices, cooked and
    crumbled
½ cup (2 ounces) shredded sharp
    Cheddar cheese
½ cup (2 ounces) shredded mozzarella
    cheese
1 unbaked (9-inch) frozen deep-dish
    pastry shell *

● **Drain** spinach well, pressing between layers of paper towels.
● **Whisk** together eggs and next 3 ingredients. Stir in spinach, crumbled bacon, and cheeses.
● **Pour** mixture into frozen pastry shell; place on a baking sheet.
● **Bake** at 375° for 40 to 45 minutes. **Yield:** 8 servings.

*Substitute ½ (15-ounce) package refrigerated piecrusts, if desired. Prepare crust according to package directions.
Marti Moran
Tallahassee, Florida

Top-Rated Menu

Fresh tomatillos, poblano chile peppers, cilantro, and familiar spices ensure cleaned plates and rave reviews for this Mexican meal.

Mexican Menu
Serves 4 to 5

Chicken Enchiladas Verde
Spanish-style rice
Mexican Pinto Beans
Grapefruit Freeze

CHICKEN ENCHILADAS VERDE

1993 Recipe Hall of Fame

Prep: 1 hour
Bake: 25 minutes

8 bone-in chicken breast halves,
    skinned
2 quarts water
1 tablespoon ground red pepper
2 teaspoons salt, divided
23 fresh tomatillos, husks removed
1 medium onion, chopped
2 garlic cloves, minced
1 tablespoon vegetable oil
2 tablespoons chopped fresh cilantro
2 cups (8 ounces) shredded Monterey
    Jack cheese, divided
1 tablespoon water
10 corn tortillas
Verde Sauce
1 (4-ounce) package crumbled feta
    cheese
Red Pepper Puree

● **Bring** first 3 ingredients and 1½ teaspoons salt to a boil in a Dutch oven. Cover, reduce heat, and simmer 30 minutes. Add tomatillos, and cook 5 more minutes. Remove chicken and tomatillos, reserving broth for Verde Sauce and Mexican Pinto Beans. Bone and shred chicken.
● **Chop** 7 tomatillos, reserving remaining tomatillos for Verde Sauce.
● **Sauté** onion and garlic in hot oil in a Dutch oven over medium-high heat until tender.
● **Add** chopped tomatillos and remaining ½ teaspoon salt. Cook 5 minutes.
● **Add** chicken, and cook 5 minutes.
● **Stir** in cilantro and 1 cup Monterey Jack cheese.
● **Sprinkle** 1 tablespoon water in tortilla package. Microwave at HIGH 1 minute.
● **Dip** each tortilla in Verde Sauce. Place about ½ cup chicken mixture down center of each tortilla; roll up. Place in a lightly greased 13- x 9-inch baking dish; top with remaining sauce, spreading to ends of tortillas.
● **Sprinkle** with remaining Monterey Jack cheese and feta cheese. Cover and chill 8 hours, if desired; let stand at room temperature 30 minutes.
● **Bake,** covered, at 425° for 25 minutes or until thoroughly heated. Serve with Red Pepper Puree. **Yield:** 4 to 5 servings.

Verde Sauce

Prep: 35 minutes
Cook: 15 minutes

4 poblano chile peppers
16 reserved cooked tomatillos
1½ cups reserved chicken broth,
      divided
1 small onion, chopped
2 garlic cloves, minced
3 romaine lettuce leaves, torn
¼ cup chopped fresh cilantro
1¼ teaspoons salt

• **Broil** peppers on an aluminum foil-lined baking sheet 5 inches from heat about 5 minutes on each side or until peppers look blistered.
• **Place** broiled peppers in a heavy-duty zip-top plastic bag; seal bag, and let stand about 10 minutes to loosen skins. Peel peppers; remove and discard seeds.
• **Process** peppers, cooked tomatillos, 1 cup chicken broth, and next 5 ingredients in a food processor or blender until mixture is smooth, stopping to scrape down sides.
• **Transfer** mixture to a saucepan; cook over medium heat 5 minutes. Slowly stir in remaining ½ cup chicken broth, and cook about 10 minutes or until sauce is thickened. **Yield:** 3 cups.

Red Pepper Puree

Prep: 5 minutes

2 (7-ounce) jars roasted red bell
      pepper, drained
½ teaspoon salt

• **Process** bell pepper and salt in a food processor or blender until smooth, stopping to scrape down sides. Cover and chill, if desired. **Yield:** 1 cup.

Note: Substitute 1 cup salsa for Red Pepper Puree, if desired.

MEXICAN PINTO BEANS

1994 Recipe Hall of Fame

Prep: 15 minutes
Soak: 1 hour
Cook: 2 hours

1 cup dried pinto beans
3 cups reserved chicken broth
3 bacon slices, diced
1 small onion, chopped
1 small green bell pepper, chopped
2 teaspoons ground cumin
2 teaspoons chili powder
¾ teaspoon salt
½ teaspoon pepper

• **Sort** and wash pinto beans; place in a large saucepan. Cover with water 2 inches above beans, and bring to a boil. Boil beans 1 minute. Cover, remove from heat, and let soak 1 hour. Drain.
• **Bring** beans, broth, and remaining ingredients to a boil. Cover, reduce heat, and simmer 2 hours. Chill, if desired; reheat over medium heat. **Yield:** 4 cups.

GRAPEFRUIT FREEZE

1993 Recipe Hall of Fame

Prep: 20 minutes
Freeze: 4 hours
Stand: 30 minutes

1½ cups sugar
1 cup water
½ cup mint leaves, chopped
1 (64-ounce) bottle Ruby Red
      grapefruit juice
Garnish: fresh mint sprigs

• **Bring** sugar and 1 cup water to a boil in a saucepan. Add chopped mint; cover and let stand 5 minutes. Pour mint mixture through a fine wire-mesh strainer into an 8-cup container; discard mint. Add grapefruit juice.
• **Divide** mixture into 2 (1-quart) freezer containers; cover and freeze at least 4 hours. Let stand 30 minutes before serving. Scrape with a spatula, or process, in batches, in a food processor. Garnish, if desired. **Yield:** 8 cups.

COOK'S NOTES

To help you serve this fabulous meal with ease, follow these tips and produce the recipes in stages. Add your favorite Spanish-style rice, and rest assured this meal will be remembered—and repeated.

Two days before
■ Prepare Red Pepper Puree; cover and chill.
■ Prepare Grapefruit Freeze.

The day before
■ Prepare Verde Sauce and Chicken Enchiladas Verde; cover and chill.
■ Prepare Mexican Pinto Beans; cover and chill.

One hour before
■ Remove enchiladas from refrigerator; let stand at room temperature 30 minutes.
■ Prepare your favorite Spanish-style rice; keep warm.

30 minutes before
■ Bake enchiladas.
■ Reheat beans.

As you serve dinner
■ Remove Grapefruit Freeze from freezer.

Quick & Easy

Check your grocery store for frozen cooked meatballs to create supper in a snap.

When most people think of meatballs, they usually think of either spaghetti or those sweet-and-sour meatballs smothered in a chili sauce-grape jelly glaze. Stirring the recipe together is quick, but forming the ground beef into balls is a chore.

But today, many different flavors of frozen cooked meatballs are available at your grocery store. The packages come with 30 to 32 meatballs to a pound. You can remove the amount needed for a recipe and then keep the remainder in the freezer. Experiment with thawing and crumbling them in place of cooked ground beef in dishes.

SPICY PARTY MEATBALLS

Prep: 5 minutes
Cook: 45 minutes

1 (12-ounce) jar cocktail sauce
1 (10.5-ounce) jar jalapeño jelly
½ small sweet onion, minced
½ (3-pound) package frozen cooked meatballs

• **Cook** first 3 ingredients in a Dutch oven over medium heat, stirring until jelly melts and mixture is smooth.
• **Stir** in meatballs. Reduce heat, and simmer, stirring occasionally, 35 to 40 minutes or until thoroughly heated. **Yield:** 4 dozen.

Tracy Sargent
Temple, Georgia

MEATBALL MINESTRONE

This minestrone and breadsticks make a satisfying combination.

Prep: 10 minutes
Cook: 30 minutes

3 garlic cloves, minced
1 tablespoon olive oil
3 (15-ounce) cans cannellini beans, undrained and divided
1 (32-ounce) container chicken broth
1 (1.4-ounce) envelope vegetable soup mix
60 to 64 frozen cooked meatballs
1 (14½-ounce) can diced tomatoes with basil, garlic, and oregano
½ teaspoon dried crushed red pepper
8 ounces uncooked rotini pasta
1 (10-ounce) package fresh spinach, torn
Garnishes: shredded Parmesan cheese, chopped fresh parsley

• **Sauté** garlic in hot oil in a stockpot over medium-high heat 1 minute. Stir in 2 cans beans and chicken broth, and bring to a boil.
• **Stir** in vegetable soup mix until dissolved. Add meatballs, tomatoes, and red pepper; return to a boil.
• **Add** rotini, and cook, stirring often, 15 minutes.
• **Stir** in remaining can beans and spinach; cook 5 more minutes. Garnish, if desired. Serve with breadsticks. **Yield:** 4 quarts.

Note: For testing purposes only, we used Knorr Vegetable Soup Mix.

Amanda Abele
Fayetteville, Arkansas

SLOPPY JOE MEATBALL HOAGIES

Prep: 10 minutes
Cook: 15 minutes

1 small sweet onion, diced
1 small green bell pepper, diced
1 tablespoon vegetable oil
1 (15.5-ounce) can sloppy joe sauce
30 to 32 frozen cooked meatballs
4 hoagie buns, split and toasted

• **Sauté** onion and pepper in hot oil in a large skillet over medium-high heat 3 minutes.
• **Add** sauce and meatballs; cook 10 more minutes or until thoroughly heated, stirring often. Spoon evenly onto hoagie buns. **Yield:** 4 servings.

MEATBALL QUESADILLAS

Prep: 10 minutes
Cook: 24 minutes

½ (16-ounce) jar spicy black bean dip
12 (8-inch) flour tortillas
30 to 32 frozen cooked meatballs, thawed and crumbled
1½ cups (6 ounces) shredded Monterey Jack cheese with peppers
1 small green bell pepper, diced
Toppings: sour cream, salsa

• **Spread** bean dip over 6 tortillas. Layer crumbled meatballs, cheese, and bell pepper evenly over bean dip. Top with remaining tortillas.
• **Cook** quesadillas in a nonstick skillet or griddle over medium heat 2 minutes on each side or until tortillas are golden and cheese is melted.
• **Cut** into 4 triangles, and serve with desired toppings. **Yield:** 4 to 6 main-dish or 10 to 12 appetizer servings.

Note: For testing purposes only, we used Guiltless Gourmet Spicy Black Bean Dip.

Sharon Jones
Birmingham, Alabama

MEATBALL LASAGNA

Prep: 15 minutes
Bake: 1 hour
Stand: 15 minutes

1 (15-ounce) container ricotta
   cheese
1 (8-ounce) container chive-and-onion
   flavored cream cheese, softened
¼ cup chopped fresh basil
½ teaspoon garlic salt
½ teaspoon coarsened pepper
1 large egg, lightly beaten
2 cups (8 ounces) shredded
   mozzarella cheese, divided
1 (3-ounce) package shredded
   Parmesan cheese, divided
2 (26-ounce) jars tomato basil pasta
   sauce
1 (16-ounce) package egg roll
   wrappers
60 to 64 frozen cooked Italian-style
   meatballs

• **Stir** together first 6 ingredients until blended.
• **Stir** in ½ cup mozzarella cheese and ½ cup Parmesan cheese; set aside.
• **Spread** 1 cup pasta sauce in bottom of a lightly greased 13- x 9-inch baking dish. Cut egg roll wrappers in half lengthwise; arrange 10 halves over pasta sauce. (Wrappers will overlap.) Top with meatballs.
• **Spoon** 3 cups pasta sauce over meatballs; sprinkle with ¾ cup mozzarella cheese.
• **Arrange** 10 wrappers evenly over mozzarella. Spread ricotta cheese mixture over wrappers; top with remaining wrappers and pasta sauce.
• **Bake** at 350° for 50 minutes. Top with remaining ¾ cup mozzarella cheese and remaining ¼ cup Parmesan cheese.
• **Bake** 10 more minutes. Let stand 15 minutes. **Yield:** 8 servings.

Note: For testing purposes only, we used Classico Tomato and Basil pasta sauce.

Susie Smith
Orlando, Florida

Overnight Breads

Yeast breads can be tricky, but the guesswork disappears with these recipes. The doughs rise overnight in the refrigerator, making it easy because the work is done the day before, explains Jan Moon of our Test Kitchens. The aroma of sweet rolls or waffles awakes sleepy eyes to morning treasures.

CRISPY WAFFLES

Prep: 10 minutes
Chill: 8 hours
Bake: 24 minutes

1 (¼-ounce) envelope active dry
   yeast
½ cup warm water (100° to 110°)
2 cups warm milk (100° to 110°)
½ cup butter or margarine, melted
1 teaspoon sugar
1 teaspoon salt
2 cups all-purpose flour
2 large eggs
¼ teaspoon baking soda

• **Combine** yeast and ½ cup warm water in a glass measuring cup; let mixture stand 5 minutes.
• **Combine** yeast mixture, milk, and next 3 ingredients in a large mixing bowl. Add flour, stirring until smooth. Cover and chill 8 hours.
• **Whisk** in eggs and baking soda.
• **Bake** in a preheated, oiled waffle iron until crisp. **Yield:** 16 (4-inch) waffles.

Carrie Treichel
Johnson City, Tennessee

CINNAMON BREAKFAST ROLLS

Cake mix and yeast contribute flavor and texture to these rolls.

Prep: 30 minutes
Rise: 1 hour
Chill: 8 hours
Stand: 30 minutes
Bake: 25 minutes

1 (18.25-ounce) package French
   vanilla cake mix
5¼ cups all-purpose flour
2 (¼-ounce) envelopes active dry
   yeast
1 teaspoon salt
2½ cups warm water (100° to 110°)
½ cup sugar
2 teaspoons ground cinnamon
½ cup butter or margarine, divided and
   melted
½ cup raisins, divided
¾ cup chopped pecans, divided
1 cup powdered sugar
3 tablespoons milk
½ teaspoon vanilla extract

• **Stir** together first 5 ingredients in a large bowl; cover and let rise in a warm place (85°), free from drafts, 1 hour.
• **Combine** ½ cup sugar and cinnamon.
• **Turn** dough out onto a well-floured surface; divide in half. Roll 1 portion into an 18- x 12-inch rectangle.
• **Brush** with half of butter; sprinkle with half of sugar mixture, half of raisins, and ¼ cup pecans.
• **Roll** up starting at long end; cut crosswise into 16 (1-inch-thick) slices. Place rolls in a lightly greased 13- x 9-inch pan. Repeat procedure with remaining rectangle. Cover and chill 8 hours.
• **Remove** from refrigerator, and let stand 30 minutes.
• **Bake** at 350° for 20 to 25 minutes or until golden; cool slightly.
• **Stir** together powdered sugar, milk, and vanilla; drizzle over rolls.
• **Sprinkle** with remaining pecans. **Yield:** 32 rolls.

Ruth H. Todd
Charlotte, North Carolina

CRANBERRY ROLLS

Prep: 40 minutes
Rise: 1 hour, 15 minutes
Chill: 8 hours
Bake: 12 minutes

2 (¼-ounce) envelopes rapid-rise yeast
¾ cup warm water (100° to 110°)
1 cup sugar, divided
3 cups all-purpose flour
6 tablespoons vegetable oil
2 large eggs
1 teaspoon salt
½ cup butter or margarine, melted
1 teaspoon ground cinnamon
1 cup sweetened dried cranberries
12 large marshmallows
1 cup powdered sugar
1 tablespoon milk
¼ teaspoon ground ginger

• **Combine** yeast and ¾ cup water in a glass measuring cup; let stand 5 minutes.
• **Beat** yeast mixture, ¼ cup sugar, and next 4 ingredients at low speed with an electric mixer until blended.
• **Turn** dough out onto a well-floured surface, and knead until smooth and elastic (about 4 minutes).
• **Cover** and let rise in a warm place (85°), free from drafts, 45 minutes or until doubled in bulk.
• **Punch** dough down; divide into 12 portions. Roll each into a 3-inch circle.
• **Brush** circles lightly with butter, reserving remaining butter.
• **Combine** remaining ¾ cup sugar and cinnamon; sprinkle evenly over circles. Place cranberries evenly in center of each circle; top with a marshmallow.
• **Pull** edges of circle to center, and pinch to seal; shape into a ball.
• **Place**, seam side down, in lightly greased muffin pans. Brush tops with reserved butter. Cover and chill 8 hours.
• **Remove** from refrigerator, and let rise in a warm place, free from drafts, 30 minutes or until doubled in bulk.
• **Bake** at 400° for 12 minutes or until lightly browned; cool slightly.
• **Stir** together powdered sugar, milk, and ginger; drizzle over rolls. **Yield:** 1 dozen.

Reba I. Haynes
Knoxville, Tennessee

Winning Desserts

Sample some of the recipes created by people who have helped make a difference in the lives of children in crisis.

How sweet it was to sample 18 desserts last October in support of Palmetto Place Children's Emergency Shelter in Columbia, South Carolina. The annual "How Sweet It Is" dessert competition raises funds for a shelter that has provided a safe environment for more than 6,000 children since 1977. Here are some of the tasty winners.

TRIPLE-LAYERED BANANA CAKE

Prep: 45 minutes
Bake: 30 minutes
Freeze: 1 hour

1 cup butter or margarine, softened
1¾ cups sugar
3 large eggs
1 teaspoon black walnut flavoring
3 cups all-purpose flour
2½ teaspoons baking soda
1 teaspoon salt
2 cups buttermilk
2 tablespoons cocoa
2 tablespoons vanilla extract
1 cup mashed bananas (about 2 small)
Buttercream Frosting
2 small bananas, sliced
8 strawberries, sliced
Garnish: drained crushed pineapple

• **Beat** butter at medium speed with an electric mixer until creamy; gradually add sugar, beating well.
• **Add** eggs, 1 at a time, beating until blended. Stir in black walnut flavoring.
• **Combine** flour, soda, and salt; gradually add to butter mixture alternately with buttermilk, beginning and ending with flour mixture. Beat until blended. Remove 2½ cups batter.
• **Stir** together 2½ cups batter, cocoa, and vanilla; pour into 1 greased and floured 9-inch round cakepan.
• **Stir** 1 cup banana into remaining batter; pour evenly into 2 greased and floured 9-inch round cakepans.
• **Bake** layers at 350° for 20 to 30 minutes or until a wooden pick inserted in center comes out clean. Cool in pans on wire racks 10 minutes.
• **Remove** from pans, and wrap in plastic wrap. Freeze 1 hour.
• **Spread** 1 banana layer with Buttercream Frosting; arrange banana slices on top.
• **Top** with chocolate layer, and spread with frosting; top with strawberries.
• **Top** with remaining banana layer; spread top and sides with frosting. Garnish, if desired. **Yield:** 1 (3-layer) cake.

Buttercream Frosting

Prep: 10 minutes

1 cup butter or margarine, softened
2 (16-ounce) packages powdered sugar
½ cup plus 2 tablespoons milk
2 teaspoons vanilla extract

• **Beat** butter at medium speed with an electric mixer until creamy; gradually add 2 cups powdered sugar, beating at low speed until blended. Add milk and vanilla, beating until blended. Gradually add remaining powdered sugar, beating until smooth. **Yield:** 5 cups.

Chef Pearl Black
Renee's Custom Catering
Irmo, South Carolina

German Chocolate Cheesecake

Prep: 30 minutes
Bake: 35 minutes
Chill: 8 hours
Cook: 7 minutes

1 cup chocolate wafer crumbs
2 tablespoons sugar
3 tablespoons butter or margarine, melted
3 (8-ounce) packages cream cheese, softened
¾ cup sugar
¼ cup cocoa
2 teaspoons vanilla extract
3 large eggs
⅓ cup evaporated milk
⅓ cup sugar
¼ cup butter or margarine
1 large egg, lightly beaten
½ teaspoon vanilla extract
½ cup chopped pecans
½ cup flaked coconut

• **Stir** together first 3 ingredients; press mixture into bottom of a 9-inch springform pan.
• **Bake** at 325° for 10 minutes. Cool.
• **Beat** cream cheese and next 3 ingredients at medium speed with an electric mixer until blended.
• **Add** eggs, 1 at a time, beating just until blended after each addition. Pour into prepared crust.
• **Bake** at 350° for 35 minutes. Loosen cake from pan, and cool. Cover and chill 8 hours.
• **Stir** together evaporated milk and next 4 ingredients in a saucepan.
• **Cook** over medium heat, stirring constantly, 7 minutes.
• **Stir** in pecans and coconut; spread over cheesecake. **Yield:** 12 servings.

Catherine Rentz
Columbia, South Carolina

Mocha Pecan Mud Pie

Prep: 8 minutes
Bake: 15 minutes
Freeze: 8 hours, 10 minutes

1 cup cream-filled chocolate sandwich cookie crumbs (12 cookies)
3 tablespoons butter or margarine, melted
1 egg white, lightly beaten
1¼ cups chopped pecans
¼ cup sugar
1 pint coffee ice cream, softened
1 pint chocolate ice cream, softened
10 cream-filled chocolate sandwich cookies, coarsely chopped

• **Stir** together cookie crumbs and butter. Press into a 9-inch pieplate. Brush with egg white.
• **Bake** at 350° for 5 minutes. Cool.
• **Place** pecans on a lightly greased baking sheet; sprinkle with sugar.
• **Bake** pecans at 350° for 8 to 10 minutes. Cool.
• **Stir** together ice creams, 1 cup cookie chunks, and 1 cup pecans; spoon into crust. Freeze 10 minutes.
• **Press** remaining cookie chunks and pecans over pie. Cover and freeze 8 hours. **Yield:** 1 (9-inch) pie.

Chef James King CEC
Jake's Famous Restaurant
Edisto Island, South Carolina

Stir-Fry Sizzle

Miso, or bean paste, has the consistency of peanut butter and comes in several flavors, colors, and textures. It adds distinction to this stir-fry.

Chicken Vegetable Stir-Fry

Prep: 20 minutes
Cook: 12 minutes

4 to 6 dried black mushrooms
1 cup hot water
4 skinned and boned chicken breast halves, cut into ½-inch-thick strips
2 tablespoons cornstarch, divided
¼ cup lite soy sauce, divided
1½ tablespoons fermented black beans or soybean miso
1 tablespoon oyster sauce
1 tablespoon dry sherry
1 teaspoon sugar
¼ cup dark sesame oil
1 large onion, chopped
2 to 3 garlic cloves, minced
6 cups shredded napa cabbage
2 tablespoons water

• **Soak** mushrooms in 1 cup hot water 15 minutes; drain mushrooms, reserving ¼ cup liquid. Chop mushrooms. Toss chicken with 1 tablespoon cornstarch and 2 tablespoons soy sauce. Mash together remaining soy sauce, reserved liquid, beans, and next 3 ingredients.
• **Heat** 2 tablespoons oil in a skillet over medium-high heat 2 minutes. Add chicken; stir-fry 5 minutes. Remove from skillet. Heat remaining oil in skillet over medium-high heat 2 minutes.
• **Add** onion; stir-fry 1½ minutes. Add garlic; stir-fry 30 seconds. Add mushrooms; stir-fry 1 minute. Add chicken and cabbage; stir-fry 30 seconds.
• **Stir** together remaining cornstarch and 2 tablespoons water until smooth; add to skillet with bean mixture. Bring to a boil; boil 1 minute. **Yield:** 4 servings.

Jim Mitchell
Homewood, Alabama

Marvelous Mirlitons

Mirlitons seem to be shrouded in mystery. In Louisiana, they're called mirlitons, but in other locales, they're referred to as chayote squash, vegetable pears, and mango squash.

Unadorned, mirlitons have the crisp flesh of a cucumber and the subtle flavor of yellow squash. As members of the cucumber family and first cousins to squash, they are all part of the giant gourd family. See "From Our Kitchen" on page 250 for more information.

MIRLITON-CORN CHOWDER

Prep: 30 minutes
Cook: 1 hour

2 tablespoons butter or margarine
4 large mirlitons, peeled, seeded, and chopped *
2 medium onions, chopped
1 red bell pepper, chopped
1 to 2 jalapeño peppers, seeded and chopped
2 garlic cloves, pressed
¼ cup all-purpose flour
1 (32-ounce) container chicken broth
1 (16-ounce) package frozen whole kernel corn
2 (4.5-ounce) cans chopped green chiles
2 cups milk
½ teaspoon salt
1 teaspoon ground cumin
½ teaspoon chili powder
2 tablespoons lime juice
Shredded Cheddar cheese (optional)
Chopped cooked bacon (optional)

• **Melt** butter in a Dutch oven over medium-high heat; add mirliton and next 4 ingredients, and sauté 5 minutes or until onion is tender. Sprinkle with flour, and cook, stirring constantly, 2 minutes. Gradually add broth, stirring constantly.
• **Stir** in corn and next 5 ingredients; cook, stirring occasionally, 45 minutes. Stir in lime juice. Ladle into bowls; sprinkle each serving with cheese and bacon, if desired. **Yield:** 14 cups.

*Substitute 4 large yellow squash or zucchini, seeded and chopped, for mirlitons, if desired.

STUFFED MIRLITONS

Prep: 1 hour, 30 minutes
Bake: 20 minutes

1 pound unpeeled, medium-size fresh shrimp
4 large mirlitons
⅓ cup minced onion
4 green onions, chopped
3 garlic cloves, minced
2 tablespoons bacon drippings
8 ounces sliced cooked ham, cut into thin strips
¾ cup soft breadcrumbs, divided
1 tablespoon Creole seasoning
¼ cup shredded Parmesan cheese

• **Peel** shrimp, and devein, if desired. Set aside.
• **Bring** mirlitons and water to cover to a boil in a Dutch oven; boil 45 to 50 minutes. Drain and cool. Cut in half lengthwise; remove seeds, and discard. Scoop out pulp, leaving ½-inch-thick shells; chop pulp, and set shells aside.
• **Sauté** onions and garlic in hot bacon drippings 5 minutes.
• **Add** shrimp and ham; cook, stirring constantly, 3 to 5 minutes or until shrimp turn pink. Stir in mirliton pulp, ½ cup breadcrumbs, and Creole seasoning; cook, stirring occasionally, 5 minutes. Stuff evenly into mirliton shells.
• **Sprinkle** with remaining ¼ cup breadcrumbs and cheese. Place in a lightly greased 13- x 9-inch baking dish.
• **Bake** at 375° for 15 to 20 minutes. **Yield:** 8 servings.

Holley Hartson Flournoy
Dallas, Texas

MARINATED MIRLITONS, ARTICHOKES, AND PEPPERS

Prep: 30 minutes
Cook: 50 minutes
Chill: 2 hours

2 (12-ounce) jars marinated artichoke hearts
6 large mirlitons *
½ cup chopped fresh basil
¼ cup chopped fresh parsley
½ cup white balsamic vinegar
2 garlic cloves, minced
1 teaspoon salt
¼ teaspoon Creole seasoning
1 (7-ounce) jar roasted red bell peppers
Mixed salad greens

• **Drain** artichokes, reserving liquid in a large bowl.
• **Bring** mirlitons and water to cover to a boil in a Dutch oven, and boil 45 to 50 minutes or until tender. Drain and cool. Peel mirlitons. Cut in half lengthwise; remove seeds, if desired. Cut mirliton halves into ¼-inch-thick slices.
• **Whisk** together reserved liquid, basil, and next 5 ingredients. Add mirliton slices, artichoke hearts, and bell pepper; toss well. Cover and chill 2 hours, stirring occasionally. Serve over salad greens. **Yield:** 4 to 6 servings.

*Substitute 6 large yellow squash or zucchini, if desired. Cut in half lengthwise; cut halves crosswise into ¼-inch-thick slices. Cook in boiling water to cover 5 minutes or until tender; drain.

Can-Do Tuna

Love the ease and economy of canned tuna but bored with the old standard recipes? Try some of these. They combine unexpected ingredients and presentations for fresh takes on this popular fish. Just like the tuna-noodle casserole we all know and love, the dishes are thrifty but still delicious. If you prefer to experiment with your own culinary creations, go ahead. With tuna at about 79 cents for a 6-ounce can, you can afford to take some chances in the kitchen.

TUNA PATTIES

Compare prices between a 12-ounce can and two 6-ounce cans of tuna—the larger cans aren't always the better buy.

Prep: 25 minutes
Cook: 16 minutes

1 (12-ounce) can tuna in spring water, drained and flaked
2 large eggs, lightly beaten
1 small sweet onion, diced
4 white bread slices, cubed
½ cup Italian-seasoned breadcrumbs
½ teaspoon Worcestershire sauce
2 dashes of hot sauce
½ teaspoon Old Bay seasoning
¼ teaspoon dry mustard
⅛ teaspoon salt
⅛ teaspoon pepper
¼ cup butter or margarine
Mixed salad greens
Mango-and-Bell Pepper Salsa

• **Stir** together first 11 ingredients. Shape mixture into 6 patties.
• **Melt** 2 tablespoons butter in a skillet over medium-high heat.
• **Cook** 3 patties 4 minutes on each side or until golden. Repeat with remaining butter and patties. Serve over salad greens, and top with Mango-and-Bell Pepper Salsa. **Yield:** 6 servings.

Charlotte Pierce
Greensburg, Kentucky

Mango-and-Bell Pepper Salsa

Prep: 20 minutes

1 large ripe mango, chopped*
½ red bell pepper, chopped
½ green bell pepper, chopped
¼ purple onion, diced
3 tablespoons chopped fresh cilantro
1 tablespoon brown sugar
1½ to 2 tablespoons white wine vinegar
1 tablespoon olive oil
⅛ teaspoon salt
⅛ teaspoon pepper

• **Combine** all ingredients, tossing gently to coat. **Yield:** 1¾ cups.

*Substitute 1 cup chopped, refrigerated mango for fresh, if desired.

Helen H. Maurer
Christmas, Florida

CURRIED TUNA-APPLE SANDWICHES

Prep: 10 minutes

¼ cup light mayonnaise
1 tablespoon lemon juice
½ teaspoon curry powder
⅛ teaspoon garlic powder
1 (6-ounce) can albacore tuna, drained
1 small Granny Smith apple, chopped
1 celery rib, chopped
¼ cup raisins
2 tablespoons diced onion
6 whole grain bread slices

• **Stir** together first 4 ingredients. Stir in tuna and next 4 ingredients.
• **Spread** mixture on whole grain bread. **Yield:** 3 sandwiches.

Janet Shogren
Fairfield Glade, Tennessee

TUNA-PASTA SALAD

Prep: 30 minutes
Cook: 10 minutes

8 ounces uncooked spaghetti, broken into pieces
4 medium tomatoes, chopped
¼ cup chopped fresh basil
¼ cup chopped fresh parsley
1 tablespoon chopped fresh oregano
2 (5-ounce) cans tuna in spring water, drained
¼ cup mayonnaise
¼ cup Caesar salad dressing

• **Cook** pasta according to package directions; rinse and drain.
• **Combine** pasta, tomato, and next 3 ingredients. Gently stir in tuna.
• **Whisk** together mayonnaise and salad dressing. Spoon over pasta mixture, and toss gently to coat. **Yield:** 4 servings.

Note: For testing purposes only, we used Ken's Steak House Caesar Dressing.

Allison Cook
Summerville, South Carolina

TUNA IN THE TIN

Choose chunk light tuna for dishes that need an assertive flavor but do not require the tuna to be in large chunks. Oil-packed tuna can be pureed as the base for a dip. Albacore is worth the added expense if chunks of tuna are the main attraction—such as in Curried Tuna-Apple Sandwiches.

Living Light

Cilantro claims center stage in these recipes, offering an earthy yet subtle character. You may think that Mexico has exclusive rights on cilantro. Turns out, the leaves of the Coriandrum sativum *plant, or coriander, are essential in Latin, Asian, Indian, and Caribbean cooking.*

If you can't find cilantro, ask your grocer to stock it, or you can purchase it at www.diamondorganics.com. Cilantro may be grown in gardens across the South. These recipes will inspire you to try this fragrant, versatile herb.

VEGETABLE STEW

Prep: 22 minutes
Cook: 30 minutes

2 poblano peppers
1 onion, chopped
2 teaspoons olive oil
1 medium butternut squash, peeled and cut into ½-inch cubes
2 garlic cloves, minced
1 (16-ounce) package frozen butter peas
3 (14½-ounce) cans reduced-sodium, fat-free chicken broth
1½ teaspoons grated fresh ginger
¼ teaspoon ground red pepper
1 (14½-ounce) can diced tomatoes, undrained
½ teaspoon salt
½ cup chopped fresh cilantro

• **Broil** peppers on an aluminum foil-lined baking sheet 5 inches from heat about 5 minutes on each side or until peppers look blistered.

• **Place** peppers in a zip-top plastic bag. Seal bag; let peppers stand 10 minutes to loosen skins. Peel peppers; remove and discard seeds. Chop peppers, and set aside.

• **Sauté** onion in hot oil in a Dutch oven over medium-high heat until onion is tender.

• **Add** squash and garlic; cook, stirring often, 15 minutes or until squash begins to soften.

• **Process** half of squash mixture in a food processor or blender until smooth, stopping to scrape down sides. Return to Dutch oven.

• **Add** chopped pepper, peas, and next 5 ingredients; cook over medium heat 15 minutes or until squash is tender.

• **Stir** in cilantro; remove from heat. **Yield:** 8 servings.

♥ Per cup: Calories 156 (10% from fat)
Fat 1.7g (sat 0.3g, mono 0.9g, poly 0.2g)
Protein 7.1g Carb 28.2g Fiber 2.8g
Chol 0mg Iron 2.5mg
Sodium 243mg Calc 70mg

CILANTRO DIP

Prep: 10 minutes
Chill: 8 hours, 30 minutes

1 (6-ounce) package reduced-fat feta cheese
1 cup fat-free milk
1 (8-ounce) package fat-free cream cheese
1 (8-ounce) can green Mexican sauce
¼ cup chopped fresh cilantro
1 garlic clove

• **Cut** feta cheese into 1-inch pieces. Place in a bowl; add milk. Cover and chill 8 hours. (Soaking reduces sodium content.) Drain.

• **Process** feta cheese, cream cheese, and remaining ingredients in a food processor until smooth, stopping to scrape down sides. Chill 30 minutes.

• **Serve** dip with baked tortilla chips or fresh vegetables. **Yield:** 1¼ cups.

Note: For testing purposes only, we used La Costeña Green Mexican Sauce.

Elisa Levy
Tallahassee, Florida

♥ Per 3 tablespoons: Calories 87 (31% from fat)
Fat 3g (sat 2g) Protein 9.6g
Carb 3g Fiber 0.1g
Chol 13mg Iron 0.1mg
Sodium 580mg Calc 193mg

CILANTRO BITES

■ Store fresh cilantro wrapped in damp paper towels in an air-filled zip-top plastic bag, or place it in a jar filled with water and cover with a plastic bag; keep in refrigerator.

■ Don't substitute dried for fresh. When hydrated, dried cilantro doesn't have the same flavor.

THAI PORK SALAD

Most of the fat in this recipe is monounsaturated, which reduces LDL, or "bad" cholesterol.

Prep: 15 minutes
Cook: 10 minutes

1 pound lean boneless pork
    chops
Vegetable cooking spray
½ cup chopped fresh cilantro
¼ cup chopped fresh mint
    leaves
3 green onions, finely chopped
1 teaspoon minced fresh
    ginger
½ teaspoon ground red pepper
½ cup fresh lime juice
1 tablespoon fish sauce
1 teaspoon sesame oil
¼ cup rice wine vinegar
2 tablespoons lite soy sauce
1 tablespoon olive oil
1 (16-ounce) package broccoli
    slaw mix
1 large cucumber, peeled and
    chopped
Hot cooked basmati rice (optional)
Garnish: fresh cilantro sprigs

• **Process** pork in a food processor until coarsely chopped.
• **Sauté** pork in a large skillet coated with cooking spray over medium-high heat 8 to 10 minutes or until meat crumbles and is no longer pink. Drain pork, and cool.
• **Combine** pork, cilantro, and next 7 ingredients.
• **Stir** together vinegar, soy sauce, and olive oil.
• **Drizzle** vinegar mixture over slaw, tossing to coat. Top salad with pork mixture; serve with cucumber, and, if desired, rice. Garnish, if desired. **Yield:** 6 servings.

Note: Fish sauce is found in Asian markets and large supermarkets.

♥ Per serving: Calories 218 (49% from fat)
Fat 11.8g (sat 3.3g, mono 5.8g, poly 1.6g)
Protein 20g Carb 9g Fiber 2.6g
Chol 57mg Iron 1.8mg
Sodium 220mg Calc 62mg

CREAM OF CILANTRO SOUP

Prep: 5 minutes
Cook: 20 minutes

1 bunch fresh cilantro
1 (32-ounce) container reduced-
    sodium, fat-free chicken broth,
    divided
2 tablespoons butter
2 tablespoons all-purpose flour
1 (8-ounce) package fat-free cream
    cheese
1 (8-ounce) container light sour
    cream
1 garlic clove, minced
¼ teaspoon salt
¼ teaspoon ground red pepper
¼ teaspoon ground cumin
Garnishes: fresh cilantro sprigs, light
    sour cream

• **Remove** stems from cilantro, and coarsely chop leaves.
• **Process** chopped cilantro and 1 cup chicken broth in a blender or food processor until blended, stopping to scrape down sides.
• **Melt** butter in a Dutch oven over medium heat; whisk in flour. Gradually add remaining 3 cups broth, whisking constantly until mixture is smooth. Boil 1 minute.
• **Stir** in cilantro mixture, cream cheese, and next 5 ingredients, and simmer soup 15 minutes. Garnish, if desired. **Yield:** 6 cups.

Victoria Tacher
Tallahassee, Florida

♥ Per cup: Calories 156 (50% from fat)
Fat 8.6g (sat 5.2g, mono 2.5g, poly 0.4g)
Protein 7.9g Carb 9.3g Fiber 1g
Chol 31mg Iron 1.6mg
Sodium 393mg Calc 177mg

MEXICAN SHRIMP COCKTAIL

Prep: 30 minutes
Cook: 3 minutes

2 pounds unpeeled, large fresh
    shrimp
6 cups water
2 to 3 tablespoons fresh lime juice
3 garlic cloves, pressed
¼ teaspoon salt
½ teaspoon pepper
1 cup ketchup
½ cup fresh lime juice
¼ cup minced sweet onion
½ to 1 teaspoon hot sauce
½ cup chopped tomato
½ cup chopped fresh cilantro
Avocado slices, lime wedges, saltine
    crackers (optional)

• **Peel** shrimp, and devein, if desired.
• **Bring** 6 cups water and next 4 ingredients to a boil in a large saucepan; add shrimp.
• **Cook** 2 to 3 minutes or just until shrimp turn pink. Drain shrimp, reserving ½ cup liquid.
• **Stir** together reserved liquid, ketchup, and next 3 ingredients.
• **Stir** in shrimp, tomato, and cilantro. Cover and chill. Serve with avocado slices, lime wedges, and saltine crackers, if desired. **Yield:** 6 servings.

Elisa Levy
Tallahassee, Florida

♥ Per serving: Calories 172 (11% from fat)
Fat 2.1g (sat 0.4g, mono 0.3g, poly 0.8g)
Protein 21.8g Carb 17.8g Fiber 1.2g
Chol 154mg Iron 3.2mg
Sodium 795mg Calc 76mg

From Our Kitchen

The Scoop on Mirlitons

■ Purchase mirlitons (also called chayote squash, mango squash, and vegetable pears) during the fall and winter months. Look for those with pale green or apple-green skin, although the colors can range from cream to dark green.

■ Choose very firm, unblemished mirlitons with skin that is fairly smooth to slightly edged, avoiding those with prickly skin. They range in weight from ½ pound to 2 pounds. The smaller ones are generally the most tender.

■ Cook mirlitons (they don't taste good raw) like you would summer squash. The fruit's firmer texture requires longer cooking times; however, the firmness makes it a better choice for stuffing.

■ Store lightly wrapped mirlitons for up to a month in the refrigerator. Don't discard the large edible seed. When boiled, it has a flavor somewhere between a lima bean and an almond. For mirliton recipes, see page 246.

Sold on Sweet Potatoes

■ Sweet potatoes lend themselves well to almost every cooking method; however, microwaving can keep them from developing their maximum sweetness.

■ These sweet spuds contain more vitamin C than white potatoes, but they have about the same calorie count. They also are a great source of vitamin A.

■ Store sweet potatoes in a cool, dark place—but not in the refrigerator. Extra-large sweet potatoes may be fibrous and stringy.

■ For smooth pies and casseroles, run cooked sweet potatoes through a food mill to remove the strings.

On Tap

Whether you're pairing beer with food or simply looking for a good thirst quencher, here's help in making the selections. Assistant Foods Editor Scott Jones gets you cooking with beer (see "A Toast to Oktoberfest" on page 238). He has found that ales are more like red wines and lagers are more like white wines. While there's a broad range of styles between the two, ales and lagers dominate the market shelves.

■ **Lagers** are light and probably the most food-friendly style of beer at a tailgating party. Lagers have more carbonation than ales, so they are considered more refreshing thirst quenchers. They're great with spicy foods such as salsa and chips. Most of our basic American beers are lagers—ambers, reds, bocks, and pilsners.

■ **Ales** are usually robust, complex, and can be slightly fruity. Varieties of ales include barley wines, amber and red ales, bitters, pale ales, porters, and stouts.

■ **Wheat beers**, or weisen (as in Heffe-weisen) are brewed with lots of wheat. They are unfiltered, full-flavored, fruity, and yeasty. These flavored beers don't fit into the ale or lager categories. Flavored beers come in a wide variety and can include everything from cherry and raspberry to chocolate. It's probably wise to buy these types as single bottles until you decide what kind you like.

Tips and Tidbits

■ Several of our readers have been looking for ham-flavored bouillon or concentrate to add more depth of flavor to foods without adding fat or calories. The brands that we use for testing purposes are Goya and Knorr. You'll find these located near the chicken and beef bouillon in the soup or seasonings section of your local supermarket.

■ We tried a new baking sheet by Dough-makers, Inc., that we like very much. This brand of baking sheets and pizza pans was developed by a couple of moms to yield baked goods that are "perfect every time." A pebbled surface allows excellent air and heat circulation and even browning. The pans are solid aluminum, so they don't rust. Doughmakers' large variety of pan sizes means that you'll find something to suit your baking needs. Pans range in price from $10 to $25. Call toll free 1-888-386-8517 or visit www.dough-makers.com.

AT MARKET

■**Pomegranate seeds** may be frozen up to a year. Extract the juice by cutting the fruit in half and squeezing it like an orange; or process seeds in a blender and strain the juice. Use the juice in salad dressings, sauces, marinades, and desserts.

■Pick up some **persimmons**. If they're large and round with a pointed base, they are Hachiyas (Japanese persimmons). Hachiyas should be soft when ripe. The small, tomato-shaped ones are Fuyu. These are still firm when ripe. Whichever you see, buy a few to try. If they're not completely ripe, put them in the freezer. The cold makes them sweeter. Freeze whole persimmons or the pureed fruit for up to a year.

■The large variety of **pears** gives you options—soft, juicy, and mellow; crisp, juicy, and sweet; or hard, slightly dry, and tart. Peel pears for cooked dishes, because the skin gets tough and turns dark with heat.

NOVEMBER

Feasting With Friends

At Loyd Hall Plantation near Cheneyville, Louisiana, Anne and Frank Fitzgerald welcome family and friends to their annual Thanksgiving gathering. Here's a scaled-down version of their menu for 50.

Holiday Feast With Friends
Serves 8

Bourbon Meatballs*

Deep-Fried Turkey   Pecan, Rice, and Crawfish Dressing*

Cranberry-Ginger Chutney

Scalloped Sweet Potatoes With Apples*

Spinach-Artichoke Casserole*

Whipped Turnip Puff*   Homemade biscuits

Simmie's Pecan Pie*

*Double these recipes to make menu serve 16.

BOURBON MEATBALLS

Prep: 5 minutes
Cook: 30 minutes

2 cups barbecue sauce
1½ cups bourbon
1 cup honey
1 cup prepared mustard
⅛ teaspoon Worcestershire sauce
1 (32-ounce) package frozen cooked
    Italian-style meatballs, thawed

● **Cook** first 5 ingredients in a Dutch oven over medium heat 5 minutes. Add meatballs; bring to a boil. Reduce heat, and simmer 25 minutes. **Yield:** 10 to 12 appetizer servings.

Anne Fitzgerald
Alexandria, Louisiana

DEEP-FRIED TURKEY
(pictured on page 265)

This fried turkey is juicy and succulent, wrapped in crisp, golden skin. Deep-frying a turkey requires care— see our tips in "From Our Kitchen" on page 300.

Prep: 40 minutes
Fry: 1 hour

1 (12- to 15-pound) turkey
2 tablespoons ground red
    pepper (optional)
4 to 5 gallons vegetable oil
Garnishes: fresh sage, parsley,
    thyme sprigs, kumquats with
    leaves

● **Remove** giblets and neck from turkey; rinse turkey with cold water. Drain cavity well; pat dry.
● **Place** turkey on fryer rod; allow all liquid to drain from turkey cavity (20 to 30 minutes).
● **Rub** outside of turkey with ground red pepper, if desired.
● **Pour** oil into a deep propane turkey fryer 10 to 12 inches from top; heat to 375° according to manufacturer's instructions over medium-low flame. Carefully lower turkey into hot oil with rod attachment.
● **Fry** 1 hour or until a meat thermometer inserted in turkey breast registers 170°. (Keep oil temperature at 340°.)
● **Remove** turkey from oil; drain and cool slightly before slicing. Garnish, if desired. **Yield:** 20 servings.

PECAN, RICE, AND CRAWFISH DRESSING
(pictured on page 265)

Creole seasoning adds a spicy kick to this rich seafood dressing.

Prep: 25 minutes
Bake: 30 minutes

1 medium onion
1 celery rib
1 green bell pepper
1 red bell pepper
1 pound lean ground beef
2 garlic cloves, minced
2 (16-ounce) packages frozen
    peeled, cooked crawfish tails,
    thawed
2 cups cooked long-grain rice
1 cup chopped pecans, toasted
¼ cup butter or margarine, cut into
    pieces
1 small bunch green onions,
    chopped
2 tablespoons Creole seasoning
½ teaspoon pepper
Chopped fresh parsley

● **Chop** first 4 ingredients.
● **Cook** vegetables, ground beef, and garlic in a Dutch oven over medium-high heat 10 minutes, stirring until beef crumbles and is no longer pink.

• **Stir** crawfish and next 6 ingredients into Dutch oven, and cook 3 minutes or until thoroughly heated.
• **Spoon** dressing mixture into a lightly greased 13- x 9-inch baking dish.
• **Bake** at 350° for 25 to 30 minutes or until lightly browned. Sprinkle with parsley. **Yield:** 8 to 10 servings.

Chef John Folse
Donaldsonville, Louisiana

CRANBERRY-GINGER CHUTNEY
(pictured on pages 1 and 265)

Prep: 10 minutes
Cook: 20 minutes
Chill: 8 hours

1 (12-ounce) package fresh
    cranberries
1½ cups sugar
1 cup fresh orange juice
2 celery ribs, chopped
1 cup golden raisins
1 medium apple, chopped
1 tablespoon grated orange
    rind
1 teaspoon minced fresh
    ginger
1 cup chopped walnuts,
    toasted

• **Bring** first 3 ingredients to a boil in a large saucepan. Reduce heat; simmer 15 minutes. Remove from heat.
• **Stir** in celery and next 4 ingredients. Cover and chill 8 hours. Stir in walnuts. **Yield:** 6 cups.

Anne Fitzgerald
Alexandria, Louisiana

A WELCOMING PARTY

At Anne and Frank Fitzgerald's annual Thanksgiving dinner, Anne stays in constant motion, arranging dishes on the buffet table, carrying food from the house, and giving hugs all around. Frank points folks toward a pitcher of his potent "lemonade," as he presides over a bubbling cauldron in which the turkey is frying. His friend Andy Anderson keeps him company, watching to see that pets and children don't wander too close to the hot oil.

"We started the party in about 1980," Anne says, "because we're such a small family—just Frank and me and our three daughters." In the beginning about 25 guests joined them, but the gathering has been as large as 300 on occasion. The number has finally settled down to a manageable 50. The Fitzgeralds invite relatives, friends, and neighbors. Anne adds, "And all of the girls' friends come. One year the girls were gone, but their friends came out of tradition."

The Fitzgeralds' guests clearly feel right at home, helping themselves to beverages, renewing acquaintances, and meandering from the backyard to the front veranda and through the early 19th-century house, which is regularly open to the public.

Most of them have been coming here to celebrate Thanksgiving for years. Fran Guthrie, Anne's cousin, drives from Arkansas for the event. Leta Adele DeFee and Mary Vizzer bring the greenery. Charles Thigpen, one of Frank's high school teachers, regales guests with tales of his mischievous pupil.

The tradition even moved North when Anne and Frank's oldest daughter, Jerianne, moved to New York. "She couldn't get home for Thanksgiving," Anne says. "She invited all these displaced Southerners—even the guys brought their favorite dishes. Jerianne said it was the most bizarre meal she'd ever seen, but they had a great time anyway."

SCALLOPED SWEET POTATOES WITH APPLES
(pictured on page 265)

Prep: 45 minutes
Bake: 1 hour

3 large sweet potatoes
3 Granny Smith apples
¾ cup firmly packed brown sugar
1 tablespoon grated orange rind
1 teaspoon salt
½ teaspoon ground cinnamon
¼ cup butter or margarine, cut up

• **Cook** sweet potatoes in boiling water to cover 45 minutes; drain and cool slightly.

• **Peel** sweet potatoes, and cut into ¼-inch-thick slices. Peel, core, and thinly slice apples into rings.
• **Combine** brown sugar and next 3 ingredients in a bowl.
• **Arrange** half of potato slices and half of apple slices in a lightly greased 13- x 9-inch baking dish.
• **Sprinkle** with half of brown sugar mixture, and dot evenly with half of butter. Repeat procedure with remaining ingredients.
• **Bake** at 350° for 1 hour. Serve warm. **Yield:** 6 to 8 servings.

Leta Adele DeFee
Alexandria, Louisiana

Spinach-Artichoke Casserole

Prep: 20 minutes
Bake: 30 minutes

2 (10-ounce) packages frozen spinach, thawed
1 (14-ounce) can artichoke hearts, drained and chopped
1 (10¾-ounce) can fat-free cream of mushroom soup, undiluted
1 (8-ounce) container reduced-fat sour cream
3 green onions, chopped
2 tablespoons all-purpose flour
1 tablespoon minced fresh parsley
¼ teaspoon Worcestershire sauce
1 tablespoon butter or margarine
1 cup sliced fresh mushrooms
2 garlic cloves, pressed
1 tablespoon lemon juice
½ teaspoon pepper
2 cups (8 ounces) shredded Monterey Jack cheese with peppers, divided

• **Drain** spinach well, pressing between layers of paper towels. Stir together spinach and next 7 ingredients.
• **Melt** butter in a skillet over medium-high heat. Add mushrooms and next 3 ingredients, and sauté 5 minutes or until mushrooms are tender.
• **Stir** mushroom mixture and 1 cup Monterey Jack cheese into spinach mixture; spoon into a lightly greased 11- x 7-inch baking dish. Sprinkle with remaining 1 cup cheese.
• **Bake** at 400° for 30 minutes. **Yield:** 8 to 10 servings.

Linnie Single
Alexandria, Louisiana

Whipped Turnip Puff

Prep: 35 minutes
Bake: 1 hour

8 medium turnips
4 large eggs, lightly beaten
2 cups soft breadcrumbs
½ cup butter or margarine, melted
2 tablespoons sugar
2 teaspoons salt
¼ teaspoon pepper

• **Peel** turnips; cut into 1-inch cubes.
• **Arrange** turnips in a steamer basket over boiling water. Cover and steam 25 minutes or until tender.
• **Mash** turnips with a potato masher; stir in eggs and remaining ingredients.
• **Spoon** mixture into a lightly greased 11- x 7-inch baking dish.
• **Bake** mixture at 375° for 1 hour. **Yield:** 8 servings.

Cissy Galloway
Alexandria, Louisiana

Simmie's Pecan Pie

Simmie Anderson has been a regular at Anne and Frank's party since her son married Melinda Fitzgerald. "I always bring pecan pie," she says with a laugh. "It's the only thing I can make!"

Prep: 5 minutes
Bake: 1 hour

3 large eggs
¾ cup sugar
1 cup dark corn syrup
3 tablespoons butter or margarine, melted
⅛ teaspoon salt
1 teaspoon vanilla extract
1½ cups chopped pecans
1 unbaked (9-inch) pastry shell

• **Stir** together eggs and sugar until blended. Stir in corn syrup and next 3 ingredients. Stir in pecans.
• **Pour** mixture into pastry shell. Place pie on a baking sheet.
• **Bake** at 400° on lower oven rack 15 minutes. Reduce oven temperature to 325°, and bake 40 to 45 minutes, shielding with aluminum foil to prevent excessive browning, if necessary. **Yield:** 1 (9-inch) pie.

Simmie Anderson
Woodworth, Louisiana

Pudding, Please

The persimmon is one of winter's rare, delicious fruits. Choose fruit that is plump and soft, with smooth, glossy skin. When ripe, persimmons will keep in the refrigerator up to three days.

Persimmon Pudding

Prep: 20 minutes
Bake: 55 minutes

2 cups persimmon pulp
½ cup butter or margarine, melted
1 cup sugar
2 large eggs
1 cup all-purpose flour
1½ teaspoons baking powder
½ teaspoon baking soda
1 teaspoon ground cinnamon
½ cup milk
½ cup buttermilk
Cinnamon-Butter Sauce

• **Stir** together first 4 ingredients until blended. Add flour and next 5 ingredients, stirring well (batter will not be smooth). Pour batter into a greased and floured 9-inch square cakepan.
• **Bake** at 350° for 50 to 55 minutes. Serve with Cinnamon-Butter Sauce. **Yield:** 6 servings.

Cinnamon-Butter Sauce

Prep: 5 minutes
Cook: 8 minutes

1 cup sugar
½ cup butter or margarine
2 tablespoons all-purpose flour
1 cup hot water
1 teaspoon ground cinnamon

• **Cook** first 4 ingredients in a saucepan over medium-high heat, stirring occasionally, 6 to 8 minutes or until thickened. Stir in cinnamon. **Yield:** 1½ cups.

Polly Frye
Alexandria, Virginia

Holiday Dinners®

Friends, family, and food make for great holidays. Come along as we enjoy a Thanksgiving dinner from our staff, share an Italian Christmas, visit a dessert party, and relish all the good things the season brings.

Jars of Joy

Start a new gift-giving tradition: homemade sauces that are simple to prepare. They offer an added bonus to the giver—no trip to the mall. Choose one of these sweet or savory recipes, or select a cherished family favorite from your files. Then dress up the results with a nice container, and rest assured that your gift is the one they'll still remember *next* Christmas.

PEPPERY BARBECUE SAUCE

Prep: 10 minutes

2   cups firmly packed brown sugar
2   tablespoons pepper
1   to 1½ teaspoons salt
4   garlic cloves, minced
4   cups ketchup
1   cup white vinegar
2   tablespoons vegetable oil
2   tablespoons prepared mustard
2   tablespoons Worcestershire sauce
2   tablespoons hot sauce

• **Stir** together all ingredients. Pour into hot sterilized jars, and seal. Store in refrigerator up to 1 month. **Yield:** 6 cups.
Scott Petrie
Phoenix, Arizona

HOT-AND-SPICY CRANBERRY-PEAR CHUTNEY

Prep: 5 minutes
Cook: 13 minutes

1½ cups fresh cranberries
1   (6-ounce) package sweetened dried cranberries
⅓   cup sugar
1   cup fresh orange juice
1   tablespoon grated fresh ginger
2   (10½-ounce) jars pear preserves
1   (10½-ounce) jar hot jalapeño jelly
1   (9-ounce) jar hot mango chutney
1   tablespoon grated orange rind

• **Bring** first 5 ingredients to a boil in a large saucepan, stirring constantly. Reduce heat, and simmer, stirring constantly, 5 minutes or until cranberry skins pop.
• **Stir** pear preserves and remaining ingredients into saucepan; simmer, stirring constantly, 5 minutes. Remove from heat; cool.
• **Pour** mixture into hot sterilized jars, and seal.
• **Store** in refrigerator up to 1 month. **Yield:** about 8 cups.

Note: For testing purposes only, we used Craisins for sweetened dried cranberries.
Janet Eilders
Sikeston, Missouri

SAFE SAUCES

Don't overlook safety when giving food gifts. Follow these tips to ensure properly handled products.

■ Sterilize jars by boiling them, covered with water, for 15 minutes. Fill while jars are still hot.

■ Refrigerate the sauces immediately, and be sure that your friends and relatives know to keep them cold. It's easy for a small gift to be lost in the holiday shuffle, so hand deliver yours. Tell the recipient to refrigerate the sauce right away.

Holiday Dinners

APPLESAUCE
(pictured on page 302)

Prep: 20 minutes
Cook: 35 minutes

12 large Granny Smith apples, peeled and coarsely chopped
1½ cups sugar
¼ cup fresh lemon juice

• **Cook** all ingredients in a Dutch oven over low heat, stirring often, 10 minutes. (Sugar will dissolve and apples will begin to break down and release juices.) Increase to medium heat, and cook, stirring often, 25 minutes or until thickened.
• **Spoon** into hot sterilized jars, and seal. Store sauce in refrigerator up to 1 month. **Yield:** about 6 cups.

Martha Jordan Newberry
Palm Bay, Florida

MEAT SAUCE FOR SPAGHETTI
(pictured on page 302)

Prep: 30 minutes
Cook: 1 hour, 10 minutes

5 pounds ground chuck
6 medium onions, diced
5 large celery ribs, diced
2 (28-ounce) cans crushed tomatoes
2 (26-ounce) cans tomato sauce
2 (12-ounce) cans tomato paste
2 (12-ounce) bottles chili sauce
2 (12-ounce) cans sliced mushrooms, drained
4 cups water
3 to 4 tablespoons sugar
2 teaspoons salt
2 teaspoons coarsely ground pepper
2 teaspoons white vinegar

• **Cook** first 3 ingredients in an 8-quart stockpot over medium heat 8 to 10 minutes, stirring until beef crumbles and is no longer pink; drain well, and return to stockpot.

• **Add** crushed tomatoes and remaining ingredients to stockpot; reduce heat to low, and cook, stirring often, 1 hour. Remove from heat, and cool.
• **Pour** into hot sterilized jars, and seal. Refrigerate up to 3 days, or freeze sauce in heavy-duty zip-top plastic bags up to 3 months (thaw in refrigerator). **Yield:** about 7 quarts.

Lewis Wimbish
Hot Springs, North Carolina

CUMBERLAND SAUCE
(pictured on page 302)

This sweet yet tart sauce has great depth of flavor. It's delicious with pork and turkey, and can be used as a glaze for ham.

Prep: 15 minutes
Cook: 25 minutes

2½ cups port wine, divided
1 (10½-ounce) jar red currant jelly
3 tablespoons light brown sugar
2 tablespoons grated orange rind
⅔ cup fresh orange juice
1½ tablespoons grated fresh ginger
2 teaspoons dry mustard
¼ teaspoon salt
¼ teaspoon ground red pepper
2½ tablespoons cornstarch

• **Bring** 2 cups wine and next 8 ingredients to a boil in a large saucepan, stirring constantly; reduce heat, and simmer, stirring often, 20 minutes.
• **Stir** together remaining ½ cup wine and cornstarch until smooth.
• **Stir** into hot mixture; bring to a boil over medium heat.
• **Boil,** stirring constantly, 1 minute. Remove from heat, and cool.
• **Pour** into hot sterilized jars, and seal. Store sauce in refrigerator up to 1 month. **Yield:** about 4 cups.

Cheri Reid
Peachtree City, Georgia

CARAMEL SAUCE
(pictured on page 302)

Prep: 5 minutes
Cook: 10 minutes

1 cup butter
2 cups sugar
2 teaspoons fresh lemon juice
1½ cups whipping cream

• **Melt** butter in a heavy saucepan over medium heat.
• **Add** sugar and lemon juice, and cook, stirring constantly, 6 to 8 minutes or until mixture turns a deep caramel color. Gradually add cream; cook, stirring constantly, 1 to 2 minutes or until smooth. Remove from heat, and cool.
• **Pour** into hot sterilized jars, and seal. Store sauce in refrigerator up to 1 month. **Yield:** about 3 cups.

Patsy Taylor
Russellville, Alabama

HEAVENLY HOT FUDGE SAUCE

Prep: 5 minutes
Cook: 10 minutes

4 (1-ounce) unsweetened chocolate squares
½ cup butter
3 cups sugar
1 (12-ounce) can evaporated milk
½ teaspoon salt

• **Melt** chocolate and butter in a large, heavy saucepan over low heat, stirring constantly.
• **Add** sugar, 1 cup at a time, alternately with evaporated milk, beginning and ending with sugar; stir constantly over medium heat 5 minutes or until smooth. Stir in salt.
• **Serve** warm, or spoon sauce into hot sterilized jars and seal. Store sauce in refrigerator up to 1 month. **Yield:** about 4 cups.

Amanda McNeal
El Paso, Texas

Progressive Dinner Party

Neighbors opened their homes to neighbors for a spirited evening of food and fun. Sample a few of the favorites these folks have passed down through families over the last 25 years.

Old-fashioned streetlights glowed, and homes were adorned as guests enjoyed Highland Circle's annual Progressive Party in Tupelo, Mississippi. Kelly Holcomb, a local interior decorator, said, "This is a special time when residents come together to celebrate the season. After fine wine, appetizers, dinner, and dessert, we gather around the piano to sing carols." Here are some of their favorites from the annual event.

CHICKEN-AND-WILD RICE CASSEROLE

Prep: 20 minutes
Bake: 20 minutes

1 (6.2-ounce) package fast-cooking
   long-grain and wild rice mix
½ cup butter or margarine
1 small onion, chopped
¼ cup all-purpose flour
1½ cups chicken broth
3 cups chopped cooked chicken
1½ cups half-and-half
1 (6-ounce) can sliced water
   chestnuts, drained
1 (4.5-ounce) jar sliced mushrooms,
   drained
1 tablespoon chopped fresh parsley
1 teaspoon salt
½ teaspoon pepper
1 (2.5-ounce) package sliced almonds

• **Cook** rice mix according to package directions; set aside.
• **Melt** butter in a Dutch oven over medium-high heat.
• **Add** onion, and sauté until tender.
• **Add** flour, and cook, stirring constantly, 1 minute.
• **Add** broth; cook, stirring constantly, 1 to 2 minutes or until mixture is thickened and bubbly. Stir in rice, chicken, and next 6 ingredients.
• **Spoon** mixture into a lightly greased 11- x 7-inch baking dish. Top casserole with almonds.
• **Bake** at 350° for 15 to 20 minutes or until casserole is thoroughly heated. **Yield:** 6 servings.

Peggy Carter
Tupelo, Mississippi

BUTTER ROLLS
(pictured on pages 1 and 264)

Prep: 15 minutes
Rise: 2 hours
Bake: 20 minutes

1 (¼-ounce) envelope active dry
   yeast
¼ cup warm water (105° to 115°)
2½ to 3 cups all-purpose flour,
   divided
¼ cup sugar
1¼ teaspoons salt
2 large eggs, divided
¼ cup milk
¼ cup butter or margarine, softened
1 tablespoon water
Sesame or poppy seeds

• **Stir** together yeast and ¼ cup warm water in a 1-cup measuring cup, and let stand 5 minutes.
• **Pulse** 1 cup flour, sugar, and salt in a food processor until blended.
• **Add** yeast mixture, 1 egg, and milk; pulse until blended. (Pulsing prevents mixture from overheating, which would kill yeast.)
• **Add** butter, 1 tablespoon at a time, pulsing until combined. Gradually add enough of remaining flour until dough is no longer sticky. (Dough should be smooth.)
• **Place** dough in a well-greased bowl, turning to grease top.
• **Cover** and let rise in a warm place (85°), free from drafts, 1 hour or until doubled in bulk. Punch dough down, and divide into fourths; shape each portion into 6 (1-inch) balls. Place balls in a lightly greased 13- x 9-inch pan.
• **Cover** and let rise in a warm place (85°), free from drafts, 1 hour.
• **Stir** together remaining egg and 1 tablespoon water; brush over rolls, and sprinkle with sesame seeds.
• **Bake** at 375° for 15 to 20 minutes or until golden brown. Freeze rolls up to 3 months, if desired. **Yield:** 2 dozen.

Note: Rolls may also be prepared with a heavy-duty mixer.

Jane Black
Tupelo, Mississippi

Thanksgiving From Our Staff

The aromas of turkey, pork loin, dressing, and sweet potatoes announced magnificent Thanksgiving meals for taste testing as our Foods staff prepared our favorite Thanksgiving recipes. Join us at everyone's favorite holiday feast.

CRISPY PECAN STICKS

Buttery pecans lend rich flavor to these cookies, which are sweetened with powdered sugar. They're great for parties because you can prepare them a couple of months ahead and store in the freezer.

Prep: 25 minutes
Bake: 15 minutes

½ cup butter, softened
¼ cup powdered sugar
2 cups all-purpose flour
¼ teaspoon salt
1 cup chopped pecans
1 tablespoon vanilla extract
1 tablespoon ice water
Powdered sugar

• **Beat** butter at medium speed with an electric mixer until creamy; gradually add ¼ cup powdered sugar, beating well.
• **Combine** flour and salt; add to butter mixture, beating at low speed until blended.
• **Stir** in pecans, vanilla, and 1 tablespoon ice water.
• **Shape** dough into 4-inch sticks, and place sticks on lightly greased baking sheets.
• **Bake** at 350° for 12 to 15 minutes or until browned.
• **Roll** in powdered sugar. Store sticks in an airtight container up to 2 weeks, or freeze up to 2 months. **Yield:** about 3 dozen.

Susan Winkler
Tupelo, Mississippi

Favorite Thanksgiving Feast
Serves 8

Orange-Dijon Pork Loin or
Maple-Plum Glazed Turkey Breast (recipe on page 285)
Cornbread Dressing
Roasted Root Vegetables   Garlic Green Beans
Sweet Onion Pudding   Butter Muffins
Caramel-Applesauce Cobbler
With Bourbon-Pecan Ice Cream

Our own styles are as varied as those of our readers. Some of us choose a casual approach; others celebrate Thanksgiving as the most formal meal of the year. But we all agree that great food—and lots of it—is a must on this day of days.

Jan Moon of our Test Kitchens staff says formality sets the tone for her family's celebration. "We all get dressed up, and Mother uses linen napkins, china, crystal, and silver. All the family members bring the dishes, assuring that the meal will be bountiful. It's the one time of year we can count on everyone being there," she says. "We're *always* together on Thanksgiving, no matter what."

The family of Vie Warshaw, another Test Kitchens staff member, has always enjoyed a casual feast. Now Vie gathers with her children, often traveling up North to her daughter's home where there might be beef tenderloin in addition to turkey. "As in most families, food is the focus of this very special day," she says. "We eat, put it away, relax for a while, then pull it out again."

Taking a cue from Vie and others, we devised a meal to be served in a casual setting. Pork loin offers a flavorful alternative or addition to turkey. And serve dinner on china with silver utensils if you prefer; it will taste wonderful either way.

Holiday Dinners

ORANGE-DIJON PORK LOIN
(pictured on page 261)

*Assistant Foods Editor
Kate Nicholson loves this recipe she
got from family friend Jo Ann Pugh
of Shreveport, Louisiana.*

*Prep: 13 minutes
Bake: 1 hour, 30 minutes*

2 teaspoons dried thyme
1 teaspoon salt
1 teaspoon rubbed sage
¼ teaspoon ground allspice
¼ teaspoon pepper
1 (4- to 5-pound) rolled boneless pork
   loin roast
Orange-Dijon Sauce

• **Combine** first 5 ingredients; rub mixture evenly over roast. Place roast in a lightly greased 13- x 9-inch pan.
• **Bake** at 325° for 1 hour. Cover and bake 30 more minutes or until a meat thermometer inserted into thickest portion registers 160°. Top with Orange-Dijon Sauce. **Yield:** 8 servings.

Orange-Dijon Sauce

Prep: 8 minutes

2 (12-ounce) jars orange marmalade
¼ cup Dijon mustard
¼ cup Worcestershire sauce
1 teaspoon ground ginger
4 large garlic cloves, minced

• **Bring** all ingredients to a boil in a small saucepan over medium heat. Serve with pork loin. **Yield:** 2 cups.

CORNBREAD DRESSING
(pictured on page 1)

*This dressing is a favorite
among our staff. Serve it
with pork roast or turkey.*

*Prep: 45 minutes
Bake: 1 hour*

2 cups cornmeal
½ cup all-purpose flour
2 teaspoons baking powder
1 teaspoon baking soda
1 teaspoon salt
1 teaspoon sugar (optional)
6 large eggs, divided
2 cups buttermilk
2 tablespoons bacon drippings or
   melted butter
½ cup butter or margarine
3 bunches green onions,
   chopped
4 celery ribs, chopped
1 (16-ounce) package herb-seasoned
   stuffing mix
5 (14½-ounce) cans chicken
   broth

• **Combine** first 5 ingredients and, if desired, sugar in a large bowl.
• **Stir** together 2 eggs and buttermilk; add to dry ingredients, stirring just until moistened.
• **Heat** bacon drippings in a 10-inch cast-iron skillet or 9-inch round cake-pan in oven at 425° for 5 minutes. Stir hot drippings into batter. Pour batter into hot skillet.
• **Bake** at 425° for 25 minutes or until cornbread is golden; cool and crumble. Freeze in large heavy-duty zip-top plastic bag up to 1 month, if desired. Thaw in refrigerator.
• **Melt** ½ cup butter in a large skillet over medium heat; add green onions and celery, and sauté until tender.
• **Stir** together remaining 4 eggs in a large bowl; stir in cornbread, onion mixture, stuffing mix, and chicken broth until blended.
• **Spoon** dressing into a lightly greased 13- x 9-inch baking dish and a lightly greased 9-inch square baking dish. Cover dressing, and freeze up to 3

months, if desired; thaw in refrigerator 8 hours.
• **Place** 13- x 9-inch dish (uncovered) and 9-inch square dish (uncovered) in oven at 350°. Bake 13- x 9-inch dish for 1 hour and 9-inch square dish for 50 minutes or until each is lightly browned. **Yield:** 12 servings.

ROASTED ROOT VEGETABLES

*The combination of colors and
flavors in these vegetables delights
Foods Editor Andria Hurst; she
serves the dish every year.*

*Prep: 15 minutes
Bake: 45 minutes*

1 (1-pound) bag parsnips
6 large turnips
2 large sweet potatoes
1 large rutabaga
6 large beets
Vegetable cooking spray
1 teaspoon salt, divided
1 teaspoon pepper, divided
2 tablespoons butter or margarine,
   melted

• **Peel** first 5 ingredients, and cut into large pieces. Coat 2 aluminum foil-lined baking sheets with cooking spray.
• **Arrange** parsnip, turnip, sweet potato, and rutabaga on a baking sheet. Lightly coat vegetables with cooking spray, and sprinkle with ¾ teaspoon salt and ¾ teaspoon pepper.
• **Arrange** beets on remaining baking sheet; lightly coat with cooking spray, and sprinkle with remaining ¼ teaspoon salt and ¼ teaspoon pepper.
• **Bake** vegetables at 425°, stirring occasionally, 35 to 45 minutes or until tender. (Pans may need to be rearranged after 15 to 20 minutes to ensure even cooking.)
• **Toss** vegetables with melted butter. **Yield:** 8 servings.

Note: We cooked the beets separately to keep them from bleeding into the other vegetables.

Holiday Dinners

GARLIC GREEN BEANS
*(pictured on facing page
and on page 1)*

*This recipe is a favorite of
Test Kitchen staffer Vie Warshaw
and her family.*

*Prep: 10 minutes
Cook: 37 minutes*

2 pounds fresh green beans, trimmed
1 cup boiling water
1 teaspoon salt
¼ cup butter or margarine
4 garlic cloves, pressed
¼ teaspoon lemon pepper
¼ cup chopped fresh parsley

• **Place** first 3 ingredients in a Dutch oven; cover and cook over medium heat 30 minutes. Drain.
• **Melt** butter in Dutch oven; add garlic and lemon pepper, and sauté mixture over medium heat 1 to 2 minutes.
• **Add** green beans; sauté 5 minutes. Sprinkle with parsley. **Yield:** 8 servings.

SWEET ONION PUDDING

*Jan Moon of our Test Kitchens
staff says this silky custard is
one of her favorites.*

*Prep: 1 hour
Bake: 30 minutes*

2 cups whipping cream
1 (3-ounce) package shredded
    Parmesan cheese
6 large eggs, lightly beaten
3 tablespoons all-purpose flour
2 tablespoons sugar
2 teaspoons baking powder
1 teaspoon salt
½ cup butter or margarine
6 medium-size sweet onions, thinly
    sliced

• **Stir** together first 3 ingredients in a large bowl. Combine flour and next 3 ingredients; gradually stir into egg mixture. Set aside.

• **Melt** butter in a large skillet over medium heat; add onion. Cook, stirring often, 30 to 40 minutes or until caramel colored. Remove onion from heat.
• **Stir** onion into egg mixture; spoon into a lightly greased 13- x 9-inch baking dish. Bake at 350° for 30 minutes or until set. **Yield:** 8 servings.

BUTTER MUFFINS
(pictured on facing page)

*Vie Warshaw's bite-size quick breads
will melt in your mouth.*

*Prep: 5 minutes
Bake: 25 minutes*

2 cups self-rising flour
1 (8-ounce) container sour cream
1 cup butter or margarine, melted

• **Stir** together all ingredients just until blended.
• **Spoon** batter into lightly greased miniature muffin pans, filling to the top.
• **Bake** at 350° for 25 minutes or until lightly browned. **Yield:** 2½ dozen.

CARAMEL-APPLESAUCE COBBLER WITH BOURBON-PECAN ICE CREAM

*This recipe was inspired by an
applesauce pie with hard sauce that
Test Kitchens staffer Mary Allen Perry
enjoyed at her grandmother's house as a
child. After devouring it, family members
may drift away from the table to doze off.*

*Prep: 45 minutes
Bake: 35 minutes*

½ cup butter or margarine
12 large Granny Smith apples, peeled
    and sliced
2 cups sugar
2 tablespoons lemon juice
1 (15-ounce) package refrigerated
    piecrusts
Bourbon-Pecan Ice Cream

• **Melt** butter in a large Dutch oven over medium-high heat.
• **Add** apple, sugar, and lemon juice; cook, stirring often, 20 to 25 minutes or until apple is caramel colored.
• **Spoon** into a shallow, greased 2-quart baking dish.
• **Roll** each piecrust to press out fold lines; cut into ½-inch strips.
• **Arrange** strips in a lattice design over filling; fold edges under. Place remaining strips on a baking sheet.
• **Bake** remaining strips at 425° for 8 to 10 minutes or until golden. Set aside to serve with cobbler.
• **Bake** cobbler at 425° for 20 to 25 minutes or until crust is golden.
• **Serve** cobbler warm with pastry strips and Bourbon-Pecan Ice Cream. **Yield:** 8 servings.

Bourbon-Pecan
Ice Cream

*Prep: 5 minutes
Freeze: 4 hours*

2 pints homemade-style vanilla ice
    cream, softened
1 cup chopped pecans, toasted
¼ cup bourbon

• **Stir** together all ingredients; freeze 4 hours. **Yield:** 2 pints.

Note: For testing purposes only, we used Blue Bell Homemade Vanilla Ice Cream.

Orange-Dijon Pork Loin, Roasted Root Vegetables, page 259; Garlic Green Beans, Butter Muffins, facing page

Pumpkin Soup With Sweet Croutons, page 296

Hot Peanuts,
page 278

Marinated
Shrimp With
Cupers,
page 279

Beef-Stuffed
Mushrooms,
page 278

Roasted Red Pepper
Bruschetta, page 278

Oven Apple Butter,
page 237

Butter Rolls,
page 257

Deep-Fried Turkey; Scalloped Sweet Potatoes With Apples; homemade biscuits; Pecan, Rice, and Crawfish Dressing; Cranberry-Ginger Chutney, pages 252-253

*Cheesy Vegetable Chowder, Anchorage Country
Store Whole Wheat Bread, page 272*

*Turkey Sandwich With
Cranberry Salsa, page 269*

*Barbecue Pork Shoulder, baked beans, Danny's Slaw,
Cheesy Potatoes and Onions, pages 274-275*

Ginger Pound Cake With Glazed Cranberry Ambrosia, facing page

Holiday Dinners

A Berry Nice Twist

A shiny scarlet berry with a refreshing tart taste has crept its way into Southern cuisine. The versatile little cranberry no longer confines itself to the traditional sauce. It's now an addition to savory dishes and desserts.

Cranberries usually come in 12-ounce packages, which yield about 3 cups whole berries. You can refrigerate them up to two months or freeze them up to a year for use anytime.

GINGER POUND CAKE WITH GLAZED CRANBERRY AMBROSIA
(pictured on facing page)

Pound cake and ambrosia are a luscious combination, but either recipe is as delectable served alone.

Prep: 10 minutes
Bake: 1 hour, 20 minutes

⅔ cup butter or margarine, softened
1 cup sugar
3 large eggs
2¼ cups all-purpose flour
1 teaspoon baking powder
1 teaspoon salt
½ cup milk
2 tablespoons minced fresh ginger
½ teaspoon vanilla extract
Glazed Cranberry Ambrosia

• **Beat** butter at medium speed with an electric mixer 2 minutes or until creamy; gradually add sugar, and beat 5 to 7 minutes. Add eggs, 1 at a time, beating just until yellow disappears.

• **Combine** flour, baking powder, and salt; add to butter mixture alternately with milk, beginning and ending with flour mixture. Beat at low speed just until blended after each addition. Stir in ginger and vanilla.
• **Pour** batter into a greased and floured 9- x 5-inch loafpan.
• **Bake** at 325° for 1 hour and 20 minutes or until a long wooden pick inserted in center comes out clean. Cool in pan on a wire rack 10 minutes; remove from pan, and cool completely on wire rack. Serve with Glazed Cranberry Ambrosia. **Yield:** 1 (9-inch) loaf.

Glazed Cranberry Ambrosia

Prep: 15 minutes
Cook: 5 minutes
Cool: 15 minutes
Chill: 8 hours

1 cup fresh or frozen cranberries, thawed
¼ cup sugar
1 tablespoon minced fresh ginger
1 tablespoon grated orange rind
5 oranges, peeled and sectioned

• **Combine** first 3 ingredients in a small saucepan; cover and cook over medium heat 2 minutes. Uncover; cook, stirring constantly, 3 more minutes or until cranberry skins pop. Remove from heat; stir in orange rind. Cool 15 minutes.
• **Stir** in orange sections, and chill 8 hours. **Yield:** 2½ cups.

TURKEY SANDWICHES WITH CRANBERRY SALSA
(pictured on page 267)

For a new twist on a turkey sandwich, slice the leftover bird and add Cranberry Salsa. This is a great way to serve a quick meal to family or friends.

Prep: 5 minutes
Broil: 6 minutes

Corn Light Bread (recipe on following page) ✳
Cranberry Salsa
1 pound thinly sliced smoked turkey
Lettuce leaves

• **Cut** Corn Light Bread into 12 slices.
• **Broil** bread slices on an ungreased baking sheet 5½ inches from heat 2 to 3 minutes on each side or until lightly toasted.
• **Spoon** ¼ cup Cranberry Salsa on 1 side of 6 bread slices, reserving remaining Cranberry Salsa for another use. Layer evenly with turkey and lettuce. Top with remaining bread slices. **Yield:** 6 servings.

✳ Substitute your favorite bread for Corn Light Bread, if desired.

Cranberry Salsa

Prep: 6 minutes
Chill: 8 hours

3 cups fresh or frozen cranberries, thawed
½ medium-size purple onion, chopped
2 jalapeño peppers, seeded and chopped
½ cup chopped fresh cilantro
½ cup honey
2 tablespoons fresh lime juice
1 tablespoon grated orange rind

• **Process** all ingredients in a food processor, pulsing 6 to 8 times or until coarsely chopped, stopping to scrape down sides. Cover and chill 8 hours. **Yield:** 2½ cups.

CORN LIGHT BREAD

Unlike the typical crusty cornbread, this bread has a cakelike texture.

Prep: 15 minutes
Stand: 10 minutes
Bake: 40 minutes
Cool: 10 minutes

2 **cups plus 1 tablespoon self-rising cornmeal, divided**
1 **cup self-rising flour**
⅓ **cup sugar**
¼ **teaspoon baking soda**
2 **cups buttermilk**
½ **cup butter or margarine, melted**
1 **large egg, lightly beaten**

• **Grease** a 9- x 5-inch loafpan, and sprinkle pan lightly with 1 tablespoon cornmeal.
• **Combine** 2 cups cornmeal and next 3 ingredients in a large bowl.
• **Add** buttermilk and remaining ingredients, stirring until blended.
• **Pour** batter into prepared pan, and let stand 10 minutes.
• **Bake** at 400° for 40 minutes or until lightly browned. Cool in pan on a wire rack 10 minutes. **Yield:** 1 (9-inch) loaf.

Bonnie Jarrell
Ashland City, Tennessee

A Greek Christmas

Paula Troupos' holiday memories are a combination of her American and Greek heritages. The Gaithersburg, Maryland, resident says, "We fasted on Christmas Eve and then went to midnight services. We broke our fast with Stuffed Cabbage Leaves and homemade bread."

Here Paula shares some recipes from her mother, Mary Yankopolus. "The recipes came down from my grandmothers," says Paula, "but my mother made them her own."

STUFFED CABBAGE LEAVES

Prep: 25 minutes
Cook: 45 minutes

12 **large cabbage leaves**
1 **tablespoon butter or margarine**
1 **medium onion, chopped**
¾ **pound ground beef**
¾ **pound ground pork**
1 **cup cooked long-grain rice**
1 **(14½-ounce) can diced tomatoes, drained**
2 **tablespoons olive oil**
2 **teaspoons salt**
1 **teaspoon pepper**
1 **teaspoon dried oregano**
1 **(32-ounce) jar sauerkraut**
1 **(32-ounce) can tomato juice**
2 **tablespoons lemon juice**

• **Cook** cabbage in boiling water to cover 8 minutes or until tender; drain. Set aside.
• **Melt** butter in a large skillet over medium heat. Add onion, and cook 5 minutes or until tender.
• **Stir** together sautéed onion, beef, and next 7 ingredients. Spoon about ½ cup meat mixture in center of each cabbage leaf; fold sides over meat mixture, and roll up.
• **Place** a thin layer of sauerkraut on bottom of a large skillet. Pour 2 cups tomato juice over sauerkraut. Top with cabbage rolls.
• **Spoon** remaining sauerkraut over cabbage rolls, and drizzle with remaining tomato juice and lemon juice.
• **Cook,** covered, over medium heat for 45 minutes or until done. **Yield:** 12 cabbage rolls.

Mary Yankopolus
Gaithersburg, Maryland

CHICKEN WITH GARLIC SAUCE

"This was a company dish, so it always showed up during the holidays," Paula says.

Prep: 10 minutes
Cook: 40 minutes

3 **to 4 pounds skinned chicken pieces**
4 **cups water**
1¼ **teaspoons salt, divided**
2 **garlic cloves, crushed**
1 **tablespoon white vinegar**
¼ **cup butter or margarine**
½ **cup all-purpose flour**
2 **large eggs, lightly beaten**
2 **tablespoons butter or margarine, melted**
¼ **teaspoon paprika**
Hot cooked rice or egg noodles

Holiday Dinners

• **Bring** chicken, 4 cups water, and 1 teaspoon salt to a boil in a Dutch oven. Reduce heat; simmer 30 minutes or until done. Drain, reserving 3 cups broth. Cover chicken, and keep warm.
• **Combine** crushed garlic and remaining ¼ teaspoon salt, forming a paste; stir in vinegar.
• **Melt** ¼ cup butter in a large skillet. Whisk in flour; cook over medium heat, whisking constantly, 1 minute. Gradually whisk in reserved broth and garlic mixture, and cook 5 minutes or until smooth and slightly thickened. Gradually whisk ½ cup hot broth mixture into eggs; add to remaining hot mixture, whisking constantly.
• **Cook** 3 minutes or until mixture reaches 160°. Spoon sauce over chicken.
• **Stir** together 2 tablespoons butter and paprika; drizzle over sauce. Serve with rice or egg noodles. **Yield:** 4 servings.

Mary Yankopolus
Gaithersburg, Maryland

BAKED MACARONI AND CHEESE

Prep: 15 minutes
Bake: 25 minutes

16 ounces uncooked large elbow
    macaroni
½ cup butter or margarine
⅓ cup all-purpose flour
2 cups milk
3 cups (12 ounces) shredded Cheddar
   cheese, divided
1 (12-ounce) container small-curd
   cottage cheese
2 large eggs, lightly beaten
1 teaspoon salt
½ cup fine, dry breadcrumbs
1 teaspoon Greek seasoning

• **Cook** pasta according to package directions; drain.
• **Melt** butter in a Dutch oven over low heat; whisk in flour until smooth.
• **Cook** 1 minute, whisking constantly. Gradually whisk in milk; cook over medium heat, whisking constantly, until mixture is thickened and bubbly.

• **Stir** in 2 cups Cheddar cheese and next 3 ingredients. Stir in pasta.
• **Spoon** mixture into a lightly greased 13- x 9-inch baking dish. Top with remaining 1 cup Cheddar cheese.
• **Combine** breadcrumbs and Greek seasoning; sprinkle over cheese.
• **Bake** at 350° for 25 minutes. **Yield:** 8 to 10 servings.

Mary Yankopolus
Gaithersburg, Maryland

A Bounty of Beverages

Spread some holiday cheer with these delicious and easy drinks. Fruit juices and ice cream are the simple foundations for scrumptious beverage recipes. Stir together a few pantry ingredients for make-ahead Lemon-Rum Slush, or cheer your soul on a moment's notice with a Currant Warmer. When ready to serve, pull out your glassware. Don't panic if pieces don't match. Glasses of different heights, colors, and shapes add pizzazz to any table.

LEMON-RUM SLUSH

Prep: 5 minutes
Freeze: 6 hours

¼ cup sugar
2 (6-ounce) cans frozen lemonade
   concentrate
2 cups water
1½ cups pineapple juice
2 cups rum

• **Combine** all ingredients, and freeze 6 hours, stirring occasionally. Remove mixture from freezer; stir until slushy. **Yield:** 7 cups.

Lemon Slush: Omit rum, and let frozen mixture stand at room temperature 20 to 30 minutes or until slushy.

PARTY APPLE PUNCH

Prep: 5 minutes
Freeze: 8 hours
Thaw: 30 minutes

3 cups sparkling apple cider
2 cups apple juice
1 cup pineapple juice
½ cup brandy (optional)

• **Combine** first 3 ingredients and, if desired, brandy; freeze 8 hours. Remove from freezer 30 minutes before serving. Place in a small punch bowl; break into chunks. Stir until slushy. **Yield:** 7 cups.

Louise W. Mayer
Richmond, Virginia

CURRANT WARMER

Prep: 10 minutes

1 (12-ounce) jar red currant jelly
1 cup water
1 (32-ounce) bottle cranberry juice
   drink
2 (12-ounce) cans unsweetened
   pineapple juice
½ cup lemon juice

• **Heat** jelly and 1 cup water in a large saucepan over medium heat, stirring often, until jelly is melted. Stir in juices, and cook until heated. **Yield:** 2 quarts.

Adelyne Smith
Dunnville, Kentucky

BRANDY CREAM

Prep: 5 minutes

2 pints vanilla ice cream, softened
½ cup brandy
⅓ cup crème de cacao
¼ cup hazelnut liqueur
¼ teaspoon ground nutmeg

• **Process** first 4 ingredients in a blender until smooth. Sprinkle servings with nutmeg; serve immediately. **Yield:** 5 cups.

Generations of Tradition

*The Plenge-Rosenberger family's cookbook,
In Grandma's Kitchen, reflects generations
of marvelous food. Enjoy these simple favorites
for a relaxed holiday meal.*

Simple Soup Supper
Serves 6 to 8

Cheesy Vegetable Chowder
Anchorage Country Store Whole Wheat Bread
Bakery apple pie

CHEESY VEGETABLE CHOWDER
(pictured on page 266)

*Prep: 15 minutes
Cook: 30 minutes*

3½ cups chicken broth
8 celery ribs, sliced
4 carrots, sliced
2 medium potatoes, peeled and cubed
1 large onion, chopped
½ teaspoon pepper
2 cups frozen whole kernel corn, thawed
¼ cup butter or margarine
¼ cup all-purpose flour
2 cups milk
2 cups (8 ounces) shredded sharp Cheddar cheese
Garnish: chopped fresh parsley

• **Bring** first 6 ingredients to a boil in a Dutch oven. Cover, reduce heat, and simmer 15 to 20 minutes or until vegetables are tender. Remove from heat, and stir in corn.
• **Melt** butter in a heavy saucepan over low heat; add flour, whisking until smooth.
• **Cook** 1 minute, whisking constantly. Gradually whisk in milk; cook over medium heat, whisking constantly, until mixture is thickened and bubbly.
• **Add** cheese, stirring until blended.
• **Stir** cheese mixture gradually into vegetable mixture.
• **Cook** over medium heat, stirring constantly, until thoroughly heated. Serve immediately. Garnish, if desired. **Yield:** 10 cups.

*Louise Watkins
Austin, Arkansas*

ANCHORAGE COUNTRY STORE WHOLE WHEAT BREAD
(pictured on page 266)

*Prep: 10 minutes
Rise: 1 hour, 45 minutes
Bake: 45 minutes*

4 cups whole wheat flour, divided
½ cup instant nonfat dry milk powder
1 tablespoon salt
2 (¼-ounce) envelopes active dry yeast
3 cups water, divided
½ cup honey
2 tablespoons butter or margarine
2 to 3 cups all-purpose flour

• **Beat** 3 cups whole wheat flour, milk powder, salt, and yeast at low speed with a heavy-duty mixer until combined.
• **Bring** 2 cups water to a boil over medium heat; add honey and butter, stirring until butter melts. Remove from heat; stir in 1 cup cold water. (Thermometer will register about 120°.) Add to flour mixture, beating at low speed 1 minute. Increase speed to medium, and beat 2 more minutes. Gradually add remaining wheat flour and enough all-purpose flour to make a soft dough.
• **Turn** dough out onto a well-floured surface, and knead until smooth and elastic (about 5 minutes). Place in a well-greased bowl, turning to grease top.
• **Cover** and let rise in a warm place (85°), free from drafts, 1 hour or until doubled in bulk.
• **Punch** dough down, and divide into 2 equal portions. Roll each portion into a 15- x 10-inch rectangle. Roll each up, jellyroll fashion, beginning with short end. Fold ends under; place each roll, seam side down, in a 9- x 5-inch loafpan.
• **Cover** and let rise in a warm place (85°), free from drafts, 45 minutes or until doubled in bulk.
• **Bake** at 375° for 40 to 45 minutes; shield with foil after 25 minutes to prevent excessive browning. **Yield:** 2 loaves.

Note: Equal amounts of whole wheat and all-purpose flour can be used.

*Marjorie Rosenberger Pierce
Louisville, Kentucky*

Celebrating With Colleagues

Enliven your office holiday gathering

with these tasty treats.

Many of the South's companies have a roster that reads like an international directory. Such is the case with Khafra Consultants Engineering headquartered in Atlanta. Because of its diverse staff, the company's annual Thanksgiving Potluck Luncheon brings a world of flavors to the table. From their global buffet of fabulous foods, the traditional Macaroni and Cheese and Sweet Potato Soufflé are some of the best we've tasted. And once you sip the Egg Nog, you'll never buy the store-bought kind again. Try this sampling of their annual office party buffet.

FRIED RICE

Henry Guo's fast and yummy
Fried Rice is a must-have
from this global buffet.

Prep: 15 minutes
Cook: 15 minutes

¼ cup vegetable oil, divided
2 large eggs
1 cup diced cooked ham
½ large red bell pepper, diced
½ large sweet onion, diced
½ cup frozen sweet green peas, thawed
3 cups cooked rice
¼ cup soy sauce
1 teaspoon chili-garlic sauce
4 green onions, sliced

● **Heat** 1 tablespoon oil in a large skillet or wok at medium-high heat 2 minutes. Add eggs, and cook 1 minute on each side or until done. Remove from skillet; chop and set aside.
● **Heat** remaining 3 tablespoons oil in skillet or wok; add ham, and stir-fry 1 to 2 minutes or until golden. Add bell pepper and onion; stir-fry 5 minutes. Add peas and next 3 ingredients; stir-fry 3 to 4 minutes or until thoroughly heated.
● **Stir** in reserved egg, and sprinkle with green onions. **Yield:** 4 servings.

Henry Guo
Atlanta, Georgia

MACARONI AND CHEESE

Prep: 20 minutes
Bake: 1 hour

16 ounces uncooked elbow macaroni
¼ cup butter or margarine
2 cups (8 ounces) shredded sharp Cheddar cheese
2 cups (8 ounces) shredded medium-sharp Cheddar cheese
½ (8-ounce) jar process cheese spread
2 (12-ounce) cans evaporated milk
4 large eggs
1 cup soft breadcrumbs
¼ cup butter or margarine, melted

● **Cook** macaroni according to package directions; drain.
● **Stir** together hot macaroni, ¼ cup butter, and next 3 ingredients. Spoon into a lightly greased 13- x 9-inch baking dish.
● **Whisk** together milk and eggs; pour over macaroni mixture.
● **Stir** together breadcrumbs and ¼ cup melted butter. Sprinkle over macaroni.
● **Bake,** covered, at 350° for 45 to 50 minutes. Uncover; bake 10 more minutes or until macaroni and cheese is set and golden. **Yield:** 10 to 12 servings.

Note: For testing purposes, we used Cheez Whiz for process cheese spread.

Violet Crawford
Atlanta, Georgia

SWEET POTATO SOUFFLÉ
(pictured on page 1)

Prep: 15 minutes
Bake: 40 minutes

1 (14½-ounce) can mashed sweet potato
1 cup sugar
¼ cup milk
1 teaspoon grated orange rind
2 tablespoons fresh orange juice
1 teaspoon vanilla extract
2 large eggs, lightly beaten
⅔ cup all-purpose flour, divided
½ cup butter or margarine, melted and divided
1 cup chopped pecans
1 cup firmly packed brown sugar

● **Stir** together first 7 ingredients, ⅓ cup flour, and ¼ cup butter; pour mixture into a lightly greased 13- x 9-inch baking dish.
● **Combine** chopped pecans, brown sugar, remaining ⅓ cup flour, and remaining ¼ cup butter; sprinkle over potato mixture.
● **Bake** at 350° for 40 minutes or until bubbly. **Yield:** 10 to 12 servings.

Verdell Rawlings
Atlanta, Georgia

EGG NOG
(pictured on page 303)

Rich, homemade Egg Nog will keep the party in good spirits.

Prep: 30 minutes
Chill: 8 hours

6 large eggs, lightly beaten
¾ cup sugar
2 cups milk
1 cup brandy
¼ cup rum
1 tablespoon vanilla extract
2 cups whipping cream
Garnishes: whipped cream, grated
    fresh nutmeg

• **Stir** together eggs and sugar in a large saucepan; gradually stir in milk.
• **Cook** over medium heat, stirring constantly, 18 to 20 minutes or until mixture thickens and coats a metal spoon. Remove from heat.
• **Stir** in brandy, rum, and vanilla. Cover and chill 8 hours.
• **Beat** 2 cups whipping cream at high speed with an electric mixer until soft peaks form; fold into chilled egg mixture. Garnish, if desired. **Yield:** 8 cups.
Val Bates
Atlanta, Georgia

Salute to the New Year

Ring in the new year with family, friends, and this hearty barbecue feast.

New Year's Barbecue Bash
Serves 10

Barbecue Pork Shoulder
Cheesy Potatoes and Onions
Baked beans   Danny's Slaw
Cornbread

As a child, Danny Henderson spent lots of time in the kitchen watching his mom cook. Today, this Huntsville, Alabama, attorney rekindles that culinary spirit with his annual New Year's Day barbecue for family and friends. "It's a chance for us to get together, think about the past year's blessings, wish each other good luck for the coming year, and spend the day eating great barbecue."

Danny has been perfecting his barbecuing techniques for nearly 15 years. He stresses the importance of supplying oxygen to the coals—especially in cold weather—to maintain the heat and keep the meat cooking evenly.

Add your favorite baked beans and cornbread for a complete meal.

BARBECUE PORK SHOULDER
(pictured on page 267)

Prep: 45 minutes
Cook: 7 hours

1 (2-pound) package hickory chunks,
    divided
2 quarts white vinegar
½ cup ground red pepper, divided
5 oranges, quartered and divided
5 lemons, quartered and divided
½ cup firmly packed brown
    sugar
¼ cup ground black pepper
2 tablespoons lemon juice
¼ cup liquid smoke
1 (7- to 8-pound) pork shoulder
    roast

• **Soak** 1 pound wood chunks in water 30 minutes to 1 hour.
• **Bring** vinegar, ¼ cup ground red pepper, 3 oranges, and 3 lemons to a boil in a Dutch oven over medium heat; cook 10 minutes. Remove from heat; cool.

Holiday Dinners

- **Combine** remaining ¼ cup ground red pepper, brown sugar, and next 3 ingredients. Rub evenly over pork.
- **Drizzle** 1 cup vinegar mixture over pork; set aside 2 cups vinegar mixture for basting, and reserve remaining mixture to fill water pan.
- **Prepare** charcoal fire in smoker; let burn 15 to 20 minutes.
- **Drain** wood chunks; place on coals. Place water pan in smoker; add vinegar mixture and remaining 2 oranges and 2 lemons to depth of fill line. Place pork on lower food rack; cover with smoker lid.
- **Cook** pork roast 6 to 7 hours or until a meat thermometer inserted into thickest part of roast registers 170°.
- **Baste** with reserved 2 cups vinegar mixture every hour after pork roast has cooked 3 hours.
- **Add** more charcoal, remaining 1 pound wood chunks, and vinegar mixture to smoker as needed. **Yield:** 10 servings.

Danny Henderson
Huntsville, Alabama

CHEESY POTATOES AND ONIONS
(pictured on page 267)

Prep: 30 minutes
Bake: 35 minutes

6 medium potatoes (3 pounds), peeled and thinly sliced
1 large onion, thinly sliced and separated into rings
1 (6-ounce) package process American cheese slices
¾ teaspoon salt, divided
¾ teaspoon pepper, divided
1 cup (4 ounces) shredded Cheddar cheese
¼ cup butter or margarine
¼ cup all-purpose flour
3 cups warm milk

- **Cook** potato in boiling water to cover 5 minutes; drain.
- **Layer** one-third of potato slices, one-third of onion slices, and one-third of cheese slices in a lightly greased 13- x 9-inch baking dish.

- **Sprinkle** with ¼ teaspoon salt and ¼ teaspoon pepper. Repeat layers twice with remaining potato, onion, cheese slices, salt, and pepper. Top with Cheddar cheese.
- **Melt** butter in a heavy saucepan over low heat; add flour, whisking until smooth.
- **Cook,** whisking constantly, 1 minute. Gradually whisk in milk until smooth. Remove from heat; pour over potato mixture.
- **Bake** at 400° for 35 minutes or until golden. Let stand 10 minutes before serving. **Yield:** 10 to 12 servings.

Danny Henderson
Huntsville, Alabama

DANNY'S SLAW
(pictured on page 267)

Prep: 20 minutes

1¼ cups sour cream
¾ cup mayonnaise
¼ to ⅓ cup grated fresh horseradish *
¼ cup cider vinegar
½ teaspoon salt
½ teaspoon celery seeds
½ teaspoon pepper
1 small savoy cabbage, shredded
1 small red cabbage, shredded

- **Stir** together first 7 ingredients in a large bowl.
- **Add** cabbage; toss well to coat. Cover and chill. **Yield:** 10 to 12 servings.

* Substitute 2 tablespoons prepared horseradish for fresh, if desired

Danny Henderson
Huntsville, Alabama

All Fired Up

When it comes to cooking, Bill Meehan of Chapel Hill, North Carolina, certainly knows his way around the kitchen. Reading cookbooks as a hobby led him to a passion for good food and entertaining. "Food should taste good," he says, "a little spice, but it should not set your mouth on fire. Just enough to enhance the flavors."

These recipes are a collection of shared ideas from friends that can be prepared in your oven during the holidays.

Hearty Holiday Menu
Serves 6

Roast Leg of Lamb
Bill's Roasted Vegetables
Bakery rolls
Chocolate Chip Cookies

ROAST LEG OF LAMB

Prep: 15 minutes
Bake: 1 hour, 35 minutes
Stand: 15 minutes

1 (5- to 6-pound) leg of lamb, trimmed
6 garlic cloves, sliced
6 fresh rosemary sprigs

- **Cut** 1-inch-deep slits, 2 to 3 inches apart, into leg of lamb. Insert a garlic slice and a small piece of rosemary into each slit. Place lamb on a rack in a roasting pan.
- **Bake** at 450° for 5 minutes. Decrease oven temperature to 350°, and bake 1 hour and 30 minutes or until a meat thermometer inserted into thickest portion registers 145° (medium rare). Remove lamb from oven, and let stand 15 minutes. **Yield:** 6 to 8 servings.

BILL'S ROASTED VEGETABLES

Serve alongside lamb, pork, or poultry entrées.

Prep: 15 minutes
Bake: 30 minutes

2 garlic bulbs
3 baking potatoes (about 1½ pounds), quartered
3 medium beets, peeled and halved
½ pound large fresh mushrooms, halved
½ pound baby carrots
1 large sweet onion, quartered
⅓ cup olive oil
2 teaspoons dried basil
2 teaspoons dried oregano
½ teaspoon salt
½ pound fresh green beans, trimmed

• **Separate** garlic bulbs into cloves; peel cloves. Toss together garlic and next 9 ingredients; place on a lightly greased 15- x 10-inch jellyroll pan. Bake at 450° for 15 minutes. Stir in green beans. Bake 15 more minutes. **Yield:** 6 servings.

CHOCOLATE CHIP COOKIES

These cookies, or "Bill's Famous Cookies" as his father refers to them, make the perfect hostess gift.

Prep: 10 minutes
Bake: 10 minutes per batch

1 cup butter or margarine, softened
1 cup sugar
1 cup firmly packed brown sugar
2 large eggs
½ teaspoon vanilla extract
2½ cups uncooked regular oats
2 cups all-purpose flour
1 teaspoon baking powder
1 teaspoon baking soda
½ teaspoon salt
1 cup (12 ounces) semisweet chocolate morsels
3 (1.55-ounce) milk chocolate candy bars, coarsely chopped
1½ cups chopped pecans

• **Beat** butter at medium speed with an electric mixer until creamy; add sugars, beating well.
• **Add** eggs and vanilla, beating until blended.
• **Process** oats in a blender or food processor until finely ground.
• **Combine** oats, flour, and next 3 ingredients. Add oats mixture to butter mixture, beating well.
• **Stir** in chocolate morsels, chopped candy bars, and pecans.
• **Shape** into 1½-inch balls, and place on baking sheets.
• **Bake** at 375° for 8 to 10 minutes or until lightly browned. Remove to wire racks to cool. **Yield:** 7 dozen.

A Toast to the Season

I find cooking to be one-third chemistry, one-third surgery, and one-third presentation," says Dr. Samuel Oliver, Jr., of Charleston, West Virginia. "If guests are relaxed and hungry, they will think anything is good when it's presented well. We eat with our eyes first," says Sam.

Serve several of these appetizers with a selection of wines to toast the season. Sam's suggestions accompany a few of the recipes.

An Appetizer Buffet
Serves 12

Caper-and-Olive Bruschetta

Chèvre-and-Avocado Terrine

Crab Polenta

Spinach and Artichokes
in Puff Pastry

Mediterranean Rollups

CAPER-AND-OLIVE BRUSCHETTA

Wine suggestions: Sangiovese, Nouveau Beaujolais, or Rioja

Prep: 10 minutes
Stand: 1 hour
Chill: 1 hour

8 plum tomatoes
½ teaspoon salt
½ cup kalamata olives, pitted and diced
3 garlic cloves, pressed
2 tablespoons extra-virgin olive oil
2 tablespoons balsamic vinegar
3 tablespoons capers
2 tablespoons chopped fresh basil
1 teaspoon sugar
½ teaspoon pepper
French baguette slices, toasted

• **Dice** tomatoes; sprinkle with salt. Let tomato stand on paper towels or in a colander 1 hour.
• **Combine** tomato, olives, and next 7 ingredients; cover and chill 1 hour. Serve on baguette slices. **Yield:** 3 cups.

CHÈVRE-AND-AVOCADO TERRINE

Prep: 20 minutes
Chill: 3 hours

5 avocados, peeled
2 tablespoons lime juice
½ teaspoon salt
8 ounces chèvre cheese, softened
½ (8-ounce) package cream cheese, softened
1 tablespoon chopped fresh cilantro
¾ cup crushed blue corn chips
¾ cup crushed red corn chips
Olive Salsa
Additional red and blue corn chips

• **Line** an 8-inch springform pan with wax paper. Combine avocado, lime juice, and salt; coarsely mash with a fork. Spread evenly in prepared pan.
• **Stir** together cheeses and cilantro until smooth; spread over avocado mixture.

Holiday Dinners

Sprinkle with crushed chips. Top evenly with Olive Salsa. Cover and chill 3 hours.
● **Unmold** and serve with additional chips. **Yield:** 12 appetizer servings.

Olive Salsa

Prep: 10 minutes

3 to 4 plum tomatoes, diced
1 (5¾-ounce) jar pimiento-stuffed
   olives, chopped
½ medium onion, diced
2 tablespoons lime juice
½ teaspoon pepper
½ teaspoon ground cumin

● **Combine** all ingredients in a bowl. **Yield:** 2 cups.

CRAB POLENTA

Wine suggestions: Gewürztraminer, Riesling, or extra-dry champagne

Prep: 5 minutes
Cook: 20 minutes
Chill: 8 hours

2 cups chicken broth
2 cups whipping cream
2 tablespoons Old Bay seasoning
1 cup yellow cornmeal
½ cup all-purpose flour
2 (6-ounce) cans crabmeat,
   drained and flaked
1 cup Asiago cheese *
¼ cup butter or margarine
Horseradish Cream

● **Bring** first 3 ingredients to a boil in a saucepan over medium-high heat. Gradually whisk in cornmeal and flour; cook mixture, whisking constantly, 10 to 12 minutes.
● **Remove** from heat, and stir in crabmeat and Asiago cheese. Pour mixture into a greased 9-inch loafpan, and chill 8 hours.
● **Unmold** polenta, and cut into ½-inch slices. Cut each slice into 2 triangles.
● **Melt** 2 tablespoons butter in a large skillet over medium-high heat; cook

half of polenta triangles in melted butter until lightly browned, turning polenta triangles once. Repeat procedure with remaining 2 tablespoons butter and polenta triangles. Serve polenta with Horseradish Cream. **Yield:** 26 appetizer servings.

*Substitute mild Cheddar or Edam cheese for Asiago, if desired.

Horseradish Cream

Prep: 3 minutes
Chill: 30 minutes

1 (8-ounce) container sour cream
1 tablespoon prepared horseradish
1 tablespoon dry mustard
2 teaspoons dried dillweed

● **Stir** together all ingredients; cover and chill 30 minutes. **Yield:** 1 cup.

SPINACH AND ARTICHOKES IN PUFF PASTRY

Offer your guests this appetizer for a festive holiday evening. Roll up the pastry sheet as you would a jellyroll. Wine suggestions: Sauvignon Blanc or Chardonnay

Prep: 20 minutes
Freeze: 30 minutes
Bake: 20 minutes per batch

1 (10-ounce) package frozen chopped
   spinach, thawed
1 (14-ounce) can artichoke hearts,
   drained and chopped
½ cup mayonnaise
½ cup grated Parmesan cheese
1 teaspoon onion powder
1 teaspoon garlic powder
½ teaspoon pepper
1 (17¼-ounce) package frozen puff
   pastry

● **Drain** spinach well, pressing between layers of paper towels.
● **Stir** together spinach, artichoke hearts, and next 5 ingredients.

● **Thaw** puff pastry at room temperature 30 minutes. Unfold pastry, and place on a lightly floured surface or heavy-duty plastic wrap.
● **Spread** one-fourth of spinach mixture evenly over pastry sheet, leaving a ½-inch border.
● **Roll** up pastry, jellyroll fashion, pressing to seal seam; wrap in heavy-duty plastic wrap. Repeat procedure with remaining pastry and spinach mixture.
● **Freeze** 30 minutes; cut into ½-inch-thick slices. (Rolls may be frozen up to 3 months.)
● **Bake** at 400° for 20 minutes or until golden brown. **Yield:** 4 dozen.

MEDITERRANEAN ROLLUPS

Tahini is a thick paste made of ground sesame seeds; it's found in the ethnic foods section of most grocery stores.

Prep: 20 minutes
Stand: 1 hour
Chill: 30 minutes

3 medium tomatoes
1 teaspoon salt
1 (16-ounce) can chickpeas,
   drained
¼ cup tahini
6 garlic cloves
⅓ cup olive oil
¼ cup lemon juice
1 teaspoon salt
4 (8-inch) flour tortillas
6 ounces feta cheese, crumbled
2 tablespoons thinly sliced fresh mint
½ teaspoon pepper
¼ teaspoon paprika

● **Seed** and dice tomatoes; sprinkle with 1 teaspoon salt. Let stand 1 hour in a wire-mesh strainer.
● **Process** chickpeas and next 5 ingredients in a food processor until smooth.
● **Spread** mixture evenly over tortillas. Sprinkle with tomato, feta, and next 3 ingredients; roll up. Chill 30 minutes.
● **Cut** each roll diagonally into 1-inch slices. **Yield:** 16 appetizer servings.

Baking From Noonday Till Dark

One day each December in the tiny city of Noonday, Texas, the clatter and chatter coming from the home of Claudia and Fred Jackson rival the sounds of Santa's workshop.

It's the day of their holiday food exchange, a 14-year tradition among good friends. "The Christmas exchange came out of conversations with friends who wanted quick meals during the holidays," Claudia explains. "We also wanted to get together to cook, laugh, visit, and share our Christmas spirit."

HOT PEANUTS
(pictured on page 263)

Prep: 11 minutes

1 to 2 tablespoons dried crushed red
   pepper
3 tablespoons olive oil
4 garlic cloves, pressed
1 (12-ounce) can cocktail peanuts
1 (12-ounce) can Spanish peanuts
1 teaspoon salt
½ teaspoon chili powder

• **Cook** crushed red pepper in hot oil in a large skillet 1 minute.
• **Stir** in garlic and peanuts; cook over medium heat, stirring constantly, 5 minutes. Remove from heat; sprinkle with salt and chili powder.
• **Drain** peanuts on paper towels; cool completely. Store in an airtight container. **Yield:** 4 cups.

Beverly Mason
Tyler, Texas

ROASTED RED PEPPER BRUSCHETTA
(pictured on page 263)

Prep: 10 minutes
Broil: 3 minutes
Cook: 25 minutes

1 (16-ounce) French bread loaf
1 medium-size purple onion, coarsely
   chopped
1 teaspoon sugar
2 tablespoons olive oil
25 small basil leaves
1 (7-ounce) jar roasted sweet red
   peppers, drained and cut into thin
   strips
1 (3-ounce) package goat cheese,
   crumbled

• **Cut** bread into 24 slices; place on baking sheets.
• **Broil** bread slices 5½ inches from heat 1 minute on each side or until golden brown. Set aside.
• **Cook** onion and sugar in hot oil in a large skillet over medium-low heat, stirring occasionally, 25 minutes. Cool.
• **Top** bread evenly with onion mixture, basil leaves, and pepper strips.
• **Sprinkle** evenly with cheese, and broil 1 minute or until cheese melts. Serve immediately. **Yield:** 24 appetizer servings.

Claudia Jackson
Noonday, Texas

BEEF-STUFFED MUSHROOMS
(pictured on page 263)

Prep: 35 minutes
Broil: 3 minutes

1 (24-ounce) package large fresh
   mushrooms (about 2 dozen)
2 tablespoons butter or margarine
2 large shallots, minced
1 garlic clove, minced
1¼ cups finely chopped cooked
   roast beef
½ teaspoon salt
¾ teaspoon pepper
¾ teaspoon chili powder
½ teaspoon anchovy paste
1 (14½-ounce) can chicken
   broth
¼ cup fine, dry breadcrumbs
Garnish: chopped fresh parsley

• **Remove** stems from mushrooms; chop stems. Set mushroom caps aside.
• **Melt** butter in a large skillet over medium-high heat; add shallots and garlic, and sauté 2 to 3 minutes.
• **Add** mushroom stems; sauté 4 minutes or until tender. Remove from heat; stir in roast beef and next 4 ingredients.
• **Bring** broth to a boil in a Dutch oven; reduce heat. Add mushroom caps in batches, and simmer each batch 3 minutes. Drain well.
• **Spoon** beef mixture evenly into mushroom caps. Sprinkle with breadcrumbs, and place on a lightly greased rack in a broiler pan.
• **Broil** stuffed mushrooms 5½ inches from heat 3 minutes. Garnish, if desired. **Yield:** 24 appetizer servings.

Claudia Jackson
Noonday, Texas

Holiday Dinners

MARINATED SHRIMP WITH CAPERS

(pictured on page 263)

Prep: 28 minutes
Chill: 8 hours

6½ cups water
2½ pounds unpeeled, medium-size
      fresh shrimp
¼ cup pickling spice
1 tablespoon salt
4 (4-inch) celery ribs with
      leaves
1 large purple onion, thinly
      sliced
8 bay leaves
1½ cups vegetable oil
¾ cup white vinegar
3 tablespoons capers, undrained
2½ teaspoons celery seeds
1½ teaspoons salt
2 teaspoons hot sauce

• **Bring** 6½ cups water to a boil; add shrimp and next 3 ingredients.
• **Cook** 3 to 5 minutes or just until shrimp turn pink. Drain shrimp, and discard celery ribs. Rinse shrimp with cold water.
• **Peel** shrimp, and devein, if desired. Place in a 13- x 9-inch dish.
• **Top** shrimp with purple onion slices and bay leaves.
• **Stir** together oil and next 5 ingredients; pour over shrimp. Cover and chill 4 to 8 hours, stirring occasionally. Discard bay leaves before serving. **Yield:** 8 to 10 appetizer servings.

Note: Claudia serves the shrimp from an attractive ice bowl. Simply stack two bowls, one slightly smaller than the other, and weigh down the center with a heavy can. Fill the outer ring with water and lemon slices. Freeze. Remove the can and both bowls. Place ice on a plate, and fill with shrimp.

Claudia Jackson
Noonday, Texas

AN ANNUAL COOKING PARTY

These friends in Noonday, Texas, team up to share casseroles, goodies, and holiday spirit. Initially, they got together to bake favorite goodies that they could share. Each baked quantities of a single recipe and left with a dozen different snacks. "It worked so well that once word got out, the group grew from 8 to 12. And we said while we were at it, we'd exchange casseroles, too," says Claudia.

For the casserole exchange, the 12 women work in teams of two. Each team selects a recipe for an entrée casserole. The requirements are that it must serve at least eight people and freeze well. Claudia masterminds the cooking assignments, approving all the recipes to ensure there are no duplications.

The Saturday before the big day, each pair makes 12 casseroles. They put them in heavy-duty disposable pans and tape the recipes and instructions to the top.

For the third and final phase of the exchange, Claudia assigns each member a snack to bring to the party. That way, the bakers can nibble finger foods throughout the day.

"It's a pretty intense two days," Peggy Heath says. "We spend all day Saturday preparing the casseroles to freeze and the snacks to take to the party."

Then on the big day—the first Sunday of December—the friends and their daughters converge at Claudia's, bearing munchies made the day before. Plus, each one brings a bag full of ingredients to prepare a Christmas treat.

Twelve cooks in one kitchen is a recipe for chaos. "There's usually flour flying everywhere," Gretta Davis says. But with its four sinks and two ovens, Claudia's kitchen is certainly equipped. "Sometimes we run next door to use my oven," Nan Bailey says. "But we don't stay there long, because no one wants to miss all the fun."

From noon until after dark, the kitchen buzzes with blenders, beaters, and the good-natured bantering of friends. "Remember the year we had puddles of pink fondant?" asks Judy Jordan Greene, ribbing her pal Polly Hitt. "I tried to make candy strawberries," explains Polly, "but the fondant never got hard."

Not everyone enjoys baking sweets, but a pretty presentation works wonders. "I'm an avid cook," Beverly Mason says, "and at Christmas I love to make things look pretty. So I might make hot buttered rum mix or hot chocolate mix and package it in pretty tins."

At the end of the day, each of these bakers takes home 12 packages of holiday sweets.

Holiday Dinners

EASY CHUT-NUT BALL

Prep: 10 minutes
Chill: 30 minutes

2 (8-ounce) packages cream cheese, softened
1 (9-ounce) jar hot mango chutney
½ teaspoon curry powder
½ teaspoon dry mustard
⅔ cup sliced blanched almonds
Assorted crackers

• **Stir** together first 4 ingredients until blended. Shape into a ball, and chill 30 minutes. Roll in almonds. Serve with crackers. **Yield:** 10 appetizer servings.

Note: For testing purposes only, we used Major Grey's Hot Mango Chutney.

Joan Hallmark
Brownsboro, Texas

MEXICAN CASSEROLE

Prep: 30 minutes
Bake: 30 minutes

4 pounds ground chuck
2 large onions, diced
3 (10¾-ounce) cans cream of chicken soup, undiluted
3 (10-ounce) cans diced tomato and green chiles
2 (15-ounce) cans ranch-style beans *
1 (16-ounce) package corn tortillas
1 (16-ounce) loaf pasteurized prepared cheese product, cubed

• **Cook** ground chuck and onion in a Dutch oven, stirring until meat crumbles and is no longer pink. Drain meat mixture; return to Dutch oven.
• **Stir** in soup, diced tomato and green chiles, and beans.
• **Layer** half of tortillas evenly into 2 lightly greased 13- x 9-inch baking dishes. Top each with one-fourth of meat mixture and one-fourth of cheese cubes. Repeat layers with remaining tortillas, meat mixture, and cheese.
• **Bake** casserole at 350° for 30 minutes or until cheese is melted. **Yield:** 12 to 16 servings.

* Substitute pinto beans for ranch-style beans, if desired.

Note: Freeze casserole up to 1 month, if desired. Thaw in refrigerator overnight, and bake as directed.

Paulette Gray
Flint, Texas

BUCKEYE BALLS

With only five ingredients, these candies are simple to make and taste divine.

Prep: 1 hour
Chill: 10 minutes

1 (16-ounce) jar creamy peanut butter
1 cup butter or margarine, softened
1½ (16-ounce) packages powdered sugar
2 cups (12 ounces) semisweet chocolate morsels
2 tablespoons shortening

• **Beat** peanut butter and butter at medium speed with an electric mixer until blended. Gradually add powdered sugar, beating until blended.
• **Shape** into 1-inch balls; chill 10 minutes or until firm.
• **Microwave** chocolate and shortening in a 2-quart glass bowl at HIGH 1½ minutes or until melted, stirring twice.
• **Dip** each ball in chocolate mixture until partially coated, and place on wax paper to harden. Store in an airtight container. **Yield:** 7 dozen.

Peggy Heath
Tyler, Texas

KING RANCH CHICKEN CASSEROLE

Prep: 35 minutes
Bake: 35 minutes

1 large onion, chopped
1 large green bell pepper, chopped
2 tablespoons vegetable oil
2 cups chopped cooked chicken
1 (10¾-ounce) can cream of chicken soup, undiluted
1 (10¾-ounce) can cream of mushroom soup, undiluted
1 (10-ounce) can diced tomato and green chiles
1 teaspoon chili powder
¼ teaspoon salt
¼ teaspoon garlic powder
¼ teaspoon pepper
12 (6-inch) corn tortillas
2 cups (8 ounces) shredded Cheddar cheese, divided

• **Sauté** onion and bell pepper in hot oil in a large skillet over medium-high heat 5 minutes or until tender.
• **Stir** in chicken and next 7 ingredients; remove from heat.
• **Tear** tortillas into 1-inch pieces; layer one-third of tortilla pieces in bottom of a lightly greased 13- x 9-inch baking dish. Top with one-third of chicken mixture and ⅔ cup cheese. Repeat layers twice.
• **Bake** at 350° for 30 to 35 minutes. **Yield:** 6 to 8 servings.

Note: Freeze casserole up to 1 month, if desired. Thaw in refrigerator overnight, and bake as directed.

Sunny's Hanukkah

Share in the Steinberg family's time of fellowship and thankfulness with this delicious menu.

Hanukkah Menu
Serves 6 to 8

Mock Chopped Liver   Crackers   Celery sticks

Baked Brisket au Jus

Potato Latkes   Applesauce   Sour cream

Sesame Asparagus

Chocolate Chip Mandelbread

"Spending family time together is the best part of Hanukkah," says Sunny Steinberg of Charleston, South Carolina. "We find new ways to tell the holiday's story each year—sometimes with pictures, sometimes with written words. The entire family participates."

The food draws family and friends together to celebrate. Sunny serves traditional dishes with a twist. All of these dishes are worthy to add to anyone's recipe file.

MOCK CHOPPED LIVER

Prep: 10 minutes
Cook: 40 minutes
Chill: 8 hours

1 cup dried lentils
2 cups chicken broth *
1 medium-size sweet onion, chopped
1 tablespoon vegetable oil
1 cup walnuts, lightly toasted
¼ teaspoon salt
½ teaspoon pepper

• **Bring** lentils and chicken broth to a boil in a large saucepan over medium heat; cover, reduce heat, and simmer, stirring occasionally, 30 minutes or until lentils are tender. Drain lentils, if necessary.
• **Sauté** chopped onion in hot oil in a large skillet over medium-high heat 5 minutes or until onion is tender.
• **Process** one-third of lentils, one-third of onion, and one-third of walnuts in a food processor, in 3 batches, until mixture is smooth, stopping to scrape down sides.
• **Stir** together lentil mixture, salt, and pepper. Line a 3-cup mold with plastic wrap. Spoon lentil mixture into mold. Cover and chill 8 hours.
• **Unmold** onto a serving plate. Serve with crackers and celery sticks. **Yield:** 3 cups.

*Substitute beef or vegetable broth for chicken broth, if desired.

BAKED BRISKET AU JUS

Prep: 10 minutes
Bake: 5 hours
Stand: 20 minutes

1 (5-pound) beef brisket
2 teaspoons salt
¼ teaspoon pepper
1 large onion, sliced
4 celery ribs
½ cup tomato paste
½ cup tomato sauce
1 tablespoon Worcestershire sauce
1 cup brewed coffee

• **Place** brisket, fat side up, in a roasting pan. Sprinkle with salt and pepper. Top with onion and celery. Stir together tomato paste, tomato sauce, and Worcestershire sauce; pour over beef.
• **Bake** at 325° for 1 hour. Cover; bake 2 more hours, basting with pan juices occasionally. Add coffee. Cover; bake 2 more hours, checking every 30 minutes for dryness. Add ¼ cup water, if needed.
• **Remove** brisket from pan; let stand 20 minutes. Thinly slice. Serve with strained pan drippings. **Yield:** 6 to 8 servings.

POTATO LATKES

Prep: 20 minutes
Fry: 20 minutes

4 large potatoes (3 to 3½ pounds)
1 large onion
¼ cup biscuit mix
2 large eggs, lightly beaten
Peanut oil

• **Peel** potatoes. Shred potatoes and onion in a food processor; drain. Combine biscuit mix and eggs; add potato and onion.
• **Pour** oil to a depth of ½ inch in a large, heavy skillet. Drop potato mixture by tablespoonfuls into hot oil, and fry, in batches, over medium heat 2 minutes on each side or until golden brown. Drain on paper towels. Serve with applesauce and sour cream. **Yield:** 10 to 12 servings.

Neapolitan Heritage

Seafood graces the table at the Scharaldi family's annual Christmas meal. "We have our big Italian dinner on Christmas Eve," says Stephen Scharaldi. "The whole family pitches in, and we start cooking early in the morning, sampling and snacking along the way."

SESAME ASPARAGUS

Prep: 5 minutes
Bake: 15 minutes

2 pounds fresh asparagus
3 tablespoons sugar
3 tablespoons sesame seeds, toasted

• **Snap** off tough ends of asparagus; arrange on a lightly greased jellyroll pan. Sprinkle with sugar.
• **Bake** at 450° for 12 to 15 minutes or to desired doneness. Sprinkle with sesame seeds. **Yield:** 6 to 8 servings.

CHOCOLATE CHIP MANDELBREAD

Sunny's niece, Dana Farbman, shared this recipe with her aunt.

Prep: 10 minutes
Bake: 35 minutes

2 cups sugar, divided
3 large eggs
1 cup vegetable oil
3¾ cups all-purpose flour
2 teaspoons baking powder
½ teaspoon salt
1 teaspoon vanilla extract
1 (6-ounce) package semisweet chocolate mini-morsels
1½ teaspoons ground cinnamon

• **Beat** 1½ cups sugar and eggs at medium speed with an electric mixer until blended. Add oil and next 4 ingredients; beat until blended. Stir in mini-morsels.
• **Divide** dough in half; shape each into a 10- x 3-inch log on lightly greased baking sheets. (Dough will be sticky. Flour hands, if necessary.)
• **Bake** at 350° for 25 to 30 minutes or until lightly browned. Cool slightly; cut diagonally into ¾-inch-thick slices.
• **Combine** remaining ½ cup sugar and cinnamon; sprinkle over slices. Bake 5 more minutes; cool completely on wire racks. **Yield:** 36 servings.

Dana Farbman
Baltimore, Maryland

Italian Christmas Eve Menu
Serves 8

Surprise Calzones	Fried Calamari
Mussels Marinara*	French bread
Shrimp Scampi*	Onion Pie
Pizza Dolce (Italian Sweet Pies)	

*Double recipes to serve 8.

SURPRISE CALZONES

The surprise? Steve's aunts place a cotton ball in one calzone. Whoever finds it has to sing a Christmas song for the family.

Prep: 45 minutes
Bake: 8 minutes

1 (15-ounce) container ricotta cheese
1 cup shredded provolone cheese
1 cup shredded Parmesan cheese
½ cup chopped fresh basil
2 garlic cloves, pressed
½ teaspoon salt
½ teaspoon pepper
2 (10.2-ounce) cans refrigerated jumbo biscuits
1 large egg
1 tablespoon water
1 (14½-ounce) can diced tomatoes, drained

• **Stir** together first 7 ingredients.
• **Split** biscuits in half; roll each half into a 4-inch circle on a lightly floured surface.
• **Whisk** together egg and 1 tablespoon water in a small bowl until blended.
• **Spoon** ricotta mixture evenly onto each circle, leaving a 1-inch border. Top evenly with tomato. Brush edges lightly with water.
• **Fold** dough over filling. Press edges with a fork to seal; prick tops.
• **Brush** calzones with egg mixture. Place calzones on lightly greased baking sheets.
• **Bake** at 450° for 6 to 8 minutes or until golden brown. (Do not overbake.) Serve immediately. **Yield:** 20 servings.

Holiday Dinners

FRIED CALAMARI

Prep: 35 minutes
Soak: 30 minutes
Fry: 5 minutes

1 (2.5-pound) package cleaned
   calamari (tubes and tentacles),
   rinsed
1½ cups all-purpose flour
¾ teaspoon salt
1½ teaspoons dried oregano
1½ teaspoons paprika
½ teaspoon pepper
Vegetable oil

● **Cut** calamari tubes into ¼-inch-thick rings. Soak calamari in cold water 30 minutes; drain. Pat calamari dry with paper towels.
● **Combine** flour and next 4 ingredients. Dredge calamari in flour mixture.
● **Pour** oil to a depth of 6 inches into a Dutch oven. Heat to 400°.
● **Fry** calamari, in batches, 1 minute, allowing oil to reach 400° before cooking next batch. Drain on paper towels. Serve immediately. **Yield:** 4 to 6 servings.

MUSSELS MARINARA

Prep: 15 minutes
Cook: 15 minutes

2 pounds fresh mussels
5 large garlic cloves, minced
2 teaspoons olive oil
1 (28-ounce) can whole Italian plum
   tomatoes, undrained
5 large fresh basil leaves, coarsely
   chopped
¼ teaspoon salt
¼ teaspoon pepper
1 (6-ounce) package fresh
   spinach
Italian bread
Garnish: chopped fresh basil

● **Scrub** mussels thoroughly with a scrub brush, removing beards. Discard any opened shells.
● **Sauté** garlic in hot oil in a Dutch oven over medium heat 1 to 2 minutes. Add

tomatoes and next 3 ingredients; simmer, stirring occasionally, 5 minutes.
● **Add** mussels and spinach; cook, covered, 5 minutes or until all mussels have opened. Remove from heat. Serve with Italian bread. Garnish, if desired. **Yield:** 4 servings.

SHRIMP SCAMPI

Prep: 35 minutes
Cook: 9 minutes

1 pound unpeeled, large fresh
   shrimp
3 large garlic cloves, minced
¼ cup olive oil
½ cup unsalted butter
¼ cup dry white wine
¼ teaspoon dried crushed red pepper
¼ cup chopped fresh parsley
8 ounces linguine, cooked

● **Peel** shrimp; devein, if desired.
● **Sauté** garlic in hot oil in a large skillet over medium heat 1 to 2 minutes.
● **Add** butter, stirring until melted. Add shrimp, and cook 1 minute.
● **Stir** in wine and red pepper; reduce heat, and simmer 1 to 2 minutes or just until shrimp turn pink. Sprinkle with parsley, and serve over linguine. **Yield:** 4 servings.

ONION PIE

Prep: 45 minutes
Bake: 30 minutes

5 large sweet onions, thinly sliced
2 tablespoons olive oil
¼ teaspoon salt
¼ teaspoon pepper
1 (15-ounce) package refrigerated
   piecrusts
15 pimiento-stuffed olives

● **Sauté** onion in hot oil in a large skillet or Dutch oven over medium-high heat 25 minutes or until golden. Stir in salt and pepper.

● **Unfold** 1 piecrust, and roll to press out fold lines. Place on a lightly greased baking sheet; roll to a 13-inch circle.
● **Spoon** onion mixture onto piecrust, leaving a 1-inch border; lightly brush border with water.
● **Roll** remaining piecrust to press out fold lines; cut into ½-inch strips.
● **Arrange** strips in a lattice design over filling; fold edges up over lattice, pressing to seal. Place olives in some of lattice openings.
● **Bake** at 375° on lower oven rack 25 to 30 minutes or until golden brown. **Yield:** 6 to 8 servings.

PIZZA DOLCE
(ITALIAN SWEET PIES)

Prep: 10 minutes
Bake: 40 minutes
Chill: 8 hours

2 (15-ounce) containers ricotta
   cheese
4 large eggs, lightly beaten
1½ cups powdered sugar
1 tablespoon grated lemon
   rind
3 tablespoons fresh lemon
   juice
⅓ cup almond liqueur
1 cup semisweet chocolate
   mini-morsels
2 (6-ounce) chocolate crumb
   crusts

● **Stir** together first 7 ingredients; pour evenly into crusts.
● **Bake** at 350° for 35 to 40 minutes or until set and golden brown. Cool on wire racks. Chill 8 hours. **Yield:** 2 pies.

The Whole Brunch

Why is it we always seem inclined toward the breakfast side of brunch? It's time we gave equal billing to the lunch side, and our recipes do just that. This whole menu, served together, is the definition of a perfect brunch.

A Versatile Brunch
Serves 8

Cranberry-Pineapple Punch
Brie-and-Sausage Breakfast Casserole
Maple-Plum Glazed Turkey Breast
Chilled Vegetable Salad
Bing Cherry-Grapefruit Salad
Blueberry Biscuits

Brie-and-Sausage Breakfast Casserole, Bing Cherry-Grapefruit Salad, and Blueberry Biscuits summon guests for breakfast, whereas Maple-Plum Glazed Turkey Breast and Chilled Vegetable Salad issue a call for lunch. Our beverage complements whatever direction you choose.

And with frenzied shopping days just around the corner, it's nice to know that all these recipes can be made ahead.

CRANBERRY-PINEAPPLE PUNCH
(pictured on page 1)

Prep: 10 minutes
Chill: 8 hours

1 (48-ounce) bottle cranberry juice drink
1 (48-ounce) can pineapple juice
½ cup sugar
2 teaspoons almond extract
1 (2-liter) bottle ginger ale, chilled

• **Stir** together first 4 ingredients until sugar dissolves. Cover mixture, and chill 8 hours.
• **Stir** in ginger ale just before serving. **Yield:** 6½ quarts.

Lynette S. Granade
Mobile, Alabama

BRIE-AND-SAUSAGE BREAKFAST CASSEROLE

Prep: 20 minutes
Chill: 8 hours
Bake: 1 hour

1 (8-ounce) round Brie*
1 pound ground hot pork sausage
6 white sandwich bread slices
1 cup grated Parmesan cheese
7 large eggs, divided
3 cups whipping cream, divided
2 cups fat-free milk
1 tablespoon chopped fresh sage or 1 teaspoon dried rubbed sage
1 teaspoon seasoned salt
1 teaspoon dry mustard
Garnishes: chopped green onions, shaved Parmesan cheese

• **Trim** and discard rind from top of Brie. Cut cheese into cubes; set aside.
• **Cook** sausage in a large skillet over medium-high heat, stirring until it crumbles and is no longer pink; drain sausage well.
• **Cut** crusts from bread slices; place crusts evenly in bottom of a lightly greased 13- x 9-inch baking dish. Layer evenly with bread slices, sausage, Brie, and grated Parmesan cheese.
• **Whisk** together 5 eggs, 2 cups whipping cream, and next 4 ingredients; pour evenly over cheeses. Cover and chill 8 hours.
• **Whisk** together remaining 2 eggs and remaining 1 cup whipping cream; pour evenly over chilled mixture.
• **Bake** at 350° for 1 hour or until casserole is set. Garnish, if desired. **Yield:** 8 to 10 servings.

*Substitute 2 cups (8 ounces) shredded Swiss cheese, if desired.
Catherine O'Brien Sturgis
Winnetka, Illinois

Holiday Dinners

MAPLE-PLUM GLAZED TURKEY BREAST

To enjoy the turkey the day you make it, let it stand 30 minutes before carving. Serve with reserved maple-plum sauce.

Prep: 15 minutes
Cook: 30 minutes
Bake: 2 hours
Chill: 8 hours

2 cups red plum jam
1 cup maple syrup
¼ cup cider vinegar
1 tablespoon grated lemon rind
2 tablespoons fresh lemon juice
1 teaspoon dry mustard
1 (5- to 5½-pound) bone-in turkey breast
½ teaspoon salt
8 fresh sage sprigs

• **Bring** first 6 ingredients to a boil in a large saucepan over medium-high heat; reduce heat to medium-low, and cook, stirring often, 25 minutes or until thickened and bubbly. Remove from heat; cool completely.
• **Reserve** 1½ cups sauce; cover and chill. Set aside remaining maple-plum sauce for basting.
• **Loosen** skin from turkey without totally detaching skin; sprinkle salt evenly under skin, and carefully place 4 sage sprigs on each side of breast. Replace skin.
• **Place** turkey in a lightly greased 11- x 7-inch baking dish.
• **Spread** ¾ cup maple-plum sauce evenly over turkey; cover loosely with aluminum foil.
• **Bake** at 325° for 1 hour; uncover and bake 1 more hour or until a meat thermometer registers 170°, basting with remaining ¾ cup maple-plum sauce every 15 minutes.
• **Remove** turkey from baking dish; cool. Wrap in plastic wrap, then aluminum foil; chill 8 hours. Serve turkey at room temperature.
• **Cook** reserved 1½ cups maple-plum sauce until thoroughly heated; serve with turkey. **Yield:** 10 servings.

Maple-Plum Glazed Turkey Tenderloins: *(pictured on page 1)* Substitute 2 (16-ounce) packages turkey tenderloins for breast, if desired. Place tenderloins on a rack in a broiler pan coated with cooking spray; sprinkle evenly with salt, omitting sage. Baste evenly with ¾ cup maple-plum sauce. Bake at 425° for 25 to 30 minutes or until done, basting often with remaining ¾ cup maple-plum sauce.

CHILLED VEGETABLE SALAD

Prep: 20 minutes
Cool: 30 minutes
Chill: 8 hours

1 cup sugar
¾ cup cider vinegar
½ cup vegetable oil
1 medium-size green bell pepper, chopped
1 medium onion, chopped
3 celery ribs, sliced
1 (7-ounce) jar diced pimiento, undrained
1 (15¼-ounce) can small sweet green peas, drained
1 (14½-ounce) can French-cut green beans, drained
1 (11-ounce) can white shoepeg corn, drained
½ teaspoon salt
¼ teaspoon pepper

• **Bring** first 3 ingredients to a boil in a small saucepan over medium heat; cook, stirring often, 5 minutes or until sugar dissolves. Remove dressing from heat, and cool 30 minutes.
• **Stir** together bell pepper and next 8 ingredients in a large bowl; gently stir in dressing. Cover and chill 8 hours. Serve salad with a slotted spoon. **Yield:** 8 cups.

Note: Salad may be refrigerated in an airtight container for several days.
Sidney Ann Allen
Shreveport, Louisiana

BING CHERRY-GRAPEFRUIT SALAD

Prep: 10 minutes
Cook: 5 minutes
Chill: 8 hours, 30 minutes

1 (26-ounce) jar refrigerated unsweetened grapefruit sections, undrained *
1 (16½-ounce) can pitted Bing cherries, undrained
⅓ cup dry sherry or dry white wine
2 (3-ounce) packages cherry gelatin
1 cup chopped pecans, toasted

• **Drain** grapefruit and cherries, reserving juices.
• **Bring** reserved juices and sherry to a boil in a medium saucepan. Remove from heat; add gelatin, and stir 2 minutes or until gelatin dissolves.
• **Chill** 30 minutes or until consistency of unbeaten egg white; stir in grapefruit, cherries, and pecans.
• **Pour** into a 6½-cup mold. Cover and chill 8 hours or until firm. Unmold onto a serving dish. **Yield:** 8 to 10 servings.

*Substitute 1½ grapefruit, sectioned, and 1⅓ cups fresh grapefruit juice (about 3 grapefruit), if desired.
Carolyn Flournoy
Shreveport, Louisiana

BLUEBERRY BISCUITS

Prep: 20 minutes
Bake: 15 minutes

½ cup frozen blueberries, thawed
2 cups all-purpose flour
2 teaspoons baking powder
¼ teaspoon baking soda
1 teaspoon salt
½ cup sugar
⅓ cup shortening
1 large egg
¾ cup buttermilk
3 tablespoons butter or margarine,
    melted
2 tablespoons sugar
¼ teaspoon ground cinnamon

• **Pat** blueberries dry with paper towels; set aside.
• **Combine** flour and next 4 ingredients in a large bowl; cut in shortening with a pastry blender until crumbly.
• **Whisk** together egg and buttermilk; add to flour mixture, stirring just until dry ingredients are moistened. Gently fold in blueberries.
• **Turn** dough out onto a lightly floured surface; knead 3 or 4 times.
• **Pat** or roll dough to ¾-inch thickness; cut with a 2¾-inch round cutter, and place on a lightly greased baking sheet.
• **Bake** at 400° for 15 minutes or until golden brown.
• **Stir** together butter, 2 tablespoons sugar, and cinnamon; brush over warm biscuits. **Yield:** 8 biscuits.

Note: Recipe can be doubled. Store biscuits in an airtight container for up to 3 weeks in freezer.

Julie Templeton
Earth, Texas

River of Sweet Dreams

Tasty confections await at a gracious gala—Libby Murphy's annual winter party in Tennessee. From simple Gentleman's Pound Cake to fancy Champagne Sabayon, there's a dessert for everyone.

Holiday Dessert Party
Serves 12 to 15

Delta Mocha Chiffon Cake   Gentleman's Pound Cake
Butter Cookies   Smoky Mountain Snowcaps
Tiramisù   Champagne Sabayon
Champagne   Coffee

DELTA MOCHA CHIFFON CAKE
(pictured on page 301)

Prep: 1 hour
Bake: 40 minutes

¾ cup boiling water
½ cup cocoa
1 teaspoon instant coffee granules
1¾ cups cake flour
1¾ cups sugar
1½ teaspoons baking soda
½ teaspoon salt
8 large eggs, separated
½ cup vegetable oil
2 teaspoons vanilla extract
½ teaspoon cream of tartar
Chocolate-Coffee Buttercream Filling
Chocolate Fudge Frosting
Garnish: chocolate-covered coffee
    beans

• **Stir** together first 3 ingredients until blended; cool.
• **Combine** flour and next 3 ingredients in a large mixing bowl. Add cocoa mixture, egg yolks, oil, and vanilla; beat at medium speed with an electric mixer until smooth.
• **Beat** egg whites and cream of tartar at high speed with an electric mixer until foamy. Fold into batter. Pour batter into 4 greased and floured 9-inch round cakepans.
• **Bake,** 2 layers at a time, at 325° for 17 to 20 minutes or until a wooden pick inserted in center comes out clean. Cool layers in pans on wire racks 10 minutes. Remove from pans; cool on wire racks covered with plastic wrap or wax paper to prevent layers from adhering to racks.
• **Spread** about ½ cup Chocolate-Coffee Buttercream Filling between layers.

Holiday Dinners

Frost with Chocolate Fudge Frosting. Garnish, if desired. Store covered in refrigerator. **Yield:** 1 (9-inch) layer cake.

Chocolate-Coffee Buttercream Filling

Prep: 10 minutes

⅔ cup butter, softened
2½ cups powdered sugar
1 tablespoon cocoa
½ cup whipping cream
2 teaspoons instant coffee granules
2 teaspoons coffee liqueur*

• **Beat** first 3 ingredients at medium speed with an electric mixer until fluffy.
• **Microwave** cream at MEDIUM (50% power) until warm (do not boil).
• **Stir** together warm whipping cream and coffee granules until granules are dissolved; cool.
• **Add** whipping cream mixture and liqueur to butter mixture, beating until smooth. **Yield:** 1¾ cups.

*Substitute 1 teaspoon vanilla extract for liqueur, if desired.

Chocolate Fudge Frosting

Prep: 10 minutes

1 cup butter, softened
⅓ cup cocoa
6 cups powdered sugar
⅓ cup milk

• **Beat** butter at medium speed with an electric mixer until creamy.
• **Add** remaining ingredients, beating until smooth. **Yield:** 3½ cups.

Note: To a make a torte, cut each cake layer in half horizontally with a serrated knife, and use ¼ cup Chocolate-Coffee Buttercream Filling between layers. Frost as directed.

Libby Murphy
Jackson, Tennessee

GENTLEMAN'S POUND CAKE
(pictured on page 304)

Prep: 25 minutes
Bake: 1 hour, 25 minutes

2 cups butter or margarine, softened
3 cups sugar, divided
8 large eggs, separated
1 cup bourbon, divided
2½ teaspoons vanilla extract
3 cups all-purpose flour
¾ cup chopped pecans, toasted
Powdered sugar

• **Beat** butter and 2 cups sugar at medium speed with an electric mixer 5 to 7 minutes. Add egg yolks, 1 at a time, beating just until yellow disappears. Stir together ½ cup bourbon and vanilla.
• **Add** flour to butter mixture alternately with bourbon mixture, beginning and ending with flour. Beat at low speed just until blended after each addition.
• **Beat** egg whites at high speed with an electric mixer until foamy. Add remaining 1 cup sugar, 1 tablespoon at a time, beating until stiff peaks form and sugar dissolves (2 to 4 minutes). Fold into batter. Sprinkle half of pecans into bottom of a greased and floured 10-inch tube pan. Fold remaining pecans into cake batter, and pour into pan.
• **Bake** at 350° for 1 hour and 25 minutes or until a long wooden pick inserted in center comes out clean. Cool cake in pan on a wire rack 10 to 15 minutes; remove from pan, and cool on wire rack.
• **Moisten** several layers of cheesecloth with remaining ½ cup bourbon; cover cake completely with cheesecloth.
• **Place** cake in an airtight container, and store in a cool place 1 week, remoistening cheesecloth as needed. Sprinkle with powdered sugar just before serving. **Yield:** 1 (10-inch) cake.

Libby Murphy
Jackson, Tennessee

Holiday Dinners

BUTTER COOKIES
(pictured on page 304)

*Use real butter for rich cookies
that will melt in your mouth.*

*Prep: 10 minutes
Chill: 8 hours
Bake: 10 minutes per batch*

1½ cups butter, softened
1¼ cups sugar
1 large egg
1 teaspoon vanilla extract
2 cups all-purpose flour
¾ cup strawberry preserves

● **Beat** butter and sugar at medium speed with an electric mixer until mixture is fluffy.
● **Add** egg and vanilla, beating well. Add flour, beating just until mixture is blended.
● **Divide** dough into 3 portions; roll each portion on wax paper into a 12-inch log. Cover and chill 8 hours.
● **Cut** each log into ½-inch-thick slices; place slices on lightly greased baking sheets.
● **Press** thumb in center of each slice to make an indentation; fill with ½ teaspoon preserves.
● **Bake** at 350° for 10 minutes or until edges are lightly browned. Remove to wire racks to cool. Freeze, if desired. **Yield:** 6 dozen.

*Josephine Murphy
Jackson, Tennessee*

SMOKY MOUNTAIN SNOWCAPS

*Prep: 25 minutes
Bake: 12 minutes per batch*

6 ounces white chocolate, chopped
¾ cup butter or margarine, softened
1 cup sugar
3 large eggs
1 teaspoon vanilla extract
3½ cups all-purpose flour
1 teaspoon baking powder
¾ teaspoon salt
⅛ teaspoon ground nutmeg
1½ cups chopped walnuts, toasted
½ cup powdered sugar

● **Melt** white chocolate in a small saucepan over low heat, stirring until chocolate is smooth.
● **Beat** butter and 1 cup sugar at medium speed with an electric mixer 5 minutes or until fluffy.
● **Add** eggs, 1 at a time, beating until blended.
● **Add** vanilla, beating well. Add melted chocolate, and beat 30 seconds.
● **Combine** flour and next 3 ingredients; add to butter mixture, beating until blended. Stir in walnuts.
● **Drop** dough by heaping tablespoonfuls onto lightly greased baking sheets.
● **Bake** at 350° for 10 to 12 minutes or until edges are lightly browned. Remove to wire racks to cool completely. Sprinkle with powdered sugar. Freeze, if desired. **Yield:** 3½ dozen.

*Libby Murphy
Jackson, Tennessee*

TIRAMISÙ

*Prep: 30 minutes
Chill: 2 hours*

8 ounces mascarpone cheese✶
½ cup sugar
2½ cups whipping cream, divided
1 cup hot water
1 tablespoon instant coffee granules
¼ cup coffee liqueur
2 (3-ounce) packages ladyfingers
1 teaspoon cocoa

● **Beat** cheese, sugar, and ½ cup whipping cream at medium speed with an electric mixer until creamy. Beat remaining cream at medium speed until soft peaks form. Fold into cheese mixture.
● **Stir** together 1 cup hot water and coffee granules until dissolved. Stir in liqueur.
● **Split** ladyfingers in half, and brush cut sides evenly with coffee mixture.
● **Arrange** one-fourth of ladyfingers in bottom of a 4-quart trifle bowl. Top with one-fourth of cheese mixture. Repeat layers 3 times. Sprinkle with cocoa. Chill at least 2 hours. **Yield:** 8 servings.

✶Substitute cream cheese, if desired.

*Libby Murphy
Jackson, Tennessee*

CHAMPAGNE SABAYON
(pictured on page 304)

Prep: 22 minutes

8 egg yolks
⅔ cup sugar
1½ cups champagne
1 pint fresh raspberries, blueberries, and strawberries

● **Whisk** egg yolks and sugar in a heavy saucepan over low heat until blended.
● **Whisk** in champagne; cook, whisking constantly, 10 minutes or until mixture reaches 160° and is thickened. Chill, if desired. Spoon champagne mixture over fresh berries. **Yield:** 2¾ cups.

*Libby Murphy
Jackson, Tennessee*

What's for Supper?

Dinner can be ready in a snap with

these five-ingredient recipes.

You have heard the expression, "gimme five." Well, we're giving you four recipes, two with variations, that require only five ingredients and take 15 minutes or less to prepare. Not only do these dishes save time, but they also simplify shopping and cleanup. Add a simple salad or side dish, and your meal is complete.

SMOTHERED HAMBURGER STEAKS

Turn this into a comfort meal with steamed rice and green beans.

Prep: 10 minutes
Cook: 47 minutes

2 pounds ground chuck
¼ cup steak sauce
1 teaspoon salt
½ teaspoon pepper
3 large onions, halved and thinly sliced
¼ cup water

• **Combine** first 4 ingredients; shape into 6 patties.
• **Cook** patties in a large nonstick skillet, in batches, over medium-high heat 3 minutes on each side. Remove patties from skillet.
• **Add** onion and ¼ cup water to skillet; cook, covered, over medium heat 15 minutes. Uncover and stir; cook 10 more minutes. Remove half of onion from skillet.
• **Return** beef patties to skillet. Top patties with reserved onion; cover, reduce heat, and simmer 10 minutes. **Yield:** 6 servings.

Sonja Dickson
Enterprise, Alabama

EASY SCALLOPED POTATOES AND CHOPS

This simple, one-skillet recipe fares well with broccoli slaw and soft dinner rolls.

Prep: 5 minutes
Cook: 35 minutes

4 (½-inch-thick) bone-in pork loin or rib chops
½ teaspoon salt
¼ teaspoon pepper
1 (5-ounce) package scalloped potatoes
1 (2-ounce) jar diced pimiento, drained

• **Sprinkle** pork with salt and pepper.
• **Cook** pork chops in a lightly greased large nonstick skillet over medium-high heat 3 minutes on each side or until browned. Remove pork chops from skillet, and set aside.
• **Prepare** scalloped potatoes (do not cook) in skillet according to package directions for the stove-top.
• **Stir** in diced pimiento, and bring to a boil, stirring occasionally. Top with pork chops. Cover, reduce heat, and simmer 20 minutes. Uncover and cook 5 more minutes or until potatoes are tender. **Yield:** 4 servings.

Percy Thompson III
Norristown, Pennsylvania

CHEESY CHICKEN PENNE

Prep: 15 minutes
Cook: 10 minutes

8 ounces uncooked penne pasta
1 (16-ounce) loaf pasteurized prepared cheese product, cubed
1 (8-ounce) container sour cream
½ cup milk
2½ cups chopped cooked chicken

• **Cook** pasta in salted water according to package directions; drain.
• **Cook** cubed cheese, sour cream, and milk over medium-low heat, stirring constantly, 5 minutes or until cheese melts. Stir in pasta and chicken, and cook until thoroughly heated. **Yield:** 4 to 6 servings.

Spicy Cheesy Chicken Penne: Substitute 2 (8-ounce) loaves pasteurized prepared cheese product with peppers for prepared cheese product.

RED RICE

Prep: 5 minutes
Cook: 35 minutes

1 (16-ounce) package smoked sausage, sliced
2 (10-ounce) cans diced tomato and green chiles
3 cups low-sodium chicken broth
2 teaspoons Creole seasoning
1½ cups uncooked long-grain rice

• **Sauté** sausage in a lightly greased Dutch oven over medium-high heat 5 minutes or until browned.
• **Stir** in tomato and green chiles, broth, and Creole seasoning; bring mixture to a boil.
• **Stir** in rice; cover, reduce heat, and simmer 25 minutes. Uncover; cook until liquid is absorbed. **Yield:** 6 servings.

Red Rice and Ham: Substitute 1 pound cooked ham, cubed, for smoked sausage. Cook as directed.

Rosie Mellis
Gardner, Massachusetts

The Cookie Queen

Each holiday season, friends and family eagerly await the arrival of Patty Vann's delicious cookie trays. Here are five of her best recipes.

PECAN PIE COOKIES
(pictured on page 303)

Prep: 30 minutes
Chill: 1 hour, 30 minutes
Bake: 16 minutes per batch

1 cup butter or margarine, softened
½ cup sugar
½ cup dark corn syrup
2 large eggs, separated
2½ cups all-purpose flour
¼ cup butter or margarine
½ cup powdered sugar
3 tablespoons dark corn syrup
¾ cup finely chopped pecans

• **Beat** 1 cup butter and sugar at medium speed with an electric mixer until light and fluffy.
• **Add** ½ cup corn syrup and egg yolks, beating well. Gradually stir in flour; cover and chill 1 hour.
• **Melt** ¼ cup butter in a heavy saucepan over medium heat; stir in powdered sugar and 3 tablespoons corn syrup.
• **Cook,** stirring often, until mixture boils. Remove from heat. Stir in pecans; chill 30 minutes.
• **Shape** pecan mixture by ½ teaspoonfuls into ¼-inch balls; set aside.
• **Shape** cookie dough into 1-inch balls; place 2 inches apart on lightly greased baking sheets. Beat egg whites until foamy; brush on dough balls.
• **Bake** at 375° for 6 minutes. Remove from oven; place pecan balls in center of each cookie. Bake 8 to 10 more minutes or until lightly browned. Cool cookies 5 minutes on baking sheets; remove to wire racks to cool completely. Freeze up to 1 month, if desired. **Yield:** 4½ dozen.

Patty Vann
Birmingham, Alabama

CRANBERRY-WALNUT SWIRLS

Prep: 15 minutes
Chill: 1 hour
Freeze: 8 hours
Bake: 15 minutes per batch

½ cup butter or margarine, softened
¾ cup sugar
1 large egg
1 teaspoon vanilla extract
1½ cups all-purpose flour
¼ teaspoon baking powder
¼ teaspoon salt
⅓ cup finely chopped fresh cranberries
½ cup ground walnuts
1 tablespoon grated orange rind

• **Beat** butter and sugar at medium speed with an electric mixer until light and fluffy.
• **Add** egg and vanilla, beating until blended. Gradually add flour, baking powder, and salt, beating until blended. Cover and chill 1 hour.
• **Combine** cranberries, walnuts, and orange rind.
• **Turn** dough out onto a lightly floured surface, and roll into a 10-inch square. Sprinkle with cranberry mixture, leaving a ½-inch border on 2 opposite sides of dough.
• **Roll** up dough, jellyroll fashion, beginning at a bordered side. Cover and freeze 8 hours.
• **Cut** roll into ¼-inch-thick slices. Place slices on lightly greased baking sheets.
• **Bake** on top oven rack at 375° for 14 to 15 minutes or until lightly browned. Freeze up to 1 month, if desired. **Yield:** 3 dozen.

Patty Vann
Birmingham, Alabama

NEAPOLITAN COOKIES
(pictured on page 303)

Prep: 20 minutes
Chill: 8 hours
Bake: 10 minutes per batch

1 cup butter or margarine, softened
1 cup sugar
1 large egg
1 teaspoon vanilla extract
2½ cups all-purpose flour
1½ teaspoons baking powder
½ teaspoon salt
1 (1-ounce) unsweetened chocolate square, melted
⅓ cup finely chopped walnuts or pecans
¼ cup finely chopped candied cherries
1 or 2 drops red liquid food coloring
⅓ cup flaked coconut
½ teaspoon rum extract

• **Beat** butter at medium speed with an electric mixer until creamy. Add sugar, beating until light and fluffy.
• **Add** egg and vanilla, beating until blended. Gradually add flour, baking powder, and salt, beating until blended.
• **Divide** dough into thirds; place each portion in a separate bowl.
• **Stir** chocolate and walnuts into 1 portion; chopped cherries and red food coloring into second portion; and coconut and rum extract into third portion.
• **Line** an 8-inch square dish with plastic wrap. Press chocolate mixture into dish. Top with rum mixture and cherry mixture, pressing gently. Cover and chill 8 hours.
• **Cut** dough evenly into 5 sections. Cut each section into ⅛-inch-thick slices. Arrange slices, 2 inches apart, on ungreased baking sheets.
• **Bake** at 375° for 8 to 10 minutes or until lightly browned. Remove to wire racks to cool. Freeze up to 1 month, if desired. **Yield:** 8 dozen.

Patty Vann
Birmingham, Alabama

TEXAS MILLIONAIRES

Patty stores these in the refrigerator instead of the freezer. Chocolate can change color when kept in the freezer.

Prep: 25 minutes
Chill: 1 hour or Freeze: 20 minutes

1 (14-ounce) package caramels, unwrapped
2 tablespoons butter or margarine
2 tablespoons water
3 cups pecan halves
1 cup (6 ounces) semisweet chocolate morsels
8 (2-ounce) vanilla candy coating squares

• **Cook** first 3 ingredients in a heavy saucepan over low heat, stirring constantly, until smooth. Stir in pecan halves. Cool in pan 5 minutes.
• **Drop** by tablespoonfuls onto lightly greased wax paper. Chill 1 hour, or freeze 20 minutes until firm.
• **Melt** morsels and candy coating in a heavy saucepan over low heat, stirring until smooth. Dip caramel candies into chocolate mixture, allowing excess to drip; place on lightly greased wax paper. Let stand until firm. **Yield:** 4 dozen.

Patty Vann
Birmingham, Alabama

BLACK-EYED SUSANS
(pictured on page 303)

Prep: 20 minutes
Bake: 8 minutes per batch
Chill: 30 minutes

½ cup butter or margarine, softened
½ cup sugar
½ cup firmly packed brown sugar
1 cup creamy peanut butter
1 large egg
1½ tablespoons warm water
1 teaspoon vanilla extract
1½ cups all-purpose flour
½ teaspoon salt
½ teaspoon baking soda
½ cup (3 ounces) semisweet chocolate morsels

CHRISTMAS COOKIES TO CRAVE

While others rush out the day after Thanksgiving to fight crowds at local malls, Associate Foods Editor Patty Vann retreats to the solitude of her kitchen to bake up her own special brand of holiday cheer. Affectionately dubbed the "Cookie Queen," Patty has been baking cookies and arranging them on decorative trays for friends and family each Christmas for nearly 20 years.

Patty bakes up to 30 different kinds of cookies over a two- to three-week period, so the trays are ready to be given out by mid-December. In 1998, a record year for the amount of trays she gave, Patty baked more than 130 dozen Christmas cookies—131½ dozen, to be exact.

Keenly aware that Patty knows who's been naughty or nice, folks are on their best behavior as the season draws near. In anticipation of the tray's arrival, her colleagues clamor around the central coffee pot like little children on Christmas morning. However, now it won't be nearly as difficult for you to get your hands on these delectable cookies, because we've asked Patty to share a few of her favorite recipes. Our hope is that by sharing her cookies, you, too, will

be able to spread a little bit of the holiday cheer Patty blesses us with each Christmas.

Here are some of Patty's tips.

■ Use shiny baking sheets; dark pans absorb more heat and can cause overbrowning.

■ Altering the suggested pan size when making bar cookies affects consistency and baking time.

■ For crisp cookies, choose the high range of the baking time. For chewy ones, pick the shorter time.

■ Cool bar cookies completely before cutting.

■ Cool cookies completely before storing. Store chewy cookies in an airtight container and crisp cookies in a jar or cookie tin.

■ An apple wedge placed in an airtight container will soften cookies that have hardened.

■ Most cookie dough can be stored in the refrigerator up to one week or the freezer up to three months.

■ Thaw frozen cookies at room temperature 10 to 15 minutes before serving.

• **Beat** butter and sugars at medium speed with an electric mixer until light and fluffy.
• **Add** peanut butter and next 3 ingredients, beating well.
• **Combine** flour, salt, and baking soda. Add to butter mixture, beating until blended.
• **Use** a cookie gun fitted with a flower-shaped disc to make cookies, following manufacturer's instructions. Place cookies on lightly greased baking sheets. Place a chocolate morsel in the center of each cookie.
• **Bake** at 350° for 8 minutes or until lightly browned. Remove to wire racks to cool. Chill 30 minutes. Freeze up to 1 month, if desired. **Yield:** 8 dozen.

Patty Vann
Birmingham, Alabama

Oranges Steal the Show

Take a fresh look at oranges. They are excellent traveling companions, cloaked in sturdy skin that keeps them flavorful for days. Use oranges in various sweet dishes and in savory ones like Orange-Glazed Cornish Hens. The tart rind provides a boost to frostings, salad dressings, chicken, and seafood dishes.

ORANGE-GLAZED CORNISH HENS

Prep: 30 minutes
Bake: 1 hour, 30 minutes

6 (1½-pound) Cornish hens
1 teaspoon salt
1 teaspoon pepper
Sausage Stuffing
½ cup water
2 large eggs, lightly beaten
1 cup orange marmalade
¼ cup orange juice
3 tablespoons honey
1 tablespoon lemon juice
¼ teaspoon ground ginger

• **Rub** hens with salt and pepper. Spoon 3 tablespoons Sausage Stuffing into each hen cavity; tie legs together, if desired. Place hens on a rack in an aluminum foil-lined roasting pan.
• **Stir** ½ cup water and eggs into remaining stuffing, and spoon into a lightly greased 13- x 9-inch baking dish. Cover and chill.
• **Stir** together marmalade and next 4 ingredients in a small saucepan. Cook over medium heat, stirring constantly, 5 minutes or until marmalade is melted.
• **Bake** hens at 350° for 30 minutes; brush with orange sauce. Bake 20 more minutes. Brush again with sauce; cover loosely with foil. Bake hens and casserole 40 minutes, uncovering casserole after 30 minutes. **Yield:** 6 servings.

Sausage Stuffing

Prep: 15 minutes
Cook: 10 minutes

1 pound ground pork sausage
3 small onions, chopped
6 green onions, chopped
4 celery ribs, chopped
1 cup coarsely chopped walnuts, toasted
1 (8-ounce) package herb-seasoned stuffing mix
1 (16-ounce) package cornbread stuffing mix
1 cup dry white wine or chicken broth
2 (14½-ounce) cans chicken broth
2 teaspoons poultry seasoning
½ teaspoon salt

• **Cook** first 4 ingredients in a large Dutch oven over medium-high heat, stirring until sausage crumbles and is no longer pink. Drain mixture well, and return to pan.
• **Stir** in walnuts and remaining ingredients. **Yield:** 12 cups.

H. W. Asbell
Tallahassee, Florida

SHRIMP IN ORANGE SAUCE

Prep: 50 minutes
Cook: 18 minutes

2 quarts water
2 pounds unpeeled, large fresh shrimp
¼ cup butter or margarine
1 small onion, diced
2 teaspoons grated orange rind
1 cup fresh orange juice
2 tablespoons orange liqueur or fresh orange juice
¼ cup whipping cream
½ teaspoon salt
¼ teaspoon pepper
1 tablespoon chopped fresh parsley
6 French bread slices, toasted

• **Bring** 2 quarts water to a boil; add shrimp, and cook 3 to 5 minutes or just until shrimp turn pink. Drain and rinse with cold water. Peel shrimp; devein, if desired.

• **Melt** butter in a large skillet over medium heat; add onion, and sauté until tender. Stir in orange rind and next 5 ingredients, and cook 6 to 8 minutes or until slightly thickened. Stir in shrimp, and cook 2 minutes or until thoroughly heated. Sprinkle with parsley, and serve over French bread. **Yield:** 6 servings.

David H. Darst
Tallahassee, Florida

Quick & Easy

When we called Ruth Varnell of Birmingham about her Mexican Meat Mix, she told us she couldn't take credit for the recipe. It came from Oscar Gomez, a friend in Tucson, Arizona. To save time when preparing Oscar's recipe, Ruth now uses a pressure cooker. (The original cooked in a Dutch oven at 200° for 12 hours.) For safety, follow the directions on your cooker.

MEXICAN MEAT MIX

This pressure cooker recipe makes 9 cups of the "meat mix." Freeze it in small portions to use in the trio of quick-to-fix dinner ideas that follow.

Prep: 15 minutes
Cook: 1 hour

1 (2½-pound) boneless chuck roast, trimmed
1 (2½-pound) boneless pork roast, trimmed
1 cup water
3 onions, chopped
1 (4.5-ounce) can chopped green chiles, undrained
1 tablespoon vegetable oil
1 (16-ounce) jar mild green salsa
¼ cup all-purpose flour
1 teaspoon salt
1 teaspoon ground cumin
¼ teaspoon garlic powder

- **Place** roasts and 1 cup water in a 6-quart pressure cooker.
- **Cover** cooker with lid, and seal securely; place pressure control over vent and tube.
- **Cook** over high heat 8 to 10 minutes or until pressure control rocks quickly back and forth. Reduce heat to medium-low; cook 40 minutes. (Pressure control will rock occasionally.)
- **Remove** from heat; run cold water over cooker to reduce pressure. Carefully remove lid so that steam escapes away from you.
- **Drain** meat, reserving juice. Pour juice into a fat strainer; let stand until fat rises to top. Reserve juice, and discard fat. Cool meat slightly, and shred.
- **Sauté** onion and green chiles in hot oil in pressure cooker 1 minute.
- **Stir** in green salsa and next 4 ingredients. Cook 1 minute over medium-low heat. Stir in reserved meat juice and shredded meat. Cook 5 minutes or until thickened. Serve on kaiser rolls with green salsa, if desired. **Yield:** 9 cups.

Oscar Gomez
Tucson, Arizona

Flautas: Pour vegetable oil to a depth of 2 inches in a large skillet; heat to 375°. Soften 30 corn tortillas, 1 at a time, by dipping in hot oil for 2 seconds. Drain on paper towels. Place 1 tablespoon Mexican Meat Mix on bottom half of each tortilla; roll tightly. Cook, seam side down, in hot oil 2 minutes on each side or until golden. Drain on paper towels. **Yield:** 10 servings.

Taco Pizza: Sauté 1 sliced purple onion in 2 teaspoons olive oil over medium heat until tender. Stir together 3 cups Mexican Meat Mix and ½ cup sour cream; spread evenly over a 16-ounce Italian bread shell. Top with onion and 1 (8-ounce) package shredded Mexican cheese blend. Place on a lightly greased baking sheet. Bake at 450° for 15 minutes. Remove from oven; top with ½ cup torn lettuce; ½ cup cherry tomatoes, halved; and 2 tablespoons chopped fresh cilantro. **Yield:** 8 servings.

Stuffed Baked Potatoes: Bake 4 large baking potatoes at 450° for 1 hour or until tender. Cut potatoes in half, and scoop out pulp, leaving ¼-inch-thick shells. Combine potato pulp; 4 cups Mexican Meat Mix; 1 (8-ounce) container sour cream; 3 green onions, sliced; 2 tablespoons chopped fresh cilantro; 1 teaspoon salt; and ½ teaspoon pepper. Spoon mixture into potato shells; sprinkle with 1 cup shredded Monterey Jack cheese with peppers. Bake at 450° for 10 minutes or until thoroughly heated. **Yield:** 4 servings.

ROAST WITH ONION-AND-MUSHROOM GRAVY

Prep: 5 minutes
Cook: 42 minutes

1 (2- to 3-pound) boneless chuck roast, trimmed
½ teaspoon pepper
1 (10¾-ounce) can cream of mushroom soup, undiluted
1 (1-ounce) envelope dry onion soup mix
2 beef bouillon cubes
2 cups water
2 tablespoons cornstarch
2 tablespoons water

- **Sprinkle** roast evenly with pepper; place in a 6-quart pressure cooker. Add mushroom soup and next 3 ingredients.
- **Cover** cooker with lid, and seal securely; place pressure control over vent and tube.
- **Cook** over medium-high heat 20 minutes or until pressure control rocks quickly back and forth. Reduce heat to medium-low; cook 20 more minutes.
- **Remove** from heat; run cold water over cooker to reduce pressure. Carefully remove lid so that steam escapes away from you.
- **Remove** roast, and keep warm. Stir together cornstarch and 2 tablespoons water; add to liquid in pressure cooker. Bring to a boil; cook 1 minute. Serve gravy with roast. **Yield:** 4 to 6 servings.

Donna M. Davidson
Waverly, New York

Soup's On

As the temperature outside drops, serving hearty greens is a great way to warm body and soul. This comforting soup is sure to take the chill off.

COLLARD GREENS SOUP

Smoked and unsmoked ham hocks can be purchased at most meat counters.

Prep: 20 minutes
Cook: 1 hour, 30 minutes

1 (8-ounce) ham hock*
2 (32-ounce) containers chicken broth
2 bacon slices, chopped
2 teaspoons olive oil
⅓ cup diced onion
2 celery ribs, diced
3 tablespoons all-purpose flour
½ cup water
2 (16-ounce) packages fresh collard greens, chopped
⅓ cup whipping cream
2 tablespoons cider vinegar
1 tablespoon hot sauce
1 teaspoon pepper

- **Bring** ham hock and broth to a boil in a Dutch oven; partially cover, reduce heat, and simmer 30 minutes.
- **Cook** bacon in hot oil in a skillet until crisp; remove bacon, and drain on paper towels, reserving drippings in skillet.
- **Sauté** onion and celery in drippings 5 minutes or until tender; add bacon.
- **Stir** together flour and ½ cup water until smooth. Stir into bacon mixture. Stir bacon mixture and collard greens into chicken broth mixture. Cover; simmer, stirring occasionally, 1 hour or until collard greens are tender.
- **Remove** ham hock; cool slightly. Remove meat; discard bone. Dice meat, and return to soup. Stir in cream and remaining ingredients. **Yield:** 15 cups.

*Substitute 8 ounces smoked turkey wings, turkey sausage, or kielbasa, if desired.

Madelyn Wallace
Apopka, Florida

Living Light

You may think you can't get meat lovers to try veggie versions of beef and sausage. But surprisingly, these meatless miracles fooled even our fussy Foods staff. Give these easy recipes a try with your finicky eaters, but don't tell them till after supper.

LOADED VEGGIE TACOS

Prep: 20 minutes
Cook: 5 minutes

1 (12-ounce) package ground beef
  substitute
1 (16-ounce) jar chipotle salsa
1 (16-ounce) jar fat-free spicy black
  bean dip
8 (10-inch) fat-free flour tortillas
1 (8-ounce) container fat-free sour
  cream
1 (8-ounce) package fat-free shredded
  Cheddar cheese
6 green onions, sliced
8 plum tomatoes, seeded and diced
4 cups shredded leaf lettuce

• **Cook** beef substitute and salsa in a large nonstick skillet over medium heat 5 minutes or until thoroughly heated.
• **Spread** bean dip evenly over 1 side of tortillas. Top evenly with beef substitute mixture, sour cream, and next 4 ingredients; roll up. Serve immediately. **Yield:** 8 servings.

♥ Per serving: Calories 333 (less than 1% from fat)
Fat 1g Protein 29g Carb 49g
Fiber 8g Chol 0mg Iron 2.3mg
Sodium 1,153mg Calc 356mg

VEGGIE SAUSAGE PIZZAS

Prep: 15 minutes
Bake: 15 minutes
Cook: 5 minutes

8 (1-inch-thick) French bread
  slices
1 sweet onion, sliced
1 medium-size green bell pepper, sliced
Vegetable cooking spray
1 cup low-fat tomato-and-basil pasta
  sauce
1 cup (4 ounces) shredded fat-free
  mozzarella cheese
1 (8-ounce) package meatless
  breakfast patties, thawed and
  crumbled
½ cup shredded Parmesan cheese

• **Bake** bread slices on a baking sheet at 425° for 5 minutes. Set aside.
• **Sauté** sliced onion and sliced bell pepper in a large nonstick skillet coated with cooking spray over medium-high heat 5 minutes.
• **Spread** pasta sauce evenly on 1 side of bread slices. Top evenly with mozzarella cheese, onion mixture, crumbled patties, and Parmesan cheese.
• **Bake** at 425° for 10 minutes or until thoroughly heated. **Yield:** 4 servings.

Rena P. Marshall
Rex, Georgia

♥ Per serving: Calories 480 (26% from fat)
Fat 14g (sat 4g, mono 3.5g, poly 4.1g)
Protein 34g Carb 43g Fiber 6g
Chol 14mg Iron 4.5mg
Sodium 1,589mg Calc 426mg

FULL-OF-VEGGIES CHILI

Prep: 20 minutes
Cook: 30 minutes

1 large sweet onion, diced
1 large green bell pepper, diced
2 garlic cloves, minced
2 tablespoons vegetable oil
1 (12-ounce) package ground beef
  substitute
1 large zucchini, diced
1 (11-ounce) can whole kernel corn,
  undrained
2 (15-ounce) cans no-salt-added
  tomato sauce
2 (10-ounce) cans diced tomato and
  green chiles, undrained
1 (15-ounce) can black beans, rinsed
  and drained
1 (15-ounce) can pinto beans, rinsed
  and drained
1 teaspoon sugar
1 (1¾-ounce) envelope Texas-style
  chili seasoning mix

• **Sauté** first 3 ingredients in hot oil in a large stockpot over medium-high heat 5 minutes or until tender.
• **Stir** in beef substitute and remaining ingredients. Bring to a boil; reduce heat. Simmer, uncovered, stirring often, 20 minutes. **Yield:** about 4 quarts.

Note: Freeze chili up to 3 months, if desired.

Pam Echeverria
Tucson, Arizona

♥ Per cup: Calories 128 (14% from fat)
Fat 2g (sat 0.4g, mono 0.6g, poly 1g)
Protein 16g Carb 19g Fiber 3g
Chol 0mg Iron 1.6mg
Sodium 547mg Calc 44mg

Try Couscous

If you like rice, you'll like couscous. The exotic-sounding name can be misleading, because couscous is just tiny pasta made from semolina wheat. Today it is popular in kitchens around the world. No special equipment is required—a pot with a lid is all you need.

ORANGE-GINGER COUSCOUS

Prep: 20 minutes
Stand: 5 minutes

1 teaspoon grated orange rind
2 cups fresh orange juice
⅓ cup sweetened dried cranberries
½ tablespoon butter or margarine
½ teaspoon salt
¼ teaspoon ground cinnamon
1 teaspoon minced fresh ginger
1 (10-ounce) package couscous
¼ cup sliced almonds, toasted

• **Bring** first 7 ingredients to a boil in a saucepan over medium heat; remove from heat.
• **Stir** in couscous. Cover and let stand 5 minutes. Fluff with a fork, and stir in almonds. **Yield:** 4 to 6 servings.

Note: For testing purposes only, we used Craisins for dried cranberries.

PAN-GRILLED SALMON

Prep: 5 minutes
Chill: 2 hours
Cook: 8 minutes

¼ cup firmly packed brown sugar
¼ cup soy sauce
4 (6-ounce) salmon steaks
Garnish: orange rind strips
Orange-Ginger Couscous (recipe above)

• **Combine** brown sugar and soy sauce in a shallow dish or heavy-duty zip-top plastic bag; add salmon. Cover or seal, and chill 2 hours. Remove salmon from marinade, discarding marinade.
• **Cook** salmon in a lightly greased skillet over medium-high heat 4 minutes on each side or until fish flakes with a fork. Garnish, if desired. Serve with Orange-Ginger Couscous. **Yield:** 4 servings.

COUSCOUS WITH RAISINS, ALMONDS, AND LEMON

Prep: 15 minutes
Cook: 35 minutes

1 (14½-ounce) can vegetable broth
¼ cup water
3 tablespoons olive oil, divided
1 (4.8-ounce) package Israeli couscous
½ cup raisins
⅓ cup chopped fresh Italian parsley
1 (2.25-ounce) package slivered almonds
1 tablespoon lemon juice
2 small celery ribs, diced
3 garlic cloves, pressed
4 skinned and boned chicken breast halves, cut into strips

• **Bring** broth, ¼ cup water, and 1 tablespoon oil to a boil in a saucepan over medium heat. Stir in couscous and seasoning packet. Cover, reduce heat, and simmer 15 minutes or until liquid is absorbed and couscous is tender. Fluff with a fork. Stir in raisins and next 4 ingredients.
• **Heat** remaining oil in a large skillet over medium heat. Add garlic; sauté 2 to 3 minutes or until tender. Add chicken; sauté 8 minutes or until browned. Spoon couscous onto a serving platter; top with chicken. **Yield:** 4 servings.

Note: For testing purposes only, we used Marrakesh Express Couscous Grande Roasted Garlic.

Ronda Carman
Houston, Texas

COUSCOUS WITH CURRANTS, PINE NUTS, AND PORK

Prep: 15 minutes
Stand: 5 minutes
Cook: 15 minutes

2 (14½-ounce) cans low-sodium fat-free chicken broth
¼ cup butter or margarine, divided
3 cups uncooked couscous
½ cup currants
½ cup pine nuts, toasted
4 green onions, thinly sliced
¼ cup chopped fresh mint
½ teaspoon grated lemon rind
1 tablespoon fresh lemon juice
2 tablespoons minced fresh dill (optional)
¾ teaspoon salt, divided
¾ teaspoon curry powder
¾ teaspoon ground red pepper, divided
4 boneless pork loin chops, cut into ½-inch cubes
½ teaspoon ground black pepper
1 tablespoon olive oil

• **Bring** broth and 3 tablespoons butter to a boil in a saucepan over medium heat; remove from heat.
• **Stir** in couscous. Cover and let stand 5 minutes; fluff with a fork.
• **Stir** in currants, next 5 ingredients, and, if desired, dill. Stir in ¼ teaspoon salt, curry, and ½ teaspoon red pepper. Keep warm.
• **Sprinkle** pork with remaining ½ teaspoon salt, remaining ¼ teaspoon red pepper, and black pepper.
• **Heat** remaining 1 tablespoon butter and oil in a skillet over medium heat. Add pork, and sauté 5 to 7 minutes. Stir into couscous. **Yield:** 4 to 6 servings.

Patsy Bell Hobson
Liberty, Missouri

Pumpkin Power

Pumpkins are good for much more than Halloween carvings. Still plentiful in November, these gourds provide the base for Pumpkin Soup With Sweet Croutons—sent in by Camilla Varner, a reader (and Southerner) living in Berlin, Germany.

Camilla tells us that she and her friend Barbara Kinkead enjoy visiting weekly open-air markets and buying seasonal produce—including fresh pumpkins. They also like many foods from other European countries, so Camilla enhances traditional recipes with ethnic flavor.

Add this soup to the menu as a surprise first course for your traditional Thanksgiving dinner.

PUMPKIN SOUP WITH SWEET CROUTONS
(pictured on page 262)

Sweet Croutons add delightful crispness to this creamy soup.

Prep: 15 minutes
Cook: 20 minutes

4 cups Pumpkin Soup Stock (recipe at right)
1 cup milk
1 tablespoon grated fresh ginger
½ teaspoon sugar
½ teaspoon salt
½ teaspoon curry powder
¼ teaspoon ground black pepper
¼ teaspoon ground cinnamon
⅛ teaspoon ground red pepper
Sweet Croutons

• **Cook** first 9 ingredients in a large saucepan over medium heat 20 minutes or until thoroughly heated. Serve with Sweet Croutons. **Yield:** 5 cups.

Note: For testing purposes only, we used Spice World ground fresh ginger in a jar.

Sweet Croutons

Prep: 5 minutes
Bake: 10 minutes

4 cups French bread cubes
3 tablespoons butter or margarine, melted
¼ cup sugar
½ teaspoon ground cinnamon

• **Toss** together bread cubes and melted butter. Combine sugar and cinnamon; add to bread cubes, tossing to coat. Spread in a single layer on a lightly greased baking sheet.
• **Bake** at 375°, stirring occasionally, for 8 to 10 minutes or until golden brown. **Yield:** 3 cups.

PUMPKIN SOUP STOCK

Prep: 40 minutes
Cook: 2 hours, 15 minutes

2 celery ribs
2 carrots
1 large onion
1 medium parsnip
1 large leek
2 garlic cloves
5 cups water
½ cup chopped fresh parsley
2 tablespoons grated fresh ginger
2 tablespoons lemon or lime juice
1 teaspoon salt
3 or 4 chicken wings
2 cups Pumpkin Puree ✱

• **Chop** first 5 ingredients; mince garlic.
• **Bring** chopped vegetables, minced garlic, 5 cups water, and next 5 ingredients to a boil in a large Dutch oven over medium heat; cover, reduce heat, and simmer 2 hours. Discard chicken wings. Stir in Pumpkin Puree.
• **Process** mixture, in small batches, in a blender or food processor until smooth, stopping to scrape down sides. Cool. Chill up to 5 days, or freeze up to 3 months. **Yield:** 10 cups.

✱Substitute 2 cups canned pumpkin for Pumpkin Puree, if desired.

Pumpkin Puree

Prep: 15 minutes
Bake: 2 hours

1 (12-pound) pumpkin
Water

• **Cut** pumpkin into fourths; remove and discard seeds and strings. Place pumpkin pieces in a large, deep roasting pan. Add water to a depth of 2 inches.
• **Bake** at 350° for 2 hours or until tender. Cool, peel, and cut into cubes.
• **Process** pumpkin cubes, in batches, in a blender or food processor until mixture is smooth, stopping to scrape down sides. Divide puree into desired portions; freeze up to 3 months. **Yield:** 12 cups.

Grandmother's Gingerbread Gathering

For Gwyn Huffman Willbanks, grandson Trey's arrival in 1985 sparked a cherished tradition—"Gingerbread Day," an annual event Gwyn hosts for cookie baking, storytelling, carol singing, and lots of hugs.

The Willbanks grandchildren and grandnieces and nephews look forward each November to receiving their invitations to join Gwyn, affectionately known as "Ditty."

Gwyn says keeping things simple and focusing on enjoyment of time together are keys to a successful gathering. To that end, she measures and mixes ingredients ahead of time for the traditional Gingerbread Men recipe she shares with us.

GINGERBREAD MEN

These cookies are so cute that they entice young and old munchers.

Prep: 30 minutes
Bake: 12 minutes per batch

2¼ cups sugar
¾ cup water
⅓ cup dark corn syrup
1½ tablespoons ground ginger
1¼ tablespoons ground cinnamon
2 teaspoons ground cloves
1¼ cups butter or margarine
1 tablespoon baking soda
1 tablespoon water
6 cups all-purpose flour
Decorations: sugar crystals, decorator frosting, red cinnamon candies

• **Cook** first 6 ingredients in a saucepan over medium heat, stirring until sugar dissolves.
• **Add** butter, stirring until melted.
• **Combine** baking soda and 1 tablespoon water; stir into sugar mixture. Pour sugar mixture into a bowl; gradually add flour, beating at medium speed with a heavy-duty electric mixer until blended.
• **Divide** dough into thirds. Roll one-third of dough to ⅛-inch thickness on a lightly floured surface (chill remaining dough). Cut with a 5½-inch gingerbread man cutter, and place on lightly greased baking sheets.
• **Bake** at 350° for 10 to 12 minutes. Cool on pan 1 minute; remove cookies to wire racks, and cool completely. Repeat procedure with remaining dough. Decorate as desired. **Yield:** 3 dozen.

Gwyn Huffman Willbanks
Pearland, Texas

GINGERBREAD JOY

"The fun really begins with the cookie decorating," Gwyn says. "It's all about encouraging each child's individuality and personal expression." Gwyn keeps things running smoothly by staggering kitchen time for the children, allowing two in at a time, and enlisting the help of another adult. Each child bakes and decorates a full sheet of cookies and receives a basket in which to carry home the goodies.

With guidelines for her annual gingerbread afternoon, Gwyn encourages grandmothers everywhere to host a memorable cookie caper. Here are her tips.

■ Make the baking activity for children only. Parents appreciate having extra holiday shopping time alone. Ask parents to return for supper, songs, and show-and-tell of each child's handiwork.

■ Plan an activity or custom that can become part of each year's gathering. Gwyn adds a single wooden toy each year to a collection she began at her first gathering in 1985.

■ If serving a meal, keep the menu simple. Serve a favorite family soup, chili, or stew.

■ Don't forget the focus of the season. Read the Christmas story. Ask youngsters to tell or re-enact the story for their parents or help arrange figures in a nativity scene.

A Taste of the South

Country ham marks the approach of the holidays, a time when family recipes offer us a taste of tradition. Our Country Ham recipe ensures a juicy, traditionally flavored ham. Serve on biscuits with or without mustard. This is our salute to those who preserve their heritage the old-fashioned way.

COUNTRY HAM

Prep: 1 hour
Soak: 24 hours
Bake: 4 hours

1 (12- to 14-pound) uncooked country ham
2 quarts cider vinegar
1 tablespoon whole cloves
Hot biscuits

• **Place** ham in a large container. Add water to cover; soak 24 hours. Drain. Scrub ham 3 or 4 times in cold water with a stiff brush, and rinse well.
• **Place** ham, fat side up, in a large roasting pan. Pour vinegar over ham; sprinkle with cloves. Cover with lid or aluminum foil.
• **Bake** at 325° for 4 hours or until a meat thermometer registers 140°. Remove from oven, and cool slightly. Slice ham, and serve with hot biscuits. **Yield:** 35 to 40 servings.

HOLIDAY HAMS

This time of year, hand-scrawled signs appear in shop windows across the South: "Cured country hams now available. Don't get left out. Buy yours today!" Those ham recipes are as different as the regions from which they come. A touch of sugar, pinch of pepper, or the bold flavor of the cure—each defines a true country ham.

Charlie Gatton of Father's Country Hams in Bremen, Kentucky, cured hams under his father's watchful eye for 33 years. Charlie has done it all—from perfecting the family cure to making home deliveries. Now he oversees a process that hasn't changed since 1945. "Sugar tones down the intense salt flavor, and aging helps tenderize the meat," says Charlie.

You can find this delicacy as whole cooked hams, uncooked hams, or packaged slices. When buying your first, look for a ham aged five to six months; it will have a milder flavor. If you crave a more concentrated flavor, a 12- to 14-month-old ham is ideal.

Regardless of your choice, tackling an uncooked ham can be overwhelming. Ask your butcher to cut a little bit off the top of the hock; doing so will give you extra room in the roasting pan. "Don't discard this moist piece of meat," advises Bob Woods of G. and W. Hamery Country Hams in Murfreesboro, Tennessee. "It provides a seasoning base for soup and beans, and the aroma is an excellent indicator of the ham's quality."

Rodman Meacham, of Meacham Country Hams in Sturgis, Kentucky, suggests removing mold (a natural part of the aging process) with elbow grease, warm water, and vinegar. After the ham has been scrubbed, soak it in a deep pot or kettle full of water to replace some of the moisture lost during curing. You'll need a large roasting pan for cooking. If your pan doesn't have a lid, heavy-duty aluminum foil will work.

It's important for the ham to cool completely before slicing, or it can crumble. Serve ham thinly sliced at room temperature for optimal flavor.

Country ham dries out quickly. Slices can be frozen up to two months or refrigerated up to two weeks. Keep the ham moist by laying excess fat on top. The ham needs to breathe, so wrap with wax paper. Then secure with foil.

Here are some places you can order country hams.

■ Father's Country Hams
P.O. Box 99
Bremen, KY 42325
1-877-525-4267 (toll free)
www.fatherscountryhams.com

■ G. and W. Hamery Country Hams
411 West Lytle Street
Murfreesboro, TN 37130
(615) 893-9712

■ Meacham Country Hams
705 O'Nan Dyer Road
Sturgis, KY 42459
1-800-552-3190
www.meachamhams.com

■ S. Wallace Edwards & Sons
P.O. Box 25
Surry, VA 23883
1-800-222-4267
www.virginiatraditions.com

The Fruitcake Tradition

Our reader files are overflowing with fruitcake recipes. Many are family traditions, handed down for generations. Ellen Jampole remembers her grandmother's White Fruitcake. She celebrates each holiday season by making this jewel as a tribute to her grandmother.

Fruitcakes require time to assemble. Chop fruit and nuts, and combine dry ingredients the night before. One secret to preparation? Grandma's deep mixing bowl and a strong stirring partner.

WHITE FRUITCAKE

Prep: 30 minutes
Bake: 2 hours

- 1 cup butter or margarine, softened
- 1 cup sugar
- 2 large eggs
- 1 teaspoon orange extract
- 1 teaspoon lemon extract
- 3 cups cake flour, divided
- 2 teaspoons baking powder
- ½ teaspoon baking soda
- ½ teaspoon salt
- ½ cup peach nectar
- 1 cup flaked coconut
- 1 cup chopped candied pineapple (about ½ pound)
- 1 cup chopped candied cherries (about ½ pound)
- 1 cup golden raisins (about ½ pound)
- 1 cup chopped crystallized ginger
- 2 cups chopped pecans, toasted
- 6 egg whites

- **Beat** butter and sugar at medium speed with an electric mixer until fluffy.
- **Add** eggs, 1 at a time, beating well after each addition. Stir in flavorings.
- **Combine** 2 cups cake flour and next 3 ingredients. Add flour mixture to butter mixture alternately with nectar, beginning and ending with flour mixture. Beat at low speed just until blended after each addition.
- **Stir** together remaining 1 cup cake flour, coconut, and next 4 ingredients. Stir fruit mixture and pecans into batter.
- **Beat** egg whites at high speed until stiff peaks form. Fold into batter.
- **Pour** batter into a greased and floured 10-inch tube pan.
- **Bake** at 275° for 2 hours or until a long wooden pick inserted in center comes out clean. Cool on a wire rack. If desired, wrap in cheesecloth, and soak with 1 cup peach brandy for 2 weeks. **Yield:** 1 (10-inch) cake.

Ellen Jampole
Cortland, New York

SHERRY-NUT FRUITCAKE

Prep: 45 minutes
Soak: 8 hours
Bake: 3 hours

- 2 cups golden raisins
- ¾ cup dry sherry
- 2 cups chopped candied pineapple (about 1 pound)
- 1½ cups chopped red candied cherries (about ¾ pound)
- 1½ cups chopped green candied cherries (about ¾ pound)
- 4 cups chopped pecans
- 3 cups all-purpose flour, divided
- ¾ cup butter or margarine, softened
- ¾ cup sugar
- ¾ cup firmly packed brown sugar
- 6 large eggs
- ¼ teaspoon salt
- 1 teaspoon ground allspice
- 1 teaspoon ground cinnamon
- ¾ teaspoon ground mace (optional)
- ¾ cup whipping cream
- 1 (10-ounce) jar strawberry preserves
- ¾ teaspoon almond extract
- ¾ teaspoon orange extract
- ¾ teaspoon vanilla extract

- **Soak** raisins in sherry 8 hours; drain.
- **Combine** pineapple, candied cherries, pecans, and 1 cup flour, tossing to coat.
- **Beat** butter at medium speed with an electric mixer until creamy; gradually add sugars, beating well. Add eggs, 1 at a time, beating well after each addition.
- **Combine** remaining 2 cups flour, salt, allspice, cinnamon, and, if desired, mace. Add to butter mixture alternately with cream, beginning and ending with flour mixture. Beat at low speed just until blended after each addition. Add preserves and flavorings, beating well. Stir in raisins and fruit mixture. Spoon into a greased and floured 10-inch tube pan.
- **Bake** at 275° for 3 hours or until a long wooden pick inserted in center comes out clean. Cool in pan on a wire rack 20 minutes; remove from pan, and cool completely on wire rack. If desired, soak cheesecloth in ⅔ cup dry sherry, wrap around cake, and place in an airtight container; refrigerate 7 to 10 days. **Yield:** 1 (10-inch) cake.

Hilda Marshall
Culpeper, Virginia

From Our Kitchen

Hold the Fat

Some recipes recommend a fat separator to remove excess fat from foods. You can accomplish the same results even if you don't have a separator cup. Most of us use the method of chilling the dish, then skimming the fat that rises to the top. If you're in a hurry (and want a cleaner way to do it), pour the liquid into a heavy-duty zip-top plastic bag. Place the bag in a tall, slim container. The fat will rise to the top. Lift the bag, without disturbing the contents, and hold it over a bowl. Snip a small hole in a bottom corner; allow the liquid to escape. Pinch the hole closed when only the fat remains; discard the bag—and the fat.

Tips and Tidbits

■ Anna Reich of Albuquerque, New Mexico, shares how she rescues drowning spoons: "To prevent a wooden spoon from sliding into a pot," writes Anna, "attach a wooden spring-type clothespin to the handle of the pot, and then clip the spoon to it."

■ This time of year, refrigerator storage space is at a premium. Pull up a chair to your open refrigerator once a week and take inventory. With a large tray at your right hand and a garbage bag at your left, you are ready to reclaim hidden goodies that were pushed out of sight and to discard leftovers past their prime. This weekly effort will save you time and money as you plan meals and shopping lists.

ON THE TURKEY PLATTER

Whether your bird is herb-stuffed and roasted, smoked, or fried, a few safe-handling tips need to be applied. Thaw the unopened turkey, breast side up, on a tray in the refrigerator. Allow one day's thawing time for every 4 pounds.

Lyda Jones, of our Test Kitchens staff, shares these tips for frying turkey, like the one on page 252.

■ Always fry turkey outdoors.

■ Remove turkey from refrigerator at least 20 minutes before frying.

■ Wipe the turkey thoroughly inside and out with paper towels. Discard the plastic doneness indicator.

■ For ease of handling, a 12- to 14-pound turkey is the largest she recommends. This is a two-person job.

■ Peanut oil or grapeseed oil are the best for frying. Fill oil no more than 6 inches from the rim of the cooker to prevent overflow.

■ Slowly lower and lift the meat three or four times into the hot oil to help evaporate any excess moisture that could cause excessive bubbling and splattering.

■ Turn off the burner before removing the turkey, so drippings won't catch fire. Cool the oil completely before you try to handle it.

■ For more information on how to prepare the best turkey ever, contact Butterball Turkey Talk-Line at 1-800-323-4848 or Reynolds Turkey Tips Line at 1-800-745-4000.

Butter

The height of baking season is upon us. When you stock up on ingredients, pause at the dairy case and choose your butter wisely. Butter and margarine contain 80 percent fat and are perfect for baking. Spreads have less than 80 percent fat and are not recommended for baked goods.

Store butter in the coldest part of the refrigerator. Place the sticks in airtight containers or bags, because butter picks up other food odors and flavors easily. Freeze in freezer bags up to six months.

To soften butter, cut it into chunks and let stand at room temperature about 15 minutes. If you are in a hurry, place the butter between sheets of wax paper, and give it a few good whacks with a rolling pin. Don't be tempted to melt butter for speed's sake. Your batter or dough will not behave properly if made with melted butter—unless the recipe specifically calls for it.

Delta Mocha Chiffon Cake, page 286

Meat Sauce for Spaghetti, Caramel Sauce,
Applesauce, Cumberland Sauce, page 256

Black-Eyed Susans, Pecan Pie Cookies,
Neapolitan Cookies, pages 290-291

Egg Nog, page 274

Butter Cookies, Champagne Sabayon,
Gentleman's Pound Cake, pages 287-288

DECEMBER

Wish Upon a Star

We're all starry-eyed over the cake on our cover. "I just love the combination of creamy white chocolate and coconut," says its creator, Jan Moon of our Test Kitchens. "And the sweetened dried cranberries inside are a fun and festive surprise."

TWINKLING STAR CAKE
(pictured on cover)

Prep: 3 hours
Bake: 30 minutes
Freeze: 2 hours
Chill: 30 minutes
Stand: 30 minutes

¾ cup butter, softened
1 (3-ounce) package cream cheese, softened
1½ cups sugar
3 large eggs
2 cups cake flour
1 teaspoon baking powder
¼ teaspoon salt
¼ cup coconut milk (not cream of coconut)
1 (6-ounce) package frozen coconut, thawed
½ teaspoon coconut extract
Nutty Cranberry Filling
White Chocolate Frosting
White sparkling sugar
Edible white glitter
Edible gold luster dust
White Chocolate Stars
Crushed rock candy (optional)

• **Beat** butter and cream cheese at medium speed with an electric mixer until fluffy; gradually add sugar, beating well. Add eggs, 1 at a time, beating until blended after each addition.
• **Combine** flour, baking powder, and salt; add to butter mixture alternately with coconut milk, beginning and ending with flour mixture. Beat at low speed until blended after each addition.

• **Stir** in coconut and coconut extract. Pour batter into 2 greased and floured 8- x 1¾-inch round cakepans.
• **Bake** at 350° for 25 to 30 minutes or until a wooden pick inserted in center comes out clean. Cool in pans on wire racks 10 minutes. Remove from pans; wrap in plastic wrap. Freeze 2 hours. (Freezing makes layers easier to cut.)
• **Cut** domed top off each cake layer, using a serrated knife.
• **Cut** each layer into 8 wedges. Arrange 5 wedges, point side out, in a star shape on a 10-inch cake plate. (See diagrams in "From Our Kitchen" on page 330.) Place about 1½ cups Nutty Cranberry Filling inside center opening of cake wedges. Spread a thin layer of filling over cake wedges. Adjust wedges to maintain star shape, pressing them into filling. Repeat procedure to form a second layer.
• **Top** each section with a cake wedge to form a third layer. (One wedge will remain; enjoy it while completing cake.) Fill center with about 1½ cups filling. Filling should be level with cake wedges. Adjust wedges to maintain star shape, pressing them into filling.
• **Spread** a thin layer of White Chocolate Frosting evenly over top and sides of cake, smoothing with a wet metal spatula. Chill 30 minutes. Set aside ½ cup frosting. Spread remaining frosting over top and sides of cake, smoothing with a wet metal spatula.
• **Sprinkle** with white sparkling sugar and edible white glitter. Spoon ½ cup frosting into a small heavy-duty zip-top plastic bag; seal. Snip a tiny hole in 1 corner of bag; outline top edge of cake.

• **Brush** edible gold luster dust accents onto piped edge, using a small paintbrush. Garnish with White Chocolate Stars and, if desired, rock candy. Store cake in refrigerator; let stand at room temperature 30 minutes before serving. **Yield:** 1 (3-layer) cake.

Nutty Cranberry Filling

Prep: 15 minutes

1 (12-ounce) package white chocolate morsels
1 cup butter, softened
1 (14-ounce) package flaked coconut
⅔ cup coconut milk (not cream of coconut)
1 (3.5-ounce) jar macadamia nuts, chopped
2 (6-ounce) packages sweetened dried cranberries, chopped

• **Microwave** white chocolate morsels in a glass bowl at HIGH 1 minute or until melted, stirring once; cool.
• **Beat** butter at medium speed with an electric mixer until fluffy; add melted white chocolate, beating until blended.
• **Stir** together coconut and coconut milk; add nuts and berries. Stir in chocolate mixture until blended. **Yield:** 5 cups.

White Chocolate Frosting

Prep: 15 minutes
Cool: 1 hour, 30 minutes

1½ cups whipping cream
2 (12-ounce) packages white chocolate morsels
4 (2-ounce) vanilla candy coating squares, chopped

• **Cook** whipping cream in a large saucepan over medium heat 3 to 4 minutes. (Do not boil.) Remove from heat; add white chocolate and candy coating, stirring until melted. Cool 1½ hours. (Mixture should reach room temperature.)
• **Beat** at medium speed with an electric mixer 4 to 5 minutes or until spreading consistency. (Do not overbeat.) **Yield:** 4½ cups.

Note: If frosting separates, reheat mixture and proceed as directed.

White Chocolate Stars

Prep: 15 minutes
Cool: 30 minutes

8 (2-ounce) vanilla candy coating
squares
Clear vanilla extract
Edible gold luster dust or pearl
luster dust
White sparkling sugar
Edible white glitter

• **Microwave** candy coating in a glass bowl at HIGH 1½ minutes or until melted, stirring twice. Pour candy coating into a wax paper-lined 8-inch square pan, spreading evenly. Cool at room temperature until firm to the touch (25 to 30 minutes).
• **Cut** into star shapes with lightly greased graduated star-shaped cutters. (Gently press each point of star, working around star until it can be removed from cutter.) Brush tops of stars with clear vanilla. Using a small, dry paintbrush, brush gold or pearl luster dust over stars. Sprinkle with sparkling sugar and glitter. **Yield:** 1 (5-inch), 1 (3½-inch), 5 (2-inch), and 15 (1-inch) stars.

Note: For testing purposes only, we used Craisins for sweetened dried cranberries and Nestle Premiere White Morsels for white chocolate morsels. Sparkling sugar, edible glitter, luster dust, and clear vanilla extract can be found at gourmet grocery stores, cake decorating supply stores, and kitchen shops. Vanilla candy coating is sold near baking chocolate in the supermarket. It is often referred to as almond bark, and it comes in vanilla and chocolate. Canned coconut milk may be found in the ethnic foods section of the supermarket. See "From Our Kitchen" on page 330 for more information.

Gathering of Stars Party Cake: Double cake layer recipe. Pour half of batter evenly into 2 greased and floured 9- x 1¾-inch round cakepans. Pour remaining batter into 2 greased and floured 6- x 1¾-inch round cakepans.

Bake at 350° for 20 to 25 minutes or until a wooden pick inserted in center comes out clean.

Halve the Nutty Cranberry Filling recipe, and spread between 9-inch layers and 6-inch layers. Place 6-inch stack on top of 9-inch stack. Frost with White Chocolate Frosting. Garnish, if desired, with sparkling sugar, glitter, and White Chocolate Stars.

Share a Sweet Wreath

Although Heather Kernan and her husband have been missionaries in South Africa for 42 years, she is still a devoted *Southern Living* reader. Her Holiday Coffee Cake Wreaths are always a big hit. "I take these to various friends," she says, "starting with the first batch, hot from the oven, on Christmas Eve. They are delicious for a quick breakfast or for a light afternoon tea following a heavy Christmas dinner."

HOLIDAY COFFEE CAKE WREATHS

Prep: 25 minutes
Rise: 1 hour, 30 minutes
Bake: 25 minutes

½ cup water
½ cup milk
½ cup butter or margarine
3½ to 4 cups all-purpose flour, divided
½ cup sugar
½ cup raisins
1 teaspoon salt
1 teaspoon ground cardamom or
cinnamon
2 (¼-ounce) envelopes rapid-rise yeast
2 large eggs, divided
1½ cups sifted powdered sugar
2 tablespoons boiling water
1 tablespoon lemon juice
¼ cup red candied cherries
¼ cup green candied cherries
12 pecan halves

• **Combine** ½ cup water, milk, and butter in a saucepan; heat, stirring constantly, until butter melts. Cool to 120° to 130°.
• **Combine** 3½ cups flour and next 5 ingredients in a large mixing bowl. Gradually add milk mixture to flour mixture, beating at high speed with an electric mixer until blended.
• **Add** 1 egg; beat at medium speed 2 minutes. Gradually stir in enough of remaining flour to make a soft dough.
• **Turn** dough onto a floured surface, and knead until smooth and elastic (about 10 minutes). Place in a well-greased bowl, turning to grease top.
• **Cover** and let rise in a warm place (85°), free from drafts, 1 hour or until doubled in bulk.
• **Punch** dough down; turn out onto a lightly floured surface. Knead lightly 4 or 5 times. Divide dough in half. Divide each half into thirds. Roll 3 portions into 20-inch-long ropes; place side by side on a greased baking sheet. Braid ropes, and shape into a ring. Pinch ends together to seal. Repeat procedure with remaining dough. Cover and let rise in a warm place (85°), free from drafts, 30 minutes. Lightly beat remaining egg, and brush over braids.
• **Bake** at 350° for 20 to 25 minutes or until wreaths sound hollow when tapped. Cool on wire racks.
• **Stir** together powdered sugar, 2 tablespoons boiling water, and lemon juice; drizzle over wreaths. Decorate with candied cherries and pecan halves. **Yield:** 2 (8-inch) wreaths.

Note: You can make these festive wreaths ahead of time and freeze them to give as gifts during the holidays. After baking, cool the wreaths and wrap tightly in aluminum foil. Place in heavy-duty zip top plastic bags, and store in the freezer. Thaw them at room temperature; then add glaze and decorations.

Heather Kernan
Nahoon Valley
East London, South Africa

Holiday Recipe Contest Winners

Fifteen readers won starring roles in
Southern Living *with these outstanding recipes.*

This year, our annual Holiday Recipe Contest was one of the most interesting ever. Readers submitted more than 5,300 wonderful recipes in hopes of taking home the Grand Prize in each of the five categories and of having their recipes featured in this issue. Some past winners have even had the opportunity to appear on television in their hometowns.

Judging the contest was exciting for the Foods staff. We sorted and discussed the recipes, eagerly anticipating tasting them. Then we sorted them once again until we narrowed the field in each category. As the fields grew smaller, the decisions became harder. We chose the best Quick Party Snacks, Entrées with Eight Ingredients or Less, Make-Ahead Main-Dish Casseroles, Easy and Fresh Sides, and Perfect Pies.

We spent an intensive (and waist-expanding) two weeks testing and retesting the recipes to select the most delicious and innovative ones. They are dishes we are confident to present to you as the best of the best. We think this year's winners fill the bill admirably.

Quick Party Snacks

Pharmacist Gloria Pleasants finds great enjoyment in creating new dishes. "I try to go for color and for something fresh and spontaneous," she says. "These were some ingredients I had on hand for the holidays."

TWO-TOMATO TAPAS

Grand Prizewinner

Prep: 20 minutes
Bake: 8 minutes

2　large plum tomatoes, seeded and chopped
12　dried tomato halves in oil, drained and chopped
1　cup (4 ounces) shredded Italian 6-cheese blend
⅓　cup crumbled Gorgonzola or blue cheese
¼　cup minced sweet onion
1　tablespoon minced fresh basil
1　teaspoon minced fresh rosemary
¼　teaspoon garlic pepper
24　baguette slices

• **Combine** first 8 ingredients. Arrange baguette slices on a baking sheet. Spoon tomato mixture evenly over slices. Bake at 350° for 7 to 8 minutes or until cheese melts. **Yield:** 24 appetizer servings.

Gloria Pleasants
Williamsburg, Virginia

CRANBERRY AMBROSIA-CREAM CHEESE SPREAD

Runner-up

Prep: 15 minutes

2　(8-ounce) packages cream cheese, softened
¼　cup powdered sugar
1　(6-ounce) package sweetened dried cranberries, divided
1　(15½-ounce) can crushed pineapple
1　(11-ounce) can mandarin oranges
1　(3½-ounce) can shredded coconut, divided
1　cup chopped pecans, toasted
8　pecan halves, toasted

• **Stir** together cream cheese and sugar until blended. Add dried cranberries, reserving ¼ cup cranberries.
• **Drain** pineapple and oranges; pat dry between layers of paper towels. Set oranges aside.
• **Stir** pineapple and coconut into cream cheese mixture, reserving ¼ cup coconut. Stir in chopped pecans. Spoon mixture into a serving bowl.
• **Sprinkle** reserved dried cranberries around edges of bowl.
• **Arrange** orange sections around inside edge of cranberries. Sprinkle reserved ¼ cup coconut in center, and top with pecan halves. Serve with gingersnaps. **Yield:** 24 appetizer servings.

Connie Cobern
Hendersonville, Tennessee

CHICKEN BITES WITH SWEET-HOT TOMATO CHUTNEY

Runner-up

Prep: 20 minutes
Bake: 12 minutes

2 skinned and boned chicken breast
   halves
¼ teaspoon lemon pepper
12 precooked bacon slices
½ cup hot mango chutney
½ cup salsa

• **Cut** each chicken breast into 12 cubes. Sprinkle with lemon pepper.
• **Cut** bacon slices in half crosswise. Wrap bacon around each chicken cube; secure with wooden picks.
• **Arrange** on a lightly greased rack in a broiler pan.
• **Bake** at 450° for 10 to 12 minutes or until bacon is crisp.
• **Process** chutney and salsa in a blender or food processor until smooth, stopping to scrape down sides. Serve with chicken bites. **Yield:** 6 to 8 appetizer servings.

Note: For testing purposes only, we used Ready Crisp precooked bacon.

Helen D. Conwell
Fairhope, Alabama

Entrées With Eight Ingredients or Less

When Diane Sparrow decided to enter the contest, there was no question what her choice of meat would be. "We live in Iowa," she says, "so beef is a favorite for us. And filets are always elegant for the holidays."

Diane enters contests frequently and reports that her husband and four grown sons have all been great recipe samplers over the years. "Because I'm always testing new things, I don't often cook the same dish twice. My husband pouts when we have something we really like. 'Guess we won't see that again,' he says." This dish is one of his favorites.

BEEF FILETS WITH STILTON-PORTOBELLO SAUCE

Grand Prizewinner

Prep: 10 minutes
Cook: 20 minutes

6 (6-ounce) beef tenderloin filets
2 teaspoons chopped fresh tarragon
½ teaspoon freshly ground pepper
5 tablespoons butter or margarine,
   divided
8 ounces portobello mushroom caps,
   sliced
⅓ cup dry red wine *
½ cup sour cream
3 ounces Stilton or blue cheese,
   crumbled and divided
Garnish: fresh tarragon sprigs

• **Rub** filets evenly with chopped tarragon and pepper.
• **Melt** 2 tablespoons butter in a large skillet over medium-high heat.
• **Cook** filets 4 to 5 minutes on each side or to desired degree of doneness. Remove from skillet, and keep warm.
• **Melt** remaining 3 tablespoons butter in skillet. Add sliced mushrooms, and sauté 3 to 4 minutes or until tender.
• **Add** wine, and cook 1 to 2 minutes, stirring to loosen particles from bottom of skillet. Stir in sour cream.
• **Sprinkle** ¼ cup cheese into sauce, stirring until melted.
• **Arrange** filets on a serving platter, and drizzle with sauce. Sprinkle with remaining cheese. Garnish, if desired. **Yield:** 6 servings.

*Substitute beef broth for wine, if desired.

Diane Sparrow
Osage, Iowa

MOROCCAN CHICKEN

Runner-up

Prep: 5 minutes
Cook: 20 minutes

4 small skinned and boned chicken
   breast halves, cut into 1-inch cubes
1 tablespoon olive oil
3 cups salsa
½ cup raisins
¼ cup sliced ripe olives
2 tablespoons honey
1 teaspoon ground cinnamon
½ teaspoon ground cumin

• **Cook** chicken in hot oil in a Dutch oven over medium-high heat 5 minutes or until chicken is done. Stir in remaining ingredients. Reduce heat to low, and simmer 15 minutes. **Yield:** 4 servings.

Marcia Walker
Toccoa, Georgia

BEEF TENDERLOIN FILETS WITH GREEN PEPPERCORN SAUCE

Runner-up

Prep: 15 minutes
Cook: 55 minutes

2 tablespoons butter or margarine
2 (8-ounce) beef tenderloin filets
2 cups Marsala wine
1 cup chicken broth
20 green peppercorns
2 cups whipping cream
⅛ teaspoon Dijon mustard

• **Melt** butter in a large skillet over medium-high heat. Add filets, and cook 6 minutes on each side or to desired degree of doneness. Remove filets from skillet, and keep warm.
• **Add** wine, broth, and peppercorns to skillet; cook 20 minutes or until liquid is reduced by half. Stir in cream and mustard; cook 20 minutes or until liquid is reduced by half. Return filets to skillet, and serve warm. **Yield:** 2 servings.

Debbie Cleveland
Verona, Wisconsin

Make-Ahead Main-Dish Casseroles

Janice Cotten developed this rich casserole the year she received a crêpe maker for Christmas. "We were living on the Gulf Coast, and lots of seafood was available," she says. "We love crab and shrimp, so I put them together in a crêpe."

SHELLFISH CRÊPES IN WINE-CHEESE SAUCE

Grand Prizewinner

Prep: 1 hour
Chill: 3 hours
Stand: 30 minutes
Bake: 20 minutes

½ cup butter or margarine, divided
2 cups chopped cooked shrimp (about 1 pound)
1 cup (8 ounces) fresh crabmeat
2 green onions, minced
¼ cup dry vermouth*
⅛ teaspoon salt
¼ teaspoon pepper
½ tablespoon butter or margarine, melted
Wine-Cheese Sauce
Crêpes
2 cups (8 ounces) shredded Swiss cheese

● Melt ¼ cup butter in a large skillet over medium-high heat. Add shrimp, crabmeat, and green onions; sauté 1 minute. Stir in vermouth, salt, and pepper. Bring to a boil, and cook 7 minutes or until most of liquid is absorbed. Remove from heat, and set aside.
● Drizzle ½ tablespoon melted butter into a 13- x 9-inch baking dish. Stir 2 cups Wine-Cheese Sauce into shrimp mixture. Spoon about 3 tablespoons shrimp mixture down center of each Crêpe. Roll up; place, seam side down, in dish. Spoon remaining Wine-Cheese

Sauce over Crêpes. Sprinkle with Swiss cheese, and dot with remaining ¼ cup butter. Cover and chill 3 hours. Let stand at room temperature 30 minutes.
● Bake at 450° for 20 minutes or until thoroughly heated. **Yield:** 12 servings.

Wine-Cheese Sauce

Prep: 10 minutes
Cook: 10 minutes

¼ cup cornstarch
¼ cup milk
⅓ cup dry vermouth*
3 cups whipping cream
¼ teaspoon salt
¼ teaspoon pepper
2 cups (8 ounces) shredded Swiss cheese

● Whisk together cornstarch and milk.
● Bring vermouth to a boil in a large skillet; cook until vermouth is reduced to 1 tablespoon. Remove from heat; whisk in cornstarch mixture.
● Add whipping cream, salt, and pepper; cook over medium-high heat, whisking constantly, 2 minutes or until mixture comes to a boil. Boil 1 minute or until thickened. Add cheese. Reduce heat; simmer, whisking constantly, 1 minute or until smooth. **Yield:** 4 cups.

*Substitute clam juice, if desired.

Crêpes

Prep: 8 minutes
Chill: 1 hour
Cook: 30 minutes

4 large eggs
2 cups all-purpose flour
¼ cup butter or margarine, melted
1 cup cold water
1 cup cold milk
½ teaspoon salt

● Process all ingredients in a blender or food processor until smooth, stopping to scrape down sides. Cover; chill 1 hour.
● Place a lightly greased 8-inch non-stick skillet over medium heat until hot.
● Pour 3 tablespoons batter into skillet; quickly tilt in all directions so that batter covers bottom of skillet.

● Cook 1 minute or until crêpe can be shaken loose from skillet. Turn crêpe, and cook about 30 seconds. Repeat procedure with remaining batter. Stack crêpes between sheets of wax paper. **Yield:** 2 dozen.

Note: Prepare casserole a day ahead, if desired. Cover and chill. Let stand at room temperature 30 minutes before baking; proceed as directed.

Janice Cotten
Clifton, Texas

HEAVENLY CHICKEN LASAGNA

Runner-up

Prep: 30 minutes
Bake: 50 minutes

1 tablespoon butter or margarine
½ large onion, chopped
1 (10½-ounce) can reduced-fat cream of chicken soup, undiluted
1 (10-ounce) container refrigerated reduced-fat Alfredo sauce
1 (7-ounce) jar diced pimiento, undrained
1 (6-ounce) jar sliced mushrooms, drained
⅓ cup dry white wine
½ teaspoon dried basil
1 (10-ounce) package frozen chopped spinach, thawed
1 cup cottage cheese
1 cup ricotta cheese
½ cup grated Parmesan cheese
1 large egg, lightly beaten
9 lasagna noodles, cooked
2½ cups chopped cooked chicken
3 cups (12 ounces) shredded sharp Cheddar cheese, divided

● Melt butter in a large skillet over medium-high heat. Add onion, and sauté 5 minutes or until tender.
● Stir in soup and next 5 ingredients. Reserve 1 cup sauce.
● Drain spinach well, pressing between layers of paper towels.
● Stir together spinach, cottage cheese, and next 3 ingredients.
● Place 3 lasagna noodles in a lightly greased 13- x 9-inch baking dish. Layer

with half each of sauce, spinach mixture, and chicken. Sprinkle with 1 cup Cheddar cheese. Repeat procedure.
• **Top** with remaining 3 noodles and reserved 1 cup sauce. Cover and chill up to 1 day ahead.
• **Bake** at 350° for 45 minutes. Sprinkle with remaining 1 cup Cheddar cheese, and bake 5 more minutes or until cheese is melted. Let stand 10 minutes before serving. **Yield:** 8 to 10 servings.

Note: For testing purposes only, we used Contadina Light Alfredo Sauce. Look for it in the dairy section of the supermarket.

Judie Fielstra
Comstock Park, Michigan

POBLANO-SHRIMP ENCHILADAS

Runner-up

Prep: 35 minutes
Bake: 25 minutes

¾ **pound unpeeled, medium-size fresh shrimp**
5 **tablespoons olive oil**
1 **large poblano chile pepper, halved and seeded**
1 **large onion, chopped**
1 **tomato, chopped**
¼ **teaspoon salt**
½ **teaspoon dried oregano**
¼ **teaspoon ground cumin**
¼ **teaspoon pepper**
½ **cup sour cream**
8 **corn tortillas**
1 **(10-ounce) can green enchilada sauce**
1½ **cups (6 ounces) shredded Monterey Jack cheese**

• **Peel** shrimp; devein, if desired. Coarsely chop shrimp, and set aside.
• **Brush** an 11- x- 7-inch baking dish with 2 tablespoons oil. Set aside.
• **Sauté** poblano pepper halves in remaining oil in a large skillet over medium-high heat until skin looks blistered. Remove from skillet, and chop.
• **Return** chopped pepper to skillet. Add onion and next 5 ingredients; sauté 4 minutes. Add shrimp, and sauté 1

minute; remove from heat, and cool 5 minutes. Stir in sour cream.
• **Heat** tortillas according to package directions. Spoon shrimp mixture down centers of tortillas; roll up. Arrange, seam side down, in prepared dish. Top with enchilada sauce; sprinkle with cheese. Cover; chill up to 1 day ahead.
• **Bake** at 350° for 25 minutes or until thoroughly heated. **Yield:** 4 servings.

Jane Allen
Austin, Texas

Easy and Fresh Sides

Persis Schlosser views cooking as one of her many artistic talents, along with calligraphy and drawing. "I read lots of cookbooks and magazines," she says. "And I come across a variety of ingredients that I'd like to try. For example, I thought about pears and raspberries together and decided to combine them in a salad."

PEAR SALAD WITH RASPBERRY CREAM

Grand Prizewinner

Pears, raspberries, and Parmesan cheese enliven this salad.

Prep: 20 minutes

¾ **cup sour cream**
¼ **cup raspberry preserves**
3 **tablespoons red wine vinegar**
⅛ **teaspoon Dijon mustard**
4 **firm, ripe pears**
2 **tablespoons lemon juice**
1 **head Bibb lettuce, torn**
1 **small head Romaine lettuce, torn**
½ **cup freshly shredded Parmesan cheese**
6 **bacon slices, cooked and crumbled**
½ **cup fresh raspberries**

• **Whisk** together first 4 ingredients. Set dressing aside.
• **Peel** pears, if desired; quarter pears. Brush with lemon juice.
• **Arrange** lettuce on 4 plates. Arrange pear quarters over lettuce. Drizzle with dressing; sprinkle with cheese, bacon, and raspberries. **Yield:** 4 servings.

Persis Schlosser
Denver, Colorado

ROASTED POTATO TRIO

Runner-up

Prep: 15 minutes
Bake: 35 minutes

2½ **pounds sweet potatoes**
2 **pounds red potatoes**
1 **pound Yukon gold potatoes**
¼ **cup butter**
¼ **cup olive oil**
⅓ **cup chopped fresh rosemary**
½ **teaspoon salt**
½ **teaspoon freshly ground pepper**

• **Cut** potatoes into ½-inch-thick slices.
• **Cook** butter, oil, and rosemary in a small saucepan over medium heat, stirring until butter is melted.
• **Brush** ¼ cup butter mixture evenly over 2 baking sheets.
• **Arrange** potato slices evenly in a single layer on prepared sheets; brush with remaining butter mixture. Sprinkle with salt and pepper.
• **Bake** at 450° for 35 minutes or until golden brown. **Yield:** 8 servings.

Kristine Snyder
Kihei, Hawaii

ISRAELI COUSCOUS SALAD WITH FENNEL AND GOAT CHEESE

Runner-up

Prep: 30 minutes

1　medium fennel bulb
½　cup olive oil
½　cup lemon juice
½　cup sliced fresh basil
½　cup chopped fresh parsley
3　garlic cloves, minced
½　teaspoon salt
½　teaspoon pepper
1　red bell pepper, diced
½　cup sliced ripe olives
1　bunch green onions, chopped
1　cup Israeli couscous, cooked
6　Bibb lettuce leaves
1　(2.5-ounce) package goat cheese, crumbled
Garnish: fresh fennel fronds

• **Trim** base from fennel bulb; cut fennel bulb into thin strips, reserving fronds for garnish, if desired.
• **Whisk** together olive oil and next 6 ingredients in a large bowl.
• **Add** fennel strips, bell pepper, olives, and green onions, tossing to coat. Add couscous, and toss lightly.
• **Arrange** lettuce leaves on 6 plates. Top with couscous mixture.
• **Sprinkle** salads with goat cheese, and garnish with fennel fronds, if desired. **Yield:** 6 servings.

Gilda Lester
Wilmington, North Carolina

Perfect Pies

Linda Morten has been cooking unusual dishes since she was a teenager. Her father was in the oil business, so she grew up in Venezuela and Southeast Asia. "We had a maid who taught me to cook Malaysian and Indian foods, and my mom was an avid cook." she explains. Linda developed this luscious pie from her favorite dessert. "I love tiramisù. I was trying to figure out a way to make it a little different, so I used a ready-made pound cake to create a different crust."

TIRAMISÙ TOFFEE TRIFLE PIE

Grand Prizewinner

Prep: 30 minutes
Chill: 8 hours

1½　tablespoons instant coffee granules
¾　cup warm water
1　(10.75-ounce) frozen pound cake
1　(8-ounce) package mascarpone or cream cheese, softened
½　cup powdered sugar
½　cup chocolate syrup
1　(12-ounce) container frozen whipped topping, thawed and divided
2　(1.4-ounce) English toffee candy bars, coarsely chopped

• **Stir** together coffee granules and ¾ cup warm water until granules are dissolved. Cool.
• **Cut** cake into 14 slices. Cut each slice in half diagonally. Place cake triangles in bottom and up sides of a 9-inch deep-dish pieplate. Drizzle coffee mixture evenly over cake.
• **Beat** mascarpone cheese, sugar, and chocolate syrup at medium speed with an electric mixer until smooth.
• **Add** 2½ cups whipped topping; beat until light and fluffy. Spread cheese mixture evenly over cake. Dollop remaining whipped topping around edges of pie. Sprinkle with candy. Chill 8 hours. **Yield:** 8 to 10 servings.

Linda Morten
Katy, Texas

MASCARPONE CREAM PIE WITH BERRY GLAZE

Runner-up

Prep: 35 minutes
Bake: 15 minutes
Chill: 8 hours

6　tablespoons butter or margarine
1　(6.75-ounce) package Bordeaux cookies, crumbled
½　cup chopped pecans
¼　cup cornstarch
2　tablespoons sugar
1½　cups whipping cream
2　egg yolks, lightly beaten
1　(8-ounce) package mascarpone cheese, softened
2　teaspoons orange liqueur or fresh orange juice
1　teaspoon vanilla extract
Berry Glaze

• **Melt** butter in a saucepan over medium-high heat. Cook 3 minutes or until golden. Stir in cookie crumbs and pecans. Press into bottom and up sides of a lightly greased 9-inch tart pan.
• **Bake** at 350° for 15 minutes until golden; cool. Combine cornstarch and sugar in a saucepan; stir in cream. Cook over medium heat, stirring, until thick and bubbly. Stir ¼ cup hot mixture into yolks; add to remaining hot mixture.
• **Cook,** stirring, 1 minute. Remove from heat. Stir in cheese, liqueur, and vanilla until smooth. Pour into crust. Spread ⅔ cup glaze over filling; chill 8 hours. Serve with glaze. **Yield:** 1 (9-inch) pie.

Berry Glaze

Prep: 10 minutes

1　cup whole-berry cranberry sauce
⅓　cup seedless blackberry jam
1½　tablespoons orange liqueur or fresh orange juice
1½　teaspoons grated orange rind

• **Cook** all ingredients in a small saucepan over medium heat 5 to 7 minutes, stirring until sauce and jam melt. Strain, discarding solids. **Yield:** about 1½ cups.

Jan Curry
Raleigh, North Carolina

FUDGY CHOCOLATE MALT-PEPPERMINT PIE

Runner-up

Prep: 45 minutes
Bake: 40 minutes
Freeze: 8 hours

½ cup butter or margarine
2 (1-ounce) unsweetened chocolate
   squares
1 (1-ounce) semisweet chocolate
   square
1 cup sugar
2 large eggs
1 teaspoon vanilla extract
¼ cup all-purpose flour
¼ cup chocolate malt mix
¼ teaspoon salt
¼ teaspoon ground cinnamon
1 cup coarsely chopped pecans
1 pint peppermint ice cream, softened
1 cup whipping cream
¼ cup powdered sugar
¼ cup crushed peppermint candy

• **Melt** first 3 ingredients in a heavy saucepan over low heat, stirring occasionally until smooth. Remove from heat, and cool.
• **Beat** chocolate mixture and sugar at medium speed with an electric mixer until blended.
• **Add** eggs and vanilla, beating until smooth. Add flour and next 3 ingredients, beating until blended.
• **Stir** in pecans. Pour into a lightly greased 9-inch pieplate.
• **Bake** at 325° for 40 minutes. Remove from oven, and cool completely on a wire rack.
• **Press** down center of crust gently. Spread ice cream over crust. Cover and freeze 8 hours.
• **Beat** whipping cream and powdered sugar at medium speed with electric mixer until soft peaks form. Spread over ice cream. Sprinkle with crushed candy. **Yield:** 1 (9-inch) pie.

Note: For testing purposes only, we used Ovaltine Chocolate Malt mix.

Carol Gillespie
Chambersburg, Pennsylvania

What's for Supper?

Kids, pizza crust, and toppings—the perfect recipe for fun. These kid-friendly, tasty recipes are as easy as one, two, three. Just provide the necessary ingredients, and then sit back and watch the magic unfold as giggles and chatter fill the kitchen. (You may need to remove the hot pizza from the oven for the youngsters.)

Looking for a quick meal during this busy season that will make the whole family happy? Enjoy one of these pizzas with a twist: Cheesy Mexican and Apple-Pineapple. Or if your kids prefer more traditional toppings, we've included an easy tomato sauce recipe to use as a base for their own pizza creations. No matter which recipe they select, the young chefs will delight in preparing supper, serving the family, and cleaning up.

APPLE-PINEAPPLE DESSERT PIZZA

Prep: 25 minutes
Bake: 12 minutes

1 (10-ounce) can refrigerated pizza
   crust
1 (15¼-ounce) can crushed
   pineapple
1 (20-ounce) can apple pie filling
1 teaspoon cornstarch
¼ teaspoon ground cinnamon
¼ teaspoon ground nutmeg
1½ cups (6 ounces) shredded sharp
   Cheddar cheese
⅔ cup all-purpose flour
½ cup firmly packed brown sugar
¼ cup butter or margarine
⅓ cup finely chopped dried
   apricots

• **Press** pizza crust into a lightly greased 11- x 7-inch baking dish.
• **Bake** at 425° for 7 minutes; cool crust slightly.
• **Drain** pineapple, reserving ⅓ cup juice. Stir together pineapple and apple pie filling.
• **Stir** together reserved pineapple juice, cornstarch, cinnamon, and nutmeg; add to pineapple mixture.
• **Spoon** pineapple mixture evenly over crust; sprinkle with cheese.
• **Combine** flour and brown sugar; cut in butter with a pastry blender until crumbly.
• **Sprinkle** flour mixture over cheese. Top with dried apricots.
• **Bake** at 450° for 10 to 12 minutes or until golden. **Yield:** 8 servings.

Mary Alice Adams
Kingsport, Tennessee

PIZZA SAUCE

Prep: 15 minutes
Cook: 1 hour, 15 minutes

1 large onion, chopped
4 garlic cloves, minced
2 tablespoons olive oil
1 (28-ounce) can diced tomatoes, undrained
1 tablespoon dried Italian seasoning
1 teaspoon salt
½ teaspoon pepper

• **Sauté** onion and garlic in hot oil in a large skillet over medium heat 10 minutes or until tender. Process tomatoes in blender or food processor until smooth; stir into onion mixture. Add Italian seasoning, salt, and pepper; bring to a boil. Reduce heat; simmer 1 hour, stirring occasionally. Cool. Process in a blender, in batches, until smooth. **Yield:** 3 cups.

Adelyne Smith
Dunnville, Kentucky

CHEESY MEXICAN PIZZA

Prep: 15 minutes
Bake: 12 minutes

1 (16-ounce) Italian bread shell
1 cup refried beans
½ cup sour cream
¼ cup black bean dip
1 (14½-ounce) can diced tomatoes
2 cups (8 ounces) shredded Cheddar cheese
1 cup (4 ounces) shredded Monterey Jack cheese with peppers

• **Place** bread shell on a baking sheet. Stir together refried beans, sour cream, and bean dip; spread over bread shell.
• **Drain** tomatoes, and pat dry with paper towels; spoon over bean mixture. Sprinkle with cheeses.
• **Bake** at 450° for 10 to 12 minutes or until cheese melts. **Yield:** 4 servings.

Note: To lighten recipe, use fat-free refried beans, fat-free or light sour cream, and reduced-fat cheeses.

Allison Cook
Summerville, South Carolina

Christmas Eve Dinner

Invite friends to share a joyful—and simple—Christmas Eve supper with your family. A little jump-start preparation will help you save precious time. Just follow the make-ahead suggestions and shortcuts.

Company's Coming
Serves 6

Orange-Cranberry Glazed Pork Tenderloins
Creamy Mashed Potatoes
Green salad or Green Beans With Shallots

ORANGE-CRANBERRY GLAZED PORK TENDERLOINS

Prepare cranberry basting sauce up to eight hours ahead; then cover and chill.

Prep: 35 minutes
Bake: 40 minutes

1 (16-ounce) can whole-berry cranberry sauce
1 teaspoon grated orange rind
⅔ cup fresh orange juice
2 teaspoons balsamic vinegar
⅛ teaspoon salt
½ teaspoon pepper
¼ teaspoon ground allspice
⅛ teaspoon ground cinnamon
⅛ teaspoon ground cloves
1½ pounds pork tenderloins, trimmed
Garnishes: fresh rosemary sprigs, whole cranberries

• **Bring** first 9 ingredients to a boil in a large saucepan. Reduce heat, and simmer, stirring occasionally, 20 minutes.
• **Place** pork in a lightly greased, shallow roasting pan.
• **Bake** at 425° for 40 minutes or until a meat thermometer inserted into thickest portion registers 160°, basting occasionally with half of cranberry mixture.
• **Slice** pork, and serve with remaining cranberry mixture. Garnish, if desired. **Yield:** 6 servings.

Joan Hadley
Charlotte, North Carolina

CREAMY MASHED POTATOES

To make this easy recipe even easier, substitute enough frozen mashed potatoes to serve six.

Prep: 25 minutes

5 pounds red potatoes, peeled and cut into 1-inch pieces
¼ teaspoon salt
1 (10-ounce) container refrigerated Alfredo sauce
½ cup butter or margarine
½ teaspoon salt
¼ teaspoon pepper

• **Cook** potato and ¼ teaspoon salt in boiling water to cover 15 to 20 minutes or until potato is tender; drain.
• **Stir** in remaining ingredients; mash with a potato masher until mixture is smooth. **Yield:** 6 servings.

Note: For testing purposes only, we used Contadina Alfredo Sauce, found in the dairy section of the supermarket.

Linda Rowan
Jonesboro, Georgia

GREEN BEANS WITH SHALLOTS

Get up to an eight-hour jump start: Steam green beans, drain, and chill in a large heavy-duty zip-top plastic bag.

Prep: 20 minutes
Cook: 15 minutes

1½ pounds fresh green beans, trimmed
3 tablespoons butter or margarine
2 small shallots, minced
1 large tomato, chopped
¼ teaspoon beef bouillon granules
¼ teaspoon salt
¼ teaspoon pepper

• **Arrange** green beans in a steamer basket over boiling water. Cover and steam 5 to 7 minutes. Plunge into ice water to stop the cooking process; drain.

• **Melt** butter in a large skillet over medium heat; add shallots, and sauté 3 minutes or until tender.
• **Add** green beans, tomato, and remaining ingredients.
• **Cook** 5 minutes or until heated. Serve immediately. **Yield:** 6 servings.

Della Taylor
Jonesborough, Tennessee

A Taste of the South

One of Editor John Floyd's fondest Christmas memories is his mother's worn brown notebook full of handwritten family recipes. As he was growing up, it served as her "cooking bible," the place where she stored her legendary divinity recipe. It was his job to push a pecan half into the middle of each piece as it cooled. This white, crumbly confection is a sweet reminiscence of the holiday season.

MRS. FLOYD'S DIVINITY

Prep: 30 minutes
Cook: 20 minutes

2½ cups sugar
½ cup water
½ cup light corn syrup
¼ teaspoon salt
2 egg whites
1 teaspoon vanilla extract
1 cup chopped pecans, toasted
Garnish: toasted pecan halves

• **Cook** first 4 ingredients in a heavy 2-quart saucepan over low heat until sugar dissolves and a candy thermometer registers 248° (about 15 minutes). Remove from heat.
• **Beat** egg whites at high speed with an electric mixer until stiff peaks form. Pour half of hot syrup in a thin stream over egg whites, beating constantly at high speed, about 5 minutes.

• **Cook** remaining half of syrup over medium heat, stirring occasionally, until a candy thermometer registers 272° (about 4 to 5 minutes). Slowly pour hot syrup and vanilla over egg white mixture, beating constantly at high speed until mixture holds its shape (about 6 to 8 minutes). Stir in chopped pecans.
• **Drop** mixture quickly by rounded teaspoonfuls onto lightly greased wax paper. Garnish, if desired. Cool. **Yield:** 4 dozen (1¾ pounds).

Louise Floyd
Selma, Alabama

MAKE IT PERFECT

Test Kitchen staffer Vie Warshaw learned the art of making divinity from her grandmother. She shares these tips in preparing this delicate candy.

Step 1: Syrup mixture should bubble on the surface. Keep an eye on the thermometer; the temperature rises quickly.

Step 2: The process used when beating egg whites is as important as cooking at the proper temperature. Start with a clean bowl. Any greasy residue can reduce the volume of beaten egg whites. When the whites are beaten properly, stiff peaks will form.

Step 3: Pour in the syrup mixture in a slow stream, beating constantly.

Step 4: Use a butter wrapper to lightly grease wax paper. Get a partner to help to drop candy. Each of you should use two teaspoons, dipping from the bottom of the bowl and working gradually to the top. (The candy starts to harden first from the bottom of the bowl.)

Shrimp Style

Al Mahfouz, owner of Bon Appétit Catering in Louisiana, uses this highly rated recipe for special occasions.

CURRY-GINGER SHRIMP

Prep: 50 minutes
Cook: 55 minutes

3 pounds unpeeled, large fresh shrimp
1 cup water
¾ cup port wine, divided
6 to 8 large garlic cloves, minced
2 tablespoons minced fresh ginger
2 teaspoons red wine vinegar
¼ cup butter or margarine, divided
¼ cup peanut oil, divided
1 teaspoon salt, divided
¼ teaspoon pepper
4 green onions, chopped
1 tablespoon curry powder
½ teaspoon hot sauce
¼ cup dry white wine
½ cup whipping cream
10 ounces fresh baby spinach
6 cups hot cooked basmati rice

• **Peel** shrimp, and devein, if desired, reserving shells; set shrimp aside. Bring shells and 1 cup water to a boil in a skillet over medium-high heat; boil 20 minutes. Strain stock, reserving ½ cup; discard remaining stock and shells.
• **Bring** ⅓ cup port wine and next 3 ingredients to a boil in a skillet over medium-high heat; boil 5 to 7 minutes or until reduced to 2 tablespoons.
• **Melt** 2 tablespoons butter with 2 tablespoons oil in a large skillet over medium-high heat. Add shrimp, ½ teaspoon salt, and pepper; sauté 6 to 8 minutes or just until shrimp turn pink. Remove from skillet, and keep warm.
• **Add** green onions, curry powder, and hot sauce to skillet; sauté over medium-high heat 1 minute. Stir in shrimp stock, remaining port wine, and white wine; cook 8 minutes or until reduced by half. Stir in cream; cook 4 minutes or until

reduced by half. Stir in reserved 2 tablespoons wine reduction and remaining butter. Add shrimp; cook until heated.
• **Sauté** spinach in remaining hot oil 1 minute; sprinkle with remaining salt. Serve with shrimp mixture and hot cooked rice. **Yield:** 6 to 8 servings.

Living Light

Double these recipes, enjoy a comforting meal tonight, and freeze the other batch for when you don't have time to cook. Freeze soups in small containers for individual portions and quick thawing.

OVEN-BAKED SPLIT PEA-AND-LENTIL SOUP

Prep: 20 minutes
Bake: 2 hours

2 (32-ounce) containers low-sodium, fat-free chicken broth
1 cup dried split peas
1 cup dried lentils
4 carrots, sliced
4 celery ribs, sliced
2 medium-size red bell peppers, chopped
2 onions, chopped
2 bay leaves
½ teaspoon salt
1½ teaspoons ground cumin
1 teaspoon pepper
¼ cup plain fat-free yogurt
¼ cup chopped cucumber

• **Combine** first 11 ingredients in an ovenproof Dutch oven.
• **Bake**, covered, at 350° for 2 hours or until peas and lentils are tender. Discard bay leaves. Serve with yogurt and cucumber. **Yield:** 8 cups.

Schley Sharpley
Atlanta, Georgia

♥ Per cup: Calories 231 (4% from fat)
Fat 0.9g (sat 0.1g, mono 0.2g, poly 0.4g)
Protein 15g Carb 40g Fiber 6.8g
Chol 0mg Iron 4.2mg
Sodium 196mg Calc 72mg

ITALIAN-STYLE BEEF-AND-PEPPERONI SOUP

Prep: 25 minutes
Cook: 45 minutes

1 pound extra-lean ground beef
1 cup sliced turkey pepperoni (3 ounces)
Vegetable cooking spray
1 cup sliced fresh mushrooms
1 green bell pepper, chopped
1 bunch green onions, chopped
2 garlic cloves, minced
1 teaspoon olive oil
2 tablespoons tomato paste
1 (28-ounce) can crushed tomatoes
4 cups low-sodium, fat-free chicken broth
1 tablespoon chopped fresh or 1 teaspoon dried basil
1 tablespoon chopped fresh or 1 teaspoon dried oregano
1 teaspoon freshly ground pepper
Garnishes: sliced fresh basil, shredded Parmesan cheese
Parmesan Toast Points (optional)

• **Cook** ground beef and turkey pepperoni in a Dutch oven coated with cooking spray over medium-high heat 8 minutes or until beef crumbles and is no longer pink. Rinse and drain beef mixture; set aside.
• **Sauté** mushrooms and next 3 ingredients in hot oil in Dutch oven 5 minutes.
• **Stir** in beef mixture, tomato paste, and next 5 ingredients. Bring to a boil; reduce heat, and simmer 30 minutes. If desired, garnish and serve with Parmesan Toast Points. **Yield:** 10 cups.

Diana Highter
Huntersville, North Carolina

♥ Per cup (not including toast points):
Calories 147 (43% from fat)
Fat 7g (sat 2.7g, mono 2.7g, poly 0.3g)
Protein 13g Carb 6.1g Fiber 0.7g
Chol 40mg Iron 1.7mg
Sodium 289mg Calc 35mg

Parmesan Toast Points: Cut 1 small sourdough loaf into thin wedges. Arrange wedges on baking sheet. Sprinkle evenly with shredded Parmesan cheese. Bake at 400° for 5 minutes or until lightly browned.

SWEET POTATO-AND-PEAR BISQUE

Prep: 15 minutes
Cook: 20 minutes

½ onion, chopped
1 teaspoon olive oil
2¼ cups low-sodium, fat-free chicken broth
¼ to ½ teaspoon dried sage
1 (15-ounce) can sweet potato pieces, drained
1 (15-ounce) can lite pear halves, undrained
¼ teaspoon salt
Spiced Croutons

• **Sauté** onion in hot oil in a saucepan over medium-high heat 7 minutes or until tender.
• **Add** broth and sage. Bring to a boil; reduce heat, and simmer 5 minutes. Cool slightly.
• **Process** broth mixture, sweet potato pieces, pear halves, and salt in a blender, in batches, (or with a handheld blender) until smooth.
• **Cook** mixture in a Dutch oven over medium-high heat 5 minutes or until thoroughly heated. Serve with Spiced Croutons. **Yield:** 4 cups.

Demetra Economos Anas
Potomac, Maryland

Spiced Croutons

Prep: 5 minutes
Bake: 15 minutes

½ (8-ounce) French bread loaf, cubed
Vegetable cooking spray
¼ teaspoon apple pie spice

• **Coat** bread cubes evenly with cooking spray. Place cubes in a zip-top plastic bag; add apple pie spice. Seal bag, and shake to coat. Arrange bread cubes on a baking sheet.
• **Bake** at 375° for 10 to 15 minutes or until browned. Cool. **Yield:** 4 servings.

♥ Per cup: Calories 262 (13% from fat)
Fat 3.7g (sat 0.5g, mono 1.2g, poly 1.3g)
Protein 5g Carb 52g Fiber 5.3g
Chol 0mg Iron 2.1mg
Sodium 386mg Calc 55mg

CHEDDAR CHEESE LOAF

Prep: 5 minutes
Bake: 45 minutes

3¾ cups reduced-fat baking mix
¾ cup reduced-fat shredded sharp Cheddar cheese
1½ cups fat-free milk
¼ cup egg substitute
⅛ to ¼ teaspoon ground red pepper
Vegetable cooking spray

• **Combine** baking mix and cheese. Add milk, egg substitute, and pepper, stirring 2 minutes or until blended.
• **Spoon** into a 9- x 5-inch loafpan coated with cooking spray.
• **Bake** loaf at 350° for 45 minutes. **Yield:** 1 loaf.

Marsha Tennant
Falmouth, Virginia

♥ Per serving: Calories 157 (20% from fat)
Fat 3.5g (sat 0.5g, mono 2g, poly 1g)
Protein 6g Carb 27g Fiber 0.9g
Chol 2mg Iron 1.3mg
Sodium 534mg Calc 122mg

QUICK BREADSTICKS

Prep: 5 minutes
Bake: 25 minutes

1 cup nonfat buttermilk
1 egg white
½ cup uncooked quick-cooking cream of wheat
½ cup all-purpose flour
1½ teaspoons baking powder
½ teaspoon salt
1½ teaspoons vegetable oil
Vegetable cooking spray

• **Stir** together first 7 ingredients until blended. Spoon batter evenly into a cast-iron corn stick pan coated with cooking spray (filling to top).
• **Bake** at 450° for 20 to 25 minutes or until golden. **Yield:** 8 sticks.

Rachel Taylor
Wadley, Alabama

♥ Per breadstick: Calories 88 (12% from fat)
Fat 1.2g (sat 0.2g, mono 0.3g, poly 0.4g)
Protein 3.5g Carb 16g Fiber 0.4g
Chol 1mg Iron 0.8mg
Sodium 246mg Calc 71mg

Quick & Easy

Half the fun of having a large turkey or ham during the holidays is enjoying a sandwich or casserole using the leftovers. These creative recipes will make tasty additions to your table.

Turkey Tetrazzini

Prep: 25 minutes
Bake: 30 minutes

3 bacon slices
1 small onion, chopped
½ green bell pepper, chopped
¼ cup milk
1 (10¾-ounce) can cream of mushroom soup, undiluted
1 (8-ounce) loaf pasteurized prepared cheese product, cubed
2 cups chopped cooked turkey or chicken
8 ounces spaghetti, cooked
1 (2-ounce) jar diced pimiento, drained

• **Cook** bacon in a large skillet until crisp; remove from skillet, reserving 2 tablespoons drippings in pan. Crumble bacon, and set aside.
• **Add** onion and bell pepper to drippings, and sauté 2 minutes or until tender. Stir in milk, soup, and cheese; cook, stirring constantly, until blended.
• **Stir** in turkey, spaghetti, and pimiento. Spoon into a lightly greased 2-quart baking dish.
• **Bake** at 375° for 30 minutes or until thoroughly heated. Sprinkle with reserved bacon. **Yield:** 4 servings.

Kim Slocumb
Lawrenceville, Georgia

Herbed Potatoes With Ham

Prep: 15 minutes
Cook: 30 minutes

2 pounds new potatoes
2 tablespoons butter or margarine
1 small leek, sliced
1 medium onion, sliced and separated into rings
1 cup chopped cooked ham
3 tablespoons all-purpose flour
2 tablespoons water
1½ cups beef broth
¼ teaspoon pepper
3 tablespoons chopped fresh parsley
3 tablespoons chopped fresh chives
1 tablespoon lemon juice
1 teaspoon chopped fresh dill or ¼ teaspoon dried dillweed
1 teaspoon chopped fresh or ¼ teaspoon dried tarragon
¼ cup shredded Parmesan cheese

• **Cook** potatoes in boiling water to cover 15 to 20 minutes or until tender; drain. Peel and slice potatoes; set aside.
• **Melt** butter in a large skillet over medium heat; add leek, onion, and ham, and sauté 5 to 7 minutes or until leek is tender.
• **Stir** together flour and 2 tablespoons water. Add flour mixture, broth, and pepper to leek mixture. Cook over medium heat, stirring occasionally, until thickened and bubbly.
• **Stir** in parsley and next 4 ingredients. Stir in potato. Sprinkle with cheese. **Yield:** 4 servings.

Nancy Crotty
Conyers, Georgia

Turkey Wraps

Prep: 25 minutes

4 (10-inch) flour tortillas
¾ cup whole-berry cranberry sauce
2 tablespoons spicy brown mustard
2 cups chopped cooked turkey
¼ cup chopped pecans, toasted
2 green onions, diced
2 tablespoons minced crystallized ginger
2 cups shredded lettuce

• **Heat** tortillas according to package directions. Combine cranberry sauce and mustard; spoon down centers of tortillas. Combine turkey and next 3 ingredients; spoon over cranberry mixture. Top with lettuce; roll up. **Yield:** 4 servings.

Janice Elder
Charlotte, North Carolina

Hot Brown Soup

Prep: 10 minutes
Cook: 15 minutes

¼ cup butter or margarine
¼ cup minced onion
¼ cup all-purpose flour
½ teaspoon garlic salt
⅛ teaspoon hot sauce
4 cups milk
1 cup (4 ounces) shredded sharp Cheddar cheese
½ cup chopped cooked ham
½ cup chopped cooked turkey
Toppings: cooked and crumbled bacon, chopped tomato, chopped fresh parsley

• **Melt** butter in a Dutch oven over medium heat; add onion. Sauté until tender. Add flour, garlic salt, and hot sauce.
• **Cook,** stirring constantly, 1 minute. Gradually stir in milk; cook until thickened and bubbly. Reduce heat; stir in cheese until melted.
• **Add** ham and turkey; cook, stirring occasionally, until thoroughly heated. (Do not boil.) Serve with desired toppings. **Yield:** 5 cups.

Paula McHargue
Richmond, Kentucky

Discover Mincemeat

Mincemeat—a tangy preserve of fruits, nuts, and spices mellowed in liquor—is good in both sweet and savory dishes.

Marilyn Rush proudly declares her Holiday Mincemeat Cheesecake has "more personality than other cakes and pies." Share her passion for mincemeat with this cheesecake or a savory fruit stuffing this season.

HOLIDAY MINCEMEAT CHEESECAKE

Prep: 30 minutes
Bake: 1 hour
Stand: 30 minutes
Chill: 8 hours

2 cups graham cracker crumbs
⅓ cup butter or margarine, melted
¼ cup sugar
½ cup cinnamon-covered raisins (optional)
3 (8-ounce) packages cream cheese, softened
1 cup sugar
4 large eggs
1 tablespoon grated orange rind
1 tablespoon fresh orange juice
1 (8-ounce) container sour cream
1 cup prepared mincemeat

• **Stir** together first 3 ingredients and, if desired, raisins. Press mixture into bottom and 1½ inches up sides of a 9-inch springform pan.
• **Beat** together cream cheese and 1 cup sugar at medium speed with an electric mixer until fluffy.
• **Add** eggs, 1 at a time, beating until blended after each addition.
• **Add** orange rind, juice, and sour cream, beating until blended. Spoon mixture into prepared crust.

• **Bake** at 350° for 1 hour or until center is firm. Turn oven off. Let cheesecake stand in oven, with oven door closed, 30 minutes.
• **Spread** mincemeat over cheesecake. Chill 8 hours. **Yield:** 12 to 14 servings.
Marilyn Rush
Sioux City, Iowa

MINCEMEAT STUFFING

Prep: 15 minutes
Bake: 40 minutes

1 (16-ounce) stale French bread loaf
3 tablespoons butter or margarine
1 large onion, chopped
2 celery ribs, chopped
2 cups prepared mincemeat
½ cup chopped pecans, toasted
⅓ cup dry white wine
3 tablespoons chopped fresh parsley
1 tablespoon chopped fresh or 1 teaspoon dried sage
1 teaspoon salt
½ teaspoon pepper
2 large eggs, lightly beaten

• **Cut** bread into 1-inch cubes; place in a large bowl, and set aside.
• **Melt** butter in a large skillet over medium heat. Add chopped onion and celery, and sauté 5 to 7 minutes or until onion is tender.
• **Add** onion mixture to bread cubes. Stir in remaining ingredients.
• **Spoon** mixture into a lightly greased 2-quart baking dish.
• **Bake** at 350° for 35 to 40 minutes or until set in center. **Yield:** 6 to 8 servings.

VARIETY OF SPICE

During the holidays, most grocery stores carry two varieties of mincemeat: the kind that's ready to use in the jar and the condensed box variety. In most recipes, either one can be used. Reconstitute the condensed variety with water, following directions on the back of the box. Store mincemeat unopened in your pantry for a year. Once opened, it can be refrigerated for up to three to four days.

Don't leave any mincemeat in the jar—try these suggestions.

■ Dollop over ice cream, and serve with a butter cookie.

■ Brush over baked ham or poultry before serving.

■ Layer between pudding or cake pieces for festive parfaits.

■ Spoon in center of baked whole apples, and serve with cream.

■ Stir into savory stuffings for flavor and moistness.

Top-Rated Menu

Elegant entertaining is easier than you think with this classic menu. Just follow "Cook's Notes" on the right.

A Top-Rated Holiday Menu
Serves 8

Chutneyed Beef Tenderloin
Roasted Vegetables
Green Bean, Walnut, and Feta Salad
Tiramisù Toffee Trifle Pie (recipe on page 312)
Wynns Cabernet-Shiraz-Merlot blend
Clos du Bois Cabernet Sauvignon

COOK'S NOTES

Follow this guide, and you'll be ready before your guests arrive.

The day before:
■ Prepare beef broth reduction, and puree vegetables for beef tenderloin; place in separate containers, and refrigerate.

■ Prepare Tiramisù Toffee Trifle Pie; refrigerate.

■ Prepare Wine Reduction Sauce; refrigerate.

2½ hours before:
■ Steam green beans; toss with onion, cheese, and walnuts. Cover and chill.

■ Prepare vinaigrette for salad. Cover and chill.

1½ hours before:
■ Prepare tenderloin.

■ Prepare vegetables for roasting; place on roasting pan. Bake tenderloin and vegetables at the same time.

■ Pour vinaigrette over salad; cover and chill. Toss before serving.

CHUTNEYED BEEF TENDERLOIN

1994 Recipe Hall of Fame

Prep: 20 minutes
Cook: 45 minutes
Bake: 40 minutes

4 cups ready-to-serve, reduced-sodium beef broth
1 onion, quartered
1 carrot, chopped
1 celery rib, chopped
1 (9-ounce) jar hot mango chutney
1 tablespoon butter or margarine, melted
1 teaspoon salt
½ teaspoon coarsely ground pepper
1 (5- to 6-pound) beef tenderloin, trimmed
Wine Reduction Sauce
3 tablespoons butter or margarine
½ teaspoon chopped fresh or
   ¼ teaspoon dried thyme
Garnishes: fresh thyme sprigs, whole shallots (see Roasted Vegetables recipe on facing page)

• **Bring** first 4 ingredients to a boil in a saucepan over medium heat. Reduce heat; simmer 40 minutes or until mixture is reduced to about 1½ cups.

• **Pour** broth reduction mixture through a wire-mesh strainer into a bowl, reserving vegetables; cover mixture, and chill, if desired.

• **Process** reserved vegetables in a food processor until smooth; cover and chill, if desired.

• **Stir** together chutney and next 3 ingredients in a bowl.

• **Spread** half of chutney mixture evenly over tenderloin.

• **Place** tenderloin on a rack in a shallow roasting pan.

• **Bake** at 450° for 20 minutes. Remove from oven, and spread remaining chutney mixture over tenderloin.

• **Bake** 10 to 20 more minutes or until a meat thermometer inserted into thickest portion registers 145° (medium-rare) to 160° (medium).

• **Remove** tenderloin from pan, and let stand 15 minutes before slicing. Remove rack from pan.

• **Add** reserved beef broth reduction to pan. Bring to a boil over medium heat, stirring to loosen browned particles from bottom of pan; pour into a large saucepan.

• **Stir** Wine Reduction Sauce and reserved vegetable puree into saucepan.

• **Bring** mixture to a boil; reduce heat, and simmer, stirring frequently, 5 minutes. Whisk in 3 tablespoons butter, 1 tablespoon at a time. Stir in chopped thyme.

• **Serve** sauce with sliced tenderloin. Garnish, if desired. **Yield:** 12 servings.

Wine Reduction Sauce

Prep: 5 minutes
Cook: 40 minutes

1 (750-milliliter) bottle Cabernet
    Sauvignon
3 small shallots, minced
1 bay leaf
3 or 4 fresh thyme sprigs

• **Bring** all ingredients to a boil in a large saucepan over medium heat. Reduce heat, and simmer until liquid is reduced to about 1 cup (40 minutes).
• **Pour** mixture through a wire-mesh strainer into a measuring cup, pressing with back of a spoon to remove all juices. Discard solids. Cover and chill, if desired. **Yield:** 1 cup.

ROASTED VEGETABLES

1998 Recipe Hall of Fame

Prep: 25 minutes
Bake: 40 minutes

2 pounds beets, peeled and
    quartered
½ cup olive oil, divided
¼ cup chopped fresh rosemary
2 teaspoons coarse-grain sea salt,
    divided
½ teaspoon pepper, divided
2 pounds carrots with tops
8 shallots
2 pounds new potatoes, halved
8 small turnips, peeled and
    quartered

• **Place** beet quarters on a 12-inch square piece of aluminum foil. Drizzle with 2 tablespoons oil; sprinkle with rosemary, ½ teaspoon salt, and ¼ teaspoon pepper. Fold up sides, forming a bowl; place bowl in 1 end of a large roasting pan.
• **Cut** tops from carrots, leaving 2-inch stems. Scrape carrots, and set aside.
• **Cut** an "X" in top of 4 unpeeled shallots; cut remaining 4 shallots in half lengthwise.
• **Toss** together carrots, shallots, potato halves, turnip, remaining 6 tablespoons

oil, remaining 1½ teaspoons salt, and remaining ¼ teaspoon pepper. Place on opposite end of roasting pan.
• **Bake** at 450° for 40 minutes or until vegetables are tender. Garnish beef tenderloin with whole shallots, if desired. **Yield:** 8 servings.

GREEN BEAN, WALNUT, AND FETA SALAD

1996 Recipe Hall of Fame

Prep: 15 minutes
Cook: 15 minutes
Chill: 2 hours

2 pounds fresh green beans,
    trimmed
1 small purple onion, thinly sliced
1 (4-ounce) package crumbled feta
    cheese
1 cup coarsely chopped walnuts or
    pecans, toasted
¾ cup olive oil
¼ cup white wine vinegar
1 tablespoon chopped fresh dill
½ teaspoon minced garlic
¼ teaspoon salt
¼ teaspoon pepper

• **Cut** green beans into thirds, and arrange in a steamer basket over boiling water. Cover and steam 15 minutes or until crisp-tender. Immediately plunge into cold water to stop the cooking process; drain and pat dry.
• **Toss** together green beans, onion, cheese, and walnuts in a large bowl. Cover and chill 1 hour.
• **Whisk** together olive oil and next 5 ingredients; cover and chill 1 hour.
• **Pour** vinaigrette over green bean mixture, cover and chill 1 hour; toss just before serving. **Yield:** 8 servings.

Fabulous Fennel

What looks similar to celery and has a flavor reminiscent of licorice? It's fennel. Cooked or raw, this versatile vegetable with feathery green leaves adds a vibrant touch to chicken, fish, and salads.

Sliced, raw fennel has a crunchy, celerylike texture and a pronounced anise taste that's a terrific addition to salads and crudités. When roasted, braised, or sautéed, the fibrous stems soften and become much more subtle in flavor. Snip the dainty leaves as a garnish or last-minute flavor boost.

When selecting fennel, look for firm bulbs that are light green to white with no signs of browning or cracking. Fennel doesn't store well, so refrigerate in a zip-top plastic bag for up to five days.

FENNEL-AND-APPLE SALAD

Prep: 20 minutes
Chill: 1 hour

1 fennel bulb
1 Granny Smith apple, thinly sliced
¼ cup chopped pecans, toasted
2 tablespoons lemon juice
2 tablespoons olive oil
⅛ teaspoon salt
⅛ teaspoon pepper
⅓ cup shredded Parmesan cheese
10 juniper berries, crushed and finely
    chopped (optional)
Garnish: fresh fennel fronds

• **Trim** base from fennel bulb; cut bulb in half, and thinly slice, reserving fennel fronds for garnish.
• **Stir** together fennel, apple, and next 5 ingredients.
• **Stir** in cheese, and, if desired, juniper berries. Cover and chill 1 hour. Garnish, if desired. **Yield:** 4 servings.

Marcus Marshall
Alpharetta, Georgia

PUREE OF WINTER VEGETABLE SOUP

Prep: 25 minutes
Cook: 40 minutes

1 fennel bulb
½ onion, chopped
2 garlic cloves, minced
1 tablespoon vegetable oil
6 cups chicken broth
4 carrots, thinly sliced
3 parsnips, thinly sliced
½ teaspoon salt
½ teaspoon ground white pepper
3 medium potatoes, peeled and cubed
½ cup half-and-half
1 (19-ounce) can cannellini beans, rinsed and drained (optional)
Curried Croutons
Garnishes: fresh fennel fronds, fennel seeds

• **Trim** base from fennel bulb; dice bulb, reserving fronds for garnish.
• **Sauté** onion and garlic in hot oil in a Dutch oven over medium-high heat 5 minutes. Stir in fennel, chicken broth, and next 4 ingredients; bring to a boil. Cover, reduce heat, and simmer 10 minutes. Add potato; cover and simmer 20 minutes or until vegetables are tender.
• **Process** soup, in batches, in a blender or food processor until smooth, stopping to scrape down sides.
• **Stir** in half-and-half and, if desired, beans; cook 5 minutes or until thoroughly heated. Serve soup with Curried Croutons, and garnish, if desired **Yield:** 12 cups.

Curried Croutons

Prep: 5 minutes
Bake: 10 minutes

½ (16-ounce) Italian bread loaf, cubed
2 tablespoons olive oil
1 teaspoon curry powder

• **Toss** bread cubes with olive oil to coat; sprinkle with curry powder. Place on a lightly greased baking sheet.
• **Bake** at 350° for 8 to 10 minutes, stirring occasionally. **Yield:** 3 cups.

Julie DeMatteo
Clementon, New Jersey

ROASTED GREEN BEANS, POTATOES, AND FENNEL

Prep: 15 minutes
Bake: 45 minutes

2 fennel bulbs
1½ pounds new potatoes, thinly sliced (about 12)
½ cup olive oil
1 teaspoon fine-grain sea salt★
1½ pounds small green beans, trimmed
½ teaspoon freshly ground pepper

• **Trim** bases from fennel bulbs, and quarter bulbs.
• **Toss** together fennel, potato, and oil in a 15- x 10-inch jellyroll pan; sprinkle with salt.
• **Bake** at 425° for 30 minutes. Add green beans, and toss gently. Bake 10 to 15 more minutes or until vegetables are lightly browned. Sprinkle with pepper, and serve hot or at room temperature. **Yield:** 8 servings.

★Substitute 1 teaspoon salt for sea salt, if desired.

Beverle Grieco
Houston, Texas

CHICKEN WITH FENNEL

Prep: 30 minutes
Cook: 30 minutes

2 fennel bulbs
Seasoning Mix, divided
6 skinned and boned chicken breast halves
3 teaspoons olive oil, divided
1 purple onion, chopped
4 large carrots, coarsely shredded
1 cup reduced-sodium chicken broth
½ cup 2% reduced-fat milk
1 tablespoon anise liqueur (optional)
Parsleyed couscous
Garnish: fresh fennel fronds

• **Trim** bases from fennel bulbs; cut bulbs into thin strips, reserving fronds for garnish.

• **Sprinkle** 3 teaspoons Seasoning Mix evenly over chicken.
• **Sauté** chicken in 2 teaspoons hot oil in a large nonstick skillet over medium-high heat 3 to 4 minutes on each side or until browned. Cut into thin slices; set aside, and keep warm.
• **Sauté** fennel, onion, and carrot in remaining 1 teaspoon hot oil in a large nonstick skillet over medium heat 5 minutes or until fennel begins to soften.
• **Stir** in chicken broth and remaining 1 teaspoon Seasoning Mix; bring to a boil. Reduce heat; simmer 8 minutes.
• **Stir** in milk and, if desired, liqueur. Top with chicken; cook 6 to 8 more minutes, or until thoroughly heated. Serve with parsleyed couscous. Garnish, if desired. **Yield:** 6 servings.

Note: For testing purposes only, we used ouzo for anise liqueur.

Seasoning Mix

Prep: 5 minutes

1 teaspoon paprika
1 teaspoon freshly ground black pepper
½ teaspoon fennel seeds, crushed
½ teaspoon dried thyme, crushed
¼ teaspoon salt
¼ teaspoon celery salt
⅛ to ¼ teaspoon ground red pepper
1 garlic clove, pressed

• **Combine** all ingredients in a bowl. **Yield:** 4 teaspoons.

Shirley DeSantis
Bethlehem, Pennsylvania

Cookie Power

Fill the hearts of your family and friends with a little of Chappy Hardy's Christmas cheer—homemade cookies.

GrandLady's Cinnamon Cookies

*Chappy's late mother,
Lady Helen Hardy, was anointed
"GrandLady" by Chappy's son, Zeph.*

*Prep: 25 minutes
Bake: 25 minutes*

¾ cup butter, softened
1 cup sugar
1 egg yolk
2 cups all-purpose flour
1 tablespoon ground cinnamon
3 cups finely chopped pecans

• **Beat** first 3 ingredients at medium speed with an electric mixer 2 to 3 minutes or until light and fluffy.
• **Add** flour and cinnamon, beating well. (Dough will be stiff.)
• **Roll** dough to ⅛-inch thickness between sheets of parchment paper. Remove top sheet of parchment, and invert dough onto a lightly greased baking sheet. Remove parchment paper, and press pecans evenly into dough.
• **Bake** at 350° for 15 minutes; reduce heat to 250°, and bake 10 more minutes. Remove from oven, and cut cookies (while dough is hot), into 3- x 1½-inch rectangles, using a pizza cutter. Cool on a wire rack. **Yield:** 3 dozen.

Note: Sprinkle cookie crumbs that remain after cutting over a bowl of vanilla ice cream.

*Chappy Hardy
New Orleans, Louisiana*

COOKIE MEMORIES

For New Orleans native Chappy Hardy, Christmas had become his least favorite time of the year—that is, until last December, when a marathon cookie-baking session melted his frosty heart and rekindled his love for the holiday season.

Between a divorce and the deaths of his parents, Chappy's once childlike enthusiasm for Christmas was long gone. So when friends from Orange Beach, Alabama, asked him to house-sit, Chappy jumped at the chance to get out of town and lay low for a week.

One of the few items to make the trip with him was his mother's old looseleaf binder full of her favorite recipes—including her beloved Cinnamon Cookies and Sand Tarts. He was determined to get in the kitchen and do justice to his mother's cookie legacy.

As Chappy baked away, he remembered several of his mother's keys to success, such as allowing the butter to come to room temperature on its own and rotating the baking sheets halfway through the baking process. He also employed his mother's oven thermometer to make sure that the cookies were baking at the correct temperature.

However, something more important than baking cookies took place in that kitchen. Chappy began to remember how much Christmas had meant to him, and he recalled the wonderful childhood bond he and his mother had shared.

As the days wore on and the cookies piled up, Chappy's malaise quickly gave way to a new heartfelt understanding of the Christmas season. His newfound happiness was difficult to contain, and practically everyone within eyesight received a tin of these very special cookies. "There's nothing better than a tasty homemade gift," Chappy says.

Sand Tarts

*We were fortunate enough
to receive a batch of these
cookies from Chappy, and we're
passing along the recipe to you.*

*Prep: 20 minutes
Bake: 14 minutes per batch*

1 cup butter, softened
2 cups all-purpose flour
½ cup powdered sugar
1 tablespoon ice water
1 teaspoon vanilla extract
¼ teaspoon salt
1 cup finely chopped pecans
Powdered sugar

• **Beat** butter at medium speed with an electric mixer until light and fluffy.
• **Add** flour and next 4 ingredients, beating well. Stir in pecans.
• **Roll** dough into 1-inch balls; roll out to 3-inch logs. Shape into crescents, and place on ungreased baking sheets.
• **Bake** at 350° for 12 to 14 minutes or until lightly browned. Cool completely on wire racks.
• **Dredge** cookies in powdered sugar. **Yield:** 3 dozen.

*Chappy Hardy
New Orleans, Louisiana*

Sephardic Hanukkah

Descendants of Spanish and Portuguese Jews are called Sephardim, after "Sephard," the Hebrew word for the Iberian Peninsula. Many Sephardic Jews prepare Spanish-influenced dishes during Hanukkah, including a variety of fried foods and sweets.

As our Foods staff sampled these recipes, we all agreed that it would be a shame to reserve these tasty dishes for only Jewish holidays. They can be enjoyed at any dinner table most any time of the year. Try these unpretentious recipes before, during, or after the holidays.

WARM GARLIC VINAIGRETTE

*Prep: 10 minutes
Cook: 5 minutes*

½ cup fresh lemon juice
2 large garlic cloves, minced
2 tablespoons olive oil
1 tablespoon water
½ teaspoon salt
½ teaspoon freshly ground pepper
1½ teaspoons chopped fresh chives
1½ teaspoons minced fresh dill
1½ teaspoons minced fresh parsley
½ teaspoon sugar

• **Cook** first 6 ingredients in a small skillet over medium heat 5 minutes. Remove from heat. Stir in remaining ingredients. Serve warm with fried fish. **Yield:** ¾ cup.

Note: Vinaigrette may also be served chilled over salad greens.

SEPHARDIC-STYLE FRIED FISH

*Prep: 8 minutes
Chill: 1 hour
Fry: 10 minutes per batch*

2½ pounds small cod fillets
1½ teaspoons coarse-grain sea salt
⅔ cup cold water
1⅓ cups all-purpose flour
4 large eggs
½ teaspoon salt
¼ to ½ teaspoon freshly ground pepper
Vegetable oil
Garnishes: lemon slices, fresh dill sprigs

• **Arrange** fish fillets in a large baking dish. Sprinkle evenly on both sides with sea salt. Pour enough cold water over fish to cover. Chill 1 hour.
• **Whisk** together ⅔ cup cold water and next 4 ingredients until smooth.
• **Drain** fish, and pat dry between layers of paper towels. Dip fish in batter, allowing excess to drip off.
• **Pour** oil to depth of 1¼ inches into a Dutch oven; heat to 370°. Fry fish, in batches, 10 minutes or until golden brown. Drain on paper towels. Serve immediately. Garnish, if desired. **Yield:** 6 to 8 servings.

*Becky Ojalvo
Medellin, Colombia*

LEEK-AND-POTATO FRITTERS

*Prep: 30 minutes
Chill: 1 hour
Cook: 4 minutes per batch*

1 large russet potato, peeled and cut into 2-inch pieces (about ½ pound)
1 teaspoon salt
2 pounds leeks, thinly sliced
4 large eggs, lightly beaten
½ cup matzo meal or fine, dry breadcrumbs
⅓ cup grated Parmesan cheese
1 teaspoon salt
¾ teaspoon freshly ground pepper
½ cup canola oil
Sour cream (optional)

• **Cook** potato and 1 teaspoon salt in a Dutch oven in boiling water to cover 20 minutes or until tender; drain. Mash potato, and set aside.
• **Cook** leeks in Dutch oven in boiling water to cover 3 minutes; drain.
• **Stir** together potato, leeks, and next 5 ingredients. Chill 1 hour. Shape into 18 patties.
• **Cook**, in batches, in hot oil in a large skillet 2 minutes on each side or until golden brown. Serve immediately with sour cream, if desired. **Yield:** 18 patties.

*Beatriz Swirsky
Sunrise, Florida*

GARLIC-DILL MAYONNAISE

Prep: 10 minutes

1 cup mayonnaise ＊
2 garlic cloves, pressed
2½ teaspoons fresh lemon juice
2 teaspoons minced fresh dill
⅛ teaspoon salt
⅛ teaspoon freshly ground pepper

• **Whisk** together all ingredients in a bowl until blended. Serve with fried fish. **Yield:** 1 cup.

＊Substitute reduced-fat mayonnaise for regular mayonnaise, if desired.

*Cory Zacharia
Miami Beach, Florida*

BETTY'S BISCOCHOS

Prep: 45 minutes
Bake: 25 minutes per batch

3 large eggs
¾ cup vegetable oil
¼ cup fresh orange juice
¾ cup sugar
1 teaspoon grated orange rind
1 tablespoon baking powder
4½ to 5 cups all-purpose flour
1 large egg, lightly beaten
¼ cup sesame seeds
¼ cup sugar

• **Beat** together first 3 ingredients with an electric mixer until blended. Add sugar and rind, beating until blended.
• **Add** baking powder, beating until blended. Gradually add flour, beating until smooth. (Add only enough flour to easily roll dough between palms of hands.) Cover; let stand 10 minutes.
• **Pinch** off a small piece of dough (about 1 tablespoon); roll into a 4-inch log. Bring ends together, making a circle. Repeat with remaining dough. (Dough may also be shaped into sticks, twists, or braids.) Brush with egg.
• **Dip** tops of half of cookies in sesame seeds. Dip tops of remaining cookies in sugar. Place on lightly greased baking sheets.
• **Bake** at 350° for 20 to 25 minutes or until golden brown. Remove to wire racks to cool. **Yield:** about 3 dozen.

Beatriz Swirsky
Sunrise, Florida

Salads and Sides

No matter how you celebrate, salads and side dishes play a big role at the holiday table. If you observe Kwanza, these recipes proclaim a bountiful harvest. If you want a new starter for the big Christmas feast, serve Peanut Soup. And even if you're not entertaining, look no further than right here to find something good for supper.

SWEET POTATO FRUIT SALAD

Prep: 15 minutes
Cook: 20 minutes
Chill: 2 hours

3 medium-size sweet potatoes (about 1½ pounds) *
1 cup mayonnaise
1 teaspoon grated lemon rind
2 tablespoons orange juice
1 tablespoon fresh lemon juice
1 tablespoon honey
2 bananas, sliced
2 medium-size red apples, diced
2 cups seedless grapes
Leaf lettuce (optional)

• **Peel** sweet potatoes, and cut into 1-inch cubes. Cook in boiling water to cover 20 minutes or until tender; drain.
• **Stir** together mayonnaise and next 4 ingredients in a large bowl; chill. Gently toss together sweet potato, banana, apple, and grapes. Cover and chill 2 hours. Serve sweet potato mixture on lettuce leaves, if desired, and serve with mayonnaise mixture. **Yield:** 6 servings.

*Substitute 1 (16-ounce) can sweet potato pieces or yam pieces, drained and cubed, if desired.

Chris Bryant
Johnson City, Tennessee

MIXED FIELD PEA SALAD

Prep: 10 minutes
Chill: 8 hours

⅓ cup red wine vinegar
3 tablespoons sugar
1 tablespoon Dijon mustard
¼ teaspoon salt
½ teaspoon dried crushed red pepper
½ small purple onion, diced
⅔ cup olive oil
6 cups assorted field peas, cooked and drained

• **Whisk** together first 6 ingredients; gradually whisk in oil.
• **Toss** mixture with peas; cover and chill 8 hours. **Yield:** 8 servings.

AMBROSIA

Prep: 30 minutes
Chill: 8 hours

8 medium navel oranges
1 (8-ounce) can crushed pineapple, drained
½ cup flaked coconut
1 cup whipping cream
2 tablespoons powdered sugar
Maraschino cherries

• **Peel** and section oranges over a bowl, reserving any juice. Stir together orange sections, juice, pineapple, and coconut. Cover and chill 8 hours.
• **Beat** whipping cream until foamy; gradually add powdered sugar, beating until soft peaks form.
• **Spoon** fruit mixture into individual dishes; top each with whipped cream and a cherry. **Yield:** 4 to 6 servings.

Note: For sweeter ambrosia, stir 2 tablespoons granulated sugar into fruit mixture.

Mary Lou Edwards
Mesa, Arizona

PEANUT SOUP

Prep: 5 minutes
Cook: 45 minutes

2 tablespoons butter or margarine
2 tablespoons grated onion
1 celery rib, minced
2 tablespoons all-purpose flour
3 cups chicken broth
½ cup creamy peanut butter
½ cup half-and-half
2 tablespoons chopped roasted peanuts

• **Melt** butter in a large saucepan over medium heat; add onion and celery, and sauté 5 minutes. Stir in flour, and cook, stirring constantly, 1 minute.
• **Add** broth; bring to a boil, stirring constantly. Reduce heat; simmer 30 minutes.
• **Stir** in peanut butter and half-and-half. Cook over low heat, stirring constantly, 3 to 4 minutes or until heated. Sprinkle with peanuts. **Yield:** about 4 cups.

Sauce Savvy

No question about it—start with a great pasta or spaghetti sauce and you have the beginnings of a culinary creation. These days there are so many prepared types to choose from that a ready-made sauce is as close as your kitchen pantry. So go ahead and explore the possibilities with these simple and savory recipes. They just might set your own creative wheels in motion.

ITALIAN BURGERS

Fennel seeds, a common ingredient in Italian sausage, add a hint of sweetness to this recipe.

Prep: 15 minutes
Grill: 18 minutes

1 pound lean ground beef
1 small onion, minced
¾ cup grated Parmesan cheese
¼ cup minced fresh parsley
1 large egg, lightly beaten
2 tablespoons dried Italian
   seasoning
¾ teaspoon pepper
½ teaspoon garlic salt
¼ teaspoon fennel seeds
4 (1-ounce) provolone cheese slices
4 English muffins, split
½ cup tomato pasta sauce
Garnish: fresh basil sprigs

• **Combine** first 9 ingredients; shape into 4 patties.
• **Grill,** covered with grill lid, over medium-high heat (350° to 400°) 7 to 8 minutes on each side or until beef is no longer pink.
• **Top** patties with cheese, and grill 1 more minute or until cheese melts.
• **Place** muffins on grill, cut sides down.
• **Grill** 1 minute or until lightly toasted. Top each muffin bottom with 2 tablespoons pasta sauce, a cheese-covered patty, and muffin tops. Garnish, if desired, and serve with your favorite potato chips. **Yield:** 4 servings.
Johnsie Ford
Rockingham, North Carolina

VEGETABLE BOLOGNESE

Prep: 30 minutes
Cook: 15 minutes

½ cup dried tomatoes
½ cup boiling water
2 medium-size sweet onions, chopped
2 small zucchini, chopped
1 medium-size green bell pepper,
   chopped
1 medium-size red bell pepper,
   chopped
1 cup sliced fresh mushrooms
2 garlic cloves, minced
2 tablespoons olive oil
1 (26-ounce) jar spicy pasta sauce
½ cup chopped fresh basil
12 ounces penne pasta, cooked

• **Stir** together dried tomatoes and ½ cup boiling water in a bowl; let stand 30 minutes. Drain, chop, and set aside.
• **Sauté** onion and next 5 ingredients in hot oil in a large skillet over medium-high heat 6 to 8 minutes or until vegetables are tender. Stir in tomatoes.
• **Stir** in pasta sauce, and bring to a boil. Reduce heat; stir in basil, and simmer, stirring occasionally, 5 minutes. Serve over hot cooked pasta. **Yield:** 6 servings.

Note: For testing purposes only, we used Newman's Own Diavolo Sauce.

EXTRA-EASY LASAGNA

The ricotta cheese layers in this lasagna will be very thin.

Prep: 15 minutes
Bake: 55 minutes
Stand: 10 minutes

1 pound lean ground beef
4 cups tomato-basil pasta sauce
6 uncooked lasagna noodles
1 (15-ounce) container ricotta cheese
2½ cups (10 ounces) shredded
   mozzarella cheese
¼ cup hot water

• **Cook** beef in a large skillet over medium heat, stirring until it crumbles and is no longer pink; drain. Stir in pasta sauce.
• **Spread** one-third of meat sauce in a lightly greased 11- x 7-inch baking dish; layer with 3 noodles and half each of ricotta cheese and mozzarella cheese.
• **Repeat** procedure; spread remaining one-third of meat sauce over mozzarella cheese. Slowly pour ¼ cup hot water around inside edge of dish. Tightly cover baking dish with 2 layers of heavy-duty aluminum foil.
• **Bake** at 375° for 45 minutes; uncover and bake 10 more minutes. Let stand 10 minutes before serving. **Yield:** 6 to 8 servings.

Note: For testing purposes only, we used Classico Tomato & Basil pasta sauce.
Phyllis Hodges
Anderson, South Carolina

PASTA SHELLS FLORENTINE

Place cooked shells in cold water to keep them from drying out while you're stuffing them.

Prep: 20 minutes
Bake: 50 minutes

2 (10-ounce) packages frozen chopped
   spinach, thawed
2 (15-ounce) containers ricotta cheese
1 cup (4 ounces) shredded Parmesan,
   Romano, and Asiago cheese blend
1 (0.4-ounce) envelope buttermilk
   Ranch-style dressing mix
2 large eggs, lightly beaten
½ teaspoon pepper
26 jumbo pasta shells, cooked
4 cups marinara sauce
1 cup (4 ounces) shredded mozzarella
   cheese
¼ cup chopped fresh basil

• **Drain** spinach well, pressing between paper towels. Stir together spinach and next 5 ingredients. Spoon into shells.
• **Spread** half of marinara sauce in a lightly greased 13- x 9-inch baking dish. Arrange shells over sauce; top with remaining sauce.
• **Bake,** covered, at 350° for 40 minutes. Uncover; sprinkle with mozzarella. Bake 5 to 10 more minutes. Sprinkle with basil. **Yield:** 6 to 8 servings.

A Season for Sideboards

Whether opulently appointed or modest in design, the sideboard plays an integral part in our holiday experience by providing the space around which we dine and celebrate.

There it stands—the sideboard—at the ready for the coming Christmas season. Most of the year, save family reunions or other special get-togethers, the sideboard hibernates—its drawers and inner spaces providing a haven for china, silver, and linen and its top providing a place to arrange heirloom candlesticks, trivets, and cherished cake pedestals.

However, on Christmas day the sideboard comes alive, taking on an almost mystical presence as it's piled high with our favorite foods. And while meats such as turkey and ham remain largely traditional, side dishes usually showcase the South's diversity of cooking styles, ingredients, and regional influences. In keeping with that spirit, these reader recipes reflect the variety of side dishes gracing family sideboards throughout the South.

GRITS AND CHEESE

Prep: 5 minutes
Cook: 18 minutes

4 cups milk
1 cup uncooked quick-cooking grits
6 (¾-ounce) spreadable cheese
    wedges
1 (8-ounce) package Gruyère cheese,
    cubed
½ cup butter or margarine
1 teaspoon salt
⅛ teaspoon pepper
¼ cup grated Parmesan cheese

• **Bring** milk to a boil in a large saucepan over medium heat; gradually stir in grits. Reduce heat; simmer, stirring occasionally, 7 minutes or until thickened.
• **Stir** in cheese wedges and next 4 ingredients; simmer, stirring occasionally, 5 minutes. Sprinkle with Parmesan cheese. **Yield:** 8 servings.

Note: For testing purposes only, we used The Laughing Cow Spreadable Cheese Collection for spreadable cheese wedges.

Sue-Sue Hartstern
Louisville, Kentucky

CABERNET CRANBERRIES

Prep: 5 minutes
Cook: 22 minutes

1¼ cups sugar
1 cup Cabernet Sauvignon
1 (12-ounce) package fresh
    cranberries
2 teaspoons grated tangerine
    rind
1 (3-inch) cinnamon stick

• **Bring** sugar and wine to a boil in a saucepan over medium-high heat.
• **Add** cranberries, tangerine rind, and cinnamon stick.
• **Return** mixture to a boil, stirring constantly.

• **Reduce** heat, and simmer, partially covered, 10 to 15 minutes or until cranberry skins pop.
• **Remove** and discard cinnamon stick. Cool slightly; serve warm, or chill 2 hours, if desired. **Yield:** 3½ cups.

Note: Sauce may be stored in refrigerator up to 2 months.

Renie Steves
Fort Worth, Texas

BLACK BEAN-AND-RICE SALAD

Prep: 25 minutes
Chill: 2 hours

½ cup canola oil
¼ cup lime juice
2 cups canned black beans, rinsed
    and drained *
2 cups cooked long-grain rice
½ cup chopped onion
¼ cup chopped fresh cilantro
1 (4-ounce) jar diced pimiento,
    drained
2 garlic cloves, pressed
½ teaspoon salt
¼ teaspoon pepper

• **Whisk** together oil and lime juice in a large bowl.
• **Add** remaining ingredients; toss to coat. Cover and chill 2 hours. **Yield:** 4 to 6 servings.

* Substitute 2 cups cooked black beans, if desired.

Linda Gassenheimer
Coral Gables, Florida

The Gift of Cheese

Each of these recipe makes two portions—ideal for enjoying, sharing, and giving. Prepare the cheese in advance, and freeze enough for when you need sensational appetizers on the spot.

When given the task of creating cheese spreads, Mary Allen Perry had a ball—but not a simple ball of cheese. The Test Kitchens pro was on a roll with three flavor medleys, but her creative zest wouldn't rest with the traditional ball. She crafted the cheese in containers and shapes we thought were perfect for holiday parties. Serve the spreads from colorful crocks, bread bowls, or braids, or mold them to suit the occasion.

SMOKY GREEN CHILE-CHEDDAR CHEESE WITH AVOCADO-MANGO SALSA

Prep: 40 minutes
Chill: 8 hours

2 **(8-ounce) packages cream cheese, softened**
2 **(8-ounce) blocks Monterey Jack cheese with peppers, shredded**
16 **ounces smoked Cheddar cheese, shredded**
6 **green onions, minced**
2 **(4.5-ounce) cans chopped green chiles, drained**
1 **(1¼-ounce) envelope taco seasoning mix**
Avocado-Mango Salsa

● **Combine** first 6 ingredients in a large bowl. Divide into 2 equal portions; shape each into a 6-inch round. Cover and chill 8 hours, or freeze up to 1 month, and thaw in the refrigerator 8 hours.
● **Place** cheese rounds on serving plates; top evenly with Avocado-Mango Salsa, and serve with tortilla chips. **Yield:** 2 cheese rounds (18 appetizer servings).

Note: Find smoked Cheddar cheese in the deli section of your grocery store.

Avocado-Mango Salsa

Prep: 20 minutes
Chill: 8 hours

¼ **cup hot jalapeño jelly**
¼ **cup fresh lime juice**
2 **large mangoes, peeled and diced✱**
2 **large avocados, diced**
1 **large red bell pepper, diced**
¼ **cup chopped fresh cilantro**

● **Whisk** together jelly and lime juice in a large bowl.
● **Add** remaining ingredients; stir until blended. Cover and chill 8 hours. **Yield:** about 5 cups.

✱Substitute 1 (26-ounce) jar refrigerated mango pieces, drained, for fresh mango, if desired.

FREEZE, PLEASE

All of these spreads can be frozen. Place the ungarnished spread in an airtight container, and freeze up to one month. Thaw in the refrigerator for eight hours. Garnish, if desired.

CHICKEN-ARTICHOKE-CHEESE SPREAD GIFT BOX

Prep: 35 minutes
Chill: 8 hours

3 **cups diced cooked chicken**
2 **(8-ounce) packages cream cheese, softened**
2 **cups shredded Parmesan cheese**
1 **(14-ounce) can artichoke hearts, drained and diced**
1 **cup finely chopped pecans, toasted**
4 **green onions, minced**
1 **tablespoon lemon juice**
½ **teaspoon salt**
1 **teaspoon seasoned pepper**
Garnishes: 7 or 8 green onion stems; 1 red chile pepper, halved

● **Stir** together first 9 ingredients in a large bowl until blended; spoon into a straight-sided 9- x 5-inch loafpan lined with plastic wrap. Cover and chill 8 hours, or freeze up to 1 month; thaw in refrigerator 8 hours.
● **Invert** chilled mixture onto a serving plate; remove plastic wrap.
● **Cut** loaf in half crosswise; place 1 cut half directly on top of remaining cut half, and smooth sides. Serve with crackers or toasted French baguette slices.
● **Garnish,** if desired, by plunging green onion stems in boiling water; plunge stems into ice water to stop the cooking process. Immediately transfer to paper towels; drain stems, and press between paper towels to dry.
● **Press** stems into sides of cheese square, beginning with 1 end of 1 stem on each side. Bring stems up and over to center of top; form loops with remaining stems. Secure stems with wooden picks. Arrange chile pepper halves on top. **Yield:** 1 gift box (24 appetizer servings).

Note: To make 2 small gift boxes, cut in half, and garnish each half, if desired.

BUTTERY BLUE CHEESE SPREAD WITH WALNUTS

Prep: 15 minutes
Chill: 8 hours

3 (8-ounce) packages cream cheese, softened
½ cup butter, softened
1 (4-ounce) package crumbled blue cheese
½ cup diced walnuts, toasted
½ cup chopped fresh chives
¼ cup cream sherry (optional)
1 (16-ounce) round bread loaf
Garnishes: toasted diced walnuts, chopped fresh chives, rosemary sprigs

• **Stir** together first 5 ingredients and, if desired, sherry in a large bowl. Cover and chill 8 hours; let stand at room temperature to soften. Or freeze cheese spread up to 1 month, and thaw in the refrigerator 8 hours.
• **Hollow** out bread loaf, leaving a 1-inch-thick shell; reserve inside of loaf for other uses.
• **Spoon** softened cheese spread into bread shell.
• **Serve** with sliced apples and pears or toasted French baguette slices. Garnish, if desired. **Yield:** about 5 cups (24 appetizer servings).

Chow Down on Chowder

As you spoon into this chowder, you'll know why Sarah and John Davis serve it to family and guests at their shore home in Alabama. We know now—we gave it our Test Kitchen's highest rating.

Although it requires some chopping, helping hands can take care of this task in minutes. With children home for the holidays, don't let them get bored. It's the perfect time to teach them some simple culinary skills and to make the task a little easier in the process.

POTATO CHOWDER WITH GREEN CHILES

Prep: 30 minutes
Cook: 45 minutes

1 large red bell pepper
4 large poblano chile peppers
5 cups chicken broth
1 large potato, peeled and cubed
1 large onion, chopped
1 jalapeño pepper, seeded and chopped
1 teaspoon salt
¼ to ½ teaspoon freshly ground pepper
¼ cup butter or margarine
⅓ cup all-purpose flour
1 teaspoon salt
1 teaspoon dry mustard
¼ to ½ teaspoon freshly ground pepper
2 cups half-and-half
1 cup milk
1 cup (4 ounces) shredded Cheddar cheese
6 bacon slices, cooked and crumbled
1 bunch green onions, chopped

• **Broil** bell pepper and chile peppers on an aluminum foil-lined baking sheet 5 inches from heat 5 minutes on each side or until peppers look blistered.
• **Place** peppers in a heavy-duty zip-top plastic bag; seal. Let stand 10 minutes to loosen skins. Peel peppers; remove and discard seeds. Coarsely chop peppers.
• **Bring** chopped roasted peppers, chicken broth, and next 5 ingredients to a boil in a Dutch oven over medium heat. Reduce heat, and simmer 15 minutes or until potato is tender.
• **Melt** butter in a heavy saucepan over low heat; whisk in flour and next 3 ingredients until smooth.
• **Cook** 1 minute, whisking constantly. Gradually whisk in half-and-half.
• **Stir** flour mixture and milk into chicken broth mixture, and cook over medium heat 8 to 10 minutes or until thickened and bubbly.
• **Sprinkle** each serving with cheese, bacon, and green onions. **Yield:** 9 cups.

Sarah Davis
Birmingham, Alabama

Everyone's a Star

Holiday parades are thrilling events for young participants. Share the magic of your favorite stars with a post-parade party full of fun and refreshments. You'll add to the twinkle in their eyes with this easy neighborhood gathering.

CHERRY SPARKLER

Prep: 10 minutes
Freeze: 8 hours

2 (6-ounce) jars red maraschino cherries, drained
2 (6-ounce) jars green maraschino cherries, drained
½ gallon distilled water
1 (2-liter) bottle cherry-flavored, lemon-lime soft drink, chilled

• **Place** 1 red or green cherry in each compartment of 4 ice-cube trays. Fill trays with distilled water, and freeze 8 hours. Serve soft drink over ice cubes. **Yield:** 8 cups.

Note: For testing purposes only, we used Cherry 7-Up for soft drink.

STARRY SNACK MIX

Prep: 5 minutes

2 (8-ounce) packages crispy cereal squares snack mix
1 (16-ounce) package raisins
1 (12-ounce) jar honey-roasted peanuts
1 (9.5-ounce) package fish-shaped Cheddar cheese crackers

• **Combine** all ingredients. Store in an airtight container. **Yield:** 15 cups.

Note: For testing purposes only, we used Bold Party Blend Chex Mix for crispy cereal squares snack mix.

From Our Kitchen

Add Flavor

You're baking more than ever this season, and now is a great time to flavor your piecrust. Add a pinch of curry or chili powder or a tablespoon of sesame seeds to the pastry for meat or chicken pies. When making sweet pies, use ground cinnamon, nutmeg, grated orange or lemon rind, or diced nuts (about ¼ cup for a single crust). If you're using a refrigerated piecrust, open it on a flat surface. Sprinkle the flavor addition evenly over crust, and blend it into the dough using a rolling pin.

Holiday Traditions

Gina L. Boyd of North Augusta, South Carolina, stumbled onto her tradition by accident. Breakfast for dinner is a family favorite for which she keeps sausage in the freezer.

"I had already made the patties and started cooking the sausage," says Gina. "The cheese grits were bubbling, and the eggs were set aside waiting for the sausage to finish. The sausage smelled wonderful and browned beautifully, and there was no fat in the pan—must be turkey sausage, I thought. When we began to eat, my son, Brandon, raved that this was the best sausage he'd ever had. My husband had a fit over it too. I took one bite and died laughing—we were eating patties of my grandmother's leftover Thanksgiving dressing. The aroma of sage made me think it was sausage. That delicious mistake is a tradition with us now. Go ahead and shape leftover dressing into little patties and freeze them. On Saturday mornings when you want a hearty breakfast without all that extra fat, reach in the freezer for that fabulous mock sausage."

"If Christmas dinner was a sentence on a page, our tradition would be the period at the end," writes Martha Barclay of Mason City, Iowa. "After the sumptuous meal and the rich plum pudding, Mother brought in a silver compote of warm, roasted, salted almonds to balance the sweetness of the dessert. The nuts announced that dinner was finished and 'all is well until another year.' We each would take a handful for crunchy good luck. It's our perfect ending to the happiest of holiday meals."

Tips and Tidbits

■ When a recipe calls for crisp bacon and clean drippings, Justin Craft, our newest Test Kitchens staff member, uses the oven. Justin places bacon strips on a rack in a shallow pan in an oven heated to 325°. In 5 to 10 minutes the bacon is evenly cooked, and the bacon drippings are then easy to collect. The bacon doesn't burn because it's not cooking in the fat.

■ "When the last of rice, potatoes, grits, or oatmeal stick to the bottom of a pot, give the item a shock of cold water," says Justin. The cold loosens the starch from the pot, making cleanup easy.

■ Betty L. Fair of Pensacola, Florida, found a use for those large, empty popcorn tins. "Arrange evergreen boughs (pine, cedar, magnolia, holly, etc.) in the tin, and tie with a big bow," writes Betty. "Place a tin near the hearth for fragrant additions near a fire. The tins make great inexpensive gifts."

CAKE TIPS

Twinkling Star Cake (page 306) takes time to make, but the result is worth it. Plan to bake one day and assemble the next.

Planning Ahead

The filling and frosting can be made two days ahead. Store in airtight containers in the refrigerator. The stars can be made several days ahead. If any break, save the pieces and remelt. Store between wax paper in a cool, dry place for up to one week.

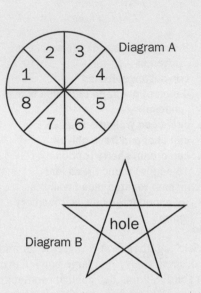

Trimming the Cake

You'll get eight wedges from each layer. (See diagram A.) To get sharp, even points, lightly freeze layers before cutting.

Trim domed top off each layer using a serrated knife, so layers will be level before assembly.

Assembling the Cake

Smooth the center filling level with each star layer. As layers are stacked, the center is filled. (See diagram B.) Make sure the points on each layer line up, and gently press the layers into the filling to maintain the star shape.

For the frosting, use completely cooled white chocolate. If it separates, remelt and start over.

Assemble the cake while layers are still cold from the freezer. Store covered in the refrigerator up to two days.

Southern Living®
Cooking School
BONUS SECTION

Come to Sunday Dinner

Gather your guests 'round the table to savor the tastes of this welcoming menu. You can entertain family or friends with ease by following the make-ahead directions in these recipes. Just remember to add a few minutes to cooking or baking times when the dishes are chilled.

Make-Ahead Sunday Dinner
Serves 6

Herb-Roasted Chicken (double recipe) or
Meat Loaf With Tomato Gravy
Double Cheddar Cheese Potatoes
Avocado-Asparagus Salad
Honey Apple Pie

HERB-ROASTED CHICKEN

Prep: 10 minutes
Bake: 1 hour

½ cup (1 stick) LAND O LAKES Butter, softened
2 shallots, diced
3 garlic cloves, minced
2 tablespoons fresh rosemary, crushed
1 (3- to 3½-pound) whole chicken
6 to 8 fresh parsley sprigs
½ teaspoon salt
¼ teaspoon pepper

● **Stir** together first 4 ingredients.
● **Loosen** skin from chicken breast without detaching it; carefully rub butter mixture over chicken, and insert parsley under skin. Rub butter mixture inside cavity.
● **Sprinkle** chicken with salt and pepper. Place chicken, breast side up, in a roasting pan. Cover and chill, if desired.
● **Bake** at 425° for 20 minutes. Reduce oven temperature to 325°, and bake 40 more minutes or until done. **Yield:** 4 servings.

MEAT LOAF WITH TOMATO GRAVY

Prep: 10 minutes
Bake: 50 minutes
Stand: 15 minutes

2 pounds ground chuck
1 (1¼-ounce) envelope taco seasoning
½ cup Italian-seasoned breadcrumbs
1 small sweet onion, diced
2 large eggs, lightly beaten
⅓ cup ketchup
1 (10-ounce) can ROTEL Mexican Festival Tomatoes & Green Chilies
½ cup (2 ounces) shredded Monterey Jack cheese
Tomato Gravy

● **Stir** together first 6 ingredients until blended. Shape into a 10- x 6-inch loaf; place in a lightly greased 13- x 9-inch pan. Cover; chill 8 hours, if desired. Top with tomatoes and green chilies.
● **Bake** at 425° for 45 to 50 minutes or until meat is no longer pink. Pour off juices. Sprinkle meat loaf with cheese; let stand 15 minutes. Serve with Tomato Gravy. **Yield:** 6 to 8 servings.

Tomato Gravy

Prep: 5 minutes
Cook: 10 minutes

3 tablespoons butter
3 tablespoons all-purpose flour
2 (10-ounce) cans ROTEL Mexican Festival Tomatoes & Green Chilies
1 (16-ounce) can tomato sauce
3 tablespoons chopped fresh cilantro
1 teaspoon sugar

● **Melt** butter in a large saucepan over medium-high heat; whisk in flour until smooth.
● **Cook,** whisking constantly, 1 minute.
● **Whisk** in tomatoes and green chilies and remaining ingredients.
● **Cook** 5 minutes or until thoroughly heated. Serve warm, or cover and chill. **Yield:** about 4½ cups.

DOUBLE CHEDDAR CHEESE POTATOES

Prep: 10 minutes
Bake: 1 hour
Stand: 10 minutes

1 (40-ounce) package frozen STOUFFER'S Family Style Favorites Scalloped Potatoes
3 cups (12 ounces) finely shredded sharp Cheddar cheese
½ small sweet onion, minced
½ (7-ounce) jar roasted sweet red peppers, drained well and diced
¼ teaspoon freshly ground pepper
1½ teaspoons Worcestershire sauce
¼ cup fine, dry breadcrumbs

• **Thaw** scalloped potatoes in refrigerator overnight.
• **Stir** together scalloped potatoes and next 5 ingredients. Spoon into a lightly greased 11- x 7-inch baking dish. Cover and chill, if desired.
• **Sprinkle** with breadcrumbs.
• **Bake** casserole at 350° for 1 hour or until deep golden brown. Let stand 10 minutes. **Yield:** 6 to 8 servings.

AVOCADO-ASPARAGUS SALAD

Prep: 12 minutes

2 pounds fresh asparagus
6 cups mixed salad greens
3 large CALIFORNIA AVOCADOS, peeled and sliced
1 cup cherry tomatoes, halved
¼ cup chopped purple onion
Oregano Vinaigrette

• **Snap** off tough ends of asparagus. Place asparagus in boiling water; let stand 2 minutes. Drain and cool. Chill, if desired.
• **Arrange** salad greens on individual plates; top evenly with asparagus, avocado, tomato, and onion.
• **Drizzle** salads with Oregano Vinaigrette. **Yield:** 6 servings.

Oregano Vinaigrette

Prep: 5 minutes

¼ cup lemon juice
1 garlic clove
1 tablespoon capers, drained
½ cup loosely packed oregano leaves
½ cup olive oil

• **Process** first 4 ingredients in a blender until smooth, stopping to scrape down sides. Turn blender on high; gradually add oil in a slow, steady stream. Cover and chill, if desired. **Yield:** about ⅔ cup.

HONEY APPLE PIE

As dinner is cooking, bake the pie and prepare the sauce so that they will be ready when you finish your meal.

Prep: 5 minutes
Bake: 1 hour, 30 minutes
Cook: 8 minutes

1 (3-pound 1-ounce) package frozen MRS. SMITH'S Deep Dish Apple Pie
1⅓ cups apple juice
¼ cup honey
1½ tablespoons cornstarch
2 teaspoons grated lemon rind
1 tablespoon butter

• **Remove** plastic overwrap from pie. Open center hole, and cut 4 to 6 slits in top crust. Place pie on aluminum foil-lined baking sheet.
• **Bake** at 375° for 1 hour and 20 minutes to 1 hour and 30 minutes, shielding top of pie with aluminum foil after 1 hour.
• **Whisk** together apple juice, honey, and cornstarch in a medium saucepan until smooth.
• **Cook** over medium heat, whisking constantly, 6 to 8 minutes or until bubbly. Stir in lemon rind and butter. Serve over pie. **Yield:** 6 servings.

Quick-Fix Desserts

The answer to that important question, "What's for dessert?" starts by keeping common ingredients in your pantry, and then adding a few of today's convenience items. Create a special twist for a frozen pecan pie by making a 12-minute vanilla custard, or turn ice cream into a decadent dessert by stirring in almonds, marshmallows, and whipped topping. All of these recipes can be prepared with ease when you have the makings in your pantry and freezer. And the next time your family asks for dessert, you'll be one step ahead.

PECAN PIE WITH CHILLED VANILLA CUSTARD

This sweet confection will tempt your taste buds.

Prep: 5 minutes
Thaw: 2 hours
Cook: 12 minutes

1 (2-pound 4-ounce) package frozen MRS. SMITH'S Southern Pecan Pie
1 cup milk
½ cup whipping cream
⅓ cup sugar
4 egg yolks
2 teaspoons vanilla extract
1 tablespoon butter or margarine

• **Remove** and discard paper circle from pecan pie. Thaw pie at room temperature 2 hours.
• **Whisk** together milk and next 3 ingredients in a heavy saucepan.
• **Cook** over low heat 10 to 12 minutes or until mixture is thickened and almost boils. Remove milk mixture from heat.
• **Stir** in vanilla and butter. Cover and chill. Serve custard over pecan pie. **Yield:** 6 to 8 servings.

Bonus Section

Best-Ever Banana Pudding

Prep: 25 minutes
Bake: 25 minutes

⅔ cup sugar
¼ cup all-purpose flour
Dash of salt
1 (14-ounce) can sweetened
    condensed milk
2½ cups milk
4 large eggs, separated
2 teaspoons vanilla extract
1 (12-ounce) package NILLA Wafers
6 large bananas
⅓ cup sugar
½ teaspoon banana extract or vanilla
    extract

● **Combine** first 3 ingredients in a heavy saucepan. Whisk together milks and egg yolks; stir into dry ingredients.
● **Cook** over medium heat, whisking constantly, until smooth and thickened. Remove from heat; stir in vanilla.
● **Arrange** one-third of wafers in bottom of a 3-quart baking dish. Slice 2 bananas; layer over wafers. Pour one-third of pudding mixture over bananas. Repeat layers of sliced bananas and pudding twice; arrange remaining wafers around edge of dish.
● **Beat** egg whites at high speed with an electric mixer until foamy.
● **Add** ⅓ cup sugar, 1 tablespoon at a time, beating until stiff peaks form and sugar dissolves. Fold in banana extract; spread over pudding, sealing to edge.
● **Bake** at 325° for 25 minutes or until golden brown. **Yield:** 8 to 10 servings.

Wedding Cookies

Prep: 11 minutes
Bake: 10 minutes per batch

½ cup (1 stick) LAND O LAKES Butter,
    softened
1 cup all-purpose flour
¼ cup sugar
1 teaspoon vanilla extract
1 cup finely chopped pecans
1 cup powdered sugar

● **Beat** butter at medium speed with an electric mixer until creamy.
● **Add** flour, sugar, and vanilla, beating until blended. Stir in pecans. (Dough will be stiff.)
● **Shape** into 1-inch balls, and place on ungreased baking sheets.
● **Bake** at 400° for 10 minutes. Remove to wire racks, and cool slightly.
● **Roll** warm cookies in powdered sugar; cool cookies completely on wire racks. **Yield:** 4 dozen.

Rocky Road Ice Cream Dessert

Prep: 10 minutes
Freeze: 4 hours

50 NILLA Wafers
¼ cup butter or margarine, melted
2 tablespoons sugar
1 (6-ounce) can whole honey-roasted
    almonds, coarsely chopped and
    divided ✱
½ gallon chocolate ice cream,
    softened
2 cups miniature marshmallows
1 (8-ounce) container frozen whipped
    topping, thawed

● **Place** vanilla wafers in a heavy-duty zip-top bag, and crush with a rolling pin. Set aside ¼ cup crumbs.
● **Stir** together remaining crumbs, butter, and sugar; press into bottom of a 9-inch springform pan.
● **Stir** together 1 cup chopped almonds, chocolate ice cream, and marshmallows; spread over crumb crust. Top with whipped topping. Cover and freeze 4 hours or until firm.
● **Sprinkle** dessert with remaining crushed wafers and ¼ cup chopped almonds. **Yield:** 12 to 14 servings.

✱Substitute 1¼ cups almonds, toasted and coarsely chopped, if desired.

Praline-Topped Pumpkin Pie

Prep: 10 minutes
Bake: 1 hour, 10 minutes

1 (2-pound 14-ounce) package
    frozen MRS. SMITH'S Homemade
    Pumpkin Pie
1 large egg, lightly beaten
2 tablespoons dark brown sugar
2 tablespoons light corn syrup
1 tablespoon butter or margarine,
    melted
1 cup chopped pecans, toasted

● **Remove** and discard paper circle from pie. Place frozen pie in pan on a baking sheet.
● **Bake** at 400° for 55 minutes.
● **Stir** together egg and next 3 ingredients until blended; stir in pecans.
● **Spread** mixture on top of pie, and bake 15 more minutes. Cool on a wire rack at least 2 hours. **Yield:** 6 servings.

Apple-Oat Snack Squares

Prep: 15 minutes
Bake: 40 minutes

3 cups BISQUICK Original All-Purpose
    Baking Mix
2 cups uncooked quick-cooking oats
⅔ cup firmly packed light brown sugar
1 teaspoon ground cinnamon
½ cup butter or margarine, cut into
    pieces
1 cup milk
1 (21-ounce) can apple fruit filling
2 tablespoons light brown sugar

● **Stir** together first 4 ingredients in a medium bowl; cut in butter with a pastry blender until crumbly.
● **Stir** in milk just until dry ingredients are moistened. Fold in fruit filling, and spoon into a lightly greased 13- x 9-inch pan. Sprinkle with 2 tablespoons brown sugar.
● **Bake** at 350° for 40 minutes or until golden. Cool on a wire rack, and cut into squares. **Yield:** 16 squares.

DOUBLE CHOCOLATE CHEWIES

Prep: 15 minutes
Bake: 9 minutes per batch

¾ cup butter or margarine, softened
1½ cups sugar
2 large eggs
1 cup all-purpose flour
¾ cup HERSHEY'S Cocoa
1 teaspoon baking powder
1 (12-ounce) package HERSHEY'S
 Semi-Sweet Chocolate Chips
1 cup chopped pecans, toasted and
 coarsely chopped

• **Beat** butter and sugar at medium speed with an electric mixer until creamy.
• **Add** eggs and next 3 ingredients, beating until blended. Stir in chocolate chips and pecans.
• **Drop** mixture by heaping tablespoonfuls onto ungreased baking sheets.
• **Bake** at 350° for 8 to 9 minutes. (Tops will be soft.) Cool cookies on baking sheet 1 minute; remove to wire racks to cool. **Yield:** 5½ dozen.

HOT FUDGE SUNDAE CAKES

Prep: 25 minutes
Bake: 20 minutes
Cook: 5 minutes

½ cup butter or margarine, softened
¾ cup sugar
2 large eggs
¾ cup all-purpose flour
½ cup HERSHEY'S Dutch Processed
 Cocoa
½ teaspoon baking soda
⅛ teaspoon salt
½ cup buttermilk
½ teaspoon vanilla extract
1 (14-ounce) can sweetened
 condensed milk
⅓ cup HERSHEY'S Dutch Processed
 Cocoa
⅓ cup milk
Vanilla ice cream
Toppings: whipped cream, chopped
 pecans, candied cherries

• **Beat** butter and sugar at medium speed with an electric mixer until blended. Add eggs, beating well.
• **Combine** flour and next 3 ingredients; add to butter mixture alternately with buttermilk, beginning and ending with flour mixture. Beat at low speed until blended after each addition.
• **Stir** in vanilla. Pour batter evenly into 12 lightly greased muffin cups.
• **Bake** at 350° for 15 to 20 minutes or until a wooden pick inserted in center comes out clean. Cool in pan 5 minutes. Remove from pan.
• **Cook** condensed milk, ⅓ cup cocoa, and milk in a medium saucepan over low heat, whisking occasionally, 5 minutes. Serve with warm cakes topped with ice cream and desired toppings. **Yield:** 12 servings.

Picnic Pleasures

These recipes are ideal for a fun excursion. A gorgeous afternoon is the only excuse you need to load up your vehicle and head out with family and friends in search of the ideal dining spot.

PORK TENDERLOIN SANDWICHES

Prep: 10 minutes
Marinate: 2 hours
Bake: 25 minutes

½ cup olive oil
8 fresh thyme sprigs
2 shallots, chopped
2 tablespoons prepared horseradish
2 teaspoons pepper
2 teaspoons salt
2 pounds PORK Tenderloin
Sourdough rolls
Thyme Mayonnaise
Lettuce
Tomato slices

• **Combine** first 6 ingredients in a large heavy duty zip-top plastic bag; seal and gently squeeze to blend ingredients.
• **Add** pork; seal bag, and chill 2 hours. Remove from marinade, discarding marinade; place pork on an aluminum foil-lined pan.
• **Broil** 6 inches from heat (with electric oven door partially open) 5 minutes. Reduce oven temperature to 425°, and bake 20 minutes.
• **Cut** pork into thin slices; cover and chill, if desired. Serve on rolls with mayonnaise. Top with lettuce and tomato. **Yield:** 6 servings.

Thyme Mayonnaise

Prep: 3 minutes

1 cup mayonnaise
1 tablespoon chopped fresh thyme
1 teaspoon lemon juice

• **Stir** together all ingredients. Cover and chill, if desired. **Yield:** 1 cup.

DOUBLE STUFFED SPINACH-AND-BACON EGGS

Prep: 25 minutes

1 (9-ounce) package frozen
 STOUFFER'S Creamed Spinach
12 hard-cooked eggs
⅓ cup instant potato flakes
½ cup mayonnaise
1 tablespoon Dijon mustard
5 bacon slices, cooked and
 crumbled
3 green onions, minced
Paprika (optional)

• **Thaw** creamed spinach in microwave at MEDIUM (50% power) 5 to 6 minutes.
• **Peel** eggs, and cut in half lengthwise. Carefully remove yolks; mash yolks and potato flakes with a fork.
• **Stir** in creamed spinach, mayonnaise, and next 3 ingredients. Stuff egg whites generously with yolk mixture.
• **Sprinkle** with paprika, if desired. Chill, if desired. **Yield:** 2 dozen.

TURTLE BARS

Prep: 10 minutes
Bake: 15 minutes
Chill: 30 minutes

1 (12-ounce) package NILLA Wafers
¾ cup butter or margarine, melted
1 (12-ounce) package semisweet chocolate morsels
1 cup pecan pieces, chopped
1 (12¼-ounce) jar caramel topping

• **Place** vanilla wafers in a large heavy-duty zip-top plastic bag; crush with a rolling pin to make fine crumbs.
• **Stir** together vanilla wafer crumbs and butter; press into bottom of a 13- x 9-inch baking dish.
• **Sprinkle** with morsels and pecans. Drizzle with caramel topping.
• **Bake** at 350° for 12 to 15 minutes. Cool in pan on a wire rack. Chill 30 minutes. Cut into 1½-inch squares. **Yield:** 4 dozen.

SWEET-AND-SPICY PECANS

Prep: 3 minutes
Stand: 10 minutes
Bake: 40 minutes

2 cups pecan halves
¼ cup KIKKOMAN Teriyaki Marinade & Sauce
2 tablespoons vegetable oil
½ teaspoon ground red pepper
2 tablespoons sugar

• **Bake** pecan halves in a 15- x 10-inch jellyroll pan at 350° for 10 minutes. Remove pecans from oven. Reduce oven temperature to 250°.
• **Stir** together teriyaki sauce, oil, and red pepper in a large bowl; add pecans, tossing to coat. Let stand 10 minutes, stirring often.
• **Remove** pecans with a slotted spoon, and arrange in an even layer in pan.
• **Bake** at 250° for 20 minutes. Sprinkle with sugar; stir and bake 10 more minutes. Cool in pan on a wire rack. Store in an airtight container. **Yield:** 2 cups.

MEXICAN MOCHA SPICE MIX

Prep: 5 minutes

1 cup HERSHEY'S Cocoa
1 cup sugar
½ cup powdered nondairy coffee creamer
2 tablespoons instant coffee granules
1 teaspoon ground cinnamon
½ teaspoon ground nutmeg

• **Combine** all ingredients in a large heavy-duty zip-top plastic bag; seal and shake to blend. To serve, spoon ¼ cup mixture into coffee mug, and stir in 1 cup hot water. **Yield:** 10 servings.

ROASTED ONION GUACAMOLE

Prep: 10 minutes
Bake: 30 minutes
Chill: 1 hour

1 large purple onion, chopped
2 garlic cloves, chopped
2 tablespoons balsamic vinegar
1 tablespoon olive oil
4 small CALIFORNIA AVOCADOS
1 tablespoon lemon juice
½ teaspoon salt
½ teaspoon dried Italian seasoning
Tortilla chips

• **Toss** together first 4 ingredients, and place on an aluminum foil-lined pan.
• **Bake** at 425° for 25 to 30 minutes or until lightly browned, stirring mixture once. Cool.
• **Peel** avocados. Mash avocados in a medium bowl; stir in onion mixture, lemon juice, salt, and Italian seasoning. Cover and chill 1 hour. Serve with chips. **Yield:** 2 cups.

Supper Solutions

Dinner served in one dish is a bonus for everyone. It gets the cook out of the kitchen fast and allows more time for your family to enjoy the meal and each other. Cleanup is quick, and leftovers are few. Just choose the supper that fits your active lifestyle.

DEEP-DISH HAMBURGER PIE

Prep: 35 minutes
Bake: 20 minutes

2 cups BISQUICK Original All-Purpose Baking Mix
⅔ cup milk
1½ cups (6 ounces) shredded Cheddar cheese, divided
1½ pounds ground beef
1 small onion, cut in half and thinly sliced
1 (8-ounce) package sliced fresh mushrooms
1 (14½-ounce) can Italian-style tomatoes, drained
1 (14-ounce) can tomato sauce
1 (14½-ounce) can French-style green beans, drained
2 teaspoons lemon pepper

• **Stir** together baking mix, milk, and ½ cup cheese. Turn dough out onto a surface sprinkled with baking mix. Shape into a ball; knead 3 or 4 times. Press dough evenly into bottom and 1 inch up sides of a 13- x 9-inch baking dish.
• **Bake** at 450° for 5 to 7 minutes.
• **Cook** beef, onion, and mushrooms in a large skillet until beef is browned, stirring until it crumbles; drain well.
• **Stir** in tomatoes and next 3 ingredients. Bring to a boil; reduce heat, and simmer 5 to 10 minutes or until slightly thickened. Spoon over biscuit crust.
• **Bake** at 350° for 15 minutes. Sprinkle with remaining 1 cup cheese, and bake 5 more minutes. **Yield:** 8 servings.

PORTOBELLO BURGERS WITH AVOCADO MAYONNAISE

To grill onion, push water-souked skewers crosswise through the whole onion at ½-inch intervals. Slice between skewers, and place skewered slices on grill.

Prep: 18 minutes
Grill: 17 minutes

6 portobello mushroom caps
2 red bell peppers, seeded and halved
1 purple onion, cut into ½-inch-thick slices
Garlic-flavored cooking-and-seasoning spray
Avocado Mayonnaise
6 hamburger buns
3 small CALIFORNIA AVOCADOS, peeled and sliced

• **Coat** mushrooms, bell peppers, and onion with cooking spray.
• **Grill** onion, covered with grill lid, over medium-high heat (350° to 400°) 8 minutes on each side.
• **Grill** mushrooms 5 minutes on each side. Place peppers on grill, skin side down; grill 4 to 5 minutes or until skin is blistered. Peel peppers; cut into strips.
• **Spread** Avocado Mayonnaise on cut sides of buns; place, cut side down, on food rack, and grill 1 minute.
• **Place** mushrooms, bell pepper strips, and onion evenly on bottom halves of buns. Top each with avocado slices and top bun halves. **Yield:** 6 servings.

Avocado Mayonnaise

Prep: 4 minutes

1 small CALIFORNIA AVOCADO, peeled and chopped
½ cup mayonnaise
2 tablespoons lemon juice
¼ cup fresh basil leaves
1 garlic clove, minced

• **Process** all ingredients in a food processor until smooth, stopping to scrape down sides. Cover and chill 2 hours, if desired. **Yield:** 1 cup.

PORK SKILLET DINNER

Prep: 15 minutes
Cook: 40 minutes

4 (½-inch-thick) PORK Rib Chops
¾ teaspoon salt, divided
¼ teaspoon pepper
3 tablespoons all-purpose flour
1 tablespoon vegetable oil
3 medium baking potatoes, cut into 1-inch cubes
4 large carrots, cut into 1-inch-thick pieces
1 small onion, chopped
1 celery rib, chopped
1 cup warm water
1 teaspoon chicken bouillon granules

• **Sprinkle** pork chops with ½ teaspoon salt and pepper; dredge in flour.
• **Brown** pork in hot oil in a large skillet over medium heat; drain. Top with potato and next 3 ingredients; sprinkle with remaining ¼ teaspoon salt.
• **Combine** 1 cup warm water and bouillon granules; pour over vegetables.
• **Cook,** covered, over medium-low heat 40 minutes or until pork is done and vegetables are tender. **Yield:** 4 servings.

CHEESE-STEAK WRAPS

Prep: 10 minutes
Cook: 12 minutes

4 (10-inch) fat-free flour tortillas
All Natural PAM Cooking Spray
1 small onion, sliced
1 small green bell pepper, sliced
1 (1-pound) package flank steak, cut into strips
1 tablespoon cornstarch
6 ounces light pasteurized prepared cheese product

• **Heat** tortillas according to package directions; keep warm.
• **Spray** a skillet with cooking spray 2 seconds; heat over medium-high heat. Add onion and bell pepper; sauté 3 minutes or until tender. Remove from skillet.
• **Toss** together steak and cornstarch.

• **Spray** a large skillet with cooking spray 2 seconds; heat over medium-high heat. Add half of steak. Sauté 2 to 3 minutes; remove from skillet, and repeat procedure.
• **Microwave** cheese in a glass bowl at HIGH 2 minutes, stirring once.
• **Place** steak strips evenly down centers of tortillas; top evenly with vegetables and melted cheese. Roll up, and serve immediately. **Yield:** 4 servings.

Note: For testing purposes only, we used Velveeta cheese product.

MUFFULETTA PIZZAS

Prep: 15 minutes
Bake: 8 minutes

2 (11¼-ounce) packages frozen STOUFFER'S French Bread Pepperoni Pizza
4 ounces thinly sliced deli baked ham
Olive Salad
2 cups (8 ounces) shredded Italian cheese blend

• **Remove** pizzas from plastic bags, and place on a glass plate. Thaw in microwave at HIGH 2 to 2½ minutes. Carefully transfer to a greased baking sheet.
• **Arrange** ham evenly on pizzas; top with Olive Salad. Sprinkle with cheese.
• **Bake** at 475° for 6 to 8 minutes or until cheese melts. **Yield:** 4 servings.

Olive Salad

Prep: 10 minutes

⅔ cup medium-size ripe olives
⅔ cup pimiento-stuffed olives
½ small red bell pepper, diced
¼ small sweet onion, diced
1 garlic clove, minced
1 tablespoon olive oil
2 teaspoons red wine vinegar

• **Place** olives in a bowl; coarsely crush olives with a fork. Stir in remaining ingredients. Cover and chill up to 5 days, if desired. **Yield:** about 1½ cups.

BONUS SECTION

MEXICAN CHICKEN SOUP

Prep: 25 minutes
Cook: 30 minutes

4 skinned and boned chicken breast
  halves, cut into bite-size pieces
1 large onion, chopped
1 tablespoon vegetable oil
2 (10-ounce) cans ROTEL Diced
  Original Tomatoes & Green Chilies
1 (10-ounce) can ROTEL Mexican
  Festival Tomatoes & Green Chilies
1 (19-ounce) can red kidney beans,
  rinsed and drained
1 (15½-ounce) can black beans,
  rinsed and drained
1 (15¼-ounce) can whole kernel corn,
  drained
2 (14½-ounce) cans chicken broth
1 to 1½ tablespoons chili powder
1 teaspoon sugar
½ teaspoon salt
⅓ cup chopped fresh cilantro
  (optional)

• **Sauté** chicken and chopped onion in
hot oil in a Dutch oven over medium-
high heat until chicken is lightly
browned.
• **Stir** in diced tomatoes and green
chilies and next 8 ingredients.
• **Bring** to a boil over medium-high
heat, stirring often. Cover, reduce heat,
and simmer 30 minutes. Sprinkle with
cilantro, if desired. **Yield:** 14 cups.

GREEN CHILIE-CHICKEN LASAGNA

Prep: 20 minutes
Bake: 30 minutes

2 (10-ounce) cans ROTEL Diced
  Original Tomatoes & Green Chilies
1 (10¾-ounce) can cream of onion
  soup, undiluted
2 cups chopped cooked chicken
6 green onions, sliced
6 (7-inch) flour tortillas
¼ cup chopped fresh cilantro
1 (8-ounce) package Monterey Jack
  cheese with peppers, shredded

• **Stir** together diced tomatoes and
green chilies and onion soup in a
saucepan until blended. Cook over
medium-high heat 6 to 8 minutes. Stir
in chicken and green onions.
• **Arrange** 2 tortillas in bottom of a
lightly greased 11- x 7-inch baking
dish, and spread one-third of tomato
mixture on top; sprinkle with one-third
of cilantro and one-third of cheese. Repeat layers twice, ending with cheese.
• **Bake** at 350° for 30 minutes. Let
stand 10 minutes before serving. **Yield:**
6 servings.

FROGMORE STEW

Prep: 15 minutes
Cook: 25 minutes

1 pound unpeeled, medium-size fresh
  shrimp
1 (16-ounce) package turkey kielbasa
1 medium onion, chopped
1 pound small new potatoes,
  quartered
1 tablespoon salt-free Cajun seasoning
4 cups water
6 frozen small ears corn
3 tablespoons KIKKOMAN Lite Soy
  Sauce
Chopped fresh parsley

• **Peel** shrimp, and devein, if desired.
Cut sausage into ¼-inch slices, and cut
each slice into quarters.
• **Sauté** sausage and onion in a Dutch
oven over medium-high heat 3 minutes.
• **Add** potato and Cajun seasoning, stir-
ring to coat. Add 4 cups water and corn.
• **Bring** to a boil. Cover, reduce heat,
and simmer 18 minutes.
• **Add** shrimp; cook 2 minutes or until
shrimp turn pink. Remove from heat;
stir in soy sauce. Sprinkle with parsley.
Remove corn, and serve on the side.
Yield: about 8 cups.

CHICKEN DUMPLING PIE

Prep: 15 minutes
Bake: 60 minutes

3 cups chopped cooked chicken or
  turkey
2 (10¾-ounce) cans cream of chicken
  soup, undiluted
1 (10½-ounce) can chicken broth,
  undiluted
1 (15-ounce) can mixed vegetables,
  drained
½ teaspoon poultry seasoning
2 cups BISQUICK Original All-Purpose
  Baking Mix
1 (8-ounce) container sour cream
1 cup milk

• **Stir** together first 5 ingredients; pour
into a greased 13- x 9-inch baking dish
or 6 to 8 individual baking dishes. Stir
together baking mix, sour cream, and
milk; pour over chicken mixture.
• **Bake** at 350° for 50 to 60 minutes or
until golden. **Yield:** 6 to 8 servings.

QUICK BLACK-EYED PEAS AND HAM

Prep: 5 minutes
Cook: 20 minutes

1 medium onion, chopped
2 tablespoons vegetable oil
2 (15-ounce) cans black-eyed peas,
  rinsed and drained
¾ cup chopped cooked ham
¼ cup KIKKOMAN Teriyaki Marinade &
  Sauce
1 teaspoon salt-free Creole seasoning
1¼ cups water
Hot cooked rice
**Toppings: chopped tomato, sliced
  green onions**

• **Sauté** chopped onion in hot oil in a
saucepan over medium-high heat 3
minutes. Add peas and next 4 ingredients. Bring to a boil; reduce heat, and
simmer, stirring occasionally, 15 minutes. Serve over rice with desired toppings. **Yield:** 4 servings.

Dinner in the Fast Lane

When the dinner bell tolls, you can whip these recipes together fast. The secrets for these quick entrées are a heavy skillet, a grill, and convenient ingredients.

BLACK-AND-BLUE SALAD

Prep: 5 minutes
Cook: 8 minutes

4 skinned and boned chicken breast halves
All Natural PAM Cooking Spray
¼ cup salt-free Cajun seasoning
2 (6-ounce) packages salad greens
2 purple onion slices, chopped
1 large tomato, cut into wedges
16 pepperoncini peppers
Low-Fat Blue Cheese Dressing

• **Spray** chicken with cooking spray 5 seconds. Coat chicken with seasoning.
• **Spray** a skillet with cooking spray 2 seconds; heat over medium-high heat.
• **Add** chicken; cook 4 minutes on each side. Cut into strips. Toss together greens and next 3 ingredients; top with chicken. Serve with dressing. **Yield:** 6 servings.

Low-Fat Blue Cheese Dressing

Prep: 10 minutes

1 (12-ounce) container low-fat cottage cheese
½ cup nonfat mayonnaise
½ cup nonfat buttermilk
4 ounces crumbled blue cheese
1 tablespoon red wine vinegar
2 teaspoons Worcestershire sauce
1 teaspoon hot sauce

• **Whisk** together all ingredients. Cover and chill, if desired. **Yield:** 3 cups.

PORK KABOBS WITH SESAME SEEDS

Serve with grilled vegetables and couscous.

Prep: 10 minutes
Grill: 8 minutes

1 pound boneless PORK Loin, sliced
2 tablespoons sesame oil
3 tablespoons soy sauce
2 tablespoons honey
1 teaspoon minced garlic
½ teaspoon hot sauce
1 teaspoon sesame seeds, toasted

• **Thread** pork loin slices evenly onto 8 (6-inch) skewers; brush with oil. Stir together soy sauce and next 4 ingredients.
• **Grill** kabobs, covered, over medium-high heat (350° to 400°) 3 to 4 minutes on each side, brushing often with soy sauce mixture. **Yield:** 4 servings.

CHICKEN, BROCCOLI, AND CAULIFLOWER CASSEROLE

Serve with fruit salad and biscuits.

Prep: 15 minutes
Bake: 15 minutes

2 (16-ounce) packages broccoli and cauliflower flowerets
4 cups boiling water
¾ cup (1½ sticks) LAND O LAKES Butter, divided
⅓ cup all-purpose flour
½ teaspoon garlic salt
¼ teaspoon freshly ground pepper
2 cups milk
2 cups (8 ounces) shredded Monterey Jack cheese with peppers
2 cups chopped cooked chicken
Paprika (optional)

• **Cook** flowerets in 4 cups boiling water 5 to 6 minutes or until crisp-tender. Drain. Toss with ¼ cup butter; arrange in a 13- x 9-inch baking dish.
• **Melt** remaining ½ cup butter in Dutch oven over medium-high heat. Add flour, garlic salt, and pepper, whisking until smooth. Cook, whisking constantly, 1 minute. Gradually add milk, whisking constantly, and cook 3 to 4 minutes or until slightly thickened.
• **Stir** in 1½ cups cheese and chicken, and pour over vegetables. Top with remaining ½ cup cheese. Sprinkle with paprika, if desired.
• **Bake** at 375° for 15 minutes or until thoroughly heated. **Yield:** 6 to 8 servings.

BLACKENED SALMON WITH MANGO SALSA

Serve with steamed green beans and sliced tomatoes.

Prep: 2 minutes
Cook: 12 minutes

2 (6-ounce) salmon fillets
All Natural PAM Cooking Spray
¼ teaspoon salt
1 tablespoon blackened seasoning
Mango Salsa

• **Spray** salmon evenly with cooking spray 5 seconds. Sprinkle salmon evenly with salt and blackened seasoning.
• **Spray** a skillet with cooking spray 2 seconds; heat over medium-high heat. Place salmon in skillet. Cook 4 to 6 minutes on each side or to desired doneness. Serve with salsa. **Yield:** 2 servings.

Mango Salsa

Prep: 10 minutes

1 large ripe mango, peeled and coarsely chopped, or 1 cup chopped jarred mango
¼ cup finely chopped purple onion
2 tablespoons chopped fresh cilantro
1 tablespoon chopped fresh mint
3 tablespoons orange juice
1 jalapeño pepper, seeded and minced
¼ teaspoon ground cumin
¼ teaspoon salt

• **Stir** together all ingredients. Cover and chill, if desired. **Yield:** 1 cup.

METRIC EQUIVALENTS

The recipes that appear in this cookbook use the standard United States method for measuring liquid and dry or solid ingredients (teaspoons, tablespoons, and cups). The information on this chart is provided to help cooks outside the U.S. successfully use these recipes. All equivalents are approximate.

METRIC EQUIVALENTS FOR DIFFERENT TYPES OF INGREDIENTS

A standard cup measure of a dry or solid ingredient will vary in weight depending on the type of ingredient. A standard cup of liquid is the same volume for any type of liquid. Use the following chart when converting standard cup measures to grams (weight) or milliliters (volume).

Standard Cup	Fine Powder (ex. flour)	Grain (ex. rice)	Granular (ex. sugar)	Liquid Solids (ex. butter)	Liquid (ex. milk)
1	140 g	150 g	190 g	200 g	240 ml
¾	105 g	113 g	143 g	150 g	180 ml
⅔	93 g	100 g	125 g	133 g	160 ml
½	70 g	75 g	95 g	100 g	120 ml
⅓	47 g	50 g	63 g	67 g	80 ml
¼	35 g	38 g	48 g	50 g	60 ml
⅛	18 g	19 g	24 g	25 g	30 ml

USEFUL EQUIVALENTS FOR DRY INGREDIENTS BY WEIGHT

(To convert ounces to grams, multiply the number of ounces by 30.)

1 oz	=	¹⁄₁₆ lb	=	30 g
4 oz	=	¼ lb	=	120 g
8 oz	=	½ lb	=	240 g
12 oz	=	¾ lb	=	360 g
16 oz	=	1 lb	=	480 g

USEFUL EQUIVALENTS FOR LENGTH

(To convert inches to centimeters, multiply the number of inches by 2.5.)

1 in					=	2.5 cm		
6 in	=	½ ft	=		=	15 cm		
12 in	=	1 ft			=	30 cm		
36 in	=	3 ft	=	1 yd	=	90 cm		
40 in					=	100 cm	=	1 m

USEFUL EQUIVALENTS FOR LIQUID INGREDIENTS BY VOLUME

¼ tsp	=							1 ml
½ tsp	=							2 ml
1 tsp	=							5 ml
3 tsp	=	1 tbls			=	½ fl oz	=	15 ml
	=	2 tbls	=	⅛ cup	=	1 fl oz	=	30 ml
	=	4 tbls	=	¼ cup	=	2 fl oz	=	60 ml
	=	5⅓ tbls	=	⅓ cup	=	3 fl oz	=	80 ml
	=	8 tbls	=	½ cup	=	4 fl oz	=	120 ml
	=	10⅔ tbls	=	⅔ cup	=	5 fl oz	=	160 ml
	=	12 tbls	=	¾ cup	=	6 fl oz	=	180 ml
	=	16 tbls	=	1 cup	=	8 fl oz	=	240 ml
	=	1 pt	=	2 cups	=	16 fl oz	=	480 ml
	=	1 qt	=	4 cups	=	32 fl oz	=	960 ml
						33 fl oz	=	1000 ml = 1 l

USEFUL EQUIVALENTS FOR COOKING/OVEN TEMPERATURES

	Fahrenheit	Celsius	Gas Mark
Freeze Water	32° F	0° C	
Room Temperature	68° F	20° C	
Boil Water	212° F	100° C	
Bake	325° F	160° C	3
	350° F	180° C	4
	375° F	190° C	5
	400° F	200° C	6
	425° F	220° C	7
	450° F	230° C	8
Broil			Grill

Menu Index

This index lists every menu by suggested occasion.
Recipes in bold type are provided with the menu.
Suggested accompaniments are in regular type.

DINNERS FOR THE FAMILY

Summer Picnic
Serves 4
page 136
Garlic-and-Wine Grilled Chicken
Vegetable Salad
Homemade Butter Rolls

Newlywed Menu
Serves 2
page 140
Cherry Tomato-Caper Salad
Cracked Pepper Salmon Fillets
Veggie Wild Rice
Easy Tropical Bananas

Summer Fish Fry
Serves 8
page 172
Fried Catfish
Home-Style Baked Beans
Creamy Sweet Slaw
Buttermilk Hush Puppies

Summer Vegetable Supper
Serves 4
page 184
Butterbeans, Bacon, and Tomatoes
Buttermilk Fried Corn   **Edna's Greens**
Cornbread   Watermelon slices

Acadian-Style Supper
Serves 4 to 6
page 194
Polly's Baked Brisket
Potato Salad
Mixed green salad   Dinner rolls

Favorite Family Fare
Serves 6
page 214
Individual Meat Loaves
Smoky Mashed Potato Bake
Steamed green beans

Mexican Menu
Serves 4 to 5
page 240
Chicken Enchiladas Verde
Spanish-style rice
Mexican Pinto Beans
Grapefruit Freeze

Hearty Holiday Menu
Serves 6
page 275
Roast Leg of Lamb
Bill's Roasted Vegetables
Bakery rolls
Chocolate Chip Cookies

Make-Ahead Sunday Dinner
Serves 6
page 332
Herb-Roasted Chicken* or
Meat Loaf With Tomato Gravy
Double Cheddar Cheese Potatoes
Avocado-Asparagus Salad
Honey Apple Pie
*Double recipe

WHEN COMPANY IS COMING

Menu for Four
Serves 4
page 20
Parmesan Cheese Bites
Lamb Chops With Minted Apples
Margaret's Creamy Grits
Steamed baby carrots
1-2-3 Blackberry Sherbet

Dallas Dinner Party
Serves 6 to 8
page 30
Barbecue Shrimp
Smoked Chicken-and-Roasted Shallot Risotto
Crunchy Romaine Toss
Champagne Vanilla Zabaglione With Fruit

Plan-Ahead Menu
Serves 4
page 32
Crunchy Romaine Toss
Pork Medaillons in Mustard Sauce
Carrot-Sweet Potato Puree
Green Beans With Caramelized Onion
Sour Cream Yeast Rolls
Hot Chocolate Deluxe   Pecan Toffee

Easy Company Dinner
Serves 8
page 96
Herb-Roasted Pork Tenderloins
Easy Romaine Toss
Best Hot Rolls

Elegant Spring Luncheon Menu
Serves 4
page 118
Gazpacho
Pesto-Chicken Cheesecakes
Quick Flatbread

Easy Make-Ahead Menu
Serves 8
page 130
Miniature Tomato Sandwiches
Cucumber Soup With Dill Cream
Crab Cakes With Sweet White Corn-and-Tomato Relish
Rice Primavera Salad
Marinated Green Bean-and-Okra Salad With Feta
French bread
Blueberry-Pecan Cobbler*
Minted Lemon Iced Tea
*Double recipe

No-Fuss Company Fare
Serves 6
page 146
Peppered Rib-Eye Steaks
Roasted Garlic-Parmesan Mashed Potatoes
Grilled Vegetable Salad
Blackberry Pudding Tarts

A Bountiful Picnic
Serves 4
page 164
Minted Tea Punch   Cheese Wafers
Corn Salsa   Tortilla chips
Grilled Chicken Salad Sandwiches
Summer Vegetable-and-Orzo Salad
Grilled Asparagus
White Chocolate Tropical Macaroons

An Appetizer Buffet
Serves 12 to 16
page 276
Caper-and-Olive Bruschetta
Chèvre-and-Avocado Tureen
Crab Polenta
Spinach and Artichokes in Puff Pastry
Mediterranean Rollups

A Versatile Brunch
Serves 8
page 284
Cranberry-Pineapple Punch
Brie-and-Sausage Breakfast Casserole
Maple-Plum Glazed Turkey Breast
Chilled Vegetable Salad
Bing Cherry-Grapefruit Salad
Blueberry Biscuits

Company's Coming
Serves 6
page 314
Orange-Cranberry Glazed Pork Tenderloins
Creamy Mashed Potatoes
Green salad or **Green Beans With Shallots**

A Top-Rated Holiday Menu
Serves 8
page 320
Chutneyed Beef Tenderloin
Roasted Vegetables
Green Bean, Walnut, and Feta Salad
Tiramisù Toffee Trifle Pie
Wynns Cabernet-Shiraz-Merlot blend
Clos du Bois Cabernet Sauvignon

MENUS FOR SPECIAL OCCASIONS

Oscar-Night Open House
Serves 10
page 56
Blue Cheese-Walnut Wafers
Taco Cheesecake
Sesame-Maple Chicken Wings

Festive Easter Menu
Serves 12 to 15
page 68
Curried Chicken Salad Spread with crackers
Honey ham on biscuits with **Beehive Butter**
Fresh Fruit Salad With Celery Seed Dressing
Steamed Asparagus With Tomato-Basil Dip
Double-Stuffed Eggs
Sunny Spring Lemonade

Passover Dinner
Serves 6
page 83
Saucy Brisket
Mushroom Matzo Kugel
Buttered brussels sprouts

Kentucky Derby Appetizer Party
Serves 12 to 16
page 106
Strawberry-Cheese Horseshoe   Crackers
Curried Chicken Pâté   Beaten biscuits
Mushrooms in Sour Cream*   Crostini
Beef Tenderloin With Henry Bain Sauce
Dinner rolls
Baby Hot Browns
Kentucky Derby Tartlets
*Double recipe

Celebration Menu
Serves 8
page 108
Prosciutto Bruschetta and Cantaloupe Chutney
Spinach Salad With Hot Citrus Dressing
Bourbon Peppered Beef in a Blanket
Creamy Chive Potatoes
Steamed green beans
Anniversary Cake

Mother's Day Dinner for Two
Serves 2
page 111
Asian Glazed Cornish Hens
Three-Cheese Mashed Potatoes
Warm Spinach-Orange Salad
Caramel-Toffee Bombe

Cinco de Mayo Brunch
Serves 8 to 10
page 122
Sangría or orange juice
Fresh Mango Salsa or **Black Bean Salsa**
Tortilla chips
Breakfast Tamales   **Huevos con Queso***
Santa Fe Grits Bake
Polvorones
*Double recipe

Game-Day Spread
Serves 12
page 210
Blue Cheese Rolls   Assorted crackers
Fried Chicken Fingers With Come Back Sauce
Black Bean Wraps   Salsa
Sweet 'n' Hot Green Beans and Carrots*
Dark Chocolate Brownies
*Double recipe

Halloween Bash
Serves 12
page 234
Bat Sandwiches
Jack-O'-Lantern Cheeseburger Pie*
Ghosts on a Stick
Candy Corn Chocolate Cakes
Fudgy Hot Cocoa
*Double recipe

Holiday Feast With Friends
Serves 8
page 252
Bourbon Meatballs
Deep-Fried Turkey   **Pecan, Rice, and Crawfish Dressing**
Cranberry-Ginger Chutney
Scalloped Sweet Potatoes With Apples
Spinach-Artichoke Casserole
Whipped Turnip Puff
Homemade biscuits
Simmie's Pecan Pie

Menus for Special Occasions (continued)

Favorite Thanksgiving Feast
Serves 8
page 258
Orange-Dijon Pork Loin or
Maple-Plum Glazed Turkey Breast
Cornbread Dressing
Roasted Root Vegetables   **Garlic Green Beans**
Sweet Onion Pudding   **Butter Muffins**
Caramel-Applesauce Cobbler With Bourbon-Pecan Ice Cream

New Year's Barbecue Bash
Serves 10
page 274
Barbecue Pork Shoulder
Cheesy Potatoes and Onions
Baked beans   **Danny's Slaw**
Cornbread

Hanukkah Menu
Serves 6 to 8
page 281
Mock Chopped Liver   Crackers   Celery sticks
Baked Brisket au Jus
Potato Latkes   Applesauce   Sour cream
Sesame Asparagus
Chocolate Chip Mandelbread

Italian Christmas Eve Menu
Serves 8
page 282
Surprise Calzones
Fried Calamari
Mussels Marinara*   French bread
Shrimp Scampi*   **Onion Pie**
Pizza Dolce (Italian Sweet Pies)
*Double recipes

Holiday Dessert Party
Serves 12 to 15
page 286
Delta Mocha Chiffon Cake
Gentleman's Pound Cake
Butter Cookies   **Smoky Mountain Snowcaps**
Tiramisù   **Champagne Sabayon**
Champagne   Coffee

Simple Menus

Easy Make-Ahead Menu
Serves 6
page 54
Marinated Chicken Strips and Vegetables
Parmesan Bread
Lemon Ice Cream

Make-Ahead Appetizer Menu
Serves 20
page 71
Shrimp Tartlets
Asparagus With Garlic Cream
Tomato-Cheese Torte   Assorted crackers
Chocolate-Almond Petits Fours

Quick Weeknight Supper
Serves 6
page 99
Creole Flounder With Lemon Couscous
Stir-Fried Broccoli
Salad greens with **Cucumber-Radish Dressing**

Supper From the Grill
Serves 6
page 126
Honey-Grilled Tenderloins
Grilled Polenta
Marinated Grilled Vegetables
Grilled Pineapple With Vanilla-Cinnamon Ice Cream

Italian Repast
Serves 4
page 166
Veal Scaloppine in Lemon Sauce
Italian Tossed Salad
Easy Tiramisù

A Simple Celebration
Serves 12
page 213
Stuffed Pork Tenderloin
Pasta Salad
Broccoli Salad

Simple Soup Supper
Serves 6 to 8
page 272
Cheesy Vegetable Chowder
Anchorage Country Store Whole Wheat Bread
Bakery apple pie

RECIPE TITLE INDEX

This index alphabetically lists every recipe by exact title.
All microwave recipe page numbers are preceded by an "M."

MONTH-BY-MONTH INDEX

This index alphabetically lists every food article and accompanying recipes by month. All microwave recipe page numbers are preceded by an "M."

GENERAL RECIPE INDEX

This index lists every recipe by food category and/or major ingredient.
All microwave recipe page numbers are preceded by an "M."